NEXUS

A RHETORICAL READER FOR WRITERS

KIM FLACHMANN
*California State University,
Bakersfield*

MICHAEL FLACHMANN
*California State University,
Bakersfield*

PEARSON

Boston   Columbus   Indianapolis   New York   San Francisco   Upper Saddle River
Amsterdam   Cape Town   Dubai   London   Madrid   Milan   Munich   Paris   Montreal   Toronto
Delhi   Mexico City   São Paulo   Sydney   Hong Kong   Seoul   Singapore   Taipei   Tokyo

Senior Acquisitions Editor: Brad Potthoff
Senior Development Editor: Marion B. Castellucci
Senior Marketing Manager: Sandra McGuire
Senior Supplements Editor: Donna Campion
Senior Media Producer: Stefanie Liebman
Associate Digital Editor: Oakley J. Clark
Associate Managing Editor: Bayani Mendoza de Leon
**Project Coordination, Text Design, and
    Electronic Page Makeup:** PreMediaGlobal
Manufacturing Buyer: Mary Ann Gloriande
Senior Cover Design Manager/Cover Designer: Nancy Danahy
Cover Images: © Photo disc, Inc.

Credits and acknowledgments borrowed from other sources and reproduced, with permission, in this textbook appear on pages 486–488.

Flachmann, Kim.
    Nexus : a rhetorical reader for writers / Kim Flachman, Michael Flachmann.
        p. cm.
    Includes bibliographical references and index.
    ISBN 978-0-205-82987-3 (alk. paper)
 1. College readers.   2. Report writing—Problems, exercises, etc.   3. English language—Rhetoric.
I. Flachmann, Michael.   II. Title.
    PE1417.F497 2011
    808.0427—dc23

                                                                                    2011028109

1 2 3 4 5 6 7 8 9 10—RRDW—14 13 12 11

www.pearsonhighered.com

ISBN-13: 978-0-205-82987-3
ISBN-10:   0-205-82987-2

Brief Contents

Rhetorical Contents

CHAPTER 11 Definition   **323**

CHAPTER 12 Cause and Effect   **371**

Thematic Contents

Family Life

Humor and Satire

Self Improvement and Personal Growth

Stages of Life

Preface

Students are reading and writing now more than ever before. They send text messages and emails all day long; they read and respond to blogs; they interact with Web sites; and they start their own Nings and Wikis without any prompting whatsoever. Granted, these are often not sustained instances of argument and persuasion, but they are brief "sound bites" of thinking, decision making, logic, and reasoning. In most cases, however, the verbal social skills of today's students do not transfer to their classroom performance. In fact, most students would say they see no connection at all between their correspondence with friends and their academic work. But what if we could provide that connection? What if we could bring their rushed, abbreviated communication skills into the classroom and build on them? Perhaps then we would really see some success in our students' reading and writing.

The purpose of *Nexus* is to do just that: to encourage students to bring their current interests, communication skills, and aspirations into their composition courses. In this way, we as instructors can help students make connections between their daily communication activities and their college writing assignments. As a result, this book starts where our students' interests lie—with engaging essays, interviews, blog conversations, Web sites, and YouTube videos that they might actually choose to interact with on their own. These "readings" are presented in a lively, multifaceted format that draws on the daily environment in which they are immersed, including electronic and visual sources that are stimulating, energizing, and directly related to topics they are studying.

Even though the format of *Nexus* is contemporary and invigorating, the content is substantive and pedagogically sound. Students are asked continually throughout this book to pull ideas from multiple forms of media and respond to them first with language and logic and then through an electronic, visual, oral, or written medium of their choice.

Approach of *Nexus*

Educational research over the past few years tells us that students learn best not through passive activities, like listening to lectures, but through active assignments in which they participate fully and energetically. If we remember 10 percent of what we hear, 20 percent of what we read, and 80 percent of what we say and do, won't our students learn most effectively if we actively involve them in the material they are studying? All of us learn best from doing or making something related to what we are studying. So why not let our students learn from the electronic and visual media they already use? This text approaches composition by teaching the traditional rhetorical modes as different ways of thinking about our contemporary world through all possible mediums. As a result, students are encouraged to practice various patterns of thought through reading and writing assignments that echo the multi-media world they inhabit.

Foundation Chapters Provide a Framework for Building Writing Skills

Four important initial chapters provide students with the basic foundation they will need to improve their thinking, reading, and writing skills:

- Chapter 1, Our Multimedia World, introduces students to the wide range of media and texts they will encounter in this book.
- Chapter 2, Reading for Understanding, explains the interactive process of reading and describes how to fully engage with both graphic and verbal texts.
- Chapter 3, Writing for Understanding, discusses various aspects of the writing process with an emphasis on the wide variety of effective approaches available to writers.
- Chapter 4, Working with Sources, demonstrates how to use sources to construct a documented essay.

Together, these four chapters provide vital information about the reading and writing processes to prepare students for reading and writing across the curriculum.

Rhetorical Modes Chapters Provide a Multi-Genre Reader for Writers

Rhetorical modes are foregrounded in the readings we chose so students can actually discover how these specific modes work in concert with others. Each modes chapter contains seven readings—four conventional models (like essays, interviews, or speeches) and three nontraditional texts (like blog conversations, images, songs, collages, and Web sites)—except for Chapter 13, Argument, which features six essays and seven nontraditional selections.

Every chapter begins with a brief explanation of thinking in that particular rhetorical mode. Then this method of thinking is highlighted throughout the chapter as a means of processing information in both reading and writing. The chapter introduction moves from a general explanation of the mode and its role in our daily lives to an exercise that helps students discover how a mode works as a pattern of thought in both reading and writing. It proceeds with an in-depth discussion of writing in the mode and then closes with an annotated student essay and a final review of the rhetorical strategy.

In every chapter, we encourage students to think rhetorically by placing their reading material in its context. To do this, we furnish additional material intended to clarify each reading:

- Before each reading, we establish the context by providing the **genre,** a brief **author biography,** and provocative **prereading questions** that students might respond to in a journal. Understanding the context will be especially useful at the end of the chapter when students complete their writing assignments.
- In the readings, **In Context** boxes provide historical background, relevant timelines, related Web sites and blogs, and links (both electronic and verbal) to other interesting sources related to the topic at hand; in addition, at the

bottom of the pages, definitions of highlighted words are provided for easy reference.

- After each reading are four sets of activities:

  - **Conversations: Collaborating in Class or Online.** These questions help students start a much larger conversation among themselves on the *Nexus* Facebook page or on a class blog or Ning about the issues raised by the reading. These questions can also be handled through class discussion if students do not have access to computers.

  - **Connections: Discovering Relationships among Ideas.** These questions are meant to inspire students to think more deeply about the subject of the reading by exploring it individually with the benefit of the online conversations they have already completed with others.

  - **Presentation: Analyzing the Writer's Craft**. These questions focus on the structure and style choices the author or artist made to create the selection.

  - **Projects: Expressing Your Own Views.** These prompts ask students to create verbal, visual, and electronic projects with the new knowledge and level of understanding they have acquired.
- **Other Resources.** This section provides students with one scholarly article and two Web sources related to the reading; these serve as the references for the research paper assignment for each selection.

- **QR Codes.** One among many cutting-edge aspects of this book is that Quick Response (QR) codes are furnished for the resources after each selection so students can quickly access the Web sites using their smartphones. These codes provide one more important connection between our students' personal and academic lives.

At the end of each of these chapters is a series of twelve **Writing Assignments**. These progress from prompts asking students to make connections among selections to others exploring the chapter's rhetorical mode to still others requiring students to combine modes and grapple with ideas at a more advanced level than they did within the chapters.

End-of-Text Resources Provide Additional Support for Writers

In the back of this text is an **Index and Glossary of Rhetorical Terms** that provides a handy reference for students as they work through the text. This resource defines and explains the boldface words that appear in each chapter.

Supplements for *Nexus*

Instructor's Resource Manual

A comprehensive *Instructor's Resource Manual* provides ideas for structuring classes, guidance for the first day of class, readability levels for the readings, more information on the reading and writing processes, multiple suggestions for approaching each reading, related discussions about these topics, and sample student answers to the postreading questions.

Nexus Facebook Page for Students

The text's Facebook page for students (www.facebook.com/NexusReader) will host conversations among students using *Nexus* from throughout the United States and Canada. They will be able to join an international discussion about the reading selection they are working on as they exchange ideas about its content and rhetorical strategies. By entering this broader conversation, students will gain a deeper and more complete understanding of their reading before they move to individual critical thinking questions and finally to writing assignments on each topic.

To encourage students to participate in the student Facebook page, instructors might consider giving them credit for their posts. In this way, students will be rewarded for entering an international conversation that deepens their understanding of the content and rhetorical strategies throughout the book. Instructors can supplement this experience with their own blog or wiki for a continuation of the conversation with their entire class.

Nexus Facebook Page for Instructors

Instructors using *Nexus* will be able to conduct their own conversations with each other and with the authors on a separate Facebook page (www.facebook.com/NexusReaderInstructor). On this site, instructors can post comments and questions about teaching the book, and the authors will offer suggestions and special resources designed for this book. The authors will also be available periodically for live discussions on this page.

MyCompLab

The only online application to integrate a writing environment with proven resources for grammar, writing, and research, MyCompLab gives students help at their fingertips as they draft and revise their essays. Instructors have access to a wide variety of assessment tools, including commenting capabilities, diagnostics and study plans, and e-portfolios. Created after years of extensive research in partnership with faculty and students across the country, MyCompLab offers a seamless and flexible teaching and learning environment built specifically for writers.

Acknowledgments

We want to acknowledge the overwhelming support we have received from Pearson on this project: for keen leadership and sustained creative energy, Brad Potthoff, Senior Acquisitions Editor; for outstanding development and editorial skills, Marion Castellucci, Senior Development Editor; for thoughtful guidance with every phase of this book from content to design, Roth Wilkofsky, President of English, Communications, and Political Science, Joe Opiela, Editorial Director, and Suzanne Phelps-Chambers, Executive Editor; for constant editorial support, Nancy Lee, Editorial Assistant; for marketing, Sandi McGuire, Senior Marketing Manager; for assistance with our Facebook page, Jean-Pierre Dufresne, Marketing Coordinator; for help with the QR codes, Oakley Clark, Associate Digital Editor; and for overseeing production, Bayani Mendoza de Leon, Associate Managing Editor. We would also like to thank Wesley Hall for handling literary permissions; Jenna Gray and Carly Bergey of PreMediaGlobal for production and image management, respectively; and Donna Campion and Teresa Ward for their work on the *Instructor's Resource Manual*.

We owe very special thanks to Lauren Martinez—our constant source of inspiration, unique ideas, and multi-media selections for this book. She is also the author of the accompanying *Instructor's Resource Manual*. In addition, we'd like to acknowledge Paul Martinez, consultant to the project throughout its development and designer of the model chapter, and Lizbett Tinoco, assistant to Lauren Martinez. In addition, we are appreciative for the innovative ideas and selections that David Babington provided. Furthermore, we want to thank Annalisa Townsend and Chris Dison for their extraordinary expertise and assistance. Finally, we are very grateful to Jeff Eagan, Abby Flachmann, Christa Hash, Matt Mason, Ty Olden, Joanie Sahagun, and Isaac Sanchez for assistance with the book's content from beginning to end.

We are especially indebted to the following instructors who reviewed the manuscript and helped us mold our ideas into a textbook that would be useful to them: Janet Alexander, Delta College; Rebecca Andrews, Southwest Texas Junior College; Juliana F. Cardenas, Grossmont College; Kathleen Combass, Santa Fe College; Derrick Conner, East Mississippi Community College; Clark Draney, College of Southern Idaho; J. Anne Dvorak, Longview Community College; Kevin Ferns, Woodland Community College; Robert G. Ford, Houston Community College; Marla Fowler, Albany Technical College; Michael Fukuchi, Barton College; Bruce Henderson, Fullerton College; Jeannine Horn, Houston Community College; Schahara Hudelson, South Plains College; Lillie Miller Jackson, Southwest Tennessee Community College; Susan A. Johnson, Sierra College; Jessica Fordham Kidd, University of Alabama; Lola A. King, Trinity Valley Community College; Rita Kranidis, Montgomery College; Alexander Kurian, North Lake College; Lucinda R. Ligget, Ivy Technical Community College of Indiana; Monique C. Logan, Southern Polytechnic State University; Ray P. Murphey, Ogeechee Technical College; Michelle Paulson, Victoria College; Amy Love Rogers, Trinity Valley Community College; Larry Silverman, Seattle Central Community College; Rosie Soy, Hudson County Community College; Barbara Urban, Central Piedmont Community College; Matt Usner, Harold Washington College; Roohi Vora, San Jose State University; Bradley A. Waltman, College of Southern Nevada; Susannah Wexler, Hudson County Community College; Courtney Huse Wika, Black Hills State University; and Connie Youngblood, Blinn College.

In preparing the IRM, we are indebted to the following writing instructors who have contributed their favorite techniques for teaching various rhetorical strategies: Sue Johnson, Sierra College; Kevin Ferns, Woodland Community College; Larry Silverman, Seattle Central Community College; Barbara Urban, Central Piedmont Community College, Levine Campus; Maria Fowler, Albany Technical College; Brad Waltman, College of Southern Nevada; Michael Fukuchi, Barton College; Michelle Paulsen, The Victoria College; Kathleen Combass, Santa Fe College.

Our final and most important debt is to our family—Laura, Christopher, Abby, Carter, and Bennett—who have always made teaching and learning enjoyable.

Kim and Michael Flachmann

Our Multimedia World

1

What an exciting time to be in college—when many different forms of media are a vital part of everyday life! Wherever you turn, another type vies for your attention. If you live off campus, you probably listen to the radio or your iPod on the way to classes; you hear ads, newscasts, and excerpts from speeches on the news; you see traffic signs, billboards, and highway warnings as you drive; when you arrive on campus, you may have time before class to check your email, comment on some Facebook posts, look briefly at a Web site a friend told you about, or watch a video on a subject you are considering for your research paper in English; then during class, you watch the carefully prepared PowerPoint slides your professor created on the topic of the day, and before class is dismissed, you access the class tutorial software online to help with your paper. But what is most astounding

is that you do all this navigation with ease, without shifting gears or preparing to deal with a new type of media at each juncture. These daily maneuvers are definitely stimulating and exhilarating, but they can also be challenging and overwhelming at times—especially when you may not be exactly sure how to think about or evaluate the various types of media bombarding you every day.

The purpose of this text is to encourage you to bring your current interests, communication skills, and aspirations into your writing class so you can build on them to think and write more clearly. As a result, this book starts with engaging essays, interviews, blog conversations, Web sites, and YouTube videos that you might actually choose to access on your own outside of class. These "readings" are presented in a lively, diverse format that mimics the multimedia environment we all currently share, including electronic and visual sources that are stimulating, energizing, and directly related to the topics you are studying. Even though the format of this book is contemporary and stimulating, its contents are based on conventional strategies that have helped millions of students become better writers. Through this combination of cutting-edge media and time-tested teaching techniques, you will be asked throughout this book to pull ideas from multiple media and respond to them—primarily in written form but also in electronic, visual, and oral projects.

Recent educational research tells us we all learn best not through passive activities such as listening to lectures, but through active assignments in which we participate fully and energetically. If we are able to remember 10 percent of what we hear, 20 percent of what we read, and 80 percent of what we say and do, won't you learn most effectively if you become actively involved in the material you are studying? And that's what we intend to do—provide resources that will fully engage you in the process of improving the way you think, read, and write.

Using Rhetorical Modes as Patterns of Thought

This text approaches composition by teaching the traditional **rhetorical modes** as different ways of thinking about our contemporary world:

- Description
- Narration
- Illustration
- Process Analysis

- Division/Classification
- Comparison/Contrast
- Definition
- Cause/Effect
- Argument

Every piece of communication, no matter what its medium, falls into at least one of these nine rhetorical modes or patterns of thought. Within this framework, we offer a variety of selections, in both written and graphic form, that address us in exciting, diverse ways. As a result, you can practice each specific method of thinking through different types of communication. So as you study each of the selections in this book, you will be working on a particular pattern of thought that will transfer quite naturally to your own writing.

As you move through this book, each chapter focuses on one rhetorical mode so you can learn how it works through example and practice. Each rhetorical pattern you study will suggest slightly different ways of seeing the world, processing information, solving problems, and structuring your writing. Each offers important ways of making sense of your immediate environment and the larger world around you. Looking closely at rhetorical strategies or specific patterns of thought will allow you to discover how our minds actually work within each mode. In a similar fashion, becoming more aware of your own thought patterns in each strategy will help you improve your basic reasoning skills as well as your reading and writing abilities.

Each chapter introduction provides instruction and exercises specifically designed to help you focus on a particular pattern of thought. When you practice each of these rhetorical patterns, you will be able to build on your previous thinking skills. As the book progresses, the rhetorical modes become more complex and require a higher degree of concentration and effort. As a result, the skills you are learning will ultimately develop into a powerful, fully realized ability to process the world around you—including reading, writing, seeing, and feeling—on an advanced analytical level.

Responding to the Readings

People read for a variety of reasons. One reader may want to be stimulated intellectually, while another seeks relaxation; one person might read to keep up with the latest developments in his or her profession, whereas the next might want to learn why a certain event happened or how something is done. The reading selections in this text fulfill all these purposes in different ways through various forms of media. They have been chosen, however, not only for their variety and interest, but for an additional, broader purpose: Reading these prose and graphic selections can help you learn to think and write more clearly. For each reading, we help you discover its effective features and qualities so you can then use them in your own written work.

Every time you read a selection in this book, you will also be preparing to develop a project based on the same rhetorical pattern. These projects include editorials, slides, essays, collages, podcasts, songs, Web sites, blogs, videos, and the like. As you read, therefore, you should pay careful attention to both content and form. Each selection in this text features one dominant pattern that is supported by others. You will see how experienced writers, illustrators, and graphic designers use carefully selected strategies to organize and communicate their ideas. In fact, the more aware you are of each author's rhetorical choices, the more skillfully you will be able to apply these strategies to your own writing.

More specifically, after you read a selection, you will be encouraged to react critically to the ideas and issues you have just encountered. Here are the stages you need to pass through to ensure that you are thinking critically or analytically.

Three Stages of Understanding

1. The **literal level** is the foundation of human understanding; it involves knowing the meanings of words and phrases as they work together to form sentences. To comprehend the statement "You must exercise to control your weight and maintain your health" on the literal level, for example, you have to know the definitions of all the words in the sentence and understand the way those words work together to make meaning.

2. **Interpretation** requires you to make connections between ideas, draw inferences from pieces of information, and reach conclusions about the material you have read. An interpretive understanding of our sample sentence might be translated into the following thoughts: "Exercising sounds like a form of medicine. I wonder if there's any correlation between the two." None of these particular thoughts is made explicit in the sentence, but each is suggested in one way or another.

3. **Critical thinking**, the most sophisticated form of reasoning, involves a type of mental activity that is crucial to success in all aspects of life. This type of thinking takes a complex idea apart, studies its parts, and reassembles the idea with a more thorough understanding of it. A critical analysis of our sample sentence might proceed in the following way: "This sentence is talking to me. It actually addresses me with the word *you*. I wonder how *my* weight and health would change if I started to exercise. I certainly want to be healthy, so I need to take this statement seriously." Students who can disassemble an issue or idea in this fashion and understand its various components more completely after reassembling them are rewarded intrinsically with a clearer knowledge of life's complexities and extrinsically with good grades. They are also more likely to earn responsible jobs with higher pay because they are able to apply this understanding effectively to all facets of their lives.

The best way to demonstrate your level of understanding is through a form of communication that suits your purpose and proves your point, which leads us to the multi-genre projects connected to each reading selection. This book asks you to refine your ability to "read" and understand many different types of media and then express yourself creatively through these same forms. In this way, your own favorite subjects and media will be your personal guides as you improve your ability to make connections through reading and writing.

Reading for Understanding

2

Reading critically begins with developing a natural curiosity about a subject and then nurturing that curiosity throughout the reading process. It means making predictions and asking questions so you stay fully engaged and involved with the reading material and you are able to understand it on the deepest, most sophisticated level possible.

Reading critically is at the core of all successful communication. Unfortunately, critical reading is not actually taught in our educational system. After elementary school, teachers simply assume that students' reading abilities progress with the complexity of their assignments. But we are learning that this assumption is shockingly untrue. We live in an age of pictures, X-boxes,

cell phones, iPads, instant messages, and e-books, which has created a culture that does not habitually support academic reading. Reading at the college level requires time and reflection. Only then will the imagination be sufficiently engaged so you can read analytically and critically and be productive citizens in our very fast-moving world. But since our culture does not naturally promote reading as an activity, you have to work diligently to become a more critical reader, which will positively affect every aspect of your life in and out of college—especially your writing ability. As you read this chapter, record in the margin or on a separate piece of paper your responses to the ideas presented so you can refer to them throughout the course.

The Reading Process

The reading process can be divided most productively into three interlocking parts that work together to help you understand as clearly as possible an author's or illustrator's purpose and meaning. This same process, which can be used to decipher both verbal and visual texts, will help you understand all the readings in this text on multiple levels. It looks like this graphically:

The Reading Process

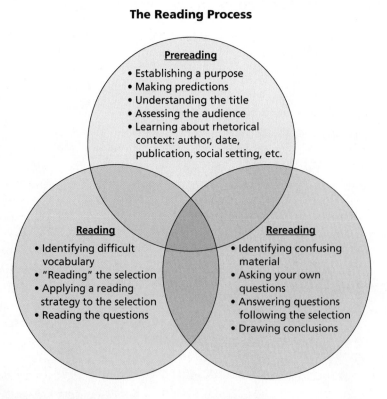

We will look closely at these elements one by one.

Prereading

The first phase of the reading process is often called **prereading** or **preparing to read**. As the title suggests, it involves preparing yourself to delve into your reading equipped with your best concentration and focus. It refers to activities that help you explore your reading material and its general subject so you can read as efficiently as possible. It also includes surveying your assignment and focusing clearly on the task ahead of you. Your mission at this stage is to stimulate your thinking before the act of reading.

Your most important responsibilities at the beginning of this process should be to focus on learning as much as you can about a selection and its context (the circumstances surrounding its development), including the title, the author, the place and year of publication, and its original audience. This background information will guide you toward making predictions and establishing a purpose for your reading. Here is a sample of this information from this text.

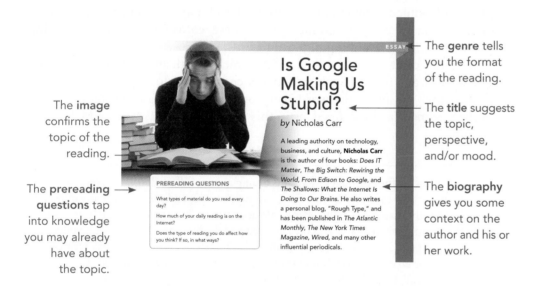

The **image** confirms the topic of the reading.

The **prereading questions** tap into knowledge you may already have about the topic.

ESSAY

Is Google Making Us Stupid?

by Nicholas Carr

A leading authority on technology, business, and culture, **Nicholas Carr** is the author of four books: *Does IT Matter, The Big Switch: Rewiring the World, From Edison to Google,* and *The Shallows: What the Internet Is Doing to Our Brains.* He also writes a personal blog, "Rough Type," and has been published in *The Atlantic Monthly, The New York Times Magazine, Wired,* and many other influential periodicals.

PREREADING QUESTIONS

What types of material do you read every day?

How much of your daily reading is on the Internet?

Does the type of reading you do affect how you think? If so, in what ways?

The **genre** tells you the format of the reading.

The **title** suggests the topic, perspective, and/or mood.

The **biography** gives you some context on the author and his or her work.

A close look at the title will usually provide important clues about the author's or illustrator's attitude toward the topic, his or her stand on an issue, or the mood of the selection. It can also furnish you with a sense of audience and purpose.

Learning as much as you can about the author of a prose piece or the creator of a graphic, along with any pertinent publication information, will generally stimulate your interest in the material and help you achieve a deeper understanding of the issues to be discussed. From some basic biographical information, for example, you can learn about the writer's/creator's age, political leanings, and profession. In other words, you can learn a great deal from a biography about the circumstances surrounding the selection's creation. The original publication information will then guide you to a sense of the intended audience.

Discovering this initial information should lead you quite naturally to ask some of your own questions on the selection you are about to encounter, thus engaging your curiosity for the duration of your reading. For example, the excerpt above from "Is Google Making Us Stupid?" not only provides background information but also engages our curiosity about the essay and its context.

Reading

Once you have previewed the material, you can start reading the selection from the beginning. The first task you should undertake is to figure out the general idea of the selection and locate vocabulary words you don't understand.

As you read, you are making meaning out of a text that someone else has written. In other words, you will be working in partnership with the author/illustrator and his or her words or graphics to make sense of the material. This will seldom happen in a single reading. In like manner, when someone reads your creations, he or she must work with your words or graphics on the page to figure out what you are saying and what your words imply. You should also try to figure out the author's primary purpose for writing the selection.

In this book, difficult vocabulary words in the reading selections are identified and defined for you at the bottom of each page. If you actually want to increase your vocabulary and incorporate these words into your own speaking and writing, you should highlight the words, compose your own lists, and/or create index cards. (You can do this electronically with an application, or "app," called Flashcard Touch.) Such activities encourage you to interact with the text in ways that will make the words your own. Blue highlighting signals words in the reading that are defined, as in this example from "Is Google Making Us Stupid?"

For me, as for others, the Net is becoming a universal medium, the conduit for most of the information that flows through my eyes and ears and into my mind. The advantages of having immediate access to such an incredibly rich store of information are many, and they've been widely described and duly applauded. "The perfect recall of silicon memory," *Wired's* Clive Thompson has written, "can be an enormous boon to thinking." But that boon comes at a price.

conduit: channel
boon: benefit

As you read these selections for the first time, you should also annotate them in some way to enhance your comprehension. This might involve making personal notes in the margin, drawing arrows from one idea to another, labeling sections of the selection, or drawing a graphic of its contents. Making notes on the material itself will keep you engaged in the process as the reading becomes more difficult and will help you remain involved as an active reader through the entire reading process.

Finally, at the end of the first reading, you should glance at the questions following the selection, which will guide your focus to the most significant material as you reread the selection. These questions lead directly to the writing assignments and projects you will address at the end of each reading.

Rereading

If you want to reach a critical understanding of a reading selection, plan to read it at least three times. To get to the deeper levels of meaning, you need to progress through the basic levels of comprehension first, which takes time and reflection.

Most students don't think reading a selection more than once is important, but the second and third readings will dramatically increase your understanding of the material. During the second reading, you should identify what is still confusing by posing three questions addressing your uncertainties. Then grapple directly with your questions by talking with your classmates, reading the material again, or asking your professor. In this way, the second reading will allow you to understand the assumptions that lie behind the words or graphics on the page and discover relationships between ideas you didn't notice in the first reading. At this stage, you are closer to critical reading, but you are not there yet. This reading helps you dig more deeply into what the author is saying and prepares you to expand your grasp of the material for your third reading.

Approaching your third reading slowly and carefully will allow you to analyze the selection and uncover your opinions on its topic. This critical reading is the highest level of comprehension and should be your goal with each selection in this book. For this reading, you should wrestle with the subject matter so you are making associations and drawing conclusions of your own that capture the essence of the reading material.

This third level of reading requires the most energy on your part because you have to produce your own questions and analyze the essay as it moves from point to point. Even though this reading takes the most energy, it is also the most rewarding because your mind gets to grapple with ideas on a level that helps you understand your reading and writing assignments more thoroughly. Ultimately, attaining this level of understanding will raise your grades in all subjects.

Finally, answer the questions following the reading and get ready to respond to the topic. You will have a variety of options to choose from, but you should be ready at this point to express your own ideas on this and other related subjects.

Once you start reading and begin to understand where you are headed, these "stages" can occur in any order you prefer. You might look up a word, argue with an idea in the first paragraph, and go back over a paragraph for a second reading—all in the first few minutes of encountering a selection. Although you may never approach any two reading projects in the same way, this chapter will help you develop your own personal reading process and guide you toward a comfortable reading ritual.

Reading Different Forms of Media

Although you need to approach verbal and graphic selections in slightly different ways, they share many of the same rhetorical features. Here is a list of Reading Essentials to apply to both words and visuals:

Reading Essentials

Subject: What is the topic or theme of the selection?

Medium: What is the selection's format or vehicle of communication: graphic, verbal, visual, auditory, etc?

Genre: What is the selection's form of communication—letter, photo, story, report, blog, drama, interview, Web site, speech, slides, collage, song, etc.?

Purpose: What is the selection's mission or purpose?

Audience: Who is the intended audience?

Context: What are the circumstances surrounding the communication?

Rhetorical strategies: What techniques does the writer/illustrator use to communicate his/her purpose: patterns, repetitions, refrains, rhythm, opposites, use of color, development of characters, setting, etc.?

Unique features: What features are exceptional or distinct from others?

Point of view/perspective: What is the angle or viewpoint of the writer or illustrator?

Effect: What is the end result?

Each of these guidelines should be applied in a slightly different way when you read either words or visuals. Here is an example of each.

Reading Prose

Here is a prose excerpt on yoga (by Maria Cristina Jimenez) that we will analyze with reference to the Reading Essentials. Read the paragraph first, and then go through the essentials one by one.

Yoga is good writing. Anyone who has walked into a yoga class has witnessed human bodies eloquently expressing themselves, pose after pose. And in this sense, writing *is* yoga. Writing is about slowing down, sitting in silence, waiting, breathing, paying attention. It is about creating an exquisite state of awareness that allows us to be fully present in the here and the now. In a broader sense, I feel as if life writes itself not just in the choices we make and in our patterns, but in our bodies, through all that we've eaten, the amount of exercise we've chosen to do or not do, the injuries we have suffered. Everything writes itself into our muscles, our bones, even into our breath. Whenever we practice yoga or sit down to write, we experience ourselves on a deeper level; we know ourselves better and improve what needs to be improved.

Reading Essentials: Yoga Paragraph

Subject: a definition of good writing

Medium: verbal

Genre: essay

Purpose: to explain the similarities between yoga and good writing; we can improve ourselves through both yoga and writing

Audience: general audience

Context: people interested in the importance of writing in our culture today; the paragraph was in a special publication of the *College Board Review* dedicated to writing.

Rhetorical Strategies: use of comparison: writing = yoga in the following ways: in the act of writing and doing yoga—slowing down, sitting in silence, waiting, breathing, paying attention, high awareness; in the basics of life—exercise, food, injuries, muscles, bones, breath

Unique Features: personal touch at end: "Whenever we practice yoga or sit down to write, we experience ourselves on a deeper level"

Point of View/Perspective: yoga instructor who understands the importance of writing

Effect: effective, convincing statement about the role of writing in our personal growth as human beings

Reading Visuals

Look closely at the following picture. Then apply the Reading Essentials to this picture as demonstrated in the paragraph above. Suggested answers are provided for you so you can check your own responses.

Reading Essentials: Yoga Image

Subject: yoga pose in a deserted area

Medium: visual

Genre: photo

Purpose: to represent solace and peace, being one with nature

Audience: general viewer/reader

Context: contemporary setting, nature, self, contemplation, quietness, starkness

Rhetorical Strategies: three natural rock formations, yoga person slightly off center, person sitting on horizon, person's clothes (white and shade of blue) in reverse order from sky (blue to white), walkway leading to seated person

Unique Features: one living person in picture, color of clothes against brown earth

Point of View/Perspective: picture taken from rear so as not to disturb the setting

Effect: calming, endless, peaceful

In the next chapter, you will see how these same essentials can be applied to the writing process.

Writing for Understanding

3

If you learn to apply your critical thinking skills to your reading, you will naturally be able to write analytically. You must process thoughts on this highest level as you read in order to produce essays and other projects on the same level. In other words, you need to "import" your reading thoughtfully in order to "export" your best possible writing. This chapter explains the intimate relationship between good writing and critical reading and will ultimately demonstrate how to apply to your own writing the valuable reading strategies discussed in Chapter 2.

Writing analytically is the flip side of reading analytically; both skills are equally important to your success in college and beyond. Ours is a culture of emails, text messages, and quickly scribbled notes posted on the refrigerator. Analytical or critical writing, however, requires concentration, focus, and reflection. Only when you fully engage with a topic, wrestle with its implications, and analyze its consequences can you produce a project or a piece of writing that represents this most sophisticated form of thinking. No other skill will prepare you so completely to compete for a job in the global marketplace. But achieving this level of writing takes time and effort.

The Writing Process

You will be most successful in your writing if you envision each writing experience as an organic process that follows a natural, repetitive cycle of prewriting, writing, and rewriting. The writing process begins the minute you get a writing assignment. It involves all the activities you do from choosing a topic to turning in a final draft, including computer searches, note taking, text messages to friends for help, and those crucial, late-night trips to Starbucks. Understanding these personal choices is just as important as knowing the details of the formal process because all these rituals have to work together to produce a final assignment on or before the designated deadline. Here is a graphic version of the writing process itself.

The Writing Process

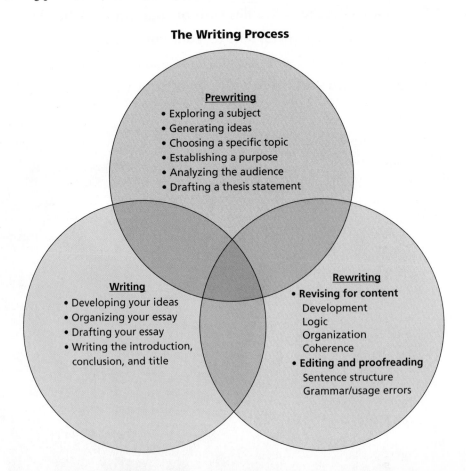

Prewriting
- Exploring a subject
- Generating ideas
- Choosing a specific topic
- Establishing a purpose
- Analyzing the audience
- Drafting a thesis statement

Writing
- Developing your ideas
- Organizing your essay
- Drafting your essay
- Writing the introduction, conclusion, and title

Rewriting
- Revising for content
  Development
  Logic
  Organization
  Coherence
- Editing and proofreading
  Sentence structure
  Grammar/usage errors

Even before the writing process can begin, you must carefully read the writing assignment, assessing all its details and directions. Here is the sample writing assignment for this chapter:

> *Facebook is a prominent part of American culture at this point in our history, and it wields a great deal of power in terms of how the world sees us. Considering all the pros and cons of social networking, what are the major decisions someone must make when setting up a Facebook page? Why are these decisions so important in establishing our electronic image?*

With this assignment in mind, let's work through a set of sample responses from our student writer, Samantha Edwards. She will demonstrate each phase of the writing process as she actually develops a draft of her essay.

Prewriting

Preparing to write, also called **prewriting**, refers to activities that help you explore a general subject, generate ideas about that subject, select a specific topic, establish a purpose, learn as much as possible about your readers, and draft a thesis statement. Your mission at this stage is to stimulate your thinking before you actually begin the act of writing.

Whenever you generate new material throughout the writing process, you are prewriting. The more ideas you generate, the more you will have to work with as you draft your essay or create your project. The most common prewriting activities are brainstorming, freewriting, and clustering.

Brainstorming

Based on free association, brainstorming involves letting one thought naturally lead to another, usually in the form of a list. You can brainstorm by yourself, with a friend, or in a group. Brainstorming allows you to set up a dialogue with yourself or others, as the act of writing down your ideas becomes a natural catalyst for other thoughts. Regardless of the method, list whatever comes to your mind about a topic—ideas, thoughts, examples, facts, anything. As with freewriting, don't worry about grammar or sentence structure.

Here is Samantha's brainstorming on the assignment above:

> *be honest*
>
> *complain about frustrating things*
>
> *be mysterious*
>
> *skip punctuation—except exclamation points*
>
> *party photo is a must*

> *act like you're popular and in demand*
>
> *include a candid photo*
>
> *add an intriguing picture of yourself*
>
> *post a group picture of yourself with good-looking people of the gender you want to date*
>
> *pictures of people of the gender you don't want to date can be less attractive than you*
>
> *add smiling pictures of yourself in interesting places*

Freewriting

Like brainstorming, freewriting involves writing down your ideas to discover what you want to say. Set a limit of five to ten minutes, and then write by free association. Write about what you are seeing, feeling, touching, thinking; write about having nothing to say; recopy the sentence you just wrote—anything to keep going. After you have generated some material, locate an idea central to your writing assignment, put it at the top of another page, and start freewriting again, letting your thoughts take shape around this new idea. This second type of preparation is called *focused freewriting* and is especially valuable when you already have a specific topic. For either type of freewriting, don't worry about sentence structure or grammar errors.

Here is Samantha's freewriting on the Facebook assignment:

> *I loved the opportunity to create my Facebook page because it let me set up a cyber self that was new to the world—and in some ways to me.*
>
> *I learned some of the ropes by listening to my friends talk about their mistakes on Facebook, and I learned that you can actually create a persona for the public that is realistic AND engaging. I knew that all decisions I made about my Facebook wall would be seen by my "friends"—old and new. I also learned what to do by making some of my own mistakes on MySpace—before I made a Facebook page. You can exercise your verbal freedom, but you have to use some restraint.*
>
> *You should definitely have an intriguing photo of yourself on your wall. Your status page lets you control the way others see you. For your status entries, you want to look like you are always in demand—don't appear to be searching desperately for a relationship, and definitely don't seem lonely in any way. This strategy will start bringing attention your way.*
>
> *Be careful to avoid pictures of yourself going through obviously awkward stages—both physically and mentally. And try very hard not to connect with any family members or family friends who might know embarrassing secrets from your past. I strongly urge you not to put up a picture of your pet or a Pokémon character in place of your own profile picture.*
>
> *Use your status updates for complaining about ridiculous commercials, difficult mothers, and other pet peeves. And don't be too honest. No one wants*

to hear the intimate details of your latest stomach upset. Play it safe and talk about well-known brand names and interesting quotations from movies like Anchorman.

Your Facebook photo album should include at least one party shot of you (especially if you are shy and on the unsociable side) and a candid shot that isn't really candid at all. After you carefully pose these pictures, choose some fun group pictures—a few with you and very good-looking people of the gender you want to date and others with less good-looking people of the gender you don't want to date.

Clustering

Clustering is a method of drawing or mapping ideas as fast as they come into your mind. Put a key word, phrase, or sentence in a circle in the center of a blank page. Next, write down and circle any related ideas that come to mind. As you add ideas, draw lines to the thoughts they come from. After two or three minutes, you will probably reach a natural stopping point. Besides generating a lot of helpful ideas, you will also have a map of your thoughts that can guide you toward a good essay. Samantha's cluster is on p. 18.

Deciding on Subject, Purpose, and Audience

The next decisions Samantha has to make involve subject, purpose, and audience. As you can tell from the tasks you have already completed, writing or creating a successful project takes careful planning. A well-designed paper or project will get the reaction from readers that its author hopes for—whether this response is to appreciate a special scene, identify with someone's grief, or leap into action. At this point, if you make some decisions about your subject, purpose, and audience before you start to write, the job of actually creating your project will be smooth and generally free of stress.

- **What is your exact subject (person, event, object, idea, etc.)?** To create a successful project, focus on a single subject, along with related thoughts and details. You may have completed prewriting activities at this point, but what will you choose as your final topic? Selecting a subject that interests you is always best because you will have more to say and you will enjoy writing much more if you know something about your topic. Here is Samantha's subject:

> *Subject: the perfect Facebook profile*

- **What is your purpose?** Your purpose is your reason for doing your project or essay. Your purpose could be to explore your feelings on a topic (to do personal writing), to tell a friend about a funny experience you had (to entertain), to explain something or share information (to inform), or to convince others of your position on a controversial issue (to persuade). Whatever your purpose,

deciding on it in advance makes completing the rest of your project much easier. Here is Samantha's purpose:

> *Purpose:* to inform

- **Who is your audience?** Your audience is made up of the people for whom your message is intended. The more you know about them, the more likely you are to accomplish your purpose. The audience for most of your writing in a college English class is your instructor, who represents what is called a "general audience"—people with an average amount of knowledge on most subjects. A general audience is a good group to aim for in all your writing unless you are given other directions. Here's how Samantha assesses her audience:

> *Audience:* readers who have a general knowledge of Facebook

Writing a Tentative Thesis Statement

By now you have a subject, purpose, and audience. You have also probably used several prewriting techniques with this subject to generate a number of thoughts that you can use in your project. At this point, you will learn how to write a **thesis statement**, which is the controlling idea for the rest of your work. It is the main point that all other details in your project will support. The decisions you have already made in this chapter will lead you to your thesis statement.

If you are writing an essay, the thesis is usually at the end of the first paragraph. Ending the introduction with your thesis lets you use the beginning of the paragraph to capture the reader's interest or give background information. For a graphic project, the thesis is implied. But it is important to have a thesis statement no matter what your proposed project is. Note that your thesis statement may change as you develop your essay or project further.

A thesis statement has two parts: a topic and your opinion about that topic.

Limited Subject	+	Your Opinion	=	Thesis Statement

Here is Samantha's thesis:

> *Through your status updates and photos, you can make yourself irresistible to your fellow Facebook-ers.*

After all this preliminary work, you are prepared to generate a draft of your essay or project.

Writing

You are now ready to write an essay or create a project based on the prewriting material you have assembled. Because you have already made several important preliminary decisions about your topic, the task of actually writing should follow naturally. At this point, you might want to think of your essay as a way of solving a problem or answering a question:

- The problem/question is posed in your writing assignment.
- The solution/answer is your essay or project.

You will now deal with the heart of the writing process: developing body paragraphs; organizing your essay; and writing the introduction, conclusion, and title. As you learned earlier in this chapter, all stages of the writing process are part of a recurring cycle that you will mold into a routine to suit your lifestyle. The more you write, the more natural this process will become for you.

Developing Body Paragraphs

The body paragraphs explain and support your thesis statement. Now that you have written your thesis statement, you need to support it with your thoughts and reasons. So the first action you need to take is to expand your list of details and ideas and group them into categories.

Samantha starts with her brainstorming list and expands it with some new ideas. She then divides her new list into two main categories:

Status updates	*Photo album*
Dos	*Essential pictures*
Don'ts	*Group pictures*
Some final advice	

All the items in her prewriting exercises fit nicely into one of these categories—although she is thinking of dividing the photo album category into two paragraphs based on the cluster she created.

Topic Sentences You now need to draft topic sentences for each of your clusters of ideas. A **topic sentence** states the controlling idea of a paragraph. The rest of a body paragraph, then, contains details that support that topic sentence. A topic sentence performs two important tasks within its paragraph: (1) it supports the essay's thesis statement, and (2) it says what the paragraph will be about. Beginning or ending a paragraph with the topic sentence gives direction to the paragraph and provides a type of road map for the reader.

Like a thesis statement, a topic sentence has two parts: a topic and a statement about that topic. The topic should be limited enough that it can be developed in a single paragraph.

Here are the topic sentences Samantha wrote for her two clusters of ideas:

Status updates:

> *Status updates are the forum for whatever you want the public to know.*

Photo album:

> *The photographic element of Facebook demands special care and artistry.*

Supporting Details Later in this text, you will learn about specific methods of developing your ideas, such as narration, dividing and classifying, defining, and arguing. But for now, we are simply going to practice generating concrete supporting details and examples that are directly related to each topic. Concrete words refer to anything you can see, hear, touch, smell, or taste, such as *cars, plants, soap, blankets, bread, cows,* and *windows.* They make writing come alive because they help the reader actually picture what the writer is talking about. Return to your list of details one more time, and add any other ideas or examples that come to your mind before you start organizing your paragraphs.

Organizing Your Ideas

To organize the ideas in your essay, you need to consider the purpose of your essay and the way each body paragraph fulfills that purpose. Then you should arrange your body paragraphs in a logical manner to achieve that purpose.

Most paragraphs and/or essays are organized in one of five ways:

1. From general to particular
2. From particular to general
3. Chronologically (by time)
4. Spatially (by physical order)
5. From one extreme to another

Let's look at these methods of organization one by one.

General to Particular The most common method of organizing an essay or paragraph is from general to particular. This method begins with a general statement and becomes more specific as it progresses, as shown in the diagram on the right.

General to Particular

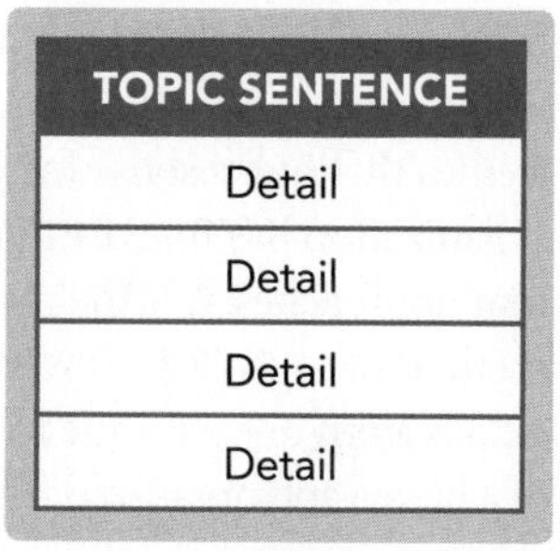

TOPIC SENTENCE
Detail
Detail
Detail
Detail

Particular to General When you reverse the first method of organization, you arrange your material from particular to general. In this case, more specific ideas start the essay or paragraph and lead up to a general statement. This type of organization is particularly effective if you suspect that your reader might not agree with the final point you intend to make. With this method, you can lead your reader to your opinion slowly and carefully, which is demonstrated in the outline here.

Particular to General

Detail
Detail
Detail
Detail
TOPIC SENTENCE

Chronological Order When you organize ideas chronologically, you are arranging them according to the passage of time—in other words, in the order in which they occurred. When you tell a story or explain how to do something, you will most often use chronological order: First this happened and then that; or first you do this, next you do that, and so on. A paragraph organized chronologically might look like this.

Chronological Order

TOPIC SENTENCE
First
Then
Next
Finally

Spatial Order Another method of arranging details is based on their relationship to each other in space. You might describe the layout of your campus from its front entrance to its back exit or the arrangement of a beautiful garden from one end to the other. Explaining a home page from top to bottom and describing a screened-in porch from inside to outside are also examples of spatial order. Beginning at one point and moving detail by detail around a specific area is the simplest way of organizing spatially, as diagrammed here.

Spatial Order

TOPIC SENTENCE
Here
There
Next
Across
Beyond

From One Extreme to Another Sometimes the best way to organize a paragraph is from one extreme to another: from most humorous to least humorous, from most difficult to least difficult, from least frustrating to most frustrating, and so on. Use whatever extremes that make sense for your topic. This method of organization has one distinct advantage over the other four approaches: It is the most flexible. When no other method of organization works, you can always arrange details from one extreme to another. Here is an outline of a paragraph organized from one extreme to another.

From One Extreme to Another

TOPIC SENTENCE
Most
Next most
Somewhat
Least

Samantha decides to organize her essay from most important to least important within two main sections. She first plans to introduce her advice on status updates. Next, she will discuss photo choices for Facebook. She now lists her details under each topic. Here is a rough outline of Samantha's plan:

> **Thesis Statement:** *Through your status updates and photos, you can make yourself irresistible to your fellow Facebook-ers.*
>
> **Topic:** *Status updates are the forum for whatever you want the public to know.*
>
> **Specific Details:**
> *be honest*
> *use some restraint*
> *don't say you are looking for someone*
> *don't say you are lonely*
> *act like you are popular and in demand*
> *complain about frustrating things*
> *share your interests*
> *praise well-known products*
> *cite quotations*
> *be mysterious*
> *skip punctuation—except exclamation points*
>
> **Topic:** *The photographic element of Facebook demands special care and artistry.*
>
> **Specific Details:**
> *party photo*
> *candid photo*
> *intriguing photo of yourself*
> *post a group picture of yourself with good-looking people of the gender you want to date*
> *pictures of people of the gender you don't want to date can be less attractive than you*
> *no pictures of you in braces, etc.*
> *add pictures of you in interesting places*

Writing the Introduction, Conclusion, and Title

The final elements of an essay are the introduction, the conclusion, and the title. You might have already written some of these parts, but you need to learn when the time is best for you to create these pieces of your essay. You could write the introduction first for one essay and at the end of your writing process for another assignment. You might know how you want to conclude from the time you begin your paper in one case, and write your conclusion just before your paper is due in another situation. For some papers, you might struggle with a title; in others, you might come up with a title when you generate your first draft. The order in which you write these three parts of an essay depends on your own personal writing process. All that matters is that your papers have a title, an introduction, several body paragraphs, and a conclusion that all work together.

Introduction The introduction of an essay is its first paragraph. It should both introduce your subject and entice your audience to read further. The introduction of an essay captures the readers' interest, gives necessary background information, and presents your thesis statement. This paragraph essentially tells readers what the essay will cover without going into detail or discussing specifics.

Writers generally use the introduction to lead up to their thesis statement. As a result, the sentences at the beginning of the introductory paragraph need to grab and hold your readers' attention. Listed here are some effective ways of starting an essay:

- Furnish a vivid description;
- Tell a brief story;
- Give a revealing fact, statistic, or definition;
- Make an interesting comparison;
- Present a dramatic example;
- Use an exciting quotation.

Samantha wrote a first draft of her introduction right after she organized all her details. She knew she would have to revise it later, but at least she got some ideas down on paper. Here is the first draft of her introduction:

> *There is no greater asset to the pursuit of blissful friendships and happily-ever-after relationships than a flawless Facebook profile. Your use of the world's greatest social networking site projects you into an intricate and wildly exciting society of potential pals and partners. Since you will be dedicating several hours a day to checking, browsing, and updating this site, you should make it work for you! You can make yourself irresistible to your fellow Facebook-ers through your status updates and photos. Just be yourself—but not too much.*

Conclusion The concluding paragraph is the final part of an essay. It brings your paper to a close. Readers should feel that all the loose ends are tied up and the point of the essay is perfectly clear. As with introductions, many different techniques can help you write a good conclusion:

- Summarize the main ideas;
- Highlight the most important issue;
- Ask a question;
- Predict the future;
- Offer a solution to a problem;
- Call readers to action.

In some cases, you might want to use several of these strategies in the concluding paragraph.

You should avoid two common problems in writing a conclusion. First, do not begin your conclusion with the words "in conclusion," "in summary," or "as you can see." Your conclusion should show—not tell—that you are at the end of your essay. Second, do not introduce a new idea. The main ideas of your essay should be in your body paragraphs. The conclusion is where you finish your essay, leaving your readers with a sense of closure or completeness.

Here is a rough outline of what Samantha wants to include in her conclusion. She is satisfied to have some basic ideas down and does not feel ready to write it yet.

> *Finding future friends and partners*
>
> *Getting invitations on Facebook*
>
> *RSVPs*

Title A title is a phrase, usually no more than a few words, that gives a hint about the subject, purpose, or focus of what is to follow. For example, the title of this book, *Nexus: A Rhetorical Reader for Writers*, suggests the way readers and writers need to come together to make meaning. In other words, that title expresses in capsule form this textbook's purpose, which is to help students become better writers by making connections between reading and writing through rhetorical modes. The title of this chapter, however, is a straightforward label of its contents: "Writing for Understanding."

Besides suggesting an essay's purpose, a good title catches an audience's attention or "hooks" readers so they want to read more. Look at some of the essay titles in this book. For example, "Sex, Lies, and Conversation" is intriguing to almost anyone. "America's Food Crisis and How to Fix It" attracts readers' attention because they will probably want to find out about this problem. "No Wonder They Call Me a Bitch" is a title that will naturally draw in most readers. "A Peek into the Future" will give rise to a lot of questions.

Do not underline or use quotation marks around your own titles. Do not put a period at the end of your title, and be sure to capitalize your titles correctly:

- The first word and last word in a title are always capitalized.
- Capitalize all other words except articles (*a, an, the*) and short prepositions (such as *in, by, on,* or *from*).

Samantha has several options for the title of her essay. At this point, she has simply recorded them on a sheet of paper:

> *How to Win Friends and Influence Facebook*
>
> *Facing Up to Your Past*
>
> *Reinventing Yourself on Facebook*
>
> *Your New Cyber Self*

SAMPLE STUDENT FIRST DRAFT

Samantha's first draft is taking shape. This is what she has so far. The essay is annotated to remind you how it developed through this chapter.

Your New Cyber Self:

How to Win Friends and Influence Facebook

INTRODUCTION

Background information

Humor

Thesis statement

1 There is no greater asset to the pursuit of blissful friendships and happily-ever-after relationships than a flawless Facebook profile. Your use of the world's greatest social networking site projects you into an intricate and wildly exciting society of potential pals and partners. Since you will be dedicating several hours a day to checking, browsing, and updating this site, you should make it work for you! Just be yourself—but not too much. You can make yourself irresistible to your fellow Facebook-ers through your status updates and photos.

BODY PARAGRAPH

Topic sentence

Details arranged from most important to least important

2 Status updates are the forum for whatever you want the public to know. Exercise your verbal freedom. With a minimum of reasonable restraints. One such restraint is not to post that you are desperately seeking that special someone. Do not post that you are desperately seeking anyone, do not even post that you are lonely. As far as the Facebook community is concerned, you are continually sought after for romantic escapades, and your social calendar is crammed. By projecting the idea that you are consistently in demand, you are well on your way to becoming so. Honest emotions like loneliness have no place in Facebook updates. Use them instead to complain about amusingly frustrating things. The category "amusingly frustrating things" does not, however, include skin abnormalities, digestive dilemmas, or other embarrassing illnesses. Keep up your end of the doctor-patient code of confidentiality, for everyone's sake. Use that glorious little box to share your interests with the

world, as long as those interests do not include anything like *World of Warcraft*, spending time with your family, or, most horrifying of all, reading anything outside of what's required for class. Praise widely relatable commodities like Starbucks, Disneyland, and Lady Gaga, which are sure to garner comments of agreement. Alternatively, use status updates to share ever-welcome quotes from the movie *Anchorman*. If you must speak seriously in your update, be sure to leave out crucial details, creating a mystique that will prompt inquiries into your well-being. Another vital truth to remember is that, in status updates, punctuation (apart from the exclamation point!) is shockingly pretentious.

3   The photographic element of Facebook demands special care and artistry. If you don't know where to begin, arrange a photo shoot with a few experienced party-goers and set up a scene featuring you having the time of your life. One or two pictures capturing moments of abandon are crucial to healthy life on Facebook. Another essential is at least one photo of you in a socially sanctioned state of intrigue. Snap a picture of yourself in pajamas, on Halloween, or at the beach. You wouldn't want your potential new friends to think you spend your entire life in shirts buttoned up to the chin, now would you? Also, be sure to include a "candid" photo—in reality, a painstakingly orchestrated and edited shot of you looking moodily into the distance. When choosing group pictures, employ caution. Post pictures of yourself with people of the gender you desire to date who are slightly more attractive then you are. People of the gender you do not seek for amorphous opportunities should only appear alongside you if they are markedly less attractive. Invite the comparison. If your friends don't fill the bill, find new ones. In addition, avoid posting pictures of your less aesthetically pleasing past (braces, pimples, and diapers leap to mind). As a further precaution, do not befriend any member of your family or family friends who may have access to the knowledge that you were ever awkward or not in total command of your bodily functions. Beyond these guidelines, fill several albums

BODY PARAGRAPH
Topic sentence

Details arranged from most important to least important

with photos of yourself grinning fetchingly with random strangers in locations of interest. I have one last note: no matter how important they are to you, resist the urge to replace your profile picture with one of a pet or Pokémon character.

CONCLUSION

Summary ⟶

Some final advice ⟶

4 Following these few guidelines will allow Facebook to help you find your future best friends and flames. Expect your text message and email inboxes to promptly overflow with invitations. Smile, enjoy, and RSVP; you've earned them by sharing your true, fairly honest, dazzling self with the online world!

Rewriting

The final stage of the writing process has two parts: revising and editing.

Revising

Revising actually starts as you are writing a draft when you change words, recast sentences, and move whole paragraphs from one place to another. Making these linguistic and organizational choices means you are constantly adjusting your content to your purpose and your audience. Revising is literally the act of "reseeing" your essay, looking at it through your readers' eyes to determine whether or not it achieves its purpose. As you revise, you should consider matters of both content and form:

Revising Checklist

- Does my thesis statement contain my subject and my opinion about that subject?
- Do my body paragraphs support my thesis statement?
- Does each body paragraph have a focused topic sentence?
- Do the details in the body paragraphs support their topic sentence?
- Is the essay organized logically?
- Is each paragraph organized logically?
- Does my introduction capture the readers' attention and build up to my thesis?
- Does the conclusion bring my essay to an interesting close?
- Is my title inviting and/or informative?

As Samantha uses this checklist to review her draft, she discovers a couple of problems. First, she decides that the idea of "amusingly frustrating things" in paragraph 2 needs some additional details to make its point. It seems slightly undeveloped compared to the other ideas in that paragraph. So she adds an explanation (in **bold**):

> Honest emotions like loneliness have no place in Facebook updates. Use them instead to complain about <u>amusingly</u> <u>frustrating things</u> **like obnoxious commercials, snooping mothers, and empty bottles of Coffemate left in the fridge.** The category "amusingly frustrating things" does not, however, include skin abnormalities, digestive dilemmas, or other embarrassing illnesses.

Second, she feels that one of the details in paragraph 3 is out of place: The sentence about making sure you don't post pictures of your less aesthetically pleasing past or befriend people with secrets about you is not about group pictures, but about individual pictures, which is the topic of the first part of the paragraph. So she moves it earlier in paragraph 3. (Changes are in **bold** below.)

> 3 The photographic element of Facebook demands special care and artistry. If you don't know where to begin, arrange a photo shoot with a few experienced party-goers and set up a scene featuring you having the time of your life. One or two pictures capturing moments of abandon are crucial to healthy life on Facebook. Another essential is at least one photo of you in a socially sanctioned state of intrigue. Snap a picture of yourself in pajamas, on Halloween, or at the beach. You wouldn't want your potential new friends to think you spend your entire life in shirts buttoned up to the chin now would you? Also, be sure to include a "candid" photo—in reality, a painstakingly orchestrated and edited shot of you looking moodily into the distance. **In addition, avoid posting pictures of your less aesthetically pleasing past (braces, pimples, and diapers leap to mind). As a further precaution, do not befriend any member of your family or family friends who may have access to the knowledge that you were ever awkward or not in total command of your bodily functions.** When choosing group pictures, employ caution. Post pictures of yourself with people of the gender you desire to date who are slightly more attractive then you are. People of the gender you do not seek for amorphous opportunities should only appear alongside you if they are markedly

less attractive. Invite the comparison. If your friends don't fill the bill, find new ones. ~~In addition, avoid posting pictures of your less aesthetically pleasing past (braces, pimples, and diapers leap to mind). As a further precaution, do not befriend any member of your family or family friends who may have access to the knowledge that you were ever awkward or not in command of your bodily functions.~~ Beyond these guidelines, fill several albums with photos of yourself grinning fetchingly with random strangers in locations of interest. I have one last note: no matter how important they are to you, resist the urge to replace your profile picture with one of a pet or Pokémon character.

Editing

Editing entails correcting mistakes in your writing so that your final draft conforms to the conventions of standard written English. Correct punctuation, spelling, and mechanics will help make your points and will encourage your readers to move smoothly through your essay from topic to topic. At this stage, you should be concerned about such matters as whether your sentences are complete, whether your punctuation is correct and effective, whether you have followed conventional rules for using mechanics, and whether the words in your essay are accurate and spelled correctly. The general checklist below, based on the twenty most common errors in freshman composition, will guide you through this phase.

Editing Checklist

1. Do all my subjects and verbs agree?
2. Have I avoided fragments?
3. Have I avoided fused sentences and comma splices?
4. Are my pronouns in the correct case?
5. Do all pronouns agree with their antecedents?
6. Are verb tenses consistent?
7. Are modifiers as close as possible to the words they modify?
8. Are all words correct?
9. Do I use apostrophes correctly?
10. Do I use commas correctly?

When applying this checklist to her essay, Samantha found a fragment (2 above), a comma splice (3 above), and two words that are incorrect (8 above). She corrected all four errors in her final draft:

Fragment:	Exercise your verbal freedom. **With a minimum of reasonable restraints.** (para. 2)
Correction:	Exercise your verbal freedom **with a minimum of reasonable restraints.**

Comma Splice:	Do not post that you are desperately seeking **anyone, do** not even post that you are lonely. (para. 2)
Correction:	Do not post that you are desperately seeking **anyone. Do** not even post that you are lonely.

Wrong Word:	Post pictures of yourself with people of the gender you desire to date who are slightly more attractive **then** you are. (para. 3)
Correction:	Post pictures of yourself with people of the gender you desire to date who are slightly more attractive **than** you are.

Wrong Word:	People of the gender you do not seek for **amorphous** opportunities should only appear alongside you if they are markedly less attractive. (para. 3)
Correction:	People of the gender you do not seek for **amorous** opportunities should only appear alongside you if they are markedly less attractive.

Finally, you should proofread your essay slowly and carefully to make sure you have not allowed any errors to slip into your final draft. In general, good writers try to let some time elapse between writing the final draft and proofreading it (at least a few hours or perhaps even a day or so). Otherwise, they find themselves proofreading their thoughts rather than their words. Some writers even profit from proofreading their papers backward—a technique that allows them to focus on individual words and phrases rather than on entire sentences.

Writing Different Forms of Media

Although verbal and visual projects have a great deal in common, as we have seen, you need to approach these two forms of media in slightly different ways. For the most part, the entire writing process can be applied to both types of media. In both cases, you need to go through a "prewriting" ritual, including exploring a subject, generating ideas, settling on a topic, establishing a purpose, analyzing your audience, and drafting a thesis statement. In a traditional essay, the thesis, or controlling idea, should be stated clearly and succinctly. But in a graphic project, the thesis is usually implied. Most media projects have a thesis, but it is embedded indirectly in the project itself.

Most of the differences between these two forms of expression occur at the writing stage. Whereas ideas are developed and organized following a particular format that meets the readers' expectations for an essay, graphic forms of media do not follow such a clear outline for presentation. But in all cases, applying the Reading

Essentials to the writing process will guide you to a focused, clear project that effectively communicates its purpose to its audience. Let's apply the Reading Essentials to Samantha's essay:

Reading Essentials: Samantha's Essay

Subject: your Facebook persona

Medium: verbal

Genre: essay

Purpose: to offer advice for setting up a Facebook page

Audience: peers

Context: our current time of increased emphasis on social networking

Rhetorical Strategies: clear purpose stated, two specific topics (status updates and photos), humorous and serious examples to support topics, thorough understanding of audience communicated through examples, logical organization

Unique features: clever title, well-timed humor mixed with useful information

Point of View/Perspective: a Facebook user, serious and humorous at the same time

Effect: entertaining and informative

Going through this "checklist" with an essay allows you to see whether your details support your thesis and whether your unique features complement your purpose. Doing this exercise will actually help you make sure all elements of your essay are aligned effectively.

When you apply these guidelines to your writing, you are actually treating it as a piece of reading and checking it before others read it. As you observed in Chapter 2, these same guidelines can be applied to a form of visual media, providing a way to double check any graphic project you have created.

Working with Sources

4

As you approach your research assignments in college, an important first step is knowing how to find sources, evaluate them, and then cite them properly in your papers. Through the library and the Internet, you can access an enormous number of sources that will help you generate paper topics, gather information, challenge your thinking, support or refute your opinions, and even make you laugh. This chapter will outline all the resources you have available to you when you need to work with sources.

Finding Sources

In today's academic world, learning how to find, assess, and use sources is a basic survival skill.

Library Sources

While working on a project with sources, you should use your library as a starting point for all your research. Through your library, you can locate books, journals, and online databases that will help you find the sources you need to complete any documented paper you are assigned.

Books   You can search for authors and subjects through your library's online catalog, listed on your library's home page, in much the same way you would search online databases or Web search engines. To locate a particular book, check your library's catalog to see if your library has the book. Find the "title" section of the catalog, and type in the title of the book or journal you need.

If you are searching for a chapter or an essay contained in a book, you should start by typing in the main book title. For example, to find the essay "The Evolution of Facebook" by David Kirkpatrick, you must type in the first three or four words of the title of the book it came from, *The Facebook Effect,* which will give you searchable titles of chapters and essays in the book. Once you have located the titles of your books in the library's catalog, you should write down the call numbers so you can find the sources in your library. Then it's just a matter of locating the book itself in the stacks. If you need help, don't hesitate to ask a librarian.

You might also use Google Books in conjunction with your college library catalog. To access Google Books, click on "more" on the Google browser and then click "Books." In many cases, you can determine the relevance of a book by searching the data provided by Google Books. In addition, Google Books will often link you to your library's catalog so you can find the book in your library.

Journals   Your library's home page is also the place to begin a search for journals and journal articles. **Journals** are scholarly publications that contain a collection of articles written by experts in a particular field to be read by others studying the same subject area. Journals are usually published by academic presses and endorsed by professional organizations. The articles in journals usually present original research and cite their sources carefully. Magazines, on the other hand, contain popular articles written by journalists and professional writers for the general public. They are published by commercial presses and rarely credit their sources. As you might suspect, most professional journals are acceptable sources for college research projects, whereas magazines generally are not.

Instructors usually expect students to use scholarly sources that have been proven reliable through rigorous screening and peer review. For example, scholarly articles are considered credible, while articles in popular periodicals, which are not screened or reviewed by professionals in the field, can be biased and/or contain inaccurate data. As a result, they are less reliable. Here is a summary of the differences between scholarly and nonscholarly sources.

Differences Between Scholarly and Nonscholarly Periodicals

SCHOLARLY	NONSCHOLARLY
Journals	Magazines
Academic articles	Popular articles
Written by experts in the field	Written by journalists/professional writers
Usually published by academic presses	Usually published by commercial presses
Credit their sources	Rarely credit their sources
Endorsed by professional organizations	Written for the general public
Professionally or peer reviewed	Not reviewed
Reliable	May be biased

When you are looking for particular journals or journal articles, access the list of Research Databases on your library's home page. From there, you can choose from a variety of online databases.

Online Research Databases The main route to journal articles for your academic papers in all disciplines is through online databases. The search engines for these databases retrieve content that is not available through more common, "surface" Web search engines, such as Google or Yahoo. You should have access to these research databases through your library's home page.

When you work with online databases, begin with a multi-disciplinary database such as EBSCOhost's *Academic Search Elite* or WilsonWeb's *OmniFile Full Text Mega*. Nearly all college libraries have at least one multi-disciplinary database. For specialized databases, check your library's Web site, which categorizes databases by both subjects and titles.

To find specific sources, type your topic into the search function of a database, limit it to the title, abstract, author, or subject field, and click "peer reviewed." The database will then display a number of books and periodical articles in a "results list." You should know, however, that popular articles might be included in "the peer-review only" results because these databases have a very loose definition of what the word "scholarly" entails. Thus, you will have to use your critical thinking skills to determine the level of scholarship of an article.

Other Electronic Sources Other electronic sources include Web sites, online magazines, e-books, software programs, newsletters, discussion groups, bulletin boards, gopher sites, podcasts, YouTube videos, blogs, newspaper articles, and email. But not all electronic sources are equally accurate and reliable. Based on your topic and purpose, you need to exercise your best judgment.

To find an electronic source related to your topic, you should go to a "surface" Web search engine of your choice. Both Yahoo and Google are examples of search engines that can save you a lot of time. For example, Google can search nearly 1.5 million sources in only a few seconds. Once you access a search engine, type in your topic as if you were searching a database. Many search engines will help you narrow your search and will provide a list of other possible topics. Most search engines have an "advanced search" option where you can specify lots of information, including domains (i.e., .com, .edu, .gov, etc.).

When the search is complete, your search engine will list the different Web sites in the order it thinks they will be most helpful to you. It will also briefly describe each Web site. After the description, you will usually find the **Uniform Resource Locator** (URL), i.e., the Web site address.

Following are notes based on three "hits" or Web sites from Google for the topic *Facebook*. Our student writer used the advanced search option to get these results and made the following note cards.

The Benefits of Facebook "Friends": Social Capital and College Students' Use of Online Social Network Sites by Nicole B. Ellison, Charles Steinfield, Cliff Lampe

The correlation between Facebook and social capital, or the ability to stay socially connected, is studied here, with the results determining that Facebook might add self-worth and self-esteem to users who were previously unsatisfied with their lives.

http://jcmc.indiana.edu/vol12/issue4/ellison.html

All Facebook: The Unofficial Facebook Resource

All Facebook gives people news and advice pertaining to their Facebook accounts. It covers everything from privacy issues to suggestions for making more friends online.

http://www.allfacebook.com/

Evaluating Sources

If you want to be certain the information you are using will be acceptable to your instructor, you should rely mainly on academic sources, which we defined at the beginning of this chapter. Found mainly through online databases, these are different from other Web sources because they have been refereed or **peer reviewed**. This means that after an author sends his or her essay to a specific publication, the editors of the publication forward the essay anonymously to readers for review. If the essays are published, they are considered valuable contributions to the field. Please note, however, that you still need to evaluate peer-reviewed sources to make sure their arguments are sound.

If you do use sources from the Web, you need to make sure you are not using biased or unreliable information, since anyone can post material on the Internet. The following guidelines will help you use Web sites intelligently.

Guidelines for Evaluating Web Sites

1. **Check the URL to determine the domain.** The endings *.com, .edu, .gov,* and *.org* are some of the most common top-level domains or categories of Web sites. The last three are generally reputable resources: *.edu* stands for "education," *.gov* for "government," and *.org* for "nonprofit organization." But you must be very careful of *.com* (which stands for "commercial") sources because anyone can purchase a *.com* site. For example, www.whitehouse.com is not a site for the President's home, as you might suspect. Instead it is a commercial financial aid site. (The White House Web site is www.whitehouse.gov.) No matter what the ending of the URL is, however, you should consider all the material on the site carefully because all Web-based material has the potential for bias.

2. **Make sure the site is providing fact and not opinion.** For academic purposes, facts and statistics are generally more useful than opinions. If you are looking for information on social networking, you don't want a site that offers lots of opinions about the subject, but no evidence to support them. Instead, you'll want to find a site that gives you examples that can be verified and supported with statistics.

3. **Pay attention to the argument a site makes.** Check to confirm that the site focuses on the subject it advertises. If you log onto a Martin Luther King, Jr. site and are inundated with racial slurs, chances are you are on a racist site. If the information does not fit the site or if the author has an obvious agenda, avoid the site altogether.

4. **Check that the site provides information about the other sides of the argument.** The best sites examine other perspectives on an argument so they can, in turn, show why one side is more valid than the others. The more opinions you can gather from a site, the more knowledgeable you will be as you form your own opinions.

These four guidelines will help you evaluate information you find on the Web.

Using Sources in Your Writing

This section will take you through the process of using sources in your academic papers. After introducing different types of sources, we will discuss how to avoid plagiarism; how to quote, paraphrase, and summarize; and how to introduce your sources.

Types of Sources

A documented paper may blend three types of material: common knowledge; someone else's data, observations, and thoughts; and your own observations and thoughts.

1. **Common knowledge.** If you are referring to such information as historical events, dates of presidents' terms, and other well-known facts, such as the effects of ultraviolet rays or smoking, you do not have to cite a source— even if you have to look the facts up. This material is called *common knowledge* because it can be found in a number of different places. For example, Samantha used this information freely because she was not borrowing anyone's original words or ideas:

    > *Students at Harvard University created Facebook in 2004. Membership was extended to students at other Ivy League universities before finally becoming open to the public in 2006. Since then, it has expanded to over 500 million users worldwide.*

2. **Someone else's data, thoughts, and observations.** If, however, you want to use someone's original research, words, or unique ideas, you must give that person credit by revealing where you found this information. This process is called *citing* or *documenting* your sources, and it involves noting in your paper where you found the information or idea. Since documented essays are usually constructed with sources that support your position, citations are an essential ingredient in any project of this type. Here is a source that Samantha quoted and cited in her paper.

    > *When speaking about Facebook, Mark Zuckerberg, one of Facebook's co-founders and CEO, is quoted as saying, "People are learning how to use the site and what's okay to share. As time goes on, people will learn what's appropriate, what's safe for them—and learn to share accordingly" (qtd. in ThinkExist.com).*

3. **Your own thoughts and observations.** These are conclusions that you draw from the sources you are reading. Our student writer, Samantha, makes the following claim based on her research and personal observations:

    > *Facebook has truly revolutionized the communication potential of this generation. Along with multitasking, the capabilities of Facebook accurately represent this group's qualities.*

Of these three types of information, you must document or cite your source only for the second type (someone else's data, thoughts, and observations). The full source would be listed at the end of the paper. Neglecting to cite your sources, whether purposeful or accidental, is a serious offense called *plagiarism*.

Avoiding Plagiarism

Plagiarism is using someone else's words or ideas as if they were your own. It comes from the Latin word *plagiarius*, meaning "kidnapper." It is a dishonest act and a serious offense in college and beyond. In student papers, plagiarism usually takes one of three forms:

1. Using the exact words from a source without quotation marks;
2. Using someone else's ideas in the form of a summary or paraphrase without citing the source;
3. Using someone else's essay as your own.

When you work with outside sources, you must give credit to the original authors of the words and ideas. That is, if you quote, paraphrase, or summarize from another source, you must provide your reader with information about that source, such as the author's name, the title of the book or article, and the details about when it was published. Whenever you use other people's words or ideas without giving them credit, you are plagiarizing.

If you are in college when you steal material from others, you can be dismissed from school. If you commit the same offense in the professional world, you can get fired and/or end up in court. So make certain you understand plagiarism as you move through this chapter. An essential first step is reading your college's policy on plagiarism, which can be found in the college catalog—online or in hard copy.

Using Direct Quotations, Paraphrases, and Summaries

As you take notes on your sources in preparation for writing your research paper, they will probably fall into one of four categories:

- **Direct quotation**—the exact words from a source;
- **Paraphrase**—a restatement in your own words of the ideas in the source;
- **Summary**—a condensed statement of your source;
- A combination of these forms.

Be sure to make a distinction in your notes between actual quotes, paraphrases, and summaries. Also, record the sources (including page and/or paragraph numbers) of all your notes so you can cite them in your essay.

To help you learn how to manage sources, this section provides a quotation and then demonstrates how to use and cite this material in different ways. The following excerpt is from "Facing Up to Facebook" by David M. Eberhardt. It was published in the journal *About Campus* in September 2007.

Original Source

> As these early connections develop, individuals can view their *friends'* or *group* pages and may discover that their peers are also stressed by the amount of reading they are suddenly confronting, frustrated by limited student parking, excited about their first weekend on campus, or feeling many other emotions common to new undergraduates. Students use statements on their *profiles* as an outlet to express their feelings, and they also express themselves through *groups* they create and join. From comments on *friends' walls,* they can also identify peers who experience similar emotions. For many students, such virtual experiences of identification and connection can be powerful steps toward feeling an early sense of belonging in their new campus community.
>
> (Eberhardt 20)

Direct Quotation If you use the exact words from a source, you must put the words in quotation marks and identify the source:

> David M. Eberhardt, in his article "Facing up to Facebook," writes about the positive effect Facebook can have on new college students' experiences: "As these early connections develop, individuals can view their friends' or group pages and may discover that their peers are also stressed by the amount of reading they are suddenly confronting, frustrated by limited student parking, excited about their first weekend on campus, or feeling many other emotions common to new undergraduates" (20).

Direct Quotation with Some Words Omitted If you want to omit a portion of a quotation, use three dots (with a space before and after each dot). This is called an *ellipsis.* Also, place brackets around any words that you add to the quotation, as in the example below.

> David M. Eberhardt, in his article "Facing up to Facebook," observes, "Students use statements on their profiles . . . [to] express themselves through groups they create and join" (20).

Paraphrase A **paraphrase** is a restatement of the main ideas of a quotation in your own words. *Paraphrase* literally means "similar phrasing," so it is usually about the same length as the original. Paraphrasing is a difficult task because you have to represent the original ideas without using the original phrasing. To force you to write the paraphrase in your own words, you might read the material, put it aside, and write a sentence or two from memory. Then compare what you wrote with the original to ensure that they are similar but not exactly the same. Taking a unique word or phrase from the original would make you guilty of plagiarism.

Even though a paraphrase is in your own words, you still need to let your readers know where you found it because it is based on someone else's ideas. A paraphrase of our original source might look like this:

> David M. Eberhardt, in his article "Facing up to Facebook," promotes the idea that college freshmen can benefit from being active in social networking Web sites. He uses examples of students sharing common fears and excitements via Facebook, defending the idea that social networking sites create stronger campus identities and promote bonding between students (20).

Summary Unlike a paraphrase, a summary is much shorter than the original. To summarize, briefly state the author's main idea in your own words. As with a paraphrase, you still need to furnish the details of your original source. Here is a summary of the Eberhardt excerpt:

> In his article "Facing up to Facebook," David M. Eberhardt asserts that Facebook can help transition students into their first years of college life (20).

Introducing Your Sources

Once you choose the sources that will most effectively help develop your thesis, you then need to learn how to seamlessly integrate them into your paper. In other words, you must introduce them before including their words or ideas by stating their names and their title or expertise. For your readers to accept the ideas contained in your sources, they need to know why you chose these people for your study. You must also show your readers that you are using evidence based on fact.

The following guidelines will help you introduce a source for the first time:

- Include the full name(s) of the author(s);
- Give the title of the source (use quotes for works inside larger works and italics for books, films, and Web site names);
- Quote or paraphrase the information you need to help build your argument.

Here are some examples of smooth, effective introductions based on Terry Judd's article entitled "Facebook Versus Email."

> Terry Judd, in "Facebook Versus Email," explains that because social networking Web sites have become so popular recently, colleges should consider using them to communicate with students (103).

> One development, asserts Terry Judd in "Facebook Versus Email," is that social networking Web sites have recently risen in popularity and colleges should consider using them to communicate with students (103).

> According to Terry Judd in "Facebook Versus Email," colleges should consider using newly popular social networking Web sites to communicate with students (103).

These model sentences offer only a few options for introducing Judd's ideas; you can probably think of many more. The main words in titles are capitalized, and commas and end punctuation—when used with quotations—go inside the quotation marks. In addition, the verbs in these examples are active choices that each expresses a slightly different meaning. Finally, you should refer to the author by last name only—"According to Judd"—the next time you use the source and mention the author.

Citing and Documenting Sources

When you document or cite your sources, you should know that requirements vary from discipline to discipline. So you need to ask your instructor about the particular documentation style he or she wants you to follow. Here are the three major documentation styles:

- **Modern Language Association (MLA),** used principally in English and humanities courses;
- **American Psychological Association (APA),** used primarily in social science courses; and
- **Chicago Manual of Style (CMS),** used in history and humanities classes.

Even though documentation styles vary somewhat from one field to another, the basic concept behind documentation is the same in all disciplines: You must give proper credit to other writers when you use their words and ideas in your own essays. You have two goals in any citation: (1) to acknowledge the author and (2) to help your reader locate the material. Citing your sources also shows your audience the extent of the reading you have done and your ability to synthesize and draw on sources to support your observations and conclusions.

When you use a source, you need to acknowledge it in two different ways:

1. In the paper directly after a quotation or idea (in-text citation)
2. At the end of the paper in a list (Works Cited, References, or Bibliographies)

Both kinds of citations are essential to the paper, and both follow very strict guidelines based on the documentation style you use.

In-text citations provide the author, page or paragraph numbers, and sometimes dates for each summary, paraphrase, or direct quotation in the body of your paper, while the **list of sources at the end of your paper** provides more complete publication information. These two types of documentation work together to provide your readers with the information they need to understand what material in your paper comes from a particular source and to locate the source itself if necessary. At the note-taking stage, you should make sure you have all the information on your sources you will need to acknowledge them properly in your paper. Having to track down missing details when you prepare your lists of works cited can be frustrating and time consuming.

MLA Citation Examples

Because most English courses require MLA documentation style, featured here are some sample MLA in-text citations that our student writer created, with the corresponding entries at the end of the paper. To find out more about citation requirements in other disciplines and to see additional citation examples in MLA style, consult the research section of a current handbook.

Book (Print) Include name of author(s), name of book, city of publication, publisher, year of publication, medium of publication (print).

In-Text Citation:	(Deal, Purinton, and Waetjen 66)

Works Cited:	Deal, Terrence E., Ted Purinton, and Daria Cook Waetjen. *Making Sense of Social Networks in Schools*. Thousand Oaks: Corwin, 2009. Print.

Note: If Samantha introduces Deal, Purinton, and Waetjen before using their material, she doesn't have to repeat the authors' names in the in-text citation.

Journal Article (Print) Include name of author, title of article, name of journal, volume number, year, page number, and medium of publication (print).

In-Text Citation:	(Page 435)

Works Cited:	Page, Ruth. "Re-examining Narrativity: Small Stories in Status Updates." *Text & Talk* 30.4 (2010): 423-444. Print.

Journal Article (Web) Include name of author, title of article, name of journal, volume number, year, page number (if any), name of database, medium of publication (Web), and date you accessed the material.

In-Text Citation:	(El-Ghoroury)

Works Cited:	El-Ghoroury, Nabil Hassan. "Social Networking Is Here to Stay." *gradPSYCH*. Mar. 2010. Web. 30 Sept. 2010.

General-Circulation Magazine (Print) Include name of author, title of article, name of magazine, date of publication, page numbers.

In-Text Citation:	(Lyons 22)

Works Cited:	Lyons, Daniel. "The High Price of Facebook." *Newsweek* 24 May 2010: 22. Print.

Web Site Include name of author, title of page, title of Web site, sponsoring organization, date of publication/last update, medium of publication (Web), and date you accessed the material. Only include a URL if the reader won't be able to find the source through a search engine.

In-Text Citation:	(*AllFacebook*)

Works Cited:	*AllFacebook*. Web Media Brands, n.d. Web. 15 June 2011.

Note: Samantha did not have all the required information, but created this citation from what she had. The abbreviation *n.d.* means "no date" of publication.

Television or Radio Broadcast Include the title of episode/segment, title of program/series, name of network, call letters and city of local station, broadcast date, and medium of reception.

In-Text Citation:	(Romo)

Works Cited:	Romo, Vanessa. "Stop Me Before I Facebook Again." *All Things Considered*. Natl. Public Radio. WGBH, Boston, 13 Dec. 2010. Radio.

When you have chosen your sources and determined that they are reliable, your last step is to consult a current handbook or Web site to help you acknowledge them correctly. Not even the best writers know the format for every source they use.

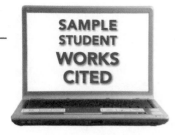

SAMPLE STUDENT WORKS CITED

Following is a partial list of sources that were cited in the examples in this chapter so you can see the formatting details we were discussing.

Edwards 4
Your last name and page number

Title centered in regular font

Works Cited

AllFacebook. Web Media Brands, n.d. Web. 15 June 2011.

Charnigo, Laurie, and Paula Barnett-Ellis. "Checking Out Facebook.com: The Impact of a Digital Trend on Academic Libraries." *Information Technology & Libraries* 26.1 (2007): 23–34. Print.

Entries alphabetical by last name

Deal, Terrence E., Ted Purinton, and Daria Cook Waetjen. *Making Sense of Social Networks in Schools*. Thousand Oaks: Corwin, 2009. Print.

One-half inch indent in all lines after the first

Eberhardt, David M. "Facing Up to Facebook." *About Campus* 12.4 (2007): 18–26. Print.

El-Ghoroury, Nabil Hassan. "Social Networking Is Here to Stay." *gradPSYCH*. Mar. 2010. JSTOR. Web. 30 Sept. 2010.

Entries double spaced

Judd, Terry. "Facebook Versus Email." *British Journal of Educational Technology* 41.5 (2010): 101–103. *Wiley InterScience*. Web. 3 Feb. 2010.

Medium of publication in each entry

Lyons, Daniel. "The High Price of Facebook." *Newsweek* 24 May 2010: 22. Print.

Page, Ruth. "Re-examining Narrativity: Small Stories in Status Updates." *Text & Talk* 30.4 (2010): 423–444. Print.

Peluchette, Joy, and Katherine Karl. "Examining Students' Intended Image on Facebook: 'What Were They Thinking?!'" *Journal of Education for Business* 85.1 (2010): 30–37. Print.

Romo, Vanessa. "Stop Me Before I Facebook Again." *All Things Considered*. Natl. Public Radio. WGBH, Boston, 13 Dec. 2010. Radio.

5 Description

Description is a major part of our daily thoughts and language. We use description in Facebook posts, job reports, and academic papers. Wanting to tell others about something we have experienced is the primary motive for description. Here are some examples:

- The faint scent of rain on a summer night;
- The sour taste of a lemon;
- The smoothness of a snake's skin;
- The beauty of the sun descending into the ocean;
- A sudden clap of thunder on a still night.

Bringing these situations to life entails choosing the exact details that will communicate a specific impression to a reader or listener. In fact, in an effective description essay, details that draw on the five senses comprise the heart of the essay and help the writer create this impression.

DEVELOPMENT STRATEGIES: DESCRIPTION
Dominant Impression
Development:
$\longrightarrow$ Sight
$\longrightarrow$ Sound
$\longrightarrow$ Smell
$\longrightarrow$ Taste
$\longrightarrow$ Touch
Conclusion

Introducing Description

Description involves capturing people, places, events, objects, and feelings in words so that a reader (or listener) can visualize and respond to them. Unlike narration, which generally presents events in a clear time sequence, description suspends its objects in time, making them exempt from the limits of chronology. Narration tells a story, while pure description contains little or no reference to action or time.

Description is one of our primary forms of self-expression; it paints a verbal picture around a dominant impression or principal effect the writer is trying to communicate. Effective description helps the reader understand or share a sensory experience through the process of *showing* rather than *telling*. *Telling* your friends, for example, that "the basketball game was filled with exciting, breath-taking moments" is not as engaging as *showing* them by saying, "The basketball game was won in the last two seconds by Monica Lopez, our rangy point guard, who hit a jumper from the top of the key over the outstretched arms of the player frantically trying to stop her." Showing your readers helps them understand your experience through as many of the five senses as possible.

Descriptions fall somewhere between two extremes:

1. Totally objective reports (with no hint of opinions or feelings), such as we might find in a dictionary or an encyclopedia, and
2. Very subjective accounts, which focus almost exclusively on personal impressions.

Objective description is principally characterized by an impartial, precise, emotionless tone, as in lab reports, marketing surveys, and medical diagnoses, in which an accurate, unbiased account is of the utmost importance. **Subjective description**, in contrast, focusing on feelings rather than on raw, objective data, is intentionally created to produce a particular sensory response in the reader or listener. Examples of subjective descriptions include a friend's opinion of your new boyfriend, a professor's analytical comments on your history paper, or a soccer coach's critique of why you lost the big game. The same golden retriever, for instance, might be described by one writer as "a water spaniel developed by Scottish hunters to retrieve birds that have been killed" (objective) and by another as "a devoted, intelligent dog who minds well and loves children" (subjective). Most descriptive writing, however, draws on both objective and subjective sources: "a friendly, intelligent breed of dog known for its skill as a retriever."

In most situations, the degree of subjectivity or objectivity in a descriptive passage depends to a large extent on the writer's purpose and intended audience. A medical patient's physician, for example, might present his or her case in a formal, scientific way to a group of medical colleagues; in a personal, sympathetic way to the person's spouse; and in financial terms to a number of potential contributors in order to solicit funds for research.

Description essays usually try to entice their readers to see a situation, event, object, or person in a specific way. As a result, writers need to provide details from as many different senses as possible. Look at the following examples:

DEVELOPMENT STRATEGIES AT WORK

Dominant Impression: a delicious dinner at my favorite restaurant

Development

⟶ **Sound/Sight:** the quiet, well-decorated dining room

⟶ **Sound/Sight:** the courteous and efficient waiter

⟶ **Smell:** the sweet, tangy aroma of their signature barbeque sauce

⟶ **Touch:** a chilled plate and fork at the salad bar

⟶ **Taste:** the delicious taste of ribs that melt in my mouth

⟶ **Touch:** the smooth texture of the vanilla bean custard dessert garnished with fresh raspberries

Conclusion

DEVELOPMENT STRATEGIES AT WORK

Dominant Impression: an enjoyable evening at a college football game

Development

⟶ **Smell:** the crisp scent of autumn in the air

⟶ **Sound:** the roar of the crowd as the team scores a touchdown

⟶ **Taste:** a stadium hot dog followed by a cold beer

⟶ **Sight:** the image of a wide receiver under a perfectly thrown pass

⟶ **Touch:** the icy feel of a metal handrail as you leave the stadium

Conclusion

Whatever your specific purpose, description is a fundamental part of almost all communication: We give and receive descriptions constantly, and our lives are continually affected by this simple yet important rhetorical technique—as a strategy on its own or a support for other rhetorical modes.

Discovering How Description Works

Following is a list of the most important elements of descriptive thinking, whether for a visual (such as a graph or a cartoon) or a prose selection. The Description Essentials listed here are equally useful as guidelines for both reading and writing.

Analyzing the graphic below will help you understand how the elements above work together to produce vivid description. If you discover on your own how this method of reasoning functions, you will be able to apply it effectively to your own reading and writing. The questions following the graphic will help you understand this rhetorical mode even more clearly than you already do.

> **Description Essentials**
>
> Dominant Impression
> Details that Show Rather than Tell
> Details that Engage the Senses
> A Consistent Point of View
> Meaningful Organization
> Logical Conclusions

1. What is this graphic's dominant impression?
2. List some details in the visual. Which are related to its dominant impression?
3. Which senses do the details engage?
4. What other visual details might support the dominant impression?
5. Are these details organized in a way that reinforces their message?
6. What conclusions can you draw from this graphic? What specific details lead you to these conclusions?

Collaborative Responses Now discuss your responses to these questions with your classmates in small groups or as an entire class. Did the diverse perspectives from other students change your "reading" of the visual? If so, in what ways?

Reading Description

As you read the cartoons, blog entries, vignettes, and essays in this chapter, pay special attention to the details the authors/illustrators use to create their impressions. In every case, the more details they provide, the more they are *showing* rather than *telling* you what they want you to know.

As you read a selection for the first time, think about how the Description Essentials work within the selection. The following questions will help you achieve this goal for both written and graphic assignments:

Description Essentials: Reading

- **Dominant Impression:** What dominant impression is the author or illustrator trying to create?
- **Details that Show Rather than Tell:** Does the author/illustrator include details that show rather than simply tell?
- **Details that Engage the Senses:** Which senses are referred to most?
- **A Consistent Point of View:** Is the writer's/illustrator's physical perspective on the subject consistent?
- **Meaningful Organization:** Does the organization of the details lead smoothly and effectively to the dominant impression?
- **Logical Conclusions:** Does the selection reach conclusions based on these details? If so, what are these conclusions?

On your second and third readings of the selection, focus on areas of ambiguity and confusion so you can deepen your comprehension.

Writing Description

Keeping the Description Essentials in mind as you move from reading to writing will help you tailor your writing to your specific purpose.

Choosing a Subject

At this point, you need to settle on a subject for your essay. Can you choose your own topic, or will your instructor assign you a subject? What are you familiar with? What interests you? If possible, choose a topic you know well or want to learn more about.

Our student writer, Suzanne Nelson, decided to describe the room where she lives. She is certainly familiar with this topic, and she knows that describing her room will make her take a hard look at her current lifestyle.

Generating Details

First, you need to generate sensory details to use in your essay. To do this, you should choose one of the prewriting options explained in Chapter 3. Record as many details concerning the writing assignment as you can think of. Then organize and analyze these details so you can write about the relationships among them.

To begin her writing process, Suzanne looks around the room and decides to draw a cluster of the details she wants to talk about in her essay.

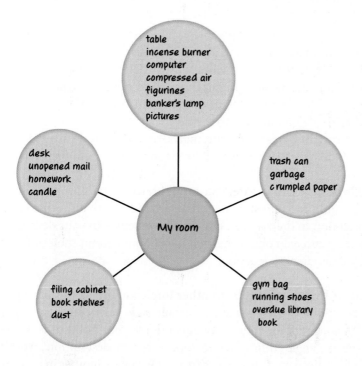

Suzanne realizes that this cluster moves naturally around her room. This method of organization would be just as useful if Suzanne were producing a visual or graphic of some kind. From this cluster, Suzanne needs to write a thesis statement that will give her project focus and direction.

Drafting a Thesis Statement

For description, your thesis statement should refer to the dominant impression you want to create. What do you want your readers to feel or think after reading your essay? The dominant impression you decide on will help you make other important choices as you write your draft. It will serve as the controlling idea for your paper and will also be the guide for choosing and organizing your examples. A thesis for a graphic or other project will not be as obvious, but will still be embedded within the project.

Suzanne's purpose is to let her readers feel like they are inside her messy room, but also to realize that she lives this way for a valid reason. Here is Suzanne's thesis:

> *My room is always more dirty than clean, and it seems to be getting worse with each passing semester.*

This statement will now give a clear purpose to Suzanne's writing.

Producing a Draft

After all this important preliminary work, developing a description essay or project should be fairly easy.

- The **introduction** presents your subject, furnishes some background, and states your dominant impression in a clear thesis.
- The **body of the paper** then provides sensory details to support your thesis statement. These details *show* rather than *tell* your readers what you want them to know. They become the primary method of organizing your essay—usually spatially from one item to the next.
- Finally, the **concluding section** summarizes the various details mentioned in the body of the paper and draws relevant conclusions from their relationships.

Selecting Details As you write, you should select details for your description with great care and precision so you leave your reader with a specific impression. Pay special attention to the way you engage all five senses in your description. You also want to make sure you omit unrelated ideas. Your careful choice of details will help control your audience's reaction.

Establishing a Point of View Another important quality of an effective descriptive essay is point of view—that is, your physical perspective on your subject. Because the organization of your essay depends on your point of view, you need to choose a specific angle from which to approach your description. Working spatially, you could move from side to side (from one wall to another in a room), from top to bottom (from ceiling to floor), or from far to near (from the farthest to the closest point in a room), or you might progress from large to small objects, from uninteresting to interesting, or from funny to serious. Whatever plan you choose should help accomplish your purpose with your particular audience.

Using Figurative Language To make your impression even more vivid, you might expand your description with figurative language, which means using words imaginatively rather than literally. The two most common forms of figurative language are *simile* and *metaphor*.

- A **simile** is a comparison between two dissimilar objects or ideas introduced by *like* or *as:* from Suzanne's essay, "My room looks as if a tornado recently ripped through it."
- A **metaphor** is an implied comparison between two dissimilar objects or ideas that is not introduced by *like* or *as:* again from our student writer, "my wasteland of a room."

Besides enlivening your writing, figurative language helps your readers understand complex or obscure objects, feelings, and ideas by comparing them to those that are more familiar.

At this point, you should use the following questions to help focus and refine your written and graphic description assignments:

Description Essentials: Writing

- **Dominant Impression:** Exactly what is your dominant impression?
- **Details that Show Rather than Tell:** What are some details from your prewriting activities that *show* rather than just *tell* about the experience you are portraying?
- **Details that Engage the Senses:** Which senses do your details refer to?
- **A Consistent Point of View:** Is your physical perspective on the subject consistent?
- **Meaningful Organization:** What order of details is most effective for the dominant impression you want to create?
- **Logical Conclusions:** What conclusions can you draw from the details you will include?

Revising and Editing

To revise and edit your essay or graphic means reviewing it to make sure it says exactly what you want it to say. Also, you should take some time to add transitions to show your readers how various items in your description are related.

Revising

Look closely at your essay or graphic as someone else might. Then answer the questions in the Revising Checklist (on page 28), which ask you focused questions about how your essay functions.

This is also the point in the writing process when you should add transitions to your essay that clarify the relationship of your details to one another. In descriptions, these are usually words and phrases that explain spatial connections. They include such words as *above, across, against, behind, below, beside, here, in, in back of, in front of, near, next to, on, over, there,* and *under.* These particular expressions will help your readers understand as clearly as possible the relationships among the items in your description.

Editing

Editing is the final phase of your writing process. It involves looking closely at your words, sentences, entire paragraphs, and any visual details to make sure they are correct. Use the Editing Checklist on page 30 to review your project for errors in grammar and usage. When you locate a potential error, consult a handbook or go to Pearson's Web-based MyCompLab for an explanation of the problem.

Also, if your instructor marks any grammar mistakes on your paper or graphic, make sure you understand them. Recognizing errors in your own writing is the most effective way of correcting them.

As you read the following student essay, "My Space" by Suzanne Nelson, refer to the Description Essentials (page 49) and the questions for reading descriptions (page 50) to help you analyze it. Then, to thoroughly understand how this student essay works, pay special attention to the margin notes and the items in each paragraph they describe.

Suzanne Nelson

Professor Flachmann

English 101

13 Sept. 2011

My Space

Subject ⟶
Background ⟶

1 From the moment I began my college career, some of my everyday responsibilities fell by the wayside. Often in a hurry to get to campus, I drop my wet towels on the bathroom floor and throw things in my room in an attempt to get dressed and review my notes before leaving for class. My friends don't even want to open the door to my room because they're afraid of the disaster they may find inside. Even I sometimes hesitate before pushing into my lair.

Thesis Statement ⟶

My room is always more dirty than clean, and it seems to be getting worse with each passing semester.

2 Walking into my room after a long day at school, I realize it's all too apparent that I haven't cleaned in a long time. I let out a small sigh as I look around, not only because my room looks as if a tornado ← Sound
recently ripped through it, but also because I can't dedicate any ← Sight
time to cleaning due to my busy schedule. My gym bag, propped up against the wall and smelling like two old sweat socks, hides a pair of ← Smell
running shoes and an overdue library book. The fine black mesh of ← Sight
the metal trashcan cannot hide the overflow of garbage spilling from its top, its base surrounded by crumpled sheets of paper and the ← Touch
metallic husks of energy bars.

3 I sit down at my desk, the main source of clutter in my wasteland ← Metaphor
of a room, and slowly shake my head at the various states of disorder it supports—unopened mail, half-finished homework, open books piled ← Sight
atop one another, and scraps of paper covered in ball-point doodles. The top shelf of the desk is rough and uneven from the hard wax drip- ← Touch
pings left by an unwatched candle long ago. An incense burner, filled with the aromatic ashes of sandalwood, needs to be dumped out and ← Smell
wiped down. I turn on my computer, which is surprisingly cleaner than the rest of the desk. This is thanks to the bottle of compressed air I use to dust the screen and keyboard whenever I can remember to do so.

4 Next to my computer are small toys and figurines in various states of chaos; they amuse me when I'm trying to work through an episode of writer's block. Looking through a day-old glass of water, ← Sight
I can barely make out the label on a yogurt container, the sweet strawberry scent it gave off days ago now battling with the earthy ← Smell
smell of mold forming at the bottom. As the late-afternoon sunlight begins to shadow the room, I reach across my desk and pull the cold ← Touch
chain on my banker's lamp. The gold and brown marbled shade casts a warm glow in the darkening room, making it much easier to see the ← Sight
text I'm trying to read. The light reflects off the glass of the numerous

Sound → picture frames on my desktop and illuminates the encouraging smiles of friends and family who continually watch me pore over books and hear me furiously type on my keyboard until late into the night.

Sight →
Smell → 5 As I swivel around in my desk chair, away from the glare of my computer, I notice the remaining piles of wreckage. The faint smell of fabric softener emanates from the pile of unfolded clothes on my unmade bed. My filing cabinet, top drawer half open like a gaping

Metaphor → mouth, waits to be fed, hungry for the paperwork that crowds my workspace. My bookshelves, one sagging under its burden and one with almost completely barren shelves, stand side-by-side next to the

Simile → desk like wooden beasts of burden patiently waiting for their loads to be evened out. Standing, I run my hand along the length of the

Touch → shelves and wince at the thick layer of grime that sticks to my finger. I obviously need to dust in here just as much as I need to vacuum. But it'll have to wait.

6 Although I realize the importance and comfort that comes from organization and cleanliness, I also understand the time con-straints faced by someone serious about his or her education. If I had

Summary → to choose between a messy room and good grades or a clean room and average grades, I know what I'd decide. With a few minutes here

Conclusion → and there I can tidy up enough to make my room livable—otherwise I can just sleep on the side of the bed with no laundry on it!

Reviewing Description

Based on the information you have learned in this chapter and the annota-tions on the student paper, show how this essay works by writing a clear, precise summary or by drawing your own outline or graphic representation of it. Label the senses on your visual. This exercise will confirm your understanding of the ele-ments of description in both reading and writing.

Raging Bulls

by Timothy Lavin

Timothy Lavin is a senior editor at *Atlantic* magazine, where he has written articles on a wide range of topics, including Barack Obama's inauguration, "the troubles" in Northern Ireland, and the U.S. government's TARP financial bailout. For the following article on running with the bulls in Pamplona, Spain, Lavin did first-hand research on the perils of this famous yearly event.

PREREADING QUESTIONS

What is your favorite tradition or celebration?

Why do you enjoy it so much?

Are there any risks connected with this ritual?

---

1   "Theese is not a joke." That's how the bartenders in Pamplona answer when you ask for tips on running with the bulls. Then they recite a litany of potential calamities—gorings, tramplings, concussions, broken ankles, beatings from an angry mob. And, of course, the big one. The bartender at a place called Txoko scribbled "1995" on a cocktail napkin, the last year someone—a young American—had died at the festival, and pointed at it. "This year, an American?" My friend and I nodded. The bartender slid his finger across his throat. "*Muerto!*"

2   Subtlety is not a salient virtue in Pamplona during the fiesta of San Fermín. For nine days each July, the city morphs into a riotous, crowd-swollen, Large Hadron Collider of a party. Bars do not close for a moment, day or night. Drums fill the night air, bands with varying dedication to their trade march to bar after bar, and troupes of dancers stagger through alleyways—everyone apparently convinced this is their last night on earth. Their famous all-white outfits seem like blank canvases on which they intend to paint a record of their drunken debauch for later reflection.

3   Entrepreneurs seem to have perfected the synthesis of selling and reveling. Like the long-haired capitalist we met on Calle San Nicolas, in the Casco Viejo neighborhood, who had set up shop with a wooden plank covered with nails. For a euro, he'd hand you a hammer. You

---

litany: series, succession
calamities: disasters
salient: strong, noticeable
debauch: indulgence

then had three chances to pound a tenpenny nail fully into the plank. This is much harder than it sounds, which I suspect is why he seemed to let everyone win, even if they completely missed. Or maybe he let everyone win because as a prize the victors got to do a shot of J&B with the proprietor, straight from his personal bottle.

4 But the fiesta is not a joke. Intimations of death animate seemingly every ritual enacted in St. Fermin's honor, religious and otherwise. The saint himself earned martyrdom—by beheading—in the second century after proselytizing too vigorously among the pagan French in Amiens. Runners rarely die during the *encierro*, the daily bull run, but on any morning they might (13 have been killed since record-keeping began). And every bull that barrels down those streets will end up dead in the ring, felled by a matador's sword during the nightly bullfights.

5 Such emotional complexity helps separate the fiesta from your average nine-day nonstop party. Edward Lewine, in *Death and the Sun*, calls it "the amazing Spanish ability to reconcile the high with the low, the grotesque with the beautiful, the morbid with the joyous, the religious with the unholy and make sense of it in a way few other cultures can."

IN CONTEXT

Pamplona, Spain

Bay of Biscay

FRANCE

Pamplona

Barcelona

PORTUGAL

MADRID

Córdoba

Cartegena

Mediterranean Sea

6 I didn't see much sense-making going on, and I suspect that enough sangria can do a lot of reconciling, but everyone in Pamplona seemed at peace with the festival's spiritual duality.

7 Once the bartender at Txoko felt sure we understood his point about the *muerto* business, he calmed down and drew an intricate map of the route that the bulls would run through the city that morning. He

If you have to do it, you have to do it

pointed out the best starting points, the corners to avoid, the tricky inclines. In two hours, we'd follow this zigzag through Pamplona's narrow, crowded streets. He offered us coffee. Finally, he shrugged and echoed nearly everyone else I had asked about the run: "If you have to do it, you have to do it."

proprietor: owner
intimations: suggestions
proselytizing: converting
vigorously: forcefully
encierro: running of the bulls
felled: cut down
intricate: complex

8   Observed from a distance, the *encierro* seems simple enough. Hemingway's description of it in *The Sun Also Rises*, which introduced most of the English-speaking world to the festival, might just as well have been about a game of marbles, if not for the sparest of nods to mortality:

> Down below the narrow street was empty. All the balconies were crowded with people. Suddenly a crowd came down the street. They were all running, packed close together. They passed along and up the street toward the bull-ring and behind them came more men running faster, and then some stragglers who were really running. Behind them was a little bare space and then the bulls galloping, tossing their heads up and down. It all went out of sight around the corner. One man fell, rolled to the gutter, and lay quiet. But the bulls went right on and did not notice him. They were all running together.

9   The morning before our run, I stood on a stone wall overlooking the final straightaway that led into the Plaza de Toros, the arena where the *encierro* concludes and the matadors later on do their dirty work. The bulls begin their death march at 8 a.m. The explosion of a ceremonial rocket announces the opening of the gates to their pen; a second report moments later indicates that all of them are loose. (A third rocket explodes when all the bulls make it to the ring, and a fourth when they're in the corral and the run is over.)

10   At about 8:03, I saw a group of wide-eyed men round the final corner, followed by six black bulls neatly escorted by some bulky, unhurried steers. After they had all entered the arena, two

IN CONTEXT

The Sun Also Rises
Ernest Hemingway's first major novel was *The Sun Also Rises*. Published in 1926, it vividly describes the running of the bulls in Pamplona from the perspective of an American tourist.

men slammed the substantial gates closed with a climactic metallic thud, in the faces of runners trying to gain last-minute entrance. Everyone clapped. Easy enough.

11   The next day, the police, without explanation, bumped us (along with perhaps a hundred other runners) off the street at our intended starting point. This meant we had to climb back in, through wooden barricades, about a hundred yards up the Calle Estafeta—closer to the bulls and farther from the relative safety of the ring.

12   As the appointed hour neared, I considered the advice the locals had dispensed the day before: Take the corners close, because the bulls will always go wide; pick a running lane and stay in it, because lane-changing leads to ugly human pileups; and, most importantly, stay down if you fall, because a bull's natural inclination is to step over things in his path—and to gore things that unexpectedly jump up in front of him. Only now did it occur to me that tips one and two would immediately enter into contradiction and that three was worthlessly counter-instinctual. Onward.

13   We walked a few blocks among the crowd. For the first time since arriving in Pamplona, I saw no one drinking. Some men bounced on the balls of their feet, soccer-style; a few stretched; many prayed, heads down, some voicing a plea famous among runners: "To San Fermin we ask, because he is our patron, to guide us through the bull run and give us his benediction. Long

IN CONTEXT

HemSpeak
Learn how to speak like a bullfighter. Go to the PBS Web site (www.pbs.org), and search "HemSpeak." Click on the Spanish words to hear pronunciations and read definitions.

---

inclination: natural desire

live San Fermin." The only laughter came from up above, on the apartment balconies that line the length of the route and fill with throngs of onlookers. I got the feeling they were all rooting against me.

14   The first rocket exploded overhead, then the next. A few seconds passed in stillness. "During the *encierro* the street feels like war," Ray Mouton writes in *Pamplona.* "The same emotions and instincts are present." Then, the crowd around me bolted almost in unison. Men were already lying on the ground beneath me when I started to run, though I don't know how. Runners in front of me looked anxiously to their rear, faces and limbs twitching like spooked deer. A persistent roar filled the narrow canyon between buildings. Then: "Toro, toro, toro, torotorotorotorotoro!"

15   In less than a minute, the bulls and steers were upon us, their clanging cowbells oddly pastoral among the urban din. They passed so closely I could have punched one in the head. We weren't being courageous; the streets are simply so narrow that a herd of bulls—1,300 pounds apiece, all muscle and horn and anger—takes up most of the available space. They rumbled by, scattering the bodies of men.

16   Eyes on the bulls, I collided with a pipe that stretched up the side of a building in front of me. I spun, cursed, regained my footing, resumed flight, and started praying. The urge to use your fellow man as a blocker is stronger than you might think. Soon, runners around us shouted that the last bull had passed. Relieved, we jogged into the arena, Deion Sanders–style, showboating for the crowd.

17   Inside, the Plaza de Toros was filled with runners high on the intoxicant of danger averted—dancing, drinking, sweaty hugging, much singing of soccer songs. I saw not one woman. The gates to the bullring stood wide open, with crowds still flowing in. This surprised me, especially considering the sudden violence with which the gates had been shut the night before. We seemed to sing with the crowd for an hour.

18   Those of us who reveled in the ring were unaware that about a minute after the first rocket launched, well before the bulls had reached us, they'd hit a sharp curve. One of them, a big black monster named Universal, had skidded into a barrier there and fallen hard. The rest of the pack had accelerated and left him behind. He'd galloped forward for a bit, slipped a few times on the slick asphalt, slammed into a few white-clad runners with his arcing horns, and then seemed to lose his bearings entirely. He spun around, looked menacingly at the crowd gathering around him, and then attacked, again and again.

> *I got the feeling they were all rooting against me*

19   A lone bull, called a *suelto,* presents the most dangerous situation in any *encierro*—bulls are by nature pack animals, and when separated they panic and lash out. About the time the

pastoral: rural
din: noise

other bulls entered the ring, Universal had started heading the wrong way back up the street, throwing bodies left and right. A group of *pastores*—professional bull handlers charged with herding stragglers—had valiantly tried to lure him back around as he charged and charged.

20   By the time they'd finally coaxed him into the ring, 13 people were on their way to the hospital—the bloodiest day of this year's festival. Two American brothers had found themselves simultaneously on the business end of Universal's horns, an apparently unprecedented feat. "Dos Hermanos," the Spanish papers called them, having great fun with it. Each went home

---

unprecedented: unmatched, exceptional

IN CONTEXT

Think You Can Handle the Running of the Bulls?

Go to Bullrunning (www.bullrunning.com/practical-guide), and click on "Can You Survive San Fermin?" Take the quiz to see if you could survive the run.

with major gore wounds. "I can't look back now and say I regret doing it," one of them later told *The Today Show*.

21   Back in the ring, none of the runners seemed aware of any of this—certainly not me. Almost five minutes had passed since the last bull had entered. But then the crowd to my right surged. A pack of men ran toward me with the spooked-deer look. Universal stomped into the center of the crowd. I hurtled over the fencing and hit the ground hard, my friend right behind me, in an act that I presume conveyed only bravery and nobility to the other onlookers.

22   The giant bull in the ring conveyed nothing but self-confidence. Snot dripped in streams from his big nostrils, and his head shook left and right on his shoulders, like a boxer before the bell rings. He twice balked as the *pastores* tried to pressure him into the corral. Both times, the crowd audibly sucked in its breath. The young men in the ring, some of them 100 feet away, flinched and scattered, and the *pastores* prodded him anew. Then he strutted into the corral, the gates clanged shut on the arena, and the final rocket burst overhead.

23   As we walked out of the plaza, three paramedics passed us, escorting a limping man. He had an orange blanket draped over his shoulders, and he held a bandage over his right eye. Blood streamed down his face. He smiled at us. *Encierro* reminds us that sometimes you can do what the hell you want. Even if it kills you.

CONVERSATIONS: Collaborating in Class or Online

1. What do revelers celebrate in Pamplona for nine days every July? What is the celebration called?

2. What details from this essay help you understand the fiesta most clearly?

3. What advice did the author get from the locals? How useful was it? Explain your answer.

4. Why does a lone bull, a *suelto*, present "the most dangerous situation in any *encierro*" (para. 19)?

CONNECTIONS: Discovering Relationships among Ideas

5. Why are the revelers focused on "intimations of death" (para. 4)?

6. What does writer Edward Lewine mean when he refers to the fiesta of San Fermin as "the amazing Spanish ability to reconcile the high with the low, the grotesque with the beautiful, the morbid with the joyous, the religious with the unholy, and make sense of it in a way few other cultures can" (para. 5)?

7. In what ways might the streets feel "like war" (para. 14), as writer Ray Mouton writes about the event?

8. How does the *encierro* remind the author that "sometimes you can do what the hell you want. Even if it kills you" (para. 23)?

PRESENTATION: Analyzing the Writer's Craft

9. Lavin starts his essay with a summary of bartenders' comments about "running with the bulls" in Pamplona. Is this an effective beginning? Explain your answer.

10. What is the author's point of view toward this subject in his essay? Is he participating in or simply observing the bull run?

11. Find at least two details that represent each of the senses (sight, sound, smell, touch, taste), and list them with their labels.

12. How are the details in this essay organized? Does this organization lead naturally to the dominant impression you think the author wants to create?

PROJECTS: Expressing Your Own Views

13. **Monologue:** Write a monologue of the thoughts the author might have had as he participated in the fiesta. Continue the monologue for the duration of the running of the bulls.

14. **Song/Poem:** Write a song or poem about an accomplishment that made you proud. Use figurative language, especially similes (comparisons of dissimilar items using "like" or "as") and metaphors (comparisons of dissimilar items not using "like" or "as") to help your readers understand your experience as fully as possible.

15. **Essay:** Describe an event that you remember fondly. Choose your details carefully to convey your dominant impression, and try to engage all five senses in your account.

16. **Research:** Read and summarize the three resources below. Generate one specific question from each resource that focuses on description. Then answer one of your questions in a documented essay, consulting these and other sources as necessary.

OTHER RESOURCES

Web Site

Bull Running—Practical Guide:
www.bullrunning.com

Audio/Video

Daily Motion—Online
Videos, Music, and Movies:
www.dailymotion.com

Search: "Nine Injured on Final Day of
Bull Running"

Click on the Video link

Academic Article

"Torophiles and Torophobes: The Politics of Bulls
and Bullfights in Contemporary Spain"

by Stanley Brandes

Anthropological Quarterly 82.3 (2009): 779–794

ONE LAST THOUGHT

People find many ways to add excitement
to their lives. Thrill-seeking activities, such
as bungee jumping or white-water rafting,
are common in the United States. Even roller
coasters offer an adrenaline rush for theme
park visitors. Have you ever participated in a
thrill-seeking activity? Do you enjoy it? Why
or why not?

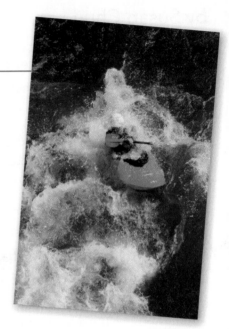

Officers Describe 9/11 in Memos

by Susan Chun

Susan Chun is the producer of Anderson Cooper's CNN cable news show titled "AC360°" and also the creator of an independent blog called "All Things CNN." She has written recent articles and blogs on the 9/11 tragedy, along with pieces on Michael Jackson's drug use, diversity in the workplace, North and South Korea, Heath Ledger's autopsy, and a number of other provocative topics.

PREREADING QUESTIONS

Write down one detail that you remember from the 9/11 national catastrophe. Then read your memories to each other in order to broaden your knowledge of the disaster.

What were you doing when you heard about the event?

How did you react to the news?

NEW YORK (CNN)—**The 2,000 pages of phone and radio transcripts from the September 11, 2001, terrorist attacks in New York City released by the Port Authority . . . include hundreds of gory and often heartbreaking typed and handwritten reports by police officers and civilian employees who survived the attacks.**

1   One police officer describes looking up at the sky and seeing the first plane head straight for the north tower of the World Trade Center.

2   "My first thought was that the aircraft was in distress," the officer wrote. "I never realized,

distress: under pressure

when I saw that plane fly over 42nd street, the disaster that was about to befall our department and our country."

3   Numerous officers wrote about the horror of seeing people jump from the upper floors.

4   "A steady stream of bodies and debris was raining down. Inspector Fields was about to run into the building, and I stopped him. A man was coming down; he hit with such force it sounded like a shotgun going off. Inspector Fields put a hand on the wall to steady himself. He said 'Oh my God,'" one police chief wrote.

He hit with such force it sounded like a shotgun going off

5   Another officer described how a group of officers ran one at a time from the sidewalk into the tower to avoid being hit by falling bodies.

6   Many of the officers escorted people out of the building minutes before the towers collapsed. One officer described hearing a noise "like a thousand freight" trains when the first tower collapsed.

7   "The air was so filled with dust that I covered my mouth and nose with my tie as I said prayers that I would be spared. After a short period of time, I emerged from underneath the truck into pitch-black darkness barely breathing. My eyes were filled with dust. I was in extreme fear for my life."

8   One officer described the gruesome sight of body parts on the ground after the collapse of the first tower.

9   The word "helpless" was used numerous times as officers described how they felt that morning. One officer described seeing injured people evacuating the tower. "I could see the panic in their eyes as they looked at me," he wrote.

10   The breakdown in communication when cell phones and radios stopped working was addressed by many officers. They described not knowing where their partners were and not being able to get through to their loved ones to tell them they were OK.

11   Despite the horrific events of that morning and the loss of 87 Port Authority police officers and employees, many expressed pride in the actions of the department that morning.

12   "We could never have foreseen this tragic event or loss of life. However, in spite of the loss and grief, we regrouped, moved forward, and kept the department running," one police sergeant wrote.

13   Nearly 3,000 people were killed that day when hijacked airplanes hit the World Trade Center in New York, the Pentagon in Virginia, and crashed into a field in Pennsylvania.

emerged: came forward

IN CONTEXT

Timeline of 9/11 Attacks (Eastern Daylight Time)

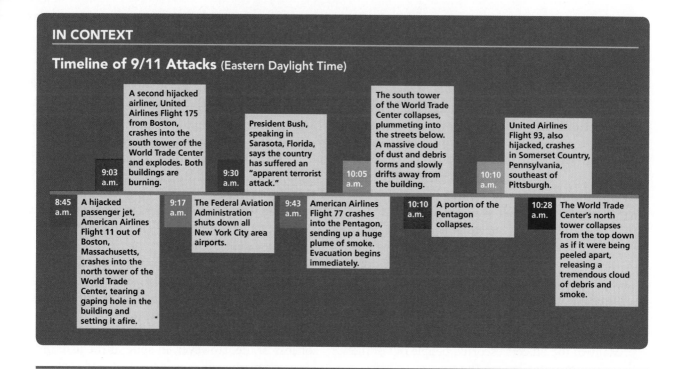

9:03 a.m. A second hijacked airliner, United Airlines Flight 175 from Boston, crashes into the south tower of the World Trade Center and explodes. Both buildings are burning.

9:30 a.m. President Bush, speaking in Sarasota, Florida, says the country has suffered an "apparent terrorist attack."

10:05 a.m. The south tower of the World Trade Center collapses, plummeting into the streets below. A massive cloud of dust and debris forms and slowly drifts away from the building.

10:10 a.m. United Airlines Flight 93, also hijacked, crashes in Somerset Country, Pennsylvania, southeast of Pittsburgh.

8:45 a.m. A hijacked passenger jet, American Airlines Flight 11 out of Boston, Massachusetts, crashes into the north tower of the World Trade Center, tearing a gaping hole in the building and setting it afire.

9:17 a.m. The Federal Aviation Administration shuts down all New York City area airports.

9:43 a.m. American Airlines Flight 77 crashes into the Pentagon, sending up a huge plume of smoke. Evacuation begins immediately.

10:10 a.m. A portion of the Pentagon collapses.

10:28 a.m. The World Trade Center's north tower collapses from the top down as if it were being peeled apart, releasing a tremendous cloud of debris and smoke.

CONVERSATIONS: Collaborating in Class or Online

1. What is the dominant impression Susan Chun is trying to create in this collection of vignettes?
2. What is the source of her notes?
3. Find a detail that covers each of the five senses in this series of recollections.
4. What details are most striking to you more than ten years after 9/11? Explain your answer.

CONNECTIONS: Discovering Relationships among Ideas

5. What themes do these accounts of the disaster cover? How accurately do these themes represent the catastrophe of 9/11?
6. What details from this news piece communicate most believably the trauma connected with this crisis?
7. What do you imagine the survivors were thinking during this crisis as they fought for their lives?
8. Are you motivated by these comments to read more on this historical event? Why or why not?

PRESENTATION: Analyzing the Writer's Craft

9. Why do you think Chun chose to feature these particular details?
10. What is Chun's point of view on this subject? Is this essay more objective or subjective in its treatment of 9/11?

11. Is this series of accounts an effective way for the author to communicate her primary message? Explain your answer.

12. How does this collection *show* rather than *tell* its audience what to think?

PROJECTS: Expressing Your Own Views

13. **Vignette:** Go to "Survivor Stories from 11 September 2001," and locate the story of one survivor. In a brief paragraph, describe that person's strategy for survival.

14. **Chat Room:** Read a strand of comments about 9/11 from 2001 along side a strand of current comments about this historic disaster. Explain how the focus of the comments has changed over the years.

15. **Essay:** Think of a "disaster" in your own life—no matter how large or small. Describe in detail how you survived this personal crisis. Use well-chosen details to create your dominant impression.

16. **Research:** Read and summarize the three resources below. Generate one specific question from each resource that focuses on description. Then answer one of your questions in a documented essay, consulting these and other sources as necessary.

OTHER RESOURCES

Web Site

The September 11 Digital Archive: http://911digitalarchive.org

Click on the Browse tab

Search the files for stories and pictures about 9/11

Academic Article

"Entertainment Wars: Television Culture after 9/11" by Lynn Spigel

American Quarterly 56.2 (2004): 235–270

Audio/Video

Free 9/11 Documentaries and Videos: www.911docs.net

Click on "9/11 Video Clips"

View at least one clip in each category

ONE LAST THOUGHT

New York Mayor Rudy Giuliani was a prominent figure in the aftermath of the 9/11 attacks. In December 2001, Giuliani was named *Time* magazine's person of the year for his ability to unify his city even in the midst of a crisis. He was quoted as saying, "New York is going to be here. And we're going to rebuild, going to be stronger than we were before. . . . I want New York to be an example to the rest of the country, and

the world, that terrorism can't stop us." What do you remember about New York's reaction to the attacks? Do you think the city could have done anything differently to help the survivors?

Longing to Die of Old Age

by Alice Walker

Alice Walker is a highly acclaimed African American author who won the Pulitzer Prize for her 1982 novel *The Color Purple*, which was later made into a movie and a Broadway musical. Like many of her other novels, such as *The Temple of My Familiar* and *Possessing the Secret of Joy*, it deals with women's struggles against a racist, sexist, and violent society.

PREREADING QUESTIONS

What is the difference between dying from a disease and dying from old age?

Which do you think would be more desirable?

What are your personal suggestions for living a long, healthy life?

1   Mrs. Mary Poole, my "4-greats" grandmother, lived the entire nineteenth century, from around 1800 to 1921, and enjoyed exceptional health. The key to good health, she taught (this woman who as an enslaved person was forced to carry two young children, on foot, from Virginia to Georgia), was never to cover up the pulse at the throat. But, with the benefit of hindsight, one must believe that for her, as

for generations of people after her, in our small farming community, diet played as large a role in her longevity and her health as loose clothing and fresh air.

2   For what did the old ones eat?

3   Well, first of all, almost nothing that came from a store. As late as my own childhood, in the fifties, at Christmas we had only raisins and perhaps bananas, oranges, and a peppermint stick, broken into many pieces, a sliver for each child; and during the year, perhaps, a half-dozen apples, nuts, and a bunch of grapes. All extravagantly expensive and considered rare. You ate *all* of the apple, sometimes, even the seeds. Everyone had a vegetable garden; a garden as large as there was energy to work it. In these gardens people raised an abundance of food: corn, tomatoes, okra, peas and beans, squash, peppers, which they ate in summer and canned for winter. There was no chemical fertilizer. No one could have afforded it, had it existed, and there was no need for it. From the cows and pigs and goats, horses, mules, and

extravagantly: excessively

fowl that people also raised, there was always ample organic manure.

4 Until I was grown, I never heard of anyone having cancer.

5 In fact, at first cancer seemed to be coming from far off. For a long time if the subject of cancer came up, you could be sure cancer itself wasn't coming any nearer than to some congested place in the North, then to Atlanta, seventy-odd miles away, then to Macon, forty miles away, then to Monticello, twenty miles away. . . . The first inhabitants of our community to die of acknowledged cancer were almost celebrities, because of this "foreign" disease. But now, twenty-odd years later, cancer has ceased to be viewed as a visitor and is feared instead as a resident. Even the children die of cancer now, which, at least in the beginning, seemed a disease of the old.

6 Most of the people I knew as farmers left the farms (they did not own the land and were unable to make a living working for the white people who did) to rent small apartments in the towns and cities. They ceased to have gardens, and when they did manage to grow a few things they used fertilizer from boxes and bottles, sometimes in improbable colors and consistencies, which they rightly suspected, but had no choice but to use. Gone were their chickens, cows, and pigs. Gone their organic manure.

7 To their credit, they questioned all that happened to them. Why must we leave the land? Why must we live in boxes with hardly enough space to breathe? (Of course, indoor plumbing seduced many a one.) Why must we buy all our food from the store? Why is the price of food so high—and so tasteless? The collard greens bought in the supermarket, they said, "tasted like water."

> *Why must we leave the land? Why must we live in boxes with hardly enough space to breathe?*

8 The United States should have closed down and examined its every intention, institution, and law on the very first day a black woman observed that the collard greens tasted like water. Or when the first person of any color observed

IN CONTEXT

Global Health

According to the World Health Organization, by the year 2020, global cancer rates are predicted to increase by 50 percent. However, they estimate that up to a third of these cancers can be prevented by healthy lifestyles, and another third are curable.

that store-bought tomatoes tasted more like unripened avocados than tomatoes.

9 The flavor of food is one of the clearest messages the Universe ever sends to human beings; and we have by now eaten poisoned warnings by the ton.

10 When I was a child growing up in middle Georgia in the forties and fifties, people still died of old age. Old age was actually a common cause of death. My parents inevitably visited dying persons over the long or short period of their decline; sometimes I went with them. Some years ago, as an adult, I accompanied my mother to visit a very old neighbor who was dying a few doors down the street, and though she was no longer living in the country, the country style lingered. People like my mother were visiting her constantly, bringing food, picking up and returning laundry, or simply stopping by to inquire how she was feeling and to chat. Her house, her linen, her skin all glowed with cleanliness. She lay propped against pillows so that by merely turning her head she could watch the postman approaching, friends and relatives arriving, and, most of

congested: crowded
improbable: unlikely

all, the small children playing beside the street, often in her yard, the sound of their play a lively music.

11   Sitting in the dimly lit, spotless room, listening to the lengthy but warm-with-shared-memories silences between my mother and Mrs. Davis was extraordinarily pleasant. Her white hair gleamed against her kissable black skin, and her bed was covered with one of the most intricately patterned quilts I'd ever seen—a companion to the dozen or more she'd stored in a closet, which, when I expressed interest, she invited me to see.

> *I thought her dying one of the most reassuring events I'd ever witnessed*

12   I thought her dying one of the most reassuring events I'd ever witnessed. She was calm; she seemed ready; her affairs were in order. She was respected and loved. In short, Mrs. Davis was having an excellent death. A week later, when she had actually died, I felt this all the more because she had left, in me, the indelible knowledge that such a death is possible. And that cancer and nuclear annihilation are truly obscene alternatives. And surely, teaching this very vividly is one of the things an excellent death is supposed to do.

13   To die miserably of self-induced sickness is an aberration we take as normal; but it is crucial that we remember and teach our children that there are other ways.

14   For myself, for all of us, I want a death like Mrs. Davis's. One in which we will ripen and ripen further, as richly as fruit and then fall slowly into the caring arms of our friends and other people we know. People who will remember the good days and the bad, the names of lovers and grandchildren, the time sorrow almost broke, the time loving friendship healed.

15   It must become a right of every person to die of old age. And if we secure this right for ourselves, we can, coincidentally, assure it for the planet. And that, as they say, will be excellence, which is, perhaps, only another name for health.

IN CONTEXT

Home Remedies

As long as sicknesses have existed, people have been using home remedies to fight them. People have used duct tape to remove warts, gin-soaked raisins to combat arthritis pain, fresh onions to reduce bruising, toothpaste to clear acne, and even cotton balls to quell hiccups. Do you use any home remedies?

indelible: lasting
annihilation: destruction
aberration: deviation, abnormality

CONVERSATIONS: Collaborating in Class or Online

1. What was Walker's great-great-great-great grandmother's secret to good health?
2. What types of food did Walker's family eat?
3. List at least one detail for each of the five senses: sight, sound, smell, taste, touch. Does Walker draw on any one sense more than the others?
4. What is Walker's dominant impression in this essay?

CONNECTIONS: Discovering Relationships among Ideas

5. According to Walker, what is the connection between eating store-bought food and staying healthy?
6. What can we learn from the flavor of our food?
7. Why was the "sound of [children's] play a lively music" (para. 10) to Walker's neighbor?
8. Why does Walker "want a death like Mrs. Davis's" (para. 14)?

PRESENTATION: Analyzing the Writer's Craft

9. Who do you think is Walker's primary audience?
10. Explain your understanding of this essay's title.
11. Why do you think Walker made paragraphs 2, 4, 9, and 13 single sentences? What purpose do they serve in this essay?
12. What is Walker's attitude toward her subject? Explain your answer, using examples from the essay.

PROJECTS: Expressing Your Own Views

13. **Ad:** Design an ad, using graphics and/or words, for organic food. Decide on a focus first; then add details that will support your dominant impression.
14. **Collage:** Create a picture collage that makes a clear statement about the relationship between health and lifestyle. Choose your pictures; then mount them in an order that makes your opinion clear.
15. **Essay:** How healthy are you? Write a description of the foods you eat and the exercise you get in a normal week. In what ways are you taking good care of yourself so that you have a chance for a long, healthy life?
16. **Research:** Read and summarize the three resources below. Generate one specific question from each resource that focuses on description. Then answer one of your questions in a documented essay, consulting these and other sources as necessary.

OTHER RESOURCES

Web Site

Organic Gardening—Living Lightly from the Ground Up: www.organicgardening.com

Academic Article

"A Cancer Risk Assessment of Inner-City Teenagers Living in New York City and Los Angeles" by Sonja N. Sax et al.

Environmental Health Perspectives 114.10 (2006): 1558–1566

Audio/Video

The Obesity Society: www.obesity.org

Search: "Hungry for Progress"

View the "Hungry for Progress—Appetite, Genes and Drugs" video

ONE LAST THOUGHT

Obesity Trends* Among U.S. Adults

(*BMI ≥30, or ~ 30 lbs. overweight for 5' 4" person)

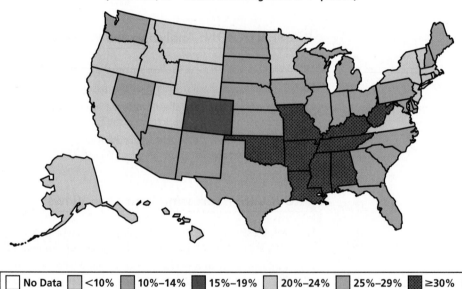

No Data | <10% | 10%–14% | 15%–19% | 20%–24% | 25%–29% | ≥30%

Obesity is one of the major health problems facing our nation today. Along with other health issues, obesity increases a person's risk of developing cardiovascular disease and diabetes. Visit Obesity Society's Web site for information about weight control. Why do you think Americans struggle with weight? How can our society change to promote healthier living?

The Ungooglable Man

by Roz Chast

A staff artist for *The New Yorker* for many years, **Roz Chast** has published over 800 of her cartoons in the magazine, most of which have chronicled what she calls "a conspiracy of inanimate objects." She has also written or illustrated over a dozen books, including *Unscientific Americans*, *Parallel Universe*, *Proof of Life on Earth*, and *The Party After You Left*.

PREREADING QUESTIONS

What do you think it means to be "ungooglable"?

Have you ever looked yourself up on the Internet? What details about your life are there?

What other types of information do you often search for on the Internet?

CONVERSATIONS: Collaborating in Class or Online

1. What is the dominant impression in this cartoon?
2. What is significant about the way this man is dressed? How does it support the impression the cartoonist is trying to convey?
3. How does the picture's background help communicate the cartoonist's message?
4. What do you make of the fact that no other people appear in this cartoon?

CONNECTIONS: Discovering Relationships among Ideas

5. What do Google and social networking Web sites have to do with personal identity in our culture today?
6. What details *show* rather than *tell* the audience important information about this type of person?
7. Based on Chast's cartoon, do you know any "ungooglable" people? Explain your answer.
8. Why is this drawing funny? Explain your answer.

PRESENTATION: Analyzing the Writer's Craft

9. What does the title of this cartoon suggest about its contents?
10. Is a cartoon the best format for the author's message? Explain your answer.
11. What specific details in this drawing reveal the cartoonist's point of view?
12. Why are some words capitalized? What pattern do they form?

PROJECTS: Expressing Your Own Views

13. **Photo Essay:** Create a photo essay about the Internet. Choose a dominant impression and select pictures or drawings that help create that impression. Then organize the pictures with the purpose of making your point.
14. **Ad:** Create an ad encouraging people to participate in some aspect of the Internet, such as Facebook, Twitter, Web courses, chat rooms, blogs, etc.
15. **Essay**: Describe your identity in relation to the Internet. Choose a dominant impression, and then use carefully chosen details to communicate that impression.
16. **Research:** Read and summarize the three resources below. Generate one specific question from each resource that focuses on description. Then answer one of your questions in a documented essay, consulting these and other sources as necessary.

OTHER RESOURCES

Web Site

Google Privacy Concerns—
Google Maps Monitoring
your Geographic Location:

www.googleprivacyconcerns.com

Academic Article

"Too Many Friends: Social Integration, Network
Cohesion and Adolescent Depressive
Symptoms" by Christina Falci and Clea
McNeely

Social Forces 87.4 (2009): 2030–2061

Audio/Video

National Public Radio: www.npr.
org

Search: "I Can't Quit You, Google"

Click on the Listen Now link

ONE LAST THOUGHT

Many people wonder what will happen to their
social networking accounts when they die. The
answer varies from site to site. Many sites do not
have policies in place in the event of a death,
while others handle them on a case-by-case
basis. Facebook gives families two choices:
They can either delete the dead user's account
or turn it into a memorial site, after providing
documentation that the user has died.

She

by Matthew Brooks Treacy

While an English major at Hampden-Sydney College in Virginia, **Matthew Brooks Treacy** wrote this essay as a class assignment in Rhetoric 101 taught by Professor Lowell Frye, who asked his students to describe a person "who should be of interest to your readers." The essay not only won a college prize for creative writing, but was also recently published in *The Norton Pocket Book of Writing by Students* (2010).

PREREADING QUESTIONS

What special qualities characterize your mother, your father, or another close family member?

Do these traits make this person strong or weak?

Which of these traits have influenced you most profoundly?

1   Mom says, "If you go a day without using your hands, you die." It's a principle that influences the way I do things. Nothing is ever futile. The most horrible chores ever devised by the devil in the days of man do not even leave me with a gutted feeling anymore, though God knows they used to. Repainting a chicken shed or lying prostrate to the sun on a steel roof is never as bad as it sounds; you've used your hands, and at least *that's* worthwhile. My mother has always shingled lessons into my mind, leaving each one slightly raised for prying up later on. There was never a day when we didn't do some meaningless household task just to pass the time. She always used her hands. On top of an adamant refusal to learn the first thing about technology, manual labor just fits her. She used her hands when She shot

futile: pointless
prostrate: face down
adamant: insistent

the groundhog who had one of her zucchinis in its mouth. She used her hands when crunching rabbits under the blunt end of a hatchet for some of the best stew in the Western hemisphere. She used her hands to hang the stockings, even when my sister and I knew better than to believe in a fat guy in a red suit. In the past I have questioned her claim of devotion to me, but there were always ethics to be spaded out of the dirt she was normally covered in, sandy values scraping the back of my neck during a rough hug before bed. Loving me is something She has always done, but with a sharp manner that hides the tenderness I sometimes cry for.

2   My Mother is not a woman so much as she is a field of energy. Mom is a force, a kind of aura that only takes human form to be that much more intimidating. An order to cut the grass is not a request but an international doctrine, and She sits at the helm of an aircraft carrier just waiting for a rebellious child to give her reason for an atomic strike. Making us cut the grass is her method of control. There lies, somewhere beneath the tile of

> **IN CONTEXT**
>
> ### Famous Quotations About Mothers
>
> "All that I am, or hope to be, I owe to my angel mother"—Abraham Lincoln
> "Let France have good Mothers, and she will have good sons."—Napoleon I
> "Men are what their mothers made them."—Ralph Waldo Emerson
> "My mother had a great deal of trouble with me, but I think she enjoyed it."—Mark Twain

our kitchen, a proverbial bag of chores just waiting to be opened, like Pandora's Box. I am in constant fear that, one day, a refusal to mow will burst that bag wide open and spill hell into my life, so I do whatever I'm told. These responsibilities have become more of a tradition than a job, so I can't mind them; God forbid I break that custom. The sun bakes me like a scone on early August days, but smiles down on the Mother weeding eggplant and the neighbors selling lemonade under an oak. She works like a madwoman in the garden and still keeps an eye on whichever unlucky child has a job outside. When all is said and done, the yard has grown to the heavens, leaving me to give it the haircut of a lifetime under the omniscient eye from amongst the bean rows. It is a task that takes a light-year, but after three hours in the field I'll gladly accept the neighbor's lemonade, no matter what's floating in it. The common image is me standing at attention and She a drill sergeant inspecting my work, looking for any surviving dandelion to give me away. I imagine She would love to find a single uncut weed to justify beating the shag out of me with the garden hose. But then, smiling a

> *My Mother is not a woman so much as she is a field of energy*

doctrine: set of guidelines
proverbial: well-known
omniscient: all-knowing

smile that would have wilted the grass anyway, She goes to get a beer and watch me finish off the front yard.

3   There are some unexplainable phenomena between the two of us. These things I've grown accustomed to but have never understood. It's all to do with her. No one else can really grasp just how weird our relationship is, because no one else has ever gone through another like it. The first clue that our mother-son bond was stronger than most was the day I came home to a chaotic scene and She immediately informed me, "Way to go baby, you let the emu out." That night I did homework in electrified silence, forcing down home-grown garden squash and awaiting her return. Finally the door screamed and I prepared for a verbal thrashing only to be greeted with a hug. Everything was forgotten. The homework lay strewn on the table and the snow fell as She unfolded a story that would eventually go down in family lore. It was not a story like the boring epics that college professors pride themselves on, but a *story*. It was like something told by five different people at Thanksgiving with sporadic interjections thrown in through mouthfuls of mashed potatoes and venison. There was a plot line, rising action, a climax, blood, and plenty of cursing. By the time she finished and I had chewed my lip raw, the escaped emu had been recaptured somehow by a turkey call and something resembling a German infantry tactic. I sat there in awe, swallowing repeatedly to wet my vocal cords back into coherence. "That's the most incredible thing I've ever heard," I managed to gasp, unable to get the image of my mom pulling a tackle on a bird from the Cretaceous period out of my mind. The amount of respect She lost for me that night was more than made up by my amazement and overwhelming love for this woman who brought down ostriches. Even being sentenced to double grass-cutting duty and cooking for a week didn't really sting that much. After all, I'd be using my hands.

4   So many times She would ruin my chances for fun. So many times I was caught when it seemed I could not be, and so many times I would be forced to dry dishes instead of climbing hay bales in the fields. Of course there will always be hay, and there will always be home. She will always be there weeping me away to college and willing me back with that same aura of power that surrounds her. Each time I will argue, but apparently dishes will never just dry themselves. And each time that I think I'm too tired to get up and turn off the dorm room TV, I will think of my mother and stumble over in the pitch black to use my hands at least one more time that day.

> ### IN CONTEXT
>
> ### The Cretaceous Period
>
> The Cretaceous period refers to a geological time between 145.5 and 65.5 million years ago.

No one else can really grasp just how weird our relationship is

emu: an American ostrich
sporadic: erratic, random

CONVERSATIONS: Collaborating in Class or Online

1. What is Treacy's dominant impression in this essay?
2. What does the author mean when he says "My mother has always shingled lessons into my mind, leaving each one slightly raised for prying up later on" (para. 1)?
3. Find at least one detail in this essay that represents each of the senses: sight, sound, smell, taste, touch.
4. Why didn't the author mind the "double grass-cutting duty and cooking for a week" (para. 3)?

CONNECTIONS: Discovering Relationships among Ideas

5. Why are hands so important to the author?
6. In what ways does manual labor suit the author's mother?
7. What does the author mean when he says, "My Mother is not a woman so much as she is a field of energy" (para. 2)?
8. Characterize Treacy's attitude toward his mother. Name five specific details that lead you to this conclusion.

PRESENTATION: Analyzing the Writer's Craft

9. Is this essay more objective or subjective? Explain your answer.
10. Why does Treacy capitalize "She" throughout the essay? How does this choice affect your thinking about the mother and her relationship to the author?
11. Treacy uses both similes (comparisons of two unlike items using "like" or "as") and metaphors (comparisons of two unlike items without using "like" or "as") in paragraph 2. Find one example of each type of figurative language, and explain how it advances his dominant impression.
12. Where does Treacy use repetition to further his point? What words does he repeat most often? What effect does this have on the reader?

PROJECTS: Expressing Your Own Views

13. **Comic Strip:** Draw a comic strip that captures some unique aspect of your family. First, consider the message you want to convey. Then choose the images that will get your point across most effectively to your readers.
14. **Vignette:** Look up your family tree or heritage, and describe a relationship represented in that tree based on either details about the people on the Internet or details from your imagination.
15. **Essay:** Write an essay about someone you respect, admire, or simply look up to. Make sure you settle on a dominant impression first and then choose the details that will convey that impression.
16. **Research:** Read and summarize the three resources below. Generate one specific question from each resource that focuses on description. Then answer one of your questions in a documented essay, consulting these and other sources as necessary.

OTHER RESOURCES

Web Site

Hands at Work: www.
handsworking.com

Academic Article

"I Like to Hoe My Own Row: A Saskatchewan
Farm Woman's Notions about Work and
Womanhood during the Great Depression"
by Cristine Georgina Bye

Frontiers: A Journal of Women Studies 26.3
(2005): 135–167

Audio/Video

National Public Radio: www.npr.
org

Search: "Farms Take Root in
Detroit's Foreclosures"

Click on the Listen Now link

ONE LAST THOUGHT

In May of 2010, CNN released a list of favorite TV moms, which includes Marge Simpson
of *The Simpsons* and Clair Huxtable of *The
Cosby Show*. Visit cnn.com, and search "The
10 Best TV Moms by Olivia Allin" to see the
breakdown. Which TV moms do you remember best? Who was your favorite and why?

Hey, Look

by Simon Rich

An American humorist who received a two-book contract from Random House prior to his graduation from Harvard University in 2007, **Simon Rich** has published *Ant Farm: And Other Desperate Situations* (2007), *Free Range Chickens* (2008), and a novel titled *Elliot Allagash* (2010). Son of the well-known *New York Times* editorialist Frank Rich, he is also a writer for the *Saturday Night Live* television show.

PREREADING QUESTIONS

Think of five events that helped form your personality during your younger years.

What has been your favorite age so far? Why does it give you the most satisfying memories?

What age are you especially looking forward to in the future? Why?

---

1 What I imagined the people around me were saying when I was …

2 **Eleven:**

"Oh, man, I can't believe that kid Simon missed that ground ball! How pathetic!"

"Wait. He's staring at his baseball glove with a confused expression on his face. Maybe there's something wrong with his glove and that's why he messed up."

"Yeah, that's probably what happened."

3 **Twelve:**

"Did that kid sitting behind us on the bus just get an erection?"

"I don't know. For a while, I thought that was the case, but now that he's holding a book on his lap it's impossible to tell."

"I guess we'll never know what the situation was."

4   **Thirteen:**

"Hey, look, that thirteen-year-old is walking around with his mom!"

"Where?"

"There—in front of the supermarket!"

"Oh, my God! That kid is *way* too old to be hanging out with his mom. Even though I've never met him, I can tell he's a complete loser."

"Wait a minute. He's scowling at her and rolling his eyes."

"Oh, yeah … and I think I just heard him curse at her, for no reason."

"I guess he's cool after all."

5   **Fourteen:**

"Why does that kid have a black 'X' on the back of his right hand?"

"I bet it's because he went to some kind of cool rock concert last night."

"Wow. He must've stayed out pretty late if he didn't have time to scrub it off."

"Yeah, and that's probably why his hair is so messy and dirty—because he cares more about rocking out than conforming to society."

"Even though he isn't popular in the traditional sense, I respect him from afar."

6   **Fifteen:**

"Hey, look, that kid is reading '*Howl*,' by Allen Ginsberg."

"Wow. He must be some kind of rebel genius."

"I'm impressed by the fact that he isn't trying to call attention to himself."

"Yeah, he's just sitting silently in the corner, flipping the pages and nodding, with total comprehension."

"It's amazing. He's so absorbed in his book that he isn't even aware that a party is going on around him, with dancing and fun."

"Why aren't any girls going over and talking to him?"

"I guess they're probably a little intimidated by his brilliance."

"Well, who *wouldn't* be?"

"I'm sure the girls will talk to him soon."

"It's only a matter of time."

7   **Sixteen:**

"Hey, look, it's that kid Simon, who wrote that scathing poem for the literary magazine."

> *"Everyone is a phony, including me."*

"You mean the one about how people are phonies? Wow—I loved that poem!"

"Me, too. Reading it made me realize for the first time that everyone is a phony, including me."

"The only person at this school who isn't a phony is Simon."

"Yeah. He sees right through us."

conforming: matching, changing to fit
comprehension: understanding
intimidated: scared, threatened

CONVERSATIONS: Collaborating in Class or Online

1. What is Rich's dominant impression in this selection?
2. What characterization is the author trying to create for each year? What details lead to these conclusions?
3. What senses does the author engage in this dialogue?
4. Why do you think the author chose these particular ages for his statement?

CONNECTIONS: Discovering Relationships among Ideas

5. Based on Rich's descriptions, explain in your own words the progression from age 11 to 16.
6. Using a single adjective, describe each age as Rich sees it.
7. How accurate are these representations for each age?
8. How does this creative piece *show* rather than *tell* the audience its primary message?

PRESENTATION: Analyzing the Writer's Craft

9. Is this an effective format for the dominant impression the author is conveying? Explain your answer.
10. Which ages are represented most accurately in your opinion? Explain your reasoning.
11. The title is repeated three times in the selection. Is this an effective strategy? Why or why not?
12. What is the author's point of view toward his subject in these vignettes? How do you know how he feels about his subject?

PROJECTS: Expressing Your Own Views

13. **NING:** Start a class NING to discuss the topic of growing up. Introduce an original entry, and respond to at least three others on this topic.
14. **Drawing:** A caricature is a picture or drawing that exaggerates one or more features of its subject. Draw a caricature of yourself at your current age. Exchange drawings with someone in the class, who will then add a humorous byline.
15. **Essay:** Describe your favorite or most memorable age in an essay. What is the main characteristic of this age for you? What details will help your readers see this time in the same way you do?
16. **Research:** Read and summarize the three resources below. Generate one specific question from each resource that focuses on description. Then answer one of your questions in a documented essay, consulting these and other sources as necessary.

OTHER RESOURCES

Web Site

Think Exist Quotations: www. Thinkexist.com

Search: "growing up"

Click on the "Quotes about: Growing up" link

Academic Article

"Nerds and Freaks: A Theory of Student **Culture** and Norms" by John H. Bishop, Matthew Bishop, Lara **Gelbwasser**, Shanna Green, and Andrea Zuckerman

Brookings Papers on Education Policy (2003): 141–199

Audio/Video

Barnes & Noble: http://media. barnesandnoble.com

Search: Billy Collins

Click on the poems you would like to hear the poet read

ONE LAST THOUGHT

Many people have a difficult time transitioning from childhood to adolescence. When did you first become aware of yourself growing up? How did moving into high school and college change you?

You Say God Is Dead? There's an app for That

by Paul Vitello

Formerly a columnist with the *Kansas City Star* and *Newsday*, **Paul Vitello** is currently a religion reporter with the *New York Times*, where he has recently published articles on sex abuse cases among Orthodox Jews, Roman Catholic sainthood, Christian Science and the modern world, Tiger Woods' apology to his family and fans, building a mosque at Ground Zero in New York, and other controversial topics.

PREREADING QUESTIONS

Do you have a cellular phone? Is it a smartphone?

Are you familiar with the App Store?

Do you have any apps? If so, what types do you have?

1   An explosion of smart-phone software has placed an arsenal of trivia at the fingertips of every corner-bar debater, with talking points on sports, politics, and how to kill a zombie. Now it is taking on the least trivial topic of all: God. Publishers of Christian material have begun producing iPhone applications that can cough up quick comebacks and rhetorical strategies for believers who want to fight back against what they view is a new strain

arsenal: weapon collection

IN CONTEXT
The Atheist Pocket Debater App

of strident atheism. And a competing crop of apps is arming nonbelievers for battle.

2   "Say someone calls you narrow-minded because you think Jesus is the only way to God," says one top-selling application introduced in March by a Christian publishing company. "Your first answer should be, 'What do you mean by narrow-minded?'"

3   For religious skeptics, the "BibleThumper" iPhone app boasts that it "allows the atheist to keep the most funny and irrational Bible verses right in their pocket" to be "always ready to confront fundamentalist Christians or have a little fun among friends."

4   The war of ideas between believers and nonbelievers has been part of the Western tradition at least since Socrates. For the most part, it has been waged by intellectual giants: Augustine, Spinoza, Aquinas, Kierkegaard, Nietzsche.

5   Yet for good or ill, combatants entering the lists today are mainly everyday people, drawn in part by the popularity of books like Richard Dawkins's "The God Delusion" and Christopher Hitchens's "God Is Not Great." The fierceness of their debate reflects the fractious talk-show culture unintentionally described so aptly in the title of the Glenn Beck best seller "Arguing With Idiots."

6   In a dozen new phone applications, whether faith-based or faith-bashing, the prospective debater is given a primer on the basic rules of engagement—how to parry the circular

argument, the false dichotomy, the ad hominem attack, the straw man—and then coached on all the likely flashpoints of contention: Why Darwinism is scientifically sound or not. The differences between intelligent design and creationism and whether either theory has any merit. The proof that America was, or was not, founded on Christian principles.

7   Users can scroll from topic to topic to prepare themselves or, in the heat of a dispute, search for the point at hand—and the perfect retort. Software creators on both sides say they are only trying to help others see the truth. But most applications focus less on scholarly exegesis than on scoring points.

8   One app, "Fast Facts, Challenges & Tactics" by LifeWay Christian Resources, suggests that in "reasoning with an unbeliever" it is sometimes effective to invoke the "anthropic principle," which posits, more or less, that the world as we know it is mathematically too improbable to be an accident. It offers an example: "The Bible's 66 books were written over a span of 1,500 years by 40 different authors on three different continents who wrote in three different languages. Yet this diverse collection has a unified story line and no contradictions."

9   "The Atheist Pocket Debater," on the other hand, asserts that because miracles like Moses's

IN CONTEXT
BibleThumper App

> *The "BibleThumper" iPhone app ... allows the atheist to keep the most funny and irrational Bible verses right in their pocket*

strident: harsh, loud
fractious: irritable
aptly: rightly
parry: avoid
anthropic principle: laws of nature
improbable: unlikely

IN CONTEXT

Logical Fallacies

FALLACY	DEFINITION	EXAMPLE
Circular Argument	The conclusion of the argument is also part of the premise.	"You can't give me a C; I'm an A student."
False Dichotomy	Two choices are presented, when there are actually other solutions.	"If today is not Tuesday, it must be Wednesday."
AD Hominem Attack	The legitimacy of the claim is rejected on the basis of an irrelevant fact about the person presenting the argument.	"I don't agree with the politician's proposed policy because she was caught cheating on her taxes."
Straw Man	One opponent misrepresents the other's argument.	"Evolution means a monkey giving birth to a human."

parting of the waters are not occurring in modern times, "it is unreasonable to accept that the events happened" at all. "If you take any miracle from the Bible," it explains, "and tell your co-workers at your job that this recently happened to someone, you will undoubtedly be laughed at."

10   These applications and others—like "One-Minute Answers to Skeptics" and "Answers for Catholics"—appear to be selling briskly, if nowhere near as fast as the top sellers among the so-called book apps in their iPhone category: ghost stories, free books, and the King James Bible.

11   Sean McDowell, the editor of "Fast Facts" and some textbooks for Bible students, said he has become increasingly aware of a skill gap between believers and nonbelievers, who he feels tend to be instinctively more savvy at arguing. "Christians who believe, but cannot explain why they believe, become 'Bible-thumpers' who seem dogmatic and insecure about their convictions," he said. "We have to deal with that."

12   "Nowadays, atheists are coming to the forefront at every level of society—from the top of academia all the way down to the level of the average Joe," added Mr. McDowell, a seminary Ph.D. candidate whose phone app was produced by the B&H Publishing Group, one of the country's largest distributors of Bibles and religious textbooks.

13   Jason Hagen may be that average guy. A musician and a real estate investor who lives in Queens, Mr. Hagen decided to write the text for "The Atheist Pocket Debater" this year after buying his first iPhone and finding dozens of apps for religious people, but none for nonbelievers like himself.

14   In creating what became the digital equivalent of a 50,000-word tract, he gleaned material from the recent anti-faith books and got the author

academia: the academic world; scholastic life

Michel Shermer's permission to reprint essays from Mr. Shermer's monthly magazine, *Skeptic*. Mr. Hagen pitched his idea to Apple, which referred him to an independent programmer who helped him develop the application; the company pays Mr. Hagen 50 cents for each download of the $1.99 app. He said a few thousand had sold.

15   What inspired him, he said, was a lifetime of frustration as the son of a fundamentalist Christian preacher in rural Virginia. "I know what people go through, growing up in the culture I grew up in," said Mr. Hagen, 39, adding that his father had only recently learned of his true beliefs. "So I tried to give people the tools they need to defend themselves, but at the same time not ridicule anybody. Basically, the people on the other side of the debate are my parents."

16   Still, some scholars consider that approach to the debate the least auspicious way of exploring the mystery of existence. "It turns it into a game," said Dr. Serene Jones, president of Union Theological Seminary, in Manhattan. "Both sides come to the discussion with fixed ideas, and you have what amounts to a contest between different types of fundamentalism."

17   Indeed, the new phone applications seem to promise hours of unrelieved, humorless argument. "When someone says, 'There is no truth,'" the Fast Facts app advises, "ask them, 'Is that true? Is it true there is no truth?' Because if it's true that there is no truth, then it's false that 'there is no truth.' "

> *If it's true that there is no truth, then it's false that "there is no truth."*

18   Mr. Hagen's atheistic app resonates with the same certitude. If Jacob saw the face of God (in Genesis 32:30) and God said, "No man shall see me and live" (in Exodus 33:20), then "which one is the liar?" he asks. His conclusion: "If we know the Bible has content that is false, how can we believe any of it?"

19   Unavailing as such exchanges may seem, they are a fact of life in parts of the country where for some people taboos against voicing doubt

have lifted for the first time. "I don't know that there are more atheists in the country, but there are definitely more people who are openly atheist, especially on college campuses," said the Rev. R. Albert Mohler Jr., president of the Southern Baptist Theological Seminary in Louisville, Ky., and author of "Atheism Remix: A Christian Confronts the New Atheists." He said students have asked him how to deal with nonbelievers.

20   "There is not one student on this campus who doesn't have at least one person in his circle of family and friends voicing these ideas," he said.

21   If smart-phone software can improve the conversation, all to the good, he said. "The app store is our new public commons." Michael Beaty, chairman of the philosophy department at Baylor University, a Christian university in Waco, Tex., was not so sure. "We'd be better off if these people were studying Nietzsche and Kant," he said.

---

auspicious: favorable

CONVERSATIONS: Collaborating in Class or Online

1. What is Vitello describing in this essay?
2. How were religious and nonreligious apps first developed?
3. What dominant impression do you think the author is trying to create in this essay?
4. What did Jason Hagen add to the religious debate?

CONNECTIONS: Discovering Relationships among Ideas

5. Why are people drawn to "faith-based" and "faith-bashing" apps?
6. What details are most interesting to you on this topic? Why do they intrigue you?
7. How does this essay show rather than tell its readers about the new apps? Be as specific as possible in your answer.
8. Do you agree with Michael Beaty that "we'd be better off if these people were studying Nietzsche and Kant"? Explain your answer.

PRESENTATION: Analyzing the Writer's Craft

9. Who do you think is Vitello's target audience?
10. Is this essay more objective or subjective? Give examples to support your answer.
11. What is Vitello's point of view toward his subject? How did you come to this conclusion?
12. The author cites excerpts from actual apps on both sides of the debate. Is this an effective strategy? Explain your answer, using examples from the essay.

PROJECTS: Expressing Your Own Views

13. **Product Description:** Write a description of a product that you would like to have, but that doesn't exist yet. This could be an app or another product. Give as many details about the product as possible. Who knows—someone might actually create it!
14. **Summary:** What current controversial topic is most interesting to you (besides the religious debate)? Summarize the essential elements of the debate over this topic, describing all the perspectives in as much detail as possible.
15. **Essay:** Write an essay describing the details from one point of view of the controversial topic you named above. Let your choice of details and their organization create your dominant impression.
16. **Research:** Read and summarize the three resources below. Generate one specific question from each resource that focuses on description. Then answer one of your questions in a documented essay, consulting these and other sources as necessary.

OTHER RESOURCES

 Web Site

Epiphenom: epiphenom.
fieldofscience.com

Academic Article

"Losing My Religion: The Social Sources of
Religious Decline in Early Adulthood" by
Jeremy E. Uecker, Mark D. Regnerus, and
Margaret L. Vaaler

Social Forces 85.4 (2007): 1667–1692

 Audio/Video

National Public Radio: www.npr.org

Search: "Religion Finds Home
On iPhones, Social Networks"

Click on the Listen Now link

ONE LAST THOUGHT

Have you ever wanted to stick
pins into a voodoo doll, cast lucky
spells, or make phone calls with an
altered voice? There are iPhone
apps for these activities and many
more. Creativity has been at the
forefront of iPhone app development since Apple began supporting third party apps in 2007.
Visit "Weird iPhone Apps" to see
more interesting applications.
What's the most interesting app
you've ever seen on a smart-
phone? Are there any apps you
would like that haven't been
developed yet?

CHAPTER WRITING ASSIGNMENTS

Write a well-developed essay in response to one of the following prompts. Consult the chapter introduction for guidance in creating your essay.

CONNECTING THE READINGS

1. "She" (Matthew Brooks Treacy) and "Hey, Look" (Simon Rich) both deal with questions of identity. Discuss at least one theme other than identity common to both of these selections.

2. What would "The Ungooglable Man" (Roz Chast) say about apps dealing with God ("You Say God Is Dead?" by Paul Vitello)? What do these selections tell us about the people they represent? Describe their similarities and differences.

3. None of the victims of 9/11 ("Officers Describe 9/11 in Memos") had the chance to die naturally of old age. What would Alice Walker ("Longing to Die of Old Age") say the terrorists deprived the 9/11 victims of?

4. Timothy Lavin ("Raging Bulls") took a huge risk to run with the bulls in Pamplona, as did the 9/11 officers ("Officers Describe 9/11 in Memos") in the line of duty. How were these experiences similar even though they took place under completely different circumstances? How were they different?

MOVING BEYOND THE READINGS

5. Describe your favorite room in the house or apartment in which you grew up.

6. What is your image on the Internet? When you "google" yourself, what do you find? Explain the accuracy of your Internet identity.

7. Is taking risks an important aspect of your life? Explain your answer. What "risks," whether major or minor, help create your self-definition?

8. Describe your ideal vacation. What would the weather be like? What amenities would your hotel offer? What other details would be part of your dream vacation?

COMBINING RHETORICAL MODES

9. Analyze the relationships some of your friends have with their parents or guardians. What are the strengths of these relationships? The weaknesses? What should they change and why?

10. In what ways is 9/11 still affecting our country? Consider all the changes we have made, and then discuss the consequences of that day in the history of America.

11. Are you conscious of the nutritional value of the foods you eat on a daily basis? How healthy is your diet? What changes would you like to make to it? How do you think these changes would affect your health?

12. Speculate on the future of phones in our society. What will they be able to do in five years? In ten years? To what extent will these changes be positive for society? In what ways will they be negative?

6 Narration

Humans are such social creatures that we cannot survive a day without narration. Telling stories helps us answer questions such as "How was your day?," "What did you do at work?," and "Why were you late?" Essentially, it gives us ways to share with others the most important details of our lives. Here are some other ways you might use narration:

- To explain how you met the person you are now dating;
- To answer a history exam question about World War II;
- To respond to an inquiry about how much time you recently spent at the gym;
- To summarize the movie you saw last night;
- To detail the events of a car accident for a police report.

Narration is storytelling that occurs in countless situations, from social networking to academic assignments. It is a necessary part of casual conversations, literature, and songs. Even diaries and biographies are based on narration. Whatever the situation, a good narrative has a purpose and supplies details that address the five Ws and one H (journalistic questions) in reference to that purpose.

DEVELOPMENT STRATEGIES: NARRATION

Purpose
Development:
⟶ Who?
⟶ What?
⟶ When?
⟶ Where?
⟶ Why?
⟶ How?
Conclusion

Introducing Narration

Narration involves telling stories that are often based on personal experience. Stories can be oral or written, real or imaginary, short or long. A good story, however, always has a particular point or purpose. Narration can be the dominant mode in an essay, where it is supported by other rhetorical strategies, or it can support another rhetorical mode (as in a persuasive essay, a historical survey, or a scientific report).

Unlike description, which generally portrays people, places, and objects in a timeless context, narration asks readers to follow a series of actions through a specific time sequence. Description often complements narration. People and their relationships must be described, for instance, before their actions can have any real meaning; similarly, places must be depicted so we can picture the setting and understand the activities in a certain scene. Just like description, narration *shows* rather than *tells* its purpose to the audience.

Narrative essays are usually intended to draw their readers into a particular event so they will see it in a specific way. As a result, writers of narrative essays need to start with a purpose, have a clear understanding of their audience, and then provide details that address the purpose by answering as many journalistic questions as possible. Look at the following examples:

DEVELOPMENT STRATEGIES AT WORK

Purpose: to show that I am financially responsible
Development
⟶ **Who?** trying to make it on my own for the first time
⟶ **What?** lots of expenses—rent, food, tuition, books, recreation, car
⟶ **When?** my first year of college
⟶ **Where?** in residence at my **college**
⟶ **Why?** because I wanted to **learn** how to balance a budget
⟶ **How?** Through trial and error—and lots of advice from others
Conclusion

DEVELOPMENT STRATEGIES AT WORK

Purpose: to prove what an awful day I had

Development

⟶ **Who?** me explaining my worst day at college so far

⟶ **What?** my alarm didn't go off; I was late for my first class; I failed a history exam; I missed lunch; my girlfriend cancelled our date; I forgot about baseball practice

⟶ **When?** my first semester in college

⟶ **Where?** on campus

⟶ **Why?** because the whole day started off wrong

⟶ **How:** I lost control of the day. I hope tomorrow will be better.

Conclusion

To write an effective narration, you should prolong the exciting parts of a story and shorten the routine facts that simply move the reader from one episode to another. If you were in a car accident on the way to work, for example, you would concentrate on the trauma you endured rather than on such boring details as what you had for breakfast and which chores you did prior to the wreck. The factual statement "I was late for work" could be made much more vivid and dramatic through the addition of some specific narrative details: "As I was driving to work at 7:30 A.M., a huge truck ran a red light and hit my car on the passenger side, hurling it to the opposite side of the street and leaving me dazed and disoriented."

Discovering How Narration Works

Here is a list of the most important elements of narrative thinking, whether for a visual (such as a graph or a cartoon) or a prose selection. These Narration Essentials are equally useful as guidelines for both reading and writing.

Narration Essentials

Purpose/Audience

Storyline

Point of View

Details Related to the Purpose

Details that Show Rather than Tell

Clear Organization

Strategic Timing

Conclusion

Analyzing the graphic below will help you understand how the elements listed here work together to produce effective, compelling narration. If you discover on your own how this method of reasoning works, you will be able to apply it effectively to your own reading and writing. The questions following the graphic will help you understand this rhetorical mode in more detail.

1. What is the purpose of this comic strip?

2. Who is Schulz's primary audience for Peanuts?

3. What is the storyline of this comic? How does Schulz create a story within a story?

4. What is the cartoonist's point of view toward his subject? What is Lucy's point of view?

5. List four details in this visual. Which are most clearly related to its purpose?

6. Which details show rather than tell the audience what to think?

7. Are these details organized in a way that reinforces their message?

8. Does the timing of the details in the comic strip add interest to the storyline?

9. What is the "conclusion" to this comic strip?

Collaborative Responses Now discuss your responses to these questions with your classmates in small groups or as an entire class. Did hearing your classmates' opinions change your "reading" of the visual in any way? If so, how?

Reading Narration

As you read the cartoons, photos, songs, and essays in this chapter, pay special attention to the details the authors/illustrators use to fulfill their purposes. Try to create a context for these details as you begin to grasp the storyline. In every case, the more details the creators provide, the more they are *showing* rather than *telling* you what they want you to know. Also, notice the timing or pacing of the details in the storyline.

Realizing how the Narration Essentials work in the selection will help you understand the piece as thoroughly as possible on a first reading. The following questions will help you achieve this goal for both written and graphic assignments:

Narration Essentials: Reading

- **Purpose/Audience:** What is the author's or illustrator's primary purpose? Who do you think is the intended audience?
- **Storyline:** Briefly summarize the storyline.
- **Point of View:** What is the point of view of the author/illustrator toward his/her subject?
- **Details Related to the Purpose:** Are the details in the selection directly related to its purpose? Explain your answer.
- **Details that Show Rather than Tell:** Does the author/illustrator include details that show rather than simply tell?
- **Clear Organization:** Does the organization lead clearly to a conclusion?
- **Strategic Timing:** Is the pacing of the storyline effective? In what ways?
- **Conclusion:** Does the selection reach a conclusion based on its details? If so, what is its conclusion?

On your second and third readings of the selection, focus on areas of ambiguity and confusion so you can deepen your comprehension.

Writing Narration

As you move from reading to writing, keep in mind the earlier list of Narration Essentials so you can tailor your writing or project to your specific purpose.

Choosing a Subject

The starting point for any project is choosing a subject. If you are allowed to select your own topic, find one you are familiar with or want to learn about. If your instructor assigns you a topic, try to develop an interest in it.

Our student writer, Chris Bertolini, decides to write about a contest he entered to win a car. He is certainly familiar with this topic, but he knows that he has to pay attention to the timing of the story so it isn't dull and uninteresting.

Generating Details

To begin, generate as many details as possible for use in your essay. To do this, you should choose one of the prewriting options explained in Chapter 3. List as many details related to this writing assignment as you can imagine. Then analyze and organize them in a way that supports the purpose of your narrative.

To begin his writing process, Chris uses the journalistic questions to make sure he covers all the important facts of his narrative:

> Who: *me, lots of other contestants, the station intern, the DJs, 22 final contestants*
>
> What: *radio contest to win a car, Whirl-Til-You-Hurl, final prize*
>
> When: *18 years old*
>
> Where: *San Diego, my home town*
>
> Why: *I was just fired from my job; I needed a new car*
>
> How: *radio stickers on my car, stalking the Surf Pig (pink and purple Cadillac), drawing, interview with DJ, my nickname (Cocky Chris), 11-day roller-coaster ride with lots of hardships, final victory!*

From these ideas, Chris needs to write a thesis statement that will give his storyline a purpose.

Drafting a Thesis Statement

For narration, your thesis statement should refer to your subject and your purpose—either directly or indirectly. What do you want your readers to feel or think after reading your essay? Your thesis statement will help you make other important choices as you write your draft. It will serve as the controlling idea for your paper and will also guide your choice of details.

Chris's purpose is to show his readers the importance of willpower, which he saves for the final paragraph. He wants his readers to feel as if they are involved in every aspect of the narrative. Here is Chris's working thesis:

> *One of the most memorable experiences was telling everyone I knew that I was going to win a contest before I had even entered it.*

This statement will now give Chris direction as he writes his first draft.

Producing a Draft

When your preliminary work is complete, you should be ready to draft your narrative essay or project following the structure of most other essays.

- The **introduction** presents your subject, furnishes some background, and states your purpose in a thesis statement.
- The **body of the paper** then provides details to support your purpose. These details become the primary means of organizing your essay—usually chronologically.
- Finally, the **concluding section** summarizes the details in the body of the paper and draws relevant conclusions from their relationships.

Organizing Your Narrative As you might suspect, the most obvious way to organize a narrative is chronologically, although more experienced writers may elect to use flashbacks (references to past actions). Your most important obligation is to have the elements of your narrative essay follow some sort of time sequence, aided by the use of clear and logical transitions (e.g., *then, next, at this point, suddenly*) that help the reader move smoothly from one event to the next.

Developing Your Essay In addition to your focus on organization, developing your essay with enough relevant details is important. The details that you choose should relay your story in a way that is engaging and believable. Instead of telling your readers about the nature of a conversation, for example, you might produce the actual dialogue that was spoken.

Establishing a Point of View Finally, the point of view of your narrator should remain consistent throughout your essay, which will give your writing a high degree of credibility. Point of view includes the (1) person, (2) vantage point, and (3) attitude of your narrator. *Person* refers to who will tell the story: an uninvolved observer, a character in the narrative, or an omniscient (all-seeing) narrator. The narrator's *vantage point* or frame of reference can be close to the action, far from the action, looking back on the past, or reporting on the present. Finally, your narrator will naturally have an *attitude,* or *personal feeling,* about the subject, which can range from positive to hostile to sarcastic to indifferent to aggravated to thankful or to any number of other emotions. Once you adopt a certain perspective in a story, you should follow it for the duration of the narrative, which will bring focus and coherence to your essay.

At this point, you should use the following questions, based on the Narration Essentials, to help focus and refine your written and graphic narration assignments:

Narration Essentials: Writing

- **Purpose/Audience:** What is your primary purpose? Who is your intended audience?
- **Storyline:** Explain your storyline.
- **Point of View:** What is your point of view toward your subject?
- **Details Related to the Purpose:** Which details from your prewriting activities are directly related to your purpose?
- **Details that Show Rather than Tell:** Which details *show* rather than *tell* your readers what you want them to know?
- **Clear Organization:** What order will achieve your purpose and lead to your conclusion?
- **Strategic Timing:** How can you pace your narrative to keep your readers' interest?
- **Conclusion:** What conclusion naturally occurs?

Revising and Editing

Revising and editing your graphic or essay involves reviewing its details to make sure they say exactly what you want them to say. At this point, you should make sure that the sequences you have developed are logical and clear to your readers.

Revising

Look closely at your essay or graphic as someone else might. Then answer the questions in the Revising Checklist (on page 28), which will help you evaluate the coherence of your composition.

Also, you should now add any transitions that will make your narrative clear and easy to follow as you show your readers how various events in your narration are related. In narrations, you need words and phrases that guide the reader smoothly through a time sequence, such as *first, next, now, then, afterward, soon, at the same time, meanwhile, immediately, later,* and *finally.* These expressions and many others will help your readers understand as clearly as possible the relationships among the elements in your narration.

Editing

Now that you have revised your content, editing is the final phase of the writing process. It involves looking closely at your words, sentences, paragraphs, and visual details to make sure they are free from errors. Use the Editing Checklist on page 30 to review your project for errors in grammar and usage. When you locate a potential error, consult a handbook or go to Pearson's Web-based MyCompLab for an explanation of the problem.

Also, if your instructor marks any grammar mistakes on your paper or graphic, make sure you understand them. Recognizing errors in your own writing is the most effective way of correcting them.

As you read the following student essay by Chris Bertolini, refer to the Narration Essentials (page 94) and the questions for reading narrations (page 96) to help you analyze it. Then, to thoroughly understand how this student essay works, pay special attention to the margin notes and the items in each paragraph they describe.

Chris Bertolini

Professor Flachmann

English 101

22 Sept. 2011

Yes I Can

1 I've often heard luck explained as preparation meeting oppor-   ⟵ Subject

tunity. This has always been true in my life. I've been told since I was   ⟵ Background a child that I could do anything I put my mind to. Because I've always believed this, I have been able to accomplish numerous goals despite obstacles that at first seemed insurmountable. One of the most memorable of these experiences was telling everyone I knew that **Thesis Statement** → I was going to win a contest before I had even entered it.

Who? → 2 I was 18 years old and had just been fired from my job as a **When?** → bank teller for making a $30,000.00 mistake. I suddenly found myself **Why?** → unemployed for the first time since I was 15, and I had bills to pay. I began working for a day-labor job while I searched for full-time work, so I was forced to drive to different locations around the city every day. **What?** → When my favorite radio station announced a competition to win a new car, I jumped at the opportunity. I plastered the radio station's stickers **How?** → all over the bumper and trunk of my ratty old automobile. I constantly listened to the station to glean clues or tips about where they were sending their giant purple and pink Cadillac, called the 'Surf Pig,' to pull over listeners who had the station's stickers on their cars. It was my goal to not only obtain a ticket into the contest, but to win a new car.

How? → 3 While driving to a new jobsite early one morning, the radio DJs told listeners where they were sending the Surf Pig. The freeway exit they claimed their intern would be driving on was less than a mile from where I was supposed to work. I decided to wait in the park- **How?** → ing lot of a convenience store directly facing the freeway off-ramp, knowing that although I'd probably be late for work, this was the opportunity I had been waiting for. After what seemed like an eternity, I watched the huge purple Cadillac cruise down the off-ramp and turn onto the road where I waited. I started my car and quickly pulled into **How?** → the street, just behind the Surf Pig. I punched the gas pedal and sped up past the purple Caddy, darting in front of it as soon as I possibly could. When the driver of the station's car saw my bumper stickers, she stuck her hand out the window and motioned for me to pull over.

Where? → 4 On the shoulder of the road, beaming from the excitement of the chase, I was presented with a large box filled with sealed envelopes. Inside each was a prize of some sort: tickets for a harbor cruise, box seats at the symphony, passes to a baseball game, and entries into the competition to win a new car. Closing my eyes, I reached into the box and grabbed an envelope. I tore open the ← What? paper and saw that I was seat number ten in the 'Whirl-Til-You-Hurl' roller coaster marathon, the competition to win a car.

5 "I won! I won a ticket! Yesssss!" I did a little dance in the hard- ← What? packed dirt, all the while crowing and hollering. The intern put a cell phone up to my ear, and I heard the DJs asking me what I had won.

6 "I won a ticket onto the roller coaster! I'm going to win the car," I exclaimed with absolute certainty.

7 "How do you know you're going to win?" one of the DJs asked.

8 "Because I'm more determined than anyone else, and I *really* need a new car," I explained.

9 "And how old are you?" they asked.

10 "I'm 18."

11 "Well, not only are you our youngest contestant, but now we know why you're so sure of yourself," they laughed. "Only someone your age is cocky enough to say you'll beat everyone else."

12 "Whether I'm 18 or 80, the fact that I'm going to win still doesn't change," I told them, slightly perturbed that they didn't understand the conviction in my voice and words.

13 "Well, we gotta give this young man a nickname," said one to the other. "What do you think about 'Cocky Chris'?" ← Who?

14 The DJs laughed and decided that because of my level of confidence and assurance, I was cocky. But nothing at that moment could dampen my spirits. I laughed along with them and agreed that "Cocky Chris" would be an appropriate nickname.

15 The "Whirl-Til-You-Hurl Contest" was a competition to see who could ride the Big Dipper rollercoaster the longest. A 100-year-old attraction still operating in San Diego, the ride is a rough wooden ← What? coaster with rib-bruising turns and breath-stealing drops. The contest

When? →
Who? →

started on a Friday afternoon with 22 contestants, some serious about winning, others just joining for fun and an afternoon of free amusement. The woman sitting next to me, a married mother of three, was only planning on staying until the end of the first evening. She had her family to get back to and couldn't dedicate more than a Friday night to winning the contest. I, on the other hand, was more than ready to stay in my seat until they handed me the keys to my shiny new vehicle.

When? →

Who? →

How? →

Why? →

16 What started out as a promotion expected to last for a weekend turned into an event that went on for 11 days. After 2,940 revolutions on the coaster, the three remaining contestants stepped off the ride to accept the keys to their brand new cars. I was one of those three. I had endured all the trials the radio station had forced upon me, from five-minute bathroom breaks every six hours, to riding blindfolded, to sleeping overnight in my seat with no pillows or blankets—and I had persevered. The resolve I had to get into the contest and my determination never to give up is what saw me through. Had I allowed myself the option to fail, it's possible I would've gotten off the coaster just like the 19 people before me had done.

How? →

17 I still believe strongly in the power of the will. On the rare occasions that I feel a goal is insurmountable, I simply think back to the moment when I held those hard-won keys in my hand and felt the warm tears of victory upon my face. And I remember that I can do anything.

Reviewing Narration

Based on the information you have learned in this chapter and the annotations on the student paper, show how this essay works by writing a clear, precise summary or by drawing your own outline or graphic representation of it. Label the five Ws and one H on your visual. This exercise will confirm your understanding of the elements of narration in both reading and writing.

Rumspringa: Amish Teens Venture into Modern Vices

by Tom Shachtman

Writer, filmmaker, and educator **Tom Shachtman** has written over thirty nonfiction books and several TV documentaries. Among his many publications are *The Inarticulate Society: Eloquence and Culture in America* (1995), *Rumspringa: To Be or Not To Be Amish* (2006), *Airlift to America* (2009), and *The Forty Years War: The Rise and Fall of the Neocons, from Nixon to Obama* (2009).

> **PREREADING QUESTIONS**
>
> At what age did you rebel—even in a small way—against your upbringing?
>
> What form did your "rebellion" take?
>
> What were the consequences of your rebellion?

1   In the gathering dusk of a warm, humid summer Friday evening in northern Indiana, small groups of Amish-born girls between the ages of sixteen and nineteen walk along straight country lanes that border flat fields of high cornstalks and alfalfa, dotted here and there with neat, drab houses set back from the roads. One pair of girls walks westward, another pair eastward toward the destination; a threesome travels due south. Although not yet baptized members of the church, these young ladies all wear traditional "plain" Amish garb: solid-colored, long-sleeved dresses with aprons over them, long stockings and black shoes; white bonnets indicative of their status as unmarried cover their long hair, which is parted in the middle and pinned up in the back. A few carry small satchels. Though they are used to exercise and walking strongly, their demeanor is demure, so

garb: clothes
indicative: representative
demure: modest

that they appear younger than non-Amish girls of the same age. The walkers pass homes where the women and children in the yards, taking in the last of the wash off clotheslines, wear no shoes, as though to better sense the warm air, grass, and dirt between their toes. Along these country lanes, while there are a few homes belonging to the "English," the non-Amish, most are owned by Old Order Amish families.

2   As the shards of sunset fade, electric lights are turned on in the English homes, but only the occasional gas lamp pierces the twilight of the Amish homesteads, illuminating buggies at rest in driveways, silhouetting horses in small pastures against high clouds, and here and there a dog and cat wandering about. No music can be heard coming from the Amish houses as the girls walk past, no faint whisper of broadcast news, no whir of air conditioners. All that disturbs the calm is the occasional animal bark, whinny, snort, or trill, and every few minutes the rapid clop-clop-clop of a horse-drawn vehicle going past; the girls' peals of laughter sound as innocent, as timeless, and as much a part of the natural surround as birds' calls.

> *All that disturbs the calm is the occasional animal bark ... and ... the rapid clop-clop-clop of a horse-drawn vehicle going past*

3   From their several directions, the walkers converge on the home of another teenage Amish girl. There they go upstairs to the bedroom shared by the young females of the family to huddle and giggle in anticipation of what is to happen later that night, after full dark. In a window visible from the lane, they position a lit gas lamp, and they leave open an adjacent side door to the house and stairway. These are signals to male Amish youth out "cruising" that there are young ladies inside who would welcome a visit and who might agree to go out courting—a part of the rumspringa, or "running-around," tradition that has been passed down in Amishdom for many generations.

4   The setting for this evening's rumspringa activities, near the town of Shipshewana and the

IN CONTEXT

Map of Shipshewana, Indiana

border between LaGrange and Elkhart counties in north-central Indiana, is similar to those in the other major areas of Old Order Amish population, Holmes and Wayne counties in Ohio, and Lancaster County in Pennsylvania; and similar rumspringa preparation scenes at young girls' homes are also enacted regularly in those areas.

5   Such activities usually go unseen by tourists, despite Shipshewana in Indiana, Berlin in Ohio, and Intercourse in Pennsylvania having become tourist destinations for millions of Americans each year. Shipshe, as the locals call their town, has only a few streets but these are lined with nearly a hundred attractive "specialty" shops that sell merchandise as likely to have been manufactured in China as crafted in Indiana.

6   East and west of the sales district, the area is rural and mostly Amish. The young ladies gathered in that upstairs bedroom, waiting for young men to come calling, work in Shipshe, Middlebury, Goshen, and other neighboring towns as waitresses, dishwashers, store clerks, seamstresses, bakers, and child-minders. All have been employed since graduating from Amish schools at age fourteen or fifteen, or leaving public schools after the eighth grade, and have been dutifully turning over most of their wages to their families to assist with household expenses. After their full days at work and before leaving their

converge: come together

homes this evening, the young ladies have also performed their chores: feeding the cows they milked earlier in the day, providing fresh bedding for the horses, assisting with housecleaning and laundry, with the preparation, serving, and clearing away of the evening meal, and caring for dozens of younger siblings.

7 In the upstairs bedroom, the girls play board games and speak of certain "hopelessly uncool" teenagers in their age cohort, girls and boys whom they have known all their lives but who are not going cruising and who seem content to spend their rumspringa years attending Sunday sings after church and volleyball games arranged by parents or church officials.

8 An hour later, when the girls have had their fill of board games, and when the parents of the house are presumed to be asleep, cars and halftrucks are heard pulling into the dirt lane. The battered, second-hand autos and pickups are parked well off the road, to be less visible to passersby in horse-drawn buggies. Out of the vehicles clamber males from sixteen to their early twenties, most of them Amish-born but at this moment trying

hard not to appear Amish, wearing T-shirts and jeans, some with long hair or crew cuts instead of Amish bowl cuts. A few English friends accompany them. The young Amish-raised men have day jobs in carpentry shops, in factories that make recreational vehicles and mobile homes, in construction, or at the animal auction and flea market in town; none are farmers, though most still live at home, some on farms and the rest on "farmettes," five- to ten-acre homesteads that have a vegetable garden and areas of pasturage for the horses and the occasional family cow.

9 The young men shine a flashlight on the upstairs room where the lamp is lit, and at that countersignal one girl comes downstairs and greets the guys, who then creep up the stairs. After introductory banter in the crowded room, the girls are invited to go with the boys, and they all troop back out to the cars, the Amish girls still in their traditional garb. A few words pass between the daughter of the house and her parents—who have not, after all, been asleep—but while these include admonitions to be careful, they do not specify that she is to come home at a particular hour. If the parents are worried about this pack of teenagers "going away" on a Friday night—perhaps not to return until Sunday evening—they do not overtly display that emotion.

10 Once the young ladies hit the cars, and the cars have pulled away from the homestead, appearances and behaviors begin to change. While riding along, each Amish girl performs at least one of many actions that have been forbidden to her throughout her childhood: lights up a cigarette, grabs a beer, switches on the rock and rap music on the car radio or CD player, converses loudly and in a flirtatious manner with members of the opposite sex.

11 Coursing past a small schoolhouse where a few of the riders attended classes in the recent past and into the small, nearly deserted center of Shipshewana—whose restaurants stop serving at 8:00 P.M.—the convoy heads south, past the auction depot, stopping

cohort: group
presumed: assumed, believed
banter: good-humored conversation

for a while on the outskirts of the business district at a gas station and convenience store. In addition to vehicle parking spaces, the station has a hitching post for horses and buggies. What these Amish teenagers seek on this visit is the convenience store's bathrooms, located next to a side door. In a bunch, the girls head into them, occupying for a while both the Gents' and the Ladies' as their male companions stand guard and graze the aisles, the older ones buying beer for them all, the younger ones springing for jerky, chips, and nuts. There are no sexually explicit magazines here at which the boys might glance, because such magazines are not carried in local stores, in deference to the wishes of the Amish and Mennonites in the area. A few young males shove quarters into a gambling machine, the Pot O Silver, which has the potential of returning them five or ten dollars for every half-dollar they put in. No one wins more than a quarter.

12   When the girls emerge from the bathrooms, only two of the eight still look Amish; the other six have been transformed. They wear jeans, T-shirts, and other mainstream American teenager outfits, some revealing their navels. Hair coverings have been removed, and a few have also let down their hair, uncut since childhood. "Ready to party," one lady avows. "Cruisin' and boozin'," another responds. The counter clerk, an older woman in Mennonite garb, seems unabashed by the changes in attire.

13   In the cars once again, cell phones—also forbidden equipment—emerge from hiding places, some from under the girls' clothing. Calls to compatriots in other vehicles, buggies as well as cars, yield the information that many dozens of Amish teenagers are now roaming the roads while trying to ascertain the location of this week's "hoedown." Soon it is identified: closer to Emma, a town three miles south of Shipshewana and not far from West-view High, the public school attended by many of the non-Amish revelers. The cars pass a young woman in a buggy heading in the direction of the party; she is smoking a cigarette and talking on her cell phone; the buggy's window flaps are open to disperse the tobacco smoke and perhaps to facilitate the cell phone connection.

14   As they would in similar settings in Holmes or Lancaster County, the young Amish on the road to a party in northern Indiana pass familiar territory composed of quiet Amish homesteads and farms, suburban-looking English homes, a few factories and assembly buildings, and some small workshops. Here is a roadside stand operated by a Yoder family; there is a quilt boutique run by a Miller family; the small-engine repair shop of a member of the Esh family is nestled on a side road but has a sign visible from the main route; over yonder is a Weaver family furniture-making factory.

15   Around midnight, scores of Amish teenagers and twentysome-things converge on the back acres of a farm south of Shipshewana, several miles from the nearest town, a third of a mile from the farmhouse, and hidden from the nearest road by a forest of cornstalks. A used-car-lot inventory of cars, trucks, buggies, bicycles, and motorcycles is already parked here. Iced coolers of beer are put out; Amish teenagers reach for bottles with both hands. Young, mechanically adept men hook up portable CD players and boom-box speakers to car batteries. Shortly, rock and rap music blasts. Heads nod and bodies sway to the beat.

16   Many of the Amish kids know the words of the most current rock songs, even of black rap recordings that speak of mayhem in inner-city ghettos and anger against whites, songs they have learned

deference: respect
compatriots: fellow-countrymen
ascertain: make certain

from listening to battery-powered radios that they bought with the first money they earned and that they have kept hidden at home. "When I'm angry at my bossy brothers," one young lady says, "I play rock on my radio; when I'm happy, I play country."

17 To have a focus for the party, the participants gather straw and brush for a bonfire. Its bright light and stark shadows crosshatch partygoers at the edges of the center, where various transactions are occurring. Most of the Amish youth are from northern Indiana, but some have come from across the state line in Michigan or from many hours away in Missouri and Ohio. There are about four hundred youth at this almost-deserted site, out of about two thousand adolescent Amish in northern Indiana. Some of the kids are what others refer to as "simmies," literally, foolish in the head, young, naive, new to rumspringa—and, most of them, willing to work hard to lose the label quickly.

18 Beer is the liquid of choice, but there are also bottles of rum and vodka, used to spike soft drinks. Some of the younger kids do not know the potency of what they are drinking, or what it might do to them. Many will be sick before long. Most guzzle to mimic the others, while gossiping about who is not there or is not drinking. This night, one young woman will wonder why she always seems to drink too much.

19 In one corner of the party, joints of marijuana are passed around, as are pipes of crank (crystal methamphetamine). Lines of cocaine are exchanged for money. A handful of the partygoers are seriously addicted, while others are trying drugs for the first time. Crank is incredibly and instantly

addictive, and it is relatively simple and cheap to make; the only ingredient used that is not available from a local hardware store, anhydrous ammonia, is a gaseous fertilizer easily stolen from tanks on farms. Those few partygoers interested in doing hard drugs gather in a different location than the majority, who prefer drinking beer or smoking pot.

20 As the party gets into full swing and beer and pot are making the participants feel no pain, a few Amish girls huddle and make plans to jointly rent an apartment in a nearby town when they turn eighteen, as some older girls have already done. Others shout in Pennsylvania Dutch and in English about how much it will cost to travel to and attend an Indianapolis rock concert and the possibilities of having a navel pierced or hair cut buzz short. One bunch of teens dances to music videos shown on a laptop computer; a small group of guys, near a barn, distributes condoms.

21 As such parties wear on, the Amish youth become even less distinguishable from their English peers, shedding their demureness, mimicking the in-your-face postures of the mainstream teen culture, with its arrogance, defiance, raucousness, inner-city-gang hand motions and exaggerated walking stances.

22 "The English girls prefer us Amish guys because we're stronger and better built and we party harder," insisted one young Amish man at a similar party. Another countered that it is because the Amish guys have more money in their pockets—the result of not having to spend much on food and shelter, since most of them are living at home. The English guys are also partial to the Amish young ladies, this young man added, because Amish girls are "more

raucousness: rowdiness, loudness

willing than English girls to get drunk." Of temptation-filled parties like this, one Amish young woman will later comment, "God talks to me in one ear, Satan in the other. Part of me wants to be Amish like my parents, but the other part wants the jeans, the haircut, to do what I want to do."

23   Couples form and head off into the darkness. Some petting goes further than exploration, and this night one of the girls who earlier walked that country lane loses her virginity. Another partygoer becomes pregnant; several weeks from now, when she realizes it, she will simply advance her wedding date so that her child, as with about 12 percent of first births among the Amish, will be born before her marriage is nine months old. This evening, as well, a few female partygoers will bring boys home, and, with their parents' cognizance, spend the night in "bed courtship," on the girls' beds but "bundled" separately.

> *A few female partygoers will bring boys home, and ... spend the night in "bed courtship"*

24   During parties like this, as the hours wear on, the boys frequently damage property. There are fistfights; one partygoer recalled a particularly bad incident in which a lad in a fit of bloody rage ripped the earring stud from another young man's ear.

25   At first light, the farm's owners and their children move about the area, to herd in and milk the cows. One farmer's daughter, spotting a partygoer about to throw up, smilingly hands her an empty pail.

IN CONTEXT

Teenage Rebellion

Teenage rebellion is a common theme in popular culture. Can you think of other examples of movies or books that deal with rebellion?

26   An hour later, the sun is fully up, but most of the exhausted partygoers in various sheltered locations around the back acres are still asleep. Undisturbed, they will wake again near noon. Some have made plans to go to a mall, twenty miles away, to shop and see a movie before continuing the party tomorrow evening in another semi-deserted location.

27   Near Shipshe, Berlin, and Intercourse, those Amish youngsters walking on the wild side of rumspringa during this weekend will party on until, late on Sunday, they return home to sober up and ready themselves for Monday and the workweek. Most have no plans to tell their parents, upon returning to the family hearth, precisely where they have been for the previous forty-eight hours or with whom they spent their "going away" time. While the parents may well ask such questions, the children feel little obligation to answer them.

cognizance: knowledge

CONVERSATIONS: Collaborating in Class or Online

1. Based on the details Shachtman furnishes throughout this essay, describe the Amish community.
2. What is "rumspringa"?
3. Where are the main Amish communities in the United States?
4. What activities have traditionally been forbidden to Amish girls?

CONNECTIONS: Discovering Relationships among Ideas

5. What primary traits characterize Amish teenagers?
6. Why do the Amish girls change their clothes when they arrive in Shipshewana?

7. What proportion of the local Amish teens participated in rumspringa on this particular night? Why do you think this percentage is so low?

8. How are Amish party activities different from parties you have attended?

PRESENTATION: Analyzing the Writer's Craft

9. What is Shachtman's purpose in this essay?

10. The author reveals detailed information about this specific night of rumspringa. What effect do these details have on your understanding of this courting ritual?

11. Does Shachtman cover all the journalistic questions? Explain your answer.

12. What is the author's point of view toward this subject? Is this an effective approach?

PROJECTS: Expressing Your Own Views

13. **Collage:** Design a collage that explains your "rebellion" from your family.

14. **Podcast:** Interview classmates about their backgrounds (religion, parents' education, parents' jobs, living conditions), and create a podcast presenting the collective background of your English class.

15. **Essay:** Write an essay on the principal social activities that make up your weekends. Describe a typical weekend; then explain why you pursue these particular activities.

16. **Research:** Read and summarize the three resources below. Generate one specific question from each resource that focuses on narration. Then answer one of your questions in a documented essay, consulting these and other sources as necessary.

OTHER RESOURCES

Web Site

Amish Country: www. amishcountry.org

Audio/Video

National Public Radio: www. npr.org

Search: "Rumspringa: Amish Teens Venture into Modern Vices"

Click on the Listen link

Academic Article

"Consenting Adults? Amish Rumspringa and the Quandary of Exit in Liberalism" by Steven V. Mazie

Perspectives on Politics 3.4 (2005): 745–759

ONE LAST THOUGHT

Amish, Hutterites, and Mennonites trace their roots to the radical reformation of Christianity in the 16th century. The Hutterites practice separatism and live and work within their own communities. Mennonites are the most modern, allowing automobiles, electricity, and running water. The Amish are best known for their simple lifestyles and plain clothing, and they do not use most modern inventions. All are considered Anabaptists, which means they reject infant baptism in favor of adult baptism. Have you ever imagined your life without modern conveniences? What aspects of a "simpler life" would you enjoy?

Academia

by David Sipress

A regular contributor to *The New Yorker*, in which he has published over 350 cartoons, **David Sipress** has also been featured in *Time*, *Playboy*, *The Washington Post*, *The Boston Review*, and many other popular magazines and newspapers. He has published eight volumes of cartoons and has illustrated several books, including *Your Cat's Just Not That Into You*.

PREREADING QUESTIONS

What do your parents or guardians do for a living?

How thoroughly do you understand their line of work?

Are your goals similar to those of your parents or guardians?

"Daddy works in a magical, faraway land called Academia."

Academia: the academic world; scholastic life

CONVERSATIONS: Collaborating in Class or Online

1. What is the storyline behind this cartoon?
2. Does the father look the part of someone who works in "Academia"? What do you think the father does in this "magical, faraway land"? List the details that suggest his role in Academia.
3. How old is the child in the cartoon? What details help you arrive at this conclusion?
4. Who is the speaker in this cartoon? How do you know?

CONNECTIONS: Discovering Relationships among Ideas

5. Why do you think the father is dressed the way he is? What does the glass of wine add to his image?
6. Why does Sipress have both figures in the drawing sitting down?
7. What do you think the child's next question might be?
8. What does the window add to the cartoonist's message?

PRESENTATION: Analyzing the Writer's Craft

9. What do you think is this cartoon's purpose?
10. Why is Academia capitalized in the line below the drawing? What does this capital letter tell us about the illustrator's point of view?
11. How do the setting and the artwork around the conversation support the author's purpose?
12. Do you think this cartoon would be more or less effective in color? Explain your reasoning.

PROJECTS: Expressing Your Own Views

13. **Drawing:** Draw a picture that represents your future profession. Exchange pictures with someone in class who will add a byline to your image.
14. **Haiku:** Write a haiku about your college experience so far. [Note: Haiku are poems of 17 syllables distributed in 3 lines (5 syllables in line 1, 7 in line 2, and 5 in line 1).]
15. **Essay:** Write a narrative essay outlining what you think a typical day will be like in your future profession. Make sure your essay has a specific purpose.
16. **Research:** Read and summarize the three resources below. Generate one specific question from each resource that focuses on narration. Then answer one of your questions in a documented essay, consulting these and other sources as necessary.

OTHER RESOURCES

Web Site

Ultrinsic: www.ultrinsic.com

Academic Article

"Stability and Change in Parental Attachment and Adjustment Outcomes During the First Semester Transition to College Life" by Marnie Hiester, Alicia Nordstrom, and Lisa M. Swenson

Journal of College Student Development 50.5 (2009): 521–538

Audio/Video

CNN: www.cnn.com

Search: "Health Files: College Drinking" Brianna Keilar

Click on the Video link

ONE LAST THOUGHT

Jerry Seinfeld did an episode of his show, *Seinfeld*, entitled "The Cartoon." In it, Elaine becomes obsessed with a political cartoon in *The New Yorker* and sets out to prove that it doesn't make sense. Do you enjoy reading cartoons? What do you think makes a cartoon funny?

I Will Never Know Why

by Susan Klebold

Susan Klebold is the mother of Dylan Klebold, who, with Eric Harris, killed 12 students and a teacher and wounded 24 others at Columbine High School in suburban Denver in the worst school massacre in United States history. Published in Oprah Winfrey's *O Magazine* more than ten years after the 1999 killings, the essay attempts to make sense of the tragedy through the eyes of a grieving mother.

PREREADING QUESTIONS

Do you remember the Columbine high school massacre?

Where were you when you heard about these shootings?

How did this tragedy change your views about life, security, and friends?

1   Just after noon on Tuesday, April 20, 1999, I was preparing to leave my downtown Denver office for a meeting when I noticed the red message light flashing on my phone. I worked for the state of Colorado, administering training programs for people with disabilities; my meeting was about student scholarships, and I figured the message might be a last-minute cancellation. But it was my husband, calling from his home office. His voice was breathless and ragged, and his words stopped my heart. "Susan—this is an emergency! Call me back immediately!"

2   The level of pain in his voice could mean only one thing: Something had happened to one of our sons. In the seconds that passed as I picked up the phone and dialed our house, panic swelled within me; it felt as though millions of tiny needles were pricking my skin. My heart pounded in my ears. My hands began shaking. I tried to orient myself. One of my boys was at school and

the other was at work. It was the lunch hour. Had there been a car accident?

3   When my husband picked up the phone, he shouted, "Listen to the television!"—then held out the receiver so I could hear. I couldn't understand the words being broadcast, but the fact that whatever had happened was big enough to be on TV filled me with terror. Were we at war? Was our country under nuclear attack? "What's happening?" I shrieked.

4   He came back on the line and poured out what he'd just learned during a distraught call from a close friend of our 17-year-old son, Dylan: There was some kind of shooting at the high school … gunmen in black trenchcoats were firing at people … the friend knew all the kids who wore trenchcoats, and all were accounted for except Dylan and his friend Eric … and Dylan and Eric hadn't been in class that morning … and no one knew where they were.

5   My husband had told himself that if he found the coat, Dylan couldn't be involved. He'd torn the house apart, looking everywhere. No coat. When there was nowhere left to look, somehow he knew the truth. It was like staring at one of those computer-generated 3-D pictures when the abstract pattern suddenly comes into focus as a recognizable image.

6   I barely got enough air in my lungs to say, "I'm coming home." We hung up without saying goodbye.

IN CONTEXT

School Shootings and Stabbings 1996–2006

7   My office was 26 miles from our house. All I could think as I drove was that Dylan was in danger. With every cell in my body, I felt his importance to me, and I knew I would never recover if anything happened to him. I seesawed between impossible possibilities, all of them sending me into paroxysms of fear. Maybe no one knew where Dylan was because he'd been shot himself. Maybe he was lying in the school somewhere injured or dead. Maybe he was being held hostage. Maybe he was trapped and couldn't get word to us. Maybe it was some kind of prank and no one was hurt. How could we think for even a second that Dylan could shoot someone? Shame on us for even considering the idea. Dylan was a gentle, sensible kid. No one in our family had ever owned a gun. How in the world could he be part of something like this?

8   Yet no matter how hard I wanted to believe that he wasn't, I couldn't dismiss the possibility. My husband had noticed something tight in Dylan's voice earlier that week; I had heard it myself just that morning. I knew that Dylan disliked his school. And that he'd spent much of the past few days with Eric Harris—who hadn't been to our house for months but who'd suddenly stayed over one night that weekend. If Eric was missing now, too, then I couldn't deny that the two of them might be involved in something bad together. More than a year earlier, they had broken into a van parked on a country road near our house. They'd been arrested and had completed a juvenile diversion program that involved counseling, community service, and classes. Their theft had shown that under each other's influence they could be impulsive and unscrupulous. Could they also—no matter how unbelievable it seemed—be violent?

Gunmen in black trenchcoats were firing at people

9   When I got home my husband told me the police were on their way. I had so much adrenaline in my system that even as I was changing

distraught: upset
paroxysms: outbursts, fits
unscrupulous: dishonest, corrupt

out of my work clothes, I was racing from room to room. I felt such an urgency to be ready for whatever might happen next. I called my sister. As I told her what was going on, I was overcome by horror, and I started to cry. Moments after I hung up the phone, my 20-year-old son walked in and lifted me like a rag doll in his arms while I sobbed into a dish towel. Then my husband shouted from the front hallway, "They're here!"

10 Members of a SWAT team in dark uniforms with bulletproof vests had arrived. I thought they were coming to help us or to get our assistance in helping Dylan; if Dylan did have a gun, maybe they were hoping we could persuade him to put it down. But it seemed that in the SWAT team's eyes, we were suspects ourselves. Years later I would learn that many of their actions that day were intended to protect us; fearing that we would hurt ourselves or that our home might have been rigged with explosives, they told us we had to leave the house. For the rest of the afternoon, we stayed outside, sitting on the sidewalk or pacing up and down our brick walk. When we needed to use the bathroom, two armed guards escorted us inside and waited by the door.

11 I do not remember how or when, but sometime that day it was confirmed that Dylan and Eric were indeed perpetrators in a massacre at the school. I was in shock and barely grasped what was happening, but I could hear the television through the open windows. News coverage announced a growing tally of victims. Helicopters began circling overhead to capture a killer's family on film. Cars lined the road and onlookers gawked to get a better view.

12 Though others were suffering, my thoughts focused on the safety of my own child. With every moment that passed, the likelihood of seeing Dylan as I knew him diminished. I asked the police over and over, "What's happening? Where's Dylan? Is he okay?" Late in the afternoon someone finally told me that he was dead but not how he died. We were told to evacuate for a few days so authorities could search our home; we found shelter in the basement of a family member's house. After a sleepless night, I learned that Dylan and Eric had killed 12 students and one teacher, and injured 24 others, before taking their own lives.

13 As a young child, Dylan made parenting easy. From the time he was a toddler, he had a remarkable attention span and sense of order. He spent hours focused on puzzles and interlocking toys. He loved origami and Legos. By third grade, when he entered a gifted program at school, he had become his father's most devoted chess partner. He and his brother acted out feats of heroism in our backyard. He played Little League baseball. No matter what he did, he was driven to win—and was very hard on himself when he lost.

14 His adolescence was less joyful than his childhood. As he grew, he became extremely shy and uncomfortable when he was the center of attention and would hide or act silly if we tried to take his picture. By junior high, it was evident that he no longer liked school; worse, his passion for learning was gone. In high school, he held a job and participated as a sound technician in school productions, but his grades were only fair. He hung out with friends, slept late when he could, spent time in his room, talked on the phone, and played video games on a computer he built. In his junior year, he stunned us by hacking into the school's computer system with a friend (a violation for which he was expelled), but the low point of that year was his arrest. After the arrest, we kept him away from Eric for several weeks, and as time passed he seemed to distance himself from Eric of his own accord. I took this as a good sign.

15 By Dylan's senior year, he had grown tall and thin. His hair was long and scraggly; under his baseball cap, it stuck out like a clown wig. He'd been accepted at four colleges and had decided

perpetrators: people involved

to go to the University of Arizona, but he'd never regained his love of learning. He was quiet. He grew irritated when we critiqued his driving, asked him to help around the house, or suggested that he get a haircut. In the last few months of senior year, he was pensive, as if he were thinking about the challenges of growing older. One day in April I said, "You seem so quiet lately—are you okay?" He said he was "just tired." Another time I asked if he wanted to talk about going away to college. I told him that if he didn't feel ready, he could stay home and go to a community college. He said, "I definitely want to go away." If that was a reference to anything more than leaving home for college, it never occurred to me.

> *I had no idea that I had just heard his voice for the last time*

16   Early on April 20, I was getting dressed for work when I heard Dylan bound down the stairs and open the front door. Wondering why he was in such a hurry when he could have slept another 20 minutes, I poked my head out of the bedroom. "Dyl?" All he said was "Bye." The front door slammed, and his car sped down the driveway. His voice had sounded sharp. I figured he was mad because he'd had to get up early to give someone a lift to class. I had no idea that I had just heard his voice for the last time.

17   It took about six months for the sheriff's department to begin sharing some of the evidence explaining what happened that day. For those six months, Dylan's friends and family were in denial. We didn't know that he and Eric had assembled an arsenal of explosives and guns. We believed his participation in the massacre was accidental or that he had been coerced. We believed that he did not intend to hurt anyone. One friend was sure that Dylan had been tricked at the last minute into using live ammunition. None of us could accept that he was capable of doing what he did.

18   These thoughts may seem foolish in light of what we now know, but they reflect what we believed to be true about Dylan. Yes, he had filled notebook pages with his private thoughts and feelings, repeatedly expressing profound alienation. But we'd never seen those notebooks. And yes, he'd written a school paper about a man in a black trench coat who brutally murders nine students. But we'd never seen that paper. (Although it had alarmed his English teacher enough to bring it to our attention, when we asked to see the paper at a parent-teacher conference, she didn't have it with her. Nor did she describe the contents beyond calling them "disturbing." At the conference—where we discussed many things, including books in the curriculum, Gen X versus Gen Y learners, and the '60s folk song "Four Strong Winds"—we agreed that she would show the paper to Dylan's guidance counselor; if he thought it was a problem, one of them would contact me. I never heard from them.) We didn't see the paper, or Dylan's other writings, until the police showed them to us six months after the tragedy.

19   In the weeks and months that followed the killings, I was nearly insane with sorrow for the suffering my son had caused and with grief for the child I had lost. Much of the time, I felt that I could not breathe, and I often wished that I would die. I got lost while driving. When I returned to work part-time in late May, I'd sit through meetings without the slightest idea of what was being said. Entire conversations slipped from memory. I cried at inappropriate times, embarrassing those around me. Once, I saw a dead pigeon in a parking lot and nearly became hysterical. I mistrusted everything—especially my own judgment.

20   Seeing pictures of the devastation and the weeping survivors was more than I could bear. I avoided all news coverage in order to function. I was obsessed with thoughts of the innocent children and the teacher who suffered because of Dylan's cruelty. I grieved for the other families, even though we had never met. Some had lost loved ones, while others were coping with severe, debilitating injuries and psychological trauma. It was impossible to believe that someone I had raised could cause so much suffering. The discovery that it could have been worse—that if their plan had

---

pensive: deep in thought
profound: deep
alienation: withdrawal, separation
debilitating: crippling

worked, Dylan and Eric would have blown up the whole school—only increased the agony.

21   But while I perceived myself to be a victim of the tragedy, I didn't have the comfort of being perceived that way by most of the community. I was widely viewed as a perpetrator or at least an accomplice since I was the person who had raised a "monster." In one newspaper survey, 83 percent of respondents said that the parents' failure to teach Dylan and Eric proper values played a major part in the Columbine killings. If I turned on the radio, I heard angry voices condemning us for Dylan's actions. Our elected officials stated publicly that bad parenting was the cause of the massacre.

22   Through all of this, I felt extreme humiliation. For months I refused to use my last name in public. I avoided eye contact when I walked. Dylan was a product of my life's work, but his final actions implied that he had never been taught the fundamentals of right and wrong. There was no way to atone for my son's behavior.

23   Those of us who cared for Dylan felt responsible for his death. We thought, "If I had been a better (mother, father, brother, friend, aunt, uncle, cousin), I would have known this was coming." We perceived his actions to be our failure. I tried to identify a pivotal event in his upbringing that could account for his anger. Had I been too strict? Not strict enough? Had I pushed too hard, or not hard enough? In the days before he died, I had

hugged him and told him how much I loved him. I held his scratchy face between my palms and told him that he was a wonderful person and that I was proud of him. Had he felt pressured by this? Did he feel that he could not live up to my expectations?

24   I longed to talk to Dylan one last time and ask him what he had been thinking. I spoke to him in my thoughts and prayed for understanding. I concluded that he must not have loved me, because love would have prevented him from doing what he did. And though at moments I was angry with him, mostly I thought that I was the one who needed his forgiveness because I'd failed to see that he needed help.

25   Since the tragedy, I have been through many hours of therapy. I have enjoyed the devotion and kindness of friends, neighbors, coworkers, family members, and strangers. I also received an unexpected blessing. On a few occasions I was contacted by the parents of some of the children killed at the school. These courageous individuals asked to meet privately so we could talk. Their compassion helped me survive.

26   Still, Dylan's participation in the massacre was impossible for me to accept until I began to connect it to his own death. Once I saw his journals, it was clear to me that Dylan entered the school with the intention of dying there. And so, in order to understand what he might have been thinking, I started to learn all I could about suicide.

27   Suicide is the end result of a complex mix of pathology, character, and circumstance that produces severe emotional distress. This distress is so great that it impairs one's ability to think and act rationally. From the writings Dylan left behind, criminal psychologists have concluded that he was depressed and suicidal. When I first saw copied pages of these writings, they broke my heart. I'd had no inkling of the battle Dylan was waging in his mind. As early as two years before the shootings, he wrote about ending his life. In one poem, he wrote, "Revenge is sorrow / death is a reprieve /

atone: make up for

pivotal: important, crucial

reprieve: release

IN CONTEXT

Suicide Information

Centers for Disease Control and Suicide Prevention Information

RISK FACTORS	PROTECTIVE FACTORS
• Family history of suicide	• Effective clinical care for mental, physical, and substance abuse disorders
• Family history of child maltreatment	
• Previous suicide attempt(s)	• Easy access to a variety of clinical interventions and support for help seeking
• History of mental disorders, particularly depression	
• History of alcohol and substance abuse	• Family and community support (connectedness)
• Feelings of hopelessness	• Support from ongoing medical and mental health care relationships
• Impulsive or aggressive tendencies	
• Cultural and religious beliefs (e.g., belief that suicide is noble resolution of a personal dilemma)	• Skills in problem solving, conflict resolution, and nonviolent ways of handling disputes
• Local epidemics of suicide	• Cultural and religious beliefs that discourage suicide and support instincts for self-preservation
• Isolation, a feeling of being cut off from other people	
• Barriers to accessing mental health treatment	
• Loss (relational, social, work, or financial)	
• Physical illness	
• Easy access to lethal methods	
• Unwillingness to seek help because of the stigma attached to mental health and substance abuse disorders or to suicidal thoughts	

life is a punishment / others' achievements are tormentations / people are alike / I am different." He wrote about his longing for love and his near obsession with a girl who apparently did not know he existed. He wrote, "Earth, humanity, HERE. that's mostly what I think about. I hate it. I want to be free … free … I thought it would have been time by now. The pain multiplies infinitely. Never stops. (yet?) I'm here, STILL alone, still in pain… ."

28   Among the items police found in his room were two half-empty bottles of Saint-John's-wort, an herb believed to elevate mood and combat mild depression. I asked one of Dylan's friends if he knew that Dylan had been taking it. Dylan told him he hoped it would increase his "motivation."

29   Each year there are approximately 33,000 suicides in the United States. (In Colorado, suicide is the second leading cause of death for people ages 15 to 34.) And it is estimated that 1 to 2 percent of suicides involve the killing of an additional person or people. I will never know why Dylan was part of that small percentage. I will never be able to explain or excuse what he did. No humiliating experience at school could justify such a disproportionate reaction. Nor can I say how powerfully he was influenced by a friend. I don't

know how much control he had over his choices at the time of his death, what factors pushed him to commit murder, and why he did not end his pain alone. In talking with other suicide survivors and attempters, however, I think I have some idea why he didn't ask for help.

30   I believe that Dylan did not want to talk about his thoughts because he was ashamed of having them. He was accustomed to handling his own problems, and he perceived his inability to do so as a weakness. People considering suicide sometimes feel that the world would be better off without them, and their reasons for wanting to die make sense to them. They are too ill to see the irrationality of their thinking. I believe it frightened Dylan to encounter something he did not know how to manage, since he had always taken pride in his self-reliance. I believe he tried to push his negative thoughts away, not realizing that bringing them out in the open was a way to conquer them.

31   In raising Dylan, I taught him how to protect himself from a host of dangers: lightning, snake

disproportionate: uneven

bites, head injuries, skin cancer, smoking, drinking, sexually transmitted diseases, drug addiction, reckless driving, even carbon monoxide poisoning. It never occurred to me that the gravest danger—to him and, as it turned out, to so many others—might come from within. Most of us do not see suicidal thinking as the health threat that it is. We are not trained to identify it in others, to help others appropriately, or to respond in a healthy way if we have these feelings ourselves.

32   In loving memory of Dylan, I support suicide research and encourage responsible prevention and awareness practices as

> *People considering suicide sometimes feel that the world would be better off without them*

well as support for survivors. I hope that someday everyone will recognize the warning signs of suicide—including feelings of hopelessness, withdrawal, pessimism, and other signs of serious depression—as easily as we recognize the warning signs of cancer. I hope we will get over our fear of talking about suicide. I hope we will teach our children that most suicidal teens telegraph their intentions to their friends, whether through verbal statements, notes, or a preoccupation with death. I hope we come to understand the link between suicidal behavior and violent behavior and realize that dealing with the former may help us prevent the latter. (According to the U.S. Secret Service Safe School Initiative, 78 percent of school attackers have a history of suicide attempts or suicidal thoughts.) But we must remember that warning signs may not always tell the story. No one saw that Dylan was depressed. He did not speak of death, give away possessions, or say that the world would be better off without him. And we should also remember that even if someone is exhibiting signs of suicide risk, it may not always be possible

to prevent tragedy. Some who commit suicide or murder-suicide are—like Eric Harris—already receiving psychiatric care.

33   If my research has taught me one thing, it's this: Anyone can be touched by suicide. But for those who are feeling suicidal or who have lost someone to suicide, help *is* available—through resources provided by nonprofits like the American Foundation for Suicide Prevention, and the American Association of Suicidology. (If you are having persistent thoughts about suicide, call the national suicide prevention lifeline at 800-273-8255 to speak with a counselor. And if you are dealing with the loss of a loved one to suicide, know that National Survivors of Suicide Day is November 21, with more than 150 conferences scheduled across the United States and around the world.)

34   For the rest of my life, I will be haunted by the horror and anguish Dylan caused. I cannot look at a child in a grocery store or on the street without thinking about how my son's schoolmates spent the last moments of their lives. Dylan changed everything I believed about my self, about God, about family, and about love. I think I believed that if I loved someone as deeply as I loved him, I would know if he were in trouble. My maternal instincts would keep him safe. But I didn't know. And my instincts weren't enough. And the fact that I never saw tragedy coming is still almost inconceivable to me. I only hope my story can help those who can still be helped. I hope that, by reading of my experience, someone will see what I missed.

telegraph: communicate
inconceivable: unbelievable

CONVERSATIONS: Collaborating in Class or Online

1. How does Klebold characterize Dylan's personality?
2. When did the author first realize that her son was dead?
3. Why did the family have to leave their house?
4. When did Klebold realize her son was one of the killers?

CONNECTIONS: Discovering Relationships among Ideas

5. In what ways do Dylan's reflections and writing assignments forecast the Columbine tragedy?

6. What was Klebold's personal reaction to the massacre? Describe her private agony.

7. How did the author finally make sense of her son's actions?

8. What does Klebold mean when she says, "Dylan changed everything I believed about my self, about God, about family, and about love" (para. 34)?

PRESENTATION: Analyzing the Writer's Craft

9. This essay starts with a close-up view of the author at work. Is this an effective beginning? Explain your answer.

10. What is Klebold's purpose in this essay?

11. How does the author pace her delivery of the details to keep her readers interested?

12. What is the author's point of view toward her subject? Does that point of view change during the course of the essay? If so, how?

PROJECTS: Expressing Your Own Views

13. **Web Site:** Search for information on the Internet about Columbine. Now that you've read this essay, what material on the Web is accurate? What is inaccurate?

14. **Poem**: Write a poem based on one of your personal experiences.

15. **Editorial**: Write an editorial about our suicide rate in the United States, expressing your opinions on the subject. Explore some reliable Internet sources if necessary.

16. **Research**: Read and summarize the three resources below. Generate one specific question from each resource that focuses on narration. Then answer one of your questions in a documented essay, consulting these and other sources as necessary.

OTHER RESOURCES

 Web Site

National Suicide Prevention Lifeline:

www.suicidepreventionlifeline.org

Academic Article

"A Columbine Study: Giving Voice, Hearing Meaning" by Carolyn Lunsford Mears

Oral History Review 35.2 (2008): 159–175

 Audio/Video

CNN: www.cnn.com

Search: "Columbine Survivor Speaks"

Click on the Video link

ONE LAST THOUGHT

In 2004, President Bush signed the Garrett Lee Smith Memorial Act into law. It provides $82 million in funding for states to provide youth suicide intervention and prevention programs. The law is named after Garrett Lee Smith, the son of Oregon Senator Gordon Smith and his wife, Sharon, who committed suicide in 2003 at the age of 21. How do you think states can best use this funding to detect and prevent teenage suicide?

Gas Station on Route 66

by Joseph Sohm

Joseph Sohm is a well-known historian, public speaker, and photographer whose book, *Visions of America,* attempts to define "democracy" through pictures taken in all fifty states. His work has been published in many prominent journals, including *National Geographic*, the *New York Times*, *The Wall Street Journal*, and *The Washington Post*. He has also created a popular music video titled *Voices for Tomorrow.*

PREREADING QUESTIONS

Have you ever visited a small town? What were the circumstances?

Have you seen any abandoned buildings? Where were they?

What connections do you have with rural communities?

CONVERSATIONS: Collaborating in Class or Online

1. What is the photograph's primary message? List the details in the photo that create this message.
2. Which details are most prominent?
3. What is the significance of the background in this picture?
4. Create a story about this picture from your imagination.

CONNECTIONS: Discovering Relationships among Ideas

5. What were these buildings? What time period do they represent? How do you know this?
6. What is the relationship between the buildings in the foreground and those in the background?
7. How do the trees in the background contrast with the buildings in the foreground?
8. What do you imagine the sign on the pole used to say?

PRESENTATION: Analyzing the Writer's Craft

9. What do you think is the photographer's purpose in this photo?
10. What is the photographer's point of view toward the subject? How did you come to this conclusion?
11. What details in the photo support the photographer's purpose?
12. What conclusions can you draw from this picture?

PROJECTS: Expressing Your Own Views

13. **Ad:** Renovate this building with an ad that will bring new life to it.
14. **Internet:** Find a picture on the Internet that tells a story completely opposite to the one suggested by this photo.
15. **Essay:** Draft a story from the picture you found in response to assignment #14.
16. **Research:** Read and summarize the three resources below. Generate one specific question from each resource that focuses on narration. Then answer one of your questions in a documented essay, consulting these and other sources as necessary.

OTHER RESOURCES

Web Site

Couch Surfing: www. couchsurfing.org

Academic Article

"Travel, Travel Writing, and the Literature of Travel" by Michael Mewshaw

South Central Review 22.2 (2005): 2–10

Audio/Video

National Geographic: www. nationalgeographic.com

Search: "Geotourism: The Future of Travel"

Click on the Video link

ONE LAST THOUGHT

In 1903, Dr. Horatio Nelson Jackson distinguished himself as the first person to drive across the country in an automobile. His trip began on May18 with a $50 bet in San Francisco and ended July 16 in New York City. Along the way, Dr. Jackson and his bicycle mechanic, Sewall K. Crocker, acquired a pit bull named Bud, but the dust proved too strong for the dog, and they eventually had to fit him with driving goggles. The car Dr. Jackson drove, a Winston called the *Vermont*, is on display in the National Museum of American History in Washington, D.C. If you could drive anywhere in the country, where would you go? Why?

After a Fall

by Garrison Keillor

Best known for his creation of the Peabody Award–winning radio program *A Prairie Home Companion*, **Garrison Keillor** began his career as a radio announcer and producer during his student days at the University of Minnesota. His show features an eclectic mix of traditional jazz and folk music, supplemented by Keillor's rambling, nostalgic, and often hilarious anecdotes about the zany inhabitants of the fictitious small town of Lake Wobegon, Minnesota.

PREREADING QUESTIONS

Have you ever been publicly embarrassed?

What types of events typically cause you to feel self-conscious?

Why do you think some people are more easily embarrassed than others?

1   When you happen to step off an edge you didn't see and lurch forward into space waving your arms, it's the end of the world for a second or two, and after you do land, even if you know you're O.K. and no bones are broken, it may take a few seconds to decide whether this is funny or not. Your body is still worked up about the fall—especially the nervous system and the adrenaline-producing areas. In fact, I am *still* a little shaky from a spill that occurred two hours ago, when I put on a jacket, walked out the front door of this house here in St. Paul, Minnesota, and for no reason whatever took a plunge down five steps and landed on the sidewalk flat on my back with my legs in the air. I am thirty-nine years old and in fairly good shape, not prone to blackouts or sudden dizziness, and so a sudden inexplicable fall comes as a big surprise to me.

2   A woman was jogging down the street—a short, muscular young woman in a gray sweat-shirt and sweatpants—stopped and asked if I was O.K. "Yeah! Fine!" I said and got right up. "I just fell, I guess," I said. "Thanks," I said. She smiled and trotted away.

3   Her smile has followed me into the house, and I see it now as a smirk, which is what it was. She was too polite to bend over and hoot and shriek and guffaw and cackle and cough and whoop and wheeze and slap her thighs and stomp on

inexplicable: strange, unexplainable

the ground, but it was there in that smile: a young woman who through rigorous physical training and feminist thinking has gradually been taking charge of her own life and ridding her attic of self-hatred and doubt and fear and mindless competitiveness and other artifacts of male-dominated culture is rewarded with the sight of a middle-aged man in a brown suit with a striped tie falling down some steps as if someone had kicked him in the pants.

4   I'm sorry if I don't consider this humorous. I would like to. I wish she had come over and helped me up and then perhaps sat on the steps with me while I calmed down. We might have got to talking about the fall and how each of us viewed it from a different perspective... .

5   I might have seen it her way, but she ran down the street, and now I can only see my side of the fall. I feel old and achy and ridiculous and cheapened by the whole experience. I understand now why my son was so angry with me a few months ago when he tripped on a shoelace and fell in the neighbor's yard—a yard where the neighbor's sheepdog had lived for years—and I cackled at him.

6   "It's not funny!" he yelled.

7   "Oh, don't be so sensitive," I said.

8   Don't be so sensitive! What a dumb thing to say! Who has the right to tell someone else how to feel? It is the right of the person who falls in the dog droppings to decide for himself or herself how he or she will feel. It's not up to a jury. The fallen person determines whether it's funny or not... .

9   Five years ago, I got on a bus with five musicians and rode around for two weeks doing shows every night. They played music; I told jokes and sang a song. One night, in the cafeteria of a junior college in southern Minnesota, we happened to draw a big crowd, and the stage—four big plywood sheets on three-foot steel legs—was moved back twenty feet to make room for more chairs. The show was late starting, the room was stuffy, the crowd was impatient, and when finally the lights dimmed and the spotlight shone on the plywood, I broke from the back door and made a run for the stage,

> *I feel old and achy and ridiculous and cheapened by the whole experience*

IN CONTEXT

In addition to hosting *A Prairie Home Companion*, Garrison Keillor also frequently writes opinion pieces for Salon.com, an online news magazine. Visit their Web site, and search "Garrison Keillor" for a directory of his recent contributions.

thinking to make a dramatic entrance and give these fine people the show they were waiting for.

10   What I could not see in the dark was the ceiling and a low concrete overhang that the stage had been moved partly under, and then the spotlight caught me straight in the eyes and I couldn't see anything. I leaped up onto the stage, and in mid-leap my head hit concrete and my right leg caught the plywood at mid-shin. I toppled forward, stuck out my hands, and landed on my hands and knees. The crowd drew a long breath. I got right up—I had been doing shows long enough to know not to lie onstage and cry in front of a paying audience—and, seeing the microphone about ten feet ahead, strode up to it and held out my arms and said, "Hello, everybody! I'm happy to be here!"

11   Then they laughed—a big thunderstorm of a laugh and a big round of applause for what they now saw had been a wonderful trick. But it wasn't funny! My neck hurt! I hurt all over! On the other hand, to see a tall man in a white suit jump directly into a ceiling and then fall down—how often does a person get to see that? Men dive off high towers through fiery hoops into tiny tanks, men rev up motorcycles and leap long rows of trucks and buses, but I am the only man in show business who takes a good run and jumps Straight Up Into Solid Concrete Using Only His Bare Head. Amazing! ...

12   Oh, it is a sad story, except for the fact that it isn't. My ceiling jump got the show off to a

---

rigorous: thorough, hard

great start. The band played three fast tunes, and I jumped carefully back onstage and did a monologue that the audience, which now *knew* I was funny, laughed at a lot. Even I, who had a headache, thought it was funny. I really did feel lucky.

13   So do I still—a tall man who fell now sitting down to write his memoirs. The body is so delicate, the skeleton so skinny; we are slick men penciled in lightly, with a wooden stick cage to protect the heart and lungs and a cap of bone over the brain. I wonder that I have survived so many plunges, so many quick drops down the short arc that leads to the ground… .

14   The first time I ever went naked in mixed company was at the house of a girl whose father had a bad back and had built himself a sauna in the corner of the basement. Donna and I were friends in college. Both of us had grown up in fundamentalist Christian homes, and we liked to compare notes on that. We both felt constricted by our upbringings and were intent on liberating ourselves and becoming more free and open and natural. So it seemed natural and inevitable one night to wind up at her house with some of her friends there and her parents gone and to take off our clothes and have a sauna.

15   We were nineteen years old and were very cool ("Take off my clothes? Well, sure. Heck, I've taken them off *dozens* of times") and were careful to keep cool and be nonchalant and not look at anybody below the neck. We got into the sauna

> **The first time I ever went naked in mixed company ›› .**

as if getting on the bus. *People do this*, I thought to myself. *There is nothing unusual about it! Nothing! We all have bodies! There is no reason to get excited! This is a normal part of life!*

16   We filed into the little wooden room, all six of us, avoiding unnecessary body contact, and Donna poured a bucket of water on the hot rocks to make steam. It was very quiet. "There's a shower there on the wall if you want to take a shower," she said in a strange, nervous voice.

17   "Hey! How about a shower!" a guy said in a cool-guy voice, and he turned on the water full blast. The shower head leaped from the wall. It was a hand-held type—a nozzle at the end of a hose—and it jumped out at us like a snake and thrashed around exploding ice-cold water. He fell back, someone screamed, I slipped and fell, Donna fell on top of me, we leaped apart, and meanwhile the nozzle danced and flew from the force of the blast of water. Donna ran out of the sauna and slipped and fell on the laundry-room floor, and another girl yelled, "God damn you, Tom!" Donna scrambled to her feet. "God! Oh, God!" she cried. Tom yelled, "I'm sorry!" Another guy laughed a loud, wicked laugh, and I tiptoed out as fast as I could move, grabbed my clothes, and got dressed. Donna grabbed her clothes. "Are you all right?" I said, not looking at her or anything. "No!" she said. Somebody laughed a warm, appreciative laugh from inside the sauna. "Don't laugh!" she yelled. "It isn't funny! It isn't the least bit funny!"

18   "I'm not laughing," I said, though it wasn't me she was angry at. I *still* am not laughing. I think it's a very serious matter, twenty years later. Your first venture as a naked person, you want it to go right and be a good experience, and then some joker has to go pull a fast one… .

19   I haven't seen you since that night, Donna. I've told the sauna story to dozens of people over the years, and they all thought it was funny but I still don't know what you think. Are you all right?

monologue: speech
fundamentalist: extreme
liberating: freeing

CONVERSATIONS: Collaborating in Class or Online

1. What is the cause of Keillor's embarrassment in this essay?
2. What role does Donna play in the situation the author depicts?
3. What did all Keillor's falls have in common?
4. What does the author mean when he says, "Who has the right to tell someone else how to feel?" (para. 8)?

CONNECTIONS: Discovering Relationships among Ideas

5. Why is "after" an important word in the title of this essay?
6. Why do you think Keillor mentions his son's fall in his narrative?
7. For Keillor, what is important about the act of falling? What do falls represent for him?
8. When he titled this essay, Keillor may have been making a reference to the Biblical fall of humankind. What do you think Keillor is saying about the relationship between his fall and the fall from grace in the Garden of Eden?

PRESENTATION: Analyzing the Writer's Craft

9. What do you think is Keillor's purpose in this essay?
10. What is his point of view toward his subject?
11. Who do you think Keillor's audience is?
12. Why does Keillor end with the question "Are you all right?"

PROJECTS: Expressing Your Own Views

13. **Script:** Write a stand-up comedy routine about embarrassing moments.
14. **Story:** Read one of Keillor's stories about Lake Wobegon on the Prairie Home Companion Web site. Then write an imaginary story of your own to add to Keillor's collection.
15. **Essay:** Write a character analysis of one of the people Keillor describes in this narrative or in the Lake Wobegon stories. What are the person's main qualities? Are these likable traits or not? Are the character's actions reasonable? Give specific examples from the story to support your opinions.
16. **Research:** Read and summarize the three resources below. Generate one specific question from each resource that focuses on narration. Then answer one of your questions in a documented essay, consulting these and other sources as necessary.

OTHER RESOURCES

Web Site

Boulder Therapist: www.
BoulderTherapist.com

Search: "Wobegon Intelligence
Test"

Click on the Wobegon Intelligence Test link

Academic Article

"Revitalizing the Oral Tradition: Stories Broadcast by Radio Parana (San, Mali)"
by Cécile Leguy

Research in African Literatures 38.3 (2007):
136–147

Audio/Video

Prairie Home Companion with
Garrison Keillor: http://prairie-home.publicradio.org

Click on any of the Audio highlights

ONE LAST THOUGHT

Radio drama, Garrison Keillor's favorite medium, has been around for decades. It developed in the 1920s and was a widespread form of entertainment by the 1940s. Stations offered broadcasts of every genre from soap operas to comedies. In 1938, Orson Wells actually convinced his listeners that an alien invasion from Mars was occurring during his radio broadcast, *The War of the Worlds*. Radio dramas began to decline in the early 1960s with the growing popularity of television. Now, most American radio dramas are available through podcasts or rebroadcasts. Have you ever heard any radio dramas? If you were going to create one, what would it be about?

Down by the Old Mill Stream

by Tell Taylor

"Down by the Old Mill Stream," a classic of America's musical heritage, was written by **Tell Taylor** in 1908 and first performed two years later by a vocal group called the Orpheus Comedy Four at a Woolworth's Store in downtown Kansas City, Missouri. Penned while Taylor was sitting on the banks of the Blanchard River in northwest Ohio, the song has sold over four million copies of its sheet music, been recorded by such legends as John Denver, and remained a staple of the repertoire of barbershop quartets for the past one hundred years.

PREREADING QUESTIONS

What is your favorite classic love story?

What are the main features of this narrative?

Is this story connected to a special time or place?

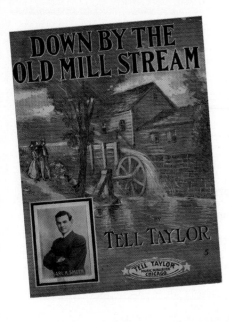

1   My darling I am dreaming of the days gone by,
    When you and I were sweethearts beneath the summer sky;
    Your hair has turned to silver the gold has faded too;
    But still I will remember, where I first met you.

2   The old mill wheel is silent and has fallen down,
    The old oak tree has withered and lies there on the ground;
    While you and I are sweethearts the same as days of yore;
    Although we've been together, forty years and more.

3   Down by the old mill stream where I first met you
    With your eyes of blue, dressed in gingham too,
    It was there I knew that you loved me true,
    You were sixteen, my village queen, by the old mill stream.

gingham: cloth with checked pattern

CONVERSATIONS: Collaborating in Class or Online

1. Briefly summarize the lyrics to this song.
2. Why do you think the writer is reminiscing about this love affair?
3. What specific details in the song help us understand the writer's feelings?
4. How do the lyrics let us know that a great deal of time has passed?

CONNECTIONS: Discovering Relationships among Ideas

5. Even though this song was written in 1908, it conveys universal feelings that most of us share today. In what ways do you identify with these lyrics?
6. How stable is the love discussed in this song? How do you know?
7. In what ways does the third verse capture the general sense of the lyrics?
8. How does growing older affect our view of the people we love?

PRESENTATION: Analyzing the Writer's Craft

9. What is Taylor's primary purpose in this song?
10. What is the songwriter's point of view in relation to his subject?
11. What one word best describes the writer's attitude in this song?
12. When you play this song, do you think the melody of the chorus goes well with the lyrics? In what ways do they complement each other?

PROJECTS: Expressing Your Own Views

13. **Song:** Write a song or poem of your own about a romantic relationship you have had. Make sure your song has a clear purpose.

14. **Commentary:** Use narration to explain the role of friends in your life. How much are they part of your self-definition? How do they fit into your lifestyle?

15. **Essay:** Of all your friends and family, which people do you need most in your life? In what ways do they fulfill your needs? What would you do without them? In a narrative essay, explain the various roles these people play in your life. Decide upon a clear purpose for your essay before you begin to write.

16. **Research:** Read and summarize the three resources below. Generate one specific question from each resource that focuses on narration. Then answer one of your questions in a documented essay, consulting these and other sources as necessary.

OTHER RESOURCES

Web Site

Parlor Songs Historical American Sheet Music Collection: http://parlorsongs.com

Click on the "Back Issues" link

Explore the May 1999 featured covers

Academic Article

"Narrative Theory as an Analytical Tool in the Study of Popular Music Texts" by David Nicholls

Music and Letters 88.2 (2007): 297–315

Audio/Video

iLike: www.ilike.com

Search: "Down by the Old Mill Stream"

Listen to clips from different artists performing this song

ONE LAST THOUGHT

"Down by the Old Mill Stream" was one of the most popular songs in the early 20th century. It quickly became a favorite of barbershop quartets, which feature four harmonizing voices and are usually performed *a cappella* (without music). Have you ever heard a quartet like this? Can you think of any songs or artists you would like to hear perform in this style?

Only Daughter

by Sandra Cisneros

Sandra Cisneros was the only daughter in a family with six sons. She earned her M.F.A. in creative writing from the University of Iowa, where she developed her unique voice as a strong and independent working-class, Mexican American woman. Her best-known book, *The House on Mango Street* (1984), is a loosely structured series of vignettes focusing on the isolation and cultural conflicts endured by Latina women in America.

PREREADING QUESTIONS

What is your family like?

What activities do you enjoy most?

Have you ever felt that your family didn't accept these activities or enjoy them as much as you did?

---

1   Once, several years ago, when I was just starting out my writing career, I was asked to write my own contributor's note for an anthology. I wrote: "I am the only daughter in a family of six sons. *That* explains everything."

2   Well, I've thought that ever since, and yes, it explains a lot to me, but for the reader's sake I should have written: "I am the only daughter in a *Mexican* family of six sons." Or even: "I am the only daughter of a Mexican father and a Mexican-American mother." Or: "I am the only daughter of a working-class family of nine." All of these had everything to do with who I am today.

3   I was/am the only daughter and *only* a daughter. Being an only daughter in a family of six sons forced me by circumstance to spend a lot of time by myself because my brothers felt it beneath them to play with a *girl* in public. But that aloneness, that loneliness, was good for a would-be writer—it allowed me time to think and think, to imagine, to read and prepare myself.

4   Being only a daughter for my father meant my destiny would lead me to become someone's wife. That's what he believed. But when I was in the fifth grade and shared my plans for college with him, I was sure he understood. I remember my father saying, "*Que bueno, mi'ja*, that's good." That meant a lot to me, especially since my brothers thought the idea hilarious. What I didn't realize was that my father thought college

was good for girls—good for finding a husband. After four years in college and two more in graduate school, and still no husband, my father shakes his head even now and says I wasted all that education.

5   In retrospect, I'm lucky my father believed daughters were meant for husbands. It meant it didn't matter if I majored in something silly like English. After all, I'd find a nice professional eventually, right? This allowed me the liberty to putter about embroidering my little poems and stories without my father interrupting with so much as a "What's that you're writing?"

6   But the truth is, I wanted him to interrupt. I wanted my father to understand what it was I was scribbling, to introduce me as "My only daughter, the writer." Not as "This is my only daughter. She teaches." *Es maestra*—teacher. Not even *profesora*.

7   In a sense, everything I have ever written has been for him, to win his approval even though I know my father can't read English words, even though my father's only reading includes the brown-ink *Esto* sports magazines from Mexico City and the bloody *¡Alarma!* magazines that feature yet another sighting of *La Virgen de Guadalupe* on a tortilla or a wife's revenge on her philandering husband by bashing his skull in with a *molcajete* (a kitchen mortar made of volcanic rock). Or the *fotonovelas,* the little picture paperbacks with tragedy and trauma erupting from the characters' mouths in bubbles.

> *somehow I could feel myself being erased*

8   A father represents, then, the public majority. A public who is disinterested in reading, and yet one whom I am writing about and for, and privately trying to woo.

9   When we were growing up in Chicago, we moved a lot because of my father. He suffered bouts of nostalgia. Then we'd have to let go of our flat, store the furniture with mother's relatives, load the station wagon with baggage and bologna sandwiches and head south. To Mexico City.

10   We came back, of course. To yet another Chicago flat, another Chicago neighborhood, another Catholic school. Each time, my father would seek out the parish priest in order to get a tuition break, and complain or boast: "I have seven sons."

11   He meant *siete hijos,* seven children, but he translated it as "sons." "I have seven sons." To anyone who would listen. The Sears Roebuck employee who sold us the washing machine. The short-order cook where my father ate his ham-and-eggs breakfasts. "I have seven sons." As if he deserved a medal from the state.

12   My papa. He didn't mean anything by the mistranslation, I'm sure. But somehow I could feel myself being erased. I'd tug my father's sleeve and whisper: "Not seven sons. Six! and one *daughter*."

13   When my oldest brother graduated from medical school, he fulfilled my father's dream that we study hard and use this—our heads, instead of this—our hands. Even now my father's hands are thick and yellow, stubbed by a history of hammer and nails and twine and coils and springs. "Use this," my father said, tapping his head, "and not this," showing us those hands. He always looked tired when he said it.

14   Wasn't college an investment? And hadn't I spent all those years in college? And if I didn't marry, what was it all for? Why would anyone go to college and then choose to be poor? Especially someone who has always been poor.

retrospect: looking back
philandering: promiscuous
bouts: short periods of time
nostalgia: longing for the past

IN CONTEXT

NEA

The National Endowment for the Arts, established in 1965, is "a public agency that offers support and funding for projects exhibiting artistic excellence." It is currently the largest source of funding for the arts in all 50 states. To learn more, visit their Web site: www.nea.gov.

15   Last year, after ten years of writing professionally, the financial rewards started to trickle in. My second National Endowment for the Arts Fellowship. A guest professorship at the University of California, Berkeley. My book, which sold to a major New York publishing house.

16   At Christmas, I flew home to Chicago. The house was throbbing, same as always; hot *tamales* and sweet *tamales* hissing in my mother's pressure cooker, and everybody—my mother, six brothers, wives, babies, aunts, cousins—talking too loud and at the same time, like in a Fellini film, because that's just how we are.

17   I went upstairs to my father's room. One of my stories had just been translated into Spanish and published in an anthology of Chicano writing, and I wanted to show it to him. Ever since he recovered from a stroke two years ago, my father likes to spend his leisure hours horizontally. And that's how I found him, watching a Pedro Infante movie on Galavision and eating rice pudding.

18   There was a glass filmed with milk on the bedside table. There were several vials of pills and balled Kleenex. And on the floor, one black sock and a plastic urinal that I didn't want to look at but looked at anyway. Pedro Infante was about to burst into song, and my father was laughing.

19   I'm not sure if it was because my story was translated into Spanish, or because it was published in Mexico, or perhaps because the story dealt with Tepeyac, the *colonia* my father was raised in and the house he grew up in, but at any rate, my father punched the mute button on his remote control and read my story.

20   I sat on the bed next to my father and waited. He read it very slowly. As if he were reading each line over and over. He laughed at all the right places and read lines he liked out loud. He pointed and asked questions: "Is this So-and-so?" "Yes," I said. He kept reading.

21   When he was finally finished, after what seemed like hours, my father looked up and asked: "Where can we get more copies of this for the relatives?"

22   Of all the wonderful things that happened to me last year, that was the most wonderful.

CONVERSATIONS: Collaborating in Class or Online

1. How many children are in Cisneros's family? How many are boys?
2. What are the differences in the way the author's father views his sons and his daughter?
3. Why does Cisneros's father always say he has seven sons? Why is this detail significant?
4. Why did Cisneros's father let her go to college? Explain your answer.

CONNECTIONS: Discovering Relationships among Ideas

5. What does Cisneros mean when she says, "I am the only daughter and *only* a daughter" (para. 3)?
6. What does her cultural heritage have to do with the fact that she is the only daughter?
7. In what way does Cisneros write for her father even though he can't read English?
8. Why was her father's reaction to her published story "the most wonderful" (para. 22) thing that happened to her last year? Why is her father's opinion so important to her?

PRESENTATION: Analyzing the Writer's Craft

9. From what point of view does Cisneros write this narrative?
10. What is her purpose in writing it?
11. Who do you think Cisneros's audience is?
12. What is the significance of her title?

PROJECTS: Expressing Your Own Views

13. **Interview:** Interview someone about his or her writing. Does the person do creative writing? Is writing difficult or easy for this person? Does he or she read a lot? Write a brief "biography" of this person focusing on his or her writing background.
14. **Internet:** Go to Cisneros's Web site (www.sandracisneros.com), and view her photo gallery. Choose one picture, and write a brief narrative about it. Turn in a copy of the picture with your story.
15. **Essay:** Write an essay telling your classmates about a time you felt out of place. Make a special effort to communicate your feelings regarding this experience. Remember to choose your details and point of view with a specific purpose in mind.
16. **Research:** Read and summarize the three resources below. Generate one specific question from each resource that focuses on narration. Then answer one of your questions in a documented essay, consulting these and other sources as necessary.

OTHER RESOURCES

Web Site

Sandra Cisneros: www. sandracisneros.com

Click on the Articles, Interviews, Reviews link

Read some of her recent postings

Academic Article

"Parental Status and Differential Investment in Sons and Daughters: Trivers-Willard Revisited" by Rosemary L. Hopcroft

Social Forces 83.3 (2005): 1111–1136

Audio/Video

5 Min Life Videopedia: www.5min.com

Search: "How a Second Generation Immigrant Opens Dialogue with Parents"

Click on the Video link

ONE LAST THOUGHT

When one of Cisneros's short stories was translated into Spanish, her father was finally able to read her writing. Translating written words is not a task for the faint of heart because mishaps like those pictured here can occur. Have you ever needed someone to translate a foreign expression for you, or are you bilingual? What difficulties might arise from reading translations? From writing translations?

CHAPTER WRITING ASSIGNMENTS

Write a well-developed essay in response to one of the following prompts. Consult the chapter introduction for guidance in creating your essay.

CONNECTING THE READINGS

1. Academia is generally viewed as a safe place to learn about life. How do you think the professor pictured in the cartoon by Sipress ("Academia") would react to the Columbine massacre ("I Will Never Know Why")?

2. In "Rumspringa," Shachtman characterizes the rebellion of a group of Amish teens as they separate from their parents to discover their own ideals and values. How would these teens react to the song "Down by the Old Mill Stream"? Why do you think they would respond in this way?

3. Garrison Keillor ("After a Fall") and Sandra Cisneros ("Only Daughter") are both well-known contemporary writers. In these essays, they deal with extremely sensitive emotional issues. Using selected details from their narratives, explain how they each cope with fragile emotions.

4. Explain how the physical desolation depicted in "Gas Station on Route 66" (Joseph Sohm) and the emotional despair in "I Will Never Know Why" (Susan Klebold) are similar. Use as many senses as possible in your comparison.

MOVING BEYOND THE READINGS

5. Write a narrative about your favorite relative. Try to characterize this person through the details of your essay.

6. Write an autobiography of yourself as a writer. When did you compose the first work you were really proud of? What genre or type of writing was it? How have you developed as a writer over the years?

7. Write a narrative about the most unusual day in your life. Decide on a particular vantage point, and make sure your essay has a specific purpose.

8. What ten items would you take with you if you were going to live alone in a deserted area? Why would you choose them? Weave these items into an interesting narrative essay that would appeal to the general reader.

COMBINING RHETORICAL MODES

9. Analyze the lyrics of your favorite song. What does it say? How do you relate to the words and ideas in the song? Why is it your favorite?

10. Compare and contrast two of your favorite photographs or works of art. What attracts you to these pictures? What are their similarities and differences?

11. Analyze the role you assume in your family (e.g., peacemaker, organizer, cook, comedian, etc.). How did you acquire this role? Why do you continue to assume these responsibilities?

12. Explain the history of how you have chosen to live your life by analyzing the causes and effects of various important decisions you have made. What do your choices say about you as a person?

7 Illustration

Giving illustrations or examples to make a point is a natural part of the way we communicate. We support our statements with illustrations on exams, through Internet conversations, and in private discussions with friends every day. Citing examples would help us accomplish all of the following tasks:

- Clarifying how much money we spend on foreign aid;
- Explaining the increase in autism in the United States;
- Showing how children acquire language;
- Persuading someone that exercise is essential to her health;
- Describing the types of problems your computer is having.

Critical thinking through illustration relies on specific examples to communicate the exact idea the speaker or writer is trying to communicate. In fact, in a successful illustration essay, the examples drive the point home by themselves. In this mode, examples stimulate, clarify, or persuade the reader or listener.

DEVELOPMENT STRATEGIES: ILLUSTRATION

Statement or Point

Development

⟶ **Example**

⟶ **Example**

⟶ **Example**

                                    Conclusion

Introducing Illustration

Working with examples gives you yet another powerful way of understanding and processing your immediate environment and the larger world around you. It involves a type of thinking that is completely different from description and narration. Using examples to think critically means finding a definite order in a series of specific, concrete, related illustrations that might not be immediately obvious to your readers.

Well-chosen examples and illustrations are an essay's building blocks. They can be drawn from your experience, your observations, and your reading. They help you *show* rather than *tell* what you mean in the following ways:

- By supplying concrete details (references to what we can see, smell, taste, hear, or touch) to support abstract ideas (such as faith, hope, understanding, and love);
- By providing specifics ("I like chocolate") to explain generalizations ("I like sweets"); and
- By giving definite references ("Turn left at the second stoplight") to clarify vague statements ("Turn in a few blocks").

Though illustrations take many forms, writers often find themselves indebted to description or narration (or some combination of the two) in order to supply enough relevant examples to achieve their rhetorical intent.

Illustration essays are written for one of three purposes: to stimulate interest, to clarify, or to persuade. Look at an example of each:

DEVELOPMENT STRATEGIES AT WORK

To Stimulate Interest

Statement: Basketball star Kobe Bryant works out a lot during his off season.

Development

⟶ **Example**: Bryant runs 50 laps each day

⟶ **Example**: He lifts weights for an hour

⟶ **Example**: He practices his jump shot for another hour

                                    Conclusion

DEVELOPMENT STRATEGIES AT WORK

To Clarify

Statement: I still have a few writing problems that I can't get rid of.

Development

⟶ **Example**: I don't understand how to write a thesis statement

⟶ **Example**: I don't develop my ideas enough

⟶ **Example**: My conclusions are boring

⟶ **Example**: I keep writing fragments

Conclusion

DEVELOPMENT STRATEGIES AT WORK

To Persuade

Statement: Americans are more health conscious today than they have been in the past.

Development

⟶ **Example**: People are buying more fresh produce at the store

⟶ **Example**: People are reading labels on food more often then they used to

⟶ **Example**: They're spending more time exercising

⟶ **Example**: They're getting more sleep

Conclusion

As you can see, the use of examples or illustrations provides a way for you to support and expand your message as you communicate in different situations. Only the inclusion of enough relevant examples will help you accomplish your purpose in writing. The guidelines discussed in this introduction will help you justify your statements and use examples effectively to support your ideas.

Discovering How Illustration Works

Here is a list of the most important elements of reasoning through illustration, whether for a visual (like a graph or a cartoon) or a prose selection. The Illustration Essentials listed here are equally useful as guidelines for both reading and writing.

Analyzing the paragraph below will help you understand the relationship between a specific point and the examples that support it. If you discover on your own how this method of reasoning works, you will be able to apply it effectively to your reading and writing. The questions following the paragraph will help you understand this rhetorical mode even more clearly.

In an essay entitled "Wallet of the Future? Your Mobile Phone," CNN makes the following statements:

> **ILLUSTRATION ESSENTIALS**
>
> Purpose or Point
> Relevant Examples
> Enough Examples
> Effective Organization
> Meaningful Conclusions

The mobile phone is staging a coup. These days, it seems that most Americans carry three things in their pockets or purses at all times: keys, a wallet, and a phone. But, in the not-too-distant future, you may be able to leave the wallet and the keys behind. Some analysts say that within five years, mobile phones in the United States will be able to make electronic payments, open doors, access subways, clip coupons, and possibly act as another form of identification. These futuristic uses for phones are becoming reality in countries like South Korea and Japan, which typically are ahead of the United States when it comes to mobile technology.

1. What is this paragraph's primary message?
2. List the examples in this paragraph. Which are directly related to the paragraph's message?
3. Are there enough examples to make the main point?
4. What other details might support the paragraph's topic sentence?
5. Are these details organized in a way that is easy to follow?
6. What conclusions can you draw from this information? What specific examples lead you to these conclusions?

Collaborative Responses Now discuss your responses to these questions with your classmates in small groups or as an entire class. How did the different perspectives from other students change your "reading" of the paragraph?

Reading Illustration

As you read the essays, cartoons, speeches, and blogs in this chapter, take time to notice the degree of specificity the writers use to make their various points. In every case, the more examples they use in their essays, the clearer their ideas are and the more we understand and are interested in what they are saying. Notice also that these writers know when to stop—when "more" becomes too much and boredom sets in for the reader.

Your initial reading of a selection is the time to pay close attention to the Illustration Essentials. You should address the following questions:

Illustration Essentials: Reading

- **Purpose or Point:** What is the author or illustrator trying to accomplish?
- **Relevant Examples:** Does the author/illustrator include relevant examples?
- **Enough Examples:** Does the author/illustrator include enough examples to make his/her point?
- **Effective Organization:** Is the reading organized so you can easily follow it?
- **Meaningful Conclusions:** Does the selection reach conclusions based on its examples? If so, what are they?

On your second and third readings of the selection, focus on areas of ambiguity and confusion so you can deepen your comprehension.

Writing Illustration

As we now consider using illustration in writing, keep the preceding list of essentials in mind as you go through the writing process for illustration.

Choosing a Subject and Audience

As with all writing, choosing a subject is the first step in producing a good essay. What do you want to write about? What do you want to say? Who will be your audience? Sometimes these guidelines are given to you. But if you can make your own choices, write on a topic that interests you and address readers who want to learn about the subject. Once you make these decisions, you can start generating examples that will form the body of your essay.

In the case of the paper you are about to read, our student writer, Manuel Garza, decided to write about competitive eating, which he recently learned about.

Generating Illustrations

Now is the time to use one of the prewriting strategies we discussed in Chapter 3. Record as many examples as you can think of that relate to your main message. Then organize and analyze these illustrations so you understand and can write about the relationships among them. Do you want to stimulate your readers' interest, clarify some information, or persuade them to think or act a certain way? Once you make these decisions, you will be able to choose the illustrations that will help you make your point most effectively.

For his paper, Manuel generates the following examples:

"speed eating"	*how to eat more efficiently*
dunking food	*strengthen jaw muscles*
rigorous practice schedule	*personal trainers*
eating strategies	*stomach elasticity*
pacing skills	*breaking, folding, and rolling food*
timing	*mental preparation*
increase stomach capacity	*will power/focus*

Next Manuel labels each item so he can determine his main topics. They fall into four main categories: (1) chewing and swallowing practice, (2) techniques for eating faster, (3) stomach elasticity, and (4) training the mind. These lists would be equally useful if Manuel were producing a visual or graphic of some kind.

"speed eating" (1)	*how to eat more efficiently (4)*
dunking food (2)	*strengthen jaw muscles (2)*
rigorous practice schedule (4)	*personal trainers (4)*
eating strategies (1)	*stomach elasticity (3)*
pacing skills (2)	*breaking, folding, and rolling food (2)*
timing (2)	*mental preparation (4)*
increase stomach capacity (3)	*will power/focus (4)*

From these categories, Manual needs to write a thesis statement that will give his project focus and direction.

Drafting a Thesis Statement

A thesis statement for an illustration essay should include the essay's topic and point. It serves as the controlling idea of your paper and will be the guide for choosing and organizing your examples. A thesis for a graphic or other project will not be as obvious, but will still be embedded in the project. For your illustration essay, do you want to stimulate your readers' interest, clarify some information, or persuade them to think or act a certain way? Once you make these decisions, you will be able to choose the illustrations that will help you make your point most effectively.

Here is Manuel's thesis:

> *Competitive eaters who want to become world champions must actually train and practice their technique to succeed in competition.*

This statement will now give focus and direction to Manuel's writing.

Producing a Draft

An illustration essay or project should be fairly straightforward to create.

- The **introduction** presents the subject(s), furnishes some background, and states the purpose of the essay in a single, clearly written thesis.
- The **body of the paper** then provides examples to support the thesis statement. These examples become the primary method of organizing the essay:
  - Spatially—from one item to the next
  - From one extreme to another—for example, from most impressive to least impressive or vice versa
  - Chronologically—from one event to another in a time sequence
- Finally, the **concluding section** summarizes the various examples cited in the body of the paper and draws relevant conclusions from their relationships.

As you will learn from reading the selections in this chapter, the careful organization of examples leads quite naturally to unity and coherence in your essays.

- **Unity** is a sense of wholeness and interrelatedness that writers achieve by making sure all their sentences are related to the essay's main idea;
- **Coherence** refers to logical development in an essay, with special attention to how well ideas grow out of one another as the essay develops.

Together, unity and coherence can help produce good writing.

At this point in the writing process, you should pay close attention to the Illustration Essentials. In fact, you can use the following questions for both written and graphic assignments:

Illustration Essentials: Writing

- **Purpose or Point:** Exactly what are you trying to say?
- **Relevant Examples:** What are the most relevant examples from your prewriting activities?
- **Enough Examples:** Do you have enough examples to make your point?
- **Effective Organization:** What order is most effective for the point you want to make?
- **Meaningful Conclusions:** What conclusions can you draw from your illustration essay?

Revising and Editing

The process of revising and editing requires you to review your essay or graphic and make certain it says exactly what you mean. Also, this is the time to add transitions to your writing that clearly show the relationship of the illustrations and examples to one another and to your central thesis.

Revising

Look closely at your essay or graphic as someone else might. Then answer the questions in the Revising Checklist (on page 28), which ask you to focus on how your essay functions.

Now is also the point in the writing process when you should add transitions to your essay that clarify the relationship of your examples to one another and to the general statement they are illustrating. In illustrations, these are usually words and phrases that explain logical connections. They include such words as *for example, in fact, in particular, namely, specifically,* and *that is.* These particular expressions will help your readers understand as clearly as possible the relationships among the items in your illustration.

Editing

To edit your work, you should look closely at words, sentences, entire paragraphs, and any visual details to make sure they are correct. Use the Editing Checklist on page 30 to review your project for errors in grammar and usage. When you locate a question or potential error, consult a handbook or go to Pearson's Web-based MyCompLab for an explanation of the problem.

Also, if your instructor marks any grammar mistakes on your paper or graphic, make sure you understand them. Recognizing errors in your own writing is the most effective way to correcting them.

As you read the following student essay, use the Illustration Essentials (page 141) and the questions for reading illustrations (page 142) to help you analyze it. Then, to thoroughly understand how this student essay works, pay special attention to the margin notes and the items in each paragraph they describe.

Manuel Garza
Professor Flachmann
English 101
22 Sept. 2011

Competitive Eating

Subject → 1 When we think about professional athletes, our minds conjure
images of sweaty men and women running through rows of tires,
muscled bodies lifting weights, and the intense looks of players on
their fiftieth wind sprint. Just as in the world of professional sports,
the world of competitive eating also features great athletes. Com-
Background → petitive eating, or "speed eating," is an activity in which participants
compete against each other to consume large quantities of food in
a short period of time. Contests are typically less than 15 minutes,
with the person consuming the most food being declared the winner. Many professional competitive eaters undergo rigorous personal
training in order to increase their stomach capacity, speed, and ef-
Thesis Statement → ficiency with various foods. Competitive eaters who want to become
world champions must actually train and practice their technique in
order to succeed in competition.

2 Because the type of food consumed varies from competition
Main Point → to competition, stomach elasticity is usually considered the key to
speed-eating success. Weeks before an event, competitive eaters
Example → train their stomachs to stretch by drinking large quantities of liq-
uid, usually water or milk, over a short period of time. Other eaters
Example → choose to expand their stomachs by consuming massive amounts of
Example → vegetables or salad, and some eaters combine the two practices by
eating vegetables and then ingesting lots of liquid.

3 Although the ability of a stomach to hold large amounts of
Main Point → food is an integral part of competitive eating, getting the food into
the stomach by chewing and swallowing is just as important. In or-
Example → der to prepare their jaws, some professional eaters will chew large
amounts of chewing gum to build jaw strength and increase their jaw

muscles' ability to stretch during the consumption of a lot of food. Along with practicing their chewing, some competitive eaters practice their swallowing with attention to pacing and timing. Certain pros will train by performing personal time trials using the contest food in order to predetermine a challenging pace for the competition. For example, a competitor may decide upon a five-count system *← Example* where he or she puts the food in the mouth, chews five times, swallows, and repeats; the pace would be something like hot dog—1 2 3 4 5, swallow; hot dog—1 2 3 4 5, swallow; and on and on until time runs out. Obviously, the type of food would have a large effect on the competitor's chewing and swallowing.

4 Along with pre-contest training, competitive eaters use a few *← Main Point* secret techniques developed over the years to help stuff food into themselves as rapidly as possible. The most basic of these methods is the water dunk. Virtually every competitor keeps a cup of water at *← Example* the table to dip the contest food into. The dunking softens and lubricates the food, which allows contestants to chew faster and swallow more easily. Although this practice is common, professional contests often enforce a limit on the amount of time competitors are allowed to dunk food, so it is important for eaters to practice this technique along with their other timed trials. Although any liquid can be used, anything that has calories will make it harder on the competitor to consume more food in the long run.

5 In addition to the water dunk, another favorite trick of profes- *← Transition* sional competitive eaters is to break the contest food into smaller, *← Example* more manageable pieces before eating it. This method allows competitors to fit more food into their mouths at once and also may cut down on chewing time. One world famous competitive eater, Takeru Kobayashi, breaks hot dogs in half when using his patented "Solo- *← Example* mon's Technique" and then stuffs both halves into his mouth at the same time. This method makes it easier to fit an entire hot dog in

Example ———▶ the mouth at once due to the length of the food in its original form. Knowing how to eat specific foods is important as well, with some pros eating their hot dogs separate from the buns, and often folding or rolling the slices when competing in a pizza-eating contest.

Summary ———▶   6 Aside from these training techniques and game-time tactics, competitive eating is largely a matter of willpower. Contestants must fight their gag reflexes and their stomach's natural adverse reaction to dumping such a large amount of food into it so quickly. But like

Conclusion ———▶ any successful athlete, the men and women who want to be world-champion professional competitive eaters must work hard to train their bodies and minds while preparing for the next challenge.

Reviewing Illustration

Based on the information you have learned in this chapter and the annotations on the student essay, show how this paper works by writing a clear, precise summary or by drawing your own outline or graphic representation of it. Label the examples on your visual. This exercise will confirm your understanding of the elements of illustration in both reading and writing.

Body Piercing

by Raquel Levine

Raquel Levine was an undergraduate student majoring in finance when "Body Piercing: Stick It Where the Sun Don't Shine" was originally published in the *McGill Tribune* under her maiden name, Kirsch. She later earned her law degree at Osgoode Hall in Toronto, where she was managing editor of *Obiter Dicta*, Canada's largest law school weekly. Levine currently works at Wolfson Law Professional Corporation in Toronto, where she specializes in corporate and commercial litigation.

PREREADING QUESTIONS

Do you have any body piercings? If so, how many?

Why did you get these piercings?

What statement do piercings generally make? Does the type of piercing change the statement?

1   Needles used to be a source of angst at the pediatrician's office. Almost any student can tell tales of kicking and screaming as a toddler. But now needles are all the rage. Not for anything illegal, but for putting holes in the body that are actually quite fashionable, otherwise known as body piercing.

2   The concept of body piercing has been around for millennia. Roman centurions, Caesar's elite, wore nipple rings as a sign of their virility and courage. Navel piercing was a symbol of royalty amongst the ancient Egyptians, and Amazonian tribal hunters and gatherers sported bullrings to intimidate their prey and appear more fearsome. However, its popularity among Westerners has soared in recent years.

3   A quick walk around campus will confirm that piercing isn't just for little girls' ears anymore. "I got my (ear) lobes pierced as a child,"

says Brianna Hersey, an art student. "It's something that girls do. Society tells you that you can do it. It's part of the traditional expected values (that society endorses)."

4   Hersey didn't stop with the ear. She also has her nose and her helix (the swell of her ear) pierced. Soon she will have her nipples pierced. She has felt unaccepted because of the prejudice against her facial piercings. "In the summer I worked at a private high school. They asked me to remove my facial piercings. Facial piercings are a representation of an alternative subculture. So if you're in a mainstream organization, they don't want to be seen as a representation of a subculture."

angst: anxiety, fear
virility: masculine strength

149

5   Richard Dupuis is a piercer at Le Slick Style Steel. He has noticed the way media has portrayed people with piercings. "There's a stigma against people with piercings," he states. "Is it going to fade? No. A lot of people have bad associations with them. In the movie *Bless the Child*, one of the hoodlums had a nose ring and an earring connected by a chain. So of course people are going to think bad things (about people with piercings)." "Younger people know that someone with a piercing isn't necessarily evil. But older people believe what they see on television. Tolerance is building, but there's room for growth."

6   Some of the hardest people to convince are parents. Chryssi Tsoupanarias, a student, got her belly button pierced, and her parents didn't take the change too easily. "My parents are kind of old fashioned when it comes to these things. I didn't think that my mom would flip out as much as she did. For a while, my parents didn't want to talk to me, but they ended up getting used to it. They eventually came around and said that I was old enough to make my own decisions."

> *There's a stigma against people with piercings*

7   When the parents of art student Lesley Hoyes saw her eyebrow ring, they weren't that upset. "They reacted so much better than I thought. I guess it's because my older sister got her belly

button pierced a while ago, so she softened them up. They were pretty mad at her," she recalled.

8   Despite criticism and family conflict, people are still avid about getting their bodies pierced. "I love it!" exclaimed Hoyes of her new eyebrow ring. "I got it done three weeks ago. It's been painless. I like my eyes, so I don't mind bringing attention to them."

9   David Abramson is a 21-year-old architecture student. Getting his nipple pierced in September of 1999 wasn't a rash decision and one that he certainly does not regret. "I'd been thinking about getting my ear or nipple done for a while before I actually did. In high school, I knew someone who had his nipple pierced, but I didn't have the guts to do it then. Then one day I said 'I'm going to do it,' and I'm really happy that I did."

10   Others had different motivations for getting something pierced. "It started off as a 'piss off the parents' device that just grew on me," explains art student Adam Fabian. "I got both my ear lobes pierced. Now I'm stretching them (with spacers). Once I get over the fear of nipple piercing, I'll probably do that too. It's a sick teen pastime."

11   Pain is a big issue when it comes to getting pierced. Many students recount tales of horror that they heard from friends about piercing jobs gone wrong. But it shouldn't be, according to

IN CONTEXT

The Pierced Ear

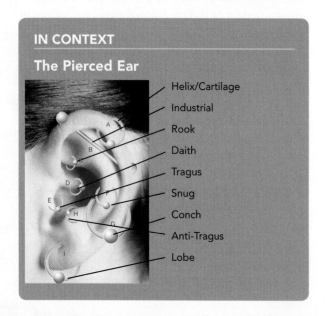

- Helix/Cartilage
- Industrial
- Rook
- Daith
- Tragus
- Snug
- Conch
- Anti-Tragus
- Lobe

stigma: mark of disgrace

IN CONTEXT

For the Sake of Culture

People all over the world engage in painful or unhealthy practices because their cultures promote them.

Chris, the resident piercer at Adrenaline. "In most spots, it's just skin. I have to get (clients) to relax," he said. "I have to put it in their heads that it's not going to hurt, because it won't. I ask them, 'If you could do it but it wouldn't hurt, would you do it?' If they say yes, then I say they should do it."

12   Another issue many are worried about is infection. Purplish gunk surrounding many navels or sore red spots on ears tend to deter some people from going near the needle. However, it is all an issue of personal hygiene, and if they are properly taken care of, piercings should not get infected too often. But Dupuis warns against overdoing the cleaning thing. "A lot of people don't know how to take care of them. If your hands are dirty and you play with your jewelry, you're going to have an infection," cautioned Dupuis. "Bacteria are going to get inside. It's important to keep clean, but also not to over clean. Then the skin gets irritated and the hole develops a discharge."

13   Tsoupanarias knows what it's like to have an infection. "Mine's all red. It's still really annoying and I've had it for almost three months. If I had known that it was going to be this much of a hassle, I wouldn't have done it. It's cool and everything, but it's really taking a long time to heal. I didn't realize how much work it would be. I really should have looked into it more before I did it."

> *I really should have looked into it more before I did it*

14   Despite the risks involved in getting piercings, many feel that the phenomenon will always be around. "Here, the biggest thing is the belly button," says Dupuis. "Nothing ever beats the belly button. Spacers are also big here. I see them here for the next ten years. In San Francisco, they've been in since the 70s."

15   Still, not everyone is jumping on the piercing bandwagon. Management student Jason Camelford expresses his dislike of the idea in general. "Even if it were painless, I wouldn't do it. I just don't like the look of it. It's not me," he says.

16   Though body piercing might not suit everybody, the reality is that it's here to stay. The good thing, as many agree, is that unlike tattoos, piercings can be removed, leaving only mild scarring as a small reminder of a societal obsession that is far from just a fad.

CONVERSATIONS: Collaborating in Class and Online

1. What is Levine's main message in this essay? Do you agree with her conclusions?
2. What is the "stigma against people with piercings" (para. 5) that the author refers to? What examples does the author offer to explain this stigma?
3. According to Levine, what are the main reasons people get body piercings?
4. Do you agree with Levine that body piercing is a "societal obsession that is far from just a fad" (para. 16)? Explain your answer.

CONNECTIONS: Discovering Relationships among Ideas

5. Using the examples Levine offers, what conclusions can you draw about the types of people who get body piercings?
6. What other inferences can you make from Levine's examples in this essay?
7. Why do you think some parents might not want their children to have body piercings?
8. What is your personal opinion of body piercings? Give some examples to explain your position.

PRESENTATION: Analyzing the Writer's Craft

9. What does the title of this essay mean? Do you think it's effective?
10. Who do you think is Levine's primary audience?
11. How does the author organize her points? Is this the best order to help her accomplish her main goals in the essay?
12. In what ways does the author use illustration to make her points?

PROJECTS: Expressing Your Own Views

13. **Collage:** Put together a collection of images or graphics that represent some of the rebellious choices young people make as they grow up. Determine an audience for your collage before you begin to design it.
14. **Interview:** Interview 5 to 10 people from different backgrounds about body piercing or tattoos. Ask all the participants the same questions. Summarize their comments as objectively as possible.
15. **Editorial:** Write an editorial explaining your views on body piercings or tattoos. Use examples to support your opinions on this topic.
16. **Research:** Read and summarize the three resources below. Generate one specific question from each resource that focuses on illustration. Then answer one of your questions in a documented essay, consulting these and other sources as necessary.

OTHER RESOURCES

Web Site
Association of Professional Piercers: www.safepiercing.org

Academic Article
"Body Piercing" by Henry Ferguson
BMJ: British Medical Journal (1999): 1627–1629

Audio/Video
CNN: www.cnn.com
Search: "No Flying with Nipple Rings"
Click on the No Flying with Nipple Rings Video link

ONE LAST THOUGHT

Although piercings and body art have gone in and out of vogue in Western society, they have existed in many different cultures and time periods. Ear piercings are the oldest and most common types of piercings—mummified remains are often discovered with earrings. Various facial piercings (lip, nose, and tongue rings) have different meanings around the world. The ancient Aztecs and Mayans used tongue piercings during religious ceremonies; in India during the 16th century, nose rings were believed to lessen the pain of childbirth; and in some African tribes, the size of a person's earrings indicates his or her societal rank. What do you think motivates people to get piercings in Western society? How do these motivations relate to their customs?

A Vision of Students Today

by Michael Wesch and Students

A professor of Cultural Anthropology at Kansas State University, **Michael Wesch** is a specialist in the emerging field of digital ethnography, which seeks to explain the effects of media on society and culture. He has made videos that have been translated into 15 languages, featured at international film festivals, and viewed by millions of people. His videos focus on such topics as rain forest natives in Papua New Guinea, cyber-phenomena, the Internet, and many other subjects within the field of popular culture. This video was done in collaboration with students in his Introduction to Cultural Anthropology class, spring 2007, at Kansas State University.

> **PREREADING QUESTIONS**
>
> How much time do you spend social networking compared to the time you spend on your schoolwork? Are you satisfied with the ratio between the two?
>
> Do you do all the assigned reading in your classes?
>
> What is the average size of your college classes?

View the entire video at www.youtube.com/watch?v=dGCJ46vyR9o before answering the questions that follow.

CONVERSATIONS: Collaborating in Class or Online

1. According to the video created by Michael Wesch and the students in his Introduction to Cultural Anthropology class at Kansas State University, what are the five most common characteristics of "Students Today"? What role do examples play in this explanation?

2. What is the main message Wesch and his students are trying to communicate?

3. What examples from the video were most shocking to you? Why did they surprise you?

4. Add two facts that you feel are missing from the video.

CONNECTIONS: Discovering Relationships among Ideas

5. What do you think motivated Wesch and his students to put this video together?

6. This YouTube video has had close to four million hits since it was produced in spring 2007. Why do you think it is so popular?

7. From your experience and observations, how accurate is the information in this video?

8. How does this video fit into the content of a cultural anthropology class?

PRESENTATION: Analyzing the Writer's Craft

9. Why do you think Wesch and his students start the video with the following Marshall McLuhan quotation: "Today's child is bewildered when he enters the 19th century environment that still characterizes the educational establishment where information is scarce but ordered and structured by fragmented, classified patterns, subjects, and schedules"? What does this quote have to do with the video's main message?

10. How did the demeanor of the students in the video help communicate their message?

11. Who do you think is the primary audience for this video?

12. In your opinion, is a video the most effective way to communicate Wesch's message?

PROJECTS: Expressing Your Own Views

13. **Video:** Many of the responses to this video were original videos. With a group of classmates, create your own video response to these YouTube images.

14. **Commercial:** Write a script for a commercial supporting or opposing the use of social networking as an effective tool for learning.

15. **Newspaper Editorial:** For your college newspaper, propose a solution to the problem that Marshall McLuhan outlines in the quotation at the beginning of this video. (See question 9 above.)

16. **Research:** Read and summarize the three resources below. Generate one specific question from each resource that focuses on illustration. Then answer one of your questions in a documented essay, consulting these and other sources as necessary.

OTHER RESOURCES

Web Site

Compact Campus: www.compact.org

Academic Article

"Making it through the First Year of College: The Role of Students' Economic Resources, Employment, and Living Arrangements" by Robert Bozick

Sociology of Education 80.3 (2007): 261–284

Audio/Video

National Public Radio: www.npr.org

Search: "Getting an Education on the Internet"

Click on the Listen Now link

ONE LAST THOUGHT

For centuries, students have been learning in classroom environments. Only recently have students had the option to take online classes, which incorporate many different forms of media and technology in learning. Visit the University of Connecticut Web site (www.uconn.edu), and search "classroom vs. online" for a comprehensive table that lists pros and cons of both classroom and online classes. Do you agree with this table? Would you add anything to it? Do you prefer taking classes online or in a classroom? Why?

When Foster Teens Find a Home

by Anita Hamilton

A feature writer for *Time* magazine, **Anita Hamilton** has published articles on a wide variety of subjects, including genetic links between migraines and depression, video gaming as an anti-dote to mental decline in the elderly, Haiti fundraising, food diaries, tattoo removal, Twitter, and many other provocative topics.

PREREADING QUESTIONS

Do you know anyone who was adopted? Are you adopted yourself?

Search the Internet for information on foster care in your hometown.

Why do you think teens are so difficult to place in foster homes?

1   When SaBreena Boyd was 11, she stood before the congregation at the New Jerusalem Full Gospel Church in Muscatine, Iowa, and asked for a new family. A member of the church's Sunday school, she had recently been placed in a foster home after her mother could no longer care for her. "I gave a speech saying that I wanted to be adopted by a Christian family, a loving family," recalls SaBreena, now 20. Stuart and Tina Juarez, a recently married couple who heard her speak that day, were impressed by SaBreena's maturity and after much soul searching decided to give the girl a home. "We just knew we had to do it," says Stuart. "We saw a child in need, we prayed about it, and everything just fell into place."

IN CONTEXT

The Adoptions and Safe Families Act

In November of 1997, President Clinton signed the Adoption and Safe Families Act into law. The ASFA is considered one of the most important changes to the U.S. adoption and foster care system in the last 20 years. In addition to helping special needs foster children become adopted, it increased government financial support for foster and adopted children. The law shifted child welfare thinking, focusing on creating safe and healthy homes for foster and adopted children rather than reuniting them with their birth parents.

2   But what seemed at first like a storybook ending for a homeless child was actually the prologue to a far more complex tale. SaBreena, a tall, serious girl, had an explosive temper. A few months after her speech, she shoved a classmate's head through a school window and broke another girl's jaw on the bus, all in one week. And after she moved in with the Juarezes in the summer of 1998, she repeatedly ran away. "We did not believe that was the same girl that spoke at the church. It was like, no way," says Stuart. Nevertheless, he and Tina decided to stick with SaBreena and formally adopted her two years later, when she was 14. But things only got worse. SaBreena became pregnant the following year and once took a large Ginsu knife from the kitchen and kept it in her room for days. "She had us all scared for the longest time," says Stuart.

3   Now married and a mother of two, SaBreena is close to her parents, but as her story shows, adopting a teen can pose all kinds of challenges for the parents and the child. Over the past few years, however, the number of 12- to 18-year-olds adopted out of foster care has risen sharply, from 6,000 in 2000 to 10,000 in 2004. That's thanks, in part, to financial incentives and intensive campaigns to persuade people to take in some of society's most unwanted children. Monthly foster-care subsidies, which used to stop after a child was adopted, now continue typically until age 18 and average about $500 a month. In addition, the federal tax credit for adopting has more than doubled, from $5,000 in 2001 to $10,630 in 2005. And both national and state websites like adoptuskids.org and cominghomekansas.org have launched online photo galleries of older kids available for adoption.

4   Child-welfare advocates applaud the trend. Young people who "age out" of foster care because they fail to get adopted by the time they turn 18 are especially at risk for homelessness, unemployment, and incarceration. "When you grow up in foster care, you just don't get the skills it takes to develop a successful adulthood," says Brenda McCreight, author of *Parenting Your Older Adopted Child*.

5   Concerned parents like the Juarezes can provide the grounding these kids need, but it can be extremely difficult for some foster teens to make the transition into a permanent family. About a quarter of adolescent adoptions fail before they're finalized vs. about 12% of adoptions overall. "You get the double whammy of teen rebellion combined with the challenge of asking the child to change their way of life, which for them is like changing their identity," says McCreight. To make such adoptions work "takes flexibility and families that are willing to give unconditional love and set limits and discipline with love," says Annie Erickson, a psychiatric social worker at the Marillac residential treatment center for troubled kids in Overland Park, Kansas.

> *SaBreena … once took a large Ginsu knife from the kitchen and kept it in her room for days*

6   More than half of all foster teens who get adopted are adopted by their foster parents. All states require prospective foster parents and those who adopt from the foster-care system to take a training program to prepare them for issues that range from coping with the horrors of sexual or physical abuse to the banalities of

prologue: introduction
Ginsu knife: specific brand of cooking knives
incentives: motivations
banalities: trite or dull rituals

eating dinner as a family or observing curfews. But parents who have taken the courses say they are only somewhat useful. "Nothing prepares you for when the child comes into your home," says Shirley Williams, who adopted two teenagers last fall. Still, a look at how some teens and families have adjusted can offer insight into what it takes to make a new life for these youngsters.

Overcoming a Lost Childhood

7   SaBreena Boyd learned to cook, clean, and take care of herself when she was just 7 because, she says, her birth mother was often too drunk or strung out on drugs to watch over her. After she moved in with the Juarezes, "I was told that I needed to try to live the rest of my childhood," says SaBreena. "But what does being a kid mean? I don't think I've ever gotten that explained to me."

8   The girl clicked right away with her adoptive dad Stuart, now 39 and a Baptist minister. Soon after she moved in, they painted her bedroom her favorite color—sky blue. And after school, Stuart would talk with her about her day. "It was me and Dad all day, every day," says SaBreena, who never met her biological father. Getting along with her new mom, Tina, a state clerical worker, also 39, was harder. Says SaBreena: "We didn't have anything to say to each other. The only time we would talk was about chores." Says Tina: "Dad was the friend. Mom was the parent."

9   Like most teens, SaBreena didn't enjoy being told to put the dishes away or leave her bedroom door unlocked. But instead of sulking when she got really mad, she would run away—sometimes for a few hours, sometimes for a few days. At first when SaBreena disappeared, the Juarezes would

> *Her birth mother was often too drunk or strung out on drugs to watch over her*

call the police and go looking for her. But "that became very old because we could never find her," says Stuart. Eventually, they began leaving a sleeping bag outside the back door as a reminder that even if she didn't want to come inside, she never had to sleep on the streets. When she did come home, the Juarezes would talk to her about what happened and either ground her or give her extra chores. One technique, suggested by counselors, was called "time in," which meant that SaBreena had to stay close to her parents and do whatever they did.

10   But then SaBreena got pregnant. "It was very shocking," says Tina. "All the values we tried to instill, for a brief moment in time went out the window." Their disappointment was so intense that they wouldn't even drive her to doctor's appointments. "We stepped back as parents," admits Stuart. When the baby girl died just a few days after she was born, SaBreena felt even more alienated from her adoptive parents and ran away again.

11   It was only when SaBreena left home a few months later to attend Iowa State University, where she is now a senior, that she was able to restore her relationship with Stuart and, for the first time, establish a true bond with Tina. "I missed her more. I used to call her all the time and say, 'Mom, I love you,'" SaBreena recalls. She drew even closer to her parents after she married and became a mother. "I get another shot at SaBreena through her daughter," says Tina. "I can establish a relationship with her on another tone."

Respecting the Outsider

12   Unlike SaBreena, Dan Knapp never ran away or openly clashed with his adoptive mother. "He never gave me a problem. He just made me proud," says Jackie Knapp, 53, a single mom who is the education director at a Christian center in Elmira, New York. Placed in foster care at age 9 after his father died and his mother was unable to care for him on her own, Dan moved in with

---

IN CONTEXT

Children Waiting to be Adopted

Of the 510,885 children in out-of-home care, almost 130,000, or 25%, are still waiting to be adopted.

Jackie and her parents the next year. Now 24, he still remembers the meeting he attended in which his birth mother told the social worker that she was relinquishing her parental rights: "I was devastated," he says. "I was hearing my mother say she doesn't want me."

13 Such feelings of abandonment by the birth family are common among older adopted kids and can make it hard for them to trust any adult. "That your mom, the person who is supposed to be there for you no matter what in life, is the first person who actually wasn't there for you—that can be very painful," says Barry Chaffkin, a co-founder of the New York City-based adoption-services agency Changing the World One Child at a Time.

14 Now a college graduate and program coordinator at a teen center in Watkins Glen, New York, Dan says that in some ways he has always felt like an outsider. When his last name was changed to Knapp, after Jackie legally adopted him when he was 14, "I expected everything to magically change, and it never did," he says. "I still felt like I was a foster kid." He recalls how upset he felt when Jackie's mother occasionally introduced him as her adopted grandson and how his cousins always seemed to get more presents than he did when the extended family exchanged gifts at Christmas time. Moreover, he says, he and Jackie "never really connected on an emotional level."

15 After Dan got his driver's license in high school, he started spending less time at home. He also stopped talking at meals or skipped them altogether. "I kind of just closed off," he says. Jackie noticed the change in him but opted for a tolerant approach. "I just took it that he's a teenager," she says. "I just kind of gave him his space."

16 Then Dan went to college, and they started instant-messaging each other to stay in touch. Although he and Jackie IM several times a week and Dan says he would like to work on their relationship, one of the few times he remembers calling Jackie Mom to her face was four years ago at church. "She was at the altar praying, and I put my arm around her, and I called her Mom. I think she cried," he says. Jackie says she knew all along that it would be hard for Dan to call her Mom. "I realized that it was because of the loss of his own mom," she says, adding, "I don't know if he'll ever really get over that, but I'm hoping."

Balancing Family Loyalties

17 Many adopted teens are torn by split allegiances to their birth and adoptive families. A tall, bubbly 16-year-old who plays drums and dreams of being a pilot or neurophysicist, Lamar Stapleton says being in foster care "taught me a lot about life. When push comes to shove, you've only got yourself and your family." And by family, he means his birth family. In November, Lamar and his younger sister, Nasia, 14, were adopted by Shirley Williams, 61, a single parent in New York City's Harlem who had already raised five of her own children.

18 Lamar, who had been in foster care since he was 4, is grateful to have a permanent home. He always calls Williams Mom, and he makes a point of hugging her every day and telling her that he loves her, but he says, "Seeing her as my mother—I don't think I can ever really do that because that would be blocking my [biological] mother out of my life." He continues to hope that he can find his missing birth mom and has even searched for her "once or twice" on the Internet. Having his sister with him helps, but sometimes the stress of

relinquishing: giving up

dueling loyalties makes him moody. "He holds a lot in. I keep telling him it's not good holding in," says Williams. Admits Lamar: "I think I have less feelings than everybody else. Being in the [foster care] system kind of dilutes your emotions. I basically have two feelings. I am either happy or angry."

19   Experts acknowledge the conflict that many adopted teens experience and say letting them maintain a relationship with their birth parents (when safe) can help provide more continuity in their tumultuous lives. "We try to help kids realize that you're not replacing one family with another. You're building on," says Chaffkin, who counsels foster kids who are considering being adopted. Tina Juarez says one of the most important lessons she learned while raising SaBreena and the two younger children whom she and Stuart have also adopted is "Don't try and take their prior life away because they'll resent you for it."

Accepting the Wild Child

20   Yevonda Graham's childhood memories are mostly the stuff of nightmares. In and out of 36 foster homes, Vonda, now 22, says she was sexually abused by relatives, molested by a foster parent, and raped as a teenager. By the time she got to the home of Dale Graham and Karla Groschelle in Whitley City, Kemtucky, at 17, she had been in eight hospitals and three group homes and had just run away from her last foster home. Arriving at the couple's house for what she expected to be yet another short-term placement, she remembers, "I was so nervous, and I was just thinking to myself, Is this going to be another bad foster home?"

21   Instead she found that for the first time in her peripatetic life, she felt at home. Karla and Dale "didn't seem fake," she says. "Usually when I'd act up, my [other] foster parents would just send me away, but they didn't. They stuck in there with me." Even when Vonda's date wrecked Karla's brand-new Durango on prom night, Vonda remembers fondly that Karla was worried more about whether Vonda was hurt than about the car. In fact, for the first several months, things

She was sexually abused by relatives, molested by a foster parent, and raped as a teenager.

went so well that one evening Vonda sat Karla and Dale down in the living room and asked whether they would adopt her even though she was about to turn 18. "I wanted a place to always come home to," she says. "In a foster home, once you're 18, you're out." Recalls Dale, a sculptor: "She said she wanted a family that would always be there for her and for somebody to walk her down the aisle when she got married. Her approach was very sincere."

22   Vonda's adoption was finalized three weeks before her 18th birthday, but she's still waiting for her happy ending. At 13 she received a diagnosis of bipolar disorder. She never stayed on the prescribed medications but did get hooked on the painkiller Oxycontin. ("I forget my problems. I forget everything," she says of her addiction.) When Karla, now 47, and Dale, 53, tried to intervene, Vonda resisted. Karla, a therapist, says Vonda once agreed to enroll in a rehab program and then checked herself out just three hours after she arrived. She was arrested in 2002 for breaking into a house to steal money for drugs and has been in and out of jail since then on

dueling: battling, fighting
dilutes: weakens
continuity: permanence
tumultuous: disorderly, chaotic
peripatetic: migrant, wandering
intervene: come between, interfere

charges including theft, identity theft, and intoxication in a public place.

23 A 2005 study by Casey Family Programs, a foster-care foundation, and Harvard Medical School found that 54% of young adults formerly in foster care as adolescents (including those who later got adopted, aged out or were reunited with their birth family) have mental-health problems, including post-traumatic stress disorder and depression. "A big part of our counseling is telling parents how to ride this roller coaster," says Kathy Boyd, supervisor of post-adoption services in Chester County, Pennsylvania. No matter how rocky things get, Boyd advises parents never to cut off communication. "Even if the child is rejecting you 100%, call, write, keep that door open so a big chasm doesn't occur and that kid is never willing to open that door again." But she also tells parents to "take care of themselves and to accept that they cannot do everything. We're careful not to lay more guilt on the parents." Karla and Dale say their home is open to Vonda as long as she stays clean. But they have also come to accept that their daughter will make the ultimate choice about how to lead her life. "All we can do is be there for her and be supportive when she's going down the right direction and try to redirect her when she's going the wrong way," says Dale. That kind of commitment is what being a parent—to any child—is all about.

Anita Hamilton, "When Foster Teens Find a Home," *Time*, May 29, 2006. Copyright Time Inc. Reprinted by permission. TIME is a registered trademark of Time Inc. All rights reserved.

CONVERSATIONS: Collaborating in Class or Online

1. What is Hamilton's main message in this essay? How do examples help her communicate that message?

2. In what ways can foster care "pose all kinds of challenges for the parents and the child" (para. 3)?

3. Why do you think more people have been willing recently to adopt teens? What additional challenges do these adoptions bring with them?

4. In your opinion, which example in this essay drove Hamilton's point home most effectively?

CONNECTIONS: Discovering Relationships among Ideas

5. What does Brenda McCreight mean when she says, "When you grow up in foster care, you just don't get the skills it takes to develop a successful adulthood" (para. 4)?

6. In what ways might foster children feel like "outsiders"?

7. Why is it important for adopted children to balance family loyalties?

8. Do you agree with Hamilton's description of "What being a parent—to any child—is all about" (para. 23)?

PRESENTATION: Analyzing the Writer's Craft

9. Hamilton divides this essay into five sections and starts each with an example. How are these examples related to the points the author is making in each section?

10. Is SaBreena's story an effective example to open this essay? Explain your answer.

11. List all the statistics that Hamilton cites. How do these figures help advance the essay's message?

12. Who do you think is this essay's intended audience?

PROJECTS: Expressing Your Own Views

13. **Image:** Define the concept of "home" in pictures and graphics.

14. **Speech:** Write a speech containing both emotional and logical appeals about the value of a supportive family.

15. **Essay:** Write an essay focusing on the advantages or disadvantages of adopting a child. Use well-chosen examples to make your point.

16. **Research:** Read and summarize the three resources below. Generate one specific question from each resource that focuses on illustration. Then answer one of your questions in a documented essay, consulting these and other sources as necessary.

OTHER RESOURCES

 Web Site

Open Adoption: www.openadoption.com/

Academic Article

"Support and Conflict in the Foster Family and Children's Well-Being: A Comparison Between Foster and Birth Children"

by Mieke Denuwelaere and Piet Bracke

Family Relations 56.1 (2007): 67–79

 Audio/Video

Operation Children: operationchildren.com

Click on either of the Video links

ONE LAST THOUGHT

Hillsides is a 100-year-old organization located in Southern California that advocates for children's rights. It creates safe places for children living in group or foster homes. Over the years, it has found creative ways to raise funds and increase awareness for these children. In 2009, Hillsides launched its "Foster Soles" auction, where celebrities donate autographed shoes that are auctioned for Hillsides' causes. Explore the Hillsides Web site (www.hillsides.org) to learn more about the organization. Have you ever been involved in a charity auction? Can you think of other creative ways that organizations like this can raise money?

How Twitter Is Hurting Students

by Geneva Reid

Geneva Reid wrote this piece for *HigherEdMorning*, a weekly subscription e-newsletter of which she is the editor. Published by PBP Media Group, it is sent to over 400,000 colleges and universities throughout the world. Its principal topics include finance, information technology, student services, enrollment, admissions, marketing, facilities, and human resources.

PREREADING QUESTIONS

What social networking sites do you visit most often?

Why do you use these forms of communication?

What are their advantages and disadvantages?

---

1   Are social networks hurting or helping your students? You might be surprised at the results of a recent study.

2   Turns out not all social networks are created equal when it comes to their effect on our brains.

3   Dr. Tracy Alloway of Scotland's University of Stirling says her study shows using Facebook stretches our "working memory" (our short-term or recent memory), while Twitter, YouTube, and text messages tend to weaken it.

4   Alloway studies working memory and has developed a training program to increase the performance of children—ages 11 to 14—who are slow learners. She found

- Keeping up to date with Facebook improved the children's IQ scores
- Playing video games—especially those that require planning and strategy—and Sudoku also were beneficial
- Using Twitter, YouTube, and text messaging does not engage enough of the brain to be helpful and actually reduces attention span.

5   "On Twitter, you receive an endless stream of information, but it's also very succinct,"

Sudoku: a logic puzzle
succinct: brief, concise

Alloway said. "You don't have to process that information."

6 She noted that Facebook requires you to keep track of past actions and then plan future actions, which stretches the working memory.

7 They might not be doing it to improve their memories, but prospective college students are increasingly using Facebook for more than just social interaction. According to a new Kaplan Test Prep and Admissions study, more than 70% of college admissions officials have received "friend requests" from students using Facebook and MySpace.

8 While it's debatable whether "friending" an admissions official gives a student an edge when applying to a given college, it's reasonable to suggest students are using social network sites to help their chances of getting into the school of their choice.

> *Not all social networks are created equal when it comes to their effect on our brains*

9 Do you interact with students on Facebook? Let us know in the comments section below.

To see the comments posted in response to this blog entry, go to the Higher Ed Morning Web site at www .higheredmorning.com, and search for "How Twitter Is Hurting Students."

CONVERSATIONS: Collaborating in Class or Online

1. What are Alloway's conclusions about the effects of different social networking venues on the "working memory"?
2. What is Reid's main point in this blog? How does she use examples to make her essay convincing?
3. What common thread runs through the responses to Reid's statement?
4. What disagreements surface in the responses?

CONNECTIONS: Discovering Relationships among Ideas

5. Do Alloway's conclusions make sense to you? Explain your answer.
6. In what ways do you keep track of information on Facebook?
7. How is Twitter different from Facebook? Which takes more concentration on your part?
8. What related skills might be affected by Alloway's findings?

PRESENTATION: Analyzing the Writer's Craft

9. In paragraph 4, Reid gives bulleted examples of Alloway's findings to prove her point. Are these examples convincing to you?
10. What is the general effect of introducing Dr. Alloway and her study?

11. Which responses do you agree with most? Explain your choices.

12. Which of the responses do you disagree with? Explain why.

PROJECTS: Expressing Your Own Views

13. **Response:** Add your response to those following the original statement.

14. **Internet:** Interview some of your peers about Facebook and Twitter, and then summarize their opinions. Draft your questions so they lead up to a viable conclusion about these social networking options.

15. **Essay:** Write an essay discussing the advantages and/or disadvantages of social networking. Make sure the examples you cite support your thesis statement.

16. **Research:** Read and summarize the three resources below. Generate one specific question from each resource that focuses on illustration. Then answer one of your questions in a documented essay, consulting these and other sources as necessary.

OTHER RESOURCES

 Web Site

Mashable: http://mashable.com

Click on the Social Media link

Academic Article

"Learning, Teaching, and Scholarship in a Digital Age"

by Christine Greenhow, Beth Robelia, and Joan E. Hughes

Educational Researcher 38.4 (2009): 246–259

 Audio/Video

YouTube: www.youtube.com

Search: "Social Networking in the Classroom by tarheelsk8tr247"

Click on the Video link

ONE LAST THOUGHT

In 2008, Ryerson University student Chris Avenir started a Facebook study group for his chemistry class. He invited classmates to post solutions and tips about their homework for the class. His instructor came across the online study group and asked the university to expel him for cheating. After an expulsion hearing, shown in this picture, the University decided to give him 0% on the 10% portion of the class that his "study group" dealt with and forced him to attend a workshop on academic integrity. He is now suing the University for $10 million, claiming he wasn't allowed proper legal representation during the expulsion hearing. Have you ever used a social networking site to study? Do you think it should be allowed? If so, do you think instructors should have access to these study groups as well?

America's Food Crisis

by Bryan Walsh

After a stint as the Tokyo bureau chief for *Time*, **Bryan Walsh** is now a staff writer for the magazine, specializing in environmental issues. Recent columns have been devoted to global warming, public health, obesity, the Avian flu, CO2 emissions, the 2010 oil spill, climate change, deforestation, "green energy," and a wide range of other scientific topics.

PREREADING QUESTIONS

What do you know about how the food you eat every day is produced?

What are your favorite foods?

Do you eat a lot of fast food?

1   Somewhere in Iowa, a pig is being raised in a confined pen, packed in so tightly with other swine that their curly tails have been chopped off so they won't bite one another. To prevent him from getting sick in such close quarters, he is dosed with antibiotics. The waste produced by the pig and his thousands of pen mates on the factory farm where they live goes into manure lagoons that blanket neighboring communities with air pollution and a stomach-churning stench. He's fed on American corn that was grown with the help of government subsidies and millions of tons of chemical fertilizer. When the pig is slaughtered, at about 5 months of age, he'll become sausage or bacon that will sell cheap, feeding an American addiction to meat that has contributed to an obesity epidemic currently afflicting more than two-thirds of the population. And when the rains come, the excess fertilizer that coaxed so much corn from the ground will be washed into the Mississippi River and down into the Gulf of Mexico, where it will help kill fish for miles and miles around. That's the state of your bacon—circa 2009.

2   Horror stories about the food industry have long been with us—ever since 1906, when Upton Sinclair's landmark novel *The Jungle* told some ugly truths about how America produces its meat. In the century that followed, things got much better, and in some ways much worse. The U.S. agricultural industry can now produce unlimited quantities of meat and grains at remarkably cheap prices. But it does so at a high cost to the environment, animals, and humans. Those hidden prices are the creeping erosion of our fertile farmland, cages for egg-laying chickens so packed that the birds can't even raise their wings, and the scary rise of antibiotic-resistant bacteria

lagoons: small bodies of water
subsidies: grants or contributions of money, often from the government
erosion: breaking down

IN CONTEXT

The Union of Concerned Scientists

A science-based nonprofit group, the Union of Concerned Scientists (UCS) was established in 1969. It works to create a safer and healthier environment by informing consumers about their purchases and lifestyle choices. They recommend using a fuel-efficient car and driving less as effective ways of helping the environment. For more information, visit their Web site at www.ucsusa.org/.

among farm animals. Add to the price tag the acceleration of global warming—our energy-intensive food system uses 19% of U.S. fossil fuels, more than any other sector of the economy.

3 And perhaps worst of all, our food is increasingly bad for us, even dangerous. A series of recalls involving contaminated foods this year—including an outbreak of salmonella from tainted peanuts that killed at least eight people and sickened 600—has consumers rightly worried about the safety of their meals. A food system—from seed to 7-Eleven—that generates cheap, filling food at the literal expense of healthier produce is also a principal cause of America's obesity epidemic. At a time when the nation is close to a civil war over health-care reform, obesity adds $147 billion a year to our doctor bills. "The way we farm now is destructive of the soil, the environment, and us," says Doug Gurian-Sherman, a senior scientist with the food and environment program at the Union of Concerned Scientists (UCS).

4 Some Americans are heeding such warnings and working to transform the way the country eats—ranchers and farmers who are raising sustainable food in ways that don't bankrupt the earth. Documentaries like the scathing *Food Inc.* and the work of investigative journalists like Eric Schlosser and Michael Pollan are reprising Sinclair's work, awakening a sleeping public to the uncomfortable realities of how we eat. Change is also coming from the very top. First Lady Michelle Obama's White House garden has so far

yielded more than 225 lb. of organic produce—and tons of powerful symbolism. But hers is still a losing battle. Despite increasing public awareness, sustainable agriculture, while the fastest-growing sector of the food industry, remains a tiny enterprise: according to the most recent data from the U.S. Department of Agriculture (USDA), less than 1% of American cropland is farmed organically. Sustainable food is also pricier than conventional food and harder to find. And while large companies like General Mills have opened organic divisions, purists worry that the very definition of *sustainability* will be co-opted as a result.

5 But we don't have the luxury of philosophizing about food. With the exhaustion of the soil, the impact of global warming, and the inevitably rising price of oil—which will affect everything from fertilizer to supermarket electricity bills—our industrial style of food production will end sooner or later. As the developing world grows richer, hundreds of millions of people will want to shift to the same calorie-heavy, protein-rich diet that has made Americans so unhealthy—demand for meat and poultry worldwide is set to rise 25% by 2015—but the earth can no longer deliver. Unless Americans radically rethink the way they grow and consume food, they face a future of eroded farmland, hollowed-out countryside, scarier germs, higher health costs—and bland taste. Sustainable food has an élitist reputation, but each of us depends on the soil, animals, and plants—and as every farmer knows, if you don't take care of your land, it can't take care of you.

> *The way we farm now is destructive of the soil, the environment, and us*

salmonella: bacteria that can lead to food poisoning
sustainable: maintainable at a certain level
scathing: damaging
philosophizing: speculating, often in a tedious or ineffective way
eroded: worn down

The Downside of Cheap

6   For all the grumbling you do about your weekly grocery bill, the fact is you've never had it so good, at least in terms of what you pay for every calorie you eat. According to the USDA, Americans spend less than 10% of their incomes on food, down from 18% in 1966. Those savings begin with the remarkable success of one crop: corn. Corn is king on the American farm, with production passing 12 billion bu. annually, up from 4 billion bu. as recently as 1970. When we eat a cheeseburger, a Chicken McNugget, or drink soda, we're eating the corn that grows on vast, monocrop fields in Midwestern states like Iowa.

7   But cheap food is not free food, and corn comes with hidden costs. The crop is heavily fertilized—both with chemicals like nitrogen and with subsidies from Washington. Over the past decade, the Federal Government has poured more than $50 billion into the corn industry, keeping prices for the crop—at least until corn ethanol skewed the market—artificially low. That's why McDonald's can sell you a Big Mac, fries, and a Coke for around $5—a bargain, given that the meal contains nearly 1,200 calories, more than half the daily recommended requirement for adults. "Taxpayer subsidies basically underwrite cheap grain, and that's what the factory-farming system for meat is entirely dependent on," says Gurian-Sherman.

8   So what's wrong with cheap food and cheap meat—especially in a world in which more than 1 billion people go hungry? A lot. For one thing, not all food is equally inexpensive; fruits and vegetables don't receive the same price supports as grains. A study in the *American Journal of Clinical Nutrition* found that a dollar could buy 1,200 calories of potato chips or 875 calories of soda but just 250 calories of vegetables or 170 calories of fresh fruit. With the backing of the government, farmers are producing more calories—some 500 more per person per day since the 1970s—but too many are unhealthy calories. Given that, it's no surprise we're so fat; it simply costs too much to be thin.

9   Our expanding girth is just one consequence of mainstream farming. Another is chemicals. No one doubts the power of chemical fertilizer to pull more crops from a field. American farmers now produce an astounding 153 bu. of corn per acre, up from 118 as recently as 1990. But the quantity of that fertilizer is flat-out scary: more than 10 million tons for corn alone—and nearly 23 million for all crops. When runoff from the fields of the Midwest reaches the Gulf of Mexico, it contributes to what's known as a dead zone, a seasonal, approximately 6,000-sq.-mi. area that has almost no oxygen and therefore almost no sea life. Because of the dead zone, the $2.8 billion Gulf of Mexico fishing industry loses 212,000 metric tons of seafood a year, and around the world, there are nearly 400 similar dead zones. Even as we produce more high-fat, high-calorie foods, we destroy one of our leanest and healthiest sources of protein.

10   The food industry's degradation of animal life, of course, isn't limited to fish. Though we might still like to imagine our food being raised by Old MacDonald, chances are your burger or your sausage came from what are called concentrated-animal feeding operations (CAFOs), which are every bit as industrial as they sound. In CAFOs, large numbers of animals—1,000 or more in the case of cattle and tens of thousands for chicken and pigs—are kept in close, concentrated conditions and fattened up for slaughter as fast as possible, contributing to efficiencies of

bu.: one bushel, a unit of measurement

monocrop: one single crop

skewed: distorted, shifted

degradation: the process by which organic substances are broken down by living organisms

scale and thus lower prices. But animals aren't widgets with legs. They're living creatures, and there are consequences to packing them in prison-like conditions. For instance: Where does all that manure go?

11   Pound for pound, a pig produces approximately four times the amount of waste a human does, and what factory farms do with that mess gets comparatively little oversight. Most hog waste is disposed of in open-air lagoons, which can overflow in heavy rain and contaminate nearby streams and rivers. "This creek that we used to wade in, that creek that our parents could drink out of, our kids can't even play in anymore," says Jayne Clampitt, a farmer in Independence, Iowa, who lives near a number of hog farms.

12   To stay alive and grow in such conditions, farm animals need pharmaceutical help, which can have further damaging consequences for humans. Overuse of antibiotics on farm animals leads, inevitably, to antibiotic-resistant bacteria, and the same bugs that infect animals can infect us too. The UCS estimates that about 70% of antimicrobial drugs used in America are given not to people but to animals, which means we're breeding more of those deadly organisms every day. The Institute of Medicine estimated in 1998 that antibiotic resistance cost the public-health system $4 billion to $5 billion a year—a figure that's almost certainly higher now. "I don't think CAFOs would be able to function as they do now without the widespread use of antibiotics," says Robert Martin, who was the executive director of the Pew Commission on Industrial Farm Animal Production.

Where does all that manure go?

13   The livestock industry argues that estimates of antibiotics in food production are significantly overblown. Resistance "is the result of human use and not related to veterinary use," according to Kristina Butts, the manager of legislative affairs for the National Cattlemen's Beef Association. But with wonder drugs losing their effectiveness, it makes sense to preserve them for as long as we can, and that means limiting them to human use as much as possible. "These antibiotics are not given to sick animals," says Representative Louise Slaughter, who is sponsoring a bill to limit antibiotic use on farms. "It's a preventive measure because they are kept in pretty unspeakable conditions."

    Such a measure would get at a symptom of the problem but not at the source. Just as the burning of fossil fuels that is causing global warming requires more than a tweaking of mileage standards, the manifold problems of our food system require a comprehensive solution. "There should be a recognition that what we are doing is unsustainable," says Martin. And yet, still we must eat. So what can we do?

Getting It Right

14   If a factory farm is hell for an animal, then Bill Niman's seaside ranch in Bolinas, California, an hour north of San Francisco, must be heaven. The property's cliffside view over the Pacific Ocean is worth millions, but the black Angus cattle that Niman and his wife Nicolette Hahn Niman raise keep their eyes on the ground, chewing contentedly on the pasture. Grass—and a trail of hay that Niman spreads from his truck

IN CONTEXT

USDA Food Pyramid

This is the current USDA food pyramid. It includes (in this order) grains, vegetables, fruits, milk, and meat & beans. Notice that the pyramid also includes daily physical activity. Visit www.mypyramid.gov for more information.

MyPyramid
STEPS TO A HEALTHIER YOU
MyPyramid.gov

GRAINS   VEGETABLES   FRUITS   MILK   MEAT & BEANS

widgets: mini computer applications
manifold: varied or diverse
contentedly: happily

periodically—is all the animals will eat during the nearly three years they'll spend on the ranch. That all-natural, noncorn diet along with the intensive, individual care that the Nimans provide their animals—produces beef that many connoisseurs consider to be among the best in the world. But for Niman, there is more at stake than just a good steak. He believes that his way of raising farm animals—in the open air, with no chemicals or drugs and with maximum care—is the only truly sustainable method and could be a model for a better food system. "What we need in this country is a completely different way of raising animals for food," says Hahn Niman, a former attorney for the environmental group Earthjustice. "This needs to be done in the right way."

There is more at stake than just a good steak

15   The Nimans like to call what they do "beyond organic," and there are some signs that consumers are beginning to catch up. This November, California voters approved a ballot proposition that guarantees farm animals enough space to lie down, stand up, and turn around. Worldwide, organic food—a sometimes slippery term but on the whole a practice more sustainable than conventional food—is worth more than $46 billion. That's still a small slice of the overall food pie, but it's growing, even in a global recession. "There is more pent-up demand for organic than there is production," says Bill Wolf, a co-founder of the organic-food consultancy Wolf DiMatteo and Associates.

16   So what will it take for sustainable food production to spread? It's clear that scaling up must begin with a sort of scaling down—a distributed system of many local or regional food producers as opposed to just a few massive ones. Since 1935, consolidation and industrialization have seen the number of U.S. farms decline from 6.8 million to fewer than 2 million—with the average farmer now feeding 129 Americans, compared with 19 people in 1940.

17   It's that very efficiency that's led to the problems and is in turn spurring a backlash, reflected not just in the growth of farmers' markets or the growing involvement of big corporations in organics but also in the local-food movement, in which restaurants and large catering services buy from suppliers in their areas, thereby improving freshness, supporting small-scale agriculture, and reducing the so-called food miles between field and plate. That in turn slashes transportation costs and reduces the industry's carbon footprint.

18   A transition to more sustainable, smaller-scale production methods could even be possible without a loss in overall yield, as one survey from the University of Michigan suggested, but it would require far more farm workers than we have today. With unemployment approaching double digits—and things especially grim in impoverished rural areas that have seen populations collapse over the past several decades—that's hardly a bad thing. Work in a CAFO is monotonous and soul-killing, while too many ordinary farmers struggle to make ends meet even as the rest of us pay less for food. Farmers aren't the enemy—and they deserve real help. We've transformed the essential human profession—growing food—into an industry like any other. "We're hurting for job creation, and industrial food has pushed people off the farm," says Hahn Niman. "We need to make farming real employment, because if you do it right, it's enjoyable work."

19   One model for how the new paradigm could work is Niman Ranch, a larger operation that Bill Niman founded in the 1990s, before he left in 2007. (By his own admission, he's a better farmer than he is a businessman.) The company has knitted together hundreds of small-scale farmers into a network that sells all-natural pork, beef, and lamb to retailers and restaurants. In doing so, it

---

connoisseurs: discerning or knowledgeable people
consolidation: combining
industrialization: a movement towards machine-based manufacturing
impoverished: poor
monotonous: boring
paradigm: concept, model

leverages economies of scale while letting the farmers take proper care of their land and animals. "We like to think of ourselves as a force for a local-farming community, not as a large corporation," says Jeff Swain, Niman Ranch's CEO.

20 Other examples include the Mexican-fast-food chain Chipotle, which now sources its pork from Niman Ranch and gets its other meats and much of its beans from natural and organic sources. It's part of a commitment that Chipotle founder Steve Ells made years ago, not just because sustainable ingredients were better for the planet but because they tasted better too—a philosophy he calls Food with Integrity. It's not cheap for Chipotle—food makes up more than 32% of its costs, the highest in the fast-food industry. But to Ells, the taste more than compensates, and Chipotle's higher prices haven't stopped the company's rapid growth, from 16 stores in 1998 to over 900 today. "We put a lot of energy into finding farmers who are committed to raising better food," says Ells.

21 Bon Appétit Management Company, a caterer based in Palo Alto, California, takes that commitment even further. The company sources as much of its produce as possible from within 150 miles of its kitchens and gets its meat from farmers who eschew antibiotics. Bon Appétit also tries to influence its customers' habits by nudging them toward greener choices. That includes campaigns to reduce food waste, in part by encouraging servers at its kitchens to offer smaller, more manageable portions. (The USDA estimates that Americans throw out 14% of the food we buy, which means that much of our record-breaking harvests ends up in the garbage.) And Bon Appétit supports a low-carbon diet, one that uses less meat and dairy, since both have a greater carbon footprint than fruit, vegetables, and grain. The success of the overall operation demonstrates that sustainable food can work at an institutional scale bigger than an élite restaurant, a small market or a gourmet's kitchen—provided customers support it. "Ultimately it's going to be consumer demand that will cause change, not Washington," says Fedele Bauccio, Bon Appétit's co-founder.

22 How willing are consumers to rethink the way they shop for—and eat—food? For most people, price will remain the biggest obstacle. Organic food continues to cost on average several times more than its conventional counterparts, and no one goes to farmers' markets for bargains. But not all costs can be measured by a price tag. Once you factor in crop subsidies, ecological damage, and what we pay in health-care bills after our fatty, sugary diet makes us sick, conventionally produced food looks a lot pricier.

23 What we really need to do is something Americans have never done well, and that's to quit thinking big. We already eat four times as much meat and dairy as the rest of the world, and there's not a nutritionist on the planet who would argue that 24-oz. steaks and mounds of buttery mashed potatoes are what any person needs to stay alive. "The idea is that healthy and good-tasting food should be available to everyone," says Hahn Niman. "The food system should be geared toward that."

24 Whether that happens will ultimately come down to all of us, since we have the chance to choose better food three times a day (or more often, if we're particularly hungry). It's true that most of us would prefer not to think too much about where our food comes from or what it's doing to the planet—after all, as Chipotle's Ells points out, eating is not exactly a "heady intellectual event." But if there's one difference between industrial

---

leverages: establishes

eschew: avoid or keep clear of

counterparts: two parts that complete each other

heady: intellectual

agriculture and the emerging alternative, it's that very thing: consciousness. Niman takes care with each of his cattle, just as an organic farmer takes care of his produce and smart shoppers take care with what they put in their shopping cart and on the family dinner table. The industrial food system fills us up but leaves us empty—it's based on selective forgetting. But what we eat—how it's raised and how it gets to us—has consequences that can't be ignored any longer.

— *With reporting by Rebecca Kaplan / New York*

CONVERSATIONS: Collaborating in Class or Online

1. What are the most serious dangers concerning the way our meat is produced?
2. What specific examples most convince you that our food production is in crisis?
3. What are the consequences of continuing to produce food as we currently do in this country?
4. How is the food production system that the Nimans use "sustainable"?

CONNECTIONS: Discovering Relationships among Ideas

5. How is global warming impacted by our production of food?
6. What are CAFOs and their dangers? Do these perils bother you personally or not? Explain your answer.
7. In what ways is our current food production based on "selective forgetting" (para. 24)?
8. Explain Gurian-Sherman's statement about our food production: "The way we farm now is destructive of the soil, the environment, and us" (para. 3) by citing examples from the essay.

PRESENTATION: Analyzing the Writer's Craft

9. Why does Walsh use the word "crisis" in his title?
10. Is the summary at the beginning of the essay effective? Why or why not?
11. How effective are the statistics in Walsh's essay? Explain your answer.
12. Walsh ends this essay with suggestions for increasing sustainable food production. Is this a good topic for the conclusion? Explain your answer.

PROJECTS: Expressing Your Own Views

13. **Ad:** Design an ad for sustainable or organic food. Choose any angle you think will most effectively reach your audience.
14. **Blog/Wiki/Ning:** Get into an ongoing Internet conversation about food production.
15. **Letter to the Editor:** Write a response to the author of this essay. Use examples from the essay and from your own experience to help make your point.
16. **Research:** Read and summarize the three resources below. Generate one specific question from each resource that focuses on illustration. Then answer one of your questions in a documented essay, consulting these and other sources as necessary.

OTHER RESOURCES

Web Site

Meat Free Mondays: www.
meatfreemondays.co.uk

Academic Article

"Environmental, Energetic, and Economic Comparisons of Organic and Conventional Farming Systems"

by David Pimentel, Paul Hepperly, James Hanson, David Douds, and Rita Seidel

BioScience 55.7 (2005): 573–582

Audio/Video

Humane Society of the United States: www.humanesociety.org

Click on the Video link

Scroll down and click on the Factory Farming channel to view a selection of videos

ONE LAST THOUGHT

In 1946, President Truman signed the National School Lunch Act into law. It uses government subsidies to provide low-cost or free lunches to students who are in need. Today, public schools serve meals to over 30 million students per day. In recent years, the government has worked to improve the quality and health of this food. The National School Lunch Program, along with numerous private organizations, educates school districts about healthier options and funds positive changes. Other associations have fought for the removal of soda and candy vending machines. Have you heard about these changes? What do you think people can do to help their local school districts?

A Bright Shining Slogan

by Elizabeth Dickinson

Elizabeth Dickinson writes for *Foreign Policy*, a bi-monthly American magazine founded in 1970 by Samuel P. Huntington and Warren Demian Manshel. It is published by the Washington Post Company. Described on its masthead as "serious, but never stuffy," it focuses on international affairs, global politics, and economics. The current editor in chief is Susan Glasser.

PREREADING QUESTIONS

Have you ever heard the expression "hearts and minds" or "body and soul"? If so, what do these terms mean to you?

Why do you think some expressions become popular and others don't?

What types of people make sayings popular?

ANTHROPOLOGY OF AN IDEA

A Bright Shining Slogan

The phrase "winning hearts and minds" has, in recent years, become indelibly associated with the challenges of an interventionist U.S. foreign policy. But the concept has had a long and circuitous life. It was first associated with democracy in the 19th century, later served as a call to national solidarity during the Great Depression, and finally became a slogan for a policy the U.S. military never quite implemented in Vietnam. As U.S. President Barack Obama fights two inherited wars and continues the daunting task of reaching out to Muslims, the concept has never been more relevant, even if the words themselves have begun to lose all meaning. —*Elizabeth Dickinson*

Greek philosopher **Plato** becomes the first to draw a clear distinction between feeling and thinking—between the **heart and the mind**. The two were referred to as separate philosophical and physiological creatures until the mid-20th century.

429-347 B.C.

Writing to a Baltimore newspaper editor, U.S. founding father **John Adams** describes the American Revolution as being "in the **minds and hearts** of the people, a change in their religious sentiments of their duties and obligations."

FEBRUARY 13, 1818

U.S. President **Franklin D. Roosevelt** uses the term frequently in his speeches to soothe a body politic battered by economic turmoil: "In these days it means to me a union not only of the states, but a union of the **hearts and minds** of the people in all the states and their many interests and purposes, devoted with unity to the human welfare of our country."

1934

The phrase gets used for the first time in its modern sense—to refer to counter-insurgency objectives—during the Malayan Emergency, an uprising by local rebel forces to oust British Colonial rule. "The answer [to defeating the insurgents] … rests in the **hearts and minds** of the Malayan people," says Gen. Sir **Gerald Templer**.

JUNE 1952

In the thick of the Cold War, "hearts and minds" creeps into U.S. counterrevolutionary rhetoric. "Perhaps most significant of all is a change in the **hearts and minds** of the people—a growing will to develop their countries," President **John F. Kennedy** tells Congress. "We can only help Latin Americans to save themselves."

APRIL 2, 1963

U.S. President **Lyndon B. Johnson** says that "ultimate victory [in Vietnam] will depend upon the **hearts and minds**" of the Vietnamese. But the policy doesn't match the rhetoric, and a brutal, escalating campaign of pacification ensues, further alienating the South Vietnamese population.

MAY 4, 1965

The Academy Award-winning Vietnam documentary, *Hearts and Minds*, helps cement the phrase's negative connotations.

1974

U.S. President **George W. Bush** justifies the invasion of Iraq by hailing the possibility of a political transformation of the Middle East. "Across the world, **hearts and minds** are opening to the message of human liberty as never before," he tells the U.N. General Assembly.

SEPTEMBER 14, 2005

Scholars begin to describe China's foreign policy, particularly in Africa, as designed to win the **"hearts and minds"** of global elites.

2006

Iranian President **Mahmoud Ahmadinejad** deploys the term in a defiant speech to the U.N.: "Would it not be easier for global powers to … win **hearts and minds** through… real promotion of justice, compassion, and peace, than through" continuing to assemble nuclear weapons?

SEPTEMBER 19, 2006

The U.S. Army and Marine Corps release a revised "Counterinsurgency Field Manual," drawing on historical counterinsurgency lessons as well as recent experience in Iraq. The manual calls for a minimal use of force. "Protracted popular war is best countered by winning the **'hearts and minds'** of the populace," it reads.

DECEMBER 15, 2006

U.S. President **Barack Obama** uses the phrase in his campaign to reset relations with both the Muslim world and Russia. "[Abiding by the Geneva Conventions]… will make us safer and will help in changing **hearts and minds** in our struggle against extremists," he says on January 9. And in Moscow six months later: "[By] mobilizing and organizing and changing people's **hearts and minds**, you then change the political landscape."

2009

indelibly: impossible to be removed
interventionist: interfering
solidarity: unity
implemented: fulfilled, carried out
daunting: intimidating
philosophical: relating to the pursuit of knowledge
physiological: characteristic of normal or healthy functioning

body politic: a group of organized citizens
counter-insurgency: retaliation to protect a governing body
ensues: follows, proceeds
connotations: overtones, suggestions
protracted: dragged on

Foreign Policy, Sept./Oct. 2009, p. 29, www.foreignpolicy.com. Copyright 2009. Reproduced with permission of Foreign Policy in the format Textbook via Copyright Clearance Center.

CONVERSATIONS: Collaborating in Class or Online

1. What role does illustration play in this chart?
2. What is the underlying message of this chart?
3. Which other quotation here uses the phrase "hearts and minds" in a way similar to President Obama's message?
4. How do the illustrations logically build up to Mr. Obama's use of the phrase? Explain your answer.

CONNECTIONS: Discovering Relationships among Ideas

5. Explain the relationship between the phrase "winning hearts and minds" and U.S. foreign policy in light of the slogans cited in this chart.
6. Discuss the origin of the phrase as outlined in the first frame (429–347 BC).
7. Summarize the progression of the phrase "hearts and minds" in your own words. Use examples from this chart to explain your summary.
8. What is the overall significance of this term?

PRESENTATION: Analyzing the Writer's Craft

9. Is a linear format the most effective way to present this material? Explain your answer.

10. The editor of this piece chose to use visuals to supplement some of the quotations. Why do you think these particular visuals were chosen? Are they effective in relation to the overall selection? Explain your answer.

11. Discuss the title of this selection. What are its connotations and complications?

12. Is Elizabeth Dickinson's opening statement an accurate summary of the sample quotations? Explain your answer.

PROJECTS: Expressing Your Own Views

13. **Song:** Write a song or poem about this phrase.

14. **Cartoon:** Design a political cartoon focusing on the history of "hearts and minds."

15. **Essay:** Write an essay about the evolution of another well-known phrase. Use illustrations to support the main point you are making about the term.

16. **Research:** Read and summarize the three resources below. Generate one specific question from each resource that focuses on illustration. Then answer one of your questions in a documented essay, consulting these and other sources as necessary.

OTHER RESOURCES

 Web Site

WordOrigins: www.wordorigins.org

Begin exploring the Web site by clicking on The Big List link

 Audio/Video

NASA: www.nasa.gov

Search: "JFK Rice Moon Speech"

Click on the Audio link

Academic Article

"Presidential Libraries: A View from the Center"

by Sharon K. Fawcett

The Public Historian 28.3 (2006): 13–36

ONE LAST THOUGHT

Many politicians use slogans and logos as part of their campaigns. President Obama's 2008 presidential campaign utilized two slogans: "Change we can believe in" and "Yes we can." His logo, seen here, is a sun-like circle rising over fields in American colors. President Obama's campaign was also notable for his extensive Internet use to rally supporters. His Web site, http://change.gov/, which provided information and links to support his campaign, was named for his slogan. Can you think of any other famous slogans? What would you want your slogan or logo to be if you were running for office?

The Multitasking Generation

by Claudia Wallis

An editor-at-large for *Time* magazine, **Claudia Wallis** specializes in essays about health, science, education, life-style, and women's and children's issues. She was also the founding editor of *Time for Kids*. She has written more than 20 cover stories for the magazine, including an investigation of such topics as "How to Make Your Kid a Better Student," "Cholesterol," and "Pills for the Mind."

PREREADING QUESTIONS

How do you define "multitasking"?

Are you aware when you are multitasking?

Can you concentrate as well when you are doing more than one task as you can when you are doing just one?

1   It's 9:30 P.M., and Stephen and Georgina Cox know exactly where their children are. Well, their bodies, at least. Piers, 14, is holed up in his bedroom—eyes fixed on his computer screen—where he has been logged onto a MySpace chat room and AOL Instant Messenger (IM) for the past three hours. His twin sister Bronte is planted in the living room, having commandeered her dad's iMac—as usual. She, too, is busily IMing, while chatting on her cell phone and chipping away at homework.

2   By all standard space-time calculations, the four members of the family occupy the same three-bedroom home in Van Nuys, California, but psychologically each exists in his or her own little universe. Georgina, 51, who works for a

display-cabinet maker, is tidying up the living room as Bronte works, not that her daughter notices. Stephen, 49, who juggles jobs as a squash coach, fitness trainer, event planner, and head of a cancer charity he founded, has wolfed down his dinner alone in the kitchen, having missed supper with the kids. He, too, typically spends the evening on his cell phone and returning e-mails—when he can nudge Bronte off the computer. "One gets obsessed with one's gadgets," he concedes.

3   Zooming in on Piers's screen gives a pretty good indication of what's on his hyperkinetic mind. O.K., there's a Google Images window open, where he's chasing down pictures of Keira Knightley. Good ones get added to a snazzy

Windows Media Player slide show that serves as his personal e-shrine to the actress. Several IM windows are also open, revealing such penetrating conversations as this one with a MySpace pal:

MySpacer: suuuuuup!!! (Translation: What's up?)
Piers: wat up dude
MySpacer: nmu (Not much. You?)
Piers: same

4   Naturally, iTunes is open, and Piers is blasting a mix of Queen, AC/DC, classic rock, and hip-hop. Somewhere on the screen there's a Word file, in which Piers is writing an essay for English class. "I usually finish my homework at school," he explains to a visitor, "but if not, I pop a book open on my lap in my room, and while the computer is loading, I'll do a problem or write a sentence. Then, while mail is loading, I do more. I get it done a little bit at a time."

5   Bronte has the same strategy. "You just multitask," she explains. "My parents always tell me I can't do homework while listening to music, but they don't understand that it helps me concentrate." The twins also multitask when hanging with friends, which has its own etiquette. "When I talk to my best friend Eloy," says Piers, "he'll have one earpiece (of his iPod) in and one out." Says Bronte: "If a friend thinks she's not getting my full attention, I just make it very clear that she is, even though I'm also listening to music."

6   The Coxes are one of 32 families in the Los Angeles area participating in an intensive, four-year study of modern family life, led by anthropologist Elinor Ochs, director of UCLA's Center on Everyday Lives of Families. While the impact of multitasking gadgets was not her original focus, Ochs found it to be one of the most dramatic areas of change since she conducted a similar study 20 years ago. "I'm not certain how the children can monitor all those things at the same time, but I think it is pretty consequential for the structure of the family relationship," says Ochs, whose work on language, interaction, and culture earned her a MacArthur "genius" grant.

7   One of the things Ochs's team of observers looks at is what happens at the end of the workday when parents and kids reunite—and what doesn't happen, as in the case of the Coxes. "We saw that when the working parent comes through the door, the other spouse and the kids are so absorbed by what they're doing that they don't give the arriving parent the time of day," says Ochs. The returning parent, generally the father, was greeted only about a third of the time, usually with a perfunctory "Hi." "About half the time the kids ignored him or didn't stop what they were doing, multitasking and monitoring their various electronic gadgets," she says. "We also saw how difficult it was for parents to penetrate the child's universe. We have so many videotapes of parents actually backing away, retreating from kids who are absorbed by whatever they're doing."

8   Human beings have always had a capacity to attend to several things at once. Mothers have done it since the hunter-gatherer era—picking berries while suckling an infant, stirring the pot with one eye on the toddler. Nor is electronic multitasking entirely new: we've been driving while listening to car radios since they became popular in the 1930s. But there is no doubt that the phenomenon has reached a kind of warp speed in the era of Web-enabled computers, when it has become

> *We also saw how difficult it was for parents to penetrate the child's universe*

etiquette: manners
consequential: important for success
perfunctory: routine

routine to conduct six IM conversations, watch *American Idol* on TV, and Google the names of last season's finalists all at once.

9   That level of multiprocessing and interpersonal connectivity is now so commonplace that it's easy to forget how quickly it came about. Fifteen years ago, most home computers weren't even linked to the Internet. In 1990 the majority of adolescents responding to a survey done by Donald Roberts, a professor of communication at Stanford, said the one medium they couldn't live without was a radio/CD player. How quaint. In a 2004 follow-up, the computer won hands down.

10   Today 82% of kids are online by the seventh grade, according to the Pew Internet and American Life Project. And what they love about the computer, of course, is that it offers the radio/CD thing and so much more—games, movies, e-mail, IM, Google, MySpace. The big finding of a 2005 survey of Americans ages 8 to 18 by the Kaiser Family Foundation, co-authored by Roberts, is not that kids were spending a larger chunk of time using electronic media—that was holding steady at 6.5 hours a day (could it possibly get any bigger?)—but that they were packing more media exposure into that time: 8.5 hours' worth, thanks to "media multitasking"—listening to iTunes, watching a DVD, and IMing friends all at the same time. Increasingly, the media-hungry members of Generation M, as Kaiser dubbed them, don't just sit down to watch a TV show with their friends or family. From a quarter to a third of them, according to the survey, say they simultaneously absorb some other medium "most of the time" while watching TV, listening to music, using the computer, or even while reading.

IN CONTEXT

The Kaiser Family Foundation

The Kaiser Family Foundation is a nonprofit organization that offers nonpartisan health care information to the public and to many policy-making organizations.

IN CONTEXT

The Pew Internet and American Life Project

The Pew Research Center is "a nonpartisan, nonprofit 'fact tank' that provides information on the issues, attitudes, and trends shaping America." The Pew Internet and American Life Project, one of seven projects that constitute the Pew Research Center, studies the way people use the Internet and its effects on various aspects of their personal and professional life.

11   Parents have watched this phenomenon unfold with a mixture of awe and concern. The Coxes, for instance, are bowled over by their children's technical prowess. Piers repairs the family computers and DVD player. Bronte uses digital technology to compose elaborate photo collages and create a documentary of her father's ongoing treatment for cancer. And, says Georgina, "they both make these fancy PowerPoint presentations about what they want for Christmas." But both parents worry about the ways that kids' compulsive screen time is affecting their schoolwork and squeezing out family life. "We rarely have dinner together anymore," frets Stephen. "Everyone is in their own little world, and we don't get out together to have a social life."

12   Every generation of adults sees new technology—and the social changes it stirs—as a threat to the rightful order of things: Plato warned (correctly) that reading would be the downfall of oral tradition and memory. And every generation of teenagers embraces the freedoms and possibilities wrought by technology in ways that shock the elders: just think about what the automobile did for dating.

13   As for multitasking devices, social scientists and educators are just beginning to assess their impact, but the researchers already have some

dubbed: called, nicknamed
wrought: brought about

strong opinions. The mental habit of dividing one's attention into many small slices has significant implications for the way young people learn, reason, socialize, do creative work, and understand the world. Although such habits may prepare kids for today's frenzied workplace, many cognitive scientists are positively alarmed by the trend. "Kids that are instant messaging while doing homework, playing games online, and watching TV, I predict, aren't going to do well in the long run," says Jordan Grafman, chief of the cognitive neuroscience section at the National Institute of Neurological Disorders and Stroke (NINDS). Decades of research (not to mention common sense) indicate that the quality of one's output and depth of thought deteriorate as one attends to ever more tasks. Some are concerned about the disappearance of mental downtime to relax and reflect. Roberts notes Stanford students "can't go the few minutes between their 10 o'clock and 11 o'clock classes without talking on their cell phones. It seems to me that there's almost a discomfort with not being stimulated—a kind of 'I can't stand the silence.'"

> *There's almost a discomfort with not being stimulated—a kind of "I can't stand this silence"*

14   Gen M's multitasking habits have social and psychological implications as well. If you're IMing four friends while watching *That '70s Show*, it's not the same as sitting on the couch with your buddies or your sisters and watching the show together or sharing a family meal across a table. Thousands of years of evolution created human physical communication—facial expressions, body language—that puts broadband to shame in its ability to convey meaning and create bonds. What happens, wonders UCLA's Ochs, as we replace side-by-side and eye-to-eye human connections with quick, disembodied e-exchanges? Those are critical issues not just for social scientists but for parents and teachers trying to understand—and do right by—Generation M.

IN CONTEXT

That '70s Show

That '70s Show is an American sitcom that ran from 1998 through 2006. Much like *Happy Days*, which was made in the '70s but took place in the '50s, *That '70s Show* was about an era decades before it was created.

---

15   Although many aspects of the networked life remain scientifically uncharted, there's substantial literature on how the brain handles multitasking. And basically, it doesn't. It may seem that a teenage girl is writing an instant message, burning a CD and telling her mother that she's doing homework—all at the same time—but what's really going on is a rapid toggling among tasks rather than simultaneous processing. "You're doing more than one thing, but you're ordering them and deciding which one to do at any one time," explains neuroscientist Grafman.

16   Then why can we so easily walk down the street while engrossed in a deep conversation? Why can we chop onions while watching Jeopardy? "We, along with quite a few others, have been focused on exactly this question," says Hal Pashler, psychology professor at the University of California at San Diego. It turns out that very automatic actions or what researchers call "highly practiced skills," like walking or chopping an onion, can be easily done while thinking about other things, although the decision to add an extra onion to a recipe or change the direction in which you're walking is another matter. "It seems that action planning—figuring out what I want to

---

implications: meanings
cognitive: relating to the mind
disembodied: disconnected

IN CONTEXT

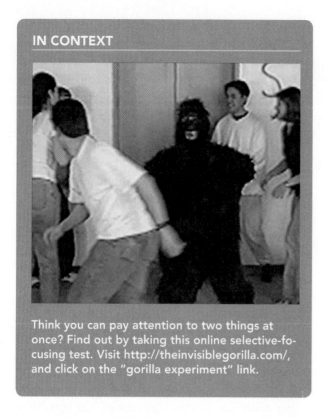

IN CONTEXT

Think you can pay attention to two things at once? Find out by taking this online selective-focusing test. Visit http://theinvisiblegorilla.com/, and click on the "gorilla experiment" link.

say in response to a person's question or which way I want to steer the car—is usually, perhaps invariably, performed sequentially" or one task at a time, says Pashler. On the other hand, producing the actions you've decided on—moving your hand on the steering wheel, speaking the words you've formulated—can be performed "in parallel with planning some other action." Similarly, many aspects of perception—looking, listening, touching—can be performed in parallel with action planning and with movement.

17   The switching of attention from one task to another, the toggling action, occurs in a region right behind the forehead called Brodmann's Area 10 in the brain's anterior prefrontal cortex, according to a functional magnetic resonance imaging (fMRI) study by Grafman's team. Brodmann's Area 10 is part of the frontal lobes, which "are important for maintaining long-term goals and achieving them," Grafman explains. "The most anterior part allows you to leave something when it's incomplete and return to the same place and continue from there." This gives us a "form of multitasking," he says, though it's actually sequential processing. Because

the prefrontal cortex is one of the last regions of the brain to mature and one of the first to decline with aging, young children do not multitask well, and neither do most adults over 60. New fMRI studies at Toronto's Rotman Research Institute suggest that as we get older, we have more trouble "turning down background thoughts when turning to a new task," says Rotman senior scientist and assistant director Cheryl Grady. "Younger adults are better at tuning out stuff when they want to," says Grady. "I'm in my 50s, and I know that I can't work and listen to music with lyrics; it was easier when I was younger."

18   But the ability to multiprocess has its limits, even among young adults. When people try to perform two or more related tasks either at the same time or alternating rapidly between them, errors go way up, and it takes far longer—often double the time or more—to get the jobs done than if they were done sequentially, says David E. Meyer, director of the Brain, Cognition and Action Laboratory at the University of Michigan: "The toll in terms of slowdown is extremely large—amazingly so." Meyer frequently tests Gen M students in his lab, and he sees no exception for them, despite their "mystique" as master multitaskers. "The bottom line is that you can't simultaneously be thinking about your tax return and reading an essay, just as you can't talk to yourself about two things at once," he says. "If a teenager is trying to have a conversation on an e-mail chat line while doing algebra, she'll suffer a decrease in efficiency, compared to if she just thought about algebra until she was done. People may think otherwise, but it's a myth. With such complicated tasks [you] will never, ever be able to overcome the inherent limitations in the brain for processing information during multitasking. It just can't be, any more than the best of all humans will ever be able to run a one-minute mile."

19   Other research shows the relationship between stimulation and performance forms a bell curve: a little stimulation—whether it's coffee or a blaring soundtrack—can boost performance, but too much is stressful and causes a fall-off. In addition, the brain needs rest and recovery time to consolidate thoughts and memories. Teenagers who fill every quiet moment with a phone call or some kind of e-stimulation may not be getting that needed reprieve. Habitual multitasking

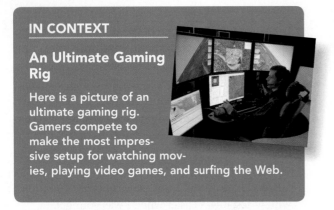

may condition their brain to an overexcited state, making it difficult to focus even when they want to. "People lose the skill and the will to maintain concentration, and they get mental antsyness," says Meyer.

20 Longtime professors at universities around the U.S. have noticed that Gen M kids arrive on campus with a different set of cognitive skills and habits than past generations. In lecture halls with wireless Internet access—now more than 40% of college classrooms, according to the Campus Computing Project—the compulsion to multitask can get out of hand. "People are going to lectures by some of the greatest minds, and they are doing their mail," says Sherry Turkle, professor of the social studies of science and technology at M.I.T. In her class, says Turkle, "I tell them this is not a place for e-mail, it's not a place to do online searches and not a place to set up IRC [Internet relay chat] channels in which to comment on the class. It's not going to help if there are parallel discussions about how boring it is. You've got to get people to participate in the world as it is."

21 Such concerns have, in fact, led a number of schools, including the M.B.A. programs at UCLA and the University of Virginia, to look into blocking Internet access during lectures. "I tell my students not to treat me like TV," says University of Wisconsin professor Aaron Brower, who has been teaching social work for 20 years. "They have to think of me like a real person talking. I want to have them thinking about things we're talking about."

22 On the positive side, Gen M students tend to be extraordinarily good at finding and manipulating information. And presumably because modern childhood tilts toward visual rather than print media, they are especially skilled at analyzing visual data and images, observes Claudia Koonz, professor of history at Duke University. A growing number of college professors are using film, audio clips and PowerPoint presentations to play to their students' strengths and capture their evanescent attention. It's a powerful way to teach history, says Koonz. "I love bringing media into the classroom, to be able to go to the website for Edward R. Murrow and hear his voice as he walked with the liberators of Buchenwald." Another adjustment to teaching Generation M: professors are assigning fewer full-length books and more excerpts and articles. (Koonz, however, was stunned when a student matter-of-factly informed her, "We don't read whole books anymore," after Koonz had assigned a 350-page volume. "And this is Duke!" she says.)

23 Many students make brilliant use of media in their work, embedding audio files and video clips in their presentations, but the habit of grazing among many data streams leaves telltale signs in their writing, according to some educators. "The breadth of their knowledge and their ability to find answers has just burgeoned," says Roberts of his students at Stanford, "but my impression is that their ability to write clear, focused and extended narratives has eroded somewhat." Says Koonz: "What I find is paragraphs that make sense internally, but don't necessarily follow a line of argument."

24 Koonz and Turkle believe that today's students are less tolerant of ambiguity than the students they taught in the past. "They demand clarity," says Koonz. They want identifiable good guys and bad guys, which she finds problematic in teaching complex topics like Hutu-Tutsi history in Rwanda. She also thinks there are political implications: "Their belief in the simple answer, put together in a visual way, is, I think, dangerous." Koonz thinks this aversion to complexity is directly related to multitasking: "It's as if they have too many windows open on their hard drive. In order to have a taste for sifting through different layers of truth, you have to stay with a topic and pursue it deeply, rather than go across the surface with your toolbar." She tries to encourage her students to find a quiet spot on campus to just think, cell phone off, laptop packed away.

25   But turning down the noise isn't easy. By the time many kids get to college, their devices have become extensions of themselves, indispensable social accessories. "The minute the bell rings at most big public high schools, the first thing most kids do is reach into their bag and pick up their cell phone," observes Denise Clark Pope, lecturer at the Stanford School of Education, "never mind that the person [they're contacting] could be right down the hall."

26   Parents are mystified by this obsession with e-communication—particularly among younger adolescents who often can't wait to share the most mundane details of life. Dominique Jones, 12, of Los Angeles, likes to IM her friends before school to find out what they plan to wear. "You'll get IMs back that say things like 'Oh, my God, I'm wearing the same shoes!' After school we talk about what happened that day, what outfits we want to wear the next day."

27   Turkle, author of the recently reissued The Second Self: Computers and the Human Spirit, has an explanation for this breathless exchange of inanities. "There's an extraordinary fit between the medium and the moment, a heady, giddy fit in terms of social needs." The online environment, she points out, "is less risky if you are lonely and afraid of intimacy, which is almost a definition of adolescence. Things get too hot, you log off, while in real time and space, you have consequences." Teen venues like MySpace, Xanga and Facebook—and the ways kids can personalize their IM personas—meet another teen need: the desire to experiment with identity. By changing their picture, their "away" message, their icon or list of favorite bands, kids can cycle through different personalities. "Online life is like an identity workshop," says Turkle, "and that's the job of adolescents—to experiment with identity."

> *Parents are mystified by this obsession with e-communication*

28   All that is probably healthy, provided that parents set limits on where their kids can venture online, teach them to exercise caution and regulate how much time they can spend with electronics in general. The problem is that most parents don't. According to the Kaiser survey, only 23% of seventh- to 12th-graders say their family has rules about computer activity; just 17% say they have restrictions on video-game time.

29   In the absence of rules, it's all too easy for kids to wander into unwholesome neighborhoods on the Net and get caught up in the compulsive behavior that psychiatrist Edward Hallowell dubs "screen-sucking" in his new book, CrazyBusy. Patricia Wallace, a techno-psychologist who directs the Johns Hopkins Center for Talented Youth program, believes part of the allure of e-mail—for adults as well as teens—is similar to that of a slot machine. "You have intermittent, variable reinforcement," she explains. "You are not sure you are going to get a reward every time or how often you will, so you keep pulling that handle. Why else do people get up in the middle of the night to check their e-mail?"

30   Many educators and psychologists say parents need to actively ensure that their teenagers break free of compulsive engagement with screens and spend time in the physical company of human beings—a growing challenge not just because technology offers such a handy alternative but because so many kids lead highly scheduled lives that leave little time for old-fashioned socializing and family meals. Indeed, many teenagers and college students say overcommitted schedules drive much of their multitasking.

31   Just as important is for parents and educators to teach kids, preferably by example, that it's valuable, even essential, to occasionally slow down, unplug, and take time to think about something for a while. David Levy, a professor at the University of Washington Information School, has found, to his surprise, that his most technophilic undergraduates—those majoring in "informatics"—are genuinely concerned about getting lost in the multitasking blur. In an informal poll of 60 students last semester, he says, the majority expressed concerns about how plugged-in they were and "the way it takes them away from other activities, including exercise, meals and sleep." Levy's students talked about difficulties concentrating and their efforts to break away, get into the outdoors and inside their head. "Although it wasn't a scientific survey," he says, "it was the first evidence I had that people in this age group are reflecting on these questions."

32   For all the handwringing about Generation M, technology is not really the problem. "The problem," says Hallowell, "is what you are not doing if the electronic moment grows too large"—too large for the teenager and too large for those parents who are equally tethered to their gadgets. In that case, says Hallowell, "you are not having family dinner, you are not having conversations, you are not debating whether to go out with a boy who wants to have sex on the first date, you are not going on a family ski trip or taking time just to veg. It's not so much that the video game is going to rot your brain, it's what you are not doing that's going to rot your life."

33   Generation M has a lot to teach parents and teachers about what new technology can do. But it's up to grownups to show them what it can't do and that there's life beyond the screen.

———————

Claudia Wallis, "genM: The Multitasking Generation," *Time*, Mar. 27, 2006. Copyright Time Inc. Reprinted by permission. TIME is a registered trademark of Time Inc. All rights reserved.

> **technophilic:** interested in technology
> **informatics:** the study of information
> **tethered:** fastened, chained

CONVERSATIONS: Collaborating in Class or Online

1. In what ways are the Coxes a typical American family? How do the examples in this essay support that perception?
2. According to the Kaiser Family Foundation, how many hours did teenagers spend per day on media in 2005? Do you think that number has increased or decreased since then? Explain your answer.
3. Why do you think it's difficult for parents to "penetrate" their child's world? (para. 7)? How do Wallis's illustrations support this statement?
4. Why is "turning down the noise" (paragraph 25) important to learning in college?

CONNECTIONS: Discovering Relationships among Ideas

5. In what ways does multitasking affect the Coxes' family life? How do illustrations help make this point?
6. Explain the dangers of "dividing one's attention into many small slices" (para. 13).
7. In what ways does understanding how the brain handles multitasking relate to our ability to learn?
8. Why do you think Wallis uses the term "Generation M"? To whom is she referring?

PRESENTATION: Analyzing the Writer's Craft

9. Wallis starts her essay with a story about a family and ends it with some advice for all families. Are these effective choices for the opening and closing of an essay? Explain your answer.

10. Explain the title of this essay. How effective is it in whetting the audience's appetite?

11. What effect do the references to experts and researchers have on Wallis's main point?

12. Does Wallis give enough examples to demonstrate "the problem" (second to last para.)? Explain your answer.

PROJECTS: Expressing Your Own Views

13. **Podcast/DVD/Video:** In a medium of your choice, make your own statement about multitasking.

14. **Web Site:** Design your own Web site for multitaskers. What type of support do they need: emotional? physical? psychological? logistical?

15. **Blog/Wiki/Ning:** Start a Blog/Wiki/Ning conversation about the advantages or disadvantages of multitasking. Then write your own commentary on the reasoning behind the thread of responses that follows.

16. **Research:** Read and summarize the three resources below. Generate one specific question from each resource that focuses on illustration. Then answer one of your questions in a documented essay, consulting these and other sources as necessary.

OTHER RESOURCES

Web Site

International Institute of Not Doing Much: http://slowdownnow.org

Academic Article

"Why Introverts Can't Always Tell Who Likes Them: Multitasking and Nonverbal Decoding" by Matthew D. Lieberman

Journal of Personality and Social Psychology 80.2 (2001): 294–310

Audio/Video

NPR: www.npr.org/

Search: "Does Multitasking Lead to a More Productive Brain?"

Click on the Listen Now link

ONE LAST THOUGHT

In January 2010, the National Safety Council released a study claiming that 28% of automobile accidents involved people talking on cell phones or texting while driving. Due to this high percentage, federal transportation officials introduced an organization called FocusDriven that provides support for people who lost loved ones to driver cell phone usage. Visit www.focusdriven.org to view the victims and the support provided. Do you ever talk on a cell phone or text while driving? What are your state's laws about driving while using cell phones?

CHAPTER WRITING ASSIGNMENTS

Write a well-developed essay in response to one of the following prompts. Consult the chapter introduction for guidance in creating your essay.

CONNECTING THE READINGS

1. How does the video "A Vision of Students Today" help us understand Wallis's essay on Generation M ("The Multitasking Generation")? What do both selections say about young adults?

2. Discuss the issue of self-esteem among teenagers today as the topic is reflected in "Body Piercing" and "When Foster Teens Find a Home."

3. How are multitasking ("The Multitasking Generation") and social networking ("How Twitter is Hurting Students") related for the current generation? At what points do these two social phenomena overlap?

4. Write a description of a hero who might solve the food crisis ("America's Food Crisis") to be added to the selection entitled "A Bright Shining Slogan."

MOVING BEYOND THE READINGS

5. What is your normal study routine? Do you study while listening to music or watching television? Where do you study? Do you read and write in different locations? What other details are part of your study ritual?

6. How are you personally participating in the greening of America? What should we do on a larger scale to save our country? Give details and examples to support your claim.

7. What role does social networking play in your life? Do you try to do other activities while you are on social networking sites? Does social networking overlap with your academic life?

8. Does multitasking play a major or minor part in your life? Give examples to explain your statement.

COMBINING RHETORICAL MODES

9. What symbolic activities, like body piercings and tattoos, have other generations participated in? What do all these activities have in common?

10. Compare multitasking habits in two different generations. What conclusions can you draw from your comparison?

11. Design a college or university that will address all the messages revealed by the Kansas State University students in "A Vision of Students Today."

12. Parenting is a difficult task, whether it involves a foster child, an adopted child, or your own biological child. What makes parenting so stressful and complicated in each of these situations? What challenges are common to all parenting situations?

Process Analysis

8

Americans love to discover how to live their lives better, faster, and more efficiently. The best-seller list is filled with books explaining how to get rich, how Facebook was started, how to dress for success, how to lose an inferiority complex, and how the stock market crashed. Here are some other typical process analysis topics:

- How Lindbergh flew across the ocean;
- Directions for assembling a bike;
- Guidelines for improving your backhand;
- An explanation of military strategies during the Civil War;
- How to accentuate your best features.

DEVELOPMENT STRATEGIES: PROCESS ANALYSIS

Overview
Development
⟶ Step 1
⟶ Step 2
⟶ Step 3
⟶ Step 4
Conclusion

A good process analysis essay can truly help the reader see an event in a totally new light. Most of us look at a bicycle already assembled or think of an important historical event without knowing how it happened. A step-by-step explanation gives the writer or speaker as well as the observer a completely new way of "seeing" the subject in question. As a result, the details of a process analysis essay or project are essentially the steps or stages of the subject at hand.

Introducing Process Analysis

A *process* is a procedure that follows a series of steps or stages; *analysis* involves taking a subject apart and explaining its components in order to understand the whole. **Process analysis**, then, explains an action or an event from beginning to end. It concentrates on either a mental or a physical operation: how to solve a math problem, how to put together a kite, how Martin Luther King, Jr. was shot, how the Internet works.

A process analysis essay can take one of two forms:

1. **Directive process analysis,** which gives directions explaining how to do something, or

2. **Informative process analysis**, which provides information about how something happened or how something works.

The first type of analysis gives directions for a task the readers might want to do themselves. Examples include how to make brownies, how to lose weight, how to save money, how to use a microscope, how to win friends, and how to ski. The explanation of the writing process at the beginning of this book is a good example of a directive analysis. It divides writing into three interrelated activities and explains how to produce an effective paper.

The second type of analysis furnishes information about what actually occurred in specific situations or how something works. Examples include how Americans reacted to 9/11, how Hollywood stars live, how the tax system works, how the movie *Avatar* was created, how Ernie Banks earned a place in the Baseball Hall of Fame, how computers work, and how the War in Iraq began. These subjects and others like them trigger a certain fascination we all have with mastering specific processes and understanding their intricate details. They all provide us with opportunities to raise our own standard of living, either by helping us learn new processes or by clarifying a knowledge of events that we can then apply to our own lives.

Process analysis essays need to be written so precisely that they result in the same outcome every time someone follows them. They are meant to inform and explain in a way that anyone can understand and/or duplicate the results. Consequently, writers must choose their words carefully and clearly specify the order of their steps in order to communicate the end result as exactly as possible. Look at the following examples:

DEVELOPMENT STRATEGIES AT WORK

Purpose: How to make a peanut butter and jelly sandwich

Development

⟶ Step 1. Get out a loaf of bread.

⟶ Step 2. Open the loaf of bread.

⟶ Step 3. Take two pieces of bread from the bread bag.

⟶ Step 4. Get out a jar of peanut butter and a jar of jelly.

⟶ Step 5. Open the jars of peanut butter and jelly.

⟶ Step 6. Get out a knife.

⟶ Step 7. Use the knife to get some peanut butter from the jar.

⟶ Step 8. Spread the peanut butter on one of the pieces of bread.

⟶ Step 9. Use the knife to get some jelly from the jelly jar.

⟶ Step 10. Spread the jelly on the other piece of bread.

⟶ Step 11. Put the pieces of bread together.

⟶ Step 12. Enjoy your creation.

Conclusion

DEVELOPMENT STRATEGIES AT WORK

Purpose: How the U.S. President is chosen

Development

⟶ Step 1. Potential candidates assemble exploratory committees.

⟶ Step 2. Potential candidates run "invisible primaries" (contests to see who can raise most campaign cash).

⟶ Step 3. States have primaries/caucuses.

⟶ Step 4. Nominees are chosen based on a majority of delegates.

(Continued)

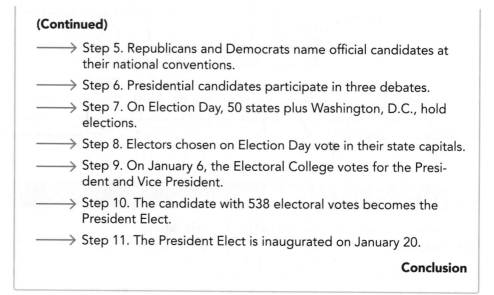

> **(Continued)**
>
> ⟶ Step 5. Republicans and Democrats name official candidates at their national conventions.
>
> ⟶ Step 6. Presidential candidates participate in three debates.
>
> ⟶ Step 7. On Election Day, 50 states plus Washington, D.C., hold elections.
>
> ⟶ Step 8. Electors chosen on Election Day vote in their state capitals.
>
> ⟶ Step 9. On January 6, the Electoral College votes for the President and Vice President.
>
> ⟶ Step 10. The candidate with 538 electoral votes becomes the President Elect.
>
> ⟶ Step 11. The President Elect is inaugurated on January 20.
>
> **Conclusion**

Whatever your specific purpose, process analysis is an essential part of our daily lives. We exchange directions with each other constantly, and sometimes the quality of our existence depends on the specificity and exactness of these directions. So learning how to produce clear, precise explanations of a process is an important communication skill.

Discovering How Process Analysis Works

To the right is a list of the most important elements of process analysis thinking, whether for a visual (like a graph or a cartoon) or a prose selection. The Process Analysis Essentials are equally useful as guidelines for both reading and writing.

Analyzing the blog below will help you understand how these elements work together to produce clear

Process Analysis Essentials

Overview
Purpose Statement
Steps of the Process or Event
Logical Organization
Description of Outcome

process analysis. If you discover on your own how this method of reasoning works, you will be able to apply it effectively to your own reading and writing. The questions following the blog will help you understand this rhetorical mode even more thoroughly than you already do.

Instructions for Starting a Blog

1   **Choose a topic that interests you.** Make sure this is a topic that you (and others) have a lot to say about and that you won't get bored with. Do some research by visiting some popular blogs that you enjoy reading.

The Basics

An Interesting Topic
Energy
Perseverance

2   **Decide on a host.** You can use a free blogging Web site like www.wordpress.com, or you can host the blog yourself. If you choose to host it yourself, you'll need to find and purchase a domain name.

3   **Design your blog.** Once you have decided where your blog will be, you can begin designing it. Try to make your blog look as appealing as possible with colorful backgrounds, photographs, and graphics. You will also need to decide whether you want your blog to be public or private.

4   **Post your first entry.** Make sure to keep your post original and unique. Encourage your guests to post comments, and then respond to their comments so your readers will stay engaged.

5   **Spread the word.** Give your blog information to your friends, family, and acquaintances. Don't get discouraged if your blog has a slow start; it usually takes five or six months for blogs to gain momentum.

1. What is the desired outcome of this process?
2. What is the purpose of this process?
3. What are the steps described here?
4. How are these steps organized?
5. How does the writer conclude the explanation of the process?

Collaborative Responses Now discuss your responses to these questions with your classmates in small groups or as an entire class. Did the diverse perspectives from other students in your class change your reading of the blog? If so, in what ways?

Reading Process Analysis

As you read the photos, Web sites, lists, and essays in this chapter, pay special attention to the details the authors/illustrators use to explain their process. You should make sure you understand the author's statement of purpose and then try to visualize each step as you continue.

As you read a selection for the first time, think about how the Process Analysis Essentials work within it. The following questions will help you achieve this goal for both written and graphic assignments:

Process Analysis Essentials: Reading

- **Overview:** What is the product or event under discussion?
- **Purpose Statement:** What is the author's/illustrator's purpose?
- **Steps of the Process or Event:** What are the main steps of the process or explanation?
- **Logical Organization:** Does the order of the steps lead to the expected outcome?
- **Description of Outcome:** Does the selection reach conclusions based on these details? If so, what are these conclusions?

On your second and third readings of the selection, focus on areas of ambiguity and confusion so you can deepen your comprehension.

Writing Process Analysis

Keeping the earlier list of Process Analysis Essentials in mind as we now move from the reading to the writing process will help you tailor your writing to your specific purpose and audience.

Choosing a Subject

As you begin the writing process, you need to settle on a subject. Will it be directive or informative? If you can choose your own subject, select a process you know very well and would enjoy telling someone else about. If you are given a subject, learn as much about it as possible before you draft your essay.

Our student writer, Juan Sanchez, decided to explain the process of snowboarding. He was recently introduced to this sport and now heads for the slopes with his board every weekend he gets the chance.

Generating Details

First of all, you need to generate a complete list of the steps of the process you will discuss. To do this, you should first write down every phase of the process. Then organize the details in a way that accurately represents (usually chronologically) the process or event.

To begin his writing process, Juan lists the steps he follows when he snowboards:

> *proper clothes*
>
> *proper equipment*
>
> *instruction—professional lessons*
>
> *ride the lift*
>
> *the first real run down the slopes*
>
> *my reward: hot chocolate*

Juan realizes that this list moves naturally through the highlights of snowboarding for the first time. This chronological method of organization would be just as useful if Juan were writing about a process or an event or if he were creating a graphic process analysis. From this list, Juan needs to write a thesis statement that will provide an overview of his process.

Drafting a Thesis Statement

To narrow your topic even more thoroughly, you should construct a thesis statement that provides an overview of the product or event you plan to discuss. This overview will give the rest of your paper a clear and specific focus. It will serve as your controlling idea and will also be the guide for choosing and organizing your details. A thesis for a graphic or other project may not be as immediately obvious, but should still be embedded within the project.

Juan's purpose is to make his readers feel as if they are learning how to snowboard right alongside him. Here is Juan's thesis:

> *I recently ventured into the world of snowboarding and found it to be an exhilarating—but occasionally embarrassing—way to have fun during the colder months of the year.*

This statement will now give a clear purpose to Juan's writing.

Producing a Draft

Well-thought-out preliminary work will lead quite naturally to a good process analysis essay or project.

- The **introduction** presents your subject and states your overview in a clear thesis.
- The **body of the paper** then presents the process or event step by step. In other words, it explains the details associated with the subject. These details become the primary method of organizing your essay—usually chronologically from one step to the next.
- Finally, the **concluding section** summarizes the various stages and the outcome mentioned in the body of the paper.

Introduction Your essay should begin with an overview of the process or event you will analyze. This initial section should introduce the subject, divide it into a set number of steps, and describe the outcome once the process is complete. Your thesis in a process analysis essay is generally a purpose statement that clearly and briefly states your approach to the procedure you will discuss: for example, "Finding an apartment to rent requires four basic steps" or "Preparation for international travel falls into three distinct stages."

Body Next, a directive or informative essay should move logically through the various stages of the process, from beginning to end. The parts of a process are most logically explained in chronological order, supported by such transitions as *first, in the beginning, then, next, after that,* and *finally.* Some processes, however, are either simultaneous, with more than one action happening at the same time, or cyclical, with continuous action and no clear starting or stopping point. Driving, for example, involves two separate and simultaneous actions that must work together: steering the car with your hands and working the pedals with your feet. In analyzing this procedure, you would probably want to describe both parts of the process separately and then explain how the hands and feet work together to move a vehicle down the road. An example of a cyclical process would be the academic terms. To explain this concept to a reader, you would need to pick a starting point, such as spring semester, and describe the entire cycle, stage by stage, from that point onward.

To generate a good process analysis paper, you need to be especially sensitive to your intended audience so they will be able to follow your explanation. The amount of information, the number of examples and illustrations, and the terms to be defined all depend on the prior knowledge and background of your readers. A writer explaining to a group of amateur gamblers how to play poker would take an entirely different approach to the subject than he or she would if the audience were a group of bona fide professional card sharks ready to enter a $1,000,000 tournament in Las Vegas. The professional poker players would undoubtedly need more sophisticated and precise explanations than their recreational counterparts, who would probably find such an approach tedious and overly complex.

Conclusion The final section of a process analysis paper should refer to the process as a whole. If, for example, the writer is giving directions on how to find a good apartment, the essay might end with an explanation and a graphic of the floor plan of a potential residence. The informative essay on international travel might offer a summary of the stages of preparation. And the essay on playing poker might finish with a photograph of the big winner with her million dollar check at the conclusion.

At this point, you should use the following questions, based on the Process Analysis Essentials, to help focus and refine your written and graphic assignments:

Process Analysis Essentials: Writing

- **Overview:** What outcome are you expecting?
- **Purpose Statement:** What purpose do you have in mind for the process analysis?
- **Steps of the Process or Event:** Which are the steps of your process or event?
- **Logical Organization:** Are these steps in chronological order?
- **Description of Outcome:** Do these steps lead naturally to your expected outcome?

Revising and Editing

Revising and editing your essay or graphic means to review it and make sure it says exactly what you want it to say. Also, you should take some time to add transitions to show your readers how various items in your process analysis are related.

Revising

Look closely at your essay or graphic as someone else might. Then answer the questions in the Revising Checklist on page 28, which ask you to focus on how your essay functions.

At this point in the writing process, you should also add carefully chosen transitions to your essay that guide your reader smoothly through the process or event you are explaining. In process essays, these are usually words or phrases that clarify chronological or sequential relationships, including *first, second, at the same time, next, meanwhile, after that, then,* and *finally.* These particular expressions will help your readers understand as clearly as possible the relationship among the details and steps in your process analysis.

Editing

Editing is the final phase of your writing process. It involves scrutinizing your words, sentences, entire paragraphs, and any visual details to make sure they are correct. Use the Editing Checklist on page 30 to review your project for errors in grammar and usage. When you locate a potential error, consult a handbook or go to Pearson's Web-based MyCompLab for an explanation of the problem.

Also, if your instructor marks any grammar mistakes on your paper or graphic, make sure you understand them. Recognizing errors in your own writing is the most effective way of correcting them.

As you read the following student essay, "Snowboarding" by Juan Sanchez, refer to the Process Analysis Essentials (page 188) and the questions for reading process analysis (page 190) to help you analyze it. Then, to thoroughly understand how this student essay works, pay special attention to the margin notes and the items in each paragraph they describe.

Juan Sanchez

Professor Flachmann

English 101

3 Oct. 2011

Snowboarding

Subject → 1 The winter sport of snowboarding is no longer an extreme pastime enjoyed by the boldest and bravest. Most ski resorts now offer lessons and rental equipment for snowboarders of all ages and **Overview of Outcome** → skill levels. I recently ventured into the world of snowboarding and found it to be an exhilarating—but occasionally embarrassing—way to have fun during the colder months of the year.

Step 1 → 2 One of the most important factors in making memories in **Explanation** → the snow is wearing the proper attire. It is imperative to have warm, breathable clothes on that will keep the cold and moisture out and keep sweat away from your body. I learned about this rule shortly after we arrived at the mountain when I stepped out of the car and quickly realized that my long-sleeve T-shirt and beanie weren't going to keep me as warm as I'd hoped. Luckily for me, one of the other members of my group had an extra pair of gloves and ski goggles she said I could use. I was so thankful to be able to feel my fingers and halt my ever-worsening snow blindness that I didn't even complain about the crazy snowman pattern on all the items.

3 After standing in a long line to buy the cheapest over-priced sweatshirt the resort sold (which also happened to have a snowman on it), I made my way to the rental shop to get the remainder of my **Step 2** →

gear. The rental shop is an important asset to all new riders because ← Explanation
it allows a novice snowboarder to try out the sport before investing a
serious amount of money. At the first Plexiglas window I was given a
helmet, at the second I was given boots, and at the third I was given
a riddle.

4 "Regular or goofy foot?" the girl with the dreadlocks and lip
ring asked me.

5 Looking around to see if anyone else found this question
strange, I leaned forward and whispered, "What does that mean?"

6 The resort employee let out a sigh and began to explain to
me that a person's lead foot is the foot they would naturally put
forward when sliding on ice or hardwood floors, or the foot that
they would step out first with after being pushed forward. If, like
most people, your left foot is your lead foot, then you are defined as
"regular foot." If your lead foot is your right, then you are, in snowboarding lingo, called "goofy foot." Understanding the question but
not having an answer, I took a couple of steps back, braced myself,
then asked the little girl behind me to push me as hard as she could.
Although I blacked out for a second when my face hit the Plexiglas
window, the rental worker said she saw me step forward with my left
foot and handed me a snowboard with the appropriate bindings. She
then high-fived the not-as-little-as-she-looked girl and went back to
work.

7 Just as getting the correct equipment is an integral part
of snowboarding, it is also important to receive instruction from a ← Step 3
professional. Even though my friends repeatedly tried to help me ← Explanation
in my newfound pastime, their laughing and joking about my lack
of athletic ability was too much of a distraction. I carried my board
to the top of the lesson hill, where I found myself surrounded by a
group of people who were experiencing similar difficulties and had
comparable skill levels. I strapped myself into my bindings and made

sure they were tight. Even though I couldn't feel my toes until hours after we left the mountain, my boots never came off once! After I was strapped in, I gently pointed my lead foot down the hill and applied pressure in the direction I wanted to travel. Closing my eyes made the experience a little more frightening, so I tried hard not to do it. I slowly began to go downhill, and my speed increased dramatically the longer I held that pose. Because I tend to scream in a high-pitched voice when I'm afraid for my life, I tried to slow down as soon as possible. After inspecting the heel or toe edge of the snowboard (the edges where the heels and toes rest, respectively), you need to judge which edge is less likely to catch in the snow and pitch you down the mountain. Because there's a lot more cushion on my rear than on my face, I prefer to lean back on the heel edge when trying to stop. After I learned how to start and stop, the instructor had us do some quick downhill races to see who had learned enough to move on. Although all those five- to ten-year-olds in my class were a talented bunch, I ended up finishing the lesson at the top of the class.

8 After gaining some proper instruction about the sport, you then have to ride the lifts up the mountainside to get to the runs you want to go down. Feeling great about my newly acquired snowboarding skills, I triumphantly headed to the ski lift to attempt my first run down the mountain. Getting on the lift is not too difficult: Just stand in the path of the lift, and wait for it to knock your legs out from under you. This forces you to sit down on the chair/bench as you are then rapidly propelled up the face of the mountain. Getting off the lift is not as easy. Because the lift is moving quickly, it is important to pay attention and be ready to leave the lift at the appropriate time. If you do not leave the lift seat fast enough, you will either be whipped off when the bench swings around to head back down the mountain, or, like me, you will end up with a very disgruntled skier in your lap.

Step 4 →

Explanation →

9 When you arrive at the top of the run, it is time for the first real ride. Check to make sure that black diamonds do not appear on the signs around you. These signify a course that only professional riders should attempt; the ski patrol gets really mad when some novice gets stuck on a slope full of powdered snow (or so I've heard). If the run says "beginner" or "bunny" on it, feel free to proceed. I rode the novice runs for hours before ever attempting the half-pipe (which the ski patrol also frowned upon).

→ Step 5
→ Explanation

10 Upon mastering the less complicated hills, you can either continue to push yourself to find more challenging runs, or, like me, you can sit in the lodge with your slushy sweatshirt, soggy beanie, and raccoon-like sunburn while enjoying a delicious hot chocolate—because, if your experience learning how to snowboard is anything like mine, you will have earned it.

→ Step 6
→ Outcome

Reviewing Process Analysis

Based on the information you have learned in this chapter and the annotations on the student essay, show how this essay works by writing a clear, precise summary or by drawing your own outline or graphic representation of it. Label the steps on your visual. This exercise will confirm your understanding of the elements of process analysis in both reading and writing.

How to Say Nothing in 500 Words

by Paul Roberts

The late **Paul Roberts** was an English professor for over 20 years, first at San Jose State College and then at Cornell University. His classic advice on writing has been anthologized in hundreds of publications and digested by millions of college students. His many publications include *Understanding Grammar* (1954), *Patterns of English* (1956), and *Understanding English* (1958).

PREREADING QUESTIONS

What are your strengths as a writer?

What problems or mistakes do you have to watch for in your writing?

What advice would you give to another student who wants to improve his or her writing?

1   It's Friday afternoon, and you have almost survived another week of classes. You are just looking forward dreamily to the weekend when the English instructor says, "For Monday you will turn in a five hundred-word composition on college football."

2   Well, that puts a good hole in the weekend. You don't have any strong views on college football one way or the other. You get rather excited during the season and go to all the home games and find it rather more fun than not. On the other hand, the class has been reading Robert Hutchins in the anthology and perhaps Shaw's "Eighty-Yard Run," and from the class discussion you have got the idea that the instructor thinks college football is for the birds. You are no fool. You can figure out what side to take.

3   After dinner you get out the portable typewriter that you got for high school graduation. You might as well get it over with and enjoy Saturday and Sunday. Five hundred words is about

two double-spaced pages with normal margins. You put in a sheet of paper, think up a title, and you're off:

Why College Football Should Be Abolished

College football should be abolished because it's bad for the school and also for the players. The players are so busy practicing that they don't have any time for their studies.

4   This, you feel, is a mighty good start. The only trouble is that it's only thirty-two words. You still have four hundred and sixty-eight to go, and you've pretty well exhausted the subject. It comes to you that you do your best thinking in the morning, so you put away the typewriter and go to the movies. But the next morning you have to do your washing and some math problems, and in the afternoon you go to the game. The English instructor turns up too, and you wonder if you've taken the right side after all. Saturday night you have a date, and Sunday morning you have to go to church. (You can't let English assignments

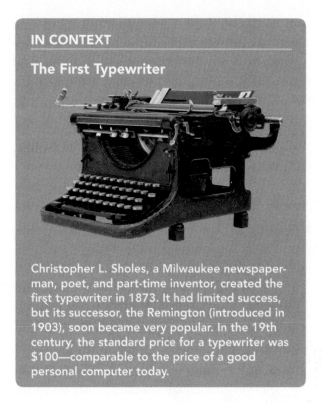

IN CONTEXT

The First Typewriter

Christopher L. Sholes, a Milwaukee newspaperman, poet, and part-time inventor, created the first typewriter in 1873. It had limited success, but its successor, the Remington (introduced in 1903), soon became very popular. In the 19th century, the standard price for a typewriter was $100—comparable to the price of a good personal computer today.

interfere with your religion.) What with one thing and another, it's ten o'clock Sunday night before you get out the typewriter again. You make a pot of coffee and start to fill out your views on college football. Put a little meat on the bones.

Why College Football Should Be Abolished

In my opinion, it seems to me that college football should be abolished. The reason why I think this to be true is because I feel that football is bad for the colleges in nearly every respect. As Robert Hutchins says in his article in our anthology in which he discusses college football, it would be better if the colleges had race horses and had races with one another, because then the horses would not have to attend classes. I firmly agree with Mr. Hutchins on this point, and I am sure that many other students would agree too.

One reason why it seems to me that college football is bad is that it has become too commercial. In the olden times when people played football just for the fun of it, maybe

college football was all right, but they do not play college football just for the fun of it now as they used to in the old days. Nowadays college football is what you might call a big business. Maybe this is not true at all schools, and I don't think it is especially true here at State, but certainly this is the case at most colleges and universities in America nowadays, as Mr. Hutchins points out in his very interesting article. Actually the coaches and alumni go around to the high schools and offer the high school stars large salaries to come to their colleges and play football for them. There was one case where a high school star was offered a convertible if he would play football for a certain college.

Another reason for abolishing college football is that it is bad for the players. They do not have time to get a college education, because they are so busy playing football. A football player has to practice every afternoon from three to six and then he is so tired that he can't concentrate on his studies. He just feels like dropping off to sleep after dinner, and then the next day he goes to his classes without having studied and maybe he fails the test.

(Good ripe stuff so far, but you're still a hundred and fifty-one words from home. One more push.)

Also I think college football is bad for the colleges and the universities because not very many students get to participate in it. Out of a college of ten thousand students only seventy-five or a hundred play football, if that many. Football is what you might call a spectator sport. That means that most people go to watch it but do not play it themselves.

(Four hundred and fifteen. Well, you still have the conclusion, and when you retype it, you can make the margins a little wider.)

These are the reasons why I agree with Mr. Hutchins that college football should be abolished in American colleges and universities.

> *He wonders how he allowed himself to get trapped into teaching English*

5   On Monday you turn it in, moderately hopeful, and on Friday it comes back marked "weak in content" and sporting a big "D." This essay is exaggerated a little, not much. The English instructor will recognize it as reasonably typical of what an assignment on college football will bring in. He knows that nearly half of the class will contrive in five hundred words to say that college football is too commercial and bad for the players. Most of the other half will inform him that college football builds character and prepares one for life and brings prestige to the school. As he reads paper after paper all saying the same thing in almost the same words, all bloodless, five hundred words dripping out of nothing, he wonders how he allowed himself to get trapped into teaching English when he might have had a happy and interesting life as an electrician or a confidence man.

6   Well, you may ask, what can you do about it? The subject is one on which you have few convictions and little information. Can you be expected to make a dull subject interesting? As a matter of fact, this is precisely what you are expected to do. This is the writer's essential task. All subjects, except sex, are dull until somebody makes them interesting. The writer's job is to find the argument, the approach, the angle, the wording that will take the reader with him. This is seldom easy, and it is particularly hard in subjects that have been much discussed: College Football, Fraternities, Popular Music, Is Chivalry Dead?, and the like. You will feel that there is nothing you can do with such subjects except repeat the old bromides. But there are some things you can do which will make your papers, if not throbbingly alive, at least less insufferably tedious than they might otherwise be.

contrive: arrange
prestige: status
bromides: clichés

Avoid the Obvious Content

7   Say the assignment is college football. Say that you've decided to be against it. Begin by putting down the arguments that come to your mind: it is too commercial, it takes the students' minds off their studies, it is hard on the players, it makes the university a kind of circus instead of an intellectual center, for most schools it is financially ruinous. Can you think of any more arguments, just off hand? All right. Now when you write your paper, make sure that you don't use any of the material on this list. If these are the points that leap to your mind, they will leap to everyone else's too, and whether you get a "C" or a "D" may depend on whether the instructor reads your paper early when he is fresh and tolerant or late, when the sentence "In my opinion, college football has become too commercial," inexorably repeated, has brought him to the brink of lunacy.

8   Be against college football for some reason or reasons of your own. If they are keen and perceptive ones, that's splendid. But even if they are trivial or foolish or indefensible, you are still ahead so long as they are not everybody else's reasons too. Be against it because the colleges don't spend enough money on it to make it worthwhile, because it is bad for the characters of the spectators, because the players are forced to attend classes, because the football stars hog all the beautiful women, because it competes with baseball and is therefore un-American and possibly Communist-inspired. There are lots of more or less unused reasons for being against college football.

9   Sometimes it is a good idea to sum up and dispose of the trite and conventional points before going on to your own. This has the advantage of indicating to the reader that you are going to be neither trite nor conventional. Something like this:

> *We are often told that college football should be abolished because it has become too commercial or because it is bad for the players. These arguments are no doubt very cogent, but they don't really go to the heart of the matter.*

10   Then you go to the heart of the matter.

Take the Less Usual Side

11   One rather simple way of getting into your paper is to take the side of the argument that most of the citizens will want to avoid. If the assignment is an essay on dogs, you can, if you choose, explain that dogs are faithful and lovable companions, intelligent, useful as guardians of the house and protectors of children, indispensable in police work—in short, when all is said and done, man's best friends. Or you can suggest that those big brown eyes conceal, more often than not, a vacuity of mind and an inconstancy of

---

IN CONTEXT

Analyzing Your Writing Style

Have you ever wondered if your writing style is similar to that of a famous author? At a Web site called "I Write Like" (http://iwl.me), you can find out. Copy and paste a sample of your writing into the text box to have it analyzed. Whose style is most like yours?

---

inexorably: tirelessly
indefensible: unforgivable
trite: unoriginal
cogent: powerful, convincing
indispensable: essential
vacuity: emptiness

purpose; that the dogs you have known most intimately have been mangy, ill-tempered brutes, incapable of instruction; and that only your nobility of mind and fear of arrest prevent you from kicking the flea-ridden animals when you pass them on the street.

12   Naturally personal convictions will sometimes dictate your approach. If the assigned subject is "Is Methodism Rewarding to the Individual?" and you are a pious Methodist, you have really no choice. But few assigned subjects, if any, will fall in this category. Most of them will lie in broad areas of discussion with much to be said on both sides. They are intellectual exercises, and it is legitimate to argue now one way and now another, as debaters do in similar circumstances. Always take the side that looks to you hardest, least defensible. It will almost always turn out to be easier to write interestingly on that side.

> *This was still funny during the War of 1812, but it has sort of lost its edge since then*

13   This general advice applies where you have a choice of subjects. If you are to choose among "The Value of Fraternities" and "My Favorite High School Teacher" and "What I Think About Beetles," by all means plump for the beetles. By the time the instructor gets to your paper, he will be up to his ears in tedious tales about a French teacher at Bloombury High and assertions about how fraternities build character and prepare one for life. Your views on beetles, whatever they are, are bound to be a refreshing change.

14   Don't worry too much about figuring out what the instructor thinks about the subject so that you can cuddle up with him. Chances are his views are no stronger than yours. If he does have convictions and you oppose him, his problem is to keep from grading you higher than you deserve in order to show he is not biased. This doesn't mean that you should always cantankerously dissent from what the instructor says; that gets tiresome too. And if the subject assigned is "My Pet Peeve,"

do not begin, "My pet peeve is the English instructor who assigns papers on 'my pet peeve.'" This was still funny during the War of 1812, but it has sort of lost its edge since then. It is in general good manners to avoid personalities.

Slip Out of Abstraction

15   If you will study the essay on college football (near the beginning of this essay), you will perceive that one reason for its appalling dullness is that it never gets down to particulars. It is just a series of not very glittering generalities: "football is bad for the colleges," "it has become too commercial," "football is big business," "it is bad for the players," and so on. Such round phrases thudding against the reader's brain are unlikely to convince him, though they may well render him unconscious.

16   If you want the reader to believe that college football is bad for the players, you have to do more than say so. You have to display the evil. Take your roommate, Alfred Simkins, the second-string center. Picture poor old Alfy coming home from football practice every evening, bruised and aching, agonizingly tired, scarcely

---

dictate: command
pious: devout, dedicated
cantankerously: in a grouchy manner
dissent: disagree
appalling: shocking

able to shovel the mashed potatoes into his mouth. Let us see him staggering up to the room, getting out his econ textbook, peering desperately at it with his good eye, falling asleep and failing the test in the morning. Let us share his unbearable tension as Saturday draws near. Will he fail, be demoted, lose his monthly allowance, be forced to return to the coal mines? And if he succeeds, what will be his reward? Perhaps a slight ripple of applause when the third-string center replaces him, a moment of elation in the locker room if the team wins, of despair if it loses. What will he look back on when he graduates from college? Toil and torn ligaments. And what will be his future? He is not good enough for pro football, and he is too obscure and weak in econ to succeed in stocks and bonds. College football is tearing the heart from Alfy Simkins and, when it finishes with him, will callously toss aside the shattered hulk.

17   This is no doubt a weak enough argument for the abolition of college football, but it is a sight better than saying, in three or four variations, that college football (in your opinion) is bad for the players.

18   Look at the work of any professional writer, and notice how constantly he is moving from the generality, the abstract statement, to the concrete example, the facts and figures, the illustrations.

If he is writing on juvenile delinquency, he does not just tell you that juveniles are (it seems to him) delinquent and that (in his opinion) something should be done about it. He shows you juveniles being delinquent, tearing up movie theatres in Buffalo, stabbing high school principals in Dallas, smoking marijuana in Palo Alto. And more than likely he is moving toward some specific remedy, not just a general wringing of the hands.

19   It is no doubt possible to be too concrete, too illustrative or anecdotal, but few inexperienced writers err this way. For most the soundest advice is to be seeking always for the picture, to be always turning general remarks into seeable examples. Don't say, "Sororities teach girls the social graces." Say, "Sorority life teaches a girl how to carry on a conversation while pouring tea, without sloshing the tea into the saucer." Don't say, "I like certain kinds of popular music very much." Say, "Whenever I hear Gerber Sprinklittle play 'Mississippi Man' on the trombone, my socks creep up my ankles."

Get Rid of Obvious Padding

20   The student toiling away at his weekly English theme is too often tormented by a figure: five hundred words. How, he asks himself, is he to achieve this staggering total? Obviously by never using one word when he can somehow work in ten.

21   He is therefore seldom content with a plain statement like "Fast driving is dangerous." This has only four words in it. He takes the thought, and the sentence becomes:

In my opinion, fast driving is dangerous.

Better, but he can do better still:

In my opinion, fast driving would seem to be rather dangerous.

elation: excitement
toil: hard work
callously: heartlessly
anecdotal: unreliable
err: make a mistake

If he is really adept, it may come out:

> *In my humble opinion, though I do not claim to be an expert on this complicated subject, fast driving, in most circumstances, would seem to be rather dangerous in many respects, or at least so it would seem to me.*

22   Thus four words have been turned into forty, and not an iota of content has been added.

23   Now this is a way to go about reaching five hundred words, and if you are content with a "D" grade, it is as good a way as any. But if you aim higher, you must work differently. Instead of stuffing your sentences with straw, you must try steadily to get rid of the padding, to make your sentences lean and tough. If you are really working at it, your first draft will greatly exceed the required total, and then you will work it down, thus:

> *It is thought in some quarters that fraternities do not contribute as much as might be expected to campus life.*
>
> *Some people think that fraternities contribute little to campus life.*
>
> *The average doctor who practices in small towns or in the country must toil night and day to heal the sick.*
>
> *Most country doctors work long hours.*
>
> *When I was a little girl, I suffered from shyness and embarrassment in the presence of others.*
>
> *I was a shy little girl.*
>
> *It is absolutely necessary for the person employed as a marine fireman to give the matter of steam pressure his undivided attention at all times.*
>
> *The fireman has to keep his eye on the steam gauge.*

24   You may ask how you can arrive at five hundred words at this rate. Simple. You dig up more real content. Instead of taking a couple of obvious points off the surface of the topic and then circling warily around them for six paragraphs, you work in and explore, figure out the details. You illustrate. You say that fast driving is dangerous, and then you prove it. How long does it take to stop a car at forty and at eighty? How far can you see at night? What happens when a tire blows? What happens in a head-on collision at fifty miles an hour?

25   Pretty soon your paper will be full of broken glass and blood and headless torsos, and reaching five hundred words will not really be a problem.

Call a Fool a Fool

26   Some of the padding in freshman themes is to be blamed not on anxiety about the word minimum but on excessive timidity. The student writes, "In my opinion, the principal of my high school acted in ways that I believe every unbiased person would have to call foolish." This isn't exactly what he means. What he means is, "My high school principal was a fool." If he was a fool, call him a fool. Hedging the thing about with "in-my-opinion's" and "it-seems-to-me's" and "as-I-see-it's" and "at-least-from-my-point-of-view's" gains you nothing. Delete these phrases whenever they creep into your paper.

> *He half suspects that he is dopey and fuzzyminded beyond the average*

27   The student's tendency to hedge stems from a modesty that in other circumstances would be commendable. He is, he realizes, young and inexperienced, and he half suspects that he is dopey and fuzzyminded beyond the average. Probably

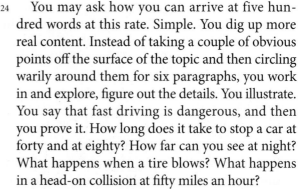

iota: bit, speck
hedge: sidestep, evade

only too true. But it doesn't help to announce your incompetence six times in every paragraph. Decide what you want to say and say it as vigorously as possible, without apology and in plain words.

28   Linguistic diffidence can take various forms. One is what we call euphemism. This is the tendency to call a spade "a certain garden implement" or women's underwear "unmentionables." It is stronger in some eras than others and in some people than others but it always operates more or less in subjects that are touchy or taboo: death, sex, madness, and so on. Thus we shrink from saying "He died last night" but say instead "passed away," "left us," "joined his Maker," "went to his reward." Or we try to take off the tension with a lighter cliché: "kicked the bucket," "cashed in his chips," "handed in his dinner pail." We have found all sorts of ways to avoid saying mad: "mentally ill," "touched," "not quite right upstairs," "feebleminded," "innocent," "simple," "off his trolley," "not in his right mind." Even such a now plain word as insane began as a euphemism with the meaning "not healthy."

29   Modern science, particularly psychology, contributes many polysyllables in which we can wrap our thoughts and blunt their force. To many writers there is no such thing as a bad schoolboy. Schoolboys are maladjusted or unoriented or misunderstood or in the need of guidance or lacking in continued success toward satisfactory integration of the personality as a social unit, but they are never bad. Psychology no doubt makes us better men and women, more sympathetic and tolerant, but it doesn't make writing any easier. Had Shakespeare been confronted with psychology, "To be or not to be" might have come out, "To continue as a social unit or not to do so. That is the personality problem. Whether 'tis a better sign of integration at the conscious level to display a psychic tolerance toward the maladjustments and repressions induced by one's lack of orientation in one's environment or—" But Hamlet would never have finished the soliloquy.

30   Writing in the modern world, you cannot altogether avoid modern jargon. Nor, in an effort to get away from euphemism, should you salt your paper with four-letter words. But you can do much if you will mount guard against those roundabout phrases, those echoing polysyllables that tend to slip into your writing to rob it of its crispness and force.

Beware of Pat Expressions

31   Other things being equal, avoid phrases like "other things being equal." Those sentences that come to you whole, or in two or three doughy lumps, are sure to be bad sentences. They are no creation of yours but pieces of common thought floating in the community soup.

32   Pat expressions are hard, often impossible, to avoid, because they come too easily to be noticed and seem too necessary to be dispensed with. No writer avoids them altogether, but good writers avoid them more often than poor writers.

33   By "pat expressions" we mean such tags as "to all practical intents and purposes," "the pure and simple truth," "from where I sit," "the time of his life," "to the ends of the earth," "in the twinkling of an eye," "as sure as you're born," "over my dead body," "under cover of darkness," "took the easy way out," "when all is said and done," "told him time and time again," "parted the best of friends," "stand up and be counted," "gave him the best years of her life," "worked her fingers to the bone." Like other clichés, these expressions were once forceful. Now we should use them only when we can't possibly think of anything else.

diffidence: shyness
maladjusted: unstable
unoriented: lost, confused
integration: mixing

34   Some pat expressions stand like a wall between the writer and thought. Such a one is "the American way of life." Many student writers feel that when they have said that something accords with the American way of life or does not they have exhausted the subject. Actually, they have stopped at the highest level of abstraction. The American way of life is the complicated set of bonds between a hundred and eighty million ways. All of us know this when we think about it, but the tag phrase too often keeps us from thinking about it.

35   So with many another phrase dear to the politician: "this great land of ours," "the man in the street," "our national heritage." These may prove our patriotism or give a clue to our political beliefs, but otherwise they add nothing to the paper except words.

Colorful Words

36   The writer builds with words, and no builder uses a raw material more slippery and elusive and treacherous. A writer's work is a constant struggle to get the right word in the right place, to find that particular word that will convey his meaning exactly, that will persuade the reader or soothe him or startle or amuse him. He never succeeds altogether—sometimes he feels that he scarcely succeeds at all—but such successes as he has are what make the thing worth doing.

> *The writer builds with words, and no builder uses a raw material more slippery and elusive and treacherous*

37   There is no book of rules for this game. One progresses through everlasting experiment on the basis of ever-widening experience. There are few useful generalizations that one can make about words as words, but there are perhaps a few.

38   Some words are what we call "colorful." By this we mean that they are calculated to produce a picture or induce an emotion. They are dressy instead of plain, specific instead of general, loud instead of soft. Thus, in place of "Her heart beat," we may write, "her heart pounded, throbbed, fluttered, danced." Instead of "He sat in his chair," we may say, "he *lounged, sprawled, coiled*." Instead of "It was hot," we may say, "It was *blistering, sultry, muggy, suffocating, steamy, wilting*."

39   However, it should not be supposed that the fancy word is always better. Often it is as well to write "Her heart beat" or "It was hot" if that is all it did or all it was. Ages differ in how they like their prose. The nineteenth century liked it rich and smoky. The twentieth has usually preferred it lean and cool. The twentieth century writer, like all writers, is forever seeking the exact word, but he is wary of sounding feverish. He tends to pitch it low, to understate it, to throw it away. He knows that if he gets too colorful, the audience is likely to giggle.

treacherous: dishonest, unfaithful

40   See how this strikes you: "As the rich, golden glow of the sunset died away along the eternal western hills, Angela's limpid blue eyes looked softly and trustingly into Montague's flashing brown ones, and her heart pounded like a drum in time with the joyous song surging in her soul." Some people like that sort of thing, but most modern readers would say, "Good grief," and turn on the television.

Colored Words

41   Some words we would call not so much colorful as colored—that is, loaded with associations, good or bad. All words—except perhaps structure words—have associations of some sort. We have said that the meaning of a word is the sum of the contexts in which it occurs. When we hear a word, we hear with it an echo of all the situations in which we have heard it before.

42   In some words, these echoes are obvious and discussible. The word *mother*, for example, has, for most people, agreeable associations. When you hear *mother* you probably think of home, safety, love, food, and various other pleasant things. If one writes, "She was like a mother to me," he gets an effect which he would not get in "She was like an aunt to me." The advertiser makes use of the associations of *mother* by working it in when he talks about his product. The politician works it in when he talks about himself.

43   So also with such words as *home, liberty, fireside,* contentment, *patriot, tenderness, sacrifice, childlike, manly, bluff, limpid.* All of these words are loaded with associations that would be rather hard to indicate in a straightforward definition. There is more than a literal difference between "They sat around the fireside" and "They sat around the stove." They might have been equally warm and happy around the stove, but *fireside* suggests leisure, grace, quiet tradition, congenial company, and *stove* does not.

44   Conversely, some words have bad associations. *Mother* suggests pleasant things, but *mother-in-law* does not. Many mothers-in-law are heroically lovable and some mothers drink gin all day and beat their children insensible, but these facts of life are beside the point. The point is that *mother* sounds good and *mother-in-law* does not.

45   Or consider the word *intellectual.* This would seem to be a complimentary term, but in point of fact it is not, for it has picked up associations of impracticality and ineffectuality and general dopiness. So also such words as *liberal, reactionary, Communist, socialist, capitalist, radical, schoolteacher, truck driver; operator, salesman,* huckster, *speculator.* These convey meaning on the literal level, but beyond that—sometimes, in some places—they convey contempt on the part of the speaker.

46   The question of whether to use loaded words or not depends on what is being written. The scientist, the scholar, try to avoid them; for the poet, the advertising writer, the public speaker, they are standard equipment. But every writer should take care that they do not substitute for thought. If you write, "Anyone who thinks that is nothing but a Socialist (or Communist or capitalist)" you have said nothing except that you don't like people who think that, and such remarks are effective only with the most naive readers. It is always a bad mistake to think your readers more naive than they really are.

Colorless Words

47   But probably most student writers come to grief not with words that are colorful or those that are colored but with those that have no

limpid: clear
contentment: satisfaction
congenial: friendly
conversely: oppositely
impracticality: uselessness
ineffectuality: unproductive
huckster: seller

color at all. A pet example is *nice*, a word we would find it hard to dispense with in casual conversation but which is no longer capable of adding much to a description. Colorless words are those of such general meaning that in a particular sentence they mean nothing. Slang adjectives like cool ("That's real cool") tend to explode all over the language. They are applied to everything, lose their original force, and quickly die.

48   Beware also of nouns of very general meaning, like *circumstances, cases, instances, aspects, factors, relationships, attitudes, eventualities,* etc. In most circumstances, you will find that those cases of writing which contain too many instances of words like these will in this and other aspects have factors leading to unsatisfactory relationships with the reader resulting in unfavorable attitudes on his part and perhaps other eventualities, like a grade of "D." Notice also what *etc.* means. It means "I'd like to make this list longer, but I can't think of any more examples."

From *Understanding English* by Paul Roberts. Copyright © 1958 by Paul Roberts. Reprinted by permission of Pearson Education, Inc.

CONVERSATIONS: Collaborating in Class or Online

1. What do you think are the main problems with the student essay on college football?
2. List the nine guidelines Roberts suggests for good writing, and explain each briefly.
3. Can you give five examples of euphemisms in current use (without repeating any of the ones Roberts uses)? Why is our society so dependent on euphemisms? What social function do they serve?
4. According to Roberts, what are "colorful words," "colored words," and "colorless words"? Add five examples of your own to each of these lists in the essay.

CONNECTIONS: Discovering Relationships among Ideas

5. To what extent do you identify with the college student described at the outset of this essay? In what ways are you different?
6. What does Roberts mean when he says, "The writer's job is to find the argument, the approach, the angle, the wording that will take the reader with him" (para. 6)?
7. Of all the guidelines presented in this essay, which is most difficult for you? Give an example from your own writing.
8. Does Roberts's essay follow his own suggestions for good writing? Why or why not? Give examples that illustrate how successfully the author pays attention to his own advice.

PRESENTATION: Analyzing the Writer's Craft

9. What is the principal purpose of this essay? Does it accomplish its purpose? Explain your answer.
10. How does Roberts organize the elements of his essay? Why does he choose this particular order? Is it effective for achieving his purpose? Why or why not?

11. Describe Roberts's intended audience in some detail. How did you come to this conclusion?

12. Analyze Roberts's use of humor throughout this essay (especially in the last paragraph). How does he raise our awareness regarding language as he makes us laugh at ourselves?

PROJECTS: Expressing Your Own Views

13. **Writing Assignment:** The student isn't the only one who needs improvement in this essay. The instructor's assignment of "a five hundred-word composition on college football" is too vague to inspire good prose. Devise a writing assignment on the topic of college sports that will get students more involved than the prompt quoted by Roberts. Include purpose, audience, and writer's role in your assignment.

14. **Analysis:** Using the guidelines Roberts suggests in this essay, analyze one of your recent papers.

15. **Essay:** In a letter to a friend who is about to start college, explain how to survive in his or her freshman writing course.

16. **Research:** Read and summarize the three resources below. Generate one specific question from each resource that focuses on process analysis. Then answer one of your questions in a documented essay, consulting these and other sources as necessary.

OTHER RESOURCES

Web Site

The Idiom Connection:
www.idiomconnection.com

Click on the 100 Most
Frequently Used Idioms link

Academic Article

"Buying In, Selling Short: A Pedagogy against the Rhetoric of Online Paper Mills"

by Kelly Ritter

Pedagogy 6.1 (2006): 25–51

Audio/Video

YouTube: www.youtube.com

Search: "The English Paper" by activeobjectx

Click on the Video link

ONE LAST THOUGHT

Do you ever see written material that is overly long and wordy? What do you think motivates people to use excessively complicated language?

www.CartoonStock.com

Assembling Furniture

by IKEA

IKEA is an international home products company based in Sweden that sells ready-to-assemble furniture. The largest home accessory retailer in the world, it was founded in 1943 by a 17-year-old student who created its initials as an acronym from his own name (**I**ngvar **K**amprad), the farm where he grew up (**E**lmtaryd), and his home parish in southern Sweden (**A**gunnaryd). The IKEA Web site, which advertises over 12,000 products, had 470 million visitors last year.

Two of its three largest stores are in Sweden, while the other is in Shenyang, China.

FREDRIK

WORKSTATION 96X62

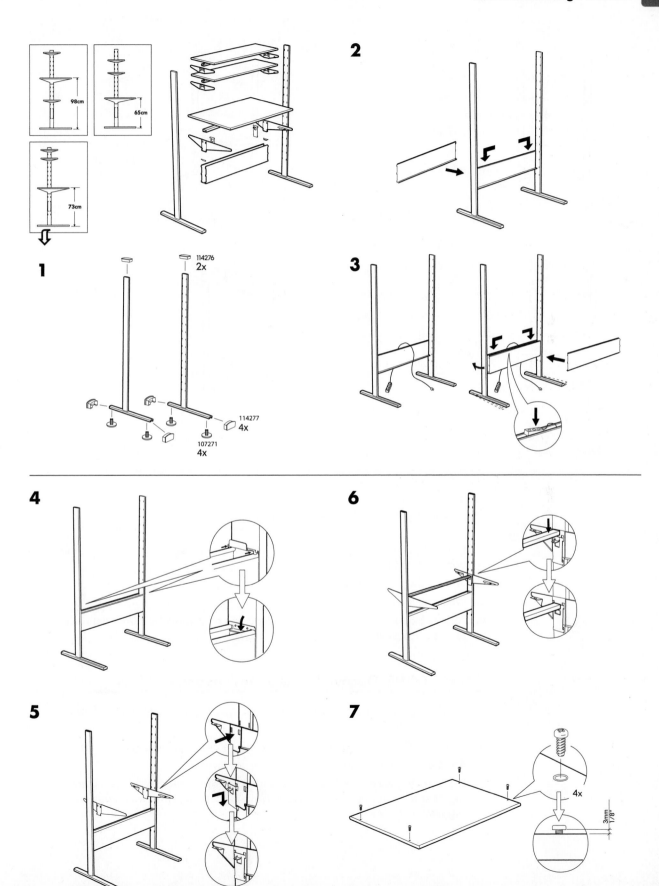

8

10

9

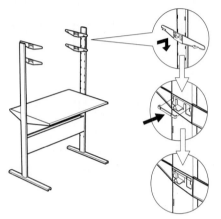

11

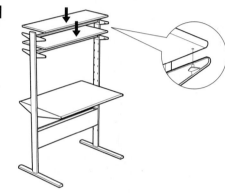

CONVERSATIONS: Collaborating in Class or Online

1. Following directions can often be difficult. What is most challenging about the directions featured here?

2. What is the process in these drawings?

3. What will the end product be?

4. After this object is assembled, how big do you think it will be? What details lead you to this conclusion?

CONNECTIONS: Discovering Relationships among Ideas

5. What products have you assembled in the past? Which were most difficult? Why were they difficult?

6. What is the artist saying by adding a caricature at the beginning of the instructions?

7. Are these directions clear to you? Explain your answer.

8. Did you ever wish that "life" came with a set of instructions? If you were putting together a list of directions for assembling a good life, what would be your top five suggestions?

PRESENTATION: Analyzing the Writer's Craft

9. Are pictures more effective than words for assembling furniture?
10. Who is the intended audience of these drawings?
11. What do the details in the drawings tell you about this process?
12. In what way is the overview on the first page intended to help the people assembling this furniture?

PROJECTS: Expressing Your Own Views

13. **Photo:** Create your own drawing of a process, exchange pictures with someone in your class, and write a summary of the process.
14. **Game:** Get into groups of three, and decide who will be the manager, the writer, and the technician. Log onto fantasticcontraption.com. Complete level 3, 5, 7, or 10 of the game, and write it up for another team. Switch seats at the computer with another team, and see if you can complete the level by following the rules each team created.
15. **Essay:** Write a detailed essay explaining a significant event in history from start to finish. Go to the Internet for ideas if necessary.
16. **Research:** Read and summarize the three resources below. Generate one specific question from each resource that focuses on process analysis. Then answer one of your questions in a documented essay, consulting these and other sources as necessary.

OTHER RESOURCES

Web Site

eHow: www.ehow.com/

Search: "How to Assemble Knock-Down Furniture"

Click on the How to Assemble Knock-Down Furniture link

Academic Article

"Diverse, Unforeseen, and Quaint Difficulties: The Sensible Responses of Novices Learning to Follow Instructions in Academic Writing"

by Karen P. Macbeth

Research in the Teaching of English 41.2 (2006): 180–207

Audio/Video

YouTube: www.youtube.com

Search: "Stop-Motion IKEA Furniture Assembly"

Click on the Video link

ONE LAST THOUGHT

IKEA, the largest furniture store in the world, was also the first retailer to sell "flat-pack" furniture, otherwise known as "knock-down" furniture. Gillis Lundgren, an IKEA employee, developed the idea when he took the legs off his table to fit it into his car. IKEA launched the first set of flat-pack furniture in 1956. Do you prefer to put your furniture together or purchase furniture that is already assembled? Why?

6 Sneaky Ways Sales Spur Spending

by Kit Yarrow

A professor of psychology and marketing at Golden Gate University in San Francisco, **Kit Yarrow** is a specialist in consumer behavior. She is the co-author of *Gen BuY: How Tweens, Teens, and Twenty-Somethings Are Revolutionizing Retail*. She has appeared on *ABC World News, Good Morning America, CNN, NPR*, and many other television news programs and maintains a blog titled "The Why Behind the Buy."

PREREADING QUESTIONS

Why do stores offer sales?

What attracts you to sales in stores?

What do you like or dislike about sales?

1   Like most Americans, Jill has a new budget. The 44-year-old San Franciscan has been working diligently for the past six months to reduce her credit card debt by skipping Starbucks and car washes, cleaning her own house, and getting her hair cut less frequently. She's managed to cut her $6,200 balance almost in half. Last week, however, Jill did something unexpected—she bought a pair of sandals for $140 (reduced from $280) and a satin trench coat for $90 (reduced from $140). "I simply couldn't resist. I don't know what came over me. They were such great deals."

2   Tanya, 23, of Alexandria, Virginia, was walking through Nordstrom on her way to meet a friend for lunch and spotted a table piled high with handbags. "It called to me! I found the cutest hobo; it was the last one; I had to buy it."

3   The song of the Shopping Sirens is a sale. Resolve is weakened, thoughts are muddled, impulse takes over, and out comes the credit card. Sales work because they hit us at a deep psychological level. We may think it's all about the deal—but there's much more to it than that.

4   Here are six different ways that sales play on emotions in very cunning ways and often inspire us to make purchases we might otherwise pass up.

5   **Fear:** Sales inspire a fear of missing out. Everyone knows sale items are limited, and this

diligently: thoroughly
muddled: confused
cunning: crafty

creates a now-or-never mentality that prompts a purchase. Like Tanya, awareness that it's the "last one" means buy it now or it's gone. Without that fear and with more time to think—a good many sale items would be left behind. This is the same mentality behind 24-hour specials and midnight madness events—when time is limited, emotions are elevated, and, well, you know the rest.

6   **Emotional Investment:** The time, energy, and engagement required to sort through a jumble of markdowns is akin to an investment. Further, finding the right color, right size, or perfect brand is like unearthing buried treasure. Our perception of an item's value and our unconscious com-

> *The hunt itself contributes to our perception of the value of the product*

mitment to purchase gets a boost when we've already made a commitment of time. Plus our sense of good fortune when we find something good after a search rubs off onto the product and increases its emotional value. In other words, the hunt itself contributes to our perception of the value of the product.

7   **Competition:** Sales create a sense of competition with other shoppers. Stacy, 33, of Chicago has been getting emails from Neiman Marcus with two-hour mid-day specials. The sales start at 11:30 and last for only two hours or until they're sold out. "I had a few minutes during lunch and checked it out—they had La Mer moisturizer for half off! That never goes on sale. But it was sold out. So now I find myself rushing to check whenever I get the email, and I've noticed that most of the things on there get sold out right away. It's like a competition to see who can get it first." Getting the best deal or a great bargain is a badge of honor of many shoppers, and the notion that they've won over others through better planning, more effort, or expertise is rewarding to many consumers. The competition can overshadow a rational evaluation of the worth of the product in that person's life. We've all seen the worst of this on the news

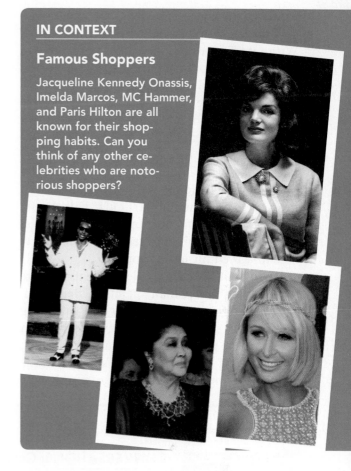

IN CONTEXT

Famous Shoppers

Jacqueline Kennedy Onassis, Imelda Marcos, MC Hammer, and Paris Hilton are all known for their shopping habits. Can you think of any other celebrities who are notorious shoppers?

when shoppers stampede retailers during Black Friday sales. A more subtle version of this phenomenon exists whenever shoppers get the sense that they've "won" rather than "bought" an item.

8   **Assumed Value:** Sales override the process of considering the value of an item. When full priced merchandise is considered, a price/value equation takes place in the minds of consumers. "Is it worth it? Is that a fair price?" When things go on sale, they're instinctively "a deal," and that process of evaluating the product's worth is often overshadowed by something like: "it used to be $400 and now it's only $200! Wow, what a great deal!" If that same product were full price at $200—shoppers

akin: similar

robust: healthy, vigorous

would go through a more lengthy thought process to determine its value to the individual. Without this process, we're also more likely to make hasty, emotional purchases.

9   **Easy Shopping:** Many shoppers move right to the sale rack—and not just because they're hungry for a bargain. Sales pare down choices—and today's shoppers are overwhelmed by choice. As Barry Schwartz has taught us all, an abundance of options can be overwhelming and mentally taxing. Research has shown that men in particular will simply leave a store when confronted with a robust selection. Sale shopping feels more comfortable to less enthusiastic shoppers.

10   **Saving not Spending:** Sales make us feel like we're saving rather than spending. Benjamin, 30, of San Francisco, recalls his wife returning home from a shopping trip positively giddy with delight at the great sales she'd found at the mall. "I kept asking her how much she's spent and she didn't have any idea, but she knew exactly how much she'd 'saved.'" Similarly, coupon clipping has made a big comeback in response to our recent economic woes. While many shoppers are using coupons to take the sting out of their weekly food expenditures, others are stocking up on items they'd otherwise avoid because they're "getting a deal."

11   While most shoppers are aware of the overt ways they rationalize purchases by taking advantage of sales, many aren't aware of the deeper ways that sales fire up our emotions and consequently override some of [our] good reasoning skills. A great sale can be a lot of fun and a terrific way to buy—as long as you know what you're up against.

———————

Reprinted with permission from *Psychology Today* Magazine (Copyright © 2009 Sussex Publishers, LLC).

robust: healthy, vigorous

CONVERSATIONS: Collaborating in Class or Online

1. Why does Yarrow call a sale "the song of the Shopping Sirens" (para. 3)?
2. Why is "resolve ... weakened" (para. 3) during a sale?
3. In your own words, what are the six ways that sales play on our emotions?
4. In what ways do sales "override some of [our] good reasoning skills" (para. 11)?

CONNECTIONS: Discovering Relationships among Ideas

5. According to Yarrow, how are time and emotions related?
6. How do "sales create a sense of competition with other shoppers" (para. 7)?
7. Why are sales appealing to most people?
8. What entices people to continue going to sales?

PRESENTATION: Analyzing the Writer's Craft

9. What is Yarrow's purpose in this essay?
10. What type of process analysis does this represent: directive or informative?
11. This essay starts with two stories. Is that an effective opening? Explain your answer.
12. What is the significance of the word "sneaky" in the title of this essay?

PROJECTS: Expressing Your Own Views

13. **Graphic:** Design a campaign to put one of the major items in the store you manage on sale. Consider what you want to achieve and how you will achieve this purpose. Also, be aware of the characteristics of most of your shoppers.

14. **Journal:** Freewrite about your shopping habits. Do you sometimes use shopping to compensate for a bad day? To reward a job well done? How sensible a shopper are you? Discuss these various issues.

15. **Essay:** Write a process analysis essay telling someone how to take a perfect photo or set up an e-album on the computer. Make sure you have a purpose, and explain each stage of the process.

16. **Research:** Read and summarize the three resources below. Generate one specific question from each resource that focuses on process analysis. Then answer one of your questions in a documented essay, consulting these and other sources as necessary.

OTHER RESOURCES

Web Site

Shopaholics Anonymous: www.shopaholicsanonymous. org

Academic Article

"What Is Advertising?" by William M. O'Barr

Advertising & Society Review 6.3 (2005)

Audio/Video

ABC News: http://abcnews. go.com

Search: "Going Out of Business"

Click on the "Beware of Going-Out-of-Business Sales" Audio link

ONE LAST THOUGHT

The Federal Trade Commission is a government agency that advocates consumers' rights. According to its Web site, the Division of Advertising Practices is a department within the FTC that "protects consumers from unfair or deceptive advertising and marketing practices." Some of their many priorities include shielding consumers from cure-all products, supervising marketing on the Internet, and advancing new advertising strategies. Have you ever seen or heard anything you thought was deceptive advertising? What rules do you think advertisers should have to adhere to?

wikiHow.com

Founded in 2005 by Jack Herrick, **wikiHow** is the world's first "collaborative on-line how-to manual." It includes cyber instructions on almost anything you might want to do, including how to string a lacrosse stick, how to perform a great French kiss, and how to treat a caterpillar sting.

PREREADING QUESTIONS

Do you think collaboration is generally effective? Why or why not?

When is individual work preferable to group work?

What do you think you might find on a Web site called wikiHow?

View the entire Web site at www.wikihow.com/Main-Page before answering the questions that follow.

CONVERSATIONS: Collaborating in Class or Online

1. Explore the wikiHow site pictured here. How could you use this site?
2. Look up a process, and introduce it to your class in your own words.

3. What roles do writing and editing play in this site?

4. How does this site compare to Wikipedia?

CONNECTIONS: Discovering Relationships among Ideas

5. Why is how-to information so popular in contemporary society?

6. What directions might you add to the wikiHow site?

7. What directions would you like to edit on this site?

8. What do you think are the most commonly searched topics on wikiHow? Why?

PRESENTATION: Analyzing the Writer's Craft

9. Do you think this is an appealing site? Explain your answer.

10. What is its purpose?

11. Who is its intended audience?

12. Does the site contain material that is more directive or informative?

PROJECTS: Expressing Your Own Views

13. **Wiki:** Make an entry on (or edit) one of the wiki sites: wikiHow or Wikipedia.

14. **Web Site:** Design the home page for a new wiki that you create.

15. **Essay:** Write a process analysis essay explaining how to undo a process. Decide on a purpose and audience before you begin.

16. **Research:** Read and summarize the three resources below. Generate one specific question from each resource that focuses on process analysis. Then answer one of your questions in a documented essay, consulting these and other sources as necessary.

OTHER RESOURCES

Web Site

Lifehacker: http://lifehacker.com/

Academic Article

"E-Learning: Is There Anything Special About the 'E'?"

by David Cook and Furman S. McDonald

Perspectives in Biology and Medicine 51.1 (2008): 5–21

Audio/Video

wikiHow: www.wikihow.com

Search: "How to Write a Research Paper"

Click on the Feb. 20, 2011, link, and watch the video after the numbered list

ONE LAST THOUGHT

MAKE is an American magazine that focuses on DIY (do it yourself) or DIWO (do it with others) projects. It provides step-by-step instructions on how to make many science-based gadgets, from small robots to remote-controlled rockets. Visit their Web site at Makezine.com. What instructions would you like to see in a magazine like this?

How Human Cloning Will Work

by Kevin Bonsor and Cristen Conger

Kevin Bonsor and **Cristen Conger** are freelance writers at the popular blog HowStuffWorks.com. They both have journalism degrees: Bonsor's from Georgia Southern University and Conger's from the University of Georgia. Previously an editor at Signature Publishing, Bonsor is now marketing manager at Thomson Reuters; Conger co-hosts the "Stuff Your Mom Never Told You" podcasts with Molly Edwards.

PREREADING QUESTIONS

What do you know about cloning?

How would you feel about having a cloned sibling or twin?

What do you think about eating meat from cloned animals?

Introduction to How Human Cloning Will Work

1   On July 5, 1997, the most famous sheep in modern history was born. Ian Wilmut and a group of Scottish scientists announced that they had successfully cloned a sheep named Dolly.

2   If you stood Dolly beside a "naturally" conceived sheep, you wouldn't notice any differences between the two. In fact, to pinpoint the only major distinguishing factor between the two, you'd have to go back to the time of conception because Dolly's embryo developed without the presence of sperm. Instead, Dolly began as a cell from another sheep that was fused via electricity with a donor egg. Just one sheep—no hanky-panky involved.

3   While Dolly's birth marked an incredible scientific breakthrough, it also set off questions in the scientific and global community about what—or who—might be next to be "duplicated." Cloning sheep and other nonhuman animals seemed more ethically benign to some than potentially cloning people. In response to

benign: harmless

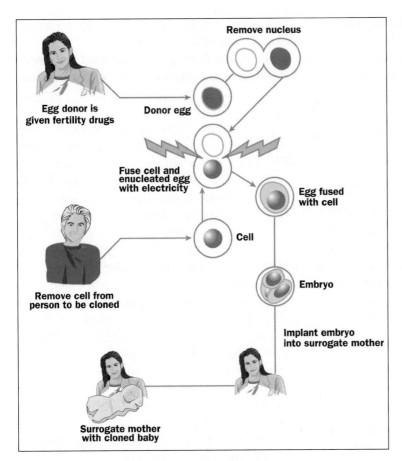

Remove nucleus

Egg donor is given fertility drugs

Donor egg

Fuse cell and enucleated egg with electricity

Egg fused with cell

Cell

Remove cell from person to be cloned

Embryo

Implant embryo into surrogate mother

Surrogate mother with cloned baby

Creating a Human Clone

7   In January 2001, a small consortium of scientists led by Panayiotis Zavos, a former University of Kentucky professor, and Italian researcher Severino Antinori said that they planned to clone a human in two years. At about the same time, news surfaced about an American couple who planned to pay $500,000 to Las Vegas-based company Clonaid for a clone of their deceased infant daughter. Neither venture produced documented success.

8   Then, in 2004, South Korean scientist Hwang Woo-suk announced that he and his research team had cloned 11 human embryos for the purpose of extracting stem cells. However, after reviewing his work, a panel at Seoul National University concluded that his findings were false. There hasn't been any confirmed human clone created to date. When discussing cloning in the sense of doing so to make a duplicate of an organism, we refer to it as reproductive cloning.

9   If human reproductive cloning proceeds, the primary method scientists will likely use is somatic cell nuclear transfer (SCNT), which is the same procedure

Just one sheep— no hanky-panky involved

that was used to create Dolly the sheep. Somatic cell nuclear transfer begins when doctors take the egg from a female donor and remove its nucleus, creating an enucleated egg. A cell, which contains DNA, is taken from the person who is being cloned. Then the enucleated egg is fused together with the cloning subject's cell using electricity. This creates an embryo, which is implanted into a surrogate mother through in vitro fertilization.

such concerns in the United States, President Clinton signed a five-year moratorium on federal funding for human cloning the same year of Dolly's arrival.

4   Today, after more than a decade since Dolly, human cloning remains in its infancy. Although cloning technology has improved, the process still has a slim success rate of 1 to 4 percent. That being said, science is headed in that direction— pending governmental restraints.

5   Scientists have cloned a variety of animals, including mice, sheep, pigs, cows, and dogs. In 2006, scientists cloned the first primate embryos of a rhesus monkey. Then, in early 2008, the FDA officially deemed milk and meat products from cloned animals and their offspring safe to eat.

6   But what would human cloning involve, and how could you take sperm out of the reproductive equation?

moratorium: ban
consortium: association, group

10   If the procedure is successful, then the surrogate mother will give birth to a baby that's a clone of the cloning subject at the end of a normal gestation period. As mentioned before, the success rate for this type of procedure is small, working in only one or two out of every 100 embryos. After all, Dolly was the result of 277 previously failed attempts.

11   On the surface, human cloning may evoke a similar reaction to the space program's race to the moon— groundbreaking accomplishment, but what could we actually glean from it? Re-engineering the human reproductive process has made many people nervous that cloning crosses the ethical boundaries of science. But we can't fully evaluate the moral dilemma without first addressing the potential benefits of human cloning.

> *Human cloning may evoke a similar reaction to the space program's race to the moon*

Cloning Uses

12   At the outset of the clone craze, some scientists and companies focused on exploiting the science-fiction aspects of the technology. For instance, Zavos and Antinori, mentioned earlier, aimed to develop cloning to aid infertile couples—to the tune of approximately $50,000 for the service. The group said that the procedure would involve injecting cells from an infertile male into an egg, which would be inserted into the female's uterus. This child would look the same as his or her father. Then there's the possibility of bringing deceased relatives back to life. A now-defunct company called Genetics Savings &

Clone performed this type of cloning for a woman's dead cat, Little Nicky, in 2004.

13   Therapeutic cloning holds the most promise of valuable medical advancement. Therapeutic cloning is the process by which a person's DNA is used to grow an embryonic clone. However, instead of inserting this embryo into a surrogate mother, its cells are used to grow stem cells. These stem cells could become the basis for customized human repair kits. They can grow replacement organs, such as hearts, livers, and skin. They can also be used to grow neurons to cure those who suffer from Alzheimer's, Parkinson's, or Rett syndrome. And since the stem cells would come from embryo clones using your own cell's DNA, your body would readily accept them. For more detailed information on stem cells, you can read How Stem Cells Work.

14   Here's how therapeutic cloning works:
- DNA is extracted from a sick person.
- The DNA is then inserted into an enucleated donor egg.
- The egg then divides like a typical fertilized egg and forms an embryo.
- Stem cells are removed from the embryo.
- Any kind of tissue or organ can be grown from these stem cells to treat various ailments and diseases.

15   To clone human embryos, however, you need eggs. If therapeutic cloning were to begin in earnest, it could increase the demand for such eggs and potentially create additional moral questions regarding the donors. Speaking of ethics, there's plenty of related debate to go around when it comes to human cloning.

Human Cloning Ethics

16   Surveys have shown that few Americans approve of cloning for reproductive purposes, although more are open to therapeutic cloning. The U.S. government has established strategic

IN CONTEXT

Cloning Plants

In the early 1900s, the term "clone" referred only to a gardening practice. Cloned plants are the result of taking a cutting, or a growing part, from one plant and putting it in soil, causing it to grow its own roots and become a separate but genetically identical plant.

glean: gather, learn
defunct: out of use

roadblocks related to human cloning, although no federal ban exists. First, the government won't fund research focused on human cloning for reproduction. Also, the FDA, which regulates public cloning research, requires anyone in the United States attempting to clone humans to first get its permission. President George W. Bush's appointed Council on Bioethics unanimously opposed cloning for reproductive purposes.

17   Certain countries abroad have stricter standards, and more than 50 have legally banned research efforts on reproductive human cloning. In Japan, human cloning is a crime punishable by up to 10 years in prison. England has allowed cloning human embryos for therapeutic use only. Many individual states have also passed laws restricting cloning.

18   While legal restrictions are one deterrent to pursuing human cloning at this time, some scientists believe today's technology just isn't ready to be tested on humans. Ian Wilmut, one of Dolly's co-creators, has even said that human cloning projects would be irresponsible. Cloning technology is still in its early stages, and nearly 98 percent of cloning efforts end in failure. The embryos are either not suitable for implanting into the uterus, or die some time during gestation or shortly after birth.

19   Those clones that do survive suffer from genetic abnormalities. Clone cells may age more rapidly, shortening their lifespan, similar to what happened with Dolly. Some clones have been born with defective hearts, lung problems, diabetes, blood vessel complications, and malfunctioning immune systems. One of the more famous cases involved a cloned sheep that was born but suffered from chronic hyperventilation caused by malformed arteries leading to the lungs.

20   Opponents of cloning point out that while we can euthanize defective clones of other animals, it's morally problematic if this happens during the human cloning process. Advocates of cloning respond that it's now easier to pick out defective embryos before they're implanted into the mother. In 2005, the United Nations attempted to pass a global ban on human cloning, but was unsuccessful due to disagreements over whether therapeutic cloning should be included. For now, human cloning remains in a stalemate from both a scientific and public policy perspective—the future of human cloning will likely depend on which side gives in first.

deterrent: obstacle
euthanize: put to death

CONVERSATIONS: Collaborating in Class or Online

1. How and why has the process of cloning been restricted since its beginnings?
2. What is "somatic cell nuclear transfer (SCNT)" (para. 9)?
3. How does therapeutic cloning work? Why is this the most promising aspect of the cloning process?
4. What are some legitimate uses of cloning?

CONNECTIONS: Discovering Relationships among Ideas

5. How might cloning help human beings in the future?
6. How does human cloning currently cross "the ethical boundaries of science" (para. 11)?
7. Why are most Americans against reproductive cloning?
8. What forms of cloning do you support, if any? What is your reasoning?

PRESENTATION: Analyzing the Writer's Craft

9. What is the purpose of this essay?

10. Why do the authors use the future tense in the title of this article?

11. Who is the essay's original audience?

12. Does the outline on therapeutic cloning clarify parts of this article? Explain your answer.

PROJECTS: Expressing Your Own Views

13. **Ad:** Design an advertisement for or against therapeutic cloning. Determine your audience before you begin.

14. **Internet:** Do some related research on stem cells, human cloning, cloning in other countries, reproductive cloning, enucleated eggs, or similar topics. Report your findings to your class, and then try to negotiate a class consensus on human cloning.

15. **Essay:** Write an essay explaining a process (such as a medical operation, a cosmetic procedure, or other related scientific process) that you feel is exceptionally important to our quality of life as humans. Establish a clear purpose and audience before you begin to write, and explain why you think it is important to our well-being.

16. **Research:** Read and summarize the three resources below. Generate one specific question from each resource that focuses on process analysis. Then answer one of your questions in a documented essay, consulting these and other sources as necessary.

OTHER RESOURCES

Web Site

Oak Ridge National Laboratory: www.ornl.gov

Search: "Cloning Fact Sheet"

Click on the "Cloning Fact Sheet" link

Academic Article

"Reproductive Cloning Combined with Genetic Modification"

by C. Strong

Journal of Medical Ethics 31.11 (2005): 654–658

Audio/Video

How Stuff Works: Science: http://howstuffworks.com

Search: "Discovery News: Tech: Human Cloning"

Click on the Video link

ONE LAST THOUGHT

The Boys From Brazil is a 1978 movie based on a novel of the same title. In this Sci-Fi thriller, an elderly Nazi hunter named Ezra Lieberman must find and stop a surviving Nazi death-camp doctor from bringing Adolf Hitler back to life through cloning. Although this is entirely a work of fiction, it brings to light legitimate questions about the ethical ramifications of human cloning. What famous, or infamous, historical figures do you think people would try to bring back to life if human cloning were scientifically possible and legal?

50 Ways to Help the Planet

from www.wireandtwine.com

The Web address **wireandtwine.com** is a site that manufactures contemporary clothes and goods. Based in Ohio, it was launched in 2008 by "a group of designers, coders, screenprinters, photographers, artists, moms, dads, and down-to-earth people" who "like to make things." Each artist in the company has chosen an organization to which they donate a portion of their profits. The company sees this gesture as "a small step in helping others and making a difference."

PREREADING QUESTIONS

What important issues surround global warming?

Do you take any positive steps toward protecting our environment? What do you do?

What environmental changes still need to be made in the United States?

PLANT A NOTION

"Going green" doesn't have to be a daunting task that means sweeping life changes. Simple things can make a difference.

The contents of this list might not be new, but they bear repeating. Sometimes it takes a few reminders for things to take root.

1. Change Your Light

If every household in the United State replaced one regular lightbulb with one of those new compact fluorescent bulbs, the pollution reduction would be equivalent to removing one million cars from the road.

Don't like the color of light? Use these bulbs for closets, laundry rooms, and other places where it won't irk you as much.

2. Turn Off Computers At Night

By turning off your computer instead of leaving it in sleep mode, you can save 40 watt-hours per day. That adds up to 4 cents a day, or $14 per year. If you don't want to wait for your computer to start up, set it to turn on automatically a few minutes before you get to work, or boot up while you're pouring your morning cup 'o joe.

3. Don't Rinse

Skip rinsing dishes before using your dishwasher, and save up to 20 gallons of water each load. Plus, you're saving time and the energy used to heat the additional water.

4. Do Not Pre-Heat the Oven

Unless you are making bread or pastries of some sort, don't pre-heat the oven. Just turn it on when you put the dish in. Also, when checking on your food, look through the oven window instead of opening the door.

5. Recycle Glass

Recycled glass reduces related air pollution by 20 percent and related water pollution by 50 percent. If it isn't recycled, it can take a million years to decompose.

6. Diaper with a Conscience

By the time a child is toilet trained, a parent will change between 5,000 and 8,000 diapers, adding up to approximately 3.5 million tons of waste in U.S. landfills each year. Whether you choose cloth or a more environmentally-friendly disposable, you're making a choice that has a much gentler impact on our planet.

7. Hang Dry

Get a clothesline or rack to dry your clothes by the air. Your wardrobe will maintain color and fit, and you'll save money.

Your favorite t-shirt will last longer too.

8. Go Vegetarian Once a Week

One less meat-based meal a week helps the planet and your diet. For example, it requires 2,500 gallons of water to produce one pound of beef. You will also save some trees. For each hamburger that originated from animals raised on rainforest land, approximately 55 square feet of forest have been destroyed.

9. Wash in Cold or Warm

If all the households in the U.S. switched from hot-hot cycle to warm-cold, we could save the energy comparable to 100,000 barrels of oil a day.

Only launder when you have a full load.

10. Use One Less Paper Napkin

During an average year, an American uses approximately 2,200 napkins—around six each day. If everyone in the U.S. used one less napkin a day, more than a billion pounds of napkins could be saved from landfills each year.

11. Use Both Sides of Paper

American businesses throw away 21 million tons of paper every year, equal to 175 pounds per office worker. For a quick and easy way to halve this, set your printer's default option to print double-sided (duplex printing). And when you're finished with your documents, don't forget to take them to the recycling bin.

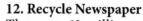

12. Recycle Newspaper

There are 63 million newspapers printed each day in the U.S. Of these, 44 million, or about 69%, of them will be thrown away. Recycling just the Sunday papers would save more than half a million trees every week.

13. Wrap Creatively

You can reuse gift bags, bows, and event paper, but you can also make some, and give your child stamps or markers to create their own wrapping paper that's environmentally friendly and extra special for the recipient.

14. Rethink Bottled Water

Nearly 90% of plastic water bottles are not recycled, instead taking thousands of years to decompose. Buy a reusable container and fill it with tap water, a great choice for the environment, your wallet, and possibly your health. The EPA's standards for tap water are more stringent than the FDA's standards for bottled water.

15. Ban Bathtime!

Have a no-bath week, and take showers instead. Baths require almost twice as much water. Not only will you reduce water consumption, but the energy costs associated with heating the water.

16. Brush Without Running

You've heard this one before, but maybe you still do it. You'll conserve up to five gallons per day if you stop. Daily savings in the U.S. alone could add up to 1.5 billion gallons—more water than folks use in the Big Apple.

17. Shower with Your Partner

Sneak in a shower with your loved one to start the day with some zest that doesn't come in a bar. Not only have you made a wise choice for the environment, but you may notice some other added . . . um . . . benefits.

18. Take a Shorter Shower

Every two minutes you save on your shower can conserve more than ten gallons of water. If everyone in the country saved just one gallon from their daily shower, over the course of

IN CONTEXT

Plastic Bottles

In addition to bottled sodas and juice, plastic water bottles make up a large part of recycled goods.

the year it would equal twice the amount of freshwater withdrawn from the Great Lakes every day.

19. Plant a Tree

It's good for the air and the land, can shade your house, and can save on cooling (plant on the west side of your home), and they can also improve the value of your property.

Make it meaningful for the whole family, and plant a tree every year for each member.

20. Use Your Cruise Control

You paid for those extra buttons in your car, so put them to work! When using cruise control, your vehicle could get up to 15% better mileage. Considering today's gasoline prices, this is a boon not only for the environment but your budget as well.

21. Second-Hand Doesn't Mean Second-Best

Consider buying items from a second-hand store. Toys, bicycles, roller blades, and other age- and size-specific items are quickly outgrown. Second hand stores often sell these items in excellent condition since they are used for such a short period of time and will generally buy them back when you no longer need them.

22. Buy Local

Consider the amount of pollution created to get your food from the farm to your table. Whenever possible, buy from local farmers or farmers' markets, supporting your local economy and reducing the amount of greenhouse gas created when products are flown or trucked in.

23. Adjust Your Thermostat

Adjust your thermostat one degree higher in the summer and one degree cooler in the winter. Each degree celsius less will save about 10% on your energy use! In addition, invest in a programmable thermostat which allows you to regulate temperature based on the times you are at home or away.

24. Invest in Your Own Coffee Cup

If you start every morning with a steamy cup, a quick tabulation can show you that the waste is piling up. Invest in a reusable cup, which not only cuts down on waste, but keeps your beverage hot for a much longer time. Most coffee shops will happily fill your own cup, and many even offer you a discount in exchange!

25. Batch Errands

Feel like you spend your whole week trying to catch up with the errands? Take a few moments once a week to make a list of all the errands that need to get done, and see if you can batch them into one trip. Not only will you be saving gasoline, but you might find yourself with much better time-management skills.

26. Turn Off Lights

Always turn off incandescent bulbs when you leave a room. Fluorescent bulbs are more affected by the number of times it is switched on and off, so turn them off when you leave a room for 15 minutes or more. You'll save energy on the bulb itself, but also on cooling costs, as lights contribute heat to a room.

27. Greener Lawn Care

If you must water your lawn, do it early in the morning before any moisture is lost to evaporation. Have a few weeds? Spot treat them with vinegar. Not sure if you should rake? Normal clippings act as a natural fertilizer, let them be. If you've waited too long, rake by hand—it's excellent exercise.

28. Picnic with a Marker

Some time in between the artichoke dip and the coleslaw, you lost track of your cup, and now there are a sea of matching cups on the table, one of which might be yours. The next time you picnic, set out permanent markers next to disposable dinnerware so guests can mark their cups and everyone will only use one.

29. Recycle Old Cell Phones

The average cell phone lasts around 18 months, which means 130 million phones will be retired each year. If they go into landfills, the phones and their batteries introduce toxic substances into our environment. There are plenty of reputable programs where you can recycle your phone, many which benefit noble causes.

30. Maintain Your Vehicle

Not only are you extending the life of your vehicle, but you are creating less pollution and saving gas. A properly maintained vehicle, clean air filters, and inflated tires can greatly improve your vehicle's performance. And it might not hurt to clean out the trunk—all that extra weight could be costing you at the pump.

31. Recycle Unwanted Wire Hangers

Wire hangers are generally made of steel, which is often not accepted by some recycling programs. So what do you do with them? Most dry cleaners will accept them back to reuse or recycle.

32. Recycle Aluminum and Glass

Twenty recycled aluminum cans can be made with the energy it takes to manufacture one brand new one.

Every ton of glass recycled saves the equivalent of nine gallons of fuel oil needed to make glass from virgin materials.

33. Telecommute

See if you can work out an arrangement with your employer that you work from home for some portion of the week. Not only will you save money and gasoline, but you get to work in your pajamas!

34. Keep Your Fireplace Damper Closed

Keeping the damper open (when you're not using your fireplace) is like keeping a 48-inch window wide open during the winter; it allows warm air to go right up the chimney. This can add up to hundreds of dollars each winter in energy loss.

35. Cut Down on Junk Mail

Feel like you need to lose a few pounds? It might be your junk mail that's weighing you down. The average American receives 40 pounds of junk mail each year, destroying 100 million trees. There are many services that can help reduce the clutter in your mailbox, saving trees and the precious space on your countertops.

36. Choose Matches Over Lighters

Most lighters are made out of plastic and filled with butane fuel, both petroleum products. Since most lighters are considered "disposable," over 1.5 billion end up in landfills each year. When choosing matches, pick cardboard over wood. Wood matches come from trees, whereas most cardboard matches are made from recycled paper.

37. Let Your Fingers do the Walking—Online

Consider if you really need a paper phone book. If not, call to stop phone book delivery and use an online directory instead. Some estimate that telephone books make up almost ten percent of waste at dump sites. And if you still receive the book, don't forget to recycle your old volumes.

38. Give It Away

Before you throw something away, think about if someone else might need it. Either donate to a charitable organization, or post it on a Web site designed to connect people and things, such as Freecycle.org.

39. Go to a Car Wash

Professional car washes are often more efficient with water consumption. If everyone in the U.S. who washes their car themselves took just one visit to the car wash, we could save nearly 8.7 billion gallons of water.

40. Plastic Bags Suck

Each year the U.S. uses 84 billion plastic bags, a significant portion of the 500 billion used worldwide. They are not biodegradable and are making their way into our oceans, and subsequently, the food chain. Stronger, reusable bags are an inexpensive and readily available option.

41. Fly with an E-Ticket

The cost of processing a paper ticket is approximately $10, while processing an e-ticket costs only $1. In the near future, e-tickets will be the only option, saving the airline industry $3 billion a year. In addition to financial savings, the sheer amount of paper eliminated by this process is commendable.

42. Download Your Software

Most software comes on a compact disc, and more than thirty billion compact discs of all types are sold annually. That's a huge amount of waste, not to mention the associated packaging. Another bonus to downloading your software is that it's often available for download at a later date when you upgrade to a new computer or are attempting to recover from a crash.

43. Stop Your Answering Machine

Answering machines use energy 24 hours a day, seven days a week. And when they break, they're just one more thing that goes into the landfill. If all answering machines in U.S. homes were eventually replaced by voice mail services, the annual energy savings would total nearly two billion kilowatt-hours.

44. Skip the Coffee Stirrer

Each year, Americans throw away 138 billion straws and stirrers. But skipping the stirrer doesn't mean drinking your coffee black. Simply put your sugar and cream in first, and then pour in the coffee, and it should be well mixed.

Determined to stir? Break off a piece of pasta from the cupboard. You can nibble after using it or throw away with less guilt.

45. Find a Better Way to Break the ICE

When a big winter storm heads our way, most of us use some sort of ice melter to treat steps and sidewalks. While this makes the sidewalks safer for people, it may pose a hazard for pets who might ingest these products. Rock salt and salt-based ice-melting products can cause health problems as well as contaminate wells and drinking water. Look for a pet-safe deicer, readily available in many stores.

46. Use Cotton Swabs with a Paperboard Spindle

Some brands of cotton swabs have a paperboard spindle while others are made of plastic. If 10% of U.S. households switched to a paperboard spindle, the petroleum energy saved per year would be equivalent to over 150,000 gallons of gasoline.

47. Pay Bills Online

By some estimates, if all households in the U.S. paid their bills online and received electronic statements instead of paper, we'd save 18.5 million trees every year, 2.2 billion tons of carbon dioxide and other greenhouse gases, and 1.7 billion pounds of solid waste.

48. Stop Paper Bank Statements

Some banks will pay you a dollar or donate money on your behalf when you cancel the monthly paper statements you get in the mail. If every household took advantage of online bank statements, the money saved could send more than 17,000 recent high school graduates to a public university for a year.

49. Use Rechargable Batteries

Each year 15 billion batteries are produced and sold, and most of them are disposable alkaline batteries. Only a fraction of those are recycled. Buy a charger and a few sets of rechargeable batteries. Although it requires an upfront investment, it is one that should pay off in no time. And on Christmas morning when all the stores are closed? You'll be fully stocked.

50. Share!

Take what you've learned, and pass the knowledge on to others. If every person you know could take one small step toward being greener, the collective effort could be phenomenal.

CONVERSATIONS: Collaborating in Class or Online

1. What items on this list (along with their statistics) were most surprising to you?
2. Which of these suggestions do you think would have the most impact if everyone did them?
3. How are these items all related to saving the planet?
4. Explain "environmentalism" in your own words.

CONNECTIONS: Discovering Relationships among Ideas

5. Find an explanation of "going green" on the Internet. Do you agree with those who say this process is important? Why or why not?

6. Which of the ideas on this list would be easiest for you to do?

7. Why do you think some people don't take responsibility for saving our environment?

8. Who benefits most from carrying out some of these simple tasks?

PRESENTATION: Analyzing the Writer's Craft

9. What is the purpose of this list?

10. Do you think this list of activities is presented in an effective way on the wireand-twine Web site? Comment on its layout, design, colors, font, material, and other features in your answer.

11. For whom was the list probably written?

12. Do you think this approach will get people to follow the suggestions or not? Explain your answer.

PROJECTS: Expressing Your Own Views

13. **Blog:** Return to the sources you found on "going green" in response to question 5, and read some of the current conversations on this topic. Enter the conversation if you feel informed enough to take part.

14. **List:** Design your own list to help solve a problem that is important to you.

15. **Essay:** Write an essay describing another current crisis in the United States, and explain how we might solve the problem(s) you identify. Have a clear purpose and audience in mind before you begin to write your essay.

16. **Research:** Read and summarize the three resources below. Generate one specific question from each resource that focuses on process analysis. Then answer one of your questions in a documented essay, consulting these and other sources as necessary.

OTHER RESOURCES

Web Site
Environmentalism: http://environmentalism.suite101.com/

Academic Article
"Bringing Green Homes within Reach: Healthier Housing for More People"
by Charles W. Schmidt

Environmental Health Perspectives 116.1 (2008): A24–A31

Audio/Video
YouTube: www.youtube.com

Search: "Total Recycling Process" by EvoWaste

Click on the Video link

ONE LAST THOUGHT

Hybrid cars are not new; vehicles with multiple power sources were available as early as 1900. However, hybrid-electric vehicles were not mass-produced until 1997 when the Toyota Prius was released in Japan. Now they are seen as a core component of the automobile industry. For a brief history of hybrids, visit www.hybridcars.com, click on the Research tab, and then on the History of Hybrid Vehicles link at the bottom of the page under Technology. Do you know anyone who drives a hybrid vehicle? Would you consider buying one? Why or why not?

What Makes a Successful Business Person?

by Murray Raphel

A successful retailer who turned a 600-square-foot infant clothing store called "Gordon's Alley" in Atlantic City into a multi-million-dollar business, **Murray Raphel** is the author of two companion books: *Selling Rules* and *Speaking Rules*. He is also one of the world's leading consultants on direct marketing, advertising, and promotion.

PREREADING QUESTIONS

How do you define the word "successful" in terms of accomplishments?

Do you consider yourself a successful person so far? Explain your answer.

Do you set your goals high and slightly out of reach or low so you can easily achieve them? Why?

1   I have a theory on doing business. If my business is good, it's not because of the weather, the time of year, or the economy. It's because of me. I'm doing something right. If my business is bad, it's not because of the weather, the time of the year, or the economy. It's because of me. I'm doing something wrong. Somebody is always buying something from somebody, so how can I make people buy from me?

2   First of all, you need confidence in yourself and your merchandise with clear goals and knowledge of the products you are selling. Only then can you inspire dedication from your staff and a willingness to buy from customers.

3   Successful business people, no matter what their industry, have been found to share similar traits. Today's world is no longer satisfied simply with success—we want to know how the successful get to the top. The Russians developed a concept called "anthropomaximology," in which they try to answer the question of why some individuals outperform others. Through the years, I've done some anthropomaximology of my own and found there are certain qualities that describe successful business people. Here are a few:

They constantly set higher goals.

4   Successful business people are mountain climbers who, having climbed one peak, look beyond to the next highest. They are the retailers who send 1,500 mailers to their customers and yield a good turnout of 100. But instead of being satisfied with 100, they ask how they can increase that number to 150 the next time.

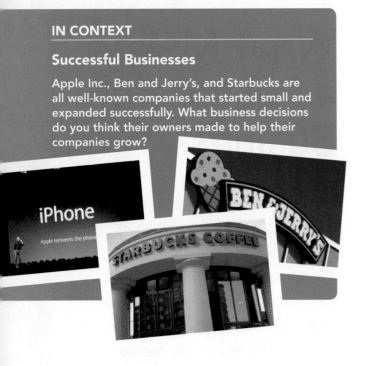

5   For example, Donald Kelley of Kelley Frame and Art Galleries, with locations in Minnesota and Wisconsin, continually tries to improve his email list. "My goal is to collect 150 new email names every month and send out a new email message to this list every two weeks."

They avoid "comfort zones."

6   To a successful person, standing still feels like going backwards. People who stay in their comfort zones do what they did before because it's "the way we've always done it." They run the same ads, buy the same merchandise in the same way, and avoid anything new, different, or unusual because they feel they might do something wrong. They blame any lack of business on the weather, the time of the year, the economy—anything except for themselves.

7   Successful gallery owners attend art shows, read catalogs, and visit other galleries in their travels. They are always searching to find unique art exclusive to their galleries. They take control of their own destinies and market their businesses as exciting destinations.

They are driven by accomplishments, not money.

8   Successful people follow the theory of Apple Computer's founder Steve Jobs, who said, "The journey is the reward." They are customer focused, not product focused. Their thrill is not the ringing of the register but the crowds responding to their mailing. For them, there is no greater high than a line outside the store before the doors open.

They solve problems rather than place blame.

9   A telephone pole blocked the view of Ron Bishop's Canadian gallery. He knew it would be difficult, if not impossible, to have the telephone pole moved. His solution was to paint the pole with an Impressionistic theme. Once it was finished, the local paper came, took a picture and wrote a story about it. "It was great publicity," said Bishop. "And then the calls started coming, asking, 'Is it for sale?'"

10   Successful gallery owners do not waste their time looking at problems and saying, "It's not our fault" or "Why didn't we. . . ." They say, "Let's look at what went wrong and realize it was a learning experience and figure out how we can make it work next time."

11   When a customer hears it will take a week or longer to have their art framed and says, "Sorry, that's too long," do you shrug your shoulders and say, "Well, that's how long it takes." Or do you think, "Hmmmm, if that's what the customer wants, how can I solve their problem?"

They look at the worst possible scenario.

12   "What's the worst possible result if we follow this plan?" they ask themselves. Then, knowing that, they decide if the risk-taking is practical.

13   However, once they make the decision, confidence, knowledge, and expertise are necessary to make it work.

---

expertise: skill

14   They understand the most harmful result and then decide if they can live with the outcome. If they can, they move ahead. Confidently.

15   Galleries that concentrate on one type of art often decide to reach into an unrelated area. Sometimes a gallery will fail in an attempt to broaden their focus, but successful performers understand even defeat is a learning experience.

16   "Every time I fail," said Thomas Edison, "I learn something." He tried 1,114 times to find a filament to stay lit in a bulb. He failed 1,113 times.

They rehearse the future as they see it.

17   "I believe our future is a one-stop shop for decorating. In addition to limited-edition prints and posters, we now offer collectibles, gift items, and small occasional furniture pieces," said Christine Knoll of the Art Gallery of Hog Hollow in Chesterfield, Mo.

18   Successful people move towards the pictures they create in their mind. They can rehearse coming actions or events as they "see" them. They are like chess players who can "feel" the next move of their opponent and have half a dozen responses ready when their time comes to move.

19   Many successful athletes will say they practice "seeing" themselves winning the race, hitting the home run, or scoring the touchdown. They actually visualize a future event which gives them the impetus to achieve the goal.

20   How many of these six characteristics are yours? The more you have, the higher degree of probability you will be doing more business next year instead of being one of the thousands of retailers listed in the obituary pages of the local paper's business news.

> *They are like chess players who can "feel" the next move of their opponent*

filament: thread, fiber
impetus: force, momentum

CONVERSATIONS: Collaborating in Class or Online

1. What does the author mean when he says, "If my business is good, it's not because of the weather, the time of year, or the economy" (para. 1)? How does this same statement apply to failure?

2. List in your own words the six characteristics of successful business people.

3. What do all the features of a successful business person have in common?

4. In what state of mind do most successful business people approach the future?

CONNECTIONS: Discovering Relationships among Ideas

5. According to the author, how are business and art related?

6. What does "rehears[ing] the future" have to do with the other five characteristics?

7. Based on the information in this essay, what does "vision" have to do with "success"?

8. In what way can defeat be "a learning experience" (para. 15) for a successful person?

PRESENTATION: Analyzing the Writer's Craft

9. What do you think Raphel's purpose is in this article?

10. Who is his intended audience?

11. The format of this essay is a list with explanations following each item. Is this an effective way to present this material? Explain your reaction.

12. Raphel supports almost every one of his listed items with representative quotations from successful people. How effective is this strategy? Explain your answer.

PROJECTS: Expressing Your Own Views

13. **Blog:** Respond to the ideas Raphel presents by going to findarticles.com and posting a comment in reference to this article.

14. **List:** Write your own formula in list form for being financially responsible.

15. **Essay:** Write a process analysis essay explaining how to be a successful student.

16. **Research:** Read and summarize the three resources below. Generate one specific question from each resource that focuses on process analysis. Then answer one of your questions in a documented essay, consulting these and other sources as necessary.

OTHER RESOURCES

Web Site

U.S. Small Business Administration: www.sba.gov/

Academic Article

"The State-Sponsored Student Entrepreneur"

by Mathew M. Mars, Sheila Slaughter, and Gary Rhoades

The Journal of Higher Education 79.6 (2008): 638–670

Audio/Video

History.com: www.history.com/

Search: "Great Minds of Business"

Click on any of the Video links to learn about successful entrepreneurs

ONE LAST THOUGHT

Creative visualization is the process of generating a mental image of something that you want to accomplish. It is similar to meditation in that visualization occurs internally and requires intense concentration. Many athletes use this strategy to prepare for competition. Visit http://Ezinearticles.com, and search "Tips for Mastering Visualization Techniques" for more information. Have you ever heard of or practiced visualization? What do you think makes it effective?

CHAPTER WRITING ASSIGNMENTS

Write a well-developed essay in response to the following prompts. Consult the chapter introduction for guidance in creating your essay.

CONNECTING THE READINGS

1. What could a successful business person ("What Makes a Successful Business Person?") learn from the sales tips in "6 Sneaky Ways Sales Spur Spending"?

2. What qualities of a good essay ("How to Say Nothing in 500 Words") do you see at work in the essay "How Human Cloning Will Work"?

3. For which topic in this section would you be most likely to consult wikiHow? Do such a search, and discuss the value of what you find.

4. Can people follow the suggestions in "50 Ways to Help the Planet" and also be successful at what they do ("What Makes a Successful Business Person?")?

MOVING BEYOND THE READINGS

5. Discuss where you think the world of the Internet will be in 10 years. What will be new? What will be improved? How will these changes affect the quality of our lives?

6. What is your favorite video game? How do you play it? Why do you like it? What are its benefits? Its drawbacks?

7. Explain how to write an excellent essay, based on Roberts's guidelines in "How to Say Nothing in 500 Words."

8. Explain your career goals and how you expect to accomplish them. How will you ensure your success?

COMBINING RHETORICAL MODES

9. What type of advertising do you think is most effective: billboards, TV ads, radio ads, newspaper or magazine ads, Internet ads, or others? In your opinion, why is this medium the most effective?

10. Make a list of "Things You Can Do Now" to be a good friend/husband/wife/daughter/son/grandson/granddaughter/grandfather/grandmother/aunt/uncle/etc. Then write an essay explaining how these "guidelines" will ensure your success in this family role.

11. Write an essay explaining how to make friends while also keeping your grades up in college.

12. Map out a comprehensive strategy that will convince high school students to go to college. What media will work best on that age group? How would you approach these students? What would be the main thrust of your approach?

9 Division and Classification

Division and classification help us bring order to our lives. Thanks to division and classification, you can find sportswear in a department store and the chapter on the Vietnam War in your history text. You also know how to organize your academic life and how to set up your kitchen cabinets. Division and classification are so natural to us that we sometimes aren't even aware we are using them. Consider the following tasks, which all involve division and classification:

- Organizing music on your iPod;
- Establishing a realistic budget;
- Writing an academic paper on types of dreams;
- Logging information in your smartphone;
- Creating a flyer on types of savings accounts at a bank.

Division and classification help us organize information so we can make sense of our complex world. Dividing large categories into smaller ones (division) and gathering many items into larger categories (classification) both help us organize a lot of information into useful groups.

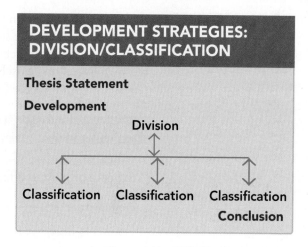

Introducing Division and Classification

Division and classification are actually mirror images of each other. **Division** is sorting and dividing something into its basic parts, such as a home into rooms or a job into various duties or responsibilities. **Classification** works in the opposite direction, moving from specifics to a cluster with common traits or from multiple subgroups to a single, more inclusive category, such as grouping furniture by room or organizing your notes for an exam. These two techniques work together as the examples show:

- A grocery store is *divided* into many sections, like produce, dairy, ethnic foods, cleaning supplies, whereas food items are *classified,* or grouped, according to categories (apples, oranges, peaches⇒produce; milk, cheese, cream⇒dairy).

- Athletics is *divided* into specific sports such as football, tennis, and hockey, while athletes are *classified* by the sport in which they participate (Tom Brady and Peyton Manning⇒football; Serena Williams and Raphael Nadal⇒tennis).

- A college is *divided* into many departments like English, communications, philosophy, and sociology, whereas courses are *classified* by the department to which they belong (Introduction to Literature and Advanced Writing⇒English; Early Childhood Development and Human Behavior⇒psychology).

Many different ways of classifying the same elements are possible. Bureau drawers vary from house to house and even from person to person; no one's kitchen is set up exactly the same way as someone else's; and drugstores have similar but not identical systems of classification. In addition, your friends probably use a method different from yours to organize their bedrooms, while two professors will probably teach the same course material in different ways. We all have distinct and uniquely logical methods of classifying the many different variables in our own lives. Look closely at the following examples:

DEVELOPMENT STRATEGIES AT WORK

Thesis Statement: Student notebooks or computer files can be useful if they are organized effectively.

Development: ⟶ Categories

History	OR	Class notes
Psychology		Notes on textbooks
English		Research notes

Conclusion

DEVELOPMENT STRATEGIES AT WORK

Thesis Statement: Our lower-division General Education requirements consist of courses from four areas.

Development

⟶ 3 Basic Skills courses
⟶ 3 Math and Science courses
⟶ 3 Arts and Humanities courses
⟶ 1 Social and Behavioral Science course

Conclusion

Division and classification give us ways to see our world more clearly. They help us make decisions by separating what we like from what we don't like and by giving us ways to arrange volumes of information that we could not understand without a useful organizing principle. They are a vital part of our existence in an ordered, civilized world.

Discovering How Division and Classification Work

On the right is a list of the most important elements of division/classification thinking, whether for a visual (like an ad or a photo) or a prose selection. These Division/Classification Essentials are equally useful as guidelines for both reading and writing.

Analyzing the chart below will help you understand how all these elements work together in division/classification. If you discover on your own how this method of reasoning functions, you will be able to apply it effectively to your own reading and writing. The questions following the graphic will help you understand this rhetorical mode even more clearly than you already do.

> ### Division/Classification Essentials
>
> Purpose
> Division/Classification into Categories
> Logical Arrangement of Categories
> Explanation of Categories
> Significance of Classification System

How People Share Content on the Web

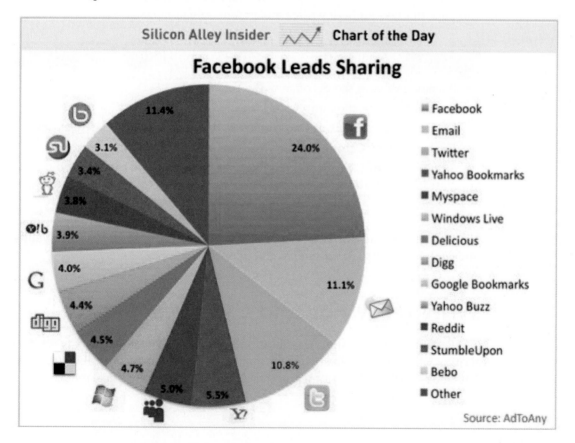

Silicon Alley Insider   Chart of the Day

Facebook Leads Sharing

- 24.0% Facebook
- 11.1% Email
- 10.8% Twitter
- 5.5% Yahoo Bookmarks
- 5.0% Myspace
- 4.7% Windows Live
- 4.5% Delicious
- 4.4% Digg
- 4.0% Google Bookmarks
- 3.9% Yahoo Buzz
- 3.8% Reddit
- 3.4% StumbleUpon
- 3.1% Bebo
- 11.4% Other

Source: AdToAny

1. What is the purpose of this chart?
2. Into what categories does the graphic artist divide the subject? How else could you divide and classify this material?
3. How are these categories arranged in the pie chart?
4. In what way are the categories explained?
5. How does the graphic artist communicate the significance of the classification system?

Collaborative Responses Now discuss your responses to these questions with your classmates in small groups or as an entire class. Did the diverse perspectives from other students in your class change your "reading" of the visual? If so, in what ways?

Reading Division and Classification

As you read the verbal and visual selections in this chapter, pay special attention to the categories the authors/illustrators use to make their points. You should ensure that you understand the author's purpose and each category that is introduced.

When you read a selection for the first time, think about how the Division/ Classification Essentials work within it. The following questions will help you accomplish this task for both written and graphic assignments:

Division/Classification Essentials: Reading

- **Purpose:** What is the purpose of the selection?
- **Division/Classification into Categories:** What are the categories introduced?
- **Logical Arrangement of Categories:** How are the categories organized?
- **Explanation of Categories:** Can you explain each category?
- **Significance of Classification System:** What is the significance of the classification system?

On your second and third readings of the selections, focus on areas of ambiguity and confusion so you can deepen your comprehension.

Writing Division and Classification

Reviewing the Division/Classification Essentials as you move from reading to writing will help you adjust your writing to your specific purpose and audience. Let's look closely at the writing process as it applies to this rhetorical mode.

Choosing a Subject

As with all projects, you need to select a subject as soon as possible. Once you have your subject, you should start to think about the categories you might use and the reason for selecting this specific set of categories.

Our student writer, Chandra Bailey, decided to discuss types of drivers she has classified over time. She thought this was a good subject for this rhetorical mode because the strategy actually saved her life.

Generating Details

First, you should complete a list of the categories you will use to explain your subject. Then use a prewriting strategy introduced in Chapter 3 to generate as many details as possible in each category.

To begin this process, Chandra chooses her four categories. She writes them down and then uses freewriting to generate ideas in each.

- *Category 1: reckless drivers*
  This type of driver endangers others in a variety of ways, they are not even aware anyone else is on the road. They blast their music and weave in and out of lanes. They don't seem to care about others and certainly don't want to share the road with anyone else. They tailgate, speed, and brake abruptly, they are ultimately very selfish.
- *Category 2: overly cautious drivers*
  These drivers are as dangerous as reckless drivers. They drive too slowly and seem to be afraid of other drivers. They accelerate too slowly and brake too early. They are aggravating and sometimes downright dangerous.
- *Category 3: road-rage drivers*
  These drivers are fueled by emotions. They are hotheads who think that everyone else is incompetent. They yell and scream, their anger is set off by such innocent events as the ways others merge and exit on the roads. I always avoid eye contact with these drivers.
- *Category 4: drivers who understand and follow the rules*
  These drivers are aware of others and their own surroundings. They are generally courteous. They want everyone on the road to be safe. They let other drivers in front of them and make sure they exit safely themselves. They also show appreciation when others do something nice for them.

Chandra realizes that she has classified drivers her entire life. Writing about this topic will help her understand the value of this pastime in her life.

Drafting a Thesis Statement

After choosing a subject and generating details, you should be ready to write a thesis statement or statement of purpose for your essay. A thesis for a visual project may not be as immediately apparent as one for an essay, but will still guide you to develop a coherent assignment.

Dividing and classifying in themselves are often not particularly interesting. But they are very useful techniques if you are trying to make a specific point. That point, or purpose, should be included in your thesis statement. Look at these two examples:

1. Today's college students can be divided into three different types.
2. Being aware of the three types of students in college today can help you find the best study groups for yourself.

Both thesis statements name a category—types of students—but only thesis statement 2 gives us a good reason to keep reading: Being aware of the three different types of students can help you survive in college.

Chandra's purpose is to convince drivers to be safe and careful as they watch out for themselves and others on the road. She includes her purpose in her thesis:

> *Being able to identify and avoid certain types of drivers has not only become part of my everyday driving routine, but it actually helped save my life.*

This statement will now provide focus and direction for the remainder of her assignment.

Producing a Draft

All this prewriting will prepare you to write a well-developed division/classification essay.

- Your **introduction** should introduce your subject and make your purpose clear in a thesis statement.
- The **body of your paper** then explains each of your categories with sufficient details in each case.
- Your **conclusion** summarizes your classification system and highlights its significance.

Developing Your Categories Since most subjects can be classified in different ways, your main task in writing a division/classification essay is to decide how you will divide your subject into categories. First, gather information to produce a list of all the possible topics. Second, decide on what basis you will divide these topics into categories.

To make your division/classification as logical as possible, take special care that your categories do not overlap and that your topics fall into one category only. If, for example, you were dividing/classifying all the jobs performed by students in your writing class, the categories of (1) indoor work and (2) outdoor work would probably be inadequate because some jobs fit into both categories. At a pizza parlor, a restaurant, or a pharmacy, for example, a delivery person's time would be split between indoor and outdoor work. So you would need to alter the classification system to avoid this problem. The categories of (1) indoor work, (2) outdoor work, and (3) a combination of indoor and outdoor work would be much more useful for this task. Making sure your categories don't overlap will help produce more readable and accurate classification essays.

Explaining each category in turn is an essential part of every division/classification essay. With division, you are trying to show what differences break the items into separate groups or types. With classification, the similarities among the items help create categories that make sense. In either case, you need to explain each category fully and provide enough details to help your readers see your subject in a new and useful way.

Organizing Your Essay Your method of organizing these categories should make sense and be easy for readers to follow. Most often, this means organizing from one extreme to another. For example, you might organize your types from most common to least common. Or you might move from least noteworthy to most noteworthy, from least serious to most serious, from largest to smallest—or the other way around. In every case, though, try to end with the category that is most memorable.

Concluding Your Essay Finally, you want to conclude your essay with a summary of your categories and a discussion of the significance of the system of classification you used. This will bring closure to your essay and leave your readers with a sense of the importance of your topic that they may not have had previously.

At this point, you should use the following questions, based on the Division/Classification Essentials, to help focus and refine your written and graphic assignments:

Division/Classification Essentials: Writing

- **Purpose:** What is your purpose?
- **Division/Classification into Categories:** What are your main categories? Why are you using these categories?
- **Logical Arrangement of Categories:** How are you organizing these categories?
- **Explanation of Categories:** Do you explain each category clearly?
- **Significance of Classification System:** Do you explain the significance of your overall classification system?

Revising and Editing

Revising and editing your essay or graphic means reviewing it to make sure it says exactly what you want it to say. Also, you should take some time to add transitions to show your readers how various items in your division/classification are related. Transitions will help your readers follow your train of thought as you move from one category to another. They will also help make your essay smooth, logical, and interesting to read.

Revising

Look closely at your essay or graphic as someone else might see it. Then answer the questions posed in the Revising Checklist on page 28, which focus on how your essay functions.

This is also the point in the writing process when you should add transitions to your essay that clarify the relationship of your details to one another. In division/classification, these are usually words and phrases that introduce and connect your categories. They include *the first category, another category, the most valuable group, next, a noteworthy classification*, and so on. These particular expressions will help your readers understand as clearly as possible the relationships among the items in your division/classification.

Editing

Editing is the final phase of your writing process. It involves reviewing your words, sentences, entire paragraphs, and any visual details to make sure they are correct. Use the Editing Checklist on page 30 to review your project for errors in grammar and usage. When you locate a potential error, consult a handbook or go to Pearson's Web-based MyCompLab for an explanation of the problem.

Also, if your instructor marks any grammar mistakes on your paper or graphic, make sure you understand them. Recognizing errors in your own writing is the most effective way of correcting them.

As you read the following student essay, refer to the Division/Classification Essentials (page 241) and the questions for reading division/classification (page 242) to help you analyze it. Then, to thoroughly understand how this student essay works, pay special attention to the margin notes and the items in each paragraph they describe.

Chandra Bailey

Professor Flachmann

English 101

21 Oct. 2011

Classifying Drivers Saved My Life

1 When first learning to drive, I was enthralled by the huge variety of people that passed me while I puttered along in the slow lane. Assuming that everyone on the road had gone through the same classes and training that I had, I was quite shocked once I got my license and began driving on the roads by myself. It didn't take me long to discover that many of the people who flew by me in blurs of color and chrome had vastly different ideas of what constituted "good driving." These drivers were easily distinguishable from one another. Being able to identify and avoid certain types of drivers has not only become part of my everyday driving routine, but it actually helped save my life.

2 The first drivers I learned to spot were the reckless ones. Weaving in and out of traffic with their music blaring, reckless drivers were those I avoided by pulling into the slow lane or exiting the road entirely. With no regard for the safety or well being of others, these types of drivers mistakenly believe they have a right to endanger the lives and property of other people who share the road with them. These selfish individuals cut other drivers off, tailgate, speed, and then brake unexpectedly because of their lack of attention and disregard for upcoming obstacles. Regardless of their rationale for doing so, reckless drivers endanger the lives of those around them by acting as if the multi-ton machine they operate is just an over-sized toy.

3 Although reckless drivers are probably the easiest to spot and avoid, the second type of driver can be just as dangerous. Drivers who are overly cautious can also be extremely hazardous and necessary to avoid. Individuals who drive too slowly, who take too long to

Subject

Division into Categories

Purpose/Thesis Statement

Category 1

Explanation of Category

Category 2

Explanation of Category

make decisions while driving, and who seem as if they're afraid of the rest of the cars on the road are just as likely to cause an accident as the reckless drivers mentioned earlier. These overly cautious vehicle operators tend to foul up lanes when merging by not accelerating quickly enough or by braking and signaling way too early before making a turn. Such hindrances to other drivers increase the likelihood of an accident and can easily change the calm composure of a normal driver into that of a raging maniac.

Category 3 →

Explanation of Category →

4 Drivers who are overtaken by "road rage" and become seething hotheads due to their perception of incompetence are the next type to watch out for. Regardless of the scenario, drivers with road rage should be given lots of room on the road. These individuals do not hesitate to make a difficult driving situation worse by yelling, screaming, cursing, gesturing, and allowing their anger to get the best of them. Simple things like merging or exiting are taken as personal affronts, which in turn gives the driver a sense of entitlement for their rage. Once the attitude begins, these types of drivers lose focus on the road and other vehicles by obsessing on the car or person who they feel has slighted them. The best resolution when dealing with a driver like this is to avoid eye contact and continue to focus on the road and obstacles in front of you.

Category 4 →

Explanation of Category →

5 Recognizing the final group of drivers, those who understand and follow the rules of the road, is also a skill I have developed over time. These drivers are not only aware of their surroundings and the other drivers around them, but are also courteous when problems arise. Considering myself to be one of these drivers, I always try to allow others to merge or change lanes whenever possible. More often than not I am thanked by a wave or a smile. Good drivers know that it is important to show appreciation for courteous behavior; someone who is recognized for good driving will often repeat his or her actions again in hopes that the favor will one day be returned.

6 Using my classification system instinctively as I was driving through the back roads of my town one night, I saw two headlights in the rearview mirror approaching uncomfortably fast. Thinking immediately that this might be a reckless, out-of-control driver, I quickly pulled onto the shoulder of the road to get out of the way. To my surprise, a late model sports car whizzed by me before I could even register what color it was. Barely able to see the vehicle's taillights receding into the darkness, I suddenly heard the screech of rubber on asphalt and saw the speeding car uncontrollably spinning off the road. The vehicle came to rest with its headlights pointed into a field, and I could hear the faint "boom" of the big bass speaker in the car. The driver walked away from the accident, but I might not have if he had hit me from behind. I believe to this day that my quick assessment of the driver's type helped me make the decision to get out of his way when I saw him behind me.   ← Significance of Classification System

7 Being a safe, courteous driver is an important responsibility.   ← Summary
But being a defensive driver is also essential. My natural instinct to classify drivers taught me indirectly to be a defensive driver. By being the type of driver who follows the rules and laws of good driving, not only did I avoid accidents and damage to my property, but I believe   ← Significance of Classification System
I also play an active role every day in making the road a better place for everyone.

Reviewing Division and Classification

Based on the information you have learned in this chapter and the annotations on the student essay, show how this essay works by writing a clear, precise summary or by drawing your own outline or graphic representation of it. Label the categories on your visual. This exercise will confirm your understanding of the elements of division/classification in both reading and writing.

No Wonder They Call Me a Bitch

by Ann Hodgman

A former food editor for *Spy* magazine and *Eating Well*, **Ann Hodgman** is the author of over 40 children's books as well as three influential cookbooks: *Beat This!*, *Beat That!*, and *One Bite Won't Kill You*. She also wrote the humorous six-book series *My Babysitter Is a Vampire* and a nonfiction memoir titled *The House of a Million Pets*.

PREREADING QUESTIONS

Have you ever been curious about something that you were reluctant to try first hand?

Why were you reluctant?

Have you ever done anything wildly out of the ordinary for you? What was it? Why did you do it?

1   I've always wondered about dog food. Is a Gaines-burger really like a hamburger? Can you fry it? Does dog food "cheese" taste like real cheese? Does Gravy Train actually make gravy in a dog's bowl, or is that brown liquid just dissolved crumbs? And what exactly *are* by-products?

2   Having spent the better part of a week eating dog food, I'm sorry to say that I now know the answers to these questions. While my dachshund, Shortie, watched in agonies of yearning, I gagged my way through can after can of stinky, white-flecked mush and bag after bag of stinky, fat-drenched nuggets. And now I understand exactly why Shortie's breath is so bad.

3   Of course, Gaines-burgers are neither mush nor nuggets. They are, rather, a miracle of beauty and packaging—or at least that's what I thought when I was little. I used to beg my mother to get them for our dogs, but she always said they were too expensive. When I finally bought a box of

cheese-flavored Gaines-burgers—after twenty years of longing—I felt deliciously wicked.

4   "Dogs love real beef," the back of the box proclaimed proudly. "That's why Gaines-burgers is the only beef burger for dogs with real beef and no meat by-products!" The copy was accurate: meat by-products did not appear in the list of ingredients. Poultry by-products did, though—right there next to preserved animal fat.

5   One Purina spokesman told me that poultry by-products consist of necks, intestines, undeveloped eggs and other "carcass remnants," but not feathers, heads, or feet. When I told him I'd been eating dog food, he said, "Oh, you're kidding! Oh, no!" (I came to share his alarm when, weeks later, a second Purina spokesman said that Gaines-burgers *do* contain poultry heads and feet—but *not* undeveloped eggs.)

6   Up close, my Gaines-burger didn't much resemble chopped beef. Rather, it looked—and

felt—like a single long, extruded piece of redness that had been chopped into segments and formed into a patty. You could make one at home if you had a Play-Doh Fun Factory.

7   I turned on the skillet. While I waited for it to heat up, I pulled out a shred of cheese-colored material and palpated it. Again, like Play-Doh, it was quite malleable. I made a little cheese bird out of it; then I counted to three and ate the bird.

8   There was a horrifying rush of cheddar taste, followed immediately by the dull tang of soybean flour—the main ingredient in Gaines-burgers. Next I tried a piece of red extrusion. The main difference between the meat-flavored and cheese-flavored extrusions is one of texture. The "cheese" chews like fresh Play-Doh, whereas the "meat" chews like Play-Doh that's been sitting out on the rug for a couple of hours.

9   Frying only turned the Gaines-burger black. There was no melting, no sizzling, no warm meat smells. A cherished childhood illusion was gone. I flipped the patty into the sink, where it immediately began leaking rivulets of red dye.

10   As alarming as the Gaines-burgers were, their soy meal began to seem like an old friend when the time came to try some canned dog foods. I decided to try the Cycle foods first. When I opened them, I thought about how rarely I use can-openers these days, and I was suddenly visited by a long-forgotten sensation of can-opener distaste. *This* is the kind of unsavory place can openers spend their time when you're not watching! Every time you open a can of, say, Italian plum tomatoes, you infect them with invisible particles of by-product.

> *Cycle-2, for adults, glistens nastily with fat, but it's passably edible*

11   I had been expecting to see the usual homogeneous scrapple inside, but each can of Cycle was packed with smooth, round, oily nuggets. As if someone at Gaines had been tipped off that a human would be tasting the stuff, the four Cycles really were different from one another. Cycle-1, for puppies, is wet and soyish. Cycle-2, for adults, glistens nastily with fat, but it's passably edible—a lot like some canned Swedish meatballs I once got in a care package at college. Cycle-3, the "lite" one, for fatties, had no specific

flavor; it just tasted like dog food. But at least it didn't make me fat.

12   Cycle-4, for senior dogs, had the smallest nuggets. Maybe old dogs can't open their mouths as wide. This kind was far sweeter than the other three Cycles—almost like baked beans. It was also the only one to contain "dried beef digest," a mysterious substance that the Purina spokesman defined as "enzymes" and my dictionary defined as "the products of digestion."

13   Next on the menu was a can of Kal Kan Pedigree with Chunky Chicken. Chunky chicken? There were chunks in the can, certainly—big, purplish-brown chunks. I forked one chunk out (by now I was becoming callous) and found that while it had no discernible chicken flavor, it wasn't bad except for its texture—like meat loaf with ground-up chicken bones.

extruded: ejected, forced out
palpated: inspected
malleable: adaptable, workable
callous: insensitive
discernible: apparent

14   In the world of canned dog food, a smooth consistency is a sign of low quality—lots of cereal. A lumpy, frightening, bloody, stringy horror is a sign of high quality—lots of meat. Nowhere in the world of wet dog foods was this demonstrated better than in the fanciest I tried—Kal Kan's Pedigree Select Dinners. These came not in a can but in a tiny foil packet with a picture of an imperious Yorkie. When I pulled open the container, juice spurted all over my hand, and the first chunk I speared was trailing a long gray vein. I shrieked and went instead for a plain chunk, which I was able to swallow only after taking a break to read some suddenly fascinating office equipment catalogues. Once again, though, it tasted no more alarming than, say, canned hash.

15   Still, how pleasant it was to turn to *dry* dog food! Gravy Train was the first I tried, and I'm happy to report that it really does make a "thick, rich, real beef gravy" when you mix it with water. Thick and rich, anyway. Except for a lingering, rancid-fat flavor, the gravy wasn't beefy, but since it tasted primarily like tap water, it wasn't nauseating either.

> *How pleasant it was to turn to* dry *dog food*

16   My poor dachshund just gets plain old Purina Dog Chow, but Purina also makes a dry food called Butcher's Blend that comes in Beef, Bacon & Chicken flavor. Here we see dog food's arcane semiotics at its best: a red triangle with a T stamped into it is supposed to suggest beef; a tan curl, chicken; and a brown S, a piece of bacon. Only dogs understand these messages. But Butcher's Blend does have an endearing slogan: "Great Meaty Tastes—without bothering the Butcher!" *You know, I wanted to buy some meat, but I just couldn't bring myself to bother the butcher. . . .*

17   Purina O.N.E. ("Optimum Nutritional Effectiveness") is targeted at people who are unlikely ever to worry about bothering a tradesperson. "We chose chicken as a primary ingredient in Purina O.N.E. for several reasonings," the long, long essay on the back of the bag announces. Chief among these reasonings, I'd guess, is the fact that chicken appeals to people who are—you know—*like us*. Although our dogs do nothing but spend eighteen-hour days alone in the apartment, we still want them to be *premium* dogs. We want them to cut down on red meat too. We also want dog food that comes in a bag with an attractive design, a subtle typeface, and no kitschy pictures of slobbering golden retrievers.

18   Besides that, we want a list of the Nutritional Benefits of our dog food—and we get it on O.N.E. One thing I especially like about this list is its constant references to a dog's "hair coat," as in "Beef tallow is good for the dog's skin and hair coat." (On the other hand, beef tallow merely provides palatability, while the dried beef digest in Cycle provides palatability *enhancement*.)

18   I hate to say it, but O.N.E. was pretty palatable. Maybe that's because it has about 100 percent more fat than, say, Butcher's Blend. Or maybe I'd been duped by the packaging; that's been known to happen before.

20   As with people food, dog snacks taste much better than dog meals. They're better looking too. Take Milk-Bone Flavor Snacks. The loving-hands-at-home prose describing each flavor is colorful; the writers practically choke on their own exuberance. Of bacon they say, "It's so good, your dog will think it's hot off the frying pan." Of liver: "The only taste your dog wants more than

rancid: rotten

arcane: secret

semiotics: signs

optimum: best

kitschy: tasteless, tacky

palatability: flavor, tastiness

exuberance: excitement

liver—is even more liver!" Of poultry: "All those farm fresh flavors deliciously mixed in one biscuit. Your dog will bark with delight!" And of vegetable: "Gardens of taste! Specially blended to give your dog that vegetable flavor he wants—but can rarely get!"

21   Well, I may be a sucker, but advertising *this* emphatic just doesn't convince me. I lined up all seven flavors of Milk-Bone Flavor Snacks on the floor. Unless my dog's palate is a lot more sensitive than mine—and considering that she steals dirty diapers out of the trash and eats them, I'm loath to think it is—she doesn't detect any more difference in the seven flavors than I did when I tried them.

22   I much preferred Bonz, the hard-baked, bone-shaped snack stuffed with simulated marrow. I liked the bone part, that is; it tasted almost exactly like the cornmeal it was made of. The mock-marrow inside was a bit more problematic: in addition to looking like the sludge that collects in the treads of my running shoes, it was bursting with tiny hairs.

23   I'm sure you have a few dog food questions of your own. To save us time, I've answered them in advance.

> Q: *Are those little cans of Mighty Dog actually branded with the sizzling word BEEF, the way they show in the commercials?*
> A: You should know by now that that kind of thing never happens.
>
> Q: *Does chicken-flavored dog food taste like chicken-flavored cat food?*
> A: To my surprise, chicken cat food was actually a little better—more chickeny. It tasted like inferior canned pâté.
>
> Q: *Was there any dog food that you just couldn't bring yourself to try?*
> A: Alas, it was a can of Mighty Dog called Prime Entree with Bone Marrow. The meat was dark, dark brown, and it was surrounded by gelatin that was almost black. I knew I would die if I tasted it, so I put it outside for the raccoons.

sludge: mud, gunk

CONVERSATIONS: Collaborating in Class or Online

1. Why did Hodgman carry out this study?
2. What were some of the primary questions the author wanted to answer?
3. What are the essay's main categories? What criteria does Hodgman use to divide her subject into these categories?
4. According to the author's investigation, which type of dog food has the healthiest ingredients?

CONNECTIONS: Discovering Relationships among Ideas

5. What initially intrigued Hodgman about dog food?
6. What did the author learn from her research?
7. In paragraphs 11 and 12, the author develops subgroups within the category of Cycle dog food. What point is she making here?
8. What role does fat play in dog food? In which brands is it most prominent?

PRESENTATION: Analyzing the Writer's Craft

9. What purpose does the word "bitch" serve in the title? Do you think this is a clever title or not? Explain your answer.

10. Hodgman starts her essay with a series of questions. Is this an effective beginning in your opinion? Why or why not?

11. In what order does the author present her categories? Why do you think she chooses this specific order?

12. What adjective best describes the author's attitude toward her subject in this essay?

PROJECTS: Expressing Your Own Views

13. **Video:** Produce a brief video that carries out some first-hand research similar to Hodgman's investigation of dog food. Divide your subject into interesting categories, then write, conduct, and film your study.

14. **Multimedia:** Working in groups, prepare a multimedia project for your class that uses division and classification to comment on a current event. Use the newspaper, *Time*, or *Newsweek* as a source for generating ideas about this project. Make sure your project has a specific purpose.

15. **Essay:** Write a division/classification essay regarding some aspect of college that will actually help you become a better student. What is your subject? What principle can you follow to divide your subject into useful categories? What purpose will this study serve?

16. **Research:** Read and summarize the three resources below. Generate one specific question from each resource that focuses on division/classification. Then answer one of your questions in a documented essay, consulting these and other sources as necessary.

OTHER RESOURCES

 Web Site

American Society for the Prevention of Cruelty to Animals: www.aspca.org

Academic Article

"Pet Ownership and Human Health: A Brief Review of Evidence and Issues"

by June McNicholas et al.

BMJ: British Medical Journal 331.7527 (2005): 1252–1254

 Audio/Video

Dog Food Reviews, Ratings, and Comparisons: http://dogfoodchat.com

Search: "How Commercial Dog Food Is Made"

Click on the Video link

ONE LAST THOUGHT

In 1860, James Spratt introduced the first processed dog food, called Spratt's Patent Meat Fibrine Dog Cakes. It was a mixture of wheat, beet root, vegetables, and beef blood. Several other companies followed suit with their own versions of dog food, but processed dog food didn't gain popularity until the 1930s, when people were looking for cheaper ways to feed their animals than table scraps. After World War II, dog food manufacturers began cooking non-human-grade food, which allowed them to use parts of animals that had previously been discarded. Since then, with clever marketing and cheap prices, manufactured dog food has become the norm for pet owners, and most people don't remember a time when they fed their animals anything else.

Do you have any animals? What do you feed them? Do you allow them to eat table scraps? Why or why not?

World Clock

by poodwaddle.com

The World Clock 2010 is maintained by **poodwaddle.com**, which provides free flash applets for blogs, Web sites, and social network profiles. Supported entirely by on-site advertising, its contents are 100 percent free. The unique status-counter clock provides real-time, constantly updated statistics for global population, causes of death, major illnesses and injuries, global warming, energy sources, crimes, food production, the national debt, and other intriguing topics.

> ### PREREADING QUESTIONS
>
> What sources do you use to keep up with significant statistics on global issues?
>
> Why do you turn to these?
>
> Do you trust these sources to stay current with important changes across the globe?

 View this Web site at http://www.poodwaddle.com/worldclock.swf before answering the questions that follow.

CONVERSATIONS: Collaborating in Class or Online

1. What categories of information does this Web site display?
2. Is your hometown listed on the World Clock time page? What time zone does your hometown fall into? Find the current time in the town of a friend or relative who lives in another time zone. What is the difference in your times?
3. According to this site, which country has the highest population?
4. What are the top three crimes in the United States? Look at these rates by the year, month, week, and day. What differences do you notice among them?

CONNECTIONS: Discovering Relationships among Ideas

5. Are you surprised by any of the global statistics connected with illnesses and injuries? If so, which ones?
6. Why do you think respiratory infections are such a serious threat to humans?
7. Why do you think the slaughter of chickens is far greater than that of other animals?
8. What results on these charts would you like to change? What could we all do to make such a changes?

PRESENTATION: Analyzing the Writer's Craft

9. Is this Web site the best way to display the messages in these charts?
10. What other format might be effective for presenting this information?
11. In what different ways could you organize the material on these lists?
12. What is most interesting to you about the presentation of this information?

PROJECTS: Expressing Your Own Views

13. **Chart:** Conduct your own survey on a statistic from this Web site. Then use division and classification to present your findings in chart form.
14. **Review:** This Web site also has a link to games. Go to this link, and play one of the games. Then write a review of the game.
15. **Essay:** Consider an important decision you had to make recently. What was the decision? What were the various choices available to you? What sources did you consult to help you make your final choice? Then write an essay using division and classification to explain how you came to this decision. Finally, analyze the choice you made and the process you went through to reach that conclusion.
16. **Research:** Read and summarize the three resources below. Generate one specific question from each resource that focuses on division/classification. Then answer one of your questions in a documented essay, consulting these and other sources as necessary.

OTHER RESOURCES

Web Site

Poodwaddle: www.poodwaddle.com

Click on the All Apps link

Audio/Video

National Public Radio: www.npr.org

Search: "'Oldest Old' Are World's Fastest Growing Age Group"

Click on the Audio link

Academic Article

"Three Measures of Longevity: Time Trends and Record Values"

by Vladimir Canudas-Romo

Demography 47.2 (2010): 299–312

ONE LAST THOUGHT

The national debt clock is a billboard on Avenue of the Americas in New York City that keeps a running total of America's national debt. Installed in 1989, it was financed by real estate developer Seymour Durst, who wanted to draw attention to the country's rising debt levels. Can you think of any other counter like this that should be made public? Where would you put it? Why?

The 10 People You'll Find in Any Gym

by Chris Sparling

Chris Sparling is a writer for thatsfit.com who publishes online articles on health and fitness. Recent essays have included "Diet Detective," "Sleep Boosts Athletic Performance," "Get Fit with a Pyramid Scheme," "5 Tips for Safe Weightlifting," "Try These Autumn Running Shoes on for Size," and "Will Eating Too Much Protein Make You Fat?"

PREREADING QUESTIONS

How often do you work out at a gym?

What regular "types" of people frequent the gym?

Do you fit in with any of these types? In what ways?

---

1 Step in any gym in any city in any state in this entire country and you're sure to find the same people. Of course not the exact same people, but the same types of people. Though their accents may differ when they yell their rep count out loud and their music selection may vary as it blares through their oversized headphones, these same people seem to magically appear in every gym throughout the nation. Some of them work out hard, some don't work out at all, and some do exercises so bizarre that it's clearly not safe to be within a fifty-foot radius of them. Who are the people in your neighborhood gym? Pretty much the same as those in everyone else's.

2 **1. The Gamma Radiation Victim**—While they aren't green (yet), these guys are so large

that they look like they could either live forever or die any second. Their clothes fit them like paint and their veins practically form roadmaps on their arms and legs. Fortunately for them, if they ever get lost on the way to their steroid dealer's house, they can use their bodies like a AAA Trip-Tic. These are also the same guys that you should never ask to spot you, because if you are struggling to bang out your last rep with what you believe to be a respectable amount of weight, they will simply lift it off you with one hand . . . and then beat up your dad with the other.

AAA Trip-Tic: map provided by the American Automobile Association

3 **2. Thomas Edison**—Stay the hell away from this guy or girl, or else you're bound to get hurt. There's truly nothing scarier in the gym than the people who feel the need to invent their own exercises. As you and everyone else go about your daily grind, these people are rolling around on a physio-ball while balancing a soft-spoken Peruvian child on their head. A common explanation for the purpose of their whacked-out maneuvers is that this new exercise is great for working their "core." The truth? It doesn't work their core at all. In fact, it doesn't work anything … except to bring utter chaos into a weight room. Get these people on a treadmill and that's when things really get dangerous.

4 **3. Sparkle Motion**—Remember the girls in college who used to get dressed to the hilt for an 8:00 AM class? Well, ten years later these same ladies are still going for cosmetic gold, primping and teasing their early morning glamour for a pre-work trip to the gym. The hair, the nails, the matching pink running shoes/zip-up sweatshirt ensemble, and even the unabashedly applied glitter lipstick … all at 5:30 in the goddamn morning. Most people with even an iota of sanity are still asleep at this hour. These glimmering gals, however, are already into their fourth cup of iced coffee and forty-third minute on the elliptical machine by this time.

> *There's truly nothing scarier in the gym than the people who feel the need to invent their own exercises*

5 **4. The "A Bit Too Personal" Trainer**—Signing-up for a gym membership in itself can be a rather daunting process for some people. When you factor in a personal training session with someone who feels the need to tell you about all of their life problems, things can quickly go from uneasy to downright weird. "That's it … one more … good … you can do it … good. … My mother died from advanced stage syphilis." Uh. . .what? Who needs to hear that? And how is that possibly motivating? I may be wrong, but I don't recall a single scene in *Rocky* where Mickey told Rocky that the reason his skin looks

IN CONTEXT

Working Out

Most gymnasts practice twice a day for at least 3 hours per session, totaling over 30 hours weekly in the gym.

so healthy is because he refuses to poop after 8:30 at night.

6 **5. Bob the Builder**—Fancy health clubs may be the only place where this guy doesn't show up, but for the rest of us whose annual gym memberships cost less than the price of a new Nissan Maxima, this unfashionably coarse fellow is a staple (Puns, kids. That's what they're called.) Sometimes it's a pair of work boots and jeans, other times it's a pair of overalls, and on some occasions it's a line of clothing seemingly purchased from the Paul Bunyon collection on QVC. How do these people work out in all those layers? The grunge epoch may have ended in the late nineties, but flannel somehow managed to survive thanks to carpenters whose parents clearly never made them put on their "play clothes" after school.

7 **6. The Unworthy Screamer**—Although it is true that the huge guys do sometimes yell while they work out, it is most times the mostly-fat-but-partially-muscled guy who feels the need to grunt and groan at the top of his lungs each time he curls a thirty-five pound dumbbell. Even

physio-ball: large rubber exercise ball
unabashedly: blatantly, without embarrassment
iota: tiny bit
daunting: intimidating, frightening
epoch: era, period

worse, when it turns out that the dying moose sounds you hear emanating from the far corner turn out to be the Herculean cries of a one hundred and fifty pound man wearing Puma sweats and a Riptide headband, banging out his last two reps of triceps extensions. Feel that burn, you annoying S.O.B.

8   **7. The Teen Titan**—Obesity rates for youths and teens are at an all time high, which is why you see fewer and fewer fat kids getting picked on today (fat is the new skinny, or at least it would seem). So, to see any teenage kids in the gym is, in and of itself, a good thing. Problems usually arise when a group of four or five teenage boys collectively decide to dive head first into a workout regimen that would make Ronnie Coleman sleep in. Their form is all out of whack and they do their best to shove around as much weight as their barely post-pubescent bodies possibly can. All goes to hell once a 45-pound plate slides off the side of the bar during an attempt at a one-rep max bench press and the other side comes crashing down onto their spleen. Even worse is when they use far too much weight on the cable crossovers and end up being violently yanked backwards like Sweetchuck in *Police Academy 2*.

> *They do their best to shove around as much weight as their barely post-pubescent bodies possibly can*

9   **8. The Doctor of Style**—Look, we all think it's very impressive that you work at a hospital.

You're clearly a very intelligent and noble person. And, depending on your particular occupation, it's likely that you probably make some serious money, too. But, is it still necessary to wear your powder blue scrubs to the gym? These people work all day long in these draw-string pants and v-neck shirts. . . . Don't they want to change out of them? They may be comfortable and they may "breathe," but that's still no excuse for wearing your work clothes in public. Do the world a favor and pick-up a pair of shorts and a T-shirt, will you please?

10   **9. Scarface**—Though he's not a cocaine drug kingpin, this guy is still to blame for leaving the weight room looking like the backroom of a bakery. Despite the fact that the signs clearly say that "Weightlifting Chalk is Not Allowed," this dusty fellow claps his hands together with pride before each set, leaving everything and everyone around him covered in a layer of white powder. Only making things worse is the industrial size weightlifting belt this guy straps around the waistband of his ultra-tight spandex shorts, essentially

emanating: emerging, coming from

forcing everyone in the gym to "say hello to his little friend."

11   **10. The Senator**—Treating each visit to the gym like a stop on a campaign trail, these types want to talk to you and everyone else about utter and complete nonsense. They never, ever shut up. Ever. Even while you attempt to finish your last five minutes of an hour run on the treadmill, or even worse, as you labor through your last set of squats, this person will find that to be the most opportune time to ask you how your family is doing or how your job is going or if you know a good place to buy deck stain. Your best attempts at ignoring them or hint dropping for them to leave you alone are about as effective as using gasoline to put out a fire. Maybe these people really should run for office.

12   Don't believe that these people are at your gym? Try looking around the next time you go and you'll see them. All of them. But if for some reason you have trouble identifying one of them from this list, well, I hate to break it to you, but that person might be you.

CONVERSATIONS: Collaborating in Class or Online

1. Explain each of Sparling's ten types of people who go to the gym.
2. Why do you think the author wrote this article about gym types?
3. Can you add any categories to Sparling's gym member types?
4. What is the significance of the author's classification system?

CONNECTIONS: Discovering Relationships among Ideas

5. Which of Sparling's types is most common at the gym? What personality traits go with the gym behavior for this group?
6. What do all the references to proper nouns (brand names, people, and places) add to this essay? Give an example to support your conclusion.
7. Why do you think people in gyms are easy to classify into groups?
8. Why do you think most of these types of people are so oblivious to their own bad behavior?

PRESENTATION: Analyzing the Writer's Craft

9. How would you describe the tone of this essay?
10. How well do the titles of his categories introduce the author's explanations? Which title do you think is most accurate? Explain your answer.
11. How does Sparling organize his categories? Is this an effective order? Explain your answer.
12. In his essay, Sparling uses several comparisons that fall into two categories: similes, which use the words "like" or "as" to compare two dissimilar items, and metaphors, which omit "like" or "as." Find three comparisons in this essay, and explain what each one adds to the selection.

PROJECTS: Expressing Your Own Views

13. **Advertisement:** Design an ad for a gym membership. Use division and classification to highlight the most attractive features of the gym.

14. **Collage:** Create a collage representing the types of people you observe at a public event—like a parade, a marathon, or a carnival. Make a statement about these types through the pictures you choose to include.

15. **Essay:** Using some of the characteristics Sparling reports, use division and classification to explain your own behavior at some public event—the gym, football games, parties, restaurants, etc.

16. **Research:** Read and summarize the three resources below. Generate one specific question from each resource that focuses on division/classification. Then answer one of your questions in a documented essay, consulting these and other sources as necessary.

OTHER RESOURCES

Web Site

National Institutes of Health: www.nih.gov

Click on the Health Information tab; click on Health Topics A–Z; click on Exercise/Physical Fitness

Academic Article

"Incentive to Exercise"

by Gary Charness and Uri Gneezy

Econometrica 77.3 (2009): 909 –931

Audio/Video

New York Times: http://www.nytimes.com/

Search: "Exercise Evolution for Baby Boomers"

Click the All Results Since 1851 tab and watch the Video

ONE LAST THOUGHT

A McDonald's quarter pounder with cheese, fries, and a soft drink contains almost 1200 calories. It would take 90 minutes of running, 120 minutes of biking, 140 minutes of stair climbing, or 190 minutes of brisk walking to burn 1200 calories. Do you eat fast food? If so, do you research the nutritional information before ordering?

The Real Threat to Americans

by St Pete for Peace

St Pete for Peace is a non-partisan anti-war group based in St. Petersburg, Florida, devoted to bringing awareness of the "atrocities our government is committing" in such countries as Afghanistan, Pakistan, Palestine, and Iraq. It also sponsors a weekly radio show focusing on topics like United States militarism, environmentalism, and other global political concerns.

PREREADING QUESTIONS

What do you think is the number-one killer in the United States?

How dominant do you think terrorism is?

What keeps certain issues in the forefront of our minds?

Nov. 2010

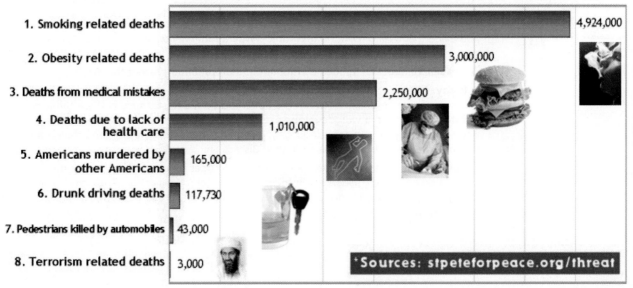

The REAL Threat to Americans

The U.S. spends about $1 trillion per year on military and homeland security, yet in the past ten years, for every American killed by an act of terrorism there were 750 killed by a medical mistake.

Number of deaths in the United States, 2000-2009, by selected cause*

1. Smoking related deaths — 4,924,000
2. Obesity related deaths — 3,000,000
3. Deaths from medical mistakes — 2,250,000
4. Deaths due to lack of health care — 1,010,000
5. Americans murdered by other Americans — 165,000
6. Drunk driving deaths — 117,730
7. Pedestrians killed by automobiles — 43,000
8. Terrorism related deaths — 3,000

*Sources: stpeteforpeace.org/threat

St Pete for Peace
StPeteforPeace.org

CONVERSATIONS: Collaborating in Class or Online

1. This chart represents a study of what killed Americans from 2000 to 2009. Which of these statistics was most surprising to you?

2. What is the leading killer of Americans? Did you guess this in your prereading journal entry?

3. Where does terrorism fall on the chart?

4. Which of these statistics is most alarming to you? Explain your response.

CONNECTIONS: Discovering Relationships among Ideas

5. Why does terrorism get more media coverage than the other threats to our country?

6. This chart shows in picture form the severity of the obesity epidemic in the United States. In what ways can we improve this statistic?

7. Why do you think we are not doing more as a country to help people stop smoking?

8. Do you believe deaths due to lack of health care will rise or fall with our new health care plans in the United States?

PRESENTATION: Analyzing the Writer's Craft

9. In your opinion, is this format the best way to present this material? Explain your answer.

10. This chart has many links built into it that explain the statistics presented here. Are you enticed to read further on any of these topics? Which ones? Why do these particular topics interest you?

11. What do the colors communicate to you?

12. Do you like the addition of visuals to each bar? Explain your answer.

PROJECTS: Expressing Your Own Views

13. **Summary:** Go to the St. Pete for Peace Web site. Choose one of the sources below the chart, and read more on that topic. Write a summary of what you discovered.

14. **Podcast:** Generate a podcast based on the summary you wrote on one of the sources for question 13. Use division and classification to present the material.

15. **Essay:** Find the 2008 version of this chart at stpeteforpeace.org/real.threat.html. Discuss the differences between the 2008 and the 2010 statistics in three different categories. Write a well-developed essay focusing on your observations. Be sure to introduce your subject adequately, using information on the site, and then draw some interesting conclusions from your discussion.

16. **Research:** Read and summarize the three resources below. Generate one specific question from each resource that focuses on division/classification. Then answer one of your questions in a documented essay, consulting these and other sources as necessary.

OTHER RESOURCES

Web Site

Nocotine Addiction and the Other Dangers of Tobacco Use: http://smoking.drugabuse.gov

Audio/Video

CBS News: www.cbsnews.com

Search: "Obesity, Death Rate"

Click on the Video link

Academic Article

"Viewpoint: Terrorism and Dispelling the Myth of a Panic Prone Public"

by Ben Sheppard, G. James Rubin, Jamie K. Wardman, and Simon Wessely

Journal of Public Health Policy 27.3 (2006): 219–245

ONE LAST THOUGHT

During Franklin Delano Roosevelt's inaugural address, he delivered the now-famous phrase "the only thing we have to fear is fear itself." He gave his speech in 1933, when the Great Depression was still deeply affecting American lives. Listen to his speech by visiting www.americanrhetoric.com and typing "FDR Inaugural Speech" in the Site Search box. How do you think that phrase relates to the St. Pete graph?

The Truth About Lying

by Judith Viorst

Author, journalist, and psychologist **Judith Viorst** is perhaps best known for her popular "Alexander" series of children's books, but she has also written such adult best sellers as *People and Other Aggravations* (1971), *Necessary Losses* (1987), and *Unexpectedly Eighty: And Other Adaptations* (2010). In addition, she has received several awards for her journalism and psychological writings.

PREREADING QUESTIONS

Explain one time when you lied. Why did you do so?

Are you ever irritated when people lie to you? Why?

Under what circumstances might lying be acceptable?

1   I've been wanting to write on a subject that intrigues and challenges me: the subject of lying. I've found it very difficult to do. Everyone I've talked to has a quite intense and personal but often rather intolerant point of view about what we can—and can never *never*—tell lies about. I've finally reached the conclusion that I can't present any ultimate conclusions, for too many people would promptly disagree. Instead, I'd like to present a series of moral puzzles, all concerned with lying. I'll tell you what I think about them. Do you agree?

Social Lies

2   Most of the people I've talked with say that they find social lying acceptable and necessary. They think it's the civilized way for folks to behave. Without these little white lies, they say, our relationships would be short and brutish and nasty. It's arrogant, they say, to insist on being so incorruptible and so brave that you cause other people unnecessary embarrassment or pain by compulsively assailing them with your honesty. I basically agree. What about you?

3   Will you say to people, when it simply isn't true, "I like your new hairdo," "You're looking much better," "It's so nice to see you," "I had a wonderful time"?

4   Will you praise hideous presents and homely kids?

5   Will you decline invitations with "We're busy that night—so sorry we can't come," when the

incorruptible: principled

IN CONTEXT

Lie Detectors

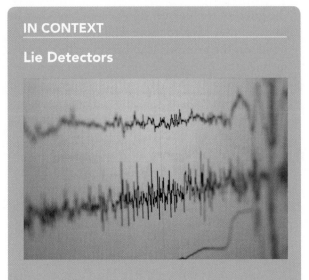

The first polygraphs, or lie detectors, were invented in the early 1900s, using blood pressure and breathing rates to measure truthfulness. Now, even though the scientific community questions their validity, polygraphs are commonly used by police departments and are sometimes admissible in court. Visit www.time.com, and search "How to Spot a Liar" to read an article describing new technologies that might someday replace the lie detector.

mellifluous comments." When others tell fibs he will not go along. He says that social lying is lying, that little white lies are still lies. And he feels that telling lies is morally wrong. What about you?

Peace-Keeping Lies

8 Many people tell peace-keeping lies; lies designed to avoid irritation or argument; lies designed to shelter the liar from possible blame or pain; lies (or so it is rationalized) designed to keep trouble at bay without hurting anyone.

9 I tell these lies at times, and yet I always feel they're wrong. I understand why we tell them, but still they feel wrong. And whenever I lie so that someone won't disapprove of me or think less of me or holler at me, I feel I'm a bit of a coward, I feel I'm dodging responsibility, I feel . . . guilty. What about you?

10 Do you, when you're late for a date because you overslept, say that you're late because you got caught in a traffic jam?

11 Do you, when you forget to call a friend, say that you called several times but the line was busy?

12 Do you, when you didn't remember that it was your father's birthday, say that his present must be delayed in the mail?

13 And when you're planning a weekend in New York City and you're not in the mood to visit your mother, who lives there, do you conceal—with a lie, if you must—the fact that you'll be in New York? Or do you have the courage—or is it the cruelty?—to say, "I'll be in New York, but sorry—I don't plan on seeing you"?

14 (Dave and his wife Elaine have two quite different points of view on this very subject. He calls her a coward. She says she's being wise. He says she must assert her right to visit New York sometimes and not see her mother. To which she always patiently replies, "Why should we have useless fights? My mother's too old to change. We get along much better when I lie to her.")

truth is you'd rather stay home than dine with the So-and-sos?

6 And even though, as I do, you may prefer the polite evasion of "You really cooked up a storm" instead of "The soup"—which tastes like warmed-over coffee—"is wonderful," will you, if you must, proclaim it wonderful?

7 There's one man I know who absolutely refuses to tell social lies. "I can't play that game," he says; "I'm simply not made that way." And his answer to the argument that saying nice things to someone doesn't cost anything is, "Yes, it does—it destroys your credibility." Now, he won't, unsolicited, offer his views on the painting you just bought, but you don't ask his frank opinion unless you want *frank*, and his silence at those moments when the rest of us liars are muttering, "Isn't it lovely?" is for the most part, eloquent enough. My friend does not indulge in what he calls "flattery, false praise and

> *He feels that telling lies is morally wrong*

credibility: integrity
unsolicited: freely, voluntarily
mellifluous: smooth

15   Finally, do you keep the peace by telling your husband lies on the subject of money? Do you reduce what you really paid for your shoes? And in general do you find yourself ready, willing, and able to lie to him when you make absurd mistakes or lose or break things?

16   "I used to have a romantic idea that part of intimacy was confessing every dumb thing that you did to your husband. But after a couple of years of that," says Laura, "have I changed my mind!"

17   And having changed her mind, she finds herself telling peace-keeping lies. And yes, I tell them too. What about you?

Protective Lies

18   Protective lies are lies folks tell—often quite serious lies—because they're convinced that the truth would be too damaging. They lie because they feel there are certain human values that supersede the wrong of having lied. They lie, not for personal gain but because they believe it's for the good of the person they're lying to. They lie to those they love, to those who trust them most of all, on the grounds that breaking this trust is justified.

19   They may lie to their children on money or marital matters.

20   They may lie to the dying about the state of their health.

21   They may lie about adultery, and not—or so they insist—to save their own hide, but to save the heart and the pride of the men they are married to.

22   They may lie to their closest friend because the truth about her talents or son or psyche would be—or so they insist—utterly devastating.

23   I sometimes tell such lies, but I'm aware that it's quite presumptuous to claim I know what's best for others to know. That's called playing God. That's called manipulation and control. And we never can be sure, once we start to juggle lies, just where they'll land, exactly where they'll roll.

24   And furthermore, we may find ourselves lying in order to back up the lies that are backing up the lie we initially told.

25   And furthermore—let's be honest—if conditions were reversed, we certainly wouldn't want anyone lying to us.

26   Yet, having said all that, I still believe that there are times when protective lies must nonetheless be told. What about you?

27   If your Dad had a very bad heart and you had to tell him some bad family news, which would you choose: to tell him the truth or lie?

28   If your former husband failed to send his monthly child-support check and in other ways behaved like a total rat, would you allow your children—who believed he was simply wonderful—to continue to believe that he was wonderful?

29   If your dearly beloved brother selected a wife whom you deeply disliked, would you reveal your feelings or would you fake it?

IN CONTEXT

Lies Parents Tell

"Santa, the Easter Bunny, and the Tooth Fairy"

"This is going to hurt me more than it will hurt you"

"Mommy and Daddy are taking a nap"

"Just tell the truth and you won't get in trouble"

"If you keep making that face, it will stick"

"Eat your vegetables and you'll grow up big and strong"

---

supersede: replace
psyche: personality
presumptuous: arrogant

30   And if you were asked, after making love, "And how was that for you?" would you reply, if it wasn't too good, "Not too good"?

31   Now, some would call a sex lie unimportant, little more than social lying, a simple act of courtesy that makes all human intercourse run smoothly. And some would say all sex lies are bad news and unacceptably protective. Because, says Ruth, "a man with an ego that fragile doesn't need your lies—he needs a psychiatrist." Still others feel that sex lies are indeed protective lies, more serious than simple social lying, and yet at times they tell them on the grounds that when it comes to matters sexual, everybody's ego is somewhat fragile.

32   "If most of the time things go well in sex," says Sue, "I think you're allowed to dissemble when they don't. I can't believe it's good to say, 'Last night was four stars, darling, but tonight's performance rates only a half.'"

33   I'm inclined to agree with Sue. What about you?

Trust-Keeping Lies

34   Another group of lies are trust-keeping lies, lies that involve triangulation, with A (that's you) telling lies to B on behalf of C (whose trust you'd promised to keep). Most people concede that once you've agreed not to betray a friend's confidence, you can't betray it, even if you must lie. But I've talked with people who don't want you telling them anything that they might be called on to lie about.

> *If her best friend is having an affair, she absolutely doesn't want to know about it*

35   "I don't tell lies for myself," says Fran, "and I don't want to have to tell them for other people." Which means, she agrees, that if her best friend is having an affair, she absolutely doesn't want to know about it.

36   "Are you saying," her best friend asks, "that if I went off with a lover and I asked you to tell my husband I'd been with you, that you wouldn't lie for me, that you'd betray me?"

37   Fran is very pained but very adamant. "I wouldn't want to betray you, so . . . don't ask me."

38   Fran's best friend is shocked. What about you?

39   Do you believe you can have close friends if you're not prepared to receive their deepest secrets?

40   Do you believe you must always lie for your friends?

41   Do you believe, if your friend tells a secret that turns out to be quite immoral or illegal, that once you've promised to keep it, you must keep it?

42   And what if your friend were your boss—if you were perhaps one of the President's men—would you betray or lie for him over, say, Watergate?

43   As you can see, these issues get terribly sticky.

44   It's my belief that once we've promised to keep a trust, we must tell lies to keep it. I also believe that we can't tell Watergate lies. And if these two statements strike you as quite contradictory, you're right—they're quite contradictory. But for now they're the best I can do. What about you?

45   Some say that truth will out and thus you might as well tell the truth. Some say you can't regain the trust that lies lose. Some say that even though the truth may never be revealed, our lies pervert and damage our relationships. Some say . . . well, here's what some of them have to say.

46   "I'm a coward," says Grace, "about telling close people important, difficult truths. I find that I'm unable to carry it off. And so if something is bothering me, it keeps building up inside till I end up just not seeing them any more."

47   "I lie to my husband on sexual things but I'm furious," says Joyce, "that he's too insensitive to know I'm lying."

48   "I suffer most from the misconception that children can't take the truth," says Emily. "But I'm starting to see that what's harder and more

---

dissemble: evade, hedge
misconception: misunderstanding

damaging for them is being told lies, is *not* being told the truth."

49 "I'm afraid," says Joan, "that we often wind up feeling a bit of contempt for the people we lie to."

50 And then there are those who have no talent for lying.

51 "Over the years, I tried to lie," a friend of mine explained, "but I always got found out and I always got punished. I guess I gave myself away because I feel guilty about any kind of lying. It looks as if I'm stuck with telling the truth."

It looks as if I'm stuck with telling the truth

52 For those of us, however, who are good at telling lies, for those of us who lie and don't get caught, the question of whether or not to lie can be a hard and serious moral problem. I liked the remark of a friend of mine who said, "I'm willing to lie. But just as a last resort—the truth's always better."

53 "Because," he explained, "though others may completely accept the lie I'm telling, I don't."

54 I tend to feel that way too.

55 What about you?

CONVERSATIONS: Collaborating in Class or Online

1. Viorst discusses four types of lies in this essay. Explain each in your own words.
2. Which types of lies are most "serious"?
3. What does Viorst mean by "Watergate lies" in paragraph 44? What is your feeling about this level of trust-keeping lies?
4. According to Viorst, what is the relationship between lying and her own self-image?

CONNECTIONS: Discovering Relationships among Ideas

5. In what ways is lying a moral problem?
6. Why do people respond in so many different ways to the issue of lying?
7. Based on your experience, what are the principal consequences of lying? Do the negative consequences outweigh the positives for you, or is the reverse true? Explain your answer in as much detail as possible.
8. How do you feel about lying? Does your opinion vary according to the types of lies you tell? Why? Explain your answer in detail.

PRESENTATION: Analyzing the Writer's Craft

9. Viorst starts by summarizing her conclusions about lying. Is this an effective beginning? Explain your answer.
10. In this essay, Viorst works with both division and classification as she arranges lies into several distinct categories. Write down the main subdivisions of her classification system; then list under each category the examples she cites. Do all her examples support the appropriate classification? How has she organized these categories?
11. Who do you think is Viorst's intended audience? What specific verbal clues in the essay help you reach this conclusion?
12. Notice that the author repeats the question "What about you?" several times. What effect does this repetition have on your response to the essay?

PROJECTS: Expressing Your Own Views

13. **Graphic:** At some time in our lives, we all tell or hear lies as Viorst defines them in this essay. Choose a particularly memorable lie (one you either told or received), and classify in a graphic format all your feelings connected with the experience.

14. **List:** Generate a list of humorous excuses related to attendance and homework. Then classify your items in categories with comical labels.

15. **Essay:** School presents a number of potential opportunities for lying. Answers to such questions as "Why is your homework late?" "Why can't you go out this weekend?" and "Why did you miss class yesterday?" can get people into or out of all sorts of trouble. Devise a useful classification system for handling these school-related dilemmas; then write an essay explaining how your classification system works and what your experiences have taught you.

16. **Research:** Read and summarize the three resources below. Generate one specific question from each resource that focuses on division/classification. Then answer one of your questions in a documented essay, consulting these and other sources as necessary.

OTHER RESOURCES

Web Site

Calculators Live: http://calculatorslive.com

Click on the Online Lie Detector link

Academic Article

"The Art of Lying—Or Risking the Wrath of Oprah"

by D. K. McCutchen

Fourth Genre: Explorations in Nonfiction 10.1 (2008): 147–151

Audio/Video

Videojug: www.videojug.com

Search: "How Can I Tell if Someone Is Lying to Me"

Click on the Video link

ONE LAST THOUGHT

Humans aren't the only creatures capable of deception. Many animals use their appearances to mislead predators. Can you figure out what creatures these are and what lies their appearances tell? Can you think of any other examples of "lies" in nature?

13 Job Interview Mistakes to Avoid

by Nathan Newberger

Nathan Newberger has been the managing editor of WorkTree.com for the past five years. He brings his expertise of over 10 years in staffing and human resources to this site, where his current focus is on jobs and careers. Previously, he worked as a recruiter and a career counselor.

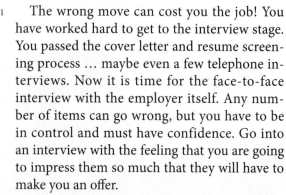

PREREADING QUESTIONS

Have you ever gone through a job interview? If so, what did you do well? What could you do better in the future?

What attitude should job seekers project during job interviews?

What do you imagine is the most common blunder made by people being interviewed?

1   The wrong move can cost you the job! You have worked hard to get to the interview stage. You passed the cover letter and resume screening process … maybe even a few telephone interviews. Now it is time for the face-to-face interview with the employer itself. Any number of items can go wrong, but you have to be in control and must have confidence. Go into an interview with the feeling that you are going to impress them so much that they will have to make you an offer.

2   The interview is the most stressful part of the job hunt for many people, because now they cannot hide behind the cover letter and resume. The real face-to-face human connection between possible employer and job candidate takes place. But for starters, if you simply follow these 13 tips below, you are on your way to interviews with results.

3   A big part of a successful interview is avoiding simple mistakes. Mistakes are deadly to the job seeker and easy to avoid if you are prepared.

4   These are the most common interview mistakes and their antidotes.

1. **Arriving late.** Get directions from the interviewer or a map. Wear a watch, and leave home early. If the worst happens and you cannot make it on time, call the interviewer and arrange to reschedule.

2. **Dressing wrong.** You make your greatest impact on the interviewer in the first 17 seconds, an impression you want to make powerfully positive. Dress right in a

conservative suit, subdued colors, little jewelry (but real gold, or silver, or pearls), low heels (polished), and everything clean and neat. Hygiene includes combed hair, brushed teeth, deodorant, and low-key scent. Check everything the night before, again before walking out the door, and once again in the restroom just before the interview.

3. **Play zombie.** OK, you are nervous. But you can still smile, right? And make eye contact, yes? Sit up, focus on the interviewer, and start responding. Enthusiasm is what the interviewer wants to see.

4. **No smoking, no gum, no drinking.** This is all comfort stuff for you, and none of it helps you here. Employers are more likely to hire non-smokers. At a lunch or dinner interview, others may order drinks. You best not.

5. **Research failure.** The interview is not the time for research. Find out the company's products and services, annual sales, structure, and other key information from the Internet, the public library, professional magazines, or former employees. Show that you are interested in working for the prospective employer by demonstrating knowledge about the company.

6. **Cannot articulate your own strengths and weaknesses.** Only you can recognize your most valuable strengths and most hurtful weaknesses. Be able to specify your major strengths. Your weaknesses, if such must

> *Good answers are to the point and usually shorter*

IN CONTEXT

Drinking on the Job

In a simulated job interview study, interviewers perceived candidates who ordered alcohol as less intelligent and less desirable, whether or not the prospective boss chose to drink. Do you think it's acceptable to drink alcohol during a job interview? Why or why not?

come up, should only be turned around to positives.

7. **Winging the interview.** Practice! Get a friend, a list of interview questions, and a tape recorder, and conduct an interview rehearsal. Include a presentation or demonstration, if that will be part of the real interview. Start with introducing yourself, and go all through an interview to saying good-bye. Write out any answers you have difficulty with, and practice until your delivery is smooth (but not slick).

8. **Talk, Talk, Talk.** Rambling, interrupting the interviewer, and answering a simple question with a fifteen-minute reply—all of these can be avoided if you have thought through and practiced what you want to communicate. Good answers are to the point and usually shorter.

9. **Failure to connect yourself to the job offered.** The job description details the company's needs. You connect your experiences, your talents, and your strengths to the description. It answers the essential reasons for the interview: "How my education/experience/talents/strengths fit your needs, and why I can do this job for you."

subdued: not bright
zombie: robot
prospective: future
articulate: explain

10. **Not asking questions—and asking too many.** Use your research to develop a set of questions that will tell you whether this is the job and the company for you. This will help you limit and focus your questions. But do not overpower the interviewer with questions about details that really will not count in the long run.

11. **Bad-mouth anyone.** Not just your present employer or former employer or the competition. You do not want to look like a complainer.

12. **Asking about compensation and/or benefits too soon.** Wait for the interviewer to bring up these issues, after the discussion of your qualifications and the company's needs and wants.

13. **Failure to ask for the job.** When the interviewer indicates the interview is over, convey your interest in the job, and ask what the next step is.

> **overpower:** overwhelm

CONVERSATIONS: Collaborating in Class or Online

1. Name three of the most common mistakes people make in job interviews, according to Newberger.
2. What specific tasks does Newberger think people should practice before a job interview?
3. How can you avoid being a "zombie" during an interview?
4. According to the author, what role should your research play in an interview?

CONNECTIONS: Discovering Relationships among Ideas

5. Why do you think most people don't ask for the job at the end of the interview?
6. Why is it important to avoid smoking, chewing gum, and drinking?
7. How can complaining get in the way of a good job interview?
8. What patterns or categories do these blunders fall into? What is the reasoning behind these patterns?

PRESENTATION: Analyzing the Writer's Craft

9. Do you think presenting these items in a numbered list is the most effective way to communicate them to an audience?
10. What is Newberger's purpose in this list?
11. What is the author's method of organization? What other order might also be effective?
12. Who is his audience?

PROJECTS: Expressing Your Own Views

13. **Blog:** Post an interview question (real or imaginary) that you would like answered. Exchange questions in class, and respond to another classmate's question.

14. **Advertisement:** Using division and classification, explain on a job site what skills and abilities you have to offer the working world. (See, for example, snagajob.com, simplyhired.com, employmentguide.com, or any of the other job-search sites available on the Internet.)

15. **Essay:** Write an essay that classifies all the jobs you are eligible for, including thorough explanations about your credentials for each job. Then present this information in some logical way in your essay.

16. **Research:** Read and summarize the three resources below. Generate one specific question from each resource that focuses on division/classification. Then answer one of your questions in a documented essay, consulting these and other sources as necessary.

OTHER RESOURCES

 Web Site

Job Interview: http://jobinterview-tips.org

Academic Article

"Exploring Boundaries of the Effects of Applicant Impression Management Tactics in Job Interviews"

by Wei-Chi Tsai, Chien-Cheng Chen, and Su-Fen Chiu

Journal of Management 31.1 (2005): 108–125

 Audio/Video

National Public Radio: http://www.npr.org

Search: "How to Hit Interview Curveballs Out of the Park"

Click on the Audio link

ONE LAST THOUGHT

Have you ever had a bad job interview? If so, you're not alone. Visit www.washingtonian.com, and search "Great Places to Work: Interview Horror Stories." Click on the Article link to read stories about job interviews gone wrong.

A Peek into the Future

by David Colker

David Colker, a staff writer for the *Los Angeles Times*, is also the assistant business editor for the newspaper. He has published recent articles on a wide range of topics, including DirecTV, Skype, Facebook, YouTube, three-dimensional television, the Apple Tablet, eBay, the iPod, digital cameras, bankruptcy, and other subjects within the field of consumer electronics and technology.

PREREADING QUESTIONS

What products or services that don't exist now do you think will be a part of our lives in five years?

What new invention would revolutionize?

How has the Internet changed your personal life over the past five years?

1   Of all the predictions made during the future-happy 1950s—when it was declared we'd soon have flying cars, robot butlers, rocket-delivered mail, and food made from wood pulp—there was one forward-looking statement that was completely validated. It was delivered by Criswell, a self-described soothsayer and TV personality, who said, "We are all interested in the future, for that is where you and I are going to spend the rest of our lives."

2   Otherwise, predicting the future, certainly in the realm of technology, is a risky endeavor. Still, billions of dollars are spent every year in trying to do just that: predict which products will spark new businesses or even whole new industries.

3   Here's a look at proposed technological wonders that are under development in the fields of energy, transportation, television, and medicine. Some are far enough along to be aimed at the near term, others are more in the pipe-dream category, but all are serious enough to be funded by corporate, government, or academic dollars.

4   Keep in mind, however, that the most important new technologies for the coming decades might not even have been thought of yet. After all, 1950s futurists didn't foresee the biggest game changer of our era—the Internet. It's where so many of us are spending much of our lives.

Energy

5   **Smart meters:** Global warming and volatile energy prices have spurred development of digital meters that provide real-time reports of energy usage. They're already in use in some parts of the country.

validated: authenticated
endeavor: undertaking, attempt
volatile: unstable

6   This year, Southern California Edison Co. will begin installing 5.3 million of them for all its residential and small-business customers. The cost: $1.63 billion, to be offset by a 1.5% rate increase until implementation is complete in 2012.

7   Once they're in place, consumers will be able to monitor their electricity use via the Internet.

8   Next up: remote-controlled thermostats and appliances. That can happen as soon as manufacturers agree to a single standard for the control chips, according to Paul Moreno of Pacific Gas & Electric Co., which is installing 9.8 million smart meters in Northern California.

> *One of the main obstacles will be skepticism about safety*

9   **Wireless electricity:** Electricity that travels through the air to power lights, computers, and other devices sounds like one of those 1950s-style fantasies. But WiTricity Corp., a company spun off from research at MIT, says it's time to cut the cord. Wireless electricity products using its technology will be available in 2011.

10   Funded by $5 million from Stata Venture Partners and Argonaut Private Equity, the company has developed a system based on a technology already used in transformers (such as the block-shaped thing on your cell phone charger).

11   In transformers, power jumps across a tiny gap between two coils. The scientists increased that distance between coils to as much as 7 feet by having them both resonate at the same frequency.

12   The energy that travels between them is in the form of a magnetic resonance that's harmless to living beings, WiTricity Chief Executive Eric Giler said.

13   "To the magnetic field," Giler said, "you look like air."

14   One of the main obstacles will be skepticism about safety. When a post about WiTricity appeared on the latimes.com technology blog, a reader who wears a pacemaker said she'd never get close to one, and a man writing from Japan wondered whether the system might "nuke someone by mistake."

Transportation

15   **Ground:** Cars are getting smarter. We drivers remain, well, about as smart as we ever were.

16   Researchers are pushing to provide drivers with better, faster information to avoid crashes and speed traffic flow.

17   One major effort is dubbed IntelliDrive. Funded by the federal government and major automobile manufacturers and overseen by the U.S. Department of Transportation, the program will begin tests of a traffic warning system in San Francisco next month.

18   Participating drivers will receive signals on their cellphones alerting them to bottlenecks approximately 60 seconds ahead. The phone will say, "Slow traffic ahead" through its speakerphone or headset, and a message will appear on its screen.

19   "We call it situational awareness," said Jim Misener, executive director of California Partners for Advanced Transit and Highways. "It's not for braking hard but for warning you in advance."

20   The operators of the program will use traffic information from several existing sources, including Caltrans, and crunch it to provide the real-time warnings. Only cellphones using Windows-based operating systems will be able to download the software to take part in the test—which leaves out iPhones and BlackBerrys, among others.

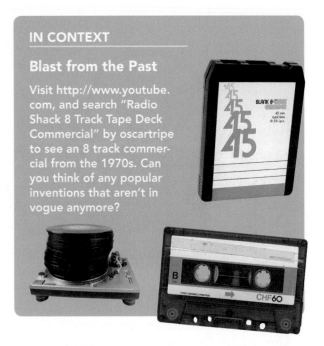

IN CONTEXT

Blast from the Past

Visit http://www.youtube.com, and search "Radio Shack 8 Track Tape Deck Commercial" by oscartripe to see an 8 track commercial from the 1970s. Can you think of any popular inventions that aren't in vogue anymore?

21 The ultimate goal is a dashboard warning system, fed by sensors in cars and along highways, to alert drivers of potential hazards all around them, including blind spots.

22 Far more radical programs take at least some control of cars away from drivers. The proposed RUF system based in Denmark is called a dual-mode program because a vehicle incorporating its design can be driven like a regular car or joined to a mass transit system reminiscent of kids' slot-car toys.

23 In that system, elevated monorail-style tracks would be built alongside major freeways, but instead of carrying trains, they'd ferry cars. Motorists would drive onto the tracks that fit into slots cut into the bottoms of their cars. That's when the automated system takes over, whisking the vehicles in single file as if they were on a fast-moving conveyor belt.

24 The RUF system's name comes from a Danish expression denoting fast movement. But in an investment brochure aimed at English speakers, inventor Palle Jensen said it could also stand for Rapid Urban Flexible.

25 No matter what the name, RUF would be a difficult sell to a city government. A study on building the system infrastructure in Los Angeles estimated the cost would be $10 billion. The proposed system can be viewed at www.ruf.dk.

26 **Commercial aviation:** NASA allocated $12.4 million in research grants last year to Boeing Co., Lockheed Martin Corp., Northrop Grumman Corp, and others to develop so-called N+3 concepts—proposed aircraft designs for three generations, aeronautically speaking, in the future. That would put them into operation in the 2030-35 period.

27 Instead of focusing on building bigger, faster commercial jets, most of these efforts are aimed at designing aircraft that will be quieter, less polluting, and more fuel efficient.

28 One NASA-funded project, which is experimenting with natural gas as fuel, is designing an aircraft that will fly at speeds approximately 10% slower than current norms.

29 Other projects are looking at biofuels. Earlier this year, Continental Airlines, Inc. powered a test flight in part with a blend of fuel derived from algae and the jatropha weed.

> *Most of these efforts are aimed at designing aircraft that will be quieter, less polluting, and more fuel efficient*

30 **Space elevator:** What if you could get to the final frontier by simply pressing an "Up" button?

31 It's in the gee-whiz category of future tech, but two university research groups have done work that could lead to elevators stretching from Earth to the edge of space.

32 At the University of Cambridge, scientists are developing carbon-based fibers far stronger than anything on the market. A practical use would be for lightweight bulletproof vests.

33 But some dreamers say it's so strong it could be used to make the ultimate elevator.

34 Meanwhile, a group at York University in Toronto says a better way to go is an inflatable tower, 9 miles high, made of already available materials filled with helium and other gases. The York team built a 2,000:1 scale model in a stairwell.

reminiscent: suggestive
jatropha: plant

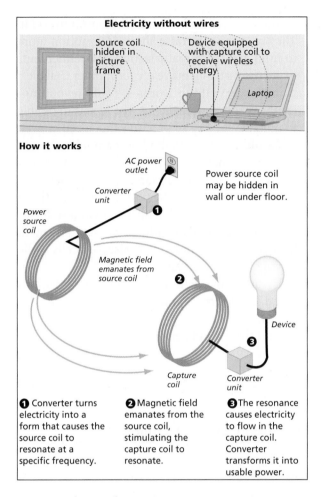

Electricity without wires

Source coil hidden in picture frame

Device equipped with capture coil to receive wireless energy

Laptop

How it works

AC power outlet

Converter unit

Power source coil may be hidden in wall or under floor.

Power source coil

Magnetic field emanates from source coil

Device

Capture coil

Converter unit

❶ Converter turns electricity into a form that causes the source coil to resonate at a specific frequency.

❷ Magnetic field emanates from the source coil, stimulating the capture coil to resonate.

❸ The resonance causes electricity to flow in the capture coil. Converter transforms it into usable power.

35 So why an elevator?

36 Because launching a vehicle from terra firma, as we now do it, is tremendously expensive and requires massive amounts of energy. An elevator would eliminate that step by delivering humans and materials to the edge of space, where the pull of gravity is far weaker. Waiting spaceships could then take over for the second leg of the journey.

37 Let's just hope the arrival and departure announcement system at this transport station in the sky would be better than at most bus stations. A year-long flight to Neptune would be no fun if you meant to instead take the red-eye to Mars.

Television

38 **3-D TV:** Plenty of experiments have been staged in presenting television programming in 3-D, but they've been novelties.

39 Manufacturers hope that high-definition imagery and electronic shutter glasses will make 3-D palatable enough to make it a regular part of viewing. Indeed, in Britain, the satellite-delivered Sky TV service said it would launch an all-3-D channel next year.

40 But is the average person ready to don dorky glasses to watch TV (without them, the 3-D picture is just a blur)? Especially when said glasses, even if digital, can bring on feelings akin to seasickness?

41 That's what happened when Panasonic Corp. showed off its new 3-D system at the Consumer Electronics Show this year. Hopefully the nausea problem will be solved before the product makes it into homes.

42 **Laser plasma:** Using a powerful, pulsed laser, Burton, Inc. in Japan has made a projector that produces 3-D images that hang in the air. So far, it can show only points of light that can be combined to spell out letters or make a geometric pattern, and glasses are needed to view them.

43 But Burton Chief Executive Hidei Kimura said the company hopes to soon demonstrate "real 3-D images inside of the closed space covered by [a] glass dome."

44 **Touchable holograms:** This is real "Star Trek" territory.

45 At the Siggraph trade show in New Orleans in August, a University of Tokyo research group demonstrated holographic images that could be touched. Sort of.

46 The images were made, as with all holograms, of light. But as you reached in to touch them, an electronic tracking system (adapted from a Wii game controller) and ultrasound generator worked together to provide a tactile sensation where the object appeared. A demonstration is at www.youtube.com/watch?v=Y-P1zZAcPuw.

47 One of the most clever demonstrations involved **holograms of raindrops** that participants could feel dropping on their hands.

48 It has been often noted that the porn industry drives a lot of the innovation in high-tech

palatable: pleasant, acceptable

don: put on

akin: similar

tactile: tangible

entertainment. No more need be said about what one day it could do with this.

Medicine

49 **Robot instruments:** At the University of Nebraska, doctors Dmitry Oleynikov and Shane Farritor developed a set of surgery instruments so small they can be inserted into the body and then remote-controlled from outside.

50 Oleynikov is used to the comparisons to the sci-fi movie "Fantastic Voyage," in which a team of doctors gets miniaturized to go inside a patient.

51 "Except with us," Oleynikov said, "the surgeon does not get shrunk."

52 One use, he said, would be to send an instrument through a patient's mouth and down the esophagus to make a small hole in the stomach. From there it could remove the gallbladder or appendix. Light could be provided by a second mini-robot.

53 The idea is to make surgery far less invasive.

54 The researchers have raised $1 million so far. They're looking to raise about $10 million more to fund greater miniaturization and refinements to get the instruments ready for human trials.

55 **Nanosurgery:** If this works, it could revolutionize the practice of medicine. The idea is to be able to practice surgery so precisely that a cell or even molecule could be repaired or manipulated.

56 It's not a new idea. In 1959, Nobel-winning physicist Richard Feynman suggested that tools be used to make smaller tools and then those tools used to make yet smaller tools and so forth.

57 Eventually, tools would be created so small, they could target individual diseased cells while leaving healthy cells alone.

58 Dreamers of the future have imagined that this could lead to triumphing over a foe as horrific as cancer.

59 And that would be a whole lot better than any flying car.

CONVERSATIONS: Collaborating in Class or Online

1. What did Criswell mean when he said, "We are all interested in the future, for that is where you and I are going to spend the rest of our lives" (para. 1)?
2. What do you think is Colker's primary purpose in this essay?
3. Which of the predictions in this essay interests you the most? Why is it interesting to you?
4. Which items does Colker say will be developed first?

CONNECTIONS: Discovering Relationships among Ideas

5. Which of the predictions in this essay will most dramatically affect our country's economy?
6. Which predictions will affect your personal lifestyle the most?
7. What main changes will wireless electricity produce in our homes?
8. Do you imagine space travel will be available to everyone during your lifetime? If so, would you prefer a space elevator or an inflatable tower? Why?

PRESENTATION: Analyzing the Writer's Craft

9. Do you think starting this essay with a reference to the predictions from the 1950s is effective? Why or why not?
10. Into what categories does Colker divide his subject? List the future changes he includes in each category. Do the examples support each subdivision? Explain your answer.

11. How did Colker organize his categories? What is his principle behind this organization?

12. Do you think referring to actual Web sites within the essay for more information on certain items is an effective strategy? Explain your answer.

PROJECTS: Expressing Your Own Views

13. **Picture or Collage:** Make a drawing, take a photograph, or create a collage focusing on a new invention that you would like to design.

14. **Multimedia:** Look up a Web site mentioned in the essay, and present your discoveries to the class in a variety of media.

15. **Essay:** Write an essay classifying your goals and ambitions for the next five years. Make sure your categories are clear and distinct; then take special care to present them in a logical order.

16. **Research:** Read and summarize the three resources below. Generate one specific question from each resource that focuses on division/classification. Then answer one of your questions in a documented essay, consulting these and other sources as necessary.

OTHER RESOURCES

 Web Site

Popular Mechanics—Automotive Care, Home Improvement: www.popularmechanics.com

Click on the Technology tab and then on Gadgets

 Audio/Video

YouTube: www.youtube.com

Search: "Touchable Holography" by Shinoda Lab

Click on the Video link

Academic Article

"Stories about the Future: From Patterns of Expectation to Pattern Recognition"

by Veronica Hollinger

Science Fiction Studies 33.3 (2006): 452–472

ONE LAST THOUGHT

Some inventions, like the wheel, have helped humankind for centuries. Others, like hat fans to cool your forehead or office chairs that double as toilets, have not been as helpful. Can you think of any inventions that are more trouble than they're worth?

www.CartoonStock.com

"This 'wheel' thing of yours—Does it have to be round or will any shape do?"

CHAPTER WRITING ASSIGNMENTS

Write a well-developed essay in response to one of the following prompts. Consult the chapter introduction for guidance in creating your essay.

CONNECTING THE READINGS

1. Write an essay explaining the patterns you see in the disease and death statistics on the World Clock site (poodwaddle.com) and "The Real Threat to Americans" (St Pete for Peace) graph. Be sure to explain your patterns and state a clear purpose for your observations.

2. Would Viorst ("The Truth about Lying") say lying is permissible in job interviews ("13 Job Interview Mistakes to Avoid")? Explain your answer in a well-developed essay.

3. Compose an essay explaining how you think the statistics in one category on the World Clock site (poodwaddle.com) will change over the next 10 years ("A Peek into the Future").

4. Obesity and eating disorders ("The Real Threat to Americans") are at the center of a lot of the problems in the United States. Write an essay explaining how these issues are related and where you predict these problems will be in 10 years ("A Peek into the Future").

MOVING BEYOND THE READINGS

5. Write an essay documenting a threat to Americans that is not listed on the St Pete for Peace chart. Explain the peril in detail, and then discuss why it is a hazard.

6. Write an essay entitled "The 10 Biggest First-Date Blunders."

7. Building on "A Peek into the Future," add some predictions in a well-developed essay of your own.

8. Divide and classify the types of people you would expect to find in a typical day at your favorite fast-food restaurant.

COMBINING RHETORICAL MODES

9. What is the value of exercise in our society? What are the main consequences of not exercising? Write an essay explaining your views on this subject in light of our current problems with obesity.

10. Do further research on one of the predictions in "A Peek into the Future" by surveying some of the links mentioned in the article. Discuss in detail the advantages and disadvantages of the potential change.

11. Explain and justify a significant time you felt compelled to lie, along with the consequences of telling this lie.

12. Write an essay entitled "The 10 Types of People You'll Find in Any College Class."

Comparison and Contrast

10

Our ability to use comparison and contrast is crucial to the quality of our lives. Our basic instincts encourage us to compare ourselves to others so we can improve the way we live. Even if we simply try to top our "personal best," comparison and contrast help us better ourselves on a daily basis. In addition, we constantly make decisions based on comparisons of one kind or another. The skillful use of comparison and contrast is clearly essential to both our personal and professional lives. Here are some ways we use this type of reasoning:

- Shopping for clothes;
- Comparing two cultures for a sociology paper;
- Choosing a major;

DEVELOPMENT STRATEGIES: COMPARISON AND CONTRAST

Purpose Statement

Development: Point by Point or Subject by Subject

Point 1	OR	**Subject A**
Subject A		Point 1
Subject B		Point 2
Point 2		Point 3
Subject A		**Subject B**
Subject B		Point 1
Point 3		Point 2
Subject A		Point 3
Subject B		
		Conclusion

- Writing a history report about the similarities and differences between the World Wars;
- Selecting a gym for our workouts.

Comparison and contrast help us establish a frame of reference so we can navigate through the larger world around us. We consistently compare ourselves and our performance to others so we can continue to function at our best.

Introducing Comparison and Contrast

Comparison and contrast help us understand one subject by seeing it in relation to another. When we *compare,* we look for similarities, and when we *contrast,* we look for differences. In reality, however, comparison and contrast are nearly always part of the same process. For this reason, we often use the word *compare* to refer to both techniques.

Comparison and contrast are most profitably applied to two items that have something in common, such as cats and dogs or cars and motorcycles. A discussion of cats and motorcycles, for example, would probably not be very interesting, because they have so little in common.

There are two ways of setting up a comparison. Look at the following examples of the two primary models of comparison/contrast:

DEVELOPMENT STRATEGIES AT WORK

Purpose Statement: Which resort would I enjoy most?

Point-by-Point Development

→ **Location**
Resort A: Bahamas
Resort B: Alaska

→ **Travel Time**
Resort A: Bahamas
Resort B: Alaska

→ **Hotel Amenities**
Resort A: Bahamas
Resort B: Alaska

→ **Regional Activities**
Resort A: Bahamas
Resort B: Alaska

Conclusion

DEVELOPMENT STRATEGIES AT WORK

Purpose Statement: Which movie should we see?

Subject-by-Subject Development

Movie A	Movie B
Storyline	Storyline
Actors	Actors
Cinematography	Cinematography
Setting	Setting

Conclusion

The basic skill of finding similarities and differences will complement your work with many other rhetorical modes. It is a pattern of thought that is essential to more complex thinking strategies, so perfecting your ability to use it is an important step in improving your critical thinking.

Discovering How Comparison and Contrast Work

To the right is a list of the key elements of comparison/contrast thinking, whether for a visual (like an ad or a photo) or a prose selection. These Comparison/Contrast Essentials are equally useful as guidelines for both reading and writing.

Analyzing the photograph below will help you understand how these elements work together in comparison/contrast. If you discover on your own how this method of reasoning functions, you will be able to apply it effectively to your own reading and writing. The questions to the left of the photo will help you understand this rhetorical mode even more clearly than you already do.

Comparison/Contrast Essentials

Purpose
Points/Subjects to Compare
Examples and Details
Logical Organization
Summary/Conclusion

1. What statement does this photo make?
2. What points of comparison are suggested in it?
3. What examples and details develop this comparison?
4. How are the points of the comparison organized?
5. How does the photographer communicate a conclusion?

Collaborative Responses Now discuss your responses to these questions with your classmates in small groups or as an entire class. Did the diverse perspectives from other students in your class change your "reading" of the visual? If so, in what ways?

Reading Comparison and Contrast

As you read the verbal and visual selections in this chapter, pay special attention to the reasons for each comparison. You should also make sure you understand the author's statement of purpose and each point that is introduced.

During your first reading of a selection, think about how the Comparison/ Contrast Essentials work within it. The following questions will help you accomplish this task for both written and graphic assignments:

Comparison/Contrast Essentials: Reading

- **Purpose:** What is the purpose of the selection?
- **Points/Subjects to Compare:** What are the points or topics to be compared?
- **Examples and Details:** What examples and details does the author use to support these points?
- **Logical Organization:** How are the points organized?
- **Summary/Conclusion:** What is the author's/illustrator's conclusion?

On your second and third readings of the selection, focus on areas of ambiguity and confusion so you can deepen your comprehension.

Writing Comparison and Contrast

Taking another look at the Comparison/Contrast Essentials as you move from reading to writing will help you adjust your writing to your specific purpose and audience. But first, let's review the writing process as it applies to this rhetorical mode.

Choosing a Subject

As with all assignments, you should select the subjects you will compare as soon as possible. Once you have your subjects, you should start to think about the points or topics you want to discuss for your subjects along with your reason for exploring this comparison.

Our student writer, Minh Hoang, decides to discuss the differences between high school and college. As a new college student, he is painfully aware of many of these discrepancies.

Generating Details

You might want to start generating ideas by listing possible points to compare. Then use a specific prewriting strategy introduced in Chapter 3 to generate as many details as possible for each point.

To begin this process, Minh decides on four points he wants to consider in his comparison of high school and college. He lists them and then uses brainstorming to generate his details and examples.

• Point 1: Attendance	
High school:	*College:*
mandatory attendance	attendance optional
courses chosen for us	choose own major
requirements set	requirements set by major
• Point 2: Accountability	
High school:	*College:*
parents help with commitments	we are on our own
parents remind us about homework	we have to remember our homework
parents wake us up	we have to wake up ourselves
• Point 3: Cost	
High school:	*College:*
free	three levels of tuition—community college, public university, private college
no job necessary	job might be necessary
• Point 4: Other Expenses	
High school:	*College:*
live at home	dorm or apartment rent
parents buy food and personal items	we buy food and personal items
books are free	books are expensive!
parents buy other supplies	we buy other supplies

Minh realizes that many of these differences really surprised him as he made the transition from high school to college. He hopes that recording these will help someone else prepare for college more efficiently than he did.

Drafting a Thesis Statement

After deciding on a subject and generating several different ideas to work with, you will be ready to write a thesis statement or statement of purpose for your essay. A thesis for a visual project may not be as immediately apparent as one for an essay, but it will still guide you to a coherent assignment.

Minh's purpose is to help other high school students understand more clearly the transition from high school to college. Here is his thesis:

Although some similarities exist between college and high school, college students are faced with a whole new set of problems and responsibilities that high school students never experience.

This statement will now provide focus and direction for the remainder of Minh's assignment.

Producing a Draft

All these preliminary decisions will prepare you to write a well-developed comparison/contrast essay.

- Your **introduction** should introduce your subjects and make your purpose clear in a thesis statement.
- The **body of your paper** explains each point with sufficient details.
- Your **conclusion** summarizes your points and draws some relevant conclusions.

Writing the Introduction The introduction of your comparison/contrast essay should (1) clearly identify your subjects, (2) explain the basis of your comparison/contrast, and (3) state your purpose and the overall limits of your particular study. Since you cannot cover all the reasons for your preference in one short essay, you must limit your subject to three or four basic points. The introduction is the place to make all these limits clear.

Organizing the Body of the Essay You can organize the body of your paper in one of four ways. The two most popular methods of organization are (1) a point-by-point, or alternating, comparison and (2) a subject-by-subject, or divided, comparison.

Although these are the two main methods of organizing a comparison/contrast essay, two other possibilities include (3) a combination of these two methods or (4) a division between the similarities and differences.

When choosing a method of organization for a comparison/contrast essay, you need to find the pattern that best suits your purpose. If you want single items to stand out in a discussion, for instance, the best choice is the point-by-point system; it is especially appropriate for long essays, but has a tendency to turn into an exercise in listing if you don't pay careful attention to your transitions. If, however, the subjects themselves (rather than the itemized points) are the most interesting feature of your essay, you should use the

1. Point by Point

MPG
Car A
Car B

HANDLING
Car A
Car B

SPECIAL EQUIPMENT
Car A
Car B

2. Subject by Subject

CAR A
MPG
Handling
Special Equipment

CAR B
MPG
Handling
Special Equipment

subject-by-subject comparison; this system is particularly good for short essays in which readers can retain what was said about one subject while they read about a second subject. You must also remember, if you choose this second method of organization, that the second (or last) subject should be in the most emphatic position because that is what your readers will remember most clearly.

The final two options for organizing a comparison/contrast essay (#3 and #4) give you some built-in flexibility so you can create emphasis and attempt to manipulate reader opinion simply by the structure of your essay.

3. Combination

SPECIAL EQUIPMENT
Car A
Car B
CAR A
MPG
Handling
CAR B
MPG
Handling

4. Similarities/Differences

SIMILARITIES
MPG
Car A
Car B
DIFFERENCES
HANDLING
Car A
Car B
SPECIAL EQUIPMENT
Car A
Car B

Using Analogies One unique form of comparison/contrast is an **analogy**, which is an extended, sustained comparison. Often used to explain something unfamiliar, abstract, or complicated by comparing it to something else that is better known, this rhetorical technique can add excitement to writing.

The process of analogy differs slightly from comparison and contrast in two important ways:

1. Comparison/contrast begins with subjects from the same class and places equal weight on both of them. On the other hand, analogy seldom explores subjects from the same class and focuses on one familiar subject in an attempt to explain another, more complex or unfamiliar one.

2. Comparison/contrast addresses both the similarities and the differences of these subjects. Analogy deals only with similarities, not differences.

A comparison/contrast essay, for example, might study two professional athletes' approaches to coping with arduous workouts by pointing out the differences in their training methods as well as the similarities. An analogy essay might use the notion of getting a root canal to reveal the pain of working out at this level.

Concluding the Essay The conclusion of a comparison/contrast essay summarizes the main points and states the deductions drawn from these points. It brings closure to your essay and reminds the reader of the important elements of your comparison.

All good comparative studies serve a specific purpose. They attempt either to examine their subjects separately or to demonstrate the superiority of one over the other. Whatever the intent, comparison/contrast essays need to be clear and logical and have a precise purpose.

You should now use the following questions, based on the Comparison/ Contrast Essentials, to help focus and refine your written and graphic assignments:

> ## Comparison/Contrast Essentials: Writing
>
> - **Purpose:** What is your purpose?
> - **Points/Subjects to Compare:** What are the main points or topics you are comparing? Why did you choose these particular points?
> - **Examples and Details:** What examples and details do you use to support these points?
> - **Logical Organization:** How do you organize these points?
> - **Summary/Conclusion:** What is your conclusion?

Revising and Editing

Revising and editing your prose or your visual means rereading and changing it so it says exactly what you want it to say. This is also the time to add some well-chosen transitions to your assignment to ensure that the readers understand how your sentences are related.

Revising

Look closely at your essay or graphic as someone else might. Then answer the questions posed in the Revising Checklist on page 28, which will ask you to focus on how your essay actually functions.

This is also the point in the writing process when you should add transitions to your essay that clarify the relationship of your details to one another. If you want to indicate comparisons, use words such as *like, as, also, in like manner, similarly,* and *in addition;* to signal contrasts, try *but, in contrast to, unlike, whereas,* and *on the one hand/on the other hand.* Using logical transitions in your comparison/contrast essays will establish clear relationships between the items in your comparisons and will also move your readers smoothly from one topic to the next.

Editing

Editing is the final phase of your writing process. It involves examining specific words, phrases, sentences, and any visual details to make sure they follow current usage rules. Use the Editing Checklist on page 30 to review your project for errors in grammar and usage. When you locate a potential error, consult a handbook or go to Pearson's Web-based MyCompLab for an explanation of the problem.

Also, if your instructor marks any grammar mistakes on your paper or graphic, make sure you understand them. Recognizing errors in your own writing is the most effective way of correcting them.

As you read the following student essay, refer to the Comparison/Contrast Essentials (page 285) and the questions for reading comparison/contrast (page 286) to help you understand and analyze it. Then, to thoroughly understand how this student essay works, pay special attention to the margin notes and the items in each paragraph they describe.

Minh Hoang

Professor Flachmann

English 101

5 Nov. 2011

High School vs. College

1 After finishing high school, many students believe that college is   ←— Background
a place where they will be able to sleep in, take only classes that interest
them, and enjoy much more freedom in their lives. Those students are
in for a serious shock when they realize that their image of college is not
as realistic as they think. Although some similarities exist between col-   ←— Purpose/Thesis Statement
lege and high school, college students are faced with a whole new set of
problems and responsibilities that high school students never have.

2 One important difference between high school and college   ←— Point 1
is that high school attendance is mandatory, whereas the decision to
pursue higher education is entirely up to the student. Not only must   ←— Explanation
students decide if they will attend college, but they must also choose   ←— Details
a focused area of study for their degree. This can be a difficult decision for many students, especially those who do not have a particular
academic goal in mind.

3 Another major difference between high school and college is   ←— Point 2
the cost. Public high schools are free, while colleges are not. Tuition   ←— Explanation
costs can vary dramatically depending on what type of higher educa-
tion a student chooses. Community colleges are most affordable; State   ←— Details
universities are more expensive than community colleges; private
universities top the list as the most costly. Unless students are receiving
scholarship money, fulfilling financial responsibilities associated with

college can be strenuous and may require a part- or full-time job to offset expenses.

Point 3 →   4 Not only can college tuition be expensive, but students must also pay for a number of other expenses seldom incurred during high

Explanation →   school. Students not living with parents or relatives must pay rent for an apartment or dorm room. They must also pay for their own neces-

Details →   sities like food, transportation, and entertainment. Books are given to you free in high school; in college, they can cost hundreds of dollars per class. Other supplies, like pens, highlighters, and sticky notes, are all items students must have, along with any specialized materials for classes. Because of these extra costs associated with a college edu-cation, students must be willing to make sacrifices in order to stretch their available budget.

Point 4 →   5 College students must not only make sacrifices and take on more responsibilities than high school students, but they must also

Explanation →   be accountable for their own actions. Students no longer have someone to make sure they do their homework or get up on time

Details →   for class. Many new university students squander their new-found freedoms by failing to attend class or turn in assignments on time. Personal accountability is another duty that college students must be more aware of than high school students.

Summary →   6 In college, students have more liberties than they did in high school. But along with these freedoms come much greater obliga-

Concluding Statement →   tions than in high school. As long as students are prepared to take on the necessary responsibilities associated with a successful college career, they can go far in their education.

Reviewing Comparison and Contrast

Based on the information you have learned in this chapter and the annota-tions on the student essay, show how this essay works by writing a clear, precise summary or by drawing your own outline or graphic representation of it. Label the topics on your visual. This exercise will confirm your understanding of the ele-ments of comparison and contrast in both reading and writing.

Grandma

by Erma Bombeck

Erma Bombeck was an American humorist who dazzled readers with a newspaper column spanning more than three decades, from 1965 to 1996. Famous for such quotations as "Insanity is hereditary. You can catch it from your kids," she also wrote a number of popular books, including *I Lost Everything in the Post-Nasal Depression*, *The Grass Is Always Greener Over the Septic Tank*, and *If Life Is a Bowl of Cherries, What Am I Doing in the Pits?*

1   The role of a grandmother has never been really defined. Some sit in rockers, some sky dive, some have careers. Others clean ovens. Some have white hair. Others wear wigs. Some see their grandchildren once a day (and it's not enough). Others, once a year (and that's too much).

2   Once I conducted an interesting survey among a group of eight-year-olds on grandmas. I asked them three questions. One, what is a grandmother? Two, what does she do? And three, what is the difference between a grandmother and a mother?

3   To the first question, the answers were rather predictable. "She's old (about eighty), helps around the house, is nice and kind, and is Mother's mother or Father's mother, depending on the one who is around the most."

4   To the second question, the answers again were rather obvious. Most of them noted grandmothers knit, do dishes, clean the bathroom, make good pies; and a goodly number reveled in the fact that Grandma polished their shoes for them.

5   It was the third question that stimulated the most reaction from them. Here is their composite of the differences between a mother and a grandmother. "Grandma has gray hair, lives alone, takes me places, and lets me go into her attic. She can't swim. Grandma doesn't spank you and stops Mother when she does. Mothers scold better and more. Mothers are married. Grandmas aren't.

6   "Grandma goes to work and my mother doesn't do anything. Mom gives me shots, but Grandma gives me frogs. Grandma lives far away. A mother you're born from. A grandmother gets married to a grandfather first, a mother to a father last.

7   "Grandma always says, 'Stay in, it's cold outside,' and my mother says, 'Go out, it's good for you.'"

8   And here's the clincher. Out of thirty-nine children queried, a total of thirty-three associated the word "love" with Grandma. One summed up the total very well with, "Grandma loves me all the time."

9   Actually this doesn't surprise me one small bit. On rare occasions when I have had my mother baby-sit for me, it often takes a snake whip and a chair to restore discipline when I get them home.

10   "Grandma sure is a neat sitter," they yawn openly at the breakfast table. "We had pizza and cola and caramel popcorn. Then we watched Lola Brooklynbridgida on the late show. After that we played Monopoly till you came home. She said when you were a kid you never went to bed. One night you even heard them play 'The Star-Spangled Banner' before the station went off."

> *It often takes a snake whip and a chair to restore discipline when I get them home*

11   "Did Grandma tell you I was twenty-eight at the time?" I snapped.

12   "Grandma said twenty-five cents a week isn't very much money for an allowance. She said we could make more by running away and joining the Peace Corps. She said you used to blow that much a week on jawbreakers."

13   "Well, actually," I said grimacing, "Grandma's memory isn't as good as it used to be. She was quite strict, and as I recall my income was more like ten cents a week, and I bought all my own school clothes with it."

14   "Grandma sure is neat all right. She told us you hid our skateboard behind the hats in your closet. She said that was dirty pool. What's dirty pool, Mama?"

15   "It's Grandma telling her grandchildren where their mother hid the skateboard."

16   "Mama did you really give a live chicken to one of your teachers on class day? And did you really play barbershop once and cut off Aunt Thelma's hair for real? Boy, you're neat!" They looked at me in a way I had never seen before.

17   Naturally I brought Mother to task for her indiscretion. "Grandma," I said, "you have a forked tongue and a rotten memory. You've got my kids believing I'm 'neat.' Now I ask you, what kind of an image is that for a mother?"

18   "The same image your grandmother gave me," she said.

19   Then I remembered Grandma. What a character.

20   In fact, I never see a Japanese war picture depicting kamikaze pilots standing erect in their helmets and goggles, their white scarves flying behind them, toasting their last hour on earth with a glass of sake that I don't think of riding to town with my grandma on Saturdays.

21   We would climb into her red and yellow Chevy coupe and jerk in first gear over to the streetcar loop, where Grandma would take her place in line between the trolley cars. Due to the rigorous concentration it took to stay on the tracks and the innumerable stops we had to make, conversation was kept to a minimum. A few times a rattled shopper would tap on the window for entrance, to which Grandma would shout angrily, "If I wanted passengers, I'd dingle a bell!"

clincher: deciding factor
indiscretion: error, mistake

22   Once, when I dared to ask why we didn't travel in the same flow of traffic as the other cars, Grandma shot back, "Laws, child, you could get killed out there." Our first stop in town was always a tire center. I could never figure this out. We'd park in the "For Customers Only" lot, and Grandma would walk through the cool building. She'd kick a few tires, but she never purchased one. One day she explained, "The day I gain a new tire is the day I lose the best free parking spot a woman ever had."

23   I don't have Grandma's guts in the traffic or her cunning. But I thought about her the other day as I sat bumper to bumper in the hot downtown traffic. "Hey, lady," yelled a voice from the next car, "wanta get in our pool? Only cost a quarter. We're putting odds on the exact minute your radiator is going to blow. You can have your choice of two minutes or fifteen seconds." Boy, Grandma would have shut his sassy mouth in a hurry.

In Case of Fire, Throw This in First

24   We had an understanding, Grandma and I. She didn't treat me like a child, and I didn't treat her like a mother. We played the game by rules. If I didn't slam her doors and sass, then she didn't spank and lecture me. Grandma treated me like a person already grown up.

25   She let me bake cookies with dirty hands . . . pound on the piano just because I wanted to . . . pick the tomatoes when they were green . . . use her clothespins to dig in the yard . . . pick her flowers to make a necklace chain. Grandma lived in a "fun" house. The rooms were so big you could skate in them. There were a hundred thousand steps to play upon, a big eave that invited cool summer breezes and where you could remain "lost" for hours. And around it all was a black, iron fence.

26   I liked Grandma the best, though, when she told me about my mama, because it was a part of Mama I had never seen or been close to. I didn't know that when Mama was a little girl a photographer came one day to take a picture of her and her sister in a pony cart. I couldn't imagine they had to bribe them into good behavior by giving them each a coin. In the picture Mama is crying and biting her coin in half. It was a dime, and she wanted the bigger coin—the nickel—given to her sister. Somehow, I thought Mama was born knowing the difference between a nickel and a dime.

27   Grandma told me Mama was once caught by the principal for writing in the front of her book, "In Case of Fire, Throw This in First." I had never had so much respect for Mama as the day I heard this.

28   From Grandma I learned that Mama had been a child and had traveled the same route I was traveling now. I thought Mom was "neat." (And what kind of an image is that for a mother?)

29   If I had it to do all over again, I would never return to Grandma's house after she had left it. No one should. For that grand, spacious house tended to shrink with the years. Those wonderful steps that I played upon for hours were broken down and rather pathetic. There was a sadness to the tangled vines, the peeling paint, and the iron fence that listed under the burden of time. The big eave was an architectural "elephant" and would mercifully crumble under the ax of urban renewal.

IN CONTEXT

Famous Grandmas

cunning: cleverness

30   Grandmas defy description. They really do. They occupy such a unique place in the life of a child. They can shed the yoke of responsibility, relax, and enjoy their grandchildren in a way that was not possible when they were raising their own children. And they can glow in the realization that here is their seed of life that will harvest generations to come.

defy: resist, refuse
yoke: bond, tie

CONVERSATIONS: Collaborating in Class or Online

1. What questions about grandmothers did Bombeck ask in her survey?
2. Summarize the answers to Bombeck's first two questions.
3. What were the children's answers to question 3?
4. What agreement did the author have with her own grandma?

CONNECTIONS: Discovering Relationships among Ideas

5. Why didn't the author want her children to perceive her as "neat"? What changed her mind?
6. What triggers Bombeck's memories of her own grandma?
7. Why did Bombeck like the stories her grandmother told her about her mother?
8. Why does the author find a sadness in her grandma's house after she left it?

PRESENTATION: Analyzing the Writer's Craft

9. What is the author's purpose in this essay?
10. Who is her intended audience?
11. Choose one adjective to label the tone of this essay. In what ways do some of the dated references contribute to this tone?
12. How does the dialogue between Bombeck and her mother further her comparison? In other words, what does it add to her essay?

PROJECTS: Expressing Your Own Views

13. **Podcast:** Create a podcast that reveals the similarities and differences between two of your family members.

14. **Photo:** Take a photo that captures the similarities or differences between two of your friends. Then write a caption for the photo.

15. **Essay:** Using this essay as a model, write an essay about your grandfather.

16. **Research:** Read and summarize the three resources below. Generate one specific question from each resource that focuses on comparison/contrast. Then answer one of your questions in a documented essay, consulting these and other sources as necessary.

OTHER RESOURCES

 Web Site

Grandparents.com: www. grandparents.com

Academic Article

"Dimensions of Grandparent-Adult Grandchild Relationships: From Family Ties to Intergenerational Friendships"

by Candace L. Kemp

Canadian Journal on Aging 24.2 (2005): 161–177

 Audio/Video

Vision: Insights and New Horizons: www.vision.org

Search: "Rent-a-Granny"

Click on the Video link

ONE LAST THOUGHT

Anna Mary Robertson Moses, better known as Grandma Moses, began a painting career in her seventies when she ran out of wallpaper while lining her parlor. To finish the room, she put up white paper and painted a rural scene. That was her first painting, known as the *Fireboard*, and it now hangs in the Bennington Museum in Vermont. Since then, her art has been widely respected and publicized. She is often cited as an example of a person who began a career later in life. Can you think of other people who became famous late in their lives?

Social Networking

by Mike Keefe

Mike Keefe has been an editorial cartoonist for the *Denver Post* since 1975. He recalls "being drawn to Richard Nixon's nose" during the Watergate crisis, after which he "came out of the closet" and became a full-time cartoonist. A frequent contributor to *USA Today*, he is also co-creator of two nationally syndicated cartoon strips, *Cooper* and *Iota*. His many books include *Running Awry*, *Keefe-Kebab*, and *The Ten-Speed Commandments*.

PREREADING QUESTIONS

Do you participate in a social networking site? Which one(s)?

Why do you enjoy this site?

What role does social networking play in your life?

CONVERSATIONS: Collaborating in Class or Online

1. What is the comparison in this cartoon?
2. What are the similarities between the two drawings?
3. What are the main differences?
4. What are some of the electronic devices depicted in this cartoon?

CONNECTIONS: Discovering Relationships among Ideas

5. What is funny about this cartoon?
6. What happened to the fire between the first and second drawings?
7. What is different about the people in these two pictures?
8. In what ways have our methods of communication changed over time?

PRESENTATION: Analyzing the Writer's Craft

9. What is Keefe's purpose in this cartoon?
10. Is this the best format for making his statement?
11. Who do you think is his intended audience?
12. Describe the tone of this cartoon in a single word.

PROJECTS: Expressing Your Own Views

13. **Ad:** Design an ad promoting your favorite social networking site.
14. **Collage:** Create a collage that makes a specific statement about social networking. Exchange collages and see if you can figure out a classmate's purpose.
15. **Essay:** Write an essay comparing and contrasting two social networking sites.
16. **Research:** Read and summarize the three resources below. Generate one specific question from each resource that focuses on comparison/contrast. Then answer one of your questions in a documented essay, consulting these and other sources as necessary.

OTHER RESOURCES

Web Site

Technolog: technolog.msnbc.msn.com

Search: "The Juiciest Gadget Rumors of CES 2011"

Academic Article

"Networks and New Media" by Jeff Rice

College English 69.2 (2006): 127–133

Audio/Video

Common Craft: www.commoncraft.com/

Search: "Social Networking in Plain English." Click on the Video link

ONE LAST THOUGHT

What if historical event had Facebook statuses? Visit http://cool-material.com/roundup/if-historical-events-had-facebook-statuses/, and view other humorous posts. Can you think of any other historical events that could have funny Facebook posts? What would the comments be?

Indecent Exposure

by Carla Power

A journalist specializing in religion, Muslim societies, global issues, and world culture, **Carla Power** has written stories for *Time*, *Newsweek*, *The New York Times*, *Vogue*, *Glamour*, *Foreign Policy Magazine*, and many other prominent periodicals. She is currently writing a book on the global Muslim women's movement.

PREREADING QUESTIONS

Have you ever visited another country? Which one(s)?

What were some similarities and differences between that country and the U.S. or between two cities you have visited (if you haven't been to another country)?

Which location did you like the best? Why?

1   Reams have been written on the differences between Islamic and Western societies, but for sheer pithiness, it's hard to beat a quip by my former colleague, a Pakistani scholar of Islamic studies. I'd strolled into his office one day to find him on the floor, at prayer. I left, shutting his door, mortified. Later he cheerfully batted my apologies away. "That's the big difference between us," he said with a shrug. "You Westerners make love in public and pray in private. We Muslims do exactly the reverse."

2   At the nub of debates over Muslim integration in the West lies the question, What's decent to do in public—display your sexuality or your faith? The French have no problem with bare breasts on billboards and TV but big problems with hijab-covered heads in public schools and government offices. Many Muslims feel just the opposite. As my friend suggested, Westerners believe that prayer is something best done in private, a matter for individual souls rather than state institutions. In the Islamic world, religion is out of the closet: on the streets, chanted five times daily from minarets, enshrined in constitutions, party platforms, and penal codes. Sexual matters are kept discreet.

3   Just how much so has become clear in recent weeks, with news of concerns for the safety of an Afghan child actor in the soon-to-be-released movie based on the best-selling novel *The Kite Runner*. Family members of Ahmad Khan Mahmidzada, whose character is raped, fear that the film will expose them to reprisals. In Afghan tribal society, sexual violation—even its portrayal in a fictional movie—can lead to dishonor, ostracism, or worse. Mahmidzada's

pithiness: briefness
quip: joke, pun
minarets: mosque towers
enshrined: preserved
reprisals: retaliations
ostracism: exclusion

IN CONTEXT

The Kite Runner

Khaled Hosseini's novel *The Kite Runner* was published in 2003. It follows two Afghani boys, Amir and Hassad, as they grow into young men. The book has been widely popular since its publication, but also criticized for its graphic language. It was made into a movie of the same title in 2007.

father told the BBC that members of his tribe "may cut my throat, they may kill me, torture me." The filmmakers, he claims, initially said they wouldn't film the rape scene. Producers deny misleading the actor and his family. The offending scene is tastefully portrayed, they say, and crucial to the plot. Still, Paramount Vantage, the film's distributor, is taking the security fears seriously. Having dispatched a retired CIA operative to Afghanistan to assess the dangers, it decided to delay the film's U.S. release by six weeks, allowing time to evacuate its child stars to the United Arab Emirates.

4 The West traditionally reveres free speech, with both sublime and ridiculous results. As *The Kite Runner's* producers hinted, it's crucial for art. It's also the backbone of ideals like democracy and human rights, as well as the protector of rather more tawdry material like reality TV and Internet porn. We reward those who reveal their private lives. When Oprah Winfrey spoke of her childhood sexual abuse, she became a goddess in a society convinced that it's good to talk. While thousands of courageous Muslims regularly speak out on taboo subjects, the reception is often not so warm. Five years ago, Mukhtar Mai, a Pakistani gang-rape victim, defied tribal custom by taking her rapists to court. In the West, she won plaudits and prizes, but in Pakistan, her legal struggle against her accused rapists continues, and she has been widely denounced as having shamed her country abroad.

5 So here is a sweeping generalization, but perhaps a useful one: Western societies are cultures of personal revelation and exposure, while Muslim cultures are traditionally structured around protecting honor and propriety. On our shrunken planet, the two codes bump up against each other, throwing the other into relief. The same era that's given us Big Brother and a cyber video of Paris Hilton *in flagrante* has also produced a striking rise of Western Muslims taking up the veil. The more of private life that Western pop culture reveals, the more that Muslim women decide to conceal. And the differences between the culture of exposure and the culture of propriety go far beyond sex and sartorial choices.

> *Muslim cultures are traditionally structured around protecting honor and propriety*

6 One of my first journalistic assignments came from an American women's magazine. During a 1994 U.N. population conference in Cairo, CNN had aired footage of the backstreet female genital mutilation of a 10-year-old Egyptian girl. Egypt's conservatives claimed that CNN and the girl's family had shamed Egypt on the world stage. A year on, I was asked to find the girl and do an update. But after a few phone calls in Cairo, I begged off the assignment: the girl was in hiding, fearing reprisals. My editors in New York assumed she'd want to "tell her story." But interviewing the girl again, I had to explain, could bring as much shame and danger as the circumcision knife.

BBC: British Broadcast Company
tawdry: cheap, tasteless
plaudits: praise
propriety: politeness
in flagrante: immoral, scandalous
sartorial: clothing, wardrobe

IN CONTEXT

Ramadan

Visit www.america.gov and search "Multicultural Ramadan" to read four young muslims' accounts of Ramadan, the Islamic month of fasting.

7   Of course, the two worlds can meet. Afghan Shah Muhammad Rais claimed that his betrayal as a domestic tyrant in the global best-seller *The Bookseller of Kabul*, by Norwegian journalist Asne Seierstad, exposed him to dishonor. So Rais did a very Western thing, launching a lawsuit against Seierstad for defamation in Norway. Then he went one better: Rais now has a deal with a Norwegian publisher for a book of his own. A spot on Oprah has to be next.

CONVERSATIONS: Collaborating in Class or Online

1. List some of the principal differences between Islamic and Western cultures.
2. How can you summarize these differences?
3. How are Muslims judged on their actions in American movies? Give an example from the essay.
4. What does Power mean when she says, "Western societies are cultures of personal revelation and exposure, while Muslim cultures are traditionally structured around protecting honor and propriety" (para. 5)?

CONNECTIONS: Discovering Relationships among Ideas

5. How is the concept of free speech construed in both Islamic and Western societies?
6. On what common ground does Power say these two cultures can meet? Give an example from the essay.
7. Are the sweeping generalizations that Power makes justified or not? Explain your answer in detail.
8. What do the references to film and other forms of media add to the essay?

PRESENTATION: Analyzing the Writer's Craft

9. What is Power's purpose in this essay?
10. Who do you think is her intended audience? What makes you think so?
11. Is an essay the best format for making her point? Why or why not?
12. Explain the title of this essay.

PROJECTS: Expressing Your Own Views

13. **Interview:** Interview someone from another country. Write up your interview, adding an introduction and conclusion based on your observations.

14. **List:** Make a list of characteristics you consider typically American. Then write a paragraph introducing your list.

15. **Essay:** Write an essay comparing and contrasting two locations that you know well. Reveal your preferences at each location through your essay.

16. **Research:** Read and summarize the three resources below. Generate one specific question from each resource that focuses on comparison/contrast. Then answer one of your questions in a documented essay, consulting these and other sources as necessary.

OTHER RESOURCES

 Web Site

Esse Quam Videri: Muslim Self Portraits: www. muslimselfportrait.info/

Click on Portraits

Academic Article

"Selling American Diversity and Muslim American Identity through Nonprofit Advertising Post 9/11"

by Evelyn Alsultany

American Quarterly 59.3 (2007): 593–622

 Audio/Video

National Public Radio: www.npr.org

Search: "The Inner Journey of Young Muslims in America"

Click on the Audio link

ONE LAST THOUGHT

Culture clash is a popular theme in modern film. Can you think of any other movies that highlight cultural differences?

Motion Gaming Review: Kinect Vs. Nintendo Wii Vs. Playstation

by Robert Workman

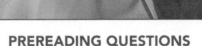

Robert Workman describes himself as a "Lover. Fighter. Gamer. Xbox ambassador. Drunk. Game-playbook.com chief. Beer enthusiast. Freelance extraordinaire. And Co-host of The Lost Levels podcast." Author of the "DCD Twitter Feed," he has written recent posts on Play Station, Sonic Adventure, and other topics of interest to game players. He wrote this article about the latest choices in motion gaming in 2010.

PREREADING QUESTIONS

Have you ever played any electronic games? Which one(s)?

What do you like about electronic games?

What do you dislike about them?

1   The Electronic Entertainment Expo (E3) has come and gone once more, but this year [2010] brought a bigger emphasis on motion-sensitive gaming than ever before. You couldn't walk five paces on the floor without running into some variation of a dancing, sporting, or racing game that required hand, foot, and body movements. That's not to say it's a bad thing, unless you're a player who's not in the greatest of shape.

2   Having been on the market for more than three years now, the Nintendo Wii is an old favorite. But with Sony gearing up to enter the market with its PlayStation Move, and Microsoft readying the Kinect (formerly known as Project Natal), consumers will soon be faced with some interesting new choices.

3   So which one is best? TechNewsDaily breaks down the positives and negatives of each. Let's start with the one that's already out. . . .

Nintendo Wii

4   Nintendo released its Wii console in late 2006, just in time for the holiday rush. It utilizes motions based on player movements to interact with characters on-screen. Some are simpler than others, depending on what the on-screen character needs to do. The system sold tremendously well in its first year, to the point that availability was bleak until Nintendo was able to catch up in manufacturing. It comes packaged with a Wii remote and analog-based Nunchuk controller, which can be connected together for dual-hand play on specific titles. It also comes packaged with a sports-oriented game called "Wii Sports," which is still the pack-in for today's black Wii console (along with Wii Sports Resort and a WiiMotion Plus accessory, which reads motion activity even more accurately than before).

"I'm sorry but we don't have athletic scholarships for video games."

www.CartoonStock.com

Ron Morgan

Positives

5   **Controllers are easy to use for all ages**—Both the Nunchuk and Wii remote are fairly simple to use. There are times you'll need to perform calibration actions or make adjustments with the Motion Bar that's packaged with the system, but it's a cinch—for adults or kids—to hook up the system, plug in your controller, sync it to your unit (two simple button presses), and get to playing.

6   **Some outstanding games**—Nintendo doesn't disappoint when it comes to creating spellbinding games, as you could probably figure out from its previous console releases. The Wii has a number of great first-party titles, including "Super Mario Galaxy 2," "Mario Kart Wii," and "Metroid Prime Trilogy." The holiday season will bring even more addictive new titles to stores, including "Goldeneye 007" (a favorite on the Nintendo 64) and "Donkey Kong Country Returns." If $50 a pop is too pricey for you, downloadable games are also available through the Wii Shop Channel for $5-$10 a game. Some of them, particularly "Cave Story" and "Excitebike," simply can't be beat.

7   **The cost is a little better**—While the Kinect accessory for the Xbox 360 will go for a whopping $149.99 and the Move accessory for the PlayStation 3 will set you back around $100 or so (after everything's bought), Nintendo has everything you need for a mere $200. That price includes the console, a controller and Nunchuk, accessories, and two hit games—Wii Sports and Wii Sports Resort.

Granted, buying extra controllers is not cheap ($40 per remote and $20 per Nunchuk), but most games allow you to pass the controller around, like the Sports games and Super Mario Galaxy 2.

Negatives

8   **Too many lackluster games**—When you have a "hot system" on your hands, developers will really make anything for it that will sell in a hurry. This usually results in a lot of shovelware, games that are better left on the shelves. The Wii is the biggest recipient of bad games to date, surpassing the PS2's stinky library with lackluster efforts from Zoo Games, Conspiracy Entertainment, and other studios. There are great games to purchase out there, but be on the lookout, because bad ones are just as easy to stumble upon.

9   **Online play is questionable**—While we applaud Nintendo for incorporating online play into some of its bigger games (including "Mario Kart Wii" and "Super Smash Bros. Brawl"), getting into a match is half the battle. You constantly have to register Friend Codes in order to add your friends to a list, a 12-digit combination that can take some time to enter. It's a lot harder than entering a simple name like you could on the PlayStation Network or Xbox Live. You can go into random matches, but to some people, racing against strangers isn't as much fun as going up against friends.

10   **The WiiMotion Plus should've come out in 2006**—The Wii remote reads movement pretty well, but it's not perfect. We've run into a number of games that didn't read your actions precisely enough, resulting in falling off a race track or performing a specific thing the wrong way. The WiiMotion Plus, a plug-in device that goes into the back of your Wii remote, improves sensitivity significantly, but you need to pay extra for it (whether it's bundled with a game or sold separately). Furthermore, Nintendo should've perfected the technology beforehand, when the system was still fresh in 2006.

---

calibration: lining up, marking
cinch: easy
lackluster: uninspiring, dull

Microsoft Kinect

11   Introduced officially this past week at the E3, the Kinect is a sleekly designed motion bar that plugs into your Xbox 360 console. It's compatible with the new slimmer Xbox 360 model, as well as older Xbox 360 units. Instead of utilizing controllers for on-screen movement, it actually reads your body with its sensor, so you are basically acting as the controller. Two players can take part in games at once, playing competitively in sports games or working together in unison to control a raft. The device is currently set for release Nov. 4 for $149.99, although a game library isn't yet fully confirmed (should be soon).

Using your body to play a video game without holding onto anything?

Positives

12   **No more sore hands from holding a controller**—Using your body to play a video game without holding onto anything? Unheard of. And yet, here's Kinect, enabling you to do just that. We have to admit, it was pretty nice being able to play a game without having to grip tightly to a controller. You can let your body do the work through such games as EA Sports Active 2 and Sonic Free Riders, without having to worry about pounding on buttons and hurting your thumbs. You'll still want to make sure you have plenty of space so you don't trip over yourself. Solve that problem and you'll love this new approach.

13   **The menu system is futuristic and cool**—Using a new touch-based menu system, Kinect changes the way you use your Xbox 360. That may be a good or bad thing, depending on how well you take to it. However, we finally get to interact with a device doing the same exact thing that Tom Cruise did in "Minority Report"—by grabbing and dragging. It may not be the flying cars we wanted, but it's still pretty.

14   **Some of the games look spiffy**—Okay, so the game library of dance titles and workout routines may not impress us, but some of the other original games coming out for the Kinect certainly do. "Child of Eden" is a mesmerizing shooting experience where your hands are the cursors, and you obliterate objects to a musical beat. "Kinect Joy Ride" looks like a ton of fun with its racing action, and "Your Shape: Fitness Evolved" tricks you into thinking that exercise is fun. Bring it.

Negatives

15   **The price**—$149.99 is a steep price to pay for a gaming device, especially considering that the console isn't included.

16   **Not all the games are winners**—Even though the Kinect will have a variety of games to choose from this holiday season, that doesn't mean they'll all be successful. When we played "Deca Sports Freedom" from Hudson Soft, for example, our movements could barely be read, even though we did exactly what it told us several times. Furthermore, titles like "Kinectimals" (a virtual pet simulator) and "Michael Jackson: The Game" look incredibly dorky, aimed more at the kiddie-teen market than the "hardcore" crowd that Microsoft usually goes for with the Xbox 360.

PlayStation Move

17   Introduced at the Game Developers Conference back in March of this year, Sony finally unveiled retail plans for the gaming controllers at E3. It's set for release on Sept. 19 [2010] in the U.S., with the motion controller set to go for $50 and a secondary navigation controller going for $40. You'll need a PS3 Eye camera as well, although you can score a bundle with the regular controller, camera, and "Sports Champions" game for $100. The Move controller, which has a glowing ping-pong-ball-attachment at one end, reads your motions via the camera and executes actions on-screen. Sony is also working to incorporate Move features in forthcoming games, including "LittleBigPlanet 2" and "The Sly Cooper Collection."

PlayStation 3 system, a regular DualShock 3 controller, the Move controller set-up, and a possible pack-in game, such as "LittleBigPlanet 2," for around $350. Considering the Xbox 360 and Kinect will set you back that same price, that's not too shabby a deal. (Sadly, it has yet to be confirmed.)

Positives

18   **Some of the games have hardcore appeal in mind**—Unlike the Kinect with its family friendly approach, Sony is going the more hardcore route with its PlayStation Move. Even though some games will appeal to all ages (like the hero-centric "Heroes On the Move" and "Sorcery"), others should draw in older gamers, such as "Time Crisis: Razing Storm" and "Killzone 3." There's something here for everyone, really.

19   **The PlayStation Move controller reads efficiently**—Unlike the questionable connectivity with some Kinect titles, the PlayStation Move seems to read well enough with the games we tried. From bowling with "Brunswick Pro Bowling" to taking care of our EyePet to taking out enemy robots in "The Shoot," we found little problem reacting to what was happening on-screen using movements.

20   **Multiple packages to choose from**—Whether you want to buy the controller by itself or in a package bundle, there are multiple options to choose from when it comes to picking up the PlayStation Move. If that isn't enough, Sony is also talking about introducing a new bundle specifically made with the Move in mind, including a 250 GB

Negatives

21   **There's a lot to set up**—Where the Kinect is one single unit and the Wii only has a couple of things to put in place, the PlayStation Move requires several components. You'll need the PS3 system, the Move controller, the Navigational controller, the PS3 Eye, and the proper software to read whatever you're doing. Based on what we've seen, it will take the longest to put into play.

22   **The ping-pong ball thing is dorky**—Although it does help read your movements, we feel a little out of place using a controller that looks like a high-tech ping pong paddle. With a multi-colored ball attached to the end of it, it almost feels as if you're conducting with a high-tech lollipop. Some of you will have no problem getting used to that, but others will feel a little out of place, as if you're holding a karaoke microphone. And trust us when we say that some people do not like that feeling.

23   **Some features take time to access**—Even though the PlayStation Move controller feels comfortable and is mostly easy to use, it'll take some time to get used to its numerous functions. The first few times we gripped it, it took a while to handle the randomly placed Home button and the on-top multi-shape buttons. Syncing it up with the navigational controller takes a few extra seconds as well—and, again, at a party, that's not the greatest thing in the world. It works, but you'll need a little patience to get through it.

CONVERSATIONS: Collaborating in Class or Online

1. Which three games is Workman evaluating in this blog?
2. What is the basis of his comparison?
3. What points does Workman compare for each subject?
4. In your opinion, what is the most striking positive and negative fact about each game?

CONNECTIONS: Discovering Relationships among Ideas

5. How important is gaming in American society?
6. Why do you think the author stresses the motion sensor feature on this blog entry?
7. Which product do you think the author prefers? What details bring you to this conclusion?
8. Which of these three products would most fully suit your needs? Explain your answer.

PRESENTATION: Analyzing the Writer's Craft

9. What is Workman's purpose in this blog?
10. Who do you think is his intended audience?
11. Is a blog the best format for this review?
12. Explain the author's principle of organization in this blog entry?

PROJECTS: Expressing Your Own Views

13. **Blog:** Write a response to the conversation on this blog: www.technewsdaily.com/motion-gaming-review-kinect-vs-nintendo-wii-vs-playstation-0741/. Then print it and bring it to class.
14. **Game:** Write a proposal for a game that could be adapted to one of the formats explained in this blog.
15. **Essay:** In a well-developed essay, compare two pastimes that you enjoy. Write a balanced comparison, but let your examples and details reveal which one you prefer.
16. **Research:** Read and summarize the three resources below. Generate one specific question from each resource that focuses on comparison/contrast. Then answer one of your questions in a documented essay, consulting these and other sources as necessary.

OTHER RESOURCES

Web Site

Entertainment Software Review Board: www.esrb.org/index-js.jsp

Academic Article

"Video Games and the Future of Learning"

by David Williamson Shaffer, Kurt R. Squire, Richard Halverson, and James P. Gee

The Phi Delta Kappan 87.2 (2005): 104–111

 Audio/Video

Tech News Daily: www.technewsdaily.com

Search: "Video: E3 2010: In Focus with Kinect"

Click on the link and watch the video

ONE LAST THOUGHT

Released in the U.S. in 1972, the Magnavox Odyssey was the first home video game system. Since then, the gaming industry has seen a decline in arcade-style games and an increase in home systems. With games like "Pong," "Pac-Man," and "Super Mario Bros," the Atari 2600 (released in 1977) and the Nintendo Entertainment System (released in 1983) were major retail successes. How much do you know about these classic games? Have you ever played any of them?

Sex, Lies, and Conversation

by Deborah Tannen

A professor of linguistics and interpersonal communication at Georgetown University, **Deborah Tannen** is best known for several books written for general audiences about the differences in the ways men and women communicate with each other: *You Just Don't Understand*, *That's Not What I Meant*, *Talking from 9 to 5*, *I Only Say This Because I Love You*, and *You're Wearing THAT?*

PREREADING QUESTIONS

Do you process information in a different way than your friends of the opposite sex do?

How do you communicate differently from these friends?

How aware are you and your friends of these differences?

1   I was addressing a small gathering in a suburban Virginia living room—a women's group that had invited men to join them. Throughout the evening, one man had been particularly talkative, frequently offering ideas and anecdotes, while his wife sat silently beside him on the couch. Toward the end of the evening, I commented that women frequently complain that their husbands don't talk to them. This man quickly concurred. He gestured toward his wife and said, "She's the talker in our family." The room burst into laughter; the man looked puzzled and hurt. "It's true," he explained. "When I come home from work I have nothing to say. If she didn't keep the conversation going, we'd spend the whole evening in silence."

2   This episode crystallizes the irony that although American men tend to talk more than women in public situations, they often talk less at home. And this pattern is wreaking havoc with marriage.

3   The pattern was observed by political scientist Andrew Hacker in the late '70s. Sociologist Catherine Kohler Riessman reports in her new book "Divorce Talk" that most of the women she interviewed—but only a few of the men—gave lack of communication as the reason for their divorces. Given the current divorce rate of nearly 50 percent, that amounts to millions of cases in the United States every year—a virtual epidemic of failed conversation.

4   In my own research, complaints from women about their husbands most often focused not on tangible inequities such as having given up the chance for a career to accompany a husband to his or doing far more than their share of daily life-support work like cleaning, cooking, social

anecdotes: stories
concurred: agreed
tangible: touchable

arrangements and errands. Instead, they focused on communication: "He doesn't listen to me," "He doesn't talk to me." I found, as Hacker observed years before, that most wives want their husbands to be, first and foremost, conversational partners, but few husbands share this expectation of their wives.

5   In short, the image that best represents the current crisis is the stereotypical cartoon scene of a man sitting at the breakfast table with a newspaper held up in front of his face, while a woman glares at the back of it, wanting to talk.

Linguistic Battle of the Sexes

6   How can women and men have such different impressions of communication in marriage? Why the widespread imbalance in their interests and expectations?

7   In the April issue of *American Psychologist*, Stanford University's Eleanor Maccoby reports the results of her own and others' research showing that children's development is most influenced by the social structure of peer interactions. Boys and girls tend to play with children of their own gender, and their sex-separate groups have different organizational structures and interactive norms.

8   I believe these systematic differences in childhood socialization make talk between women and men like cross-cultural communication, heir to all the attraction and pitfalls of that enticing but difficult enterprise. My research on men's and women's conversations uncovered patterns similar to those described for children's groups.

9   For women, as for girls, intimacy is the fabric of relationships, and talk is the thread from which it is woven. Little girls create and maintain

friendships by exchanging secrets; similarly, women regard conversation as the cornerstone of friendship. So a woman expects her husband to be a new and improved version of a best friend. What is important is not the individual subjects that are discussed but the sense of closeness, of a life shared, that emerges when people tell their thoughts, feelings, and impressions.

10   Bonds between boys can be as intense as girls', but they are based less on talking, more on doing things together. Since they don't assume talk is the cement that binds a relationship, men don't know what kind of talk women want, and they don't miss it when it isn't there.

> *Men don't know what kind of talk women want*

11   Boys' groups are larger, more inclusive, and more hierarchical, so boys must struggle to avoid the subordinate position in the group. This may play a role in women's complaints that men don't listen to them. Some men really don't like to listen, because being the listener makes them feel one-down, like a child listening to adults or an employee to a boss.

12   But often when women tell men, "You aren't listening" and the men protest, "I am," the men are right. The impression of not listening results from misalignments in the mechanics of conversation. The misalignment begins as soon as a man and a woman take physical positions. This became clear when I studied videotapes made by psychologist Bruce Dorval of children and adults talking to their same-sex best friends. I found that at every age, the girls and women faced each other directly, their eyes anchored on each other's faces. At every age, the boys and men sat at angles to each other and looked elsewhere in the room, periodically glancing at each other. They were obviously attuned to each other, often mirroring

systematic: structured
hierarchical: orderly, ranked
subordinate: lower-ranking
misalignments: confusion

MEN ARE FROM MARS, *Women Are from Venus*

A Practical Guide for Improving Communication and Getting What You Want in Your Relationships

JOHN GRAY, Ph.D.

each other's movements. But the tendency of men to face away can give women the impression they aren't listening even when they are. A young woman in college was frustrated: Whenever she told her boyfriend she wanted to talk to him, he would lie down on the floor, close his eyes, and put his arm over his face. This signaled to her, "He's taking a nap." But he insisted he was listening extra hard. Normally, he looks around the room, so he is easily distracted. Lying down and covering his eyes helped him concentrate on what she was saying.

13   Analogous to the physical alignment that women and men take in conversation is their topical alignment. The girls in my study tended to talk at length about one topic, but the boys tended to jump from topic to topic. The second-grade girls exchanged stories about people they knew. The second-grade boys teased, told jokes, noticed things in the room and talked about finding games to play. The sixth-grade girls talked about problems with a mutual friend. The sixth grade boys talked about 55 different topics, none of which extended over more than a few turns.

Listening to Body Language

14   Switching topics is another habit that gives women the impression men aren't listening, especially if they switch to a topic about themselves. But the evidence of the 10th-grade boys in my study indicates otherwise. The 10th-grade boys sprawled across their chairs with bodies parallel and eyes straight ahead, rarely looking at each other. They looked as if they were riding in a car, staring out the windshield. But they were talking about their feelings. One boy was upset because a girl had told him he had a drinking problem, and the other was feeling alienated from all his friends.

15   Now, when a girl told a friend about a problem, the friend responded by asking probing questions and expressing agreement and understanding. But the boys dismissed each other's problems. Todd assured Richard that his drinking was "no big problem" because "sometimes you're funny when you're off your butt." And when Todd said he felt left out, Richard responded, "Why should you? You know more people than me."

16   Women perceive such responses as belittling and unsupportive. But the boys seemed satisfied with them. Whereas women reassure each other by implying, "You shouldn't feel bad because I've had similar experiences," men do so by implying, "You shouldn't feel bad because your problems aren't so bad."

> *The boys tended to jump from topic to topic*

17   There are even simpler reasons for women's impression that men don't listen. Linguist Lynette Hirschman found that women make more listener-noise, such as "mhm," "uhuh," and "yeah," to show "I'm with you." Men, she found, more often give silent attention. Women who expect a stream of listener noise interpret silent attention as no attention at all.

18   Women's conversational habits are as frustrating to men as men's are to women. Men who expect silent attention interpret a stream of listener

analogous: similar, related
alignment: position
belittling: demeaning

noise as overreaction or impatience. Also, when women talk to each other in a close, comfortable setting, they often overlap, finish each other's sentences and anticipate what the other is about to say. This practice, which I call "participatory listenership," is often perceived by men as interruption, intrusion and lack of attention.

19 A parallel difference caused a man to complain about his wife, "She just wants to talk about her own point of view. If I show her another view, she gets mad at me." When most women talk to each other, they assume a conversationalist's job is to express agreement and support. But many men see their conversational duty as pointing out the other side of an argument. This is heard as disloyalty by women and refusal to offer the requisite support. It is not that women don't want to see other points of view, but that they prefer them phrased as suggestions and inquiries rather than as direct challenges.

20 In his book "Fighting for Life," Walter Ong points out that men use "agonistic" or warlike, oppositional formats to do almost anything; thus discussion becomes debate, and conversation a competitive sport. In contrast, women see conversation as a ritual means of establishing rapport. If Jane tells a problem and June says she has a similar one, they walk away feeling closer to each other. But this attempt at establishing rapport can backfire when used with men. Men take too literally women's ritual "troubles talk," just as women mistake men's ritual challenges for real attack.

The Sounds of Silence

21 These differences begin to clarify why women and men have such different expectations about communication in marriage. For women, talk creates intimacy. Marriage is an orgy of closeness: you can tell your feelings and thoughts and still be loved. Their greatest fear is being pushed away. But men live in a hierarchical world, where talk maintains independence and status. They are on guard to protect themselves from being put down and pushed around.

22 This explains the paradox of the talkative man who said of his silent wife, "She's the talker." In the public setting of a guest lecture, he felt challenged to show his intelligence and display his understanding of the lecture. But at home, where he has nothing to prove and no one to defend against, he is free to remain silent. For his wife, being home means she is free from the worry that something she says might offend someone, or spark disagreement, or appear to be showing off; at home she is free to talk.

23 The communication problems that endanger marriage can't be fixed by mechanical engineering. They require a new conceptual framework about the role of talk in human relationships. Many of the psychological explanations that have become second nature may not be helpful, because they tend to blame either women (for not being assertive enough) or men (for not being in touch with their feelings). A sociolinguistic approach by which male-female conversation is seen as cross-cultural communication allows us to understand the problem and forge solutions without blaming either party.

24 Once the problem is understood, improvement comes naturally, as it did to the young woman and her boyfriend who seemed to go to sleep when she wanted to talk. Previously, she had accused him of not listening, and he had refused to change his behavior, since that would be

---

intrusion: invasion
requisite: essential
rapport: bond, unity
paradox: contradiction

admitting fault. But then she learned about and explained to him the differences in women's and men's habitual ways of aligning themselves in conversation. The next time she told him she wanted to talk, he began, as usual, by lying down and covering his eyes. When the familiar negative reaction bubbled up, she reassured herself that he really was listening. But then he sat up and looked at her. Thrilled, she asked why. He said, "You like me to look at you when we talk, so I'll try to do it." Once he saw their differences as cross-cultural rather than right and wrong, he independently altered his behavior.

25   Women who feel abandoned and deprived when their husbands won't listen to or report daily news may be happy to discover their husbands trying to adapt once they understand the

> *"Women see conversation as a ritual means of establishing rapport"*

place of small talk in women's relationships. But if their husbands don't adapt, the women may still be comforted that for men, this is not a failure of intimacy. Accepting the difference, the wives may look to their friends or family for that kind of talk. And husbands who can't provide it shouldn't feel their wives have made unreasonable demands. Some couples will still decide to divorce, but at least their decisions will be based on realistic expectations.

26   In these times of resurgent ethnic conflicts, the world desperately needs cross-cultural understanding. Like charity, successful cross-cultural communication should begin at home.

resurgent: renewed

CONVERSATIONS: Collaborating in Class or Online

1. Who initially observed the pattern of men talking more than women in public, but less at home?
2. According to Tannen, what does "failed conversation" (para. 3) have to do with the divorce rate?
3. What is the basis of friendships between girls? Why is this ritual so important to them?
4. What binds males together?

CONNECTIONS: Discovering Relationships among Ideas

5. According to Tannen, what is the relationship between children's play groups and communication in a marriage?
6. What does Tannen's research reveal about the eye movements of men and women when they are listening to each other?
7. How do men and women deal with problems within their gender groups?
8. What does Tannen mean when she says, "Like charity, successful cross-cultural communication should begin at home" (para. 26)?

PRESENTATION: Analyzing the Writer's Craft

9. What is Tannen's purpose in this essay?
10. Who do you think is her intended audience?
11. How do Tannen's references to other experts affect your reading of her essay?
12. List the main points Tannen compares in this essay. Then explain her method of organization.

PROJECTS: Expressing Your Own Views

13. **Collage:** Create a collage of either men's or women's preferred activities.
14. **Slide Show:** Make a slide show pantomiming the research that Tannen presents in this essay.
15. **Essay:** In a well-developed essay, explore one other major difference between men and women.
16. **Research:** Read and summarize the three resources below. Generate one specific question from each resource that focuses on comparison/contrast. Then answer one of your questions in a documented essay, consulting these and other sources as necessary.

OTHER RESOURCES

 Web Site

Education.com:
www.education.com

Click on the Education A-Z tab

Search: "Gender Differences"

 Audio/Video

Top Documentary Films: http://topdocumentaryfilms.com

Search: "Killing Us Softly 3"

Click on the Video link

Academic Article

"Barbie Against Superman: Gender Stereotypes and Gender Equity in the Classroom"

by Aksu Bengü

Journal of Language and Linguistic Studies 1.1 (2005): 12–21

ONE LAST THOUGHT

Researchers in the mid-nineties determined that voice intonation had an important effect on memory retention. They studied 120 subjects and found that most remembered information when it was presented to them in a variety of pitches and rates of speed, although subjects rated the speakers in those instances as significantly less likable than other speakers. Do you find that you relate better to monotone speakers or to people who use a variety of pitches and speeds? Why?

Smoking Ads

by Lucky Strike and New York Department of Health

The first advertisement below, "Be Happy, Go Lucky," was created in 1950 by the Lucky Strike Company. The "Lucky Strike" brand was founded in 1871 by R. A. Patterson of Richmond, Virginia, who began selling cut-plug chewing tobacco and later marketed cigarettes. The brand was bought in 1905 by the American Tobacco Company to compete with the R. J. Reynolds Company's "Camel" cigarette. The second ad featuring

Ronaldo Martinez entitled "Nothing Will Ever Be the Same" was part of the "Ronaldo Campaign" produced by the New York City Department of Health and Mental Hygiene in 2010.

PREREADING QUESTIONS

Do you smoke or have you ever smoked?

Why did you decide to smoke or not smoke?

What prompted you to quit or continue smoking?

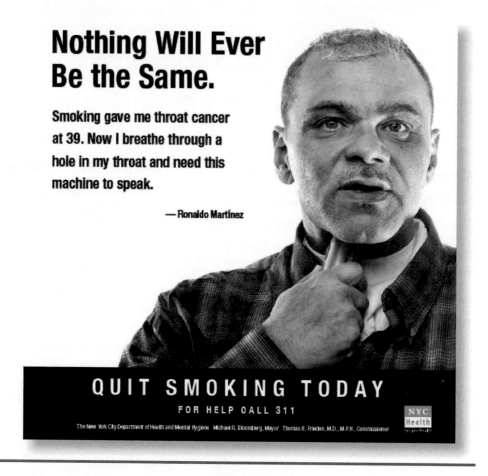

Nothing Will Ever Be the Same.

Smoking gave me throat cancer at 39. Now I breathe through a hole in my throat and need this machine to speak.

—Ronaldo Martínez

QUIT SMOKING TODAY
FOR HELP CALL 311

The New York City Department of Health and Mental Hygiene   Michael R. Bloomberg, Mayor   Thomas R. Frieden, M.D., M.P.H., Commissioner

NYC Health

CONVERSATIONS: Collaborating in Class or Online

1. What words are in bold print in each ad?
2. Write a thesis statement for each ad.
3. Summarize the words in each ad.
4. What do the pictures add to the message in each?

CONNECTIONS: Discovering Relationships among Ideas

5. Which ad draws more on emotions?
6. Which ad is older? How do you know?
7. Why is a mail carrier pictured in the Lucky Strike ad?
8. Are these ads both effective in getting their messages across? Explain your answer.

PRESENTATION: Analyzing the Writer's Craft

9. What is the purpose of each of these ads?
10. How does each layout (color, design, pictures, typeface) communicate the ad's message?
11. Who do you think is the intended audience of each ad?
12. In what ways are the two ads similar?

PROJECTS: Expressing Your Own Views

13. **Ad:** Create an ad for quitting a specific activity or habit. What do you want the focus of your ad to be? What is your purpose?

14. **Web Site:** Design a Web site that features various bad habits with links to information about controlling them.

15. **Essay:** Write a well-developed essay comparing your current daily routine with your routine in high school. How are they different? How are they the same? What observations can you make from the patterns you discover in your essay?

16. **Research:** Read and summarize the three resources below. Generate one specific question from each resource that focuses on comparison/contrast. Then answer one of your questions in a documented essay, consulting these and other sources as necessary.

OTHER RESOURCES

Web Site

Centers for Disease Control and Prevention: www.cdc.gov/tobacco

Academic Article

"Taxes, Cigarette Consumption, and Smoking Intensity"

by Jérôme Adda and Francesca Cornaglia

The American Economic Review 96.4 (2006): 1013–1028

Audio/Video

World News: http://wn.com/

Search: "The Golden Age of Cigarette Advertising"

Click on the Video link

ONE LAST THOUGHT

The Tobacco Master Settlement Agreement of 1998 was a settlement between the four largest U.S. tobacco companies, 46 state governments, and five U.S. territories. In addition to reimbursing the states for tobacco-related health care costs, the companies agreed to restrict certain tobacco marketing practices. They also agreed to fund an anti-smoking public education group, which in turn is responsible for a smoking prevention campaign. Do you think it's appropriate that tobacco companies help fund groups who campaign against their products? Why or why not?

How E-Books Will Change Reading and Writing

by Lynn Neary

A National Public Radio correspondent on books and publishing, **Lynn Neary** began her media career in 1982 as a newscaster on *Morning Edition* and as the weekend host of *All Things Considered*. She developed NPR's first religion beat and has covered such stories as welfare reform, the Republican resurgence in congress, breast cancer treatment, public housing, and prison inmates.

PREREADING QUESTIONS

Have you ever read an e-book?

How is it different from a traditional book?

Which do you prefer? Why?

1   Ten years ago, few imagined that by decade's end, people would be reading novels on cell phones. A lot has changed in the book world.

2   "Over the last couple of years, I've really noticed if I sit down with a book, after a few paragraphs, I'll say, 'You know, where're the links? Where's the e-mail? Where's all the stuff going on?'" says writer Nicholas Carr. "And it's kind of sad."

3   Carr says he's thought of himself as a serious reader all his life, but in an article in *The Atlantic*, he argued that the Internet is training us to read in a distracted and disjointed way. But does that mean writers will have to change the way they write to capture the attention of an audience accustomed to this new way of reading? Carr thinks the answer is yes, and he looks to the past to make his point.

4   "When printed books first became popular, thanks to Gutenberg's press, you saw this great expansion of eloquence and experimentation," says Carr. "All of which came out of the fact that here was a technology that encouraged people to read deeply, with great concentration and focus. And as we move to the new technology of the screen . . . it has a very different effect, an

disjointed: disconnected, disorganized
accustomed: familiar, used to

almost opposite effect, and you will see a retreat from the sophistication and eloquence that characterized the printed page."

5   As digital platforms proliferate, writers are trying to figure out how to use them. Novelist Rick Moody recently wrote a story on the social networking site Twitter. Moody says he got intrigued by the idea of writing in abbreviated form to fit within the 140-character limitations of each Twitter post.

6   "I began to see that trying to write within this tiny little frame, 140 characters, was kind of like trying to write haiku. It's very poetical in its compaction, and it kind of got under my skin, and I kept thinking, 'Wouldn't it be fun to try and work with this?'" Moody says.

7   His flirtation with Twitter was not entirely successful. The delivery of the story went awry, and some industry insiders were bombarded with repetitive tweets. Still, Moody doesn't regret the experiment. But he does have doubts about Twitter's literary potential.

8   "It forced me to try to imply more narrative than I could actually include in the piece, because I was so stuck in this little box. It's hard to have

> *You will see a retreat from the sophistication and eloquence that characterized the printed page*

dialogue between characters in the confines of the Twitter box," Moody says. "That was all fun. Whether I think Twitter is going to be a great vehicle for fiction, I'd say no."

9   A lot of writers are trying their hand at Twitter books—both on the Web and in print—but *Time* magazine book reviewer Lev Grossman thinks it's a passing fad. Asked what might have some staying power, Grossman suggests the cell phone novel. Written on cell phones and meant to be read on them, many of these books are bestsellers in Japan. The authors are usually young women, and romance is the main theme.

10   "They tend to be narratively very propulsive [and] not very interested in style and beautiful language," Grossman says. "There tends to be a lot of drama and melodrama, sex and violence. They grab your attention, and they don't really let it go."

11   Apart from Twitter books and cell phone novels, Grossman, who is also a novelist, says the real challenge for writers is electronic-book readers like the Kindle. He says the increasingly popular devices force people to read books in a different way.

12   "They scroll and scroll and scroll. You don't have this business of handling pages and turning them and savoring them." Grossman says that particular function of the e-book leads to a certain kind of reading and writing: "Very forward moving, very fast narrative . . . and likewise you don't tend to linger on the language. When you are seeing a word or a sentence on the screen, you tend to go through it, you extract the data, and you move on."

13   Grossman thinks that tendency not to linger on the language also affects the way people react to a book when they are deciding whether to buy it: More purchases will be based on brief excerpts.

IN CONTEXT

The First Printing Press

Johannes Gutenberg began working on the printing press in 1436. He was the first person to make type out of durable metals and is also credited with using oil-based inks, which last much longer than the previously used water-based variety.

---

proliferate: multiply, grow
haiku: short Japanese poem
propulsive: active, forward moving

14   "It will be incumbent on novelists to hook readers right away," says Grossman. "You won't be allowed to do a kind of tone poem overture; you're going to want to have blood on the wall by the end of the second paragraph. And I think that's something writers will have to adapt to, and the challenge will be to use this powerfully narrative form, this pulpy kind of mode, to say important things."

15   Grossman, Moody, and Carr all believe that traditional books will still be around for a long time and that some of the changes that may occur in writing will be more evolutionary than revolutionary. But it's hard to know, says Carr, whether traditional books—and the people who read and write them—will have much influence on the culture in the future.

16   "The real question is," wonders Carr, "is that segment of the population going to just dwindle and be on the periphery of the culture rather than at the center, which is where printed books have stood for centuries now?"

17   Perhaps we'll have to wait another 10 years to find out.

> **incumbent:** necessary
> **pulpy:** cheap and sensational
> **periphery:** outside

CONVERSATIONS: Collaborating in Class or Online

1. What does Neary say is the main difference between e-books and printed books?
2. How might e-books affect writers?
3. What are "Twitter books" and "cell phone novels"?
4. According to Neary, why is it "incumbent on novelists to hook readers right away" (para. 14) and keep their attention?

CONNECTIONS: Discovering Relationships among Ideas

5. How does the way we read affect professional writers?
6. What does Neary mean when she says that some of the changes we will see in writing "will be more evolutionary than revolutionary" (para. 15)?
7. Do you think traditional books will be part of our culture in the future? In what capacity?
8. How do you think the Kindle, iPad, and other devices will change the way we read and write?

PRESENTATION: Analyzing the Writer's Craft

9. What is Neary's purpose in this article?

10. This essay actually leaves us with more questions than answers about the transition from traditional books to e-books. Is this a useful approach to the topic?

11. Who is Neary's intended audience?

12. Is the final sentence of this essay an effective ending? Why or why not?

PROJECTS: Expressing Your Own Views

13. Narrative: With a friend, write a continuous cell-phone story, going back and forth between your phones several times.

14. Poem: Write a poem about books that will fit on Twitter (140 characters).

15. Essay: In a well-developed essay, compare your reading habits between high school and college.

16. Research: Read and summarize the three resources below. Generate one specific question from each resource that focuses on comparison/contrast. Then answer one of your questions in a documented essay, consulting these and other sources as necessary.

OTHER RESOURCES

Web Site

Free eBooks by Project Gutenberg: www.gutenberg.org/wiki/Main_Page

Academic Article

"Usability and Usefulness of eBooks on PPCs: How Students' Opinions Vary Over Time"

by Paul Lam, Shun Leung Lam, John Lam, and Carmel McNaught

Autralasian Journal of Educational Technology 25.1 (2009): 30–44

Audio/Video

Video: http://vimeo.com/

Search: "Why eBooks? An Overview for Niche Publishers and Indie Authors"

Click on the Video link

ONE LAST THOUGHT

The increased popularity of e-books brings with it the foreseeable increase of illegal downloading. Pirated electronic books have already become an issue for major publishing companies, which report potential revenue losses in the millions. What do you think publishing companies can do to protect their assets from online theft? What is a suitable punishment for people who choose to download books illegally?

CHAPTER WRITING ASSIGNMENTS

Write a well-developed essay in response to the following prompts. Consult the chapter introduction for guidance in creating your essay.

CONNECTING THE READINGS

1. What do you think Workman ("Motion Gaming Review") and Neary ("How e-Books Will Change Reading and Writing") could learn from each other? How will we all have to cooperate as we move into the future of gaming and e-books?

2. How do you think social networking practices ("Social Networking") might be affected by the gender differences outlined by Tannen in "Sex, Lies, and Conversation"?

3. Discuss the principal differences between Islamic and Western cultures ("Indecent Exposure") compared to those between men and women in communication ("Sex, Lies, and Conversation"). Which would be most easily solved? Which will be impossible to solve? Which are more serious and/or more permanent? What conclusions can you draw from your discussion of these issues?

4. What might a typical grandma ("Grandma") say about smoking ads (Smoking Ads)? What do we know now about the dangers of tobacco that she probably didn't know?

MOVING BEYOND THE READINGS

5. What role do relatives play in your life? Do you welcome this involvement in your personal affairs? Which relative plays the most important role in your life? How is this role different from the involvement of your other relatives?

6. Write an objective review of a piece of equipment you use regularly by comparing it to similar products.

7. Analyze your family rituals in reference to those of another family. What do you do that is similar? What is different?

8. Which current ads seem most appealing and effective to you? What products are they selling? Write an essay explaining what you think is the most effective approach to advertising. Feel free to discuss any medium (TV, Internet, magazines, billboards, etc.).

COMBINING RHETORICAL MODES

9. Have you read any e-textbooks? What was your experience with them? How do they affect your study habits? Do you learn differently with e-books? If you haven't actually used an e-book, how do you think you will respond to them?

10. Where do you predict social networking will be in 10 years? What will we be doing then that we aren't doing now? Will you welcome these changes or not?

11. What is the value of gaming in our culture? What needs does it satisfy? Why is it interesting to some and not to others?

12. What are three of your current pastimes? Of these three, which is your favorite? Why is it your favorite? What role does it play in your self-image? Explain how this activity is an important part of your self-definition.

Definition

11

Clear communication depends on our understanding of a common set of definitions. If we did not work from shared definitions, we would not be able to carry on coherent conversations, write clear academic papers, or understand any form of media. Functioning from a mutual understanding of words and phrases helps us work with each other in a variety of important ways. Here are some examples:

- Writing a job description for the classified ads;
- Starting a paper for a criminal justice class with a definition of criminal law;
- Discussing the qualities of a great wide receiver with your Fantasy Football friends;

DEVELOPMENT STRATEGIES: DEFINITION

Purpose of Definition
Development
⟶ Category
⟶ Etymology
⟶ Synonym
⟶ Negation
                    Conclusion

- Defining the financial structure of a third-world country for your economics class;
- Agreeing on the definition of a low-budget dinner with your date.

Definitions are building blocks in communication that help us function from a shared understanding of terms and ideas. They give us a foundation to build on—in both reading and writing.

Introducing Definition

Definition is the process of explaining a word, an object, or an idea. A good definition focuses on the meaning of the term as well as on what qualities set it apart from similar words or concepts. Definitions help us understand basic concrete terms (*iPad, hamburger, table*), discuss events in our lives (*dance recital, graduation, basketball game*), and grasp complex ideas (*fame, democracy, friendship*). Definitions force us to consider meanings and associations that are interesting as well as informative.

Definitions can vary greatly. They can be as short as one word (a "mole" is a spy) or as long as an essay or even a book. Words or ideas that require such extended definitions are usually abstract, complex, and/or controversial. Think, for example, how difficult it might be to define an abstract idea like *courage* compared to concrete words such as *book* or *desk*. Definitions can also be *objective* (very precise and often dry) or *subjective* (interspersed with personal opinions), and they can be used to instruct, to entertain, or to achieve a combination of these two goals.

Look at the following notes for a definition paper:

DEVELOPMENT STRATEGIES AT WORK

Purpose
What is the role of cell phones in our lives?

Development
⟶ **Category:** a hand-held technology device
⟶ **Etymology:** from "cellular," referring to the network of "cells" or base stations required for two-way radio telecommunications systems
⟶ **Synonym:** mobile phone
⟶ **Negation:** not a standard home telephone or a cordless portable phone

                    Conclusion

DEVELOPMENT STRATEGIES AT WORK

Purpose

What does freedom mean to our citizens?

Development

⟶ **Category:** type of mental and physical behavior

⟶ **Etymology:** from the Old English "freo," meaning "free" or "unrestrained"

⟶ **Synonym:** liberty, independence

⟶ **Negation:** not restrictive or suppressive

Conclusion

Clear definitions give readers and writers a mutual starting point in the shared responsibility for successful communication. Definition is also a pattern of thought that can work jointly with other rhetorical modes to explain complex concepts and issues on the analytical level. It is, therefore, an essential aspect of critical thinking.

Discovering How Definition Works

On the right is a list of the key elements of definitional thinking, whether for a visual (like a collage or a cartoon) or a prose selection. The Definition Essentials offered here are equally useful as guidelines for reading and writing.

Analyzing the graphic below will help you realize how these elements work together to create a useful definition. If you discover on your own how this method of reasoning functions, you will be able to apply it effectively to your own reading and writing. The questions following the cartoon will help you understand this rhetorical mode even more clearly than you already do.

1. What is the purpose of this cartoon?

2. How is "negation" (saying what the word is *not*) used in this visual?

Definition Essentials

Purpose

Category, Etymology, Synonym, Negation

Examples

Other Rhetorical Modes

Logical Organization

Summary/Conclusion

'There aren't any icons to click. It's a chalk board."

3. What details in this picture lead to an understanding of a chalk board?

4. What other rhetorical modes support this definition?

5. How does the layout of this cartoon emphasize the chalk board?

6. How does the illustrator bring closure to the message?

Collaborative Responses   Now discuss your responses to these questions with your classmates in small groups or as an entire class. Did the diverse perspectives from other students in your class change your "reading" of the visual? If so, in what ways?

Reading Definitions

As you read the prose and graphic selections in this chapter, pay special attention to the purpose for each definition. You should also make sure you understand the author's or illustrator's approach to each definition, along with his or her method of organization.

During your first reading of a selection, think about how the Definition Essentials work within the reading. The following questions will help you accomplish this task for both written and graphic assignments:

Definition Essentials: Reading

- **Purpose:** What is the purpose of the selection?
- **Category, Etymology, Synonym, Negation:** How are these strategies used in the "reading"?
- **Examples:** What examples does the author or illustrator use to explain the definition?
- **Other Rhetorical Modes:** What other rhetorical modes support the definition?
- **Logical Organization:** How is the definition organized?
- **Summary/Conclusion:** What is the author's/illustrator's conclusion?

On your second and third readings of the selection, focus on areas of ambiguity and confusion so you can deepen your comprehension.

Writing Definitions

Taking another look at the Definition Essentials as you move from reading to writing will help you adjust your writing to your specific purpose and audience. But first, let's review the writing process as it applies to this rhetorical mode.

Choosing a Subject

As with all assignments, you should select the subject you will define as soon as possible. Choosing a word or idea that can be defined and explained from several different angles is best so you have the potential to write a lively extended definition. Once you have chosen your subject, you should start to think about the strategies you want to use in your definition as well as the significance of your definition.

Our student writer, Isabel Caldwell, decides to define what makes up a county fair. She recently attended her own county fair and wanted to share the exhilaration she felt with others.

Generating Details

You might want to start generating ideas by listing possible approaches to this topic. Then, use a specific prewriting strategy introduced in Chapter 3 to generate as many details as possible for each point.

To begin this process, Isabel decides on five points she wants to consider in her definition. She lists them and then draws a cluster of their relationships (see page 328) to generate some examples.

> *Essential elements of the fair*
>
> *Games*
>
> *Food*
>
> *Agricultural competitions*
>
> *Rides*

Isabel has gone to her county fair for years, but she did not realize how valuable it is in her community until she started writing this essay. She now sees the fair as part of her local culture and can't imagine her town without it.

Drafting a Thesis Statement

After choosing a subject and generating lots of ideas for your paper, you are ready to write a thesis statement. At this point, you need to give your readers a working definition so they have a mental hook on which to hang the explanations in the rest of your essay. Also include the purpose of your essay in your thesis statement. A thesis for a graphic project may not be as immediately apparent as one for an essay, but it will still guide you to a coherent assignment.

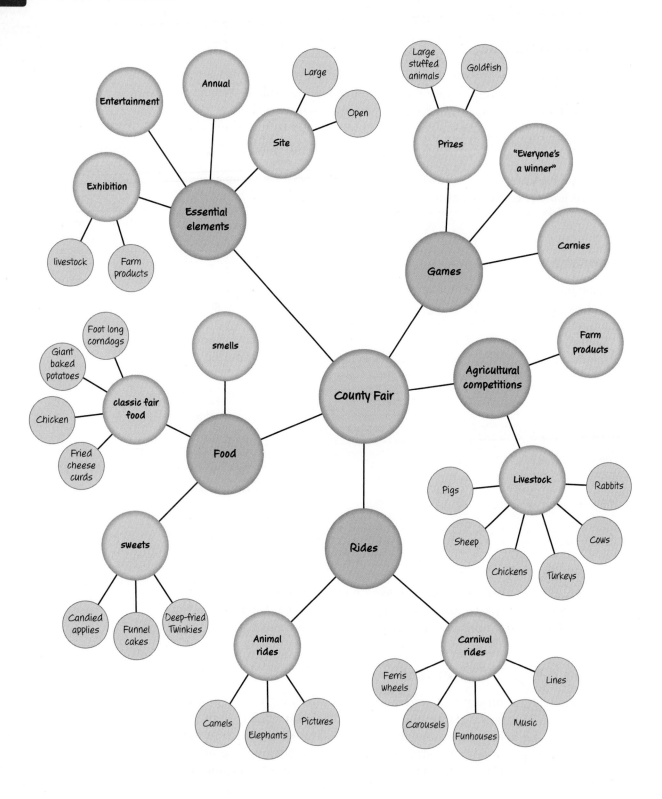

Isabel's purpose is to emphasize the importance of a county fair within the context of an entire community. Here is her thesis:

> *Part carnival, part agricultural competition, and part food extravaganza, the county fair aims to please both young and old every year.*

This statement will now provide focus and direction for the remainder of Isabel's assignment.

Producing a Draft

All these preliminary decisions will prepare you to write a well-developed definition essay.

- Your **introduction** should introduce your subject and make your purpose as clear as possible in a thesis statement.
- The **body of your paper** then defines your topic with well-chosen strategies and a sufficient number of examples.
- Your **conclusion** then summarizes the points you have made and draws some relevant conclusions.

Extended definitions seldom follow a set pattern of development or organization. Instead, as you will see from the examples in this chapter, they draw on a number of different techniques to help explain a word, object, term, concept, or phenomenon. Category, etymology, synonym, and negation are four common ways to develop a definition.

1. **Category.** Defining a term by **category** is a formal type of definition which one might find in a dictionary. Defining by category has two parts: the class or general category that the word belongs to and the way the word is different from other words in that group. For example, *brain* might be defined as "the organ that controls the nervous system." The general category is *organ*, and it is different from other organs (heart, lungs, stomach, liver, and so on) because it controls the nervous system.

2. **Etymology.** Introducing a word's **etymology,** which involves discussing the linguistic origin and development of a word, is a second method for expanding a definition essay. This strategy includes the word's derivation, original meaning, and usages. The word *brain* is derived from the Old German and Dutch word "bregen," which means "forehead." As the cerebral cortex and center of the nervous system, it controls all the other organ systems of the body. Tracing a word's origin often illuminates its current meaning and usage as well. This information can generally be found in any good dictionary or encyclopedia.

3. **Synonym.** When you define by using a **synonym** you furnish readers with a similar word or a short explanation through synonyms. Synonyms

for *brain* include *mind, intelligence, head,* or *intellect.* Synonyms give your readers another perspective on the word, event, or idea you are defining.

4. **Negation.** Another approach to defining a term is to explain what it is *not,* or to define it by **negation**. That is, you define a term by contrasting it with something else. So a *brain* is not a *stomach* or a *liver* or a *lung.* Again, you are furnishing your readers with just one more option for understanding the subject of your essay.

In addition to these four strategies for developing your definitions, nearly every definition essay can be improved by adding well-chosen examples, which can show your definition in action. They also put your personal imprint on the essay.

Being Objective or Subjective Definitions can be *objective* (strictly factual, as in a dictionary definition) or *subjective* (combined with personal opinions). An extended definition is usually more subjective than objective because in it you are providing your personal opinions about a word or concept. You are explaining to your readers your own meaning with examples to support your perspective, which is what makes your essay interesting. If your readers wanted a purely objective definition, they could simply go to a dictionary.

Using Other Rhetorical Modes As you continue to develop your definition essay, you should look at your word or idea in as many different ways as possible. The other rhetorical strategies you have already studied in this book can help you accomplish this goal. Perhaps a description, a short narrative, or a comparison will expand your definition even further and make your word or idea come alive. Writers also frequently use definition to support other rhetorical modes.

Organizing Your Essay Now you need to figure out the most logical way to organize your definition essay. You might move from particular to general or from general to particular. Or you might arrange your ideas from one extreme to another, such as from most important to least important, least dramatic to most dramatic, or most familiar to least familiar. In some cases, you might organize your definition chronologically or spatially. Or you could organize part of your essay one way and the rest another way. What's important is that you move in some logical fashion from one point to another so your readers can follow your train of thought.

You should now use the following questions, based on the Definition Essentials, to help focus and refine your written and graphic assignments:

Definition Essentials: Writing

- **Purpose:** What is your purpose?
- **Category, Etymology, Synonym, Negation:** How do you plan to use these strategies in your essay?

- **Examples:** What examples will you use to explain the definition?
- **Other Rhetorical Modes:** What other rhetorical modes will support your definition?
- **Logical Organization:** How will you organize the definition?
- **Summary/Conclusion:** How will you conclude the essay?

Revising and Editing

Revising and editing your verbal or visual project means rereading and rewriting the material so it says exactly what you want to communicate. This is also the time to link your sentences with some well-chosen transitions to ensure the readers understand how your ideas are related.

Revising

Look closely at your essay or graphic as someone else might see it. Most importantly, make sure it says what you intend to say. Then answer the questions posed in the Revising Checklist on page 28, which focus your attention on how your essay functions.

This is also the point in the writing process when you should add transitions to your essay that clarify the relationship of your details to one another. In definition, these words and phrases will depend on the development strategies you use in your essay. They should evolve naturally from what you are trying to communicate. Transitions will help your readers follow your thinking as you move from one point to the next. They will also make your essay coherent and enjoyable to read.

Editing

Editing is the final phase of your writing process. It involves looking closely at specific words, phrases, sentences, and any visual details to ensure that they follow current usage rules. Use the Editing Checklist on page 30 to review your project for errors in grammar and usage. When you locate a potential error, consult a handbook or go to Pearson's Web-based MyCompLab for an explanation of the problem.

Also, if your instructor marks any grammar mistakes on your paper or graphic, make sure you understand them. Recognizing errors in your own writing is the most effective way of correcting them.

As you read the following student essay, refer to the Definition Essentials (page 325) and the questions for reading definitions (page 326) to help you comprehend and analyze it. Then to thoroughly understand how this student essay works, pay special attention to the margin notes and the items in each paragraph they describe.

Isabel Caldwell

Professor Flachmann

English 101

13 Sept. 2011

A Day at the Fair

Significance →
Purpose →
Thesis Statement →

1 Many people don't understand the significance of the county fair. An age-old gathering that brings agriculture, food, and entertainment together in one exciting place, it is a destination that includes something for everyone in the family. Part carnival, part agricultural competition, and part food extravaganza, the county fair aims to please both young and old every year.

Topic 1 →
Definition →
Explanation using Cause/Effect →

2 Certain essential elements constitute a county fair. An exhibition of livestock and farm products often combined with entertainment and held annually by a county or state in a particular location are the basic characteristics of a county fair. These fairs are held at an open and accessible location—fairgrounds, stadiums, and arenas being the most common. A big site is necessary because of the large number of people and animals a county fair must accommodate.

Topic 2 →
Explanation using Cause/Effect →

3 Because county fairs often have an emphasis on agricultural competitions, visitors are able to see numerous specimens of livestock and farm products. Children of all ages, especially those in clubs like 4-H, show their animals off to judges and

spectators alike hoping to win a blue first-place ribbon. Ticket holders to the fair can walk through the livestock yard and see a variety of animals such as pigs, sheep, cows, and chickens, but they might catch a glimpse of turkeys, rabbits, or guinea pigs too.   ← Examples

4 In addition to farmyard animals, visitors to the county fair   ← Topic 3
can often see unique creatures in the fairground's ride area. For   ← Explanation using Illustration
a small fee, parents can perch their children atop camels and elephants or pose with exotic specimens of snakes, alligators,   ← Examples
or armadillos. These rides provide perfect photo ops for friends and family.

5 Next, no county fair is complete without quintessential   ← Topic 4
carnival rides like Ferris wheels, giant slides, carousels, and fun-   ← Examples
houses. Dizzying lights and music accompany most of the offer-
ings, which help complete the county fair experience. These rides   ← Explanation using Description
are popular with children and adults alike, and many fairgoers spend the majority of their time waiting in line for the opportunity to enjoy the exhilaration of these thrill-producing roller coasters and rides.

6 Another significant factor in defining a county fair is the   ← Topic 5
food. The smells of numerous savory concoctions float through   ← Explanation using Illustration
the festivities, and the selections are practically endless. Fairgo-
ers can gorge themselves on classic fare like foot-long corndogs,   ← Examples
barbequed corn-on-the-cob, giant baked potatoes, or rotisserie chicken, but can also taste more intriguing dishes like fried cheese curds or falafel. After finishing one of the many main dish choices, revelers can then decide to surrender to their sweet tooth by purchasing one of the numerous varieties of desserts found only at the fair, such as candied apples, funnel cakes, cotton candy, kettle   ← Examples
corn, and, of course, the infamous deep-fried Twinkies, Snickers, and Oreos.

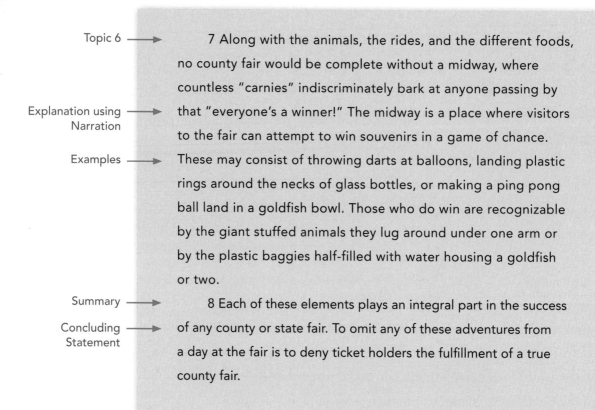

Topic 6 → 7 Along with the animals, the rides, and the different foods, no county fair would be complete without a midway, where countless "carnies" indiscriminately bark at anyone passing by

Explanation using Narration → that "everyone's a winner!" The midway is a place where visitors to the fair can attempt to win souvenirs in a game of chance.

Examples → These may consist of throwing darts at balloons, landing plastic rings around the necks of glass bottles, or making a ping pong ball land in a goldfish bowl. Those who do win are recognizable by the giant stuffed animals they lug around under one arm or by the plastic baggies half-filled with water housing a goldfish or two.

Summary → 8 Each of these elements plays an integral part in the success

Concluding Statement → of any county or state fair. To omit any of these adventures from a day at the fair is to deny ticket holders the fulfillment of a true county fair.

Reviewing Definition

Based on the information you have learned in this chapter and the annotations on the student essay, show how this essay works by writing a clear, precise summary or by drawing your own outline or graphic representation of it. Label the strategies on your visual. This exercise will confirm your understanding of the elements of definition in both reading and writing.

When Is It Rape?

by Nancy Gibbs

An essayist and editor-at-large for *Time*, **Nancy Gibbs** has written over 100 cover stories for the magazine. She is also a frequent guest on the *Today Show*, *Good Morning America*, *Charlie Rose*, and many other popular television programs and has co-authored, with Michael Duffy, the *New York Times* bestseller, *The Preacher and the Presidents: Billy Graham in the White House.*

PREREADING QUESTIONS

How would you define *date rape*?

When did this term come into vogue in our society?

Approximately what percentage of women do you think will be victims of this form of crime during their lifetimes?

1   Be careful of strangers and hurry home, says a mother to her daughter, knowing that the world is a frightful place but not wishing to swaddle a child in fear. Girls grow up scarred by caution and enter adulthood eager to shake free of their parents' worst nightmares. They still know to be wary of strangers. What they don't know is whether they have more to fear from their friends.

2   Most women who get raped are raped by people they already know—like the boy in biology class, or the guy in the office down the hall, or their friend's brother. The familiarity is enough to make them let down their guard, sometimes even enough to make them wonder afterward whether they were "really raped." What people think of as "real rape"—the assault by a monstrous stranger lurking in the shadows—accounts for only 1 out of 5 attacks.

3   So the phrase "acquaintance rape" was coined to describe the rest, all the cases of forced sex between people who already knew each other, however casually. But that was too clinical for headline writers, and so the popular term is the narrower "date rape," which suggests an ugly ending to a raucous night on the town.

4   These are not idle distinctions. Behind the search for labels is the central mythology about rape: that rapists are always strangers and victims are women who ask for it. The mythology is hard to dispel because the crime is so rarely exposed. The experts guess—that's all they can do under the circumstances—that while 1 in 4 women will be raped in her lifetime, less than 10% will report the assault, and less than 5% of the rapists will go to jail.

raucous: rowdy, wild
dispel: eliminate

5   When a story of the crime lodges in the headlines, the myths have a way of cluttering the search for the truth. The tale of Good Friday in Palm Beach landed in the news because it involved a Kennedy, but it may end up as a watershed case, because all the mysteries and passions surrounding date rape are here to be dissected. William Kennedy Smith met a woman at a bar, invited her back home late at night, and apparently had sex with her on the lawn. She says it was rape, and the police believed her story enough to charge him with the crime. Perhaps it was the bruises on her leg; or the instincts of the investigators who found her, panicked and shaking, curled up in the fetal position on a couch; or the lie-detector tests she passed.

6   On the other side, Smith has adamantly protested that he is a man falsely accused. His friends and family testify to his gentle nature and moral fiber and insist that he could not possibly have committed such a crime. Maybe the truth will come out in court—but regardless of its finale, the case has shoved the debate over date rape into the minds of average men and women. Plant the topic in a conversation, and chances are it will ripen into a bitter argument or a jittery sequence of pale jokes.

7   Women charge that date rape is the hidden crime; men complain it is hard to prevent a crime they can't define. Women say it isn't taken seriously; men say it is a concept invented by women who like to tease but not take the consequences. Women say the date-rape debate is the first time the nation has talked frankly about sex; men say it is women's unconscious reaction to the excesses of the sexual revolution. Meanwhile, men and women argue among themselves about the "gray area" that surrounds the whole murky arena of sexual relations, and there is no consensus in sight.

> *A romantic encounter is a context in which sex could occur*

8   In court, on campus, in conversation, the issue turns on the elasticity of the word *rape*, one of the few words in the language with the power to summon a shared image of a horrible crime.

9   At one extreme are those who argue that for the word to retain its impact, it must be strictly defined as forced sexual intercourse: a gang of thugs jumping a jogger in Central Park, a psychopath preying on old women in a housing complex, a man with an ice pick in a side street. To stretch the definition of the word risks stripping away its power. In this view, if it happened on a date, it wasn't rape. A romantic encounter is a context in which sex *could* occur, and so what omniscient judge will decide whether there was genuine mutual consent?

10   Others are willing to concede that date rape sometimes occurs, that sometimes a man goes too far on a date without a woman's consent. But this infraction, they say, is not as ghastly a crime as street rape, and it should not be taken as seriously. The *New York Post*, alarmed by the Willy Smith case, wrote in a recent editorial, "If the sexual encounter, *forced or not*, has been preceded by a series of consensual activities—drinking, a trip to the man's home, a walk on a deserted beach

adamantly: stubbornly
consensus: agreement
elasticity: flexibility
omniscient: all-knowing
concede: admit

at 3 in the morning—the charge that's leveled against the alleged offender should, it seems to us, be different than the one filed against, say, the youths who raped and beat the jogger."

11 This attitude sparks rage among women who carry scars received at the hands of men they knew. It makes no difference if the victim shared a drink or a moonlit walk or even a passionate kiss, they protest, if the encounter ended with her being thrown to the ground and forcibly violated. Date rape is not about a misunderstanding, they say. It is not a communications problem. It is not about a woman's having regrets in the morning for a decision she made the night before. It is not about a "decision" at all. Rape is rape, and any form of forced sex—even between neighbors, co-workers, classmates, and casual friends—is a crime.

12 A more extreme form of that view comes from activists who see rape as a metaphor, its definition swelling to cover any kind of oppression of women. Rape, seen in this light, can occur not only on a date but also in a marriage, not only by violent assault but also by psychological pressure. A Swarthmore College training pamphlet once explained that acquaintance rape "spans a spectrum of incidents and behaviors, ranging from crimes legally defined as rape to verbal harassment and inappropriate innuendo."

13 No wonder, then, that the battles become so heated. When innuendo qualifies as rape, the definitions have become so slippery that the entire subject sinks into a political swamp. The only way to capture the hard reality is to tell the story.

14 A 32-year-old woman was on business in Tampa last year for the Florida supreme court.

Stranded at the courthouse, she accepted a lift from a lawyer involved in her project. As they chatted on the ride home, she recalls, "he was saying all the right things, so I started to trust him." She agreed to have dinner, and afterward, at her hotel door, he convinced her to let him come in to talk. "I went through the whole thing about being old-fashioned," she says. "I was a virgin until I was 21. So I told him talk was all we were going to do."

15 But as they sat on the couch, she found herself falling asleep. "By now, I'm comfortable with him, and I put my head on his shoulder. He's not tried anything all evening, after all." Which is when the rape came. "I woke up to find him on top of me, forcing himself on me. I didn't scream or run. All I could think about was my business contacts and what if they saw me run out of my room screaming rape.

16 "I thought it was my fault. I felt so filthy. I washed myself over and over in hot water. Did he rape me?, I kept asking myself. I didn't consent. But who's gonna believe me? I had a man in my hotel room after midnight." More than a year later, she still can't tell the story without a visible struggle to maintain her composure. Police referred the case to the state attorney's office in Tampa, but without more evidence it decided not to prosecute. Although her attacker has admitted that he heard her say no, maintains the woman, "he says he didn't know that I meant no. He didn't feel he'd raped me, and he even wanted to see me again."

17 Her story is typical in many ways. The victim herself may not be sure right away that she has been raped, that she had said no and been physically forced into having sex anyway. And the rapist commonly hears but does not heed the protest. "A date rapist will follow through no matter what the woman wants because his agenda is to get laid," says Claire Walsh, a Florida-based consultant on sexual assaults. "First comes the dinner, then a dance, then a drink, then

innuendo: hint, insinuation
prosecute: take to court
heed: pay attention

the coercion begins." Gentle persuasion gives way to physical intimidation, with alcohol as the ubiquitous lubricant. "When that fails, force is used," she says. "Real men don't take no for an answer."

18   The Palm Beach case serves to remind women that if they go ahead and press charges, they can expect to go on trial along with their attacker, if not in a courtroom then in the court of public opinion. *The New York Times* caused an uproar on its own staff not only for publishing the victim's name but also for laying out in detail her background, her high school grades, her driving record, along with an unattributed quote from a school official about her "little wild streak." A freshman at Carleton College in Minnesota, who says she was repeatedly raped for four hours by a fellow student, claims that she was asked at an administrative hearing if she performed oral sex on dates. In 1989 a man charged with raping at knife-point a woman he knew was acquitted in Florida because his victim had been wearing lace shorts and no underwear.

> *"Gentle persuasion gives way to physical intimidation, with alcohol as the ubiquitous lubricant"*

19   From a purely legal point of view, if she wants to put her attacker in jail, the survivor had better be beaten as well as raped, since bruises become a badge of credibility. She had better have reported the crime right away, before taking the hours-long shower that she craves, before burning her clothes, before curling up with the blinds down. And she would do well to be a woman of shining character. Otherwise the strict constructionist definitions of rape will prevail in court. "Juries don't have a great deal of sympathy for the victim if she's a willing participant up to the nonconsensual sexual intercourse," says Norman Kinne, a prosecutor in Dallas. "They feel that many times the victim

has placed herself in the situation." Absent eyewitnesses or broken bones, a case comes down to her word against his, and the mythology of rape rarely lends her the benefit of the doubt.

20   She should also hope for an all-male jury, preferably composed of fathers with daughters. Prosecutors have found that women tend to be harsh judges of one another—perhaps because to find a defendant guilty is to entertain two grim realities: that anyone might be a rapist and that every woman could find herself a victim. It may be easier to believe, the experts muse, that at some level the victim asked for it. "But just because a woman makes a bad judgment, does that give the guy a moral right to rape her?" asks Dean Kilpatrick, director of the Crime Victim Research and Treatment Center at the Medical University of South Carolina. "The bottom line is, Why does a woman's having a drink give a man the right to rape her?"

21   Last week the Supreme Court waded into the debate with a 7-to-2 ruling that protects victims from being harassed on the witness stand with questions about their sexual history. The Justices, in their first decision on "rape shield laws," said an accused rapist could not present evidence about a previous sexual relationship with the victim unless he notified the court ahead of time. In her decision, Justice Sandra Day O'Connor wrote that "rape victims deserve heightened protection against surprise, harassment, and unnecessary invasions of privacy."

22   That was welcome news to prosecutors who understand the reluctance of victims to come forward. But there are other impediments to justice as well. An internal investigation of the Oakland police department found that officers ignored a quarter of all reports of sexual assaults or

coercion: force
ubiquitous: prevalent
acquitted: freed, released
waded: walked difficultly

attempts, though 90% actually warranted investigation. Departments are getting better at educating officers in handling rape cases, but the courts remain behind. A New York City task force on women in the courts charged that judges and lawyers were routinely less inclined to believe a woman's testimony than a man's.

23   The present debate over degrees of rape is nothing new: All through history, rapes have been divided between those that mattered and those that did not. For the first few thousand years, the only rape that was punished was the defiling of a virgin, and that was viewed as a property crime. A girl's virtue was a marketable asset, and so a rapist was often ordered to pay the victim's father the equivalent of her price on the marriage market. In early Babylonian and Hebrew societies, a married woman who was raped suffered the same fate as an adulteress—death by stoning or drowning. Under William the Conqueror, the penalty for raping a virgin was castration and loss of both eyes—unless the violated woman agreed to marry her attacker, as she was often pressured to do. "Stealing an heiress" became a perfectly conventional means of taking—literally—a wife.

24   It may be easier to prove a rape case now, but not much. Until the 1960s it was virtually impossible without an eyewitness; judges were often required to instruct jurors that "rape is a charge easily made and hard to defend against; so examine the testimony of this witness with caution." But sometimes a rape was taken very seriously, particularly if it involved a black man attacking a white woman—a crime for which black men were often executed or lynched.

25   Susan Estrich, author of *Real Rape*, considers herself a lucky victim. This is not just because she survived an attack 17 years ago by a stranger with an ice pick, one day before her graduation from Wellesley. It's because police, and her friends, believed her. "The first thing the Boston police

asked was whether it was a black guy," recalls Estrich, now a University of Southern California law professor. When she said yes and gave the details of the attack, their reaction was, "So, you were really raped." It was an instructive lesson, she says, in understanding how racism and sexism are factored into perceptions of the crime.

26   A new twist in society's perception came in 1975, when Susan Brownmiller published her book *Against Our Will: Men, Women and Rape*. In it she attacked the concept that rape was a sex crime, arguing instead that it was a crime of violence and power over women. Throughout history, she wrote, rape has played a critical function. "It is nothing more or less than a conscious process of intimidation, by which *all men* keep *all women* in a state of fear."

27   Out of this contention was born a set of arguments that have become politically correct wisdom on campus and in academic circles. This view holds that rape is a symbol of women's vulnerability to male institutions and attitudes. "It's sociopolitical," insists Gina Rayfield, a New Jersey psychologist. "In our culture men hold the power, politically, economically. They're socialized not to see women as equals."

28   This line of reasoning has led some women, especially radicalized victims, to justify flinging around the term rape as a political weapon, referring to everything from violent sexual assaults to inappropriate innuendos. Ginny, a college senior who was really raped when she was 16, suggests that false accusations of rape can serve a useful purpose. "Penetration is not the only form of violation," she explains. In her view, rape is a subjective term, one that women must use to draw attention to other, nonviolent, even nonsexual forms of oppression. "If a woman did falsely accuse a man of rape, she may have had reasons

> **IN CONTEXT**
>
> **Rape Crisis Centers**
>
> As a result of feminist movements that originated in the 1970s, Rape Crisis Centers (RCCs) were created. Today, the National Sexual Assault Hotline (1-800-656-HOPE) works with over 1,100 RCCs to provide emotional assistance and information for rape victims.

subjective: based on personal opinion

to," Ginny says. "Maybe she wasn't raped, but he clearly violated her in some way."

29   Catherine Comins, assistant dean of student life at Vassar, also sees some value in this loose use of "rape." She says angry victims of various forms of sexual intimidation cry rape to regain their sense of power. "To use the word carefully would be to be careful for the sake of the violator, and the survivors don't care a hoot about him." Comins argues that men who are unjustly accused can sometimes gain from the experience. "They have a lot of pain, but it is not a pain that I would necessarily have spared them. I think it ideally initiates a process of self-exploration. 'How do I see women?' 'If I didn't violate her, could I have?' 'Do I have the potential to do to her what they say I did?' Those are good questions."

> *How exactly should consent be defined and communicated?*

30   Taken to extremes, there is an ugly element of vengeance at work here. Rape is an abuse of power. But so are false accusations of rape, and to suggest that men whose reputations are destroyed might benefit because it will make them more sensitive is an attitude that is sure to backfire on women who are seeking justice for all victims. On campuses where the issue is most inflamed, male students are outraged that their names can be scrawled on a bathroom-wall list of rapists and they have no chance to tell their side of the story.

31   "Rape is what you read about in *The New York Post* about 17 little boys raping a jogger in Central Park," says a male freshman at a liberal-arts college, who learned that he had been branded a rapist after a one-night stand with a friend. He acknowledges that they were both very drunk when she started kissing him at a party and ended up back in his room. Even through his haze, he had some qualms about sleeping with her: "I'm fighting against my hormonal instincts, and my moral instincts are saying, 'This is my friend and if I were sober, I wouldn't be doing this.'" But he went ahead anyway. "When you're drunk, and there are all sorts of ambiguity, and the woman says 'Please, please' and then she says no sometime later, even in the middle of the act, there

still may very well be some kind of violation, but it's not the same thing. It's not rape. If you don't hear her say no, if she doesn't say it, if she's playing around with you—oh, I could get squashed for saying it—there is an element of say no, mean yes."

32   The morning after their encounter, he recalls, both students woke up hung over and eager to put the memory behind them. Only months later did he learn that she had told a friend that he had torn her clothing and raped her. At this point in the story, the accused man starts using the language of rape. "I felt violated," he says. "I felt like she was taking advantage of me when she was very drunk. I never heard her say 'No!,' 'Stop!,' anything." He is angry and hurt at the charges, worried that they will get around, shatter his reputation, and force him to leave the small campus.

33   So here, of course, is the heart of the debate. If rape is sex without consent, how exactly should consent be defined and communicated, when and by whom? Those who view rape through a political lens tend to place all responsibility on men to make sure that their partners are consenting at every point of a sexual encounter. At the extreme, sexual relations come to resemble major surgery, requiring a signed consent form. Clinical psychologist Mary P. Koss of the University of Arizona in Tucson, who is a leading scholar on the issue, puts it rather bluntly: "It's the man's

IN CONTEXT

RAINN: The Rape, Abuse and Incest National Network

Tori Amos and Christina Ricci are both spokespeople for RAINN, the Rape, Abuse and Incest National Network. Founded by Scott Berkowitz in 1994, RAINN is the largest anti-sexual assault organization in the country.

qualms: doubts

penis that is doing the raping, and ultimately he's responsible for where he puts it."

34 Historically, of course, this has never been the case, and there are some who argue that it shouldn't be—that women too must take responsibility for their behavior and that the whole realm of intimate encounters defies regulation from on high. Anthropologist Lionel Tiger has little patience for trendy sexual politics that make no reference to biology. Since the dawn of time, he argues, men and women have always gone to bed with different goals. In the effort to keep one's genes in the gene pool, "it is to the male advantage to fertilize as many females as possible, as quickly as possible and as efficiently as possible." For the female, however, who looks at the large investment she will have to make in the offspring, the opposite is true. Her concern is to "select" who "will provide the best set up for their offspring." So, in general, "the pressure is on the male to be aggressive and on the female to be coy."

35 No one defends the use of physical force, but when the coercion involved is purely psychological, it becomes hard to assign blame after the fact. Journalist Stephanie Gutmann is an ardent foe of what she calls the date-rape dogmatists. "How can you make sex completely politically correct and completely safe?" she asks. "What a horribly bland, unerotic thing that would be! Sex is, by nature, a risky endeavor, emotionally. And desire is a violent emotion. These people in the date-rape movement have erected so many rules and regulations that I don't know how people can have erotic or desire-driven sex."

36 Nonsense, retorts Cornell professor Andrea Parrot, co-author of *Acquaintance Rape: The Hidden Crime.* Seduction should not be about lies, manipulation, game playing, or coercion of any kind, she says. "Too bad that people think that the only way you can have passion and excitement and sex is if there are miscommunications and one person is forced to do something he or she doesn't want to do." The very pleasures of sexual encounters should lie in the fact of mutual comfort and consent: "You can hang from the ceiling, you can use fruit, you can go crazy and have really wonderful sensual erotic sex, if both parties are consenting."

37 It would be easy to accuse feminists of being too quick to classify sex as rape, but feminists are to be found on all sides of the debate, and many protest the idea that all the onus is on the man. It demeans women to suggest that they are so vulnerable to coercion or emotional manipulation that they must always be escorted by the strong arm of the law. "You can't solve society's ills by making everything a crime," says Albuquerque attorney Nancy Hollander. "That comes out of the sense of overprotection of women, and in the long run that is going to be harmful to us."

38 What is lost in the ideological debate over date rape is the fact that men and women, especially when they are young, and drunk, and aroused, are not very good at communicating. "In many cases," says Estrich, "the man thought it was sex, and the woman thought it was rape, and they are both telling the truth." The man may envision a celluloid seduction, in which he is being commanding, she is being coy. A woman may experience the same event as a degrading violation of her will. That some men do not believe a woman's protests is scarcely surprising in a society so drenched with messages that women have rape fantasies and a desire to be overpowered.

39 By the time they reach college, men and women are loaded with cultural baggage, drawn from movies, television, music videos, and "bodice ripper" romance novels. Over the years they have watched Rhett sweep Scarlett up the stairs in *Gone With the Wind;* or Errol Flynn, who was charged twice with statutory rape, overpower a protesting heroine who then melts in his arms;

coy: shy, modest
onus: burden, responsibility
celluloid: movie, film

or Stanley rape his sister-in-law Blanche du Bois while his wife is in the hospital giving birth to a child in *A Streetcar Named Desire*. Higher up the cultural food chain, young people can read of date rape in Homer or Jane Austen, watch it in *Don Giovanni* or *Rigoletto*.

40   The messages come early and often, and nothing in the feminist revolution has been able to counter them. A recent survey of sixth- to ninth-graders in Rhode Island found that a fourth of the boys and a sixth of the girls said it was acceptable for a man to force a woman to kiss him or have sex if he has spent money on her. A third of the children said it would not be wrong for a man to rape a woman who had had previous sexual experiences.

41   Certainly cases like Palm Beach, movies like *The Accused* and novels like Avery Corman's *Prized Possessions* may force young people to re-examine assumptions they have inherited. The use of new terms, like "acquaintance rape" and "date rape," while controversial, has given men and women the vocabulary they need to express their experiences with both force and precision. This dialogue would be useful if it helps strip away some of the dogmas, old and new, surrounding the issue. Those who hope to raise society's sensitivity to the problem of date rape would do well to concede that it is not precisely the same sort of crime as street rape, that there may be very murky issues of intent and degree involved.

42   On the other hand, those who downplay the problem should come to realize that date rape is a crime of uniquely intimate cruelty. While the body is violated, the spirit is maimed. How long will it take, once the wounds have healed, before it is possible to share a walk on a beach, a drive home from work or an evening's conversation without always listening for a quiet alarm to start ringing deep in the back of the memory of a terrible crime?

> *A fourth of the boys and a sixth of the girls said it was acceptable for a man to force a woman to kiss him or have sex if he has spent money on her*

Nancy Gibbs, "When Is It RAPE?" *Time*, June 3, 1991. Copyright Time Inc. Reprinted by permission. TIME is a registered trademark of Time Inc. All rights reserved.

maimed: wounded, mutilated

CONVERSATIONS: Collaborating in Class or Online

1. According to statistics, what types of people are responsible for most rapes?
2. What does Gibbs mean when she says, "What they don't know is whether they have more to fear from their friends" (para. 1)?
3. According to this essay, what percentage of women will be raped during their lifetimes? What percentage of these crimes is reported?
4. How does anthropologist Lionel Tiger explain the difference between men's and women's attitudes toward sex?

CONNECTIONS: Discovering Relationships among Ideas

5. Why are the rape victims on trial as much as their attackers?
6. According to Gibbs, how are "racism and sexism . . . factored into perceptions of the crime" (para. 25)?
7. How are movies and novels related to date rape? How do some romance novels glorify rape?
8. What does Gibbs mean when she says, "Date rape is a crime of uniquely intimate cruelty" (para. 42)?

PRESENTATION: Analyzing the Writer's Craft

9. Why does Gibbs cite the William Kennedy Smith case in her essay?

10. What other narratives does Gibbs introduce to support her point of view? Are they effective choices for clarifying her definition? Cite two stories that were especially persuasive to you.

11. This essay was first published on June 24, 2001, but it remains an essential part of our conversations about date rape. In what areas have we made progress since this essay was published?

12. How does Gibbs organize her definition essay?

PROJECTS: Expressing Your Own Views

13. **Podcast:** Interview at least five of your peers on the issues surrounding date rape. Prepare a thoughtful set of questions before you begin. Then compile the facts and opinions you learned into an informative, interesting podcast.

14. **Poem:** Write a poem about true love. Be sure to establish a specific purpose before you begin to write.

15. **Editorial:** Write an editorial for your college newspaper expressing your views on the issue of date rape.

16. **Research:** Read and summarize the three resources below. Generate one specific question from each resource that focuses on definition. Then answer one of your questions in a documented essay, consulting these and other sources as necessary.

OTHER RESOURCES

Web Site

Rape Crisis Center: Serving Children, Women, and Men: http://rapecrisis.com

Academic Article

"The Wrong of Rape"

by David Archard

The Philosophical Quarterly 57.228 (2007): 374–393

Audio/Video

CBS New: www.cbsnews.com

Search: "Date Rape Common in College"

Click on the Video link

ONE LAST THOUGHT

Rape is a major problem in South Africa. The Community of Information, Empowerment, and Transparency interviewed 4,000 women and found that one in three said they had been raped in the last year. The Medical Research Council estimates that 500,000 rapes are committed annually in South Africa, with more than 25% of men admitting to the crime. In 2006, a South African woman named Sonnet Ehlers invented Rape-aXe, an anti-rape female condom, after a victim said, "If only I had teeth down there." Blades on the inside of the device attach themselves to the attacker's penis and have to be removed surgically, often leading to arrest. The invention has been criticized for its medieval-style violence. If you owned a store in South Africa, would you carry this product? Why or why not?

Augmented Reality: Coming to a Device Near You

by Mark Sullivan

As the Senior Editor of PC World, Mark Sullivan is on the cutting edge of developments in the world of technology. PC World.com, which won the 2004 and 2005 Jesse H. Neal Award for Best Web Site, helps businesses keep up with technological changes that keep them competitive.

PREREADING QUESTIONS

How far do you think technology will take our society during your lifetime?

What do you think Augmented Reality is?

How do you use social networking sites? In what ways?

View the entire video at www.pcworld.com/article/182182/augmented_reality_coming_to_a_device_near_you.html before answering the questions that follow.

CONVERSATIONS: Collaborating in Class or Online

1. Define *Augmented Reality* (AR) in your own words.
2. How is AR related to the use of smartphones?
3. What does AR have to do with contact lenses?
4. Summarize the content of the video.

CONNECTIONS: Discovering Relationships among Ideas

5. From your understanding of the material in the video and the accompanying statement, how does the app "Nearest Places" work?

6. How might smartphones and wireless communication projected on reality take us to places we can't imagine right now?

7. Beyond the examples in the video, what other situations might be enhanced by AR?

8. What immediate aspects of your daily routine would be most affected by AR?

PRESENTATION: Analyzing the Writer's Craft

9. How do Mark Sullivan and his demeanor or image in the video help communicate the definition of Augmented Reality? Explain your answer.

10. How effective was the combination of words and pictures in the video?

11. Do you think opening with a definition of AR is effective? Explain your answer.

12. Explain how Sullivan organizes his examples? How does this order clarify AR?

PROJECTS: Expressing Your Own Views

13. **Slide Show:** Create a slide show that presents your definition of Augmented Reality. What aspects of our lives will be most affected by this technology?

14. **Photo:** Find another example of AR on the Internet. How does the example illustrate the definition in this selection? Explain your answer in detail.

15. **Essay:** Write an essay predicting and defining one other technological change that might take place in the next five years. What are its details? Why will it occur?

16. **Research**: Read and summarize the three resources below. Generate one specific question from each resource that focuses on definition. Then answer one of your questions in a documented essay, consulting these and other sources as necessary.

OTHER RESOURCES

Web Site
Augmented Reality: AR Apps Phones and Games: www.augmentedreality.org

Academic Article
"Remix: The Art and Craft of Endless Hybridization"
by Michele Knobel and Colin Lankshear

Journal of Adolescent & Adult Literacy 52.1 (2008): 22–33

Audio/Video
TAT: The Astonishing Tribe: www.tat.se
Click on the Videos tab, and watch the Horizon 2D-3D Map video

ONE LAST THOUGHT

4-D films are interactive movie experiences that combine 3-D film with physical effects, such as wind, mist, odors, lights, and even vibrating seats. *Honey, I Shrunk the Audience* is a well-known 4-D film that ran from 1998-2010 at several Disney theme parks. Have you ever seen a movie in 4-D? What special effects would be most entertaining to you at a 4-D film?

The Millennials

by Pew Research Center

The following article was written by the **Pew Research Center**, a non-partisan "fact tank" based in Washington, D.C., that provides polls, public opinion research, and national surveys on issues, attitudes, and trends shaping America and the world. Originally founded in Philadelphia in 2004, it is funded by the Pew Charitable Trusts.

PREREADING QUESTIONS

What specific characteristics separate your generation from others?

How accurately do these qualities describe you?

If you could create a label for your generation, what would it be?

1   Generations, like people, have personalities, and Millennials—the American teens and twenty-somethings who are making the passage into adulthood at the start of a new millennium—have begun to forge theirs: confident, self-expressive, liberal, upbeat, and open to change.

2   They are more ethnically and racially diverse than older adults. They're less religious, less likely to have served in the military, and on track to become the most educated generation in American history.

3   Their entry into careers and first jobs has been badly set back by the Great Recession, but they are more upbeat than their elders about their own economic futures as well as about the overall state of the nation.

4   They embrace multiple modes of self-expression. Three-quarters have created a profile on a social networking site. One in five has posted a video of themselves online. Nearly four in ten have a tattoo (and for most who do, one is not enough; about half of those with tattoos have two to five, and 18% have six or more). Nearly one in four has a piercing in some place other than an earlobe—about six times the share of older adults who've done this. But their look-at-me tendencies are not without limits. Most Millennials have placed privacy boundaries on their social media profiles. And 70% say their tattoos are hidden beneath clothing.

5   Despite struggling (and often failing) to find jobs in the teeth of a recession, about nine in ten either say that they currently have

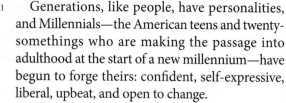

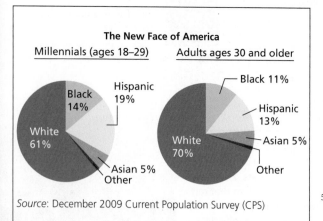

The New Face of America

Millennials (ages 18–29)

Hispanic 19%
Black 14%
White 61%
Asian 5%
Other

Adults ages 30 and older

Black 11%
Hispanic 13%
White 70%
Asian 5%
Other

Source: December 2009 Current Population Survey (CPS)

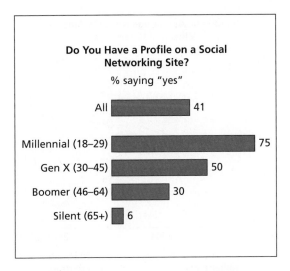

Do You Have a Profile on a Social Networking Site?

% saying "yes"

All	41
Millennial (18–29)	75
Gen X (30–45)	50
Boomer (46–64)	30
Silent (65+)	6

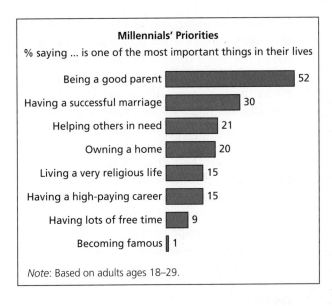

Millennials' Priorities

% saying … is one of the most important things in their lives

Being a good parent	52
Having a successful marriage	30
Helping others in need	21
Owning a home	20
Living a very religious life	15
Having a high-paying career	15
Having lots of free time	9
Becoming famous	1

Note: Based on adults ages 18–29.

enough money or that they will eventually meet their long-term financial goals. But at the moment, fully 37% of 18- to 29-year-olds are unemployed or out of the workforce, the highest share among this age group in more than three decades. Research shows that young people who graduate from college in a bad economy typically suffer long-term consequences—with effects on their careers and earnings that linger as long as 15 years.

6 Whether as a by-product of protective parents, the age of terrorism, or a media culture that focuses on dangers, they cast a wary eye on human nature. Two-thirds say, "You can't be too careful" when dealing with people. Yet they are less skeptical than their elders of government. More so than other generations, they believe government should do more to solve problems.

7 They are the least overtly religious American generation in modern times. One in four are unaffiliated with any religion, far more than the share of older adults when they were ages 18 to 29. Yet not belonging does not necessarily mean not believing. Millennials pray about as often as their elders did in their own youth.

8 Only about six in ten were raised by both parents—a smaller share than was the case with older generations. In weighing their own life priorities, Millennials (like older adults) place parenthood and marriage far above career and financial success. But they aren't rushing to the altar. Just one in five Millennials (21%) are

married now, half the share of their parents' generation at the same stage of life. About a third (34%) are parents, according to the Pew Research survey. In 2006, more than a third of 18 to 29-year-old women who gave birth were unmarried. This is a far higher share than was the case in earlier generations.

9 Millennials are on course to become the most educated generation in American history, a trend driven largely by the demands of a modern knowledge-based economy, but most likely accelerated in recent years by the millions of 20-somethings enrolling in graduate schools, colleges, or community colleges in part because they can't find a job. Among 18- to 24-year-olds, a record share—39.6%—was enrolled in college as of 2008, according to census data.

> *Millennials are on course to become the most educated generation in American history*

10 They get along well with their parents. Looking back at their teenage years, Millennials report having had fewer spats with mom

spats: small arguments

or dad than older adults say they had with their own parents when they were growing up. And now, hard times have kept a significant share of adult Millennials and their parents under the same roof. About one-in-eight older Millennials (ages 22 and older) say they've "boomeranged" back to a parent's home because of the recession.

11   They respect their elders. A majority says that the older generation is superior to the younger generation when it comes to moral values and work ethic. Also, more than six in ten say that families have a responsibility to have an elderly parent come live with them if that parent wants to. By contrast, fewer than four in ten adults ages 60 and older agree that this is a family responsibility.

12   Despite coming of age at a time when the United States has been waging two wars, relatively few Millennials—just 2% of males— are military veterans. At a comparable stage of their life cycle, 6% of Gen Xer men, 13% of Baby Boomer men, and 24% of Silent men were veterans.

13   Politically, Millennials were among Barack Obama's strongest supporters in 2008, backing him for president by more than a two-to-one ratio (66% to 32%) while older adults were giving just 50% of their votes to the Democratic nominee. This was the largest disparity between younger and older voters recorded in four decades of modern election-day exit polling. Moreover, after decades of low voter participation by the young, the turnout gap in 2008 between voters under and over the age of 30 was the smallest it had been since 18- to 20-year-olds were given the right to vote in 1972. But the political enthusiasms of Millennials have since cooled—for Obama and his message of change, for the Democratic Party, and, quite possibly, for politics itself. About half of Millennials say the president has failed to change the way Washington works, which had been the central promise of his candidacy. Of those who say

> *They are still more likely than any other age group to identify as Democrats*

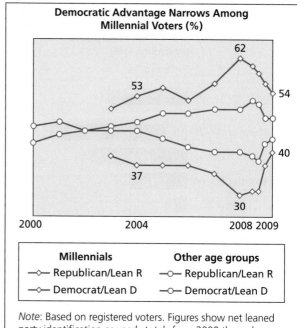

Democratic Advantage Narrows Among Millennial Voters (%)

62
53   54
37
40
30

2000   2004   2008 2009

Millennials	Other age groups
–◇– Republican/Lean R	–○– Republican/Lean R
–◇– Democrat/Lean D	–○– Democrat/Lean D

Note: Based on registered voters. Figures show net leaned party identification as yearly totals from 2000 through 2008 and quarterly for 2009.

Source: Pew Research Center surveys

this, three in ten blame Obama himself, while more than half blame his political opponents and special interests.

14   To be sure, Millennials remain the most likely of any generation to self-identify as liberals; they are less supportive than their elders of an assertive national security policy and more supportive of a progressive domestic social agenda. They are still more likely than any other age group to identify as Democrats. Yet by early 2010, their support for Obama and the Democrats had receded, as evidenced both by survey data and by their low level of participation in recent off-year and special elections.

Our Research Methods

15   This Pew Research Center report profiles the roughly 50 million Millennials who currently span the ages of 18 to 29. It's likely that when

receded: decreased

What's in a Name?

Generational names are the handiwork of popular culture. Some are drawn from a historic event; others from rapid social or demographic change; others from a big turn in the calendar.

The Millennial generation falls into the third category. The label refers to those born after 1980–the first generation to come of age in the new millennium.

Generation X covers people born from 1965 through 1980. The label long ago overtook the first name affixed to this generation: the Baby Bust. Xers are often depicted as savvy, entrepreneurial loners.

The Baby Boomer label is drawn from the great spike in fertility that began in 1946, right after the end of World War II, and ended almost as abruptly in 1964, around the time the birth control pill went on the market. It's a classic example of a demography-driven name.

The Silent generation describes adults born from 1928 through 1945. Children of the Great Depression and World War II, their "Silent" label refers to their conformist and civic instincts. It also makes for a nice contrast with the noisy ways of the anti-establishment Boomers.

The Greatest Generation (those born before 1928) "saved the world" when it was young, in the memorable phrase of Ronald Reagan. It's the generation that fought and won World War II.

Generational names are works in progress. The Zeitgeist changes, and labels that once seemed spot-on fall out of fashion. It's not clear if the Millennial tag will endure, although a calendar change that comes along only once in a thousand years seems like a pretty secure anchor.

future analysts are in a position to take a fuller measure of this new generation, they will conclude that millions of additional younger teens (and perhaps even pre-teens) should be grouped together with their older brothers and sisters. But for the purposes of this report, unless we indicate otherwise, we focus on Millennials who are at least 18 years old.

16   We examine their demographics, their political and social values, their lifestyles and life priorities, their digital technology and social media habits, and their economic and educational aspirations. We also compare and contrast Millennials with the nation's three other living generations—Gen Xers (ages 30 to 45), Baby Boomers (ages 46 to 64), and Silents (ages 65 and older). Whenever the trend data permit, we compare the four generations as they all are now—and also as older generations were at the ages that adult Millennials are now.

17   Most of the findings in this report are based on a new survey of a national cross-section of 2,020 adults (including an oversample of Millennials), conducted by landline and cellular telephone from Jan. 14 to 27, 2010; this survey has a margin of error of plus or minus 3.0 percentage points for the full sample and larger percentages for various subgroups. The report also draws on more than two decades of Pew Research Center surveys, supplemented by our analysis of Census Bureau data and other relevant studies.

Some Caveats

18   A few notes of caution are in order. Generational analysis has a long and distinguished place in social science, and we cast our lot with those scholars who believe it is not only possible but often highly illuminating to search for the unique and distinctive characteristics of any given age group of Americans. But we also know this is not an exact science.

19   We acknowledge, for example, that there is an element of false precision in setting hard chronological boundaries between the generations. Can we say with certainty that a typical 30-year-old adult is a Gen Xer while a typical 29-year-old adult is a Millennial? Of course not. Nevertheless, we must draw lines in order to carry out the statistical analyses that form the core of our research methodology. And our boundaries—while admittedly too crisp—are not arbitrary. They are based on our own research findings and those of other scholars.

20   We are mindful that there are as many differences in attitudes, values, behaviors, and

caveats: warnings
arbitrary: random

lifestyles within a generation as there are between generations. But we believe this reality does not diminish the value of generational analysis; it merely adds to its richness and complexity. Throughout this report, we will not only explore how Millennials differ from other generations, we will also look at how they differ among themselves.

The Millennial Identity

21   Most Millennials (61%) in our January 2010 survey say their generation has a unique and distinctive identity. That doesn't make them unusual, however. Roughly two-thirds of Silents, nearly six in ten Boomers and about half of Xers feel the same way about their generation.

> *But Millennials have a distinctive reason for feeling distinctive*

22   But Millennials have a distinctive reason for feeling distinctive. In response to an open-ended follow-up question, 24% say it's because of their use of technology. Gen Xers also cite technology as their generation's biggest source of distinctiveness, but far fewer—just 12%—say this. Boomers' feelings of distinctiveness coalesce mainly around work ethic, which 17% cite as their most prominent identity badge. For Silents, it's the shared experience of the Depression and World War II, which 14% cite as the biggest reason their generation stands apart.

23   Millennials' technological exceptionalism is chronicled throughout the survey. It's not just their gadgets—it's the way they've fused their social lives into them. For example, three-quarters of Millennials have created a profile on a social networking site, compared with half of Xers, 30% of Boomers and 6% of Silents. There are big generation gaps, as well, in using wireless technology, playing video games, and posting self-created videos online. Millennials are also more likely than older adults to say technology makes life easier and brings family and friends closer together (though the generation gaps on these questions are relatively narrow).

What Makes Your Generation Unique?

Millennial	Gen X	Boomer	Silent
1. Technology use (24%)	Technology use (12%)	Work ethic (17%)	WW II, Depression (14%)
2. Music/Pop culture (11%)	Work ethic (11%)	Respectful (14%)	Smarter (13%)
3. Liberal/tolerant (7%)	Conservative /Trad'l (7%)	Values/Morals (8%)	Honest (12%)
4. Smarter (6%)	Smarter (6%)	"Baby Boomers" (6%)	Work ethic (10%)
5. Clothes (5%)	Respectful (5%)	Smarter (5%)	Values/Morals (10%)

Note: Based on respondents who said their generation was unique/distinct. Items represent individual open-ended responses. Top five responses are shown for each age group. Sample sizes for sub-groups are as follows: Millennials, n=527; Gen X, n=173; Boomers, n=283; Silent, n=205.

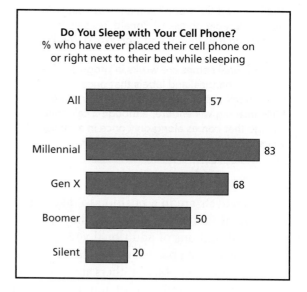

Do You Sleep with Your Cell Phone?
% who have ever placed their cell phone on or right next to their bed while sleeping

All	57
Millennial	83
Gen X	68
Boomer	50
Silent	20

coalesce: join together

Work Ethic, Moral Values, Race Relations

24 Of the four generations, Millennials are the only one that doesn't cite "work ethic" as one of their principal claims to distinctiveness. A nationwide Pew Research Center survey taken in 2009 may help explain why. This one focused on differences between young and old rather than between specific age groups. Nonetheless, its findings are instructive.

25 Nearly six in ten respondents cited work ethic as one of the big sources of difference between young and old. Asked who has the better work ethic, about three-fourths of respondents said that older people do. By similar margins, survey respondents also found older adults have the upper hand when it comes to moral values and their respect for others.

26 It might be tempting to dismiss these findings as a typical older adult gripe about "kids today." But when it comes to each of these traits—work ethic, moral values, respect for others—young adults agree that older adults have the better of it. In short, Millennials may be a self-confident generation, but they display little appetite for claims of moral superiority.

27 That 2009 survey also found that the public—young and old alike—thinks the younger generation is more racially tolerant than their elders. More than two decades of Pew Research surveys confirm that assessment. In their views about interracial dating, for example, Millennials are the most open to change of any generation, followed closely by Gen Xers, then Boomers, then Silents.

28 Likewise, Millennials are more receptive to immigrants than are their elders. Nearly six in ten (58%) say immigrants strengthen the country, according to a 2009 Pew Research survey; just 43% of adults ages 30 and older agree.

29 The same pattern holds on a range of attitudes about nontraditional family arrangements, from mothers of young children working outside the home, to adults living together without being married, to more people of different races marrying each other. Millennials are more accepting than older generations of these more modern family arrangements, followed closely by Gen Xers. To be sure, acceptance does not in all cases translate into outright approval. But it does mean Millennials disapprove less.

A Gentler Generation Gap

30 A 1969 Gallup survey, taken near the height of the social and political upheavals of that turbulent decade, found that 74% of the public believed there was a "generation gap" in American society. Surprisingly, when that same question was asked in a Pew Research Center survey last year—in an era marked by hard economic times but little if any overt age-based social tension—the share of the public saying there was a generation gap had risen slightly to 79%.

gripe: complaint
overt: obvious, apparent

Weighing Trends in Marriage and Parenthood, by Generation

% saying this is a bad thing for society

	Millennial	Gen X	Boomer	Silent
More single women deciding to have children	59	54	65	72
More gay couples raising children	32	36	43	55
More mothers of young children working outside the home	23	29	39	38
More people living together w/o getting married	22	31	44	58
More people of different races marrying each other	5	10	14	26

Note: "Good thing", "Doesn't make much difference", and "Don't know" responses not shown.

The Satisfaction Gap

% saying they are satisfied with the way things are going in this country today

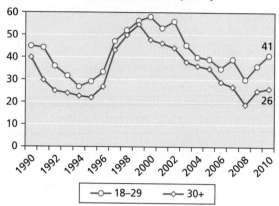

Source: Pew Research Center surveys

31　But as the 2009 results also make clear, this modern generation gap is a much more benign affair than the one that cast a shadow over the 1960s. The public says this one is mostly about the different ways that old and young use technology—and relatively few people see that gap as a source of conflict. Indeed, only about a quarter of the respondents in the 2009 survey said they see big conflicts between young and old in America. Many more see conflicts between immigrants and the native born, between rich and poor, and between black and whites.

32　There is one generation gap that has widened notably in recent years. It has to do with satisfaction over the state of the nation. In recent decades, the young have always tended to be a bit more upbeat than their elders on this key measure, but the gap is wider now than it has been in at least twenty years. Some 41% of Millennials say they are satisfied with the way things are going in the country, compared with just 26% of those ages 30 and older. Whatever toll a recession, a housing crisis, a financial meltdown, and a pair of wars may have taken on the national psyche in the past few years, it appears to have hit the old harder than the young.

33　But this speaks to a difference in outlook and attitude; it's not a source of conflict or tension. As they make their way into adulthood, Millennials have already distinguished themselves as a generation that gets along well with others, especially their elders. For a nation whose population is rapidly going gray, that could prove to be a most welcome character trait.

benign: harmless
psyche: spirit

CONVERSATIONS: Collaborating in Class or Online

1. Who are the Millennials? Where did this label come from?
2. What are the defining characteristics of this group?
3. Based on the information furnished here, what is the most striking difference between Millennials and their parents?
4. What are the main features of the four generations the Pew Research Center names in this essay?

CONNECTIONS: Discovering Relationships among Ideas

5. In what ways are the Millennials "on track to become the most educated generation in American history" (para. 2)?
6. Why do you think students graduating into a bad economy "suffer long-term consequences" (para. 5)? What consequences do you think they will suffer?

7. Which of the characteristics that the Pew Research Center outlines in this article is most surprising to you? Explain your answer.

8. Why do you think Millennials get along well with their elders?

PRESENTATION: Analyzing the Writer's Craft

9. What is the Pew Research Center's purpose in this essay?

10. Who do you think was its original audience?

11. How is this essay organized? Do you think this arrangement was effective? Explain your answer in detail.

12. How do the visuals support the prose in this essay? Explain your answer.

PROJECTS: Expressing Your Own Views

13. **Comic Strip:** Create a comic strip that captures the essence of your generation.

14. **Photo Essay:** Create a photo essay that highlights the dominant features of the four generations the Pew Research Center compares in this essay.

15. **Essay:** Write an essay defining yourself in reference to the article's discussion of the four most recent generations. How do you see yourself in relation to the comparisons made here? Are these findings accurate from your point of view?

16. **Research:** Read and summarize the three resources below. Generate one specific question from each resource that focuses on definition. Then answer one of your questions in a documented essay, consulting these and other sources as necessary.

OTHER RESOURCES

Web Site

Beloit College: www.beloit.edu

Search: "Mindset list"

Click on the Mindset List link

and then on a year that interests you

Audio/Video

CBS News: www.cbsnews.com

Search: "The Millennials Are Coming"

Click on the Video link

Academic Article

"Millennials in the Workplace: A Communication Perspective on Millennials' Organizational Relationships and Performance"
by Karen K. Myers and Kamyab Sadaghiani

Journal of Business and Psychology 25.2 (2010): 225–238

ONE LAST THOUGHT

Generationism is the idea that specific generations have traits exclusive to them. People use these traits to separate and define different generations. What qualities that your generation shares do you embrace? Which do you reject? Which prepare you to be successful in life?

Fans as Authors

by Andres Salazar and
Paul Martinez

Andres Salazar grew up in Little Rock, Arkansas. He attended Roosevelt School of the Arts, where he specialized in theater and visual life drawing, then earned a Bachelor of Science at University of California, Santa Barbara, in Molecular Biology. In addition to working on a number of independent film projects, he enjoys writing TV spec scripts. **Paul Martinez** works as a graphic designer and web designer for an advertising agency in California. He has written and illustrated various comic books, including his own web comic,

The Adventures of the 19XX, an adventure story that takes place in the 1930s.

PREREADING QUESTIONS

What is the last novel you read?

Would you like to change any part of that novel? If so, what would you change?

What do you suppose fan fiction is?

1   Ever watch a movie and wish it had turned out differently? Would you like to create new characters in a popular TV show or put a different spin on those who already exist? Perhaps you'd like to submit a script for an episode of your favorite sitcom. Well, here's your chance. Enter the new and exciting world of fan fiction, which means "fiction" written by "fans" of a well-known novel, movie, television show, or other forms of media. In the following interview, Andres Salazar and Paul Martinez define "fan fiction" and "spec scripts" and explain how we can become authors of these new artistic genres.

What is fan fiction?

2   **ANDRES:** Fan fiction is amateur fiction written by fans. It's a story that takes place in a universe that's already been established by another writer. It's amateur writing about characters that we all already know.

3   **PAUL:** And it's important to note the word *amateur* because the people who get paid to write stories are professional writers; the ones who do it as an unpaid hobby really make up the bulk of fan fiction authors.

What separates fan fiction from professional writing?

4   **ANDRES:** Fan fiction authors write for fun. Anyone can be a fan fiction writer, but not everyone gets paid for their work, like professionals do. That's part of the reason the term has so many negative connotations now. A lot of people, when they hear "fan fiction," think of

genres: types of writing
connotations: implications

sub-par, amateurish writing, though this is not always an accurate description of their efforts.

5   **PAUL:** Part of those negative connotations also come from the fact that fan fiction is so easy to write now with the accessibility of the Internet. Literally anyone can write about anything they want and post it on a fan fiction Website like www.fantiction.net.

How did fan fiction originate?

6   **PAUL:** Fan fiction really got its start in the '60s with the sci-fi genre. The original *Star Trek* had fanzines that included some fan fiction. It grew again when the Internet took off, mostly because people finally had a new, exciting way to share their stories with others who had similar interests.

Another way for fans to share stories is through a genre called "spec scripts." Exactly what are those?

7   **ANDRES:** The term "spec script" actually stands for "speculative screenplay." Spec scripts are non-commissioned scripts that people write for television shows or movies. Writers aren't hired to produce these scripts; rather, they choose to write them on their own. People submit them as resume builders or for the chance they'll eventually be made into a film or movie. Spec scripts are almost like calling cards for writers.

> **A lot of people write spec scripts for TV shows to get writing jobs**

8   **PAUL:** A lot of people write spec scripts for TV shows to get writing jobs, even if their scripts are never produced.

What fan fiction or spec scripts have you read or written?

9   **ANDRES:** I've read a lot of scripts. I read specs that I want to learn from. The best way to learn is to read. I've read spec scripts for *West Wing*, *Sopranos*, *Breaking Bad*, *Justified*, *White Collar*, *30 Rock*, *Modern Family*, and *Entourage*, to name just a few. I've written spec scripts for *Breaking Bad* and *The Office*. I find it easier to write scripts for shows that I watch on a regular basis.

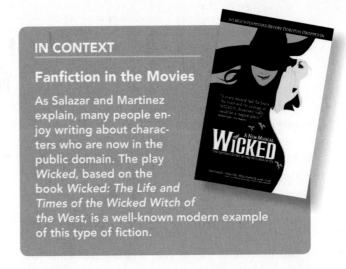

IN CONTEXT

Fanfiction in the Movies

As Salazar and Martinez explain, many people enjoy writing about characters who are now in the public domain. The play *Wicked*, based on the book *Wicked: The Life and Times of the Wicked Witch of the West*, is a well-known modern example of this type of fiction.

10   **PAUL:** I've written some *G.I. Joe* fan fiction too. One story I wrote involved Duke, Snake Eyes, and Dusty in a three-part narrative about the downfall of the G.I. Joes—Cobra defeats them, but then they come back to beat Cobra at the end. I also like writing shorter fan fiction stories; I do a lot with *Star Trek: The Next Generation* and *Star Trek: Voyager*.

Why do people enjoy writing fan fiction or spec scripts?

11   **PAUL:** It's cathartic to play out these scenes you wish had happened in the originals. Or you can continue shows that got cancelled before you were ready to see them go, like *Firefly* or *Buffy the Vampire Slayer*. Both have huge fan fiction bases. Another growing fan fiction outlet is Harry Potter; fan fiction writers on the Internet are attempting to keep Harry and his Hogwarts buddies alive and well in the world of the imagination.

12   **ANDRES:** Spec scripts are a good way to get jobs too. Your script, even if it's unproduced, is your résumé. Whether you want to work in TV or movies, you have to write to get jobs. How do you get your scripts into people's hands? That's the $8 million question.

---

accessibility: availability

fanzines: fan club magazines

non-commissioned: not solicited

Are there any legal ramifications of writing fan fiction or spec scripts?

13   **ANDRES:** Absolutely. Most big publishers and creators turn a blind eye to them, but you can be prosecuted if you try to *sell* fan fiction when someone owns the rights to the characters you use.

What are some pros and cons of writing fan fiction or spec scripts?

14   **ANDRES:** One negative is that you are restricted by the characters that already exist; you cannot grow creatively as a writer doing only fan fiction. If you're just writing fictional stories with someone else's characters, say *Twilight*, you can't mature as much as if you had created the characters on your own. Also, there's a lot of competition in the spec script field. It's not easy to write a script and get a job. It takes an immense amount of work.

15   **PAUL:** It's good, though, to work with fleshed-out characters, so it's easier than starting from scratch. Your characters are immediately recognizable, so you already have this built-in fan-base, especially for characters in the public domain.

Where do you find or display fan fiction or spec scripts?

16   **ANDRES:** Online. The fan fiction world is huge on the Internet. You will find web rings and communities with enormous followings online. There's a show called *Jericho* that was cancelled in 2008, and there are still new stories and scripts being written for it. There probably will be for years to come. It keeps the franchise alive.

17   **PAUL:** I have friends who write spec scripts, and sometimes we share them with each other. I have read a ton of my friends' stories. We help each other generate ideas and revise our plots.

What are some fan fiction success stories?

18   **PAUL:** There are entire genres that are professional fan fiction. One example is *The Wizard of Oz*. The characters from Oz exist in comic books, novels, and even theater.

19   **ANDRES:** Even really well-known stuff, like Alan Moore's *League of Extraordinary Gentlemen*, is essentially fan fiction because it's based on literary characters from the public domain.

20   **PAUL:** Jane Austen's work has recently been expanded, too, with books like *Pride and Prejudice and Zombies* and *Sense and Sensibility and Sea Monsters*.

Do you have any advice for people who want to write fan fiction or spec scripts?

21   **ANDRES:** I think there are two things you have to do to be a writer: you have to read and you have to write. You need to pay attention to format and structure; if you want to write an hour drama, you need to understand what a five-act story is. You need to know how that structure is written. You must know that on page 12 or 13 you're going to have an act break. You need to know when to put in a dilemma and when you need a red herring or a turn.

22   **PAUL:** You should also know a lot about the characters you're using. Be intimately familiar with them before you try to write about them. But I agree with Andres: You have to read and write a lot. The more you do it, the better your writing will be.

> **franchise:** license to use a specific product

CONVERSATIONS: Collaborating in Class or Online

1. Define *fan fiction* in your own words.
2. What is the origin of fan fiction?
3. In what ways are spec scripts "almost like calling cards for writers"?
4. Explain two potential problems or drawbacks associated with fan fiction.

CONNECTIONS: Discovering Relationships among Ideas

5. In what ways does the Internet foster the development of fan fiction?
6. What program, book, or movie not mentioned in this interview would be a good source for fan fiction writers?
7. Why do you think readers enjoy sharing fan fiction?
8. In what ways could fan fiction be a useful source of publicity for the authors of the original sources?

PRESENTATION: Analyzing the Writer's Craft

9. What is the purpose of this interview?
10. What standard features of definition appear in this selection?
11. Outline this interview, and explain how the questions are organized.
12. Does this explanation inspire you to find out more about fan fiction? Explain your answer.

PROJECTS: Expressing Your Own Views

13. **Collage:** Find a single photo, drawing, or Internet image that captures your concept of recreational reading. Exchange artwork with a classmate and write a caption for your partner's visual.
14. **Video/Podcast:** Work in pairs to write and act out a story. One person should begin making a video of an original narrative. When the first person is ready to turn the storyline over to his or her partner, the second person should take the camera and finish the story. (Props and costumes are optional.)
15. **Fiction:** Produce your own fan fiction by rewriting a section of a novel, essay, TV program, live production, or movie. First, establish which details you want to change. Then decide how you want to change them. Give a brief introduction to your revision so we understand the situation in the original.
16. **Research:** Read and summarize the three resources below. Generate one specific question from each resource that focuses on definition. Then answer one of your questions in a documented essay, consulting these and other sources as necessary.

OTHER RESOURCES

Web Site

FanFiction.Net: www.fanfiction.net

Click on a genre to find examples of fanfiction

Academic Article

"Fan Fiction Online: Engagement, Critical Response and Affective Play through Writing" by Angela Thomas

Australian Journal of Language and Literacy 29.3 (2006): 226–239

Audio/Video

YouTube: www.youtube.com

Search: "Thundercats Movie Trailer" by WormyT

Click on the Video link to watch a fanfiction movie trailer

ONE LAST THOUGHT

Ronald Moore is a screenwriter and television producer who got his start writing fan fiction. In 1988, he wrote a script for *Star Trek: The Next Generation* that caught the attention of the show's producers. They liked his work so much that they aired his episode, "The Bonding," in the third season. He went on to write for many television shows, including *Star Trek: Deep Space Nine, Star Trek: Voyager* and *Battlestar Galactica*. Have you ever participated in a fan fiction conversation? Are you interested in developing any fan fiction yourself?

The Art of the Handshake

by Tom Chiarella

A writer-at-large and fiction editor at *Esquire*, **Tom Chiarella** has contributed more than one hundred articles to that magazine since 1996, along with dozens of others to the *New Yorker*, the *London Observer*, *Forbes*, and *Oprah Magazine*. Referred to by *Sports Illustrated* as "the best golf writer you've never heard of," he has also published three books: *Foley's Luck*, *Writing Dialogue*, and *Thursday's Game*.

> ### PREREADING QUESTIONS
>
> What message does your handshake send to others?
>
> What are the main characteristics of a good handshake?
>
> Do you find that you judge people on their handshakes? If so, how?

1   A perfunctory gesture? Hardly. It defines you. It defines the exchange. A hands-on study of a subtle craft.

2   The hand is an intimate body part. Its very shape and condition tell a lot about who you are. I've always hated my hands. They're meaty and fat, the very definition of a paw. In college I worked several jobs—cleaning dumpsters, pitchforking rocks out of a freshly tilled soccer field, carrying ten-gallon buckets of hot pitch across the roof of a large shopping mall—that built up a very nice, very manly set of calluses. My father used to check them by shaking my hand from time to time. He liked it when they were nasty rough, though his were always ultra-smooth. To him, this seemed to define the gap between us. I was a kid who worked his vacations because he needed the money; he was a boss who skipped his by choice.

3   Shaking hands, it follows, is an intimate act, though this might not be agreed upon outside the discussion board for obsessive hand-washers. But if a kiss is intimate, why not a handshake? The other night I was watching some half-assed TV show in which a guy kissed a girl, then looked at her and said, "You're a good kisser." I groaned. My teenage son was there, cutting a peach into little pieces, not paying much attention. "A kiss is not that easy," he said. He doesn't talk much, but I could tell he was speaking from experience—recent experience. "It's not like a handshake or anything."

4   So true, my little man, so true. A kiss is not like a handshake. It's far *easier* than a handshake.

perfunctory: routine, automatic
pitch: tar

A kiss you perform mostly in private, again and again. Why wouldn't you get better?

5 But a good handshake—now that is a subtle business.

6 Truth be told, a man who has a good handshake can do any goddamned thing he wants. I'm not saying he will; I'm saying he can. He can work a room—one person to the next, shaking with strangers, with old colleagues, with huge men and tiny women alike—with his hand. People remember him; they listen to him. Men like this are followed.

7 The good handshake demands a particularly strong command of several **divergent** elements of influence in a single gesture, in one small-ish moment, in order to connect with a person whom (presumably) you have never met before. Think of the components: a swift, elegant movement toward the waiting hand, wise use of the eyes, the considered grip strength, even the rhythm of the shake is important. All that and you have to speak, too; you have to be engaged enough to **muster** a question, remember a name, acknowledge some common experience while you grip, shake, and release.

8 Isn't a handshake just another grim layer of social obligation? Isn't there a reason it's called glad-handing? Well, for a person who's interested in influence, social obligation is more of a tool than a barrier, one that demands use and examination. And it's only glad-handing if the shake is cheap, insincere. So I went forth, spending the better part of two months searching out the perfect handshake while crafting a better one for myself.

9 In that period, I shook hands with a candidate for county commissioner, two priests, three general contractors, an ice-cream salesman, a U. S. senator, a typewriter repairman, a dry cleaner, three women playing shorthanded bridge at a sandwich shop, seven of my son's friends, my ex-wife, her new husband, a woman selling jelly at a New York State Thruway stop, six bellmen, one hotel desk clerk, a concierge, four maitre d's, a guy who runs a moving company, a sawmill operator, two cops, one

IN CONTEXT

Greetings

We use many greetings besides handshakes to say hello or goodbye. Can you think of any others?

professional card dealer, a mathematician, a biologist, a "sandwich artist," the captain of the Maid of the Mist IV, two parking valets, one waiter, two waitresses, a yogi, and three NBA players. In the process I had my arm rotated like a piston on a steam engine and my shoulder jerked practically out of its socket. I received seven shake-appendant gangster hugs. My hand was brushed, crushed, scratched, and double squeezed.

10 I found that if I held on just two beats longer than usual, people stopped what they were saying and eyeballed me. They saw me. This worked particularly well with people who were working for me—the desk clerks, the bellmen, the valets, the concierge. I knocked down at least one suite upgrade with that alone. I also discovered that if I gradually increased the pressure of a shake, people would automatically smile. Really. It was like I was blowing up some balloon in their face. Unless you went at it too hard. And once I had them smiling, then, well, I had them.

11 And the people I saw every day? The ones I work with or buy my coffee from? With them

> *A man who has a good handshake can do any goddamned thing he wants*

divergent: different
muster: raise

I learned to be quick and efficient. They liked a shake, sure, but they didn't want to mess around with it. In and out. Keep a rhythm. Let them know you're there for them.

12   The people I met only once, like the senator? Or the yogi? I wanted them to remember me. I gave them the business. I reached out slowly, without looking down, gripped, and gave my own little doorknob twist at the wrist, playful but not bouncy, holding it until the very end of what I had to say, until the very last syllable dropped away. It cracked the senator up. The yogi did a double take.

13   One thing to know about the range of handshakes: It's a menagerie, a bunch of animals, each replete with its own characteristics, tendencies, and warning signs. Figure out what sort of animal you are dealing with, deconstruct the handshake, and you can tell a lot about what's about to happen.

14   A long, deep shake by a hand that is a bit too large for you, a bit too clammy, one that lingers, with an undifferentiated grip strength, fingers on your wrist just a little too long? That's your son's Pop Warner coach. Well, he shakes like an alligator. Filthy animal. Alligators lie under the water, like dead logs, till they flip their jaws up and crush an egret in one flashing movement. A guy like that is just acting like he's calm, because he knows people expect that he's too big and too strong for his own good. He is. I'm not talking about the fish grip, the one that a really big guy gives you because he's just a little jumpy about people being afraid of him. Those guys let go as soon as you do. Different animal. I'm talking about alligators. I once interviewed Kyle Turley, then the left tackle for the Saints, famous for throwing his helmet across the field in anger. He slipped me a big-time gator—slow and scaly—and I just knew he was pretending to be small for me.

15   There are people who shake like a sparrow, making their hand smaller than it needs to be, lighting upon the other person's hand rather than gripping it. This is a lousy shake. It conveys the commitment of a bird that lives its entire life caught in the posture of scanning the physical world for predators. If you are going to lift your hand from your side in the first place, then get in

there. Apply pressure. Dwell in it a bit.

16   And then there are the Big Cats. Cool name, but these guys aren't animals at all. They're salesmen, and their handshakes tell you so. They show strength—extra-firm grip, an insistent rhythm, a bizarre enthusiasm—but it is more of a reminder of what they want from you than it is a statement of self. These are the kinds of guys who learned their handshake in a seminar somewhere. They might use two hands—one for the shake, the other to grasp the bend of your elbow unnecessarily. Note to Big Cats: An accent like this should be reserved for moments that matter—funerals, state dinners, the closing of estates.

17   My best handshake is a sidewinder—coming in with my wrist cocked a bit, swinging my hand on a little orbit from the hip. I use it when I'm happy to see people. I found that once I paid attention to it, I was pulling the other person closer, just a bit, by turning his hand toward me with just the subtlest pinch of domination.

18   A handshake sets the tone. I like to dominate a little, to define things a bit at the start, so I do my little doorknob twist, or I pull the person in for a little hug. That is my way; it doesn't have to be yours. Just don't look at the other person's hand while you're reaching; that's a tell, a sure sign of insecurity. Look at his face, his eyes; concentrate on what he is showing you.

19   The one handshake I most remember was my father's when I went to visit him in a nursing-care center in Albany, where he was recovering from a stroke. He was in his wheelchair when I got there, facing the window. I reached over his shoulder to

menagerie: collection
replete: filled

touch his hands, and he pulled me around for a look and a shake.

20 "Pop," I said, reaching out and taking his hand. It was smooth as ever, though a little loose. I gave him the extra pressure, a bit of a sidewinder pull, and bent down for a kiss. "Wow, nice grip," he said. "Your hands are soft. You must be making real money." I told him I was doing okay. I asked how he was, and he allowed that he'd been better. He told me he loved the trees where he lived now. Didn't I like the trees? I turned for a look, but it was hard to see, because he held my grip. I have learned that sometimes you don't let go.

CONVERSATIONS: Collaborating in Class or Online

1. Why did Chiarella's father want his son's hands to be rough?
2. Do you agree with the author that a kiss is easier than a handshake?
3. According to Chiarella, what are the major components of a handshake?
4. What did the author learn from his search for the perfect handshake?

CONNECTIONS: Discovering Relationships among Ideas

5. How does a handshake define you?
6. Why does the author think someone with a good handshake can do anything he or she wants?
7. How do handshakes help Chiarella predict what is about to happen?
8. How did the author change his handshake during this experimental period?

PRESENTATION: Analyzing the Writer's Craft

9. What is Chiarella's purpose in this essay?
10. Who do you think was his original audience?
11. How would you classify the tone of this essay?
12. Chiarella ends with a paragraph about shaking his dad's hand, which is similar to the topic of his first paragraph. What effect does the final paragraph have on the essay? How does it change the author's emotional message?

PROJECTS: Expressing Your Own Views

13. **Ad:** Define yourself in an ad for the classified section of a newspaper with which you are familiar.
14. **Video:** Create a video representing the many unique ways people greet each other in different countries. You might have to research this as you create your video.
15. **Essay:** Write an essay explaining a social act that is just as revealing as a handshake. How does this act help define people?
16. **Research:** Read and summarize the three resources below. Generate one specific question from each resource that focuses on definition. Then answer one of your questions in a documented essay, consulting these and other sources as necessary.

OTHER RESOURCES

Web Site

Stop Handshaking: http://
stophandshaking.com

Audio/Video

ibeatyou: www.ibeatyou.com

Click the Competitions tab, and
view Best Secret Handshake

Click the Entries tab to view more handshakes

Academic Article

"The Handshake" by Brett Kahr

American Imago 63.3 (2006): 359–369

ONE LAST THOUGHT

Time Magazine recently published
the article "Are Hugs the New Handshakes?" in which the two greetings
are compared. Although he's not credited with starting the trend, President
Obama has certainly furthered the hugging movement, spreading them all over
the country during his campaign and
after he took office. Do you prefer hugs
or handshakes? What social situations
would make you change your answer?
Why?

THE FULL
FRONTAL
Total body con-
tact, heart to heart
embrace and firm
spaces. For par-
ents, children, and
good friends

THE ASS-OUT
HUG
Nothing touches
below the shoul-
ders. Reserved
for the office, bad
dates, and refer-
ences to Vince
Vaughn

THE HIP-HOP
HUG
A.k.a the man hug
and the hetero
hug. Shake with
right hand and hug
with left, with slaps
on the back

What Is a Sport?

by Kim Flachmann and Michael Flachmann

The following photo essay was compiled by the authors of this text. It includes pictures from 12 different "athletic" activities: soccer, race car driving, windsurfing, poker, judo, the one-man luge, billiards, sumo wrestling, BMX (bicycle motocross), basketball, snowboarding, and cheerleading. While some would define all of these as "sports," others would disagree. Which of these do you consider a sport? Why?

PREREADING QUESTIONS

How would you define a "sport"?

What are some controversial sports?

Do you think the label "sports" is misused in any ways? If so, how?

Soccer

Race Car Driving

Windsurfing

One-Man Luge

Sumo Wrestling

Judo

Snowboarding

Poker

Billiards

Basketball

BMX (Bicycle Motocross)

Cheerleading

CONVERSATIONS: Collaborating in Class or Online

1. In your opinion, what are the essential characteristics of a "sport"?
2. Which of the "sports" in this photo essay are questionable? Why would you put them in this category?
3. Which sports do you enjoy? Do you think other people would consider them "sports"?
4. How do organizations like the Olympics or your school's athletics department influence your definition of a sport?

CONNECTIONS: Discovering Relationships among Ideas

5. How do sports help define people?
6. What sports are most interesting to you?
7. Do you care that sports are classified and defined properly? Why or why not?
8. How are sports and confidence related for you?

PRESENTATION: Analyzing the Writer's Craft

9. How are the photos organized in this essay? Why do you think they are organized in this way?

10. Which of these photos make you want to experience that sport?

11. What role do the colors in the photos play in your impression of the sports in this essay?

12. What is the relationship between sports and good health?

PROJECTS: Expressing Your Own Views

13. **Collage:** Make a sports collage of the activities that interest you as a spectator. Try to show through pictures why these sports appeal to you.

14. **Survey:** Take a survey on your campus asking whether or not the questionable sports in this essay are "real" sports. Write a summary of your survey results.

15. **Essay:** Write an essay defining yourself in relation to the hobbies and/or sports that you pursue. What makes you different from others in this regard? How are you alike?

16. **Research:** Read and summarize the three resources below. Generate one specific question from each resource that focuses on definition. Then answer one of your questions in a documented essay, consulting these and other sources as necessary.

OTHER RESOURCES

Web Site

History of Sports: www.historyofsports.net

Academic Article

"Do Sports Build or Reveal Character?—An Exploratory Study at One Service Academy"

by Joseph P. Doty and Angela Lumpkin

Physical Educator 67.1 (2010): 18–32

Audio/Video

National Public Radio: www.npr.org

Search: "Women Sports Reporters Still Fighting For Respect"

Click on the Listen Now link

ONE LAST THOUGHT

Technology has improved some sports, but not all of them. Can you name some technological devices that complement athletic activities? Are there any that detract from athletics?

www.CartoonStock.com

You Wanna Take This Online?

by Jeff Chu

A graduate of Princeton and the London School of Economics, **Jeff Chu** began his journalistic career as a London-based staff correspondent at *Time Magazine*, for which he wrote stories on African refugees, Arab women's rights, and the James Bond film franchise, among other topics. Now a senior editor at *Fast Company Magazine*, he specializes in articles on business, urban affairs, and philanthropy.

PREREADING QUESTIONS

Were you ever bullied when you were younger?

What experience have you had with cyber-bullying—either through your own involvement or through friends?

What do you know about the recent suicides connected with cyberbullying: 15-year-old Phoebe Prince, who killed herself after months of cyber-threats, or Rutgers college student Tyler Clementi, who jumped off a bridge after his roommate posted a video of Tyler's sex life?

1   What does 13-year-old Taylor Hern ♥? Lots of things: the actor Ewan McGregor, the color pink, the band My Chemical Romance, her boyfriend Alex. You would know all that if you visited her Xanga, a blog/home-page hybrid that is the modern teen's public and interactive equivalent of a diary. You could even leave a comment on her Xanga or send her an "eProp" if, say, you ♥ Ewan McGregor too.

2   On April 18, Taylor, who is about to enter eighth grade at Lost Mountain Middle School in Kennesaw, Georgia, got an instant message (IM) from her friend Sydney Meyer that said, "OMG [Oh, my God] OMG OMG go to your xanga." Someone using the screen named lmmsgirlsgot2hell had left Taylor a comment that read, "Go to my Xanga, bitch." Taylor did—and found a List of Hos. Her name was on it. The list was hurtful, but Taylor says she wasn't as bothered as other girls. "A bunch of the cheerleading chicks spazzed," she says. "Me and all my friends thought it was stupid. Who would actually make time in their schedule to do something like that?"

3   Turns out, many of her peers would. Technology has transformed the lives of teens, including the ways they pick on one another. If parents and teachers think it's hard to control mean girls and bullying boys in school, they haven't reckoned with cyberspace. Cyberbullying can mean anything from posting pejorative items like the List of Hos to spreading rumors by e-mail

pejorative: insulting, derogatory

to harassing by instant message. It was experienced in the preceding two months by 18% of 3,700 middle schoolers surveyed by researchers at Clemson University. Their study is scheduled to be presented at this month's American Psychological Association meeting. The phenomenon peaks at about age 13; 21% of eighth-graders surveyed reported being cyberbullied recently. And incidents of online bullying are like roaches: for every one that's reported, many more go unrecorded. "Our statistics are conservative," says Clemson psychologist Robin Kowalski. "Part of the problem is kids not recognizing that what's happening is a form of bullying."

4 Online bullying follows a gender pattern that's the opposite of what happens off-line, the Clemson study found. On playgrounds and in school hallways, boys are the primary perpetrators and victims; online, girls rule. Nearly a third of the eighth-grade girls surveyed reported being bullied online in the previous two months, compared with 10% of the boys; 17% of the girls said they had bullied online, but only 10% of the boys said they had. Such stats get an eye roll from teens. "Girls make up stuff and sooooooo much drama," Taylor said (by IM, of course). "Drama queens."

5 On the Internet, you can wear any mask you like—and that can be harrowing for the victim of a cyberbully. A few weeks after the List of Hos

> *On the Internet, you can wear any mask you like—and that can be harrowing for the victim of a cyberbully*

was posted, Taylor's classmate Courtney Katasak got an IM from someone using the screen name ToastIsYummy. Courtney thought it might be a friend with a new screen name, so she asked, WHO IS THIS? ToastIsYummy responded with teasing lines and a link to a porn site. "Then they kept sending me these inappropriate messages," she says. "I blocked the screen name so they couldn't talk to me, but I didn't know who this person was or what they were trying to do. It freaked me out."

6 "Anonymity emboldens the person doing it—and it increases the fear factor for the victim," says Kowalski. Parry Aftab, founder of an online nonprofit called WiredSafety.org says teens "are exploring who they are—and they role-play by being mean, horrible, and hateful in ways they would never be offline." Aftab recalls meeting a New Jersey 13-year-old with a preppie-perfect appearance—khakis, button-down shirt, penny loafers complete with pennies—and a creepy hobby of making online death threats against strangers. He would gather information from chat rooms or people's websites, then threaten them as if he knew them. Says Aftab: "He said to me, 'I would never do anything in real life. I'm a good kid. But I can do it online because it doesn't matter.'"

7 Actually, it does. When a cyberbully lashes out, it can be a sign of emotional or psychological problems. And cyberbullying is viral. The Clemson study found that kids who are victimized

harrowing: upsetting, distressing

"seem to be heavily involved in bullying others," says psychologist Sue Limber. In the real world, physical intimidation may keep those who are bullied from retaliating, but that's not a problem online. "Cyberbullying can also lead to other forms of victimization," Limber says. If someone insults a classmate on a Xanga, the effects could include ostracization at school. "Passing notes or writing on lockers was nothing," says Limber. "This takes public to a whole other level."

8   It can be especially embarrassing since cyberbullying often has sexual overtones. "It's raging hormones, and 13 is the heart of it," says Aftab. "We tell adults they can't operate heavy machinery under the influence. These kids are under the influence of hormones 24/7."

9   A parent's instinctive response may be to apply an electronic tourniquet, cutting off a teen's access. But experts agree that severing online links is not the solution. "The Internet is no longer just an advantage. A child is at a disadvantage not having it," says Brittany Bacon, an FBI-trained WiredSafety.org volunteer. She says teens need to learn boundaries and manners in cyberspace just as they must in other venues of society.

> *Cyberbullying often has sexual overtones*

10   It's also the parents' responsibility to be aware of a child's life online. "Kids know so much about the computer that some parents just throw up their hands," says Patti Agatston, a counselor with Cobb County Schools' prevention-intervention program in Georgia. "Don't do that," she says. Instead, parents

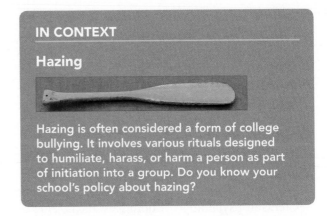

IN CONTEXT

Hazing

Hazing is often considered a form of college bullying. It involves various rituals designed to humiliate, harass, or harm a person as part of initiation into a group. Do you know your school's policy about hazing?

should keep their eyes open. "Parents are totally clueless that some of this even exists," Aftab says.

11   Taylor Hern's mother Caryn counts herself in that number. "I am absolutely an idiot when it comes to that kind of stuff," she says. But Taylor's cyberbullying experience convinced Hern that she had to get Net-savvy. She has signed up for lessons from an expert: her son David, who is 19. "You read about what kids do to other kids, but you don't think it's going to happen to yours," she says. "Who knows what happens online after I go to bed at 10? I need to find out."

Jeff Chu, "You Wanna Take This Online?" *Time*, August 1, 2005. Copyright TIME INC. Reprinted by permission. TIME is a registered trademark of Time Inc. All rights reserved.

ostracization: rejection
tourniquet: a device used to constrict something

CONVERSATIONS: Collaborating in Class or Online

1. Based on the information provided in this essay, define cyberbullying in your own words.
2. Who is Taylor Hern?
3. Through what form of technology does Taylor communicate with her peers?
4. According to the Clemson University study, when does cyberbullying peak in the lives of our children? What percentage of them are involved in cyberbullying at this age?

CONNECTIONS: Discovering Relationships among Ideas

5. Why do you think Taylor was not as upset as some of her friends about being included on a list of Hos? What does this say about her character?

6. Why do you think kids don't recognize this type of persecution online as bullying?

7. Why do you think anonymity makes a person bolder and more aggressive than he or she might be in person?

8. In what ways is cyberbullying "viral" (para. 7)?

PRESENTATION: Analyzing the Writer's Craft

9. What is the purpose of Chu's definition?

10. How does the author organize his essay?

11. Do the statistics that the author cites help him accomplish his purpose? In what way?

12. Chu embeds his definition of cyberbullying in a real-life situation. Is this an effective approach to this particular topic? Why or why not?

PROJECTS: Expressing Your Own Views

13. **Drawing:** Think of a safe place you could go—either imaginary or real—if you were bullied. What does it look like? Why is it safe? Write a brief description of this place; then draw a picture of it, focusing on its special features.

14. **Web Site or Blog:** Design a Web site or a blog that discusses manners and boundaries online.

15. **Essay:** Write an essay proposing a solution to the serious problem of bullying in our schools—whether online or in person. How can we begin to solve this problem? What are some of the obstacles we face in this crisis?

16. **Research:** Read and summarize the three resources below. Generate one specific question from each resource that focuses on definition. Then answer one of your questions in a documented essay, consulting these and other sources as necessary.

OTHER RESOURCES

Web Site

STOP cyberbullying: www.stopcyberbullying.org

Academic Article

"Online Communication and Adolescent Relationships" by Kaveri Subrahmanyam and Patricia Greenfield

The Future of Children 18.1 (2008): 119–146

Audio/Video

Stop Bullying: Speak Up: www.cnn.com/SPECIALS/2010/bullying

Click on any of the Video links

ONE LAST THOUGHT

Bully Beatdown is an MTV reality show on which "bullies" are confronted by their victims and mixed martial arts (MMA) star Jason "Mayhem" Miller. Miller challenges the bully to fight an MMA fighter and potentially win $10,000. But every time the bully has to "tap out" or give up, he loses $1000. Do you think this is an effective way to deal with bullies? Why or why not?

CHAPTER WRITING ASSIGNMENTS

Write a well-developed essay in response to the following prompts. Consult the chapter introduction for guidance in creating your essay.

CONNECTING THE READINGS

1. As virtual reality yields to augmented reality ("Augmented Reality (AR): Will It Change Your Life?"), what new dangers besides cyberbullying ("You Wanna Take This Online?") might be lurking within this new electronic environment? Are we prepared to handle these hazards? Write an essay explaining your predictions on this topic.

2. What do sports ("What Is a Sport?") and fanfiction ("What Is Fanfiction?") have in common? How are they different? Discuss their various advantages and disadvantages in a well-developed essay.

3. As more and more of the social interaction for the Millennials ("The Millennials") goes online, what will take the place of the handshake ("The Art of the Handshake") in the world of the Internet? Write an essay discussing this issue.

4. In what ways can rape ("When Is It Rape?") and cyberbullying ("You Wanna Take This Online") be related? What are the similarities and differences between them? How can we use what we know about one to reduce the threat of the other?

MOVING BEYOND THE READINGS

5. Write an essay defining love. You could discuss all types of love or limit your explanation to a few types. How does the current technological age fit into your definition?

6. Come up with an original name for your generation, and justify your label in a clear, logical essay.

7. Write an essay entitled "The Meaning of the Kiss" that discusses the social role of the kiss in our culture.

8. Design a new sport with a full set of rules that you explain in a well-developed essay.

COMBINING RHETORICAL MODES

9. Write an essay comparing men's and women's attitudes on a controversial issue like sex that affects them in significant ways. How different are their views on this issue? How similar? Do the differences or similarities cause any problems for either gender? How can we solve these problems?

10. Why do you think spousal abuse, date rape, and child abuse are on the rise in the U.S.? What can we do to curb these crimes? What suggestions do you have for helping us regain control of these problems?

11. In an essay, discuss the relationship you see between virtual sports and real sports. Do they benefit each other in any way? Do they detract from one another? How can we use them both wisely to solve some of the problems in society today?

12. In what ways are the Millennials changing our country's culture? Are these changes for the better or worse? Do you think these changes will be permanent? Explain your answers.

Cause and Effect

Cause and effect is a type of reasoning we use every day, often without realizing it. It is part of a natural curiosity we are born with. Wanting to know why things happen is one of our earliest, most basic instincts. In fact, thinking about causes and effects is not only part of human nature but also an advanced mental process and the basis for most decisions we make in life. Consider the following examples:

- An election campaign advertising the reasons a candidate would be an effective senator;
- An academic paper that analyzes the causes and effects of eating disorders;
- A traffic school course that explains why driving defensively is important;

> **DEVELOPMENT STRATEGIES:**
> **CAUSE AND EFFECT**
>
> **Statement of Purpose**
> **Development**
>
> Cause ⟶ Effect
>
> Cause ⟶ Event ⟶ Effect
>
> Cause ⟶ Effect
> **Conclusion**

- A lecture from your mother outlining the consequences of spending more money than you earn;
- A letter of complaint about a faulty microwave oven.

All these cause and effect scenarios have a progression of several causes and outcomes. Cause and effect thinking analyzes the relationship between events and actions. It explains why an event took place and shows what else happened or might happen as a result of that event.

Introducing Cause and Effect

Cause and effect analysis requires us to look for connections among various causes and effects and then analyze our findings. As the name implies, this rhetorical mode has two separate components: *cause* and *effect*. A particular essay, for example, might concentrate on cause (Why do you drive a Chevy?), on effect (What are the resulting advantages and disadvantages of driving a Chevy?), or on some combination of the two. In analyzing causes, we search for circumstances that may have prompted a single event; to determine effects, we look for occurrences that took place after a particular event and resulted from that event.

Like process analysis, cause and effect makes use of our ability to analyze. Whereas process analysis addresses *how* something happens, causal analysis discusses *why* it happened and *what* the result was. A process analysis paper, for example, might explain how to advertise more effectively to increase sales; a cause and effect study would show that three specific elements contributed to an increase in sales, which in turn prompted several different effects:

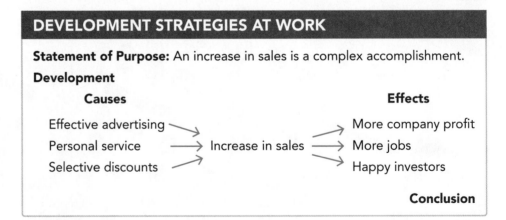

DEVELOPMENT STRATEGIES AT WORK

Statement of Purpose: An increase in sales is a complex accomplishment.
Development

     Causes   **Effects**

Effective advertising ⟶
Personal service ⟶ Increase in sales ⟶ More company profit / More jobs / Happy investors
Selective discounts ⟶

          Conclusion

The study of causes and effects, therefore, provides many diverse and helpful ways for us to examine and clarify our views of the world, including remote and immediate causes, causal chains, and immediate and ultimate effects.

Remote and Immediate Causes

The most accurate and effective causal analysis results from finding the "remote" causes as well as those that are more obvious or "immediate." For example, Olivia Benson on *Law and Order: Special Victims Unit* would have been out of a job if she stopped her investigation at the immediate cause of death (gunshot wound) rather than searching for the remote causes as well:

⟶ Cause: Drug overdose of girlfriend
⟶ Cause: Angry boyfriend
⟶ Cause: Gang violence
⟶ Cause: Gunshot wound to drug dealer
             ⟶ Effect: Death of drug dealer

Causal Chains

A **causal chain** occurs when the result of one action is the cause of another. A good example of this pattern of reasoning is the following:

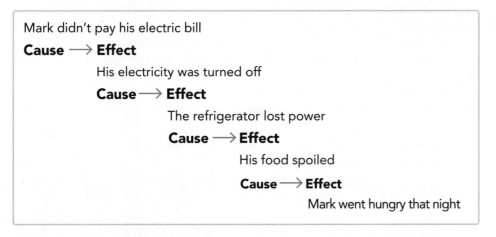

Mark didn't pay his electric bill
Cause ⟶ **Effect**
          His electricity was turned off
          Cause ⟶ **Effect**
                    The refrigerator lost power
                    Cause ⟶ **Effect**
                              His food spoiled
                              Cause ⟶ **Effect**
                                        Mark went hungry that night

Writing a "causal chain" essay is relatively easy since you will simply move through the sequence of events as you develop your paper.

Immediate and Ultimate Effects

Similarly, a cause can have immediate results and, later on, ultimate results. For example, voters would be easy to manipulate if they considered only the immediate effects of a tax increase rather than the ultimate benefits that would result:

Additional costs to individuals

More jobs

Passage of local proposition ⟶ Tax increase → Better education

Additional state revenue

Fewer people on welfare

Fewer people unemployed

Ultimately, the discovery of all the relevant causes and effects of an event or an action will lead to a better understanding of our lives and the world around us.

Discovering How Cause and Effect Works

On the right is a list of the most important elements of cause and effect analysis, whether for a visual (like a graph or a cartoon) or a prose selection. The Cause/Effect Essentials listed here are equally useful as guidelines for both reading and writing.

Analyzing the cartoon below will help you understand the relationship between causes and effects. If you discover on your own how this method of reasoning works, you will be able to apply it to your own reading and writing. Examine the cartoon and answer the questions that follow.

Cause/Effect Essentials

Purpose
All Relevant Causes
All Relevant Effects
Concrete Evidence
Valid Conclusions

1. What is this cartoon's primary message? How did you determine this?

2. What do you think were some of the immediate causes of the conversation in this cartoon?

3. What will be the effects if the boy goes outside and "plays" with his laptop?

4. What are the larger, more remote social implications connected with this cartoon?

5. What details support these implications?

"You're right. I should go outside and play. Buy me a laptop, and I will."

www.CartoonStock.com

6. Do you think this cartoon is funny? Why or why not?

7. What conclusions can you draw from this cartoon? What evidence leads you to these conclusions?

Collaborative Responses Now discuss your responses to these questions with your classmates in small groups or as an entire class. How did the different perspectives from the other students in your class change your "reading" of the cartoon?

Reading Cause and Effect

As you read and analyze the cartoons, essays, graphs, and blogs in this chapter, pay special attention to the cause and effect relationships the authors and illustrators use to create their messages. In every case, focusing on cause and effect reasoning in these selections will guide you to a deep understanding of their content.

As you read a selection for the first time, think about how the Cause/Effect Essentials work within the selection. The following questions will help you achieve this goal for both written and graphic assignments:

Cause/Effect Essentials: Reading

- **Purpose:** What primary purpose is the author or illustrator trying to accomplish?
- **All Relevant Causes:** What remote and immediate causes does the selection discuss?
- **All Relevant Effects:** Does the author/illustrator discover all the immediate and ultimate effects?
- **Concrete Evidence:** Does the "reading" provide detailed evidence to prove its point?
- **Valid Conclusions:** Does the selection reach legitimate conclusions? If so, what are they?

On your second and third readings of the selection, focus on areas of ambiguity and confusion so you can deepen your comprehension.

Writing Cause and Effect

Keeping the Cause/Effect Essentials in mind as you move from reading to writing will help you use the most effective features of this mode in your projects.

Choosing a Subject

First, you must choose a subject for your essay or project. Is your instructor assigning a topic, giving you some options, or letting you select your own subject?

Our student writer, Marta Ruelas, wants to learn more about obesity in the United States. She believes her discoveries about this topic will help her lead a healthier life.

Generating Details

For this type of analysis, you need to generate all the causes and effects directly related to your topic. To do this, you should choose one of the prewriting options explained in Chapter 3. Record as many details concerning the writing assignment as you can think of. Then organize and analyze these ideas or events so you understand the relationships among them: What happened first? What followed? Did one event cause the other? What were the consequences? What are all the relevant causes? The relevant effects? Which are the most important? The most immediate or remote?

Our student writer, Marta, started with a list of causes and effects that she wanted to investigate. Here is her list:

Fast food	*Hard work*
Frantic lifestyle	*Availability of fast food*
Large portions	*Technology*
Bad eating habits	*Calories in soda*
Little or no exercise	*Sedentary activities*
Cheap food	*Video games*
Demanding jobs	

Next Marta sorts and labels each item so she can determine her main topics.

Fast food	*Sedentary activities*
Large portions	*Fast lifestyle*
Bad eating habits	*Little or no exercise*
Cheap food	*Technology*
Availability of fast food	*Video games*
Calories in soda	

These lists would be equally useful if Marta were producing a visual or graphic of some kind. From this list, Marta needs to generate a thesis statement that will give her project focus and direction.

Drafting a Thesis Statement

A thesis for a cause and effect essay or project should clearly specify the relationships between the causes and/or effects you will discuss, which will be the writer's statement of purpose. For example, here is Marta's thesis:

> *The problem of obesity in America is directly related to poor eating habits and a sedentary lifestyle.*

This statement gives focus and direction to Marta's writing.

Producing a Draft

Despite its apparent complexity, a cause and effect essay is relatively simple to organize:

- The **introduction** generally presents the subject(s) and states the purpose of the analysis in a single, clearly written thesis statement.
- The **body of the paper** then explores causes, effects, or both causes and effects in a carefully planned progression.
- Finally, the **concluding section** summarizes the various cause/effect relationships established in the body of the paper and clearly states the conclusions that can be drawn from those relationships.

Mapping Your Ideas Although cause and effect essays follow a logical order, their structure is often quite complex. A particular situation will often have numerous causes and many different effects. Your job is to identify all these elements, including their relationship to one another, as you begin to write.

To identify the remote and immediate causes and effects, Marta decides to diagram her ideas.

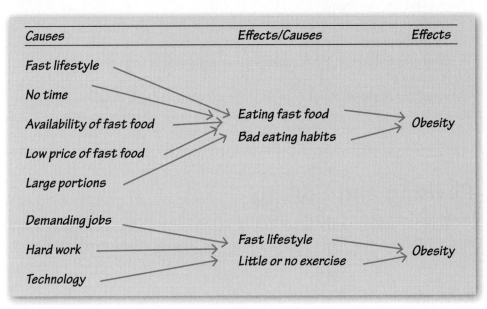

Now she has to decide how she will organize her essay.

Organizing Your Essay After you have identified the cause/effect relationships for your essay, you are ready to organize your ideas. You can discuss causes, effects, or both causes and effects in one of the following sequences:

- Chronologically—from causes to effects (a causal chain)
- From one extreme to another—for example, from most important to least important causes
- From remote to immediate—or vice versa
- From most obvious to least obvious—or vice versa

Marta decided to organize her essay from most obvious to least obvious. So she wrote about the problems inherent in fast food before dealing with our lifestyle in America.

Avoiding *Post Hoc, Ergo Propter Hoc* Reasoning This Latin expression literally means "After this, therefore because of this." In cause/effect reasoning, it is a fallacy to link events just because one comes after the other when, in fact, no causal relationship exists between them. One classic example is this: Just because Jason gets up every morning before the sun rises doesn't mean that the sun comes up *because* Jason is awake. In another situation, if a power failure follows a fireworks display, this doesn't necessarily mean that the display *caused* the power failure.

This point in the writing process is an ideal time for you to focus once again on the Cause/Effect Essentials. In fact, you can use the following questions for both written and graphic assignments:

Cause/Effect Essentials: Writing

- **Purpose:** Exactly what are you trying to accomplish?
- **All Relevant Causes:** What are all the causes involved? Label them "immediate" or "remote."
- **All Relevant Effects:** What are the related results? Label them "immediate" or "ultimate."
- **Concrete Evidence:** What concrete evidence makes your points most effectively?
- **Valid Conclusions:** What legitimate conclusions can you draw from your evidence?

Revising and Editing

To revise and edit your essay or graphic means to review it and make sure it says exactly what you want it to say. Also, you should take some time to add transitions to show your readers how various items in your cause/effect analysis are related.

Revising

Look closely at your essay or graphic as someone else might. Most importantly, make sure it says what you intend to say. Then answer the questions posed in the Revising Checklist on page 28, which focus your attention on how your essay functions.

This is also the point in the writing process when you should add transitions to your essay that clarify the relationship of your ideas to one another and to the general notion you are analyzing. In cause/effect analyses, these are usually words and phrases that explain causal connections: *one cause, another cause, the first result, another result, the main reason, the most important cause, then, next, because, as a result,* and *for this reason.* These particular expressions will help your readers understand as clearly as possible the relationships among the items in your analysis and also guide your readers as smoothly as possible through your essay.

Editing

Editing is the final phase of your writing process. It involves looking closely at your words, sentences, entire paragraphs, and any visual details to make certain they are correct. Use the Editing Checklist on page 30 to review your project for errors in grammar and usage. When you locate a potential error, consult a handbook or go to Pearson's Web-based MyCompLab for an explanation of the problem.

Also, if your instructor marks any grammar mistakes on your paper or graphic, make sure you understand them. Recognizing errors in your own writing is the most effective way of correcting them.

SAMPLE STUDENT ESSAY

As you read the following student essay, refer to the Cause/Effect Essentials (page 374) and the questions for reading cause/effect (page 375) to help you analyze it. Then, to thoroughly understand how this student essay works, pay special attention to the margin notes and the items in each paragraph they describe.

Marta Ruelas

Professor Flachmann

English 101

15 April 2012

Obesity in America

1 America is getting fatter. Two-thirds of Americans are over-weight, with many in that group classified as obese ("Obesity and Overweight"). Cheap, unhealthy food can be found on almost every street corner in America in the form of fast-food restaurants and convenience stores. The number of hours Americans spend watching television has also increased dramatically since its introduction in the 1950s. The prevalence of video gaming systems and the Internet in most American households is another reason our lives have become

— Background

Purpose/Thesis Statement ——▶ so inactive. The problem of obesity in America is directly related to poor eating habits and a sedentary lifestyle.

Immediate Cause ——▶ 2 Because such a variety of food is available for a minimal

Immediate Effect ——▶ amount of money, fast food has become available to anyone at any-

Immediate Cause ——▶ time. This is not a good thing. Because this food is so cheap and the drive-thrus are so accessible, more and more Americans are choosing

Immediate Effect ——▶ to eat fast food rather than cook meals at home. This is detrimental in numerous ways. Instead of preparing our own meals, we rely on

Immediate Effect ——▶ the mass-produced unhealthy options from the fast-food industry, not fully realizing that what we are eating is chock-full of preserva-tives, trans-fats, and excessive amounts of salt. Consuming these

Ultimate Effect ——▶ items leads to obesity, which in turn causes many health problems such as diabetes, high blood pressure, and heart disease.

Remote Cause ——▶ 3 Not only has the quality of food fallen in recent years, but

Remote Cause ——▶ portion sizes have increased as well, which is a dangerous combina-

Ultimate Effect ——▶ tion that is potentially harmful to consumers. So we are eating poor quality food, and we are eating more of it. A prime example of this is the question we hear almost every time we go through a fast-food

Example ——▶ drive thru: "Would you like that combo small, medium, or super-sized?" Now, at most any fast-food place, we can get large fries and a large soda to wash down our 1,000-calorie burger. Consumers don't realize that they are getting much more than they pay for when

Immediate Effects ——▶ they increase the size of their meal—more excess fat and salt along with a cool, refreshing cup of refined sugar that contains absolutely

Ultimate Effect ——▶ no nutritional value. This means that we are increasing our caloric in-take and our consumption of unhealthy meals at an alarming rate.

Immediate Cause ——▶ 4 Soda is definitely another culprit in the obesity epidemic. Most Americans drink soda throughout the day, seldom thinking

Remote Cause ——▶ about how bad it is for them. Soda pop is made with refined sugar (mostly corn syrup) that offers no nutritional value to our bodies. In

Immediate Effects ——▶ fact, consuming excess amounts of sugar can often lead to fatigue, muscle weakness, insulin resistance (a precursor to diabetes), and a host of other health problems (Pleis 10). The empty calories from sugar contain no nutrients or vitamins and are either burned off quickly or stored as fat. — Ultimate Effects

5 Along with our poor eating habits, Americans are exercising less than ever before. — Immediate Cause / Immediate Effect

With the hurried pace of our modern culture, we are finding it more and more difficult to exercise. — Remote Cause

Add to this the technological advances in recent years, and we have a recipe for disaster. Family members come home, tired from work and school, and they want to relax. — Immediate Cause

They turn on the television, a video game, or the computer. — Immediate Effects

No longer content to walk or bike with friends, we communicate through mobile phones, text messages, and social networking sites. — Ultimate Effects

6 Americans need to start eating healthier and exercising more. Most of us are basically uninformed about what we are consuming and why we ought to exercise. Americans need to start preparing their own meals while keeping a close eye on their fat and salt intake. They need to eat healthy food and increase their heart rates by getting regular exercise. — Summary (with Proposed Ultimate Effects)

Most important, they must understand that our country is not prepared for the consequences brought on by an epidemic of unhealthy, overweight people. — Concluding Statement

Works Cited

"Obesity and Overweight 2009." *Centers for Disease Control*. Centers for Disease Control, 18 Jan. 2010. Web. 10 May 2010.

Pleis, J. R., J. W. Lucas, and B. W. Ward. "Summary Health Statistics for U.S. Adults: National Health Interview Survey, 2008." National Center for Health Statistics. *Vital Health Statistics* 10 (242). Dec. 2009. Print.

Reviewing Cause and Effect Analysis

Based on the information you have learned in this chapter and the annotations on the student essay, explain how this essay works by drawing your own outline or graphic representation of it. Label the causes and effects on your visual. This exercise will confirm your understanding of the elements of cause and effect in both reading and writing.

What Evolutionary Psychology Says About Social Networking

by Michael Rogers

Michael Rogers is a "futurist-in-residence" at the New York Times Company, where he writes articles on media and technology. He also runs a speaking, writing, and consulting business called "Practical Futurist," which he founded in 2004. He was previously the technology guru at *Newsweek* and vice president of the new media division at the *Washington Post*. His article "What Evolutionary Psychology Says about Social Networking" was originally published in an MSNBC column on September 10, 2007.

PREREADING QUESTIONS

Approximately how many "friends" do you have? Do they fall into different categories? How many are you close to? What purpose do the others serve in your social network?

Why do so many people socialize on the Internet? What are the advantages and disadvantages of this type of networking?

Do you enjoy hearing stories about other people's lives?

1   The Internet world is relentlessly enthusiastic in its embrace of the latest and greatest, and this year's new flavor has been social networking. Between MySpace, Facebook, LinkedIn, Twitter, Bebo, and scores of lesser start-ups, social networking seems poised to take over the Internet. Indeed, some digerati have suggested that Facebook, by allowing developers to write mini-applications called widgets, might become the new Internet.

2   However, from push technology to Pets.com, the former Information Superhighway is littered with the digital corpses of the next big thing. The Internet is the early adopters' ultimate paradise, an all-you-can-eat buffet table of novel software gadgets, and it's dangerous to rely on the enthusiasms of the blogosphere to determine the longevity of any new Web phenomenon. But social networking may be in a class by itself—for reasons that go back long even before human memory.

digerati: the elite of the computer industry and online communities
widgets: mini computer applications
blogosphere: all blogs and their interconnections

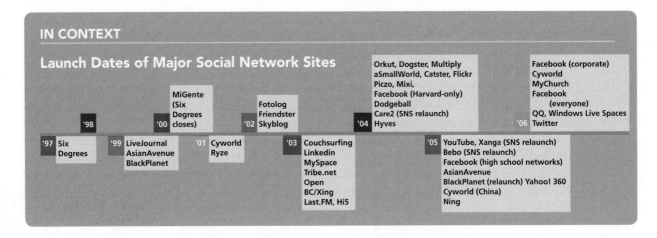

IN CONTEXT

Launch Dates of Major Social Network Sites

'97	'98	'99	'00	'01	'02	'03	'04	'05	'06

- **'97** Six Degrees
- **'98**
- **'99** LiveJournal, AsianAvenue, BlackPlanet
- **'00** MiGente (Six Degrees closes)
- **'01** Cyworld, Ryze
- **'02** Fotolog, Friendster, Skyblog
- **'03** Couchsurfing, Linkedin, MySpace, Tribe.net, Open BC/Xing, Last.FM, Hi5
- **'04** Orkut, Dogster, Multiply, aSmallWorld, Catster, Flickr, Piczo, Mixi, Facebook (Harvard-only), Dodgeball, Care2 (SNS relaunch), Hyves
- **'05** YouTube, Xanga (SNS relaunch), Bebo (SNS relaunch), Facebook (high school networks), AsianAvenue, BlackPlanet (relaunch) Yahoo! 360, Cyworld (China), Ning
- **'06** Facebook (corporate), Cyworld, MyChurch, Facebook (everyone), QQ, Windows Live Spaces, Twitter

3   A decade ago, Robin Dunbar, the British anthropologist, wrote a book called "Gossip, Grooming and the Evolution of Language." Dunbar is one of the more influential practitioners of evolutionary psychology—looking at how the human animal behaved in our earliest ancestral environments, long before civilization, for clues about why we are the creatures we are today. It's a fascinating book that suggests both why social networking is so popular and where it may be headed.

4   Dunbar begins with the premise that back when our Paleolithic ancestors were still more monkey than human, understanding one's place in the group hierarchy was exceedingly important. Compared to other creatures, primates are unusually social animals. And thus knowledge about relationships—who's mating with whom, who became allies, who just had a fight—was crucial for primates to maintain or advance their place in the pack. It was, Dunbar suggests, the birth of gossip. But before language evolved, how was gossip transmitted?

5   Dunbar speculated that the early hominids maintained and communicated their relationships via the mutual grooming behavior we still see in lower primates. Baboons and chimpanzees spend 20 percent of their time grooming one another. But grooming, Dunbar argues—besides tidying one's fur and feeling good—was a way to establish and maintain friendships, determine the hierarchy within the tribe, and signal one's social connections to other tribe members. One might almost say that grooming was the first social networking application.

6   But there's more to Dunbar's theory. He speculates that at some point, our early ancestors' tribes began to get too big for even the most energetic primate to get around to grooming everyone. And thus language emerged to replace grooming as a means of conveying social relationships. (It's not clear which came first—language or the larger tribe size—but they grew in tandem.) An exchange of personal information with language was far quicker than a 20-minute grooming session, and a single individual could converse with several others at one time. So rather than the traditional anthropologic explanation that language evolved among males to coordinate hunting, Dunbar proposed that language evolved as a way to maintain and identify social relationships. And we haven't stopped gossiping since.

Grooming was the first social networking application

7   Gossip's primitive significance may explain the unending appeal of celebrity journalism. We're still watching the behavior of the alpha males and females in our tribe, only now we identify them as Brad and Angelina. (They do look awfully large on the silver screen.) In a sense, our gossip appetite is a bit like another bit of programming we inherited from our hard-living primate ancestors: the urge that tells us to consume all the food we can when it's available. Today, of course, surrounded by fat and sugar, that dietary programming rapidly leads many of us to excess poundage. With professionally produced gossip now as readily available as fast food, it may be only natural that we overdose on that as well.

Paleolithic: a prehistoric era distinguished by the development of the first stone tools

hominids: a primate of a family (Hominidae) that includes humans and their fossil ancestors

8   Web-based social networking fills the same need on a personal level: it is an incredibly efficient gossip engine, with an unprecedented ability to establish the precise nature of relationships. (Limited profiles and privacy settings provide plenty of signals as to who's close and who is closer.) That's an age-old attraction that's not going away. But there's another element of social networking that may be something altogether new.

9   It stems from Dunbar's observation that, with the new tools of language, humans managed to increase their group size significantly from the 50 or so members that characterize baboon and chimpanzee groupings. But over the last 10,000 years or so, we seem to have hit another ceiling for an optimum group size in which members are reasonably in touch. That number is about 150, a figure supported by examples that range from the size of Neolithic villages to military units to corporate management theory. Organizations, of course, get bigger than that, but as they do they change character: bureaucracies, levels of authority, social stratification begin to emerge. Dunbar theorizes that this may be due to the limits of how many individuals one can converse with, based on the acoustics of speech, and still have time to take care of life's essentials.

10 So the obvious question about Internet-based social networking is whether we humans are once again increasing the size of our effective groups. Is this an evolutionary shift that—while certainly not as significant as the advent of spoken language—will ultimately change the way we operate as social creatures? Will anthropologists of some distant era look back and say that this was the moment when humans once again created much larger social networks than we were able to maintain in the past? Or perhaps in the end we'll discover that, once again, about 150 "friends" is as far as our capacities can take us.

11 Whether or not Dunbar's decade-old theory about language's origin in gossip is correct, it's a fascinating way to think about what's important in human communication. And it suggests that with social software, we're for the first time arranging the Internet in a way that makes sense to the deeper inclinations of our brains. While we're only in the very earliest days, this new twist may well be the beginning of the Internet as it is meant to be.

MSNBC.com, September 10, 2007. Copyright 2007 by MSNBC Interactive News, LLC. Reproduced with permission of MSNBC Interactive News, LLC in the format Textbook via Copyright Clearance Center.

CONVERSATIONS: Collaborating in Class or Online

1. This essay focuses on both causes and effects. Write out the essay's thesis, and list the causes and effects connected with that thesis. Then circle the real causes. Does the author put more stress on causes or effects? Why do you think this is so?

2. What do you believe the author means when he says, "Facebook … might become the new Internet" (para. 1)? According to the information in this article, how realistic do you think this prediction is?

3. What does the timeline of social networking sites tell us about our instinctive need to gossip? According to Michael Rogers, in what ways is gossiping about relationships a basic necessity of human existence?

4. Robin Dunbar claims, "language evolved as a way to maintain and identify social relationships" (para. 6). What do you think he means by this statement?

CONNECTIONS: Discovering Relationships among Ideas

5. Based on the information in this essay, what is the relationship between evolutionary psychology and gossip? Which is the cause, and which is the effect?

6. How are grooming and social networking related? What other social processes are involved in this relationship?

7. According to Dunbar, understanding their place in the "group hierarchy" (para. 4) was extremely important to the primates. Is this process still important today? What is the role of this process in human communication in our world today?

8. What is Rogers implying in this essay about the future of social networking?

PRESENTATION: Analyzing the Writer's Craft

9. Rogers uses several analogies or comparisons in his first two paragraphs. List these comparisons, and then discuss which ones you find most effective.

10. The author introduces Robin Dunbar early in the essay and then quotes him throughout the essay. What does Dunbar's expertise add to Rogers's argument?

11. What does Rogers's reference to celebrity journalism contribute to the essay?

12. The author ends his essay with a series of questions that ask us to consider whether or not we are redefining human communication and our role as social creatures. Is this an effective ending to this essay or not? Add one more question to his list of inquiries.

PROJECTS: Expressing Your Own Views

13. **Podcast/DVD/Video:** In a medium of your choice, make your own statement about the importance of social networking in today's world.

14. **Web Site:** Design a fictitious Web site that explains the most important aspects of human communication and why they are important.

15. **Blog/Wiki/Ning:** Start a Blog, Wiki, or Ning conversation about how social networking helps us learn "why we are the creatures we are today" (para. 3). Then write your own commentary on the reasoning behind the thread of responses that occurred.

16. **Research:** Read and summarize the three resources below. Generate one specific question from each resource that focuses on cause/effect reasoning. Then answer one of your questions in a documented essay, consulting these and other sources as necessary.

OTHER RESOURCES

Web Site

International Network for Social Network Analysis: www.insna.com

Under the About SNA tab, click on the What is Social Network Analysis link

Academic Article

"Alone in the Crowd: The Structure and Spread of Loneliness in a Large Social Network"

by John T. Cacioppo, James H. Fowler, and Nicholas A. Christakis

Journal of Personality and Social Psychology 97.6 (2009): 977–991

Audio/Video

YouTube: www.youtube.com

Search: "The Business of Social Networks" by Rocketboom

Click on the Video link

ONE LAST THOUGHT

This comic by Mikhaela B. Reid explores the phenomenon of blogs being optioned for books, television, and movies. While some highly entertaining blogs have turned into successful films, such as 2009's *Julie & Julia*, the number of blogs that are probably not worth reading far outweighs those that we might find entertaining enough to watch unfold on our TV screens. Do you have a blog? If so, what is it about? If not, what would you consider as a good topic for a blog?

Read at Your Own Risk

by Roz Chast

Roz Chast is a staff cartoonist for the *New Yorker*, to which she has contributed over a thousand cartoons since 1979. Her most recent book is *Theories of Everything: Selected, Collected, and Health-Inspected Cartoons, 1978–2006*. She also illustrated *The Alphabet from A to Y with Bonus Letter Z* written by Steve Martin.

PREREADING QUESTIONS

When did you read your first entire book? What was it?

What books and magazines have you read recently?

Do you like to read? Why or why not?

The Read-At-Your-Own-Risk Bookstore" by Roz Chast. Copyright 2002 by Roz Chast, used with permission of The Wylie Agency LLC.

CONVERSATIONS: Collaborating in Class or Online

1. What role does cause and effect reasoning play in this cartoon?
2. What is the general tone of this cartoon?
3. Which message in this cartoon is most humorous? What makes it funny?
4. Why would anyone want "pasteurized, homogenized, and sterilized books"?

CONNECTIONS: Discovering Relationships among Ideas

5. How do the signs on the windows explain the name of the bookstore?

6. Where do you imagine this storefront might be? What in the drawing brings you to this conclusion?

7. In what ways are the signs in this cartoon similar to signs in other stores? What is the reason for these types of signs?

8. What is the significance of the sign on the door? Is that the most effective place for that sign? Why or why not?

PRESENTATION: Analyzing the Writer's Craft

9. What do you like or dislike about the cartoonist's artistic style?

10. What does the woman in front of the bookstore add to the cartoon?

11. Which of the cartoonist's artistic elements attract the most attention? Why do you think this is so?

12. How do the different types of handwriting on the signs help make the cartoon funny?

PROJECTS: Expressing Your Own Views

13. **Script:** Develop this cartoon into a conversation between two or more people talking about reading.

14. **Billboard:** Design a billboard with your own message about the benefits of reading.

15. **Survey/Essay:** Develop a questionnaire about people's reading habits. Phrase your questions so you can discover the reasons behind these habits. Then write up the results of your survey for your class.

16. **Research:** Read and summarize the three resources below. Generate one specific question from each resource that focuses on cause and effect reasoning. Then answer one of your questions in a documented essay, consulting these and other sources as necessary.

OTHER RESOURCES

Web Site

Internet Archive: www.archive.org

Explore the many public domain works you can download for free or view on the Internet

Academic Article

"Cartoon Violence and Freedom of Expression" by David Keane

Human Rights Quarterly 30.4 (2008): 845–875

Audio/Video

National Public Radio: www.npr.org

Search: "'Reading Rainbow' Reaches Its Final Chapter"

Click on the Listen Now link

ONE LAST THOUGHT

Bookselling began with handwritten manuscripts copied by scribes. High demand for Islamic and Christian texts increased the production of books until primitive forms of printing arose. Modern bookselling is again in a state of flux with the growing popularity of electronic books. Do you ever buy books? Do you prefer shopping online, in chain stores, or in local bookstores? Explain your preference.

Black Men and Public Space

by Brent Staples

Brent Staples is an author and member of the editorial board for the *New York Times,* for which he writes essays on politics and culture. His principal publications include *Parallel Time: Growing Up in Black and White* (1995) and *An American Love Story* (1999). His article "Black Men and Public Space" was originally published in the September 1986 issue of *Ms. Magazine* under the title "Just Walk on By: A Black Man Ponders His Power to Alter Public Space," then later reprinted in *Harper's Magazine* (December 1986) under its current title.

PREREADING QUESTIONS

What are your deepest fears? What triggers these fears?

Are you always in control of the image you project? Explain your answer.

What problems in society would you like to solve? Why do you want to solve these problems? Who will benefit most from these solutions?

1   My first victim was a woman—white, well dressed, probably in her early twenties. I came upon her late one evening on a deserted street in Hyde Park, a relatively affluent neighborhood in an otherwise mean, impoverished section of Chicago. As I swung onto the avenue behind her, there seemed to be a discreet, uninflammatory distance between us. Not so. She cast back a worried glance. To her, the youngish black man—a broad six feet two inches with a beard and billowing hair, both hands shoved into the pockets of a bulky military jacket—seemed menacingly close. After a few more quick glimpses, she picked up her pace and was soon running in earnest. Within seconds she disappeared into a cross street.

2   That was more than a decade ago. I was twenty-two years old, a graduate student newly arrived at the University of Chicago. It was in the echo of that terrified woman's footfalls that I first began to know the unwieldy inheritance I'd come into—the ability to alter public space in ugly ways. It was clear that she thought herself the quarry of a mugger, a rapist, or worse. Suffering a bout of insomnia, however, I was stalking sleep, not defenseless wayfarers. As a softy who is scarcely

discreet: cautious
unwieldy: awkward, difficult to control
quarry: prey, intended victim

able to take a knife to a raw chicken—let alone hold one to a person's throat—I was surprised, embarrassed, and dismayed all at once. Her flight made me feel like an accomplice in tyranny. It also made it clear that I was indistinguishable from the muggers who occasionally seeped into the area from the surrounding ghetto. That first encounter, and those that followed, signified that a vast, unnerving gulf lay between nighttime pedestrians—particularly women—and me. And I soon gathered that being perceived as dangerous is a hazard in itself. I only needed to turn a corner into a dicey situation, or crowd some frightened, armed person in a foyer somewhere, or make an errant move after being pulled over by a policeman. Where fear and weapons meet—and they often do in urban America—there is always the possibility of death.

3 In that first year, my first away from my hometown, I was to become thoroughly familiar with the language of fear. At dark, shadowy intersections, I could cross in front of a car stopped at a traffic light and elicit the thunk, thunk, thunk of the driver—black, white, male, or female—hammering down the door locks. On less traveled streets after dark, I grew accustomed to but never comfortable with people crossing to the other side of the street rather than pass me. Then there were the standard unpleasantries with policemen, doormen, bouncers, cabdrivers, and others whose business it is to screen out troublesome individuals before there is any nastiness.

4 I moved to New York nearly two years ago, and I have remained an avid night walker. In central Manhattan, the near-constant crowd cover minimizes tense one-on-one street encounters. Elsewhere—in SoHo, for example, where sidewalks are narrow and tightly spaced buildings shut out the sky—things can get very taut indeed.

5 After dark, on the warrenlike streets of Brooklyn where I live, I often see women who fear the worst from me. They seem to have set their faces on neutral, and with their purse straps strung across their chests bandolier-style, they forge ahead as though bracing themselves against being tackled. I understand, of course, that the danger they perceive is not a hallucination. Women are particularly vulnerable to street violence, and young black males are drastically overrepresented among the perpetrators of that violence. Yet these truths are no solace against the kind of alienation that comes of being ever the suspect, a fearsome entity with whom pedestrians avoid making eye contact.

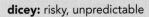

I understand, of course, that the danger they perceive is not a hallucination

6 It is not altogether clear to me how I reached the ripe old age of twenty-two without being conscious of the lethality nighttime pedestrians attributed to me. Perhaps it was because in Chester, Pennsylvania, the small, angry industrial town where I came of age in the 1960s, I was scarcely noticeable against a backdrop of gang warfare, street knifings, and murders. I grew up one of the good boys, had perhaps a half-dozen fistfights. In retrospect, my shyness of combat has clear sources.

7 As a boy, I saw countless tough guys locked away; I have since buried several, too. They were babies, really—a teenage cousin, a brother of twenty-two, a childhood friend in his mid-twenties—all gone down in episodes of bravado played out in the streets. I came to doubt the

dicey: risky, unpredictable

foyer: lobby

SoHo: trendy New York neighborhood; an abbreviation of "South of Houston Street"

warrenlike: similar to a rabbit hole, a maze

bandolier: a belt worn over the shoulder and diagonally across the chest

lethality: danger, deadliness

virtues of intimidation early on. I chose, perhaps unconsciously, to remain a shadow—timid, but a survivor. The fearsomeness mistakenly attributed to me in public places often has a perilous flavor. The most frightening of these confusions occurred in the late 1970s and early 1980s, when I worked as a journalist in Chicago. One day, rushing into the office of a magazine I was writing for with a deadline story in hand, I was mistaken for a burglar. The office manager called security and, with an ad hoc posse, pursued me through the labyrinthine halls, nearly to my editor's door. I had no way of proving who I was. I could only move briskly toward the company of someone who knew me.

8   Another time I was on assignment for a local paper and killing time before an interview. I entered a jewelry store on the city's affluent Near North Side. The proprietor excused herself and returned with an enormous red Doberman pinscher straining at the end of a leash. She stood, the dog extended toward me, silent to my questions, her eyes bulging nearly out of her head. I took a cursory look around, nodded, and bade her good night.

9   Relatively speaking, however, I never fared as badly as another black male journalist. He went to nearby Waukegan, Illinois, a couple of summers ago to work on a story about a murderer who was born there. Mistaking the reporter for the killer, police officers hauled him from his car at gunpoint and but for his press credentials would probably have tried to book him. Such episodes are not uncommon. Black men trade tales like this all the time.

10   Over the years, I learned to smother the rage I felt at so often being taken for a criminal.

IN CONTEXT

Racial Profiling

The American Civil Liberties Union, or the ACLU, is a non-profit organization that defends Americans' civil rights through litigation and legislative lobbying. Visit their Web site at www.aclu.org and search "Racial Profiling" to see the ACLU's most recent work in this area.

Not to do so would surely have led to madness. I now take precautions to make myself less threatening.

11   I move about with care, particularly late in the evening. I give a wide berth to nervous people on subway platforms during the wee hours, particularly when I have exchanged business clothes for jeans. If I happen to be entering a building behind some people who appear skittish, I may walk by, letting them clear the lobby before I return, so as not to seem to be following them. I have been calm and extremely congenial on those rare occasions when I've been pulled over by the police.

12   And on late-evening constitutionals, I employ what has proved to be an excellent tension-reducing measure: I whistle melodies from Beethoven and Vivaldi and the more popular classical composers. Even steely New Yorkers hunching toward nighttime destinations seem to relax, and occasionally they even join in the tune. Virtually everybody seems to sense that a mugger wouldn't be warbling bright, sunny selections from Vivaldi's Four Seasons. It is my equivalent of the cowbell that hikers wear when they know they are in bear country.

perilous: frightening
labyrinthine: like a place filled with intricate passageways
cursory: brief
skittish: easily frightened

CONVERSATIONS: Collaborating in Class or Online

1. What is Staples's primary purpose in this essay? Record his thesis, and diagram the causes and effects he introduces to make his point before you enter a conversation about this essay.

2. What does Staples mean when he says "being perceived as dangerous is a hazard in itself" (para. 2)? Name some of the "hazards" connected with this observation.

3. According to Staples, what are some signals of fear among pedestrians after dark? What do these signals say collectively? Why do they involve Staples?

4. What types of "tales" do Black men trade? Why are these stories common?

CONNECTIONS: Discovering Relationships among Ideas

5. How does Staples deal inwardly and outwardly with the role of "accomplice in tyranny" (para. 2) that has been thrust upon him?

6. Who are the various victims of the experiences Staples describes? Explain the consequences of each set of victims you identify.

7. What does Staples do to show people he is harmless? What are his reasons for this behavior?

8. In what ways is whistling classical tunes like wearing a cowbell in bear country?

PRESENTATION: Analyzing the Writer's Craft

9. Why do you think Staples opens this essay with references to his "victims" in paragraph 1? Is this an effective beginning for his main point?

10. Who do you think was Staples's original audience for this essay? What details point to this conclusion?

11. What is Staples implying in his essay about black men? What led you to this answer?

12. What effect does Staples's reference in paragraph 2 to the place "where fear and weapons meet" have on the rest of the essay? How would introducing that reference later change the impact of the essay?

PROJECTS: Expressing Your Own Views

13. **Blog:** Start a blog conversation that studies the relationship between certain ethnic groups and violence. Look up some relevant data on the Internet. What conclusions can you draw?

14. **Podcast/Video:** Tell a story without words about a "close encounter" of yours. Cover both the causes and effects of this encounter in your story.

15. **Newspaper Article:** As a concerned citizen, you have been asked to write an opinion piece on victims in American society. What groups are most often victimized in the U.S.? Why are they treated in this way? End your article with a proposal for changing the situations you describe.

16. **Research:** Read and summarize the three resources below. Generate one specific question from each resource that focuses on cause/effect reasoning. Then answer one of your questions in a documented essay, consulting these and other sources as necessary.

OTHER RESOURCES

Web Site

The New York Times: www.nytimes.com

Search: "Brent Staples" to read some of his other articles

Academic Article

"Racism versus Professionalism: Claims and Counter-claims about Racial Profiling"

by Vic Satzewich and William Shaffir

Canadian Journal of Criminology and Criminal Justice 51.2 (2009): 199–226

Audio/Video

ABC News: www.abcnews.go.com

Search: "Attack Sparks Racial Profiling Debate"

Click on the Video link

ONE LAST THOUGHT

Supporters of racial profiling argue that even though the practice is undesirable and sometimes distasteful, it can help law enforcement officers work more effectively. Critics contend that it is discriminatory, and personal rights are violated when officers profile according to race. Do you think racial profiling is a viable tool or a harmful strategy for law enforcement use? Have you or anyone you know ever been profiled? Can you think of any famous examples of racial profiling? In your opinion, were they justified?

How High Will It Go? The Superspike Scenario

by The McKinsey Global Institute

This article was written by a team of contributors at the **McKinsey Global Institute**, a worldwide management consulting firm. The Institute, which is the company's economics research arm, studies global markets, consumption, productivity, and the impact of technology on the world economic marketplace. Graphics for the article were created by Katherine Yester at *Foreign Policy Magazine*.

PREREADING QUESTIONS

What do you know about the oil industry?

What types of energy does oil generate in the U.S.?

How do you personally rely on oil in your daily life?

1   Just months after 2008's expensive summer at the pump, oil prices plummeted—hitting a low of $32.40 per barrel in December 2008. Consumers and industrial users, hit hard by the financial crisis, scaled back on all types of petroleum products. Months of concern over tight supplies were washed away by a glut of cheap oil.

2   Yet as signs of recovery have begun to appear, volatile oil prices have started to more or less tick up again, prompting many to wonder what might happen once economic recovery truly begins. Could the world see another oil spike? The likely answer: yes.

3   In the first half of this decade, oil prices per day tended to rise when global spare capacity—the difference between supply and demand—fell to 3 million barrels per day or lower. This is not the case today; projected levels for summer 2009 were at their highest since the 1980s, more than twice the 3 million mark. Recent price hikes can likely be attributed to OPEC, the cartel of oil-producing countries that has imposed strict production quotas and taken spare capacity offline. Traders, who see scarce oil on the horizon again, could also be pushing up prices in ominous anticipation.

OPEC: Organization of the Petroleum Exporting Countries, a group that protects the interests of countries that export petroleum

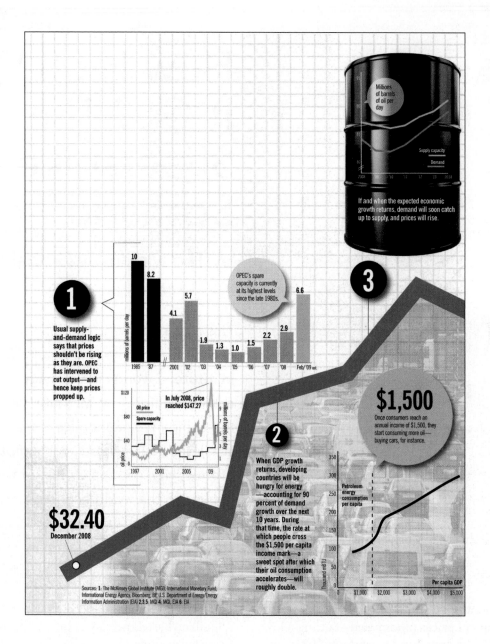

Millions
of barrels
of oil per
day

Supply capacity
Demand

2008   '10   '11   '12   '13   2014

If and when the expected economic
growth returns, demand will soon catch
up to supply, and prices will rise.

1

Usual supply-
and-demand logic
says that prices
shouldn't be rising
as they are. OPEC
has intervened to
cut output—and
hence keep prices
propped up.

10
8.2
5.7
4.1
1.9   1.3   1.0   1.5   2.2   2.9   6.6

millions of barrels per day

1985   '87   2001   '02   '03   '04   '05   '06   '07   '08   Feb/'09 est.

OPEC's spare
capacity is currently
at its highest levels
since the late 1980s.

3

$1,500

Once consumers reach an
annual income of $1,500, they
start consuming more oil—
buying cars, for instance.

$120

In July 2008, price
reached $147.27

Oil price
Spare capacity

$80

$40

oil price

0

1997   2001   2005   '09

millions of barrels per day

9
7
5
3
1

2

When GDP growth
returns, developing
countries will be
hungry for energy
—accounting for 90
percent of demand
growth over the next
10 years. During
that time, the rate at
which people cross
the $1,500 per capita
income mark—a
sweet spot after which
their oil consumption
accelerates—will
roughly double.

$32.40

December 2008

350
300
250   Petroleum
        energy
200   consumption
        per capita
150
100
50
0

Thousand mBTU

Per capita GDP

0    $1,000 $2,000 $3,000 $4,000 $5,000

Sources: 1: The McKinsey Global Institute (MGI): International Monetary Fund,
International Energy Agency, Bloomberg, BP, U.S. Department of Energy/Energy
Information Administration (EIA) 2,3,5: MGI 4: MGI, EIA 6: EIA

4   The traders might have the right idea. If oil demand grows as quickly as expected when the world economy recovers, OPEC's spare capacity could be gone within five years. And since the world relies increasingly on unconventional sources of oil (think tar sands), it will take time and money to bring more supply online. Until then, the world will be left with only demand-side measures—such as boosting energy efficiency and cutting back on use—to control prices. These, too, will require time, money, and changes in behavior. Meanwhile, prices will rise to clear the market.

5   All the ingredients are in place for another spike, perhaps as early as 2012, depending on the timing of the economic recovery. Prices could fly up as they did in late 2007 through mid-2008, when they reached nearly $150 per barrel.

tar sands: naturally occurring mixtures of sand or clay, water, and a dense form of petroleum called bitumen

GDP: Gross domestic product, a measure of a country's economy

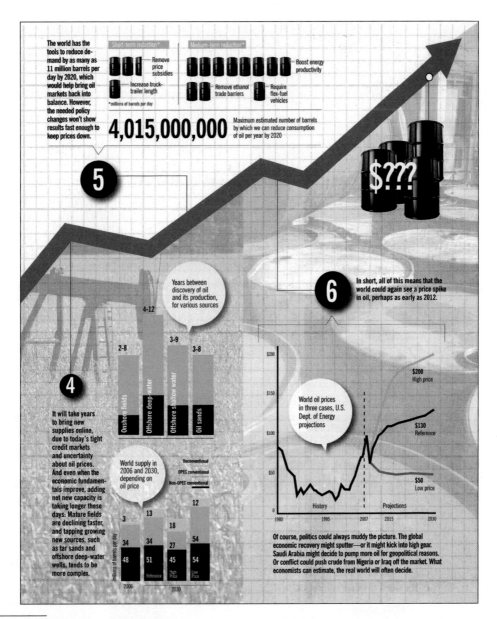

By The McKinsey Global Institute, graphics by Katherine Yester, *Foreign Policy*, September/October 2009, pp. 96–97. Copyright 2009. Reproduced with permission of Foreign Policy in the format Textbook via Copyright Clearance Center.

Subsidies: government grants
Flex-fuel vehicles: alternative fuel vehicles

CONVERSATIONS: Collaborating in Class or Online

1. This series of graphs tells a very complex story about the oil industry. Explain Graphs 1 through 5 in your own words.

2. According to the information here, what are the main reasons oil prices increase? What causes them to decline?

3. What does the author mean by the phrase "When GDP growth returns" (Graph 2)? What is the significance of this statement in reference to the price of oil?

4. According to these graphs, how do OPEC quotas affect oil prices?

CONNECTIONS: Discovering Relationships among Ideas

5. How can the world reduce its demand for oil? Explain the primary actions required based on the graphs provided here.

6. When will demand for oil catch up to supply (Graph 3)? What will make this happen?

7. What does the number 4,015,000,000 refer to in Graph 5? What are the consequences of this number in the oil industry for the year 2020?

8. Why could the world see a rapid spike in oil prices in the near future?

PRESENTATION: Analyzing the Writer's Craft

9. How does the visual layout of these graphs help you understand them?

10. What people and organizations would be most interested in these graphs?

11. Which of the graphs do you think is easiest to understand? Why?

12. What does a graph accomplish that another format could not? In your opinion, is this the most effective way of displaying such information? Explain your answer.

PROJECTS: Expressing Your Own Views

13. **Blog/Wiki/Ning:** Find more information about world oil production, and enter an existing Internet conversation about oil. Exchange at least five posts with others on the site. Print your conversation for class discussion.

14. **YouTube Video:** Research one of the causes or effects associated with oil prices and create a brief video of your findings. Make sure you show a clear relationship between one specific market variable and the current price of oil.

15. **Graph/Essay:** Choose one of the predictions for 2012 in Graph 6, draw a hypothetical Graph 7, and write an essay explaining your graph.

16. **Research:** Read and summarize the three resources below. Generate one specific question from each resource that focuses on cause/effect reasoning. Then answer one of your questions in a documented essay, consulting these and other sources.

OTHER RESOURCES

Web Site

American Petroleum Institute: www.api.org

Academic Article

"Causes and Consequences of the Oil Shock of 2007–08" by James D. Hamilton

Brookings Papers on Economic Activity Spring (2009): 215–261

Audio/Video

History.com: www.history.com

Search: "Oil Drilling Ships"

Click on the Modern Marvels Video link

ONE LAST THOUGHT

Large oil spills, such as the Exxon Valdez in Alaska and the Deepwater Horizon in the Gulf of Mexico, can upset ecosystems for generations. Would you support higher gas prices to ensure better precautions and help with cleanups? Would you pay $10/gal? $8/gal? How much would you pay to make certain that oil is extracted safely? Why is that price your limit?

Does Thinking Make It So?

by Erin O'Donnell

Erin O'Donnell, a staff writer for *Harvard Magazine*, has published essays on a number of intriguing topics, including male vs. female brain development ("When Minnie Turns Mickey"), male birth control pills ("Slowing Sperm"), how liberals and conservatives differ in brain chemistry ("Twigs Bent Left or Right"), immigration ("Latinos Nix Violence"), and global weather ("Climate Change Solutions"). The article "Does Thinking Make It So?" was originally published in the January–February 2009 issue of *Harvard Magazine*.

PREREADING QUESTIONS

Has your mind ever convinced you that you were sick when you were not (or vice versa)?

How are the mind and body related in terms of your health?

What does the power of "positive thinking" mean to you?

1   In a world that prizes medical science and blames illness on factors such as genes, viruses, bacteria, or poor diet, certain perplexing cases stand out. Consider babies in orphanages who have had all their physical needs met, yet fail to develop because they lack a strong connection to another person. Or the roughly 200 women in Cambodia with perfectly healthy eyes who became blind after they were forced to watch as loved ones were tortured and killed. Or Mr. Wright, a man whose tumors "melted like snowballs on a hot stove" when he was given Krebiozen, an experimental drug that he believed would cure his cancer, but was later declared to be worthless by the American Medical Association.

2   These cases underscore the powerful idea that the mind matters in sickness and health. Judging by the millions of Americans who use mind-body modalities such as yoga, meditation, qi gong, and massage to fight diseases like cancer, it's an idea that many accept.

3   But why do we believe in the mind-body link in the first place? Anne Harrington, professor of the history of science and chair of the

qi gong: Chinese meditative practice

397

IN CONTEXT

Anne Harrington

Anne Harrington believes that stories connect us to our cultures. In an interview on the Paula Gordon show, Harrington said, "Not only do stories tell us how to behave in the world, they also tell us how to feel in the world."

department [at Harvard University], says we're only partially convinced by laboratory studies revealing which of these therapies do and don't work. "Science is only part of what has created mind-body medicine and sustains it today," she notes. In her recent history, *The Cure Within*, she argues that we're also persuaded by stories, especially a key set of narratives that humans have told about the mind and body through history. These stories, she says, help us make sense of complicated experiences like illness and suffering.

> *Stories ... help us make sense of complicated experiences like illness and suffering*

4   For example, the cultural power of some mind-body ideas becomes clear when you trace them back to their roots in religion. Groups such as the Christian Scientists drew from the New Testament the message that strong faith can yield miracle cures, and Harrington shows how this led eventually to self-help bestsellers about the therapeutic effects of positive thinking.

5   In the secular arena, she continues, post-World War II anxieties produced stories about the ways our minds leave us vulnerable to illness, including "the idea that we live in a world that we weren't made to endure, that taxes our energies beyond our capacity." At the center of that narrative she places physical and emotional stress, a relatively new concept that was formulated near the end of the 1940s by the Czech biochemist Hans

Selye, who borrowed the term from metallurgy. The concept subsequently gained traction as psychiatrists studied traumatized soldiers and, later, overworked executives, especially those with Type A personalities (thought to be prone to heart attacks). During the decades since then, Harrington says that concern about stress and the illnesses it may trigger have escalated.

6   But these laments centered on modern life have also yielded some hopeful mind-body stories: "efforts to narrate our way out of the darkness," in Harrington's words. For instance, one type of narrative maintains that we can stay healthy or even heal ourselves through strong relationships. Another set of stories finds promise in the healing practices of Eastern cultures, an interest that burgeoned with the Beatles' trip to India to seek the spiritual guidance of the Maharishi Mahesh Yogi; was sustained by the late 1970s discovery—by Mind/Body Medical Institute associate professor of medicine Herbert Benson—of the meditation-derived "relaxation response" to counter stress, and continues to be the subject of Harvard research: for example, scientists are studying MRI scans of the brains of meditating Tibetan monks.

7   Harrington says that it's useful to consider when we find these mind-body stories most convincing. "It's often when we're let down by the mainstream medical narrative of Western society"—which values concrete solutions and statistics. Such an approach fails to help chronically ill patients grapple with questions like "Why did this happen to me?" Mainstream medicine, Harrington continues, "often will answer that there is no reason or that in

Christian Scientists: members of a religion that advocates the healing power of prayer

secular: non-religious

metallurgy: the study of metals

Type A personalities: highly ambitious and competitive individuals

MRI scan: technique that uses magnetic forces to obtain detailed images of the body

effect the reason is dumb bad luck. Mind-body medicine is a tempting alternative for patients in such moments because it is all about connecting the 'why, where, and what now' of an illness back to a person's biography." Mind-body narratives give us a vocabulary for complex experiences like discontent and hope, she adds. "Stories can do things that science can't."

CONVERSATIONS: Collaborating in Class or Online

1. What specific cause/effect relationship is O'Donnell studying in this essay? Diagram the causes and effects that are part of the mind-body connection.
2. What are "mind-body stories" (para. 6)? According to Harrington, what role do they play in medicine?
3. In what ways does our mind leave us "vulnerable to illness" (para. 5)? Explain this implicit connection in detail.
4. What role does meditation play in mind-body medicine?

CONNECTIONS: Discovering Relationships among Ideas

5. What does the author mean by the statement "the mind matters in sickness and health" (para. 2)? According to O'Donnell, what is the relationship between sickness and health?
6. According to O'Donnell, what is the relationship between stress and mind-body narratives?
7. In what ways do stories "tell us how to feel in the world" (Anne Harrington)?
8. Do you think stories can ever "do things that science can't" (para. 7)?

PRESENTATION: Analyzing the Writer's Craft

9. Why does O'Donnell introduce Harrington and her ideas into the essay? What impact do they have on the author's thesis?
10. O'Donnell begins this essay with several examples before stating a main point. Is this an effective opening? Explain your answer.
11. Do you think the title of this essay is effective? Does it capture the essence of the author's statement? Explain your answer in detail.
12. Who do you think was O'Donnell's original audience for this essay? What details support this answer?

PROJECTS: Expressing Your Own Views

13. **Graphic:** Create a collage or take a photo that represents your view of the mind's relationship with the body. Which of the two is most dominant in your own life? Give evidence of your reasoning in pictures. Then present it to the class with an explanation.
14. **Song/Poem:** Compose lyrics or a poem focusing on your view of the role stories can play in medicine. Set them to music if you can.

15. **Essay:** Think of a mind-body story from your own experience, and analyze its causes and effects in a well-developed essay.

16. **Research:** Read and summarize the three resources below. Generate one specific question from each resource that focuses on cause/effect reasoning. Then answer one of your questions in a documented essay, consulting these and other sources as necessary.

OTHER RESOURCES

Web Site

National Library of Medicine: www.nlm.nih.gov

Search: "mind body"

Audio/Video

National Public Radio: www. npr.org

Search: "The Mind's Control Over Healing"

Click on the Listen Now link

Academic Article

"The Placebo Effect: Illness and Interpersonal Healing"

by Franklin G. Miller, Luana Colloca, and Ted J. Kaptchuk

Perspectives in Biology and Medicine 52.4 (2009): 518–539

ONE LAST THOUGHT

The earliest examples of firewalking, or walking on hot coals, are reported in India around 1200 BC. People have practiced firewalking in many cultures and for many reasons, including as a rite of passage or a confidence building exercise. Proponents of the activity consider it an example of "mind over matter," but modern physicists believe that it is actually not as difficult as it was once believed to be. Can you think of any other potentially dangerous "mind over matter" activities? Would you ever try them? Why or why not?

On Reality TV, Less Sleep Means More Drama

by Joel Rose

Joel Rose is a feature writer for National Public Radio, where some of his more recent stories have included "In Pa., College Students Reflect on Obama's First Year" (1/17/10), "When Fair Use Isn't Fair" (2/13/10), "Remembering Ragtime" (1/19/10), "Is Obama's Pastor Anti-Gay" (4/2/08), and "Levi Johnston's Rise in Media Examined" (9/3/09). "On Reality TV: Less Sleep Means More Drama" originally aired on NPR's "Morning Edition," May 14, 2008, hosted by Steve Inskeep.

PREREADING QUESTIONS

Have you ever been deprived of sleep? What were the circumstances?

What does sleep deprivation do to you? How do you feel and act?

How long can you go with only a few hours of sleep per night?

1   Stay close to your television or your TiVo, because tonight, millions of viewers find out whether Anya or Fatima or Whitney walks away with the title of "America's Next Top Model." Big news. And the winner may decide to celebrate with a nap. Former contestants on reality TV shows say producers routinely deprived them of sleep in order to heighten the drama. Joel Rose reports.

2   **JOEL ROSE:** Former "Project Runway" contestant Jay McCarroll says it took him a few days to catch on.

3   **Mr. JAY McCARROLL (Former Contestant. "Project Runway"):** Well, they work you till, like, midnight or one. Before you know it, it's four days later, and you're like, wait, I've slept a total of 11 hours in the past week.

4   **ROSE:** McCarroll says he tried to take naps during filming, but the lack of sleep really came across on TV.

TiVo: a brand of digital video recorders for television

5 **Mr. McCARROLL:** Oh, my. I was having such trauma at the machines, and I was cursing at them.

(Soundbite of TV show, "Project Runway")

6 **Mr. McCARROLL:** You know, you're a fat [censored].

7 **UNIDENTIFIED MAN #1:** Jay.

8 **Mr. McCARROLL:** What?

9 **UNIDENTIFIED MAN #1:** It's cool. Just chill. (unintelligible)

10 **ROSE:** In the end, McCarroll endured three weeks of sleep deprivation, well enough to win the first season of "Project Runway." But he says some of the other contestants couldn't handle it.

11 **Mr. McCARROLL:** It makes people crazy. It puts people on edge. It makes them irritable, screaming.

12 **ROSE:** This is not so different from what actual sleep researchers observe in the lab. Mary Carskadon at Brown University says sleep-deprived people tend to be emotionally volatile.

13 **Prof. MARY CARSKADON (Brown University):** So, you have little girls on their sleepovers giggling themselves silly. But you also have people who have short tempers or who easily cry—I guess all things that do make for high drama.

14 **ROSE:** In other words, sleep deprivation makes for good TV. And apparently, "Project Runway" isn't the only reality show that's figured this out. Here's a clip from a recent episode of "Top Chef."

(Soundbite of TV show, "Top Chef")

15 **UNIDENTIFIED MAN #2:** Okay, so I just did a check in after the chefs have been cooking all night long. They're clearly exhausted, and I think that's going to be a major factor.

16 **UNIDENTIFIED MAN #3:** I'm just so tired that I can't bring myself to stress about anything other than hold on to that cake for dear life, because if it smashes, I'm going to therapy.

17 **ROSE:** "Top Chef' and "Project Runway" are produced by a company called Magical Elves, which did not respond to our requests for an interview. It looks like "America's Next Top Model" may also be depriving its cast members of their beauty rest. Former contestant Victoria Marshman told the blog IvyGate that sleep deprivation made the girls, quote, "physically ill and mentally insane."

> *It makes people crazy. It puts people on edge. It makes them irritable, screaming*

18 **Prof. CARSKADON:** I don't want to say that it's unethical, but maybe it is.

19 **ROSE:** Sleep researcher, Mary Carskadon.

20 **Prof. CARSKADON:** There's documentation that sleep deprivation has been used as torture in prisoner of war settings.

21 **Mr. LINCOLN HIATT (Executive Producer, "Solitary"):** I wouldn't call it torture. Sleep deprivation is a producer's ally on almost any show.

22 **ROSE:** Lincoln Hiatt is the executive producer of "Solitary" on the Fox Reality Channel. The premise is that nine guests are held in solitary confinement and subjected to the whims of an unseen, mechanical-sounding woman named Val.

(Soundbite of TV show, "Solitary")

23 **VAL (Computer Voice/Host, "Solitary"):** I find that depriving my guests of sleep makes them pliable. It helps me to discover their physical, mental, and emotional limitations.

unintelligible: incapable of being understood

volatile: easily changing from one mood or interest to another

ally: friend

pliable: flexible, easy to manipulate

IN CONTEXT

Sleep Deprivation

Long-term sleep deprivation has been linked to more than just higher TV ratings:

Effects of
Sleep deprivation

- Irritability
- Cognitive impairment
- Memory lapses or loss
- Impaired moral judgement
- Severe yawning
- Hallucinations
- Symptoms similar to ADHD
- Impaired immune system

- Increased heart rate variability
- Risk of heart disease

- Decreased reaction time and accuracy
- Tremors
- Aches

Other:
- Growth suppression
- Risk of obesity
- Decreased temperature

- Risk of diabetes Type 2

24   **Mr. HIATT:** These people come in wanting to be tested. And if a tool like sleep deprivation makes somebody more raw, you know, that's valid in that exploration of, you know, what your personal limits are.

25   **ROSE:** Lincoln Hiatt says contestants can leave the show any time they want. All they have to do is push the little red button that takes them out of the running for the $50,000 prize.

CONVERSATIONS: Collaborating in Class or Online

1. What is the purpose of this interview? How do you know?
2. What role does Jay McCarroll play in Joel Rose's research on reality TV?
3. What do "Project Runway," "Top Chef," and "America's Next Top Model" have in common? Why do producers think they are successful?
4. Why do you think reality TV is so popular?

CONNECTIONS: Discovering Relationships among Ideas

5. According to the interview, how are sleep deprivation and "high drama" related?
6. Do you think depriving reality show contestants of sleep is unethical, as Carskadon suggests? Explain your reasoning.
7. List all the effects of sleep deprivation introduced in this essay. How is each related to reality TV?
8. Do you agree with Rose that "sleep deprivation makes for good TV"?

PRESENTATION: Analyzing the Writer's Craft

9. Is the opening announcement before this interview catchy? Explain your answer.
10. In what ways does the expertise of Professor Carskadon bring credibility to this piece?
11. In your opinion, to what extent does this interview achieve its purpose?
12. What effect does the prisoner of war reference have on the rest of the essay? Explain your answer in detail.

PROJECTS: Expressing Your Own Views

13. **TV Show:** Devise your own reality show, and write a detailed explanation of what your concept would add to our current choices on television. What would its ultimate effects be on the general public? What would make this show a success?
14. **Presentation:** Go to the Web site of a reality show you know. Find out five facts or details about the show and think about the reasons behind them. Then present your findings to your class.

15. **Essay:** Ask three people their opinions about reality shows. Do they watch them? Do they enjoy them? What do they like about these shows? How long do they think this television genre will last? Then write an article for your local newspaper about the comments you received.

16. **Research:** Read and summarize the three resources below. Generate one specific question from each resource that focuses on cause/effect reasoning. Then answer one of your questions in a documented essay, consulting these and other sources as necessary.

OTHER RESOURCES

 Web Site

Reality TV World: www. realitytvworld.com

 Audio/Video

ABC News: www.abcnews. go.com

Search: "Growing Up on Reality TV"

Click on the Video link

Academic Article

"Fallen Women in Reality TV: A Pornography of Emotion"

by Rachel E. Dubrofsky

Feminist Media Studies 9.3 (2009): 353–368

ONE LAST THOUGHT

In 2009, Tom Sparks, 33, died after competing as a contestant on the ABC reality show *Wipeout*. Although producers pulled him from the competition after an injury, the game show was investigated for not detecting a pre-existing condition. How rigorous do you think TV physical screenings should be? Do you think ABC should be held responsible for Sparks's death?

Skin Deep: Seeking Self-Esteem Through Surgery

by Camille Sweeney

Camille Sweeney is a journalist and frequent contributor to the *New York Times*. Her recent articles have included "Always the Quiet Ones: Does My Daughter's Shyness Need to be Fixed?" (11/9/09), "Twittering From the Cradle" (9/10/08), "More Fun Than Root Canals: It's the Dental Vacation" (2/7/08), and "Pheromones and Pharaohs" (7/29/09). "Seeking Self Esteem Through Surgery" was originally published in the *New York Times* on January 14, 2009.

PREREADING QUESTIONS

Have you or someone you know ever had cosmetic surgery?

What do you think are the top three reasons people have cosmetic surgery?

How do you think cosmetic surgery and self-esteem are related?

---

1   When 18-year-old Kristen of River Edge, New Jersey, began to develop curves at 15, she was disappointed that breasts didn't follow. "They never grew," said Kristen. "I didn't feel like a woman."

2   And, in fact, at 15, Kristen wasn't yet a woman. But to someone raised in a culture of celebrity obsession and makeover TV shows—not to mention the fact that when Kristen was 16, her mother and older sister had received breast implants—she believed a shapely bust line was her due. So, last May, as a high school graduation gift from her parents, Kristen underwent breast augmentation surgery with

saline implants, approved by the Food and Drug Administration for people 18 and older. "I just wanted to look normal, and now I do," said Kristen, whose family members asked that their last name not be used.

3   To the rigors of teenage grooming—waxing, plucking, body training, and skin care regimens that were once the province of adults—add cosmetic surgery, which is fast becoming a mainstream option among teenagers. But with this popularity, some experts are concerned that the underlying motivation for many of the young people seeking surgery—namely, self-esteem—is being disregarded in the drive to look, as Kristen puts it, "normal."

4   The latest figures from the American Society for Aesthetic Plastic Surgery show that the number of cosmetic surgical procedures performed on youths 18 or younger more than tripled over a 10-year period, to 205,119 in 2007 from 59,890 in 1997. This includes even more controversial procedures: liposuctions rose to 9,295 from 2,504, and breast augmentations increased nearly sixfold, to 7,882 from 1,326. (The latter two procedures have been associated with the deaths of two 18-year-olds: Amy Fledderman of Pennsylvania, who died in 2001 of fat embolism syndrome after undergoing liposuction, and Stephanie Kuleba of Florida, who died last spring from complications because of anesthesia used during a breast augmentation and inverted nipple surgery.)

5   At this point, the recession is apparently having little effect on teenage cosmetic surgery. While figures aren't available for 2008, reports from doctors suggest that parents are keeping their commitments for procedures that are covered by insurance only if considered reconstructive, and that can be costly if they aren't covered. The most frequent procedure, oroplasty, or ear reshaping, costs an average of $3,000, while rhinoplasty costs $4,500, according to the American Society for Aesthetic Plastic Surgery. These costs can be twice as much in the New York area.

6   "If parents have bought into the concept, if they're supportive of a procedure for their child, they seem to be going through with it despite the economy," said Dr. Alan Gold, a plastic surgeon in Great Neck, New York, and president of the society. In fact, one of the most popular times for procedures for young patients is winter break, and several doctors said they noticed no drop in the number of adolescent patients last month.

7   Critics say that with plastic surgery becoming more common, parents are more likely to find themselves having to learn how to say no to a son or daughter with a tarnished self-image who is begging for the same quick surgical fix that the parents themselves may have had. "Our children are barraged with images of ideal women and men that aren't even real, but computer composites," said Jean Kilbourne, co-author of *So Sexy, So Soon*, a book on teenagers and pre-teenagers. "These girls and boys can't compete. The truth is, no one can. And it leaves teens feeling more inadequate than ever and a lot of parents unsure as to the right thing to do."

8   Dr. Frederick Lukash, a plastic surgeon in New York City and Long Island who specializes in treating adolescents, said, "Unlike adults who may elect cosmetic surgery for that 'wow' factor to stand out in a crowd, to be rejuvenated and get noticed, kids have a different mantra. They do it to fit in."

IN CONTEXT

The American Society for Aesthetic Plastic Surgery

Founded in 1967, the American Society for Aesthetic Plastic Surgery is a group of surgeons who are committed to the advancement of cosmetic surgery. They focus on research, education, and safety in their profession.

Food and Drug Administration: FDA, government agency that regulates the safety of food, tobacco, cosmetic, and medicinal products

province: the extent of one's activities

fat embolism syndrome: when fat enters the circulatory system and causes blockage

oroplasty: ear surgery

rhinoplasty: nose surgery

barraged: consistently bombarded with

9   Still, some parents are at least as concerned about their children's discomfort with their appearance as their children are. Jill Marks, whose 11-year-old daughter Julia is a rhinoplasty patient of Dr. Lukash's, said that when Julia was 6 she started taking her to doctors, including ear, nose, and throat specialists, to find out what could be done about her crooked nose. "I knew she was having a hard time with it physically, but also emotionally," Ms. Marks said. "I'd see her in the bathroom pushing her nose to make it straighter. Some kids would ask her, 'Why's your nose so crooked?' I didn't want her to have to go through that anymore."

10   A recent survey of more than 1,000 girls in the United States ages 8 to 17 sponsored by the Dove Self-Esteem Fund—which has a partnership with the Girl Scouts of the U.S.A and is linked to Dove's Campaign for Real Beauty, a program aimed at changing narrow cultural definitions of beauty—showed that 7 in 10 girls surveyed believed that when it came to issues including beauty and body image, they did not "measure up."

> *7 in 10 girls surveyed believed that when it came to issues including beauty and body image, they did not "measure up"*

Only 10 percent found themselves to be "pretty enough." "It's clear there is an epidemic of low self-esteem among girls," said Ann Kearney-Cooke, director of the Cincinnati Psychotherapy Institute, adviser to Dove's study, and author of the book *Change Your Mind, Change Your Body*. "I work with a lot of teens on body image," Dr. Kearney-Cooke said. "I have girls who say they want lipo when really what they need is to learn how to exercise and diet. If a girl thinks no waist, big breasts, and chiseled features is the only definition of beautiful, I try and teach them to recognize the narrow view of what's considered acceptable appearance in our culture and how to challenge that view."

11   Apart from the fact that what may be considered less than ideal at 15 or 16 may change over

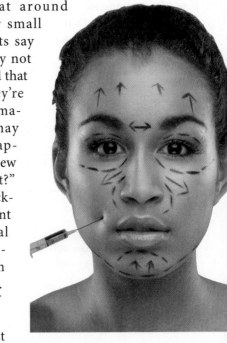

time—baby fat around a chin, say, or small breasts—experts say adolescents may not fully understand that the change they're making is permanent. "They may not be any happier with their new look. Then what?" asks Diana Zuckerman, president of the National Research Center for Women and Families. "And even if all goes well first with breast implant surgery, for example, it may require follow-up procedures. And we know how wrong breast implants can go with breast pain, ruptures, hardening, even a strange sloshing sound that sometimes occurs with saline implants."

12   But plastic surgeons say that as body parts develop at different rates in different people, the opportunity to transform a teenager with low self-esteem and a crooked nose into someone with self-confidence is often justified because a well-timed operation could prevent destructive behaviors, including eating disorders, bullying, and self-mutilation. "There are general guidelines we follow with regard to physical development, but we take each candidate on an individual basis," said Dr. Richard D'Amico, a plastic surgeon in Englewood, New Jersey. "Someone can develop at an accelerated or slowed-down rate. And, of course, levels of maturity vary." Michael Laudisio, now 22, of Massapequa, New York, admits he might not have been mature enough to understand the full implications when his ears were pinned at age 10, but he said his family's decision to

self-mutilation: causing injury to oneself

do it changed his life profoundly. "I had really big ears like no one else and was teased about it all the time," he said. "That surgery made me free."

13 But it can be a very fine line between corrective surgery and cosmetic, and even within a family there can be vastly differing opinions. "I've had mothers dragging their daughters in to have something done, and of course, if the teen is not on board, I'll suggest another appropriate course

of action," said Dr. D'Amico, adding, "You don't get self-esteem from a scalpel."

CONVERSATIONS: Collaborating in Class or Online

1. Why do you think Sweeney wrote this essay? What is her thesis?
2. What does "normal" (para. 2) mean to Kristen in this essay? What are the causes of being "normal" for her? The effects?
3. According to Dr. Frederick Lukash, why do teenagers elect to have cosmetic surgery?
4. In what ways are our children bombarded by "computer composites" of people (para. 7)? According to the author, what effect does this experience have on teens?

CONNECTIONS: Discovering Relationships among Ideas

5. In what ways can cosmetic surgery be beneficial to teenagers?
6. What is the connection between the Heidi Montag graphic at the end of the essay and the content of the essay?
7. What is the relationship between self-esteem and cosmetic surgery? Is this relationship the same, in your opinion, for all age groups?
8. What do you think accounts for the dramatic increase in cosmetic surgeries since 2007?

PRESENTATION: Analyzing the Writer's Craft

9. Do you think Kristen's story is an effective beginning to this essay? Why or why not?
10. Give the essay an alternate title.
11. What is the "fine line" between corrective and cosmetic surgery (last paragraph)? Why do you think Sweeney brings this distinction up at the end of the essay?
12. Why do you think Sweeney ends her essay by saying "You don't get self-esteem from a scalpel" (para. 13)? What does this statement mean to you?

PROJECTS: Expressing Your Own Views

13. **Interview:** Interview someone concerning his/her views on the causes and/or effects of cosmetic surgery. Write out a transcript of your interview and a summary of your observations.
14. **Graphic:** Draw a graphic (diagram, cartoon, picture, or computer-generated image) of your view of the relationship between self-esteem and cosmetic surgery.

15. **Essay:** Using one of your Conversations above (questions 1–4), write a well-developed essay focusing on the consequences of teenage cosmetic surgery.

16. **Research:** Read and summarize the three resources below. Generate one specific question from each resource that focuses on cause/effect reasoning. Then answer one of your questions in a documented essay, consulting these and other sources as necessary.

OTHER RESOURCES

Web Site

The American Society for Aesthetic Plastic Surgery: www.surgery.org

Audio/Video

CBS News: www.cbsnews.com

Search: "Plastic Surgery for Pets"

Click on the Video link

Academic Article

"Children's Bodies, Parents' Choices"
by Susan Gilbert

Hastings Center Report 39.1 (2009): 14–15

ONE LAST THOUGHT

Reality star Heidi Montag recently underwent a flurry of plastic surgeries in one day, which attracted nationwide media scrutiny. How much surgery is too much? Do you think this attention was fair? Why or why not?

CHAPTER WRITING ASSIGNMENTS

Write a well-developed essay in response to one of the following prompts. Consult the chapter introduction for guidance in creating your essay.

CONNECTING THE READINGS

1. On what points would Rogers ("What Evolutionary Psychology Says about Social Networking") and O'Donnell ("Does Thinking Make It So?") agree about our minds controlling our bodies? Where would they disagree?

2. What would Staples ("Black Men and Public Space") and Sweeney ("Skin Deep") say are the three most important social values in our country that have changed over the past 10 years? What would they agree are the causes of these changes? The effects?

3. What do you think Chast ("Read at Your Own Risk") and Rose ("On Reality TV") would say about literacy in the U.S. today? How would they predict literacy will change in the next five years?

4. How would O'Donnell ("Does Thinking Make It So?"), Rose ("On Reality TV"), and Sweeney ("Skin Deep") characterize our culture in the U.S. today? What would they say makes Americans who we are?

MOVING BEYOND THE READINGS

5. What are your predictions for social networking during the next five years? Where do you think this cultural phenomenon is headed? And why will it go there?

6. What TV shows do you watch most often? Why do you prefer these shows over others?

7. How do people know they are "middle class" in the U.S.? What five adjectives would you use to describe people in that category? What are some of their principal behavioral characteristics? Why do you think they share these traits?

8. What are your favorite Internet sites? Why do you like them so much?

COMBINING RHETORICAL MODES

9. Write your "reading autobiography" or history of your experiences with reading from your first memories to the present. What were your earliest memories of reading, and what types of books and articles do you read now? What are your reasons for the reading choices you have made over the years? How has the material you read influenced you as a person?

10. Write your "writing autobiography" or history of your experiences with writing from your first memories to the present. What were your earliest experiences with writing, and how do you feel about writing now? What are the main reasons you feel that way?

11. What are the differences between any two generations that interest you (Grandparents and parents? Great-grandparents and children? Etc.?) What are the reasons behind these differences?

12. How can you explain the continuing rise in oil prices? Go to www.wtrg.com/prices.htm or http://news.yahoo.com/s/ap/oil_prices, and discuss with your classmates the data presented on these sites. What future predictions can you make based on this information?

Argument

Argument may be our most useful form of communication because it helps us get what we want in life. The main reason people use this rhetorical mode is to persuade others to take action or share their points of view on an issue. In fact, anyone who wants something from someone else, ranging from grant money for a civic project to a new computer for a birthday, must use some form of argument to get what he or she desires. Thus argument is not a shouting match or fight, but a well-reasoned statement on a debatable issue. In essence, argument is a fundamental part of our lives. Here are some examples of this important rhetorical strategy in action:

- A letter to persuade your former classmates to attend their high school reunion;
- An essay for your English class arguing for or against new immigration laws;

- A request to a bank asking to forgive a late fee;
- A paper for a psychology course arguing for the influence of either nature or nurture;
- A billboard promoting a political candidate.

You can use three main types of strategies to persuade others when you are constructing an argument:

- Logical appeals or *logos* (facts and reasoning);
- Emotional appeals or *pathos* (vivid descriptions, stories, images, and details); and
- Ethical appeals or *ethos* (your own credibility and experience).

These three approaches to argument give us a solid foundation to work from in both reading and writing.

Introducing Argument

You are in the realm of argument when you deal with complex, debatable issues about which multiple views are possible. Although reason and logic are the focus of this chapter, you will also need to learn how to use emotional and ethical appeals as skillfully as possible to create effective arguments. An extremely sophisticated form of reasoning, argumentative writing requires you to present your views on an issue in a convincing way. Writers of successful arguments adjust their use of the three appeals to their particular purpose and audience in order to persuade their readers. Argument and persuasion are taught together because good arguments are usually persuasive.

Logical Appeals

An appeal to logic, which relies on reason and intellect to make its point, is most effective when you are expecting your readers to disagree with your argument. This type of appeal can help change your readers' opinions or influence their future actions through the sheer strength of logical thinking. Once you make a claim or statement, you need to support it with well-chosen examples or evidence. If you want to argue, for example, that convicted criminals cannot be rehabilitated while in prison, you could cite statistics illustrating that many of them commit repeat offenses after they have served their time and return to society.

Emotional Appeals

Emotional appeals, on the other hand, attempt to arouse your readers' feelings, instincts, senses, and biases in an attempt to get them to agree with your argument. Used most profitably when your readers already side with you, this approach generally validates, reinforces, and/or incites your readers to share your feelings or ideas. For example, in order to encourage lawmakers to create more effective rehabilitation programs for prisoners, you might describe a recent tragic incident involving a robber who served his time, was released from prison, and soon thereafter robbed a bank, killing a guard at the entrance during his escape. By focusing on such vivid emotional details as the anguish of the guard's family, his role in his church, and his two small children, you can build a powerful essay that would seize readers' attention and be much more effective than a dull recitation of impersonal facts and nationwide statistics.

Ethical Appeals

Ethical appeals, the third strategy writers often use to persuade their readers, involves cultivating a sincere, honest tone that helps establish your reputation as a reliable, credible person who is well informed on the topic under discussion. In fact, you can think of the ethical appeal as trying to get your readers to answer "yes" to the question "Would you buy a used car from this person?" Whether you are trying to "sell" readers shampoo or hate crime legislation, gay marriage or tougher prison terms for repeat offenders, the more honest and believable you and your sources are, the better chance you have of convincing your audience. This approach is often used in conjunction with logical and emotional appeals to create an argument that will result in minimal resistance from its readers.

Differing Viewpoints and Common Ground

As you gather evidence for your argument, you should acknowledge and refute dissenting viewpoints that are in opposition to your own stance. In addition to discrediting the opposition, you also might want to include some **common ground**, mutual assumptions or points of agreement you share with your readers. By doing this, you will make them realize that you actually have some viewpoints in common, and your readers might be more likely to consider your argument. Using these two approaches within an argument paper will make your argument broader and stronger as your reasoning unfolds.

The Appeals at Work

Look at the following examples of logical, emotional, and ethical appeals in two arguments related to college students.

DEVELOPMENT STRATEGIES AT WORK

Debatable Statement: Students should choose a major early in their college career.

Development

→ **Logical:** Lets students know their exact required courses and prerequisites

→ **Logical:** Lets students start major courses in their first two years

→ **Logical:** Encourages students to bond early with others in their major

→ **Logical:** Lets students compete early for apprenticeships related to their major

→ **Logical:** Forces students to focus earlier on their futures

→ **Emotional:** Students who choose a major in their first year say they feel more control over their academic lives

→ **Emotional:** Students who delayed choosing a major claim they lost a sense of purpose and did not bond with any group of peers

→ **Ethical:** Our Dean of Students claims that most students who declare a major in their first year complete college in four to five years

Conclusion: Persuasion

DEVELOPMENT STRATEGIES AT WORK

Debatable Statement: Students should work while going to college.

Development

→ **Logical:** Studies say 15 hours/week of work actually improves academic performance

→ **Logical:** Extra money helps with school expenses

→ **Logical:** Apprenticeships or jobs can help students select a major

→ **Logical:** Apprenticeships/jobs let students build a network for future employment

→ **Emotional:** Students feel good about helping pay for their own education

→ **Emotional:** Students gain the respect of their parents

→ **Ethical:** The author of this essay is working during college to gain experience

Conclusion: Persuasion

The success or failure of an argument is easily determined: If the people addressed change their actions or attitudes in favor of the writer or speaker, the argument has been successful.

Discovering How Argument Works

On the right is a list of the principal elements of argumentative thinking, whether for a visual or a prose selection. These Argument Essentials are equally useful as guidelines for both reading and writing.

Analyzing the graphic below will help you realize how these elements work together to create an effective argument. If you discover on your own how this method of reasoning functions, you will be able to apply it effectively to your own reading and writing. The questions will help you understand this rhetorical mode even more clearly than you already do.

> **Argument Essentials**
>
> Debatable Thesis Statement
> Significance
> Evidence
> Appeals: Logical, Emotional, Ethical
> Opposing Viewpoints
> Common Ground
> Logical Organization
> Summary/Conclusion

1. How would you express the thesis statement of this ad?
2. What is the significance of this statement?
3. What evidence does the advertiser use to create this visual argument?
4. What appeals (logical, emotional, ethical) are at work in this ad?
5. What dissenting viewpoints are shown/implied?
6. What common ground (that is, points of agreement between advertiser and reader) can you find in this ad?
7. Based on the layout of the details in this graphic, what elements are featured?
8. How does the artist bring this graphic to a conclusion?

PEACE CORPS

Cultivate fresh ideas and help them take root.

Live, learn, and work with a community overseas.
Be a Volunteer.
peacecorps.gov

Collaborative Responses Now discuss your responses to these questions with your classmates in small groups or as an entire class. Did the diverse perspectives from other students in your class change your "reading" of the visual? If so, in what ways?

Reading Arguments

As you read the prose and graphic selections in this chapter, pay special attention to the details and evidence presented in each argument. You should also make sure you understand the author's/illustrator's approach to the argument, along with his or her method of organization.

Reading and writing arguments effectively calls for high-level thought processes that will ensure your success in all that you do. On your first reading of each selection, the following questions will help you accomplish this task for both written and graphic assignments:

Argument Essentials: Reading

- **Debatable Thesis Statement:** What is the main argument?
- **Significance:** What is the significance of this argument?
- **Evidence:** What evidence is presented to support this argument?
- **Appeals: Logical, Emotional, Ethical:** What specific appeals are at work in this selection?
- **Opposing Viewpoints:** What differing viewpoints are represented?
- **Common Ground:** What assumptions or values that the readers might share are mentioned?
- **Logical Organization:** How is the argument organized?
- **Summary/Conclusion:** What is the author's/illustrator's conclusion?

On your second and third readings of the selection, focus on areas of ambiguity and confusion so you can deepen your comprehension.

Writing Arguments

Taking another look at the Argument Essentials as you move from reading to writing will help you adjust your argument to your specific purpose and audience. But first, let's review the writing process as it applies to this rhetorical mode.

Choosing a Subject

As with all assignments, you should select your subject as soon as possible. When you write an argument essay, choose a subject about which you can make a debatable claim. In addition, if you have strong feelings about it, you will more easily gather evidence and convince your readers of your point of view. Keep in mind, however, that your readers might feel just as strongly about another side of the issue. No matter what your topic, you need to be open-minded and willing to consider all viewpoints. Finally, you should only consider a subject that can be adequately developed in the space assigned to you.

Our student writer, Tyrone Johnson, decides to write about our antiquated academic schedule in kindergarten through high school because it no longer serves the needs of today's students.

Generating Details

You might want to start generating ideas by listing free-flowing thoughts on your topic. Then, use one of the prewriting strategies introduced in Chapter 3 to generate as many details as possible for each point.

To begin this process, Tyrone lists three groups that are affected by outdated elementary, junior high, and high school academic year schedules: parents, teachers, and students. As Tyrone starts recording his ideas, he realizes that the traditional school year is causing more problems than he initially thought. Here is his list so far:

Parents	Teachers	Students
problems w/childcare	time lost	most important
household chores	always behind	lose skills
stress	no pay	can't keep up in fall
need rest	students lose skills in summer	continuous learning necessary
cleaning up—futile	low test scores	summer reading
	review necessary	might lose ground permanently
	catching up	
	stress	

Drafting a Thesis Statement

After choosing a subject and generating some ideas for your paper, you should be ready to compose a thesis statement, which means you must take a stand for or against an action or an idea. In other words, your thesis statement should be a debatable claim, meaning that it can be argued or challenged and will not be met with agreement by everyone who reads it. Your thesis statement should introduce your subject and state your opinion about that subject, which will serve as the controlling idea or purpose for your entire paper. A thesis for a graphic project will be implied rather than stated, but it will still guide you to a coherent assignment.

Tyrone's thesis names his topic and states his opinion about that topic:

> *The original rationale for students being free during the summer months is no longer applicable to most families; as a result, students, teachers, and parents are suffering from an antiquated school calendar.*

This statement will now provide focus and direction for the remainder of the assignment.

Producing a Draft

All these preliminary decisions will prepare you to write a well-developed argument essay.

- Your **introduction** should introduce your subject, including any necessary background information, and make your point of view as clear as possible in a thesis statement.
- The **body of your paper** provides evidence to support your point of view, including opposing points of view and rebuttal. It will generally consist of a combination of logical, emotional, and ethical appeals—all leading to some final summation or recommendation.
- Your **conclusion** then summarizes the evidence you have marshaled and draws relevant conclusions.

Your Audience   You will be able to engineer your best support if you know your readers' opinions, feelings, and background before you begin writing. All the rest of the decisions you will make, including how to approach your topic, will be dictated by these characteristics. Just as with a good speech, the more you know about your audience, the better argument you can construct.

Evidence   When you write an argument essay, you need to make sure your argument is significant and you have taken into account any dissenting viewpoints. The evidence that you bring to bear on your topic is the best gauge of these factors. Without solid evidence, your essay is nothing more than opinion; with it, your essay can be much more powerful and persuasive. If you supply convincing evidence, your readers will not only understand your position but may even be persuaded by it.

Evidence can consist of facts, statistics, statements from authorities, and examples or personal stories. Examples and stories can be based on your own observations, experiences, and reading; but your personal opinions, by themselves, are not evidence. The evidence you choose should be relevant and sufficient to prove your thesis. You can also develop your ideas with the writing strategies you've learned in Chapters 5 through 12. Comparison/contrast, definition, and cause/effect can be particularly beneficial in building an argument. You should feel free to use any combination of evidence and writing strategies that will help support your thesis statement.

Opposing Views and Rebuttal   In addition to stating and supporting your position, anticipating and responding to opposing or dissenting views are also important. Presenting only your side of the argument leaves at least half of the story untold—the opposing viewpoints. When you acknowledge opposing arguments and address them, you are increasing your chances of convincing your reader.

Common Ground Pointing out common ground between you and your audience is also an effective strategy. **Common ground** refers to points of agreement between two opposing positions. For example, one person might be in favor of legalizing marijuana and another strongly opposed, but they might find common ground—agreement—in the need to keep other drugs out of everyone's hands. Locating some common ground is possible in almost every situation. When you agree with your opponent on certain points, your reader sees you as a fair and credible person.

Inductive versus Deductive Reasoning To develop a well-constructed *logical* argument, you have two principal patterns available to you: *inductive reasoning* or *deductive reasoning.* The first encourages readers to make what is called an "inductive leap" from several particular examples to a single generalization. The detectives on *Law and Order*, for instance, function almost exclusively on inductive logic. They view a crime scene, gather forensic and situational evidence, and draw their conclusions based solidly on the evidence. Used most often by detectives, scientists, and lawyers, the process of inductive reasoning asks the audience to think logically by moving systematically from an assortment of selected evidence to a rational and ordered conclusion.

In contrast, deductive reasoning moves its audience from a broad, general statement to particular examples supporting that statement. In writing such an essay, you would present your thesis statement about a crime scene first and then offer clear, orderly evidence to support that belief. Although the mental process we go through in creating a deductive argument is quite sophisticated, it is based on a three-step form of reasoning called a **syllogism**, which most logicians believe is the foundation of logical thinking. The traditional syllogism has the following components:

> *A major premise:* All humans have fears.
>
> *A minor premise:* Criminals are humans.
>
> *A conclusion:* Therefore, criminals have fears.

As you might suspect, this type of reasoning is only as accurate as its original premises, so you need to be sure your premises are true so your argument will be valid.

Fallacies In constructing a logical argument, you should also take great care to avoid fallacies in reasoning, which occur most often when you use faulty evidence, when you misrepresent your evidence, or when you cite evidence that is irrelevant to your argument. Avoiding fallacies is important because readers who discover a fallacy or problem in logic are likely to question your intelligence, credibility, and perhaps even your interpretation of other evidence. Listed on page 87 are the most common fallacies that signal faulty reasoning in student writing. To recognize other fallacies, consult a current handbook.

As a writer, you have the ultimate responsibility to find credible evidence and present it in a well-reasoned, convincing way. If you build your argument on true statements and accurate evidence, your essay will be effective, and your argument is likely to be persuasive.

Organization Most arguments are organized from general to particular, from particular to general, or from one extreme to another. When you know that your readers already agree with you, arranging your details from general to particular or from most to least important is usually most effective. With this order, you are building on your readers' enthusiasm and loyalty as you advance your thesis. If you suspect that your audience does not agree with you, reverse the organization of your evidence and arrange it from particular to general or from least to most important. In this way, you can lead your readers step by step through your reasoning in an attempt to align them with your thinking on the topic.

The concluding paragraph of an argument essay should restate your main assertion (in terms slightly different from your original statement) and offer some constructive recommendations about the problem you have been discussing (if you haven't already done so). This section of your paper should clearly bring your argument to a close in one final attempt to move your audience to accept or act on the viewpoint you have presented.

By the end of your essay, you want your audience to agree with you. So you should organize your essay in such a way that your readers can easily follow it. The number of your paragraphs may vary, depending on your assignment and/or your topic, but the following outline shows the order in which the features of an argument essay are most effective:

Argument Outline

Introduction
   Background information
   Introduction of subject and its significance
   Debatable thesis

Body (These elements of argument can appear in different sequences in the essay.)
   Reasons and evidence: Inductive or deductive
   Common ground
   Opposing viewpoints
   Rebuttal: Response to dissenting viewpoints

Conclusion
   Restatement of your position
   Call for action or agreement

You should now use the following questions, based on the Argument Essentials, to help focus and refine your written and graphic assignments:

Argument Essentials: Writing

- **Debatable Thesis Statement:** What is your main argument?
- **Significance:** What is the significance of your argument?
- **Evidence:** What evidence do you present to support your argument?
- **Appeals: Logical, Emotional, Ethical:** What specific appeals are at work in your essay?

- **Opposing Viewpoints:** What differing viewpoints do you represent?
- **Common Ground:** What shared assumptions and/or values do you mention in your argument?
- **Logical Organization:** How is your argument organized?
- **Summary/Conclusion:** What is your conclusion?

Revising and Editing

Revising and editing your verbal or visual project means rereading and rewriting the material so it says exactly what you want it to say. This is also the time to strengthen the connections between your sentences by adding some well-chosen transitions, which will help your readers follow your thinking as you move from one point to the next. They will also make your essay coherent and enjoyable to read.

Revising

Look closely at your essay or graphic as someone else might see it. Most importantly, make sure it says what you intend to say. Then answer the questions posed in the Revising Checklist on page 28, which focus your attention on how your essay functions.

Now is also the point in the writing process when you should add transitions to your essay that clarify the relationship of your ideas to one another and to the general argument you are constructing. In arguments, these are usually words and phrases that explain logical connections. Some, such as *first, second, in addition,* and *finally*, signal your main points. Others, such as *however, nevertheless, yet*, and *still*, mark opposing arguments. And other useful transitions simply show changes in direction as they guide your readers thorough your reasoning: *as a result, in brief, for these reasons, in other words, in short, overall, for example*, and *therefore*. These particular expressions will help your readers understand as clearly as possible the relationships among the points in your argument.

Editing

Editing is the final phase of your writing process. It involves looking closely at specific words, phrases, sentences, and any visual details to make sure they follow current usage rules. Use the Editing Checklist on page 30 to review your project for errors in grammar and usage. When you locate a potential error, consult a handbook or go to Pearson's Web-based MyCompLab for an explanation of the problem.

Also, if your instructor marks any grammar mistakes on your paper or graphic, make sure you understand them. Recognizing errors in your own writing is the most effective way of correcting them.

As you read the following student essay, refer to the Argument Essentials (page 415) and the questions for reading arguments (page 416) to help you understand and analyze it. Then, to fully appreciate how this student essay works, notice the marginal notes highlighting the features of a good argument.

Tyrone Johnson

Professor Flachmann

English 101

24 Sept. 2011

Do We Need to Reset the Academic Calendar?

Common Ground → 1 As our society progresses, so must our traditions. Often we are reluctant to change thoughts and ideals that we have held our entire lives. But when times change, we must reassess the validity *Introduction of Subject* → and rationale behind our past decisions. Here in the U.S., it is time for us to reconsider the role of public schools and how our current school year calendar is ineffective and outdated. More specifically, it is time for all publicly funded education to be held year-round. The *Significance of Subject* → original rationale for students being free during the summer months *Debatable Thesis* → is no longer applicable to most families; as a result, teachers, parents, and students are suffering from this antiquated school calendar.

Background Information → 2 In the earlier days of the United States, many people's livelihoods derived from the family farm. School-aged children needed to be free during the summer months to help their parents and siblings work in the fields in order to guarantee food for the winter. But in *Dissenting Viewpoints* → today's world, many more people live in cities, and small family farms *Common Ground* → are not nearly as common. Since we all want our children to compete *Restatement of Thesis* → in the global job market, we need to reconsider the current structure of attending school only nine months out of the year, which is not ultimately beneficial to teachers, parents, or students.

3 Teachers might find the summer break difficult to deal with in several significant ways. First, they do not get paid for three months, which is a financial strain and an added stress on their summer budget. When teachers do return to teach in the fall, their students may have lost knowledge and skills. This means that teachers must spend a significant amount of time reviewing and bringing students up to speed before beginning new material. This can create a teaching environment in which instructors are always trying to catch up during the year, which may result in students missing important concepts and performing poorly on standardized tests—a bad reflection on the teachers, the students, and the school.   ← Topic 1 / Evidence (Logical) / Evidence (Logical) / Evidence (Logical)

4 Many parents also suffer from the traditional school schedule because finding daycare for school children during the summer months is difficult and expensive. Since both parents are in the workforce in most households, securing daycare for their school-aged children while the parents are at work is a necessity. A summer break from school provides unwelcome stress and strain on parents. Actually, the summer months can be disastrous even for households with a stay-at-home parent. What a parent used to be able to accomplish while the kids were at school must now be done with the children at home. Grocery shopping can be a huge ordeal with kids in tow, and cleaning up is practically pointless because another mess is bound to follow with kids creating constant chaos in the house. These additional stressors could be avoided by rethinking the traditional yearly school schedule.   ← Topic 2 / Evidence (Logical) / Evidence (Emotional) / Evidence (Logical) / Evidence (Emotional)

5 Most important, however, students suffer academically from having three months off during the summer. Unless parents are organizing study sessions at home and insisting that their children read throughout the summer, most students come back to school in the fall at a serious disadvantage. After three months without instruction, students often forget essential lessons from the previous school year because they have not had an opportunity to actively use the   ← Topic 3 / Evidence (Logical)

knowledge and skills they learned. Systematic practice of skill sets is an integral feature of learning. If students do not continually use what they have learned, they are likely to forget it. If skills and knowledge are lost over the summer, students must relearn material, which ultimately detracts from time needed to learn new skills in the next school year and can cause a student to fall permanently behind.

Evidence (Emotional) ──→

6 Admittedly, summer breaks can bring some positive results. Teachers in K-12 are able to retool their teaching skills and take a calm, well-deserved rest; parents can see their kids more often and go on exciting family excursions with them; and students' minds get necessary relaxation. But we need to look past these creature comforts and put the development of our youngest citizens first in our minds.

Dissenting Viewpoints ──→

Common Ground ──→

7 For American students to become more competitive in the world, we need to increase their educational opportunities, starting with our school schedules. Since the current academic schedule is based on an outmoded agrarian economy, everyone would benefit if schools began year-round instruction. Teachers would earn salaries all year and wouldn't have to spend time reviewing material; parents wouldn't have to pay for daycare during the summer months; and students would not suffer from large gaps of time between instruction. Because of these advantages, it is time for us to reconsider the traditional school schedule and make a long-overdue change to year-round instruction.

Response to Dissenting Viewpoints ──→

Restatement of Position ──→

Call to Action ──→

Reviewing Argument

Based on the information you have learned in this chapter and the annotations on the student essay, show how this essay works by writing a clear, precise summary or by drawing your own outline or graphic representation of it. Label the categories on your visual. This exercise will confirm your understanding of the elements of argument in both reading and writing.

Is Google Making Us Stupid?

by Nicholas Carr

A leading authority on technology, business, and culture, **Nicholas Carr** is the author of four books: *Does IT Matter, The Big Switch: Rewiring the World, From Edison to Google,* and *The Shallows: What the Internet Is Doing to Our Brains.* He also writes a personal blog, "Rough Type," and has been published in *The Atlantic Monthly, The New York Times Magazine, Wired,* and many other influential periodicals.

PREREADING QUESTIONS

What types of material do you read every day?

How much of your daily reading is on the Internet?

Does the type of reading you do affect how you think? If so, in what ways?

1   "Dave, stop. Stop, will you? Stop, Dave. Will you stop, Dave?" So the supercomputer HAL pleads with the implacable astronaut Dave Bowman in a famous and weirdly poignant scene toward the end of Stanley Kubrick's *2001: A Space Odyssey.* Bowman, having nearly been sent to a deep-space death by the malfunctioning machine, is calmly, coldly disconnecting the memory circuits that control its artificial " brain." "Dave, my mind is going," HAL says, forlornly. "I can feel it. I can feel it."

2   I can feel it, too. Over the past few years I've had an uncomfortable sense that someone, or something, has been tinkering with my brain, remapping the neural circuitry, reprogramming the memory. My mind isn't going—so far as I can tell—but it's changing. I'm not thinking the way I used to think. I can feel it most strongly when I'm reading. Immersing myself in a book or a lengthy article used to be easy. My mind would get caught up in the narrative or the turns of the argument, and I'd spend hours strolling through long stretches of prose. That's rarely the case anymore. Now my concentration often starts to drift after two or three pages. I get fidgety, lose the thread, begin looking for

implacable: merciless, ruthless
forlornly: hopelessly

something else to do. I feel as if I'm always dragging my wayward brain back to the text. The deep reading that used to come naturally has become a struggle.

3   I think I know what's going on. For more than a decade now, I've been spending a lot of time online, searching and surfing and sometimes adding to the great databases of the Internet. The Web has been a godsend to me as a writer. Research that once required days in the stacks or periodical rooms of libraries can now be done in minutes. A few Google searches, some quick clicks on hyperlinks, and I've got the telltale fact or pithy quote I was after. Even when I'm not working, I'm as likely as not to be foraging in the Web's info-thickets reading and writing emails, scanning headlines and blog posts, watching videos and listening to podcasts, or just tripping from link to link to link. (Unlike footnotes, to which they're sometimes likened, hyperlinks don't merely point to related works; they propel you toward them.)

> *The Net seems to be . . . chipping away my capacity for concentration and contemplation*

4   For me, as for others, the Net is becoming a universal medium, the conduit for most of the information that flows through my eyes and ears and into my mind. The advantages of having immediate access to such an incredibly rich store of information are many, and they've been widely described and duly applauded. "The perfect recall of silicon memory," *Wired's* Clive Thompson has written, "can be an enormous boon to thinking." But that boon comes at a price. As the media theorist Marshall McLuhan pointed out in the 1960s, media are not just passive channels of information. They supply the stuff of thought, but they also shape the process of thought. And what the Net seems to be doing is chipping away my capacity for concentration and contemplation. My mind now expects to take in information the way the Net distributes it: in a swiftly moving stream of particles. Once I was a scuba diver in the sea of words. Now I zip along the surface like a guy on a Jet Ski.

5   I'm not the only one. When I mention my troubles with reading to friends and acquaintances—literary types, most of them—many say they're having similar experiences. The more they use the Web, the more they have to fight to stay focused on long pieces of writing. Some of the bloggers I follow have also begun mentioning the phenomenon. Scott Karp, who writes a blog about online media, recently confessed that he has stopped reading books altogether. "I was a lit major in college and used to be [a] voracious book reader," he wrote. "What happened?" He speculates on the answer: "What if I do all my reading on the web not so much because the way I read has changed (i.e., I'm just seeking convenience), but because the way I THINK has changed?"

6   Bruce Friedman, who blogs regularly about the use of computers in medicine, also has described how the Internet has altered his mental habits. "I now have almost totally lost the ability to read and absorb a longish article on the web or in print," he wrote earlier this year. A pathologist who has long been on the faculty of the University of Michigan Medical School, Friedman elaborated on his comment in a telephone conversation with me. His thinking, he said, has taken on a "staccato" quality, reflecting the way he quickly scans short passages of text from many sources online. "I can't read *War and*

pithy: concise
conduit: channel
boon: benefit
voracious: eager, avid

Peace anymore," he admitted. "I've lost the ability to do that. Even a blog post of more than three or four paragraphs is too much to absorb. I skim it."

7 Anecdotes alone don't prove much. And we still await the long-term neurological and psychological experiments that will provide a definitive picture of how Internet use affects cognition. But a recently published study of online research habits, conducted by scholars from University College London, suggests that we may well be in the midst of a sea change in the way we read and think. As part of the five-year research program, the scholars examined computer logs documenting the behavior of visitors to two popular research sites, one operated by the British Library and one by a U.K. educational consortium, that provide access to journal articles, e-books, and other sources of written information. They found that people using the sites exhibited "a form of skimming activity," hopping from one source to another and rarely returning to any source they'd already visited. They typically read no more than one or two pages of an article or book before they would "bounce" out to another site. Sometimes they'd save a long article, but there's no evidence that they ever went back and actually read it. The authors of the study report

> It is clear that users are not reading online in the traditional sense; indeed there are signs that new forms of "reading" are emerging as users "power browse" horizontally through titles, contents pages, and abstracts going for quick wins. It almost seems that they go online to avoid reading in the traditional sense.

8 Thanks to the ubiquity of text on the Internet, not to mention the popularity of text-messaging on cell phones, we may well be reading more today than we did in the 1970s or 1980s, when television was our medium of choice. But it's a different kind of reading, and behind it lies a different kind of thinking—perhaps even a new sense of the self. "We are not only what we read," says Maryanne Wolf, a developmental psychologist at Tufts University and the author of *Proust and the Squid: The Story and Science of the Reading Brain.* "We are how we read." Wolf worries that the style of reading promoted by the Net, a style that puts

IN CONTEXT

The MTV Generation

Teens raised in the 1980s are sometimes referred to as the MTV Generation because they spent larger amounts of time watching television  than any previous generations. Lauren Lipton's 1991 article in the *LA Times*, entitled "The Shaping of a Shapeless Generation: Does MTV Unify a Group Known Otherwise For its Sheer Diversity," explains, "Much has been written about the so-called 'Baby Buster Generation'—the fairly anonymous group of 20ish young adults struggling to separate themselves from the shadow of the baby boomers. . . . The group's newest moniker, 'the MTV Generation,' might be the most accurate description yet. For while much has been made about the generation's lack of a single unifying theme or experience, its members seem to have one thing in common: music videos."

"efficiency" and "immediacy" above all else, may be weakening our capacity for the kind of deep reading that emerged when an earlier technology, the printing press, made long and complex works of prose commonplace. When we read online, she says, we tend to become "mere decoders of information." Our ability to interpret text, to make the rich mental connections that form when we read deeply and without distraction, remains largely disengaged.

9 Reading, explains Wolf, is not an instinctive skill for human beings. It's not etched into our genes the way speech is. We have to teach our minds how to translate the symbolic characters we see into the language we understand. And the media or other technologies we use in learning and practicing the craft of reading play an important part in shaping the neural circuits inside our

consortium: organization
ubiquity: presence
etched: engraved

brains. Experiments demonstrate that readers of ideograms, such as the Chinese, develop a mental circuitry for reading that is very different from the circuitry found in those of us whose written language employs an alphabet. The variations extend across many regions of the brain, including those that govern such essential cognitive functions as memory and the interpretation of visual and auditory stimuli. We can expect as well that the circuits woven by our use of the Net will be different from those woven by our reading of books and other printed works.

10   Sometime in 1882, Friedrich Nietzsche bought a typewriter—a Malling-Hansen Writing Ball, to be precise. His vision was failing, and keeping his eyes focused on a page had become exhausting and painful, often bringing on crushing headaches. He had been forced to curtail his writing, and he feared that he would soon have to give it up. The typewriter rescued him, at least for a time. Once he had mastered touch-typing, he was able to write with his eyes closed, using only the tips of his fingers. Words could once again flow from his mind to the page.

IN CONTEXT

Friedrich Nietzsche

Friedrich Nietzsche was a 19th-century German philosopher and philologist. He is best known for his ideas about existentialism and postmodernism.

11   But the machine had a subtler effect on his work. One of Nietzsche's friends, a composer, noticed a change in the style of his writing. His already terse prose had become even tighter, more telegraphic. "Perhaps you will through this instrument even take to a new idiom," the friend wrote in a letter, noting that, in his own work, his " 'thoughts' in music and language often depend on the quality of pen and paper."

12   "You are right," Nietzsche replied, "our writing equipment takes part in the forming of our thoughts." Under the sway of the machine, writes the German media scholar Friedrich A. Kittler, Nietzsche's prose "changed from arguments to aphorisms, from thoughts to puns, from rhetoric to telegram style."

13   The human brain is almost infinitely malleable. People used to think that our mental meshwork, the dense connections formed among the 100 billion or so neurons inside our skulls, was largely fixed by the time we reached adulthood. But brain researchers have discovered that that's not the case. James Olds, a professor of neuroscience who directs the Krasnow Institute for Advanced Study at George Mason University, says that even the adult mind "is very plastic." Nerve cells routinely break old connections and form new ones. "The brain," according to Olds, "has the ability to reprogram itself on the fly, altering the way it functions."

> *The Internet . . . [is] becoming our map and our clock, our printing press and our typewriter, our calculator and our telephone, and our radio and TV*

14   As we use what the sociologist Daniel Bell has called our "intellectual technologies"—the tools that extend our mental rather than our physical capacities—we inevitably begin to take on the qualities of those technologies. The mechanical clock, which came into common use in the 14th century, provides a compelling example. In *Technics and Civilization*, the historian and cultural critic Lewis Mumford described how the clock "disassociated time from human events and helped create the belief in an independent world of mathematically measurable sequences." The "abstract framework of divided time" became "the point of reference for both action and thought."

15   The clock's methodical ticking helped bring into being the scientific mind and the scientific

---

terse: abrupt
aphorisms: sayings

man. But it also took something away. As the late MIT computer scientist Joseph Weizenbaum observed in his 1976 book, *Computer Power and Human Reason: From Judgment to Calculation*, the conception of the world that emerged from the widespread use of timekeeping instruments "remains an impoverished version of the older one, for it rests on a rejection of those direct experiences that formed the basis for, and indeed constituted, the old reality." In deciding when to eat, to work, to sleep, to rise, we stopped listening to our senses and started obeying the clock.

16   The process of adapting to new intellectual technologies is reflected in the changing metaphors we use to explain ourselves to ourselves. When the mechanical clock arrived, people began thinking of their brains as operating "like clockwork." Today, in the age of software, we have come to think of them as operating "like computers." But the changes, neuroscience tells us, go much deeper than metaphor. Thanks to our brain's plasticity, the adaptation occurs also at a biological level.

17   The Internet promises to have particularly far-reaching effects on cognition. In a paper published in 1936, the British mathematician Alan Turing proved that a digital computer, which at the time existed only as a theoretical machine, could be programmed to perform the function of any other information-processing device. And that's what we're seeing today. The Internet, an immeasurably powerful computing system, is subsuming most of our other intellectual technologies. It's becoming our map and our clock, our printing press and our typewriter, our calculator and our telephone, and our radio and TV.

18   When the Net absorbs a medium, that medium is re-created in the Net's image. It injects the medium's content with hyperlinks, blinking ads, and other digital gewgaws, and it surrounds the content with the content of all the other media it has absorbed. A new e-mail message, for instance, may announce its arrival as we're glancing over the latest headlines at a newspaper's site. The result is to scatter our attention and diffuse our concentration.

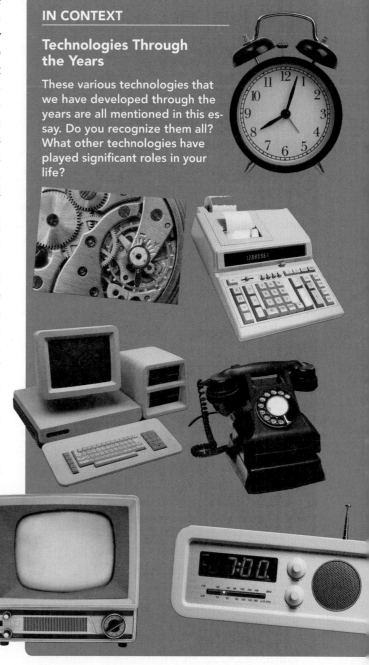

19   The Net's influence doesn't end at the edges of a computer screen, either. As people's minds become attuned to the crazy quilt of Internet media, traditional media have to adapt to the audience's new expectations. Television programs add text crawls

subsuming: absorbing
gewgaws: showy things

and pop-up ads, and magazines and newspapers shorten their articles, introduce capsule summaries, and crowd their pages with easy-to-browse info-snippets. When, in March of this year, *The New York Times* decided to devote the second and third pages of every edition to article abstracts, its design director, Tom Bodkin, explained that the "shortcuts" would give harried readers a quick "taste" of the day's news, sparing them the "less efficient" method of actually turning the pages and reading the articles. Old media have little choice but to play by the new-media rules.

20   Never has a communications system played so many roles in our lives—or exerted such broad influence over our thoughts—as the Internet does today. Yet, for all that's been written about the Net, there's been little consideration of how, exactly, it's reprogramming us. The Net's intellectual ethic remains obscure.

21   About the same time that Nietzsche started using his typewriter, an earnest young man named Frederick Winslow Taylor carried a stopwatch into the Midvale Steel plant in Philadelphia and began a historic series of experiments aimed at improving the efficiency of the plant's machinists. With the approval of Midvale's owners, he recruited a group of factory hands, set them to work on various metalworking machines, and recorded and timed their every movement as well as the operations of the machines. By breaking down every job into a sequence of small, discrete steps and then testing different ways of performing each one, Taylor created a set of precise instructions—an "algorithm," we might say today—for how each worker should work. Midvale's employees grumbled about the strict new regime, claiming that it turned them into little more than automatons, but the factory's productivity soared.

22   More than a hundred years after the invention of the steam engine, the Industrial Revolution had at last found its philosophy and its philosopher. Taylor's tight industrial choreography—his "system," as he liked to call it—was embraced by manufacturers throughout the country and, in time, around the world. Seeking maximum speed, maximum efficiency, and maximum output, factory owners used time-and-motion studies to organize their work and configure the jobs of their workers. The goal, as Taylor defined it in his celebrated 1911 treatise, *The Principles of Scientific Management*, was to identify and adopt, for every job, the "one best method" of work and thereby to effect "the gradual substitution of science for rule of thumb throughout the mechanic arts." Once his system was applied to all acts of manual labor, Taylor assured his followers, it would bring about a restructuring not only of industry but of society, creating a utopia of perfect efficiency. "In the past the man has been first," he declared; "in the future the system must be first."

> **"In the past the man has been first . . . ; in the future the system must be first"**

23   Taylor's system is still very much with us; it remains the ethic of industrial manufacturing. And now, thanks to the growing power that computer engineers and software coders wield over our intellectual lives, Taylor's ethic is beginning to govern the realm of the mind as well. The Internet is a machine designed for the efficient and automated collection, transmission, and manipulation of information, and its legions of programmers are intent on finding the "one best method"—the perfect algorithm—to carry out every mental movement of what we've come to describe as "knowledge work."

24   Google's headquarters, in Mountain View, California—the Googleplex—is the Internet's high church, and the religion practiced inside its walls is Taylorism. Google, says its chief

automatons: robots

executive, Eric Schmidt, is "a company that's founded around the science of measurement," and it is striving to "systematize everything" it does. Drawing on the terabytes of behavioral data it collects through its search engine and other sites, it carries out thousands of experiments a day, according to the *Harvard Business Review*, and it uses the results to refine the algorithms that increasingly control how people find information and extract meaning from it. What Taylor did for the work of the hand, Google is doing for the work of the mind.

25   The company has declared that its mission is "to organize the world's information and make it universally accessible and useful." It seeks to develop "the perfect search engine," which it defines as something that "understands exactly what you mean and gives you back exactly what you want." In Google's view, information is a kind of commodity, a utilitarian resource that can be mined and processed with industrial efficiency. The more pieces of information we can "access" and the faster we can extract their gist, the more productive we become as thinkers.

26   Where does it end? Sergey Brin and Larry Page, the gifted young men who founded Google while pursuing doctoral degrees in computer science at Stanford, speak frequently of their desire to turn their search engine into an artificial intelligence, a HAL-like machine that might be connected directly to our brains. "The ultimate search engine is something as smart as people—or smarter," Page said in a speech a few years back. "For us, working on search is a way to work on artificial intelligence." In a 2004 interview with *Newsweek*, Brin said, "Certainly if you had

> ### IN CONTEXT
>
> #### Google's Searching Technology
>
> In 1996, when Larry Page and Sergey Brin launched Google, the other available search engines used a technology that counted how many times the search terms appeared on pages. Google's searching technology, called PageRank, instead analyzed the relationships among Web sites to create a more accurate search engine.

all the world's information directly attached to your brain or an artificial brain that was smarter than your brain, you'd be better off." Last year, Page told a convention of scientists that Google is "really trying to build artificial intelligence and to do it on a large scale."

27   Such an ambition is a natural one, even an admirable one, for a pair of math whizzes with vast quantities of cash at their disposal and a small army of computer scientists in their employ. A fundamentally scientific enterprise, Google is motivated by a desire to use technology, in Eric Schmidt's words, "to solve problems that have never been solved before," and artificial intelligence is the hardest problem out there. Why wouldn't Brin and Page want to be the ones to crack it?

28   Still, their easy assumption that we'd all "be better off" if our brains were supplemented, or even replaced, by an artificial intelligence is unsettling. It suggests a belief that intelligence is the output of a mechanical process, a series of discrete steps that can be isolated, measured, and optimized. In Google's world, the world we enter when we go online, there's little place for the fuzziness of contemplation. Ambiguity is not an opening for insight but a bug to be fixed. The human brain is just an outdated computer that needs a faster processor and a bigger hard drive.

29   The idea that our minds should operate as high-speed data-processing machines is not only built into the workings of the Internet, it is the network's reigning business model as well. The faster we surf across the Web—the more links we click and pages we view—the more opportunities Google and other companies gain to collect information

about us and to feed us advertisements. Most of the proprietors of the commercial Internet have a financial stake in collecting the crumbs of data we leave behind as we flit from link to link—the more crumbs, the better. The last thing these companies want is to encourage leisurely reading or slow, concentrated thought. It's in their economic interest to drive us to distraction.

30   Maybe I'm just a worrywart. Just as there's a tendency to glorify technological progress, there's a countertendency to expect the worst of every new tool or machine. In Plato's *Phaedrus*, Socrates bemoaned the development of writing. He feared that, as people came to rely on the written word as a substitute for the knowledge they used to carry inside their heads, they would, in the words of one of the dialogue's characters, "cease to exercise their memory and become forgetful." And because they would be able to "receive a quantity of information without proper instruction," they would "be thought very knowledgeable when they are for the most part quite ignorant." They would be "filled with the conceit of wisdom instead of real wisdom." Socrates wasn't wrong—the new technology did often have the effects he feared—but he was shortsighted. He couldn't foresee the many ways that writing and reading would serve to spread information, spur fresh ideas, and expand human knowledge (if not wisdom).

31   The arrival of Gutenberg's printing press, in the 15th century, set off another round of teeth gnashing. The Italian humanist Hieronimo Squarciafico worried that the easy availability of books would lead to intellectual laziness, making men "less studious" and weakening their minds. Others argued that cheaply printed books and broadsheets would undermine religious authority, demean the work of scholars and scribes, and spread sedition and debauchery. As New York University professor Clay Shirky notes, "Most of the arguments made against the printing press were correct, even prescient." But, again, the doomsayers were unable to imagine the myriad blessings that the printed word would deliver.

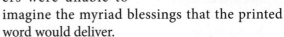

> *The kind of deep reading that a sequence of printed pages promotes is valuable . . . for the intellectual vibrations those words set off within our own minds*

32   So, yes, you should be skeptical of my skepticism. Perhaps those who dismiss critics of the Internet as Luddites or nostalgists will be proved correct, and from our hyperactive, data-stoked minds will spring a golden age of intellectual discovery and universal wisdom. Then again, the Net isn't the alphabet, and although it may replace the printing press, it produces something altogether different. The kind of deep reading that a sequence of printed pages promotes is valuable not just for the knowledge we acquire from the author's words but for the intellectual vibrations those words set off within our own minds. In the quiet spaces opened up by the sustained, undistracted reading of a book, or by any other act of contemplation, for that matter, we make our own associations, draw our own inferences and analogies, foster our own ideas. Deep reading, as Maryanne Wolf argues, is indistinguishable from deep thinking.

33   If we lose those quiet spaces or fill them up with "content," we will sacrifice something important not only in our selves but in our culture. In a recent essay, the playwright Richard Foreman eloquently described what's at stake:

> I come from a tradition of Western culture, in which the ideal (my ideal) was the complex, dense, and "cathedral-like" structure of the highly educated and articulate personality—a man or woman who carried inside themselves a personally constructed and unique version of the entire heritage of the West. [But now]

sedition: rebellion, disorder
debauchery: immorality
prescient: psychic

I see within us all (myself included) the replacement of complex inner density with a new kind of self—evolving under the pressure of information overload and the technology of the "instantly available."

34 As we are drained of our "inner repertory of dense cultural inheritance," Foreman concluded, we risk turning into "'pancake people'—spread wide and thin as we connect with that vast network of information accessed by the mere touch of a button."

35 I'm haunted by that scene in *2001*. What makes it so poignant, and so weird, is the computer's emotional response to the disassembly of its mind: its despair as one circuit after another goes dark, its childlike pleading with the astronaut—"I can feel it. I can feel it. I'm afraid"—and its final reversion to what can only be called a state of innocence. HAL's outpouring of feeling contrasts with the emotionlessness that characterizes the human figures in the film, who go about their business with an almost robotic efficiency. Their thoughts and actions feel scripted, as if they're following the steps of an algorithm. In the world of *2001*, people have become so machinelike that the most human character turns out to be a machine. That's the essence of Kubrick's dark prophecy: as we come to rely on computers to mediate our understanding of the world, it is our own intelligence that flattens into artificial intelligence.

repertory: collection

CONVERSATIONS: Collaborating in Class or Online

1. How does the author claim his mind is changing?
2. How do hyperlinks differ from footnotes?
3. In what ways is the Internet a "universal medium" (para. 4)?
4. According to James Olds, how is the mind "plastic" (para. 13)?

CONNECTIONS: Discovering Relationships among Ideas

5. How do the media "shape the process of thought" (para. 4), as Marshall McLuhan put it?
6. Do you agree with Maryanne Wolf that we are actually creating a new sense of the "self" with our contemporary reading habits? Explain your answer.
7. How does Google treat information as a commodity? What are the results of this mindset?
8. Why do Internet companies want us to resist "leisurely reading or slow, concentrated thought" (para. 29)? How do they benefit from our more distracted reading habits?

PRESENTATION: Analyzing the Writer's Craft

9. What is the debatable issue in this essay?
10. Find three pieces of evidence (one from each category—logical, emotional, ethical) that Carr uses to support his argument. How effective is each? Explain your answer.
11. At the end of paragraph 3, Carr compares the depth of his reading to "a guy on a Jet Ski" when he used to be "a scuba diver in the sea of words." Does this comparison explain what is happening to the author's concentration? Is this an effective way to explain the changes he believes his mind is going through? How does this comparison further Carr's argument?
12. Do you think the people and the detailed examples Carr introduces in his essay are an effective way to prove his point? Explain your answer.

PROJECTS: Expressing Your Own Views

13. **Podcast:** Use the Internet to discover how the development of writing, the arrival of Gutenberg's printing press, and the Internet are all related to each other. How are these "inventions" alike? How are they different? What consequences did each create? Write a brief podcast with your responses to these questions.

14. **Collage:** Using clip art or pictures from magazines, create a collage that defines you in the midst of our 21st-century technology. Be conscious of whether you are presenting yourself in a good or bad light.

15. **Essay:** Write an essay discussing the role of the Internet in our lives at present and then forecasting its role over the next five years, arguing for or against its potential to help us progress as a society.

16. **Research:** Read and summarize the three resources below. Generate one specific question from each resource that focuses on argument. Then answer one of your questions in a documented essay, consulting these and other sources as necessary.

OTHER RESOURCES

Web Site

The Search Engine List:
www.thesearchenginelist.com

Academic Article

"Music to Our Eyes: Google Books, Google Scholar, and the Open Content Alliance"

by Kirstin Dougan

Libraries and the Academy 10.1 (2010): 75–93

Audio/Video

National Public Radio:
www.npr.org

Search: "What Happens When People Migrate to the Internet?"

Click on the Listen Now link

ONE LAST THOUGHT

In response to Carr's article, writer David Wolman published an article in *Wired* magazine entitled "The Critics Need a Reboot. The Internet Hasn't Led Us Into a New Dark Age." Wolman opens his article by outlining the numerous technologies that were predicted to destroy our lives: "When in doubt, blame the latest technology. Socrates thought the advent of writing would wreak havoc on the powers of the mind. Christian theologians denounced the printing press as the work of the devil. The invention of the telephone was supposed to make letter-writing extinct, and the arrival of the train—and later the car and plane—was going to be the death of community." He goes on to argue that the solution to Carr's problem lies in educating people to distinguish "knowledge from garbage." Access the article by visiting www.wired.com and searching for the title. Do you agree more with Wolman or Carr? Why?

Watering Little Sprout

by Kristy-Anne Glubish

This picture, entitled "Watering Little Sprout," was taken in 2009 by **Kristy-Anne Glubish**, one of the world's top photographers with pictures published in *Time*, *Wired*, *Rhythm Magazine*, and many other well-known periodicals. Her images have accompanied recent articles on a wide variety of topics, including special needs children, sexual satisfaction, Mennonite women, health and fitness, train trips in British Columbia, and anti-smoking campaigns.

> ### PREREADING QUESTIONS
>
> What do you do to help save the environment?
>
> How are you more "green" this year than you were last year?
>
> What else can you do to help save the earth?

CONVERSATIONS: Collaborating in Class or Online

1. What statement do you think this picture is making?
2. What visual details contribute to this message?
3. What is in the background in this photo?
4. What is the central focus of this image?

CONNECTIONS: Discovering Relationships among Ideas

5. What do all the materials on the ground have in common?
6. What is the photographer trying to convince the viewer to think or do?
7. What other images might convey the same or similar arguments?
8. What personal associations do you make with this photo?

PRESENTATION: Analyzing the Writer's Craft

9. What different arguments could this photograph support?
10. Which elements in the photo would be most effective with each argument you suggest?
11. What do the colors in the picture contribute to the main argument?
12. In your opinion, how effective is the photo?

PROJECTS: Expressing Your Own Views

13. **Web Site:** Design a Web site dedicated to ecology. What will the tabs on this site be? What will be its focus? What are some of its messages?
14. **Game:** Create a game that helps children understand the importance of recycling. Who will be your primary audience? What will be the specific focus of your game?
15. **Essay:** Many different types of projects are currently attempting to save the planet. But all campaigns are not equally effective. Write an essay arguing for or against a particular type of conservation effort. What is your reasoning? On what evidence do you base your conclusions?
16. **Research:** Read and summarize the three resources below. Generate one specific question from each resource that focuses on argument. Then answer one of your questions in a documented essay, consulting these and other sources as necessary.

OTHER RESOURCES

Web Site

Earth Day Network: http: // earthday.net

Academic Article

"The Problem of Consumption"

by Peter Dauvergne

Global Environmental Politics 10.2 (2010): 1–10

Audio/Video

National Public Radio: www.npr.org

Search: "The Green Movement Turns Black and Brown"

Click on the Audio link

ONE LAST THOUGHT

Keep America Beautiful's
Crying Indian (1971)

National Geographic's
Afghan Girl (1985)

Raising the Flag on Iwo
Jima (1945)

People have been using powerful imagery to influence public perception for decades. Here are three examples of images from different eras that have lingered in the public's consciousness years after they were first shown. Can you think of any other images that are clearly meant to affect our feelings about a certain topic?

Now You Take "Bambi" or "Snow White"—That's Scary!

by Stephen King

One of America's most prolific and highly celebrated writers of horror, suspense, and science fiction, **Stephen King** has sold over 350 million copies of his novels and short stories. Among his most popular books are *Carrie*, *Salem's Lot*, *The Shining*, *The Dark Tower* (a series), *Firestarter*, *Christine*, and *Cujo*. Many of his novels have been made into movies and television shows.

PREREADING QUESTIONS

Which classic children's stories do you remember most vividly?

Which didn't you like?

What are the reasons for your preferences?

1   Read the story synopsis below and ask yourself if it would make the sort of film you'd want your kids watching on the Friday—or Saturday—night movie:

2   A good but rather weak man discovers that, because of inflation, recession, and his second wife's fondness for overusing her credit cards, the family is tottering on the brink of financial ruin. In fact, they can expect to see the repossession men coming for the car, the almost new recreational vehicle, and the two color TVs any day; and a pink warning-of-foreclosure notice has already arrived from the bank that holds the mortgage on their house.

3   The wife's solution is simple but chilling: Kill the two children, make it look like an accident, and collect the insurance. She browbeats her husband into going along with this homicidal scheme. A wilderness trip is arranged, and while wifey stays in camp, the father leads his two children deep into the Great Smoky wilderness. In the end, he finds he cannot kill them in cold blood; he simply leaves them to wander around until, presumably, they die of hunger and exposure.

browbeats: badgers

4   The two children spend a horrifying three days and two nights in the wilderness. Near the end of their endurance, they stumble upon a back-country cabin and go to it, hoping for rescue. The woman who lives alone there turns out to be a cannibal. She cages the two children and prepares to roast them in her oven as she has roasted and eaten other wanderers before them. The boy manages to get free. He creeps up behind the woman as she stokes her oven and pushes her in, where she burns to death in her own fire.

5   You're probably shaking your head no, even if you have already recognized the origin of this bloody little tale (and if you didn't, ask your kids: they probably will) as "Hansel and Gretel," a so-called fairy tale that most kids are exposed to even before they start kindergarten. In addition to this story, with its grim and terrifying images of child abandonment, children lost in the woods and imprisoned by an evil woman, cannibalism, and justifiable homicide, small children are routinely exposed to tales of mass murder and mutilation ("Bluebeard"), the eating of a loved one by a monster ("Little Red Riding-Hood"), treachery and deceit ("Snow White"), and even the specter of a little boy who must face a black-hooded, ax-wielding headsman ("The 500 Hats of Bartholomew Cubbins," by Dr. Seuss).

6   I'm sometimes asked what I allow my kids to watch on the tube, for two reasons: First, my three children, at ten, eight, and four, are still young enough to be in the age group that opponents of TV violence and horror consider to be particularly impressionable and at risk; and second, my seven novels have been popularly classified as "horror stories." People tend to think those

two facts contradictory. But . . . I'm not sure that they are.

7   Three of my books have been made into films, and at this writing, two of them have been shown on TV. In the case of *Salem's Lot*, a made-for-TV movie, there was never a question of allowing my kids to watch it on its first run on CBS; it began at nine o'clock in our time zone, and all three children go to bed earlier than that. Even on a weekend, and even for the oldest, an eleven o'clock bedtime is just not negotiable. A previous TV Guide article about children and frightening programs mentioned a three-year-old who watched *Lot* and consequently suffered night terrors. I have no wish to question any responsible parent's judgment—all parents raise their children in different ways—but it did strike me as passingly odd that a three-year-old should have been allowed to stay up that late to get scared.

> *He creeps up behind the woman as she stokes her oven and pushes her in, where she burns to death in her own fire*

8   But in my case, the hours of the telecast were not really a factor, because we have one of those neat little time machines, a videocassette recorder. I taped the program and, after viewing it myself, decided my children could watch it if they wanted to. My daughter had no interest; she's more involved with stories of brave dogs and loyal horses these days. My two sons, Joe, eight, and Owen, then three, did watch. Neither of them seemed to have any problems, either while watching it or in the middle of the night—when those problems most likely turn up.

9   I also have a tape of *Carrie*, a theatrical film first shown on TV about two and a half years ago.

IN CONTEXT

Violence on TV

According to the A. C. Nielsen Co., the average child spends 1,680 minutes, or 28 hours, per week watching television. By the time the average child has finished elementary school, he or she has seen over 8,000 murders on TV.

---

treachery: betrayal, deceit
specter: ghost

I elected to keep this one on what my kids call "the high shelf" (where I put the tapes that are forbidden to them), because I felt that its depiction of children turning against other children, the lead character's horrifying embarrassment at a school dance, and her later act of homicide would upset them. *Lot*, on the contrary, is a story that the children accepted as a fairy tale in modern dress.

10   Other tapes on my "high shelf" include *Night of the Living Dead* (cannibalism), *The Brood* (David Cronenberg's film of intergenerational breakdown and homicidal "children of rage" who are set free to murder and rampage), and *The Exorcist*. They are all up there for the same reason: They contain elements that I think might freak the kids out.

11   Not that it's possible to keep kids away from everything on TV (or in the movies, for that matter) that will freak them out; the movies that terrorized my own nights most thoroughly as a kid were not those through which Frankenstein's monster or the Wolfman lurched and growled, but the Disney cartoons. I watched Bambi's mother shot and Bambi running frantically to escape being burned up in a forest fire. I watched, appalled, dismayed, and sweaty with fear, as Snow White bit into the poisoned apple while the old crone giggled in evil ecstasy. I was similarly terrified by the walking brooms in *Fantasia* and the big, bad wolf who chased the fleeing pigs from house to house with such grim and homicidal intensity. More recently, Owen, who just turned four, crawled into bed with my wife and me. "Cruella DeVille is in my room," he said. Cruella DeVille is, of course, the villainess of *101 Dalmatians*, and I suppose Owen had decided that a woman who would want to turn puppies into dogskin coats might also be interested in little boys. All these films would certainly get G ratings if they were produced today, and frightening excerpts of them have been shown on TV during "the children's hour."

12   Do I believe that all violent or horrifying programming should be banned from network TV? No, I do not. Do I believe it should be telecast only in the later evening hours, TV's version of the "high shelf"? Yes, I do. Do I believe that children should be forbidden all violent or horrifying programs? No, I do not. Like their elders, children have a right to experience the entire spectrum of drama, from such warm and mostly unthreatening programs as *Little House on the Prairie* and *The Waltons* to scarier fare. It's been suggested again and again that such entertainment offers us a catharsis—a chance to enter for a little while a scary and yet controllable world, where we can express our fears, aggressions, and possibly even hostilities. Surely no one would suggest that children do not have their own fears and hostilities to face and overcome; those dark feelings are the basis of many of the fairy tales children love best.

13   Do I think a child's intake of violent or horrifying programs should be limited? Yes, I do, and that's why I have a high shelf. But the pressure groups who want to see all horror (and anything smacking of sex, for that matter) arbitrarily removed from television make me both uneasy and angry. The element of Big Brotherism inherent in such an idea causes the unease; the idea of a bunch of people I don't even know presuming to dictate what is best for my children causes the anger. I feel that deciding such things myself is my right—and my responsibility.

depiction: portrayal
appalled: horrified
catharsis: release
arbitrarily: randomly

CONVERSATIONS: Collaborating in Class or Online

1. After reading this essay, what do you think of the violence in the famous fairy tales mentioned in paragraph 5?
2. Why does King let his young children watch horror films? Do you agree with his stance on this issue?
3. What purpose do horror films serve in our lives?
4. What does "Big Brotherism" refer to in this essay? Why does this notion make the author "uneasy and angry" (para. 13)?

CONNECTIONS: Discovering Relationships among Ideas

5. Were you frightened when you were young by any of the children's stories listed in paragraph 5?
6. How do you think your initial reactions to these stories affected you later in life? Explain your answer in detail.
7. How do we all benefit from different forms of catharsis in our lives?
8. What do you think scares kids the most in movies?

PRESENTATION: Analyzing the Writer's Craft

9. King starts his essay with a gruesome synopsis of a very popular fairy tale. Is this an effective beginning for this essay? Which appeal is he using in this case?
10. What do you think King's primary argument is in this essay?
11. Who do you think is King's intended audience? Who might be the dissenters in this audience?
12. Outline King's argument against banning "violent and horrifying" TV programs (paras. 12–13). How is it organized? Is this an effective order for the claim he is trying to make?

PROJECTS: Expressing Your Own Views

13. **Story:** Write a children's story without any scary elements.
14. **Critique:** Write a review of your favorite fairy tale. Emphasize what you like best about it in your critique, and try to persuade your readers to share your response.
15. **Essay:** In essay form, explain your general response to scary movies. Do you like or dislike them? Use well-chosen evidence to convince your readers to see this type of entertainment as you do.
16. **Research:** Read and summarize the three resources below. Generate one specific question from each resource that focuses on argument. Then answer one of your questions in a documented essay, consulting these and other sources as necessary.

OTHER RESOURCES

Web Site

The Internet Movie Database:
www.imdb.com/chart/horror

Audio/Video

StephenKing.com:
www.stephenking.com/

Click on the Multimedia link for access to Stephen King's latest video and audio samples

Academic Article

"Grownups Are Not Afraid of Scary Stuff, but Kids Are: Young Children's and Adults' Reasoning about Children's, Infants', and Adults' Fears"

by Liat Sayfan and Kristin Hansen Lagattuta

Child Development 79.4 (2008): 821–835

ONE LAST THOUGHT

Urban legends are modern stories of questionable authenticity that appear mysteriously and spread quickly. The Vanishing Hitchhiker (in which a hitchhiker inexplicably disappears from a car), the Kidney Heist (involving someone being ambushed, anesthetized, and waking up missing one kidney), and the Hook (detailing the near-miss of an attack on a young couple by a dangerous, escaped mental patient with a hook in place of one hand) are all examples of these popular stories. Many television shows have attempted to verify or explain urban legends, including *Beyond Belief: Fact or Fiction*, *Mostly True Stories: Urban Legends Revealed*, and *Mythbusters*. A few Web sites are even devoted to researching these stories: See http://www.snopes.com and http://tafkac.org/. Have you ever heard or repeated an urban legend? Why do you think such stories become popular?

Center for Immigration Studies

The **Center for Immigration Studies** is dedicated to researching immigration into the U.S. The Center provides data to help our country make informed decisions about immigration. It is supported by private foundations, government grants, and individual donors.

PREREADING QUESTIONS

Are you an immigrant to the U.S. or do you personally know an immigrant?

Why do you think people immigrate to the U.S.?

What would be some of the difficulties associated with leaving your home country?

View this Web site at www.cis.org before answering the questions that follow.

CONVERSATIONS: Collaborating in Class or Online

1. Go to the home page for the Center for Immigration Studies (www.cis.org), and list three of the topics featured on that page.

2. What can you learn about the content of this site by surveying the home page?

3. Considering the posted articles, policies, and videos, which items are most interesting to you from this site?

4. Read one segment and summarize its contents in three sentences.

CONNECTIONS: Discovering Relationships among Ideas

5. Name two items that you agree with on the cis.org site.

6. Name two items that you disagree with on the cis.org site.

7. Find a Web site that represents another perspective on immigration. What is the central difference between the two sites?

8. Choose one of the cis.org videos, and explain how it supports the message and mission of the site.

PRESENTATION: Analyzing the Writer's Craft

9. Is this Web site inviting to you? Why or why not?

10. Identify a debatable issue on this Web site?

11. Which of the three argumentative appeals is most effective on this site? Explain your answer.

12. Are the topics on this site well suited to its purpose? Explain your answer.

PROJECTS: Expressing Your Own Views

13. **Interview:** Interview two people who have come to the U.S. from another country. Find out why they came here, what entices them to stay, what they like about the U.S., and what they miss about their country of origin. Craft interesting, well-phrased questions before you conduct your interview. Then reproduce your interview, and add an introduction and conclusion that highlight your findings.

14. **Web Site:** Design a Web site featuring the 10 top reasons to live in the U.S.

15. **Essay:** Write an argument in response to one of the segments on this site. Search the Internet for more details on this issue if necessary.

16. **Research:** Read and summarize the three resources below. Generate one specific question from each resource that focuses on argument. Then answer one of your questions in a documented essay, consulting these and other sources as necessary.

OTHER RESOURCES

Web Site

U.S. Citizenship and Immigration Services: www.uscis.gov

Academic Article

"Immigration and the American Century" by Charles Hirschman

Demography 42.4 (2005): 595–620

Audio/Video

History.com: www.history.com

Search: "Immigrant Success"

Click on the Video link

ONE LAST THOUGHT

Many natural-born American citizens know less about their government and its history than immigrants who have studied for the U.S. naturalization exam. Take an interactive citizenship quiz at www.history.com/ by searching "Citizenship Quiz" to see how much you know.

Letter From Birmingham Jail

by Martin Luther King, Jr.

An American clergyman and social activist, **Dr. Martin Luther King, Jr.** (1929–1968) was a prominent leader in the U.S. civil rights movement. Perhaps best known for his nonviolent protest tactics, his 1963 March on Washington, and his iconic "I Have a Dream" speech, he became in 1964 the youngest person in history to receive the Nobel Peace Prize for his efforts to end racial discrimination through civil disobedience.

PREREADING QUESTIONS

What particular problem in society bothers you the most? Why?

What suggestions do you have for dealing with it?

Do you think these suggestions, if implemented, would cause their own problems?

My Dear Fellow Clergymen:

1   While confined here in the Birmingham city jail, I came across your recent statement calling present activities "unwise and untimely." Seldom do I pause to answer criticism of my work and ideas. If I sought to answer all the criticisms that cross my desk, my secretaries would have little time for anything other than such correspondence in the course of the day, and I would have no time for constructive work. But since I feel that you are men of genuine good will and that your criticisms are sincerely set forth, I want to try to answer your statement in what I hope will be patient and reasonable terms.

2   I think I should indicate why I am here in Birmingham, since you have been influenced by the view which argues against "outsiders coming in." I have the honor of serving as President of the Southern Christian Leadership Conference, an organization operating in every southern state, with headquarters in Atlanta, Georgia. We have some eighty-five affiliated organizations across the South, and one of them is the Alabama Christian Movement for Human Rights. Frequently we share staff, educational and financial resources with our affiliates. Several months ago the affiliate here in Birmingham asked us to be on call to engage in a nonviolent direct-action program if such were deemed necessary. We readily consented, and when the hour came we lived up to our promise. So I, along with several members of my staff,

445

am here because I was invited here. I am here because I have organizational ties here.

3 But more basically, I am in Birmingham because injustice is here. Just as the prophets of the eighth century B.C. left their villages and carried their "thus saith the Lord" far beyond the boundaries of their home towns and just as the Apostle Paul left his village of Tarsus and carried the gospel of Jesus Christ to the far corners of the Greco-Roman world, so am I compelled to carry the gospel of freedom beyond my own home town. Like Paul, I must constantly respond to the Macedonian call for aid.

4 Moreover, I am cognizant of the interrelatedness of all communities and states. I cannot sit idly in Atlanta and not be concerned about what happens in Birmingham. Injustice anywhere is a threat to justice everywhere. We are caught in an inescapable network of mutuality, tied in a single garment of destiny. Whatever affects one directly, affects all indirectly. Never again can we afford to live with the narrow, provincial "outside agitator" idea. Anyone who lives inside the United States can never be considered an outsider anywhere within its bounds.

5 You deplore the demonstrations taking place in Birmingham. But your statement, I am sorry to say, fails to express a similar concern for the conditions that brought about the demonstrations. I am sure that none of you would want to rest content with the superficial kind of social analysis that deals merely with effects and does not grapple with underlying causes. It is unfortunate that demonstrations are taking place in Birmingham, but it is even more unfortunate that the city's white power structure left the Negro community with no alternative.

6 In any nonviolent campaign there are four basic steps: collection of the facts to determine whether injustices exist; negotiation; self-purification; and direct action. We have gone through all these steps in Birmingham. There can be no gainsaying the fact that racial injustice engulfs this community. Birmingham is probably the most thoroughly segregated city in the United States. Its ugly record of brutality is widely known. Negroes have experienced grossly unjust treatment in the courts. There have been more unsolved bombings of Negro homes and churches in Birmingham than in any other city in the nation. These are the hard, brutal facts of the case. On the basis of these conditions, Negro leaders sought to negotiate with the city fathers. But the latter consistently refused to engage in good-faith negotiation.

7 Then, last September, came the opportunity to talk with leaders of Birmingham's economic community. In the course of the negotiations, certain promises were made by the merchants—for example, to remove the stores humiliating racial signs. On the basis of these promises, the Reverend Fred Shuttlesworth and the leaders of the Alabama Christian Movement for Human Rights agreed to a moratorium on all demonstrations. As the weeks and months went by, we realized that we were the victims of a broken promise. A few signs, briefly removed, returned; the others remained.

8 As in so many past experiences, our hopes had been blasted, and the shadow of deep

cognizant: aware of
agitator: rebel
deplore: disapprove of
grapple: deal with
gainsaying: denying
moratorium: suspension

disappointment settled upon us. We had no alternative except to prepare for direct action, whereby we would present our very bodies as a means of laying our case before the conscience of the local and the national community. Mindful of the difficulties involved, we decided to undertake a process of self-purification. We began a series of workshops on nonviolence, and we repeatedly asked ourselves, "Are you able to accept blows without retaliation?" "Are you able to endure the ordeal of jail?" We decided to schedule our direct-action program for the Easter season, realizing that except for Christmas, this is the main shopping period of the year. Knowing that a strong economic withdrawal program would be the by-product of direct action, we felt that this would be the best time to bring pressure to bear on the merchants for the needed change.

9   Then it occurred to us that Birmingham's mayoralty election was coming up in March, and we speedily decided to postpone action until after Election Day. When we discovered that the Commissioner of Public Safety, Eugene "Bull" Connor, had piled up enough votes to be in the run-off, we decided again to postpone action until the day after the run-off so that the demonstrations could not be used to cloud the issues. Like many others, we waited to see Mr. Connor defeated, and to this end we endured postponement after postponement. Having aided in this community need, we felt that our direct-action program could be delayed no longer.

10   You may well ask, "Why direct action? Why sit-ins, marches, and so forth? Isn't negotiation a better path?" You are quite right in calling for negotiation. Indeed, this is the very purpose of direct action. Nonviolent direct action seeks to create such a crisis and foster such a tension that a community which has constantly refused to negotiate is forced to confront the issue. It seeks so to dramatize the issue that it can no longer be ignored. My citing the creation of tension as part of the work of the nonviolent-resister may sound rather shocking. But I must confess that I am not afraid of the word "tension." I have earnestly opposed violent tension, but there is a type

> *To . . . rise from the dark depths of prejudice and racism to the majestic heights of understanding and brotherhood*

IN CONTEXT

Eugene "Bull" Connor

A safety commissioner from Birmingham, Alabama, Eugene "Bull" Connor fought against integration using fire hoses, attack dogs, and even a small tank. His forceful, often violent approach backfired when videos of his methods were aired nationally, thereby showing the nation firsthand how desperately change was needed.

of constructive, nonviolent tension which is necessary for growth. Just as Socrates felt that it was necessary to create a tension in the mind so that individuals could rise from the bondage of myths and half-truths to the unfettered realm of creative analysis and objective appraisal, we must see the need for nonviolent gadflies to create the kind of tension in society that will help men rise from the dark depths of prejudice and racism to the majestic heights of understanding and brotherhood.

11   The purpose of our direct-action program is to create a situation so crisis-packed that it will inevitably open the door to negotiation. I therefore concur with you in your call for negotiation. Too long has our beloved Southland been bogged down in a tragic effort to live in monologue rather than dialogue.

12   One of the basic points in your statement is that the action that I and my associates have taken in Birmingham is untimely. Some have asked, "Why didn't you give the new city administration time to act?" The only answer that I can give to this query is that the new Birmingham administration must be prodded about as much as the outgoing one, before it will act. We are sadly mistaken if we feel that the election of Albert Boutwell as mayor will bring the millennium to Birmingham. While

query: question
prodded: poked

Mr. Boutwell is a much more gentle person than Mr. Connor, they are both segregationists, dedicated to maintenance of the status quo. I have hoped that Mr. Boutwell will be reasonable enough to see the futility of massive resistance to desegregation. But he will not see this without pressure from devotees of civil rights. My friends, I must say to you that we have not made a single gain in civil rights without determined legal and nonviolent pressure. Lamentably, it is an historical fact that privileged groups seldom give up their privileges voluntarily. Individuals may see the moral light and voluntarily give up their unjust posture; but as Reinhold Niebuhr has reminded us, groups tend to be more immoral than individuals.

13   We know through painful experience that freedom is never voluntarily given by the oppressor; it must be demanded by the oppressed. Frankly, I have yet to engage in a direct-action campaign that was "well timed" in view of those who have not suffered unduly from the disease of segregation. For years now I have heard the word "Wait!" It rings in the ear of every Negro with piercing familiarity. This "Wait" has almost always meant "Never." We must come to see, with one of our distinguished jurists, that "justice too long delayed is justice denied."

Privileged groups seldom give up their privileges voluntarily

14   We have waited for more than 340 years for our constitutional and God-given rights. The nations of Asia and Africa are moving with jet-like speed toward gaining political independence, but we still creep at horse-and-buggy pace toward gaining a cup of coffee at a lunch counter. Perhaps it is easy for those who have never felt the stinging darts of segregation to say, "Wait." But when you have seen vicious mobs lynch your mothers and fathers at will and drown your sisters and brothers at whim; when you have seen hate-filled policemen curse, kick, and even kill your black brothers and sisters; when you see the vast majority of your twenty million Negro brothers smothering in an airtight cage of poverty in the midst of an affluent society; when you suddenly find your tongue twisted and your speech stammering as you seek to explain to your six-year-old daughter why she can't go to the public amusement park that has just been advertised on television and see tears welling up in her eyes when she is told that Funtown is closed to colored children, and see ominous clouds of inferiority beginning to form in her little mental sky, and see her beginning to distort her personality by developing an unconscious bitterness toward white people; when you have to concoct an answer for a five-year-old son who is asking, "Daddy, why do white people treat colored people so mean?"; when you take a cross-country drive and find it necessary to sleep night after night in the uncomfortable corners of your automobile because no motel will accept you; when you are humiliated day in and day out by nagging signs reading "white" and "colored," when your first name becomes "nigger," your middle name becomes "boy" (however old you are), and your last name becomes "John," and your wife and mother are never given the respected title "Mrs."; when you are harried by day and haunted by night by the fact that you are a Negro, living constantly at tiptoe stance, never quite knowing what to expect next, and are plagued with inner fears and outer resentments; when you are forever fighting a degenerating sense of "nobodiness," then you will understand why we find it difficult to wait. There comes a time when the cup of endurance runs over and men are no longer willing to be plunged into the abyss of despair. I hope, sirs, you can understand our legitimate and unavoidable impatience.

15   You express a great deal of anxiety over our willingness to break laws. This is certainly a legitimate concern. Since we so diligently urge people to obey the Supreme Court's decision of 1954 outlawing segregation in the public schools, at first glance it may seem rather paradoxical for us consciously to break laws. One may ask, "How can you advocate breaking some laws and obeying others?" The answer lies in the fact that there are two types of laws: just and unjust. I would be

ominous: threatening
concoct: make up, prepare
abyss: void

IN CONTEXT

St. Augustine

St. Augustine, or Augustine of Hippo, lived from 354 to 430, and his writings on philosophy and theology helped shape Western Christianity. He believed that humans desperately need Jesus's grace to be free, and his work influenced the notions of original sin and justifiable war.

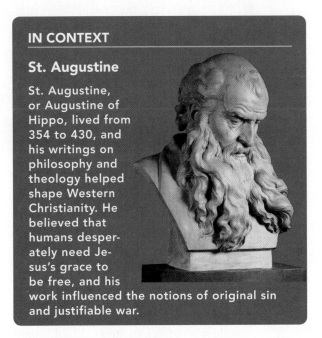

the first to advocate obeying just laws. One has not only a legal but a moral responsibility to obey just laws. Conversely, one has a moral responsibility to disobey unjust laws. I would agree with St. Augustine that "an unjust law is no law at all."

16 Now, what is the difference between the two? How does one determine whether a law is just or unjust? A just law is a man-made code that squares with the moral law or the law of God. An unjust law is a code that is out of harmony with the moral law. To put it in the terms of St. Thomas Aquinas: An unjust law is a human law that is not rooted in eternal law and natural law. Any law that uplifts human personality is just. Any law that degrades human personality is unjust. All segregation statutes are unjust because segregation distorts the soul and damages the personality. It gives the segregator a false sense of superiority and the segregated a false sense of inferiority. Segregation, to use the terminology of the Jewish philosopher Martin Buber, substitutes an "I-it" relationship for an "I-thou" relationship and ends up relegating persons to the status of things. Hence segregation is not only politically, economically, and sociologically unsound, it is morally wrong and sinful. Paul Tillich has said that sin is separation. Is not segregation an existential expression of man's tragic separation, his awful estrangement, his terrible sinfulness? Thus

is it that I can urge men to obey the 1954 decision of the Supreme Court, for it is morally right; and I can urge them to disobey segregation ordinances, for they are morally wrong.

17 Let us consider a more concrete example of just and unjust laws. An unjust law is a code that a numerical or power majority group compels a minority group to obey but does not make binding on itself. This is difference made legal. By the same token, a just law is a code that a majority compels a minority to follow and that it is willing to follow itself. This is sameness made legal.

18 Let me give another explanation. A law is unjust if it is inflicted on a minority that, as a result of being denied the right to vote, had no part in enacting or devising the law. Who can say that the legislature of Alabama which set up that state's segregation laws was democratically elected? Throughout Alabama all sorts of devious methods are used to prevent Negroes from becoming registered voters, and there are some counties in which, even though Negroes constitute a majority of the population, not a single Negro is registered. Can any law enacted under such circumstances be considered democratically structured?

19 Sometimes a law is just on its face and unjust in its application. For instance, I have been arrested on a charge of parading without a permit. Now, there is nothing wrong in having an ordinance which requires a permit for a parade. But such an ordinance becomes unjust when it is used to maintain segregation and to deny citizens the First Amendment privilege of peaceful assembly and protest.

20 I hope you are able to see the distinction I am trying to point out. In no sense do I advocate evading or defying the law, as would the rabid segregationist. That would lead to anarchy. One who breaks an unjust law must do so openly, lovingly, and with a willingness to accept the penalty. I submit that an individual who breaks a law that conscience tells him is unjust and who willingly accepts the penalty of imprisonment in order to arouse the conscience of the community over its injustice, is in reality expressing the highest respect for law.

rabid: extreme

21   Of course, there is nothing new about this kind of civil disobedience. It was evidenced sublimely in the refusal of Shadrach, Meshach, and Abednego to obey the laws of Nebuchadnezzar, on the ground that a higher moral law was at stake. It was practiced superbly by the early Christians, who were willing to face hungry lions and the excruciating pain of chopping blocks rather than submit to certain unjust laws of the Roman Empire. To a degree, academic freedom is a reality today because Socrates practiced civil disobedience. In our own nation, the Boston Tea Party represented a massive act of civil disobedience.

22   We should never forget that everything Adolf Hitler did in Germany was "legal" and everything the Hungarian freedom fighters did in Hungary was "illegal." It was "illegal" to aid and comfort a Jew in Hitler's Germany. Even so, I am sure that, had I lived in Germany at the time, I would have aided and comforted my Jewish brothers. If today I lived in a Communist country where certain principles dear to the Christian faith are suppressed, I would openly advocate disobeying that country's anti-religious laws.

23   I must make two honest confessions to you, my Christian and Jewish brothers. First, I must confess that over the past few years I have been gravely disappointed with the white moderate. I have almost reached the regrettable conclusion that the Negro's great stumbling block in his stride toward freedom is not the White Citizen's Councilor or the Ku Klux Klan, but the white moderate, who is more devoted to "order" than to justice; who prefers a negative peace which is the absence of tension to a positive peace which is the presence of justice; who constantly says, "I agree with you in the goal you seek, but I cannot agree with your methods of direct action"; who paternalistically believes he can set the timetable for another man's freedom; who lives by a mythical concept of time and who constantly advises the Negro the wait for a "more convenient season." Shallow understanding from people of good will is more frustrating

Lukewarm acceptance is much more bewildering than outright rejection"

than absolute misunderstanding from people of ill will. Lukewarm acceptance is much more bewildering than outright rejection.

24   I had hoped that the white moderate would understand that law and order exist for the purpose of establishing justice and that when they fail in this purpose they become the dangerously structured dams that block the flow of social progress. I had hoped that the white moderate would understand that the present tension in the South is a necessary phase of the transition from an obnoxious negative peace, in which the Negro passively accepted his unjust plight, to a substantive and positive peace, in which all men will respect the dignity and worth of human personality. Actually, we who engage in nonviolent direct action are not the creators of tension. We merely bring to the surface the hidden tension that is already alive. We bring it out in the open, where it can be seen and dealt with. Like a boil that can never be cured so long as it is covered up but must be opened with all its ugliness to the natural medicines of air and light, injustice must be exposed, with all the tension its exposure creates, to the light of human conscience and the air of national opinion, before it can be cured.

25   In your statement you assert that our actions, even though peaceful, must be condemned because they precipitate violence. But is this a logical assertion? Isn't this like condemning a robbed man because his possession of money precipitated the evil act of robbery? Isn't this like condemning Socrates because his unswerving commitment to truth and his philosophical inquiries precipitated the act by the

misguided populace in which they made him drink hemlock? Isn't this like condemning Jesus because his unique God-consciousness and never-ceasing devotion to God's will precipitated the evil act of crucifixion? We must come to see that, as the federal courts have consistently affirmed, it is wrong to urge an individual to cease his efforts to gain his basic constitutional rights because the quest may precipitate violence. Society must protect the robbed and punish the robber.

26   I had also hoped that the white moderate would reject the myth concerning time in relations to the struggle for freedom. I have just received a letter from a white brother in Texas. He writes, "All Christians know that the colored people will receive equal rights eventually, but it is possible that you are in too great a religious hurry. It has taken Christianity almost two thousand years to accomplish what it has. The teachings of Christ take time to come to earth." Such an attitude stems from a tragic misconception of time, from the strangely irrational notion that there is something in the very flow of time that will inevitably cure all ills. Actually, time itself is neutral; it can be used either destructively or constructively. More and more I feel that the people of ill will have used time much more effectively than have the people of good will. We will have to repent in the generation not merely for the hateful words and actions of the bad people, but for the appalling silence of the good people. Human progress never rolls in on wheels of inevitability; it comes through the tireless efforts of men willing to be co-workers with God, and without this hard work, time itself becomes an ally of the forces of stagnation. We must use time creatively, in the knowledge that the time is always ripe to do right. Now is the time to make real the promise of democracy and transform our pending national elegy into a creative psalm of brotherhood. Now is the time to lift our national policy from the quicksand of racial injustice to the solid rock of human dignity.

27   You speak of our activity in Birmingham as extreme. At first I was rather disappointed that fellow clergyman would see my nonviolent efforts as those of an extremist. I began thinking about the fact that I stand in the middle of two opposing forces in the Negro community. One is a force of complacency, made up in part of Negroes who, as a result of long years of oppression, are so drained of self-respect and a sense of "somebodiness" that they have adjusted to segregation; and in part of a few middle-class Negroes who, because of a degree of academic and economic security and because in some ways they profit by segregation, have become insensitive to the problems of the masses. The other force is one of bitterness and hatred, and it comes perilously close to advocating violence. It is expressed in the various black nationalist groups that are springing up across the nation, the largest and best-known being Elijah Muhammad's Muslim movement. Nourished by the Negro's frustration over the continued existence of racial discrimination, this movement is made up of people who have lost faith in America, who have absolutely repudiated Christianity, and who have concluded that the white man is an incorrigible "devil."

IN CONTEXT

Elijah Muhammad

Elijah Muhammad, who lived from 1897 to 1975, was an activist and religious leader who influenced many African Americans, including Malcolm X, Muhammad Ali, and Martin Luther King, Jr.

---

hemlock: poisonous potion
perilously: dangerously

28   I have tried to stand between these two forces, saying that we need emulate neither the "do-nothingism" of the complacent nor the hatred and despair of the black nationalist. For there is the more excellent way of love and nonviolent protest. I am grateful to God that, through the influence of the Negro church, the way of nonviolence became an integral part of our struggle.

29   If this philosophy had not emerged, by now many streets of the South would, I am convinced, be flowing with blood. And I am further convinced that if our white brothers dismiss as "rabble-rousers" and "outside agitators" those of us who employ nonviolent direct action, and if they refuse to support our nonviolent efforts, millions of Negroes will, out of frustration and despair, seek solace and security in black-nationalist ideologies—a development that would inevitably lead to a frightening racial nightmare.

30   Oppressed people cannot remain oppressed forever. The yearning for freedom eventually manifests itself, and that is what has happened to the American Negro. Something within has reminded him of his birthright of freedom, and something without has reminded him that it can be gained. Consciously or unconsciously, he has been caught up by the Zeitgeist, and with his black brothers of Africa and his brown and yellow brothers of Asia, South America, and the Caribbean, the United States Negro is moving with a sense of great urgency toward the promised land of racial justice. If one recognizes this vital urge that has engulfed the Negro community, one should readily understand why public demonstrations are taking place. The Negro has many pent-up resentments and latent frustrations, and he must release them. So let him march; let him make prayer pilgrimages to the city hall; let him go on freedom rides—and try to understand why he must do so. If his repressed emotions are not released in nonviolent ways, they will seek expression through violence; this is not a threat but a fact of history. So I have not said to my people, "Get rid of your discontent." Rather, I have tried to say that this normal and healthy discontent can be channeled into the creative outlet of nonviolent direct action. And now this approach is being termed extremist.

IN CONTEXT

Abraham Lincoln

President Abraham Lincoln is also known as the Great Emancipator for his role in freeing American slaves during the Civil War.

31   But though I was initially disappointed at being categorized as an extremist, as I continued to think about the matter I gradually gained a measure of satisfaction from the label. Was not Jesus an extremist for love: "Love your enemies, bless them that curse you, do good to them that hate you, and pray for them which despitefully use you and persecute you." Was not Amos an extremist for justice: "Let justice roll down like waters and righteousness like an ever-flowing stream." Was not Paul an extremist for the Christian gospel: "I bear in my body the marks of the Lord Jesus." Was not Martin Luther an extremist: "Here I stand; I cannot do otherwise, so help me God." And John Bunyan: "I will stay in jail to the end of my days before I make a butchery of my conscience." And Abraham Lincoln: "This nation cannot survive half slave and half free." And Thomas Jefferson: "We hold these truths to be self-evident, that all men are created equal. . . ." So the question is not whether we will be extremists, but what kind of extremists we will be. Will we be extremists for hate or for love? Will we be extremists for the preservation of injustice or for the extension of justice? In that dramatic scene on Calvary's hill, three men were crucified. We must never forget that all three were crucified for the same crime—the crime of extremism. Two were extremists for immorality and thus fell below their environment. The other, Jesus Christ, was an extremist for love, truth, and goodness, and thereby rose above his environment. Perhaps the South, the nation, and the world are in dire need of creative extremists.

emulate: imitate
Zeitgeist: spirit of the times

32 I had hoped that the white moderate would see this need. Perhaps I was too optimistic; perhaps I expected too much. I suppose I should have realized that few members of the oppressor race can understand the deep groans and passionate yearnings of the oppressed race and still fewer have the vision to see that injustice must be rooted out by strong, persistent, and determined action. I am thankful, however, that some of our white brothers in the South have grasped the meaning of this social revolution and committed themselves to it. They are still all too few in quantity, but they are big in quality. Some—such as Ralph McGill, Lillian Smith, Harry Golden, James McBride Dabbs, Ann Braden, and Sarah Patton Boyle—have written about our struggle in eloquent and prophetic terms. Others have marched with us down nameless streets of the South. They have languished in filthy, roach-infested jails, suffering the abuse and brutality of policemen who view them as "dirty nigger-lovers." Unlike so many of their moderate brothers and sisters, they have recognized the urgency of the moment and sensed the need for powerful "action" antidotes to combat the disease of segregation.

33 Let me take note of my other major disappointment. I have been so greatly disappointed with the white church and its leadership. Of course, there are some notable exceptions. I am not unmindful of the fact that each of you has taken some significant stands on this issue. I commend you, Reverend Stallings, for your Christian stand on this past Sunday in welcoming Negroes to your worship service on a non-segregated basis. I commend the Catholic leaders of this state for integrating Spring Hill College several years ago.

34 But despite these notable exceptions, I must honestly reiterate that I have been disappointed with the church. I do not say this as one of those negative critics who can always find something wrong with the church. I say this as a minister of the gospel who loves the church; who was nurtured in its bosom; who has been sustained by its spiritual blessings; and who will remain true to it as long as the cord of life shall lengthen.

35 When I was suddenly catapulted into the leadership of the bus protest in Montgomery, Alabama, a few years ago, I felt we would be supported by the white church. I felt that the ministers, priests, and rabbis of the South would be among our strongest allies. Instead, some have been outright opponents, refusing to understand the freedom movement and misrepresenting its leaders; all too many others have been more cautious than courageous and have remained silent behind the anesthetizing security of stained-glass windows.

36 In spite of my shattered dreams, I came to Birmingham with the hope that the white religious leadership of this community would see the justice of our cause and, with deep moral concern, would serve as the channel through which our just grievances could reach the power structure. I had hoped that each of you would understand. But again I have been disappointed.

37 I have heard numerous southern religious leaders admonish their worshipers to comply with a desegregation decision because it is the law, but I have longed to hear white ministers declare, "Follow this decree because integration is morally

Many others have . . . remained silent behind the anesthetizing security of stained-glass windows

catapulted: thrown unexpectedly

right and because the Negro is your brother." In the midst of blatant injustices inflicted upon the Negro, I have watched white churchmen stand on the sideline and mouth pious irrelevancies and sanctimonious trivialities. In the midst of a mighty struggle to rid our nation of racial and economic injustice, I have heard many ministers say, "Those are social issues, with which the gospel has no real concern." And I have watched many churches committhemselves to a completely otherworldly religion, which makes a strange, un-Biblical distinction between body and soul, between the sacred and the secular.

38   I have traveled the length and breadth of Alabama, Mississippi, and all the other southern states. On sweltering summer days and crisp autumn mornings, I have looked at the South's beautiful churches with their lofty spires pointing heavenward. I have beheld the impressive outlines of her massive religious-education buildings. Over and over I have found myself asking, "What kind of people worship here? Who is their God? Where were their voices when the lips of Governor Barnett dripped with words of interposition and nullification? Where were they when Governor Wallace gave a clarion call for defiance and hatred? Where were their voices of support when bruised and weary Negro men and women decided to rise from the dark dungeons of complacency to the bright hills of creative protest?"

39   Yes, these questions are still in my mind. In deep disappointment I have wept over the laxity of the church. But be assured that my tears have been tears of love. Yes, I love the church. How could I do otherwise? I am in the rather unique position of being the son, the grandson, and the great-grandson of preachers. Yes, I see the church as the body of Christ. But, oh! How we have blemished and scarred that body through social neglect and through fear of being nonconformists.

40   There was a time when the church was very powerful in the time when the early Christians rejoiced at being deemed worthy to suffer for what they believed. In those days, the church was not merely a thermometer that recorded the ideas and principles of popular opinion, it was a thermostat that transformed the mores of society. Whenever the early Christians entered a town, the people in power became disturbed and immediately sought to convict the Christians for being "disturbers of the peace" and "outside agitators." But the Christians pressed on in the conviction that they were "a colony of heaven," called to obey God rather than man. Small in number, they were big in commitment. They were too God-intoxicated to be "astronomically intimidated." By their effort and example they brought an end to such ancient evils as infanticide and gladiatorial contests.

41   Things are different now. So often the contemporary church is a weak, ineffectual voice with an uncertain sound. So often it is an arch-defender of the status quo. Far from being disturbed by the presence of the church, the power structure of the average community is consoled by the church's silent—and often even vocal—sanction of things as they are.

42   But the judgment of God is upon the church as never before. If today's church does not recapture the sacrificial spirit of the early church, it will lose its authenticity, forfeit the loyalty of millions, and be dismissed as an irrelevant social club with no meaning for the twentieth century. Every day I meet young people whose disappointment with the church has turned into outright disgust.

43   Perhaps I have once again been too optimistic. Is organized religion too inextricably bound to the status quo to save our nation and the world? Perhaps I must turn my faith to the inner spiritual church, the church within the church, as the true *ekklesia* and the hope of the world. But again

> **IN CONTEXT**
>
> **Clarion**
>
> A clarion is a type of trumpet used by cavalries during times of war.

pious: devout, religious
laxity: neglectfulness
ekklesia: Greek word for the early Christian church

I am thankful to God that some noble souls from the ranks of organized religion have broken loose from the paralyzing chains of conformity and joined us as active partners in the struggle for freedom. They have left their secure congregations and walked the streets of Albany, Georgia, with us. They have gone down the highways of the South on tortuous rides for freedom. Yes, they have gone to jail with us. Some have been dismissed from their churches, have lost the support of their bishops and fellow ministers. But they have acted in the faith that right defeated is stronger than evil triumphant. Their witness has been the spiritual salt that has preserved the true meaning of the gospel in these troubled times. They have carved a tunnel of hope through the dark mountain of disappointment.

44   I hope the church as a whole will meet the challenge of this decisive hour. But even if the church does not come to the aid of justice, I have no despair about the future. I have no fear about the outcome of our struggle in Birmingham, even if our motives are at present misunderstood. We will reach the goal of freedom in Birmingham and all over the nation, because the goal of America is freedom. Abused and scorned though we may be, our destiny is tied up with America's destiny. Before the pilgrims landed at Plymouth, we were here. Before the pen of Jefferson etched the majestic words of the Declaration of Independence across the pages of history, we were here. For more than two centuries our forebears labored in this country without wages; they made cotton king; they built the homes of their masters while suffering gross injustice and shameful humiliation—and yet out of bottomless vitality they continued to thrive and develop. If the inexpressible cruelties of slavery could not stop us, the opposition we now face will surely fail. We will win our freedom because the sacred heritage of our nation and the eternal will of God are embodied in our echoing demands.

> *Our destiny is tied up with America's destiny*

45   Before closing I feel impelled to mention one other point in your statement that has troubled me profoundly. You warmly commended the Birmingham police force for keeping "order" and "preventing violence." I doubt that you would have so warmly commended the police force if you had seen its dogs sinking their teeth into unarmed, nonviolent Negroes. I doubt that you would so quickly commend the policemen if you were to observe their ugly and inhumane treatment of Negroes here in the city jail; if you were to watch them push and curse old Negro women and young Negro girls; if you were to see them slap and kick Negro men and young boys; if you were to observe them, as they did on two occasions, refuse to give us food because we wanted to sing our grace together. I cannot join you in your praise of the Birmingham police department.

46   It is true that the police have exercised a degree of discipline in handling the demonstrations. In this sense they have conducted themselves rather "nonviolently" in public. But for what purpose? To preserve the evil system of segregation. Over the past few years, I have consistently preached that nonviolence demands that the means we use must be as pure as the ends we seek. I have tried to make clear that it is wrong to use immoral means to attain moral ends. But now I must affirm that it is just as wrong, or perhaps even more so, to use moral means to preserve immoral ends. Perhaps Mr. Connor and his policemen have been rather nonviolent in public, as was Chief Pritchett in

Albany, Georgia, but they have used the moral means of nonviolence to maintain the immoral end or racial injustice. As T.S. Eliot has said, "The last temptation is the greatest treason: To do the right deed for the wrong reason."

47 I wish you had commended the Negro sit-inners and demonstrators of Birmingham for their sublime courage, their willingness to suffer, and their amazing discipline in the midst of great provocation. One day the South will recognize its real heroes. They will be the James Merediths, with the noble sense of purpose that enables them to face jeering and hostile mobs and with the agonizing loneliness that characterizes the life of the pioneer. They will be old, oppressed, battered Negro women, symbolized in a seventy-two-year-old woman in Montgomery, Alabama, who rose up with a sense of dignity and with her people decided not to ride segregated buses and who responded with ungrammatical profundity to one who inquired about her weariness: "My feets is tired, but my soul is at rest." They will be the young high school and college students, the young ministers of the gospel and a host of their elders, courageously and nonviolently sitting in at lunch counters and willingly going to jail for conscience' sake. One day the South will know that when these disinherited children of God sat down at lunch counters, they were in reality standing up for what is best in the American dream and for the most sacred values in our Judaeo-Christian heritage, thereby bringing our nation back to those great wells of democracy which were dug deep by the founding fathers in their formulation of the Constitution and the Declaration of Independence.

48 Never before have I written so long a letter. I'm afraid it is much too long to take your precious time. I can assure you that it would have been much shorter if I had been writing from a comfortable desk, but what else can one do when he is alone in a narrow jail cell other than write long letters, think long thoughts, and pray long prayers?

49 If I have said anything in this letter that overstates the truth and indicates an unreasonable impatience, I beg you to forgive me. If I have said anything that understates the truth and indicates my having a patience that allows me to settle for anything less than brotherhood, I beg God to forgive me.

50 I hope this letter finds you strong in the faith. I also hope that circumstances will soon make it possible for me to meet each of you, not as an integrationist or a civil-rights leader, but as a fellow clergyman and a Christian brother. Let us all hope that the dark clouds of racial prejudice will soon pass away and the deep fog of misunderstanding will be lifted from our fear-drenched communities, and in some not too distant tomorrow the radiant stars of love and brotherhood will shine over our great nation with all their scintillating beauty.

> *Let us all hope that the dark clouds of racial prejudice will soon pass away*

Yours for the cause of Peace and Brotherhood,
Martin Luther King, Jr.

CONVERSATIONS: Collaborating in Class or Online

1. What does King mean when he says, "Injustice anywhere is a threat to justice everywhere" (para. 4)?

2. What are the four basic steps of nonviolent action? Have King and his colleagues tried these tactics? What were the results?

3. According to King, what is the difference between just and unjust laws (para. 16)? How does the author use this difference in his argument?

4. Martin Luther King talks about three disappointments in this letter. What is the nature of these disappointments? How does he deal with them?

CONNECTIONS: Discovering Relationships among Ideas

5. This letter has been reprinted thousands of times because it is an extraordinary example of argument. Which parts of this letter appeal to you most strongly? Explain your answer in detail. Why do you think this letter is still famous today?

6. What does the author mean by "nobodiness" (para. 14) and "somebodiness" (para. 27)?

7. What does King mean when he accuses the "white moderate" of becoming "the dangerously structured dams that block the flow of social progress" (para. 24)?

8. In paragraph 31, King compares his approach on segregation to that of Martin Luther, Abraham Lincoln, Thomas Jefferson, and others. What does this comparison accomplish in his letter?

PRESENTATION: Analyzing the Writer's Craft

9. This letter was written in 1963 to eight Southern clergymen. What do we learn from King's references about their frame of mind? Are there other groups of people who would benefit from reading this letter today? Who are they? What would they learn?

10. What is King's point of view in this essay? Is it an effective approach to his subject? Where in the letter does he alter this point of view?

11. Find two examples in this letter of each of the three appeals: logical, emotional, and ethical. How do these appeals strengthen King's argument?

12. In paragraph 14, King builds momentum by putting all the examples of prejudice that he cites in parallel grammatical structure, meaning they all start with the same word or part of speech. What effect does this technique have on the topic of this paragraph? Find one other example of parallel structure in the letter.

PROJECTS: Expressing Your Own Views

13. **Collage:** Make a collage depicting moments from the time of segregation in the United States. Craft a thesis before you put together the collage so your project has a purpose.

14. **Letter:** Mimicking King's tone, write a letter that addresses some problem in society that bothers you. Be sure you consider the problem from all angles as you draft your letter.

15. **Essay:** To understand why this letter has been popular for almost 50 years, look closely at King's use of the three major appeals: logos, ethos, and pathos. First, review the details of these strategies in the chapter introduction. Once you feel you understand each approach, highlight in three different colors as many examples of each as you can find in King's letter. Then, analyze your findings in an essay: Which appeal is most common in this letter? How do these appeals support his purpose in this letter? How does each type of appeal work on the reader? Draw your own conclusions about the effectiveness and lasting success of this letter from your analysis.

16. **Research:** Read and summarize the three resources below. Generate one specific question from each resource that focuses on argument. Then answer one of your questions in a documented essay, consulting these and other sources as necessary.

OTHER RESOURCES

Web Site

The Martin Luther King Jr. Center for Nonviolent Social Change: www.thekingcenter.org

Audio/Video

History.com: www.history.com/ Search: "Martin Luther King, Jr."

Click on the Videos link to watch videos dedicated to Martin Luther King, Jr.

Academic Article

"Doing Time: King's 'Letter from Birmingham Jail'"

by Edward Berry

Rhetoric & Public Affairs 8.1 (2005): 109–131

ONE LAST THOUGHT

Martin Luther King, Jr.'s "Letter from Birmingham Jail" was a response to a 1963 letter entitled "A Call for Unity," which was written by eight white clergymen and published in a local newspaper. The eight writers urged King's demonstrators to cease their forceful civil actions and instead use the court systems to fight for their rights. Read the full text of their letter by visiting www.stanford.edu and searching "Statement by Alabama Clergymen." What differences can you see between King's letter and the clergymen's? Who presents a better argument? Why?

After You've Gone

by Turner Layton and Henry Creamer

One of the most famous songs of the early blues era, "After You've Gone" was composed by **Turner Layton** in 1918, with lyrics by **Henry Creamer**. It was recorded by such popular artists as Louis Armstrong, Ella Fitzgerald, Benny Goodman, Frank Sinatra, and Bessie Smith—the most popular blues singer of the 1920s and 1930s—whose version is reprinted here.

PREREADING QUESTIONS

Have you ever broken up with someone?

If you didn't want to break up, what would you do to try to change the mind of your partner?

Why are romantic relationships often so fragile?

Now listen honey while I'm saying
How can you tell me that you're going away?
Don't say that we must part
Don't break my aching heart

You know I've loved you true for many years
Loved you night and day
How can you leave me, can't you see my tears?
So listen while I say

After you've gone, and left me crying
After you've gone, there's no denying
You'll feel blue, you'll feel sad
You'll miss the dearest pal you ever had
There'll come a time, now don't forget it
There'll come a time, when you'll regret it
Some day, when you grow lonely

Your heart will break like mine and you'll want me
    only
After you've gone, after you've gone away
After you've gone, left me crying
After you've gone, there's no denying
You'll feel blue, you'll feel sad
You'll miss the best pal you ever had

Lord, there'll come a time, now don't forget it
There'll come a time, when you'll regret it
Some day, when you grow lonely
Your heart will break like mine and you'll want me
    only
After you've gone, after you've gone away
[http://www.songlyrics.com/bessie-smith/
    after-you-ve-gone-lyrics/]

CONVERSATIONS: Collaborating in Class or Online

1. Restate this argument in your own words. What is its main point?
2. What do you think the lyricist wants to accomplish in this song?
3. Do the lyrics communicate a sense of urgency? Which specific words and/or phrases set this tone?
4. In what ways will the person to whom the song is addressed be sad and lonely?

CONNECTIONS: Discovering Relationships among Ideas

5. Is a song the best medium for communicating this message? Explain your answer.
6. What other forms of communication would also be effective?
7. What is the tone of this song?
8. Why is the singer sure his/her "ex" will miss him/her?

PRESENTATION: Analyzing the Writer's Craft

9. These lyrics address the ex-lover directly. Is this an effective approach in this song? Explain your answer.
10. Why do you think Creamer wrote this song? Who do you think is his target audience?
11. Which of the rhetorical appeals is most prevalent in this song? Is that an effective emphasis? Explain your answer.
12. Listen to Bessie Smith's recording of the song on YouTube: www.youtube.com/watch?v=VCDOr6au_H8. In what ways does the melody complement the lyrics?

PROJECTS: Expressing Your Own Views

13. **Song/Poem:** From the point of view of the other person in this relationship, write a song or poem in response to this song.
14. **Twitter Message:** Condense the message in this song to no more than a 140-character Tweet.
15. **Essay:** Write a well-developed essay arguing for or against something you want to change in a relationship of yours (with a family member, with a boyfriend or girl-friend, or with a friend). Give any necessary background before you explain the situation; then offer your argument for a change.
16. **Research:** Read and summarize the three resources below. Generate one specific question from each resource that focuses on argument. Then answer one of your questions in a documented essay, consulting these and other sources as necessary.

OTHER RESOURCES

Web Site

Notable Names Database:
www.nndb.com

Search: "Bessie Smith"

Click on the Bessie Smith link

Academic Article

"Formulaic Composition in the Blues: A View
from the Field"

by David Evans

Journal of American Folklore 120.478 (2007):
482–499

Audio/Video

Old Time Jazz On Line: www.jazz-
on-line.com

Click on Bessie Smith's link to
listen to samples of her music

ONE LAST THOUGHT

Influences of the blues can be found throughout popular culture. Muddy
Water's "Hoochie Coochie Man" has been covered more than 25 times by
such artists as the Allman Brothers, Jimi Hendrix, and Supertramp. In 2004,
Eric Clapton released the album *Me and Mr. Johnson* as a tribute to blues
singer Robert Johnson. The White Stripes incorporated parts of Son House's
"John the Revelator" into their song "Cannon" in 1999. Even the video
game *Bioshock 2*, released in 2010, features Bessie Smith's song "Nobody
Knows You When You're Down and Out."

Depression in College Students

by Alissa Steiner

Originally from San Francisco, **Alissa Steiner** was a double major in Communications and Music at the University of California, Davis, when she won a 2008 creative writing contest with her essay "Depression in College Students." She currently lives in England, where she is completing a Masters in Media and Communications at the London School of Economics.

PREREADING QUESTIONS

What do you know about depression?

Have you ever had any experience with depression—either in yourself or in someone you know?

Why do you think depression is so common among college students?

1   Nima Shaterian was the 2004–05 student body president at Tamalpais High School in Mill Valley, California. He starred in plays, wrote volumes of poetry, and played the piano. I knew Nima—he was a year behind me in school and a friend of my sister. I heard him speak at his graduation, awing the audience with his wisdom and his wit. As I had, Nima went on to study at UC Davis, where he made friends easily and was known for being charismatic, friendly, funny, and bright. Nobody guessed that on January 3, 2006—the day before he planned to return to Davis for winter quarter of his freshman year—he would shoot himself to death. Seven hundred people attended his memorial, all trying to understand why someone so popular, gifted, and warm would want to end his life.

2   Nima is one of the 11 UC Davis students who committed suicide between 2000 and 2006.

3   Depression and suicide are major issues not only here in Davis but also at college campuses nationwide. A striking number of college students are being diagnosed with depression, and that number is consistently rising. A study by the American College Health Association in 2005 showed that

> *A striking number of college students are being diagnosed with depression*

wit: humor

15 percent of college students around the country have been professionally diagnosed with depression, up from 10 percent in 2000 (Stone).

4 Understanding depression, its symptoms and its consequences, can help us identify and help friends and family members who may be suffering. Also, if counseling services on college campuses were able to better publicize and reach out to students, perhaps more students could get the help they need before it is too late.

Recognizing Depression

5 Depression is an illness that inhibits a person's ability and desire to function normally day to day. People who suffer from depression typically experience a loss of interest in once-pleasurable things, along with sadness, irritability, fatigue, weight changes (loss or gain), inability to sleep, and feelings of hopelessness and despair. The symptoms of depression can be easy to mistake for moodiness or stress, and students who suffer from those symptoms often fail to get help in time.

6 Depression is caused by chemical changes in the brain. The brain sends out neurotransmitters between cells to regulate mood. In depression, these chemical messages aren't delivered correctly between brain cells, disrupting communication. When this happens, people lose access to their positive moods, and they feel anxious, stressed, and depressed. In addition, research in genetics has shown that people can inherit a vulnerability to brain chemistry changes related to depression. When someone has a stressful or traumatic experience, that vulnerability may be triggered and can lead to the onset of a mental illness. The hormonal changes experienced during the teen years can also cause chemical changes in the brain that inhibit neurotransmitters, meaning that depression is not merely a passing condition. College students need to recognize both the causes and the symptoms of depression so that they can get help if they need it or seek guidance about how to help a friend who is depressed.

Triggering Factors

7 College is a time when students often experience a variety of pressures that can initiate

IN CONTEXT

Are You Depressed?

Take a Depression Test at http://depression.about.com/ by clicking on the Am I Depressed? link.

depression, leaving college students at a higher risk than other age groups to develop mental illnesses. Diana Hill, a doctoral intern at the UC Davis Center for Counseling and Psychological Services (CAPS), attributes the high number of depressed students to the challenge of balancing multiple life demands. While in college, students often juggle school, work, extracurricular activities, family, relationships, and friends, among other things. "Students have to play all these roles at once and often feel a lack of support in that process," says Hill. She also notes that students may not have fully developed the coping skills needed to deal with the stress of all the transitions they make during their college years.

8 According to Hill, the stress starts at the very beginning—the shock of leaving the support of family life at home for independence can be enough to traumatize a student. And once college students are in school, more pressures abound. Demands are increasing for students to earn advanced degrees in order to have top careers, and students must achieve high grades so that the top graduate schools will admit them. Such heavy workloads and competition can certainly play on a student's psyche. In addition to

> *The shock of leaving the support of family life at home for independence can be enough to traumatize a student*

psyche: mind

academic stress, many students must also finance their own educations. Working to support themselves while trying to keep up academically is difficult and can fuel anxiety and hopelessness. Finally, many students take on new kinds of relationships for the first time during college, and the instability caused by the building and breaking of interpersonal bonds lends itself to feelings of depression and anxiety. All of these stressors can easily trigger depression, especially in students who are genetically predisposed.

9   Hill identifies another reason for the increase in students experiencing depression and seeking therapy—the recent advance in psychopharmacology. "Over time, we are seeing more cases of people making it to college who have been depressed earlier in life and had good treatment," she says. In effect, students who in the past may not have been capable of attending universities are able to further their educations. When these students are exposed to college-related stressors, they often find themselves re-experiencing depression and anxiety. Some will seek treatment once again, though others may not.

Depression at Its Darkest: Suicide

10   Depression in college students can have devastating consequences; over the course of a single year, 1 in 12 college students in the United States will make a suicide plan, and about 15 of every 100,000 college students die each year from suicide. It is the second leading cause of death among college students, second only to accidents. Massachusetts Institute of Technology (MIT) chancellor Phillip Clay stated, "Indeed, the death of a student is one of the most painful losses a college community can suffer" ("Elizabeth Shin"). MIT, which has a reputation of being an academic pressure cooker, recorded 12 suicides between 1990 and 2000 ("Elizabeth Shin").

> *Depression in college students can have devastating consequences*

11   The most shocking of these suicides was that of Elizabeth Shin, an MIT sophomore who set herself on fire in her dorm room in 2000. On the surface, she was popular and lively, busy and self-motivated. She was an accomplished musician, athlete, and student who had many friends in her dorm. But she dreamt of death, of escaping the pressures she put on herself to feel worthy, productive, and loved. She told her suicidal thoughts to some roommates and friends, who feared for her life. And though she shared with various counselors at the MIT counseling center that she was regularly cutting her wrists, having suicidal fantasies, and not eating, they neglected to tell her parents or admit her to a hospital. On April 9, 2000, Elizabeth confessed to a friend and a counselor that she had seriously contemplated sticking a knife in her chest. Two days later, her dormmates heard Elizabeth crying and smelled smoke coming from her locked room before immediately calling for help. The fire squad found her engulfed in flames, flailing on the floor in the middle of her room. On April 14, Elizabeth died in the hospital of third-degree burns that covered 65 percent of her body.

12   Elizabeth's death brought national attention to the state of students' mental health. In an article in the *New York Times Magazine*, Deborah Sontag wrote that colleges and universities were sharpening "an evolving national conversation about a more demanding, more needy and more troubled student body. Colleges are grappling to minister to what administrators describe as

flailing: swinging

an undergraduate population that requires both more coddling and more actual mental health care than ever before."

Looking Out For Each Other

13   So what can we do for a friend who is in crisis or appears to be mentally unhealthy? The first step is acknowledging that friend's feelings. Expressing concern for our friend's well-being, while at the same time validating that it might be hard for them to speak out about their feelings, is crucial. As Hill phrases it, "the first piece with friends is listening, offering support, and knowing that if someone doesn't want to seek help, all you can do is try to support him or her." Should a friend appear to be a threat to himself or herself, or to others, the problem should be addressed immediately. Hill recommends in such situations that concerned students either come into CAPS themselves or bring their friend in directly.

14   I will never know for certain why my classmate Nima took his life. Maybe if he and his friends had been more aware of counseling services on campus, he or they would have sought out support. Perhaps he did not realize that what he was feeling was far more common than it seemed.

15   If students are better educated about what depression is and how to detect it, they may be quicker to seek out someone to talk to and possibly less likely to consider suicide as a solution. For though the college years may be commonly referred to as the best four years of a person's life, they are packed with turmoil. Hopefully, as universities come to realize the importance of students' mental health in academic functioning, they will make funding their counseling services a priority. Perhaps then fewer college students will suffer needlessly—or take their own lives.

Sources

Birch, Kristi. "College Level Coping." Arts & Sciences Magazine, John Hopkins University Fall/Winter 2005.

Depression.com. <http://www.depression.com.>

"Elizabeth Shin." Wikipedia: Free Online Encyclopedia. <http://en.wikipedia.org/wiki/Elizabeth_Shin>.

Hill, Diana. Personal Interview, 30 November 2007.

iFred—International Foundation for Research and Education on Depression. <http://www.iFred.org>.

Kennedy, Talia. "UC Regents Hear Plan to Prevent Suicide." The California Aggie 29 September 2006.

Liebermensch, Hagar. Personal Interview, 3 December 2007.

Polonik, Wolfgang & Shahar Sunsani. "Counseling and Psychological Services Unit Visit 2006–2007." Student Services and Fees Administrative Advisory Committee 22 February 2007.

Ryan, Joan. "The Darkness Behind his Perfect Smile." The San Francisco Chronicle 15 January 2006: B-1.

Sontag, Deborah. "Who was Responsible for Elizabeth Shin?" The New York Times Magazine 28 April 2002 <http://query.nytimes.com/gst/fullpage.html?sec=health&res=9F00EED7113FF93BA15757C0A9649C8B63>.

Stone, Gigi. "Depression, Suicide Stalk College Students." World News Tonight. ABC News. 2 October 2005 <http://abcnews.go.com/WNT/Health/story?id=1188772>.

"Youth Suicide Fact Sheet." American Association of Suicidology. <http://www.suicidology.org>.

coddling: pampering, fussing over

CONVERSATIONS: Collaborating in Class or Online

1. What university did Alissa Steiner attend? What was the suicide rate at her university between 2000 and 2006?
2. What are the main symptoms of depression?
3. What does "balancing multiple life demands" (para. 7) have to do with some cases of depression?
4. Why is college a time that can trigger depression?

CONNECTIONS: Discovering Relationships among Ideas

5. Why is recognizing the symptoms of depression especially important for college students?
6. Why do you think the suicide rate is so high among college students?
7. How does Steiner think we can reduce the number of college suicides?
8. How could health education classes and programs affect the depression rate among students?

PRESENTATION: Analyzing the Writer's Craft

9. The author starts her essay with a true story about a student named Nima Shaterian. Is this an effective beginning for the essay?
10. What is the debatable issue Steiner addresses in this essay?
11. Of the three traditional appeals (logical, emotional, and ethical), which does the author rely on most? Give an example of each, and explain its effectiveness.
12. This author used details about the Elizabeth Shin story from Wikipedia, which is not generally a very reliable source. But this story has a significant role in this essay. Why do you think the author included the story of Elizabeth Shin in her essay? In your opinion, is Wikipedia an adequate source for Steiner's purpose here?

PROJECTS: Expressing Your Own Views

13. **Interview:** Interview at least five students on your campus about their lives in college: What pressures are they experiencing? Do they feel they can succeed in college? Is their family supportive of their college work? Are they balancing a job outside of classes? Then summarize your interviews in a succinct statement with references to particular comments from those who participated.
14. **Poster:** Create an ad for the counseling program at your college or university. What will it offer? How could it improve the quality of life for all students?
15. **Essay:** Write an essay identifying a problem on your campus and proposing a solution to it. Spend some time establishing the extent of the dilemma and then presenting a realistic solution to it.
16. **Research:** Read and summarize the three resources below. Generate one specific question from each resource that focuses on argument. Then answer one of your questions in a documented essay, consulting these and other sources as necessary.

OTHER RESOURCES

Web Site

National Institute of Mental Health: www.nimh.nih.gov/

Scroll down to the Mental Health Information box, and click on the Depression link

Academic Article

"Depression and College Stress among University Undergraduates: Do Mattering and Self-Esteem Make a Difference?"

by Sarah K. Dixon and Sharon E. Robinson Kurpius

Journal of College Student Development 49.5 (2008): 412–424

Audio/Video

Health Guru: http://college. ealthguru.com/

Search: "Deep Depression on Campus"

Click on the Video link

ONE LAST THOUGHT

Many studies have linked time spent watching television to depression. Why do you think this connection has been made? Do you think different types of television shows affect viewers differently? Why or why not?

Multiple Viewpoints: Global Warming

The concept of global warming is the center of a debate over the future of our planet. In the following cluster of readings, you are invited to consider an essay, a cartoon, and a video that each offer a different perspective on this controversial topic. Together, they will help you come to your own conclusions about this important issue in our culture today.

PREREADING QUESTIONS

What do you know about global warming?

Are you aware of the consequences of climate change?

Why is this topic so controversial?

ESSAY

Public Opinion Stunner: Washpost-ABC Poll Finds Strong Support for Global Warming Reductions Despite Relentless Big Oil and Anti-Science Attacks

by Daniel J. Weiss

Daniel J. Weiss is a senior fellow at the Center for American Progress (CAP), a liberal think-tank dedicated to transforming progressive ideas into public policy. An expert in energy and environmental policy, Weiss leads the center's clean energy and climate advisory campaign. He came to CAP after working for 16 years at the Sierra Club, where he was the political director.

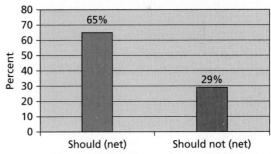

Do you think the federal government should or should not regulate the release of greenhouse gasses from sources like power plants, cars, and factories in an effort to reduce global warming?

Source: Washington Post/ABC Poll, Dec 13, 2009. Sample: 1003 adults.

1   Today's new *Washington Post*-ABC News Poll demonstrates yet again that the American people want action to "regulate the release of greenhouse gases from sources like power plants, cars, and factories in an effort to reduce global warming." Respondents supported this statement by more than two to one (65 percent favor, 29 percent oppose). This poll was conducted December 10–13 at the height of the trumped up brouhaha over stolen emails from a British climate research institution. These findings are consistent with the Associated Press-Stanford University poll released on Tuesday.

2   The WP-ABC poll found that three of five Americans would support reductions in greenhouse gas pollution even if it "raised your monthly expenses by 10 dollars a month." And 55 percent would still support reductions if it "raised your monthly energy expenses by 25 dollars a month."

3   Three federal government estimates predict that households would have an overall "purchasing power loss" of $7–$13 per month, which includes

brouhaha: ruckus

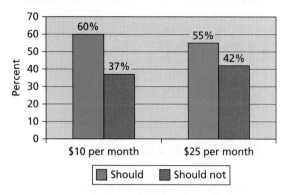

"Should the government regulate greenhouse gasses even if it increased your monthly energy bill by…"

all goods and services, not just energy costs. And none of these estimates include the economic benefits of action or the huge costs of inaction. In other words, the poll shows that the projected costs of domestic global warming pollution reductions are well within the range of the amount that two-thirds of the public are willing to pay.

4   As Climate Progress documents nearly every day, the scientific debate over the existence of global warming has been settled, despite what Sen. Jim Inhofe (R-OK) and other climate deniers might claim. Every day there are new data or evidence that global warming is here and having an impact on our planet. The only questions are the speed and severity of the impacts and whether humans can promptly reduce their global warming pollution enough to stave off the worst impacts of climate change.

5   Despite this scientific consensus, big oil companies and global warming deniers are doing their best to undermine this scientific consensus by raising questions in the public's mind about scientific uncertainty. The media have allowed this debate to focus on distractions like the stolen emails, converting the discussion to a case of "he said, she said" rather than cover the much

projected: expected

more relevant global warming threat and economic opportunities. The strategy of raising enough questions about settled science to cause public uncertainty is the same approach the tobacco industry employed for years to prevent adoption of restrictions on tobacco use even though scientists and doctors determined that smoking cigarettes causes cancer and other serious diseases.

6   The WP-ABC News poll reflects the partial success of this strategy. It found that 36 percent of respondents believe that "most scientists agree with one another about whether or not global warming is happening," while 62 percent "think there is a lot of disagreement among scientists on this issue." One could theorize that this could reflect the effectiveness of deniers' efforts to use the stolen emails to undermine the public's acceptance of the global warming consensus.

7   Interestingly, there is little evidence of this occurrence. The public's perception of the degree of scientific agreement has varied relatively little over the last dozen years. Various polls have asked this question over the last twelve years, and

Household Cost Estimates of American Clean Energy and Security Act, H.R. 2454

Study	Average Household Purchasing Power Impact per month
Congressional Budget Office	$13
Energy Information Administration	$12
Environmental Protection Agency	$7

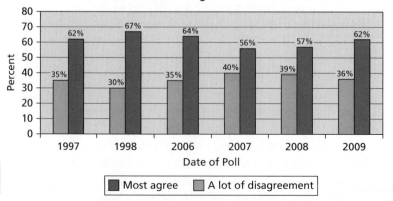

"Do you think most scientists agree with one another about whether or not global warming is happening or do you think there is a lot of disagreement on this issue?"

the answers ranged from 30 to 40 percent who believe that there is scientific agreement, while 56 to 67 percent believe there is not consensus. And the numbers are identical in a 1997 Ohio State University poll and this new WP-ABC poll—35-62 percent in the former, and 36-62 percent in the latter.

8   Despite the public's uncertainty about scientific agreement, they still overwhelmingly favor action. Half the respondents in the WP-ABC poll "strongly" believe that the government should require pollution reductions, while only one fifth of respondents strongly oppose such action (50 percent to 20 percent).

9   The just released Washington Post-ABC poll yet again reinforces that Americans overwhelmingly want the government to reform our energy programs to create jobs, cut pollution, and increase American energy independence. It's up to the United States Senate to respond to this *vox populi* early in 2010.

Originally published on ThinkProgress.org, December 18, 2009.

vox populi: popular opinion

CARTOON

"No Plastic Bags, Please"

by R. J. Matson

R. J. Matson is an editorial cartoonist at the *St. Louis Post-Dispatch* and the *New York Observer* whose work has also appeared in such well-known periodicals as *The New Yorker*, *The Nation*, *Mad Magazine*, *The Washington Post*, and *Rolling Stone*. He has also done cover art for 19 CDs released by "Capitol Steps," a political comedy troupe.

"NO PLASTIC BAGS, PLEASE. I DON'T WANT TO CONTRIBUTE TO GLOBAL WARMING!"

An Inconvenient Truth

by Davis Guggenheim

Davis Guggenheim is an American film director who has produced *Training Day*, *The Shield*, *NYPD Blue*, *ER*, and many other movies and television series. In 2006, he directed *An Inconvenient Truth*, which chronicled former Vice President Al Gore's campaign to educate people about global warming. The film earned over $50 million at the box office and won the 2006 Academy Award for Best Documentary Feature.

By far the most terrifying film you will ever see.

 View this trailer at **www.spike.com/video/Inconvenienttruth/2718952** before answering the questions that follow this group of readings.

CONVERSATIONS: Collaborating in Class or Online

1. According to Guggenheim's trailer, when did the 10 hottest years occur? Which has been the hottest so far?
2. Who does Weiss say is still raising questions about the existence of global warming?
3. What does Al Gore mean when he says at the end of Guggenheim's trailer, "Our ability to live is what is at stake"?
4. Explain the global warming cartoon in your own words.

CONNECTIONS: Discovering Relationships among Ideas

5. Which of the assertions from Guggenheim's video was most convincing to you?
6. Why do you think Americans want to reduce greenhouse gas pollution even if it raises their monthly expenses (Weiss)?
7. Why do you think people generally favor action in reference to global warming (Weiss, para. 8)?
8. Where does this cartoon fall in the debate over global warming?

PRESENTATION: Analyzing the Writer's Craft

9. Is a video format an effective medium for Gore to promote his argument? Explain your answer.

10. What does Weiss's comparison of the media's treatment of global warming and tobacco add to his argument? In what ways?

11. What do you think Weiss's purpose is in writing his essay? Who do you think is his primary audience? Explain your answer.

12. What is the most prominent feature of the global warming cartoon? Is this a good choice for promoting the cartoon's argument?

PROJECTS: Expressing Your Own Views

13. **Video:** Create a video of an environmental problem that is important to you. Start with a clear impression; help your viewers see the problem the way you do; then suggest a solution to conclude your video.

14. **Chart:** Search for information on the Internet about a pollution issue that interests you. Create a chart that represents the extent of the problem with the intention of convincing people to solve it.

15. **Essay:** Write an essay that tries to persuade your readers to take action against some issue that you believe is ultimately unhealthy. First, argue that a certain problem exists. Then, convince your readers to take some specific action against this dilemma. Check your essay for coherence and logic.

16. **Research:** Read and summarize the three resources below. Generate one specific question from each resource that focuses on argument. Then answer one of your questions in a documented essay, consulting these and other sources as necessary.

OTHER RESOURCES

Web Site

U.S. Environmental Protection Agency: www.epa.gov/climatechange

Academic Article

"The Polls—Trends"
by Matthew Nisbet and Teresa Myers
Public Opinion Quarterly 71.3 (2007): 444–470

Audio/Video

National Aeronautics and Space Administration: http://climate.nasa.gov

Search: "Top Ten Climate Movies"

Click on the Climate Reel to watch some of NASA's short videos about earth's climate

ONE LAST THOUGHT

After the September 11 attacks, the U.S. grounded all commercial flights for a three-day period. Even a week after 9/11, air travel had not completely returned to normal. During that short period, scientists noticed that variations in high and low global temperatures increased—that is, we experienced higher highs and lower lows. People who are concerned about global warming use this information as evidence that even our air travel affects global temperatures. The other side argues that nature's resiliency will allow the Earth to repair itself and bounce back from any potential damage. Can you think of any other scientific evidence that can be used to support opposing arguments about global warming?

Multiple Viewpoints: Privacy Issues in Our Culture Today

Who can be safe in this new age of computer hackers, sexting, social networking sites, Internet dating, and a myriad of other online perils? The digital world offers many seductive pleasures and opportunities, which are represented here in a blog on online privacy, an ad on identify theft, and an essay on privacy and the Internet. As a group of "readings," they will guide you to an informed opinion on the subject of privacy.

Online Privacy Fears Are Real

by Bob Sullivan

Author of the popular blog *The Red Tape Chronicles*, **Bob Sullivan** is a journalist specializing in technology crime and consumer fraud. He writes a regular column for MSNBC.com and appears frequently on such NBC news programs as *The Today Show*, *NBC Nightly News*, and *CNBC*. He has also written three best-selling books: *Your Evil Twin*, *Gotcha Capitalism*, and *Stop Getting Ripped Off*.

1   A 20-year-old woman stalked through the Internet and killed. Thousands of e-commerce customers watching as their credit card numbers are sold online for $1 apiece. Internet chat rooms where identities are bought, sold, and traded like options on the Chicago Board of Trade. These are the horror stories dredged up by privacy advocates who say the Net's threat to personal privacy can't be dismissed as mere paranoia. And, they say, we've only seen the tip of the iceberg.

2   Internet privacy is a murky, complicated issue full of conflicting interests, misinformation, innuendo, and technology snafus. On the face of it, e-commerce companies and privacy advocates are locked in stalemate. Websites want to know all they can about you; consumers generally want to share as little as possible.

3   Complicating matters further are criminals who break into Websites, steal the information, and use it for personal gain.

4   Advertising firms, who stand to gain as much as any from personal data collection, have absorbed the brunt of complaints from privacy critics. But Rick Jackson, once a marketer and now CEO of privacy technology firm Privada Inc, thinks ad firms like DoubleClick are serving as an unwitting smokescreen for the real privacy problems.

5   "There are a lot more people tracking you than you think," Jackson said. "The data world is a very powerful and lucrative marketplace with a lot of players involved." For evidence, he points to a Washington Post story that revealed that 11 pharmaceutical companies—including Pfizer Inc., SmithKline Beecham PLC, Glaxo Wellcome PLC—had formed an alliance and were tracking every click consumers made across their sites, then comparing notes. Consumers were never told.

6   "Everybody points to advertising. That's just the tip of the iceberg," Jackson said. "We as consumers don't have any knowledge of what really goes on out there."

7   At its heart, the Internet privacy problem is a paradox.

8   The Net was born as an open research tool and thus was never designed to allow privacy or security. But at the same time, the Net seems to offer perfect anonymity, and most users behave as if they cannot be seen. Who hasn't said or done something online that we wouldn't do in the "real world"?

9   Warnings about revealing personal information online may sound obvious, but they often go

> *Thousands of e-commerce customers watching as their credit card numbers are sold online for $1 apiece*

---

dredged: searched
snafus: bad situations caused by incompetence
lucrative: profitable
anonymity: secrecy

unheeded—warnings such as "Don't post notes in newsgroups or chat rooms you wouldn't want your future boss—or spouse—to read." Still, spend two minutes and you'll find notes from Internet users in health support groups who are shocked to discover their supposedly private discussions about prostate cancer are now full-text searchable from a Website.

10   In fact, according to the Pew Internet & American Life Project, 36 percent of Net users have sought online support for health, family, and mental health issues, and 24 percent of those have signed in with their real name and email address. Every question they've asked and every statement they've made is now stored on a hard drive somewhere.

11   Even the experts don't have control. Jackson was a victim of identity theft earlier this year. He recouped all his financial losses, but said it was "a big emotional issue for me. Somebody's out there ruining my reputation." Super cyber-sleuth Richard Smith, now chief technical officer at the non-profit Privacy Foundation, had someone run up credit card bills under his name recently, too.

12   "They used my FAX number as the home phone number in the application, and I started getting all these calls: 'When are you going to pay your bills?'" Smith said.

13   Most of the horror stories from the online privacy realm stem from criminals. The most dramatic involves a 20-year-old Nashua, N.H., woman named Amy Boyer who was stalked with help from the Internet and then murdered Oct. 15, 1999. The killer, who committed suicide immediately, had purchased Boyer's social security number for $45 from an online information firm, according to a Website authored by Boyer's stepfather detailing

the murder. Congressional lawmakers are now considering legislation that would make the sale of social security numbers illegal, which has been dubbed the "Amy Boyer law."

14   But there are plenty of other scary tales from the world of Internet privacy. Earlier this year, a hacker posted tens of thousands of credit card numbers stolen from CD Universe on a Website; he offered to share more for $1 apiece. Later, an MSNBC investigation revealed dozens of Internet Relay Chat rooms where stolen personal profiles—names, addresses, phone numbers, and credit card numbers—are bought, sold, and traded out in the open.

15   But privacy concerns don't always arise from criminal activity. Privacy advocate and well-known spam fighter Ian Oxman was surprised earlier this year how easily he was able to track down the former owner of a used car he had just purchased. Oxman discovered some concealed damage to the car and wanted to learn if it had been in an accident. Armed with the car's Vehicle Identification Number, he was able to look up the original title owner through an online database on the state of Illinois' Website.

> *Increasingly, Internet users find themselves asking someone "How did you find me?"*

16   "I called her up and said 'You don't know who I am but I'm driving the car you sold.' She talked to me, but at the end said, 'How did you find me'?" Oxman recalls.

17   Increasingly, Internet users find themselves asking someone "How did you find me?" The experience can change the privacy topic from a government policy issue into a highly personal problem.

18   "A lot of people think about privacy but don't really care until something happens to them personally," said Beth Givens, director of the Privacy Rights Clearinghouse. "It's like freedom.

cyber-sleuth: Internet investigator, detective

IN CONTEXT

The Privacy Rights Clearinghouse

The Privacy Rights Clearinghouse is a nonprofit consumer advocacy organization based in San Diego, California. Its two-part mission is to inform consumers about privacy issues and advocate for consumers who have privacy-related complaints. Visit its Website at http://www. privacyrights.org.

You don't appreciate it until it's gone. If you are a victim of identity theft, you experience a change of world view; you realize how little control you have over your world."

19   While most of the drama of Net privacy comes from crime, almost all the public debate has centered around Web companies collecting data for marketing purposes. Stories of companies abusing this information are actually hard to come by; most of the complaints center on what happens if the Web company were careless or ill intentioned.

20   Still, even the hint that data are being collected surreptitiously can create a firestorm of bad publicity for a technology company. Both heavyweights Microsoft and Intel have been forced to turn off features that would have allowed either company to track its customers across the Internet. RealNetworks, maker of popular video software, was twice accused of surreptitiously telling its programs to "phone home" and tattle on users' surfing habits to the firm. Mattel Interactive had to admit it embedded phone-home software called "Broadcast" in its Reader Rabbit software. Surf Monkey, which prevents children from accessing inappropriate sites, also transmits data like user IP addresses back to its maker.

21   DoubleClick Inc, an advertising network that tracks users anonymously as they move around the Internet, is really the lightning rod for such criticism. It was sued earlier this year after it revealed plans to match a real-world mass mailing marketing list with its anonymous database of Internet users, which would have revealed the Web users' identities. It has since backed off the plans.

22   And Doubleclick is hardly the only firm to land in court over privacy issues. The Federal Trade Commission sued now-bankrupt Toysmart.com

after it planned to liquidate its customer database to the highest bidder. And the Missouri state attorney general sued online drugstore More.com when one of his staff members was solicited by a third-party contact lens seller after registering at the Website. More.com's privacy policy at the time said it did not share private information with third parties, a particular sticking point for privacy advocates.

23   This battle between consumers and e-commerce sites wages on, and at least according to one independent analyst, consumers are losing the tug of war. Economist Simon Smelt, who runs survey firm SimplyQuick.com, says most privacy policies on many Websites are "slipping,"—meaning offering consumers less protection. In a June survey, most of the top 90 sites surveyed had polices indicating personal information would not be shipped to third parties. A follow-up survey in November revealed that most site policies now indicate firms retain the right to sell the information to outside parties, leaving the burden on consumers to "opt out." In fact, only 30 percent of the 90 sites surveyed guarantee they won't sell information—and More. com was one of those. Smelt suggested that increasing financial pressures are leading e-commerce sites to see personal data "as a resource itself."

24   "The sense of unease consumers have about privacy online is in a sense justified," Smelt said. "At the end of a day, a privacy policy is really about a guarantee . . . and there are fewer guarantees to go around now."

25   While Web companies argue they need personal information to offer individualized service, privacy advocates point to surveys that show the perceived privacy invasion actually hurts business.

26   The National Fraud Information Center recently completed a study in which one quarter of all respondents said they hadn't purchased anything on-line in the past year because they were afraid their personal information would be misused in some way. Another study by the group shows Web users are more concerned about privacy than health care, crime, and even taxes.

surreptitiously: secretly, sneakily

27   But not everyone agrees the digital, online world is so fraught with peril. In fact, some argue that Internet privacy discussions are rarely placed in proper context—and that personal information is no more at risk online than offline.

28   "There's far less information available about people on the Net than there is about anybody who uses a credit card," said Russ Cooper, security expert. He thinks privacy advocates sometimes create unnecessary fear about the Internet. "The guy with the database has the same access to your information whether the data is sent through Amazon online or Barnes & Noble in the physical world."

29   "What are we afraid of when we do the same kind of stuff in the real world? We give away an awful lot of privacy in the real world on a regular basis. Why is this hyped up when we talk about the Net?"

30   But Givens, from the Privacy Rights Clearinghouse, disagrees, saying the problem from cybercriminals is hardly 21st-century hype, since stealing digital information is so much easier than tapping phone calls or grabbing letters from a mailbox. It's also much more thorough.

31   "If you have the technical know-how, you're able to capture a lot more of an individual's personal communication than you can with a wire tap or through stealing [regular] mail," Givens said. That's why the FBI's Carnivore system, which allows agents to trap and read emails intended for a suspect, raises so much ire among privacy advocates.

32   Meanwhile, the technological Pandora's box opened by Web marketing firms also creates a series of problems unique to the digital age, Givens says. "How would you feel if you were in the mall and someone followed you around with a camera, noting every item you looked at," Givens said. "I'm amazed that there's this set of values out there in these companies that thinks it's Okay to capture data about one's meanderings on the Web and attempt to make money off them without consent."

> *Who hasn't said or done something online that we wouldn't do in the "real world"*

33   There is little debate that receiving uninvited communications is one of the consequences of connecting all the world's people online. Another consequence: having your name placed in an ever-increasing number of databases that can be accessed by an ever-increasing number of companies—and hackers.

34   But Jackson hopes companies such as Privada, which he now heads, will find a way to strike a balance between targeted sales and invasion of privacy. Privada acts as a third party that allows Web surfers to receive accurately targeted advertising pitches, while preserving the anonymity of the consumer.

35   But he holds no illusions that the effort to preserve privacy is easy or sure to succeed. "We've completely lost control over our information. We've got to quickly do something different," he said. "Do I have to worry about the fact that my 8-year-old is growing up in this digital world and his life is being tracked more than any generation? If he goes for a job, will they find something that happened in his teen-aged years or in his health background and then take that job away from him?" He has about 10 years to find out. The rest of us might not have quite so long.

To discuss this blog entry, go to the MSNBC site at www.msnbc.com, and search for "Online Privacy Fears Are Real."

peril: danger

Identity Theft

by Guard Dog Identity Solutions

Established to address the fastest growing financial threat to Americans, **Guard Dog**

Identity Solutions has developed programs to help secure the 11.1 million victims per year of compromised identity, including the loss of social security numbers, credit cards, and other personal information.

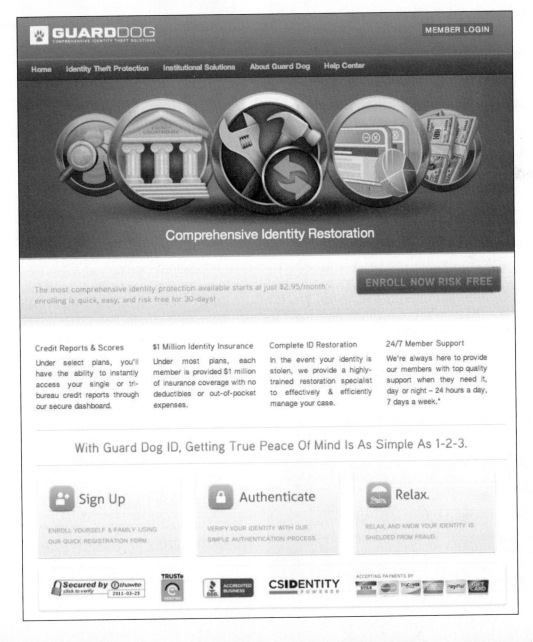

Privacy, Facebook, and the Future of the Internet

by Marshall Kirkpatrick

"Privacy, Facebook and the Future of the Internet" was written and published by **Marshall Kirkpatrick** on ReadWriteWeb, a popular weblog providing technology news, reviews, and analysis that is syndicated daily by *The New York Times*. Kirkpatrick is the co-editor and lead writer at the site, which is one of the most widely read technology blogs in the world.

1   Today is the 3rd annual international Data Privacy Day, and a whole bunch of companies are listed on the organization's website as participants. Google, Microsoft, even Walmart. Facebook is not listed as a participant and has stirred up a lot of controversy with changes to its privacy policy lately.

2   Why are these corporations singing out loud about protecting our personal privacy? According to the website, "Data Privacy Day is an international celebration of the dignity of the individual expressed through personal information." More than dignity, this is about building trust with consumers so that these companies can do things with our personal data. Some of those are things we might like, a lot. Aggregate data analysis and personal recommendation could be the foundation of the next step of the Internet. Unfortunately, Facebook's recent privacy policy changes put that future at risk by burning the trust of hundreds of millions of mainstream users.

3   Facebook's privacy changes were bad for two reasons: because they violated the trust of hundreds of millions of users, putting many of them at risk where they had felt safe before, and because by burning that trust in the first major social network online, the next generation of online innovation built on top of social network user data is put at risk.

4   Had Facebook opened up access to user data through users' consent—then access to those data would be a whole different story. As is, the privacy change was unclear and pushed through without user choice concerning some key data, putting the whole concept of users sharing their data at risk.

How Facebook Changed

5   This past December, Facebook did an about-face on privacy. . . . For years the company had

IN CONTEXT

Data Privacy Day

Data Privacy Day is a national holiday that falls on January 28. The day is designed to promote data privacy education. Visit http://dataprivacyday.org to learn more.

aggregate: collective

based its core relationship with users on protecting their privacy, making sure the information they posted could only be viewed by trusted friends. Privacy control "is the vector around which Facebook operates," Zuckerberg told me in an interview two years ago. 350 million people around the world signed up for that system.

6   Facebook's obsession with privacy slowed down the work of people who wanted to build cool new features or find important social patterns on top of all the connections we users make between people, places, and things on the site. (Marshall shared a link to The San Francisco Giants with Alex, for example.)

7   Those geeky cries in the wilderness to set the data free, for users to be allowed to take their data with them ("data portability") from one website to another? Not going to happen at Facebook, founder Mark Zuckerberg said, due to privacy concerns.

8   Aggregate data analysis? Facebook as a living census unlike any the world has ever seen? Back off, sociologists, you can't access aggregate Facebook user data due to . . . privacy concerns, the company

said. Facebook staff did team with a few outside academics they knew and studied the Facebook data themselves. They published some charts about racial demographics on Facebook, concluding that everything was peachy-keen and only getting better on the social network. But if you thought an army of independent analysts could glean some objective insights into the contemporary human condition out of Facebook, you were wrong.

9   Then in December, things changed. Facebook began prompting users to re-evaluate their privacy settings. Public was the new default and some fields on a user's profile were suddenly and irrevocably made visible to the web at large. Your photo, your list of friends, and your interests as expressed through fan page subscriptions could no longer be set to private.

10   Sorry, 350 million people who signed up for the old system. When Facebook said in the fine print that it reserved the right to change its policies, the company really meant it.

11   The changes were responded to with an international wave of confusion and indignation. News stories were written all around the world about Facebook's privacy changes—they're still being written today. Yesterday the Canadian government announced it was launching its second investigation in six months into Facebook's privacy policies.

Did Facebook Break the Future of the Internet?

12   Is it naive to think that things you post on the Internet are really "private?" Many people say it is, but that was core to the value proposition that Facebook grew up on.

13   Presumably the companies working together on International Data Privacy Day don't believe that privacy online is a lost cause.

14   In fact, trusting that your private data will remain private could be a key requirement for everyday, mainstream users to be willing to input all the more of their personal data into systems that would build value on top of that data.

---

vector: course, direction
glean: collect, gather
irrevocably: irreversibly
indignation: offense

15   Facebook is the first system ever that allowed hundreds of millions of people around the world to input information about their most personal interests, no matter how minor.

16   Will that information serve as a platform for developers to build applications and for social observers to tell us things about ourselves that we never could have seen without a bird's eye view? That would be far more likely if more people trusted the systems they input their data into.

17   Think of Mint's analysis of your spending habits over time. Think of Amazon's product recommendations. Think of Facebook's friend recommender. Think of the mashup between U.S. census data and mortgage loan data that exposed the racist practice of real-estate Redlining in the last century.

18   Personal recommendations and the other side of that same coin—large-scale understanding of social patterns—could be the trend that defines the next era of the internet just like easy publishing of content has defined this era.

19   Imagine this kind of future:

You say, "Dear iPad (or whatever), I'm considering inviting Jane to lunch at The Observatory on Thursday. What can you tell me about that? Give me the widest scope of information possible."

Then your Web 3.0-enabled iPad (or whatever) says to you, "Jane has not eaten Sushi in the past 6 weeks but has 2 times in the year so far. [Location data] The average calorie count of a lunch meal at that location is 250 calories, which would put you below your daily goal. [Nutrition data online.] Please note that there is a landmark within 100 yards of The Observatory for which the Wikipedia page is tagged with 3 keywords that match your recent newspaper reading interest-list and 4 of Jane's. *Furthermore.* . . .

"People who like sushi and that landmark also tend to like the movie showing at a theatre down the street. Since you have race and class demographics turned on, though, I can also tell you that college-educated black people tend to give that director's movies unusually bad reviews. Click here to learn more."

20   That's what the future of the Internet could look like. That sounds great to me. Think that vision of the future sounds crazy? How long ago was it that it sounded crazy to think a day would come when you typed little notes into your computer about how you felt and all your friends and family saw them?

21   But how many people will trust this new class of systems enough to contribute meaningfully to them, now that they've been burned by Facebook?

22   On International Data Privacy Day, it's good to consider the possible implications of Facebook's actions not just on users in the short term, but on the larger ecosystem of online development and innovation over time.

> **mashup:** web application that combines data from more than one source

---

CONVERSATIONS: Collaborating in Class or Online

1. Are you concerned about companies buying and selling your identity information as Sullivan reports? Explain your answer.

2. Why are advertising companies more interested in customer information than other types of companies are (Sullivan)?

3. Exactly how did Facebook violate its initial privacy agreement with its customers (Kirkpatrick)?

4. How is this ad on the Guard Dog home page related to the two articles in this cluster?

CONNECTIONS: Discovering Relationships among Ideas

5. Why do companies want your contact information? How do they get it (Sullivan) ?

6. Why is the "Internet privacy problem" a paradox (Sullivan, para. 7)?

7. How do Facebook's violations of privacy issues put future online privacy at risk (Kirkpatrick)?

8. Which features are most persuasive on the Guard Dog home page? Why are they so compelling?

PRESENTATION: Analyzing the Writer's Craft

9. What is the purpose of Sullivan's essay? Who is his primary audience?

10. Are the headings in Kirkpatrick's essay helpful in guiding you through the essay? If so, in what ways?

11. What is the first feature of the Guard Dog ad that you noticed? Is it effective in promoting the company's product? Explain your answer.

12. What are the primary appeals (logical, emotional, or ethical) that are at work in each selection?

PROJECTS: Expressing Your Own Views

13. **Flow Chart or Graphic Plan:** Design a flow chart or graphic plan for protecting a relationship that is important to you (friend, family, boyfriend, girlfriend). What should be the course of action if everything is going well? What should happen when you fight? When someone gets hurt? When the entire relationship is at risk? How can you protect each other? How can you consistently save the relationship and get back to where you want to be with each other? Try to capture as many of these elements as possible in some sort of graphic plan of action.

14. **Letter:** Write a letter to a social networking site explaining how you expect them to protect your personal and financial information. Before you write a draft, decide exactly what you want to accomplish with this letter. After you compose your draft, revise it with that purpose in mind.

15. **Essay:** Write an essay advocating a realistic approach to identity theft that will address even more serious risks of this sort in the future. What do you think these future risks will be? How can we best protect ourselves from them? Outline a thorough plan that would be realistic and appealing to consumers.

16. **Research:** Read and summarize the three resources below. Generate one specific question from each resource that focuses on argument. Then answer one of your questions in a documented essay, consulting these and other sources as necessary.

OTHER RESOURCES

Web Site
OnGuard Online: www.onguardonline.gov

Academic Article
"The Evolution (or Devolution) of Privacy"
by Debbie V. S. Kasper
Sociological Forum 20.1 (2005): 69–92

Audio/Video
National Public Radio: www.npr.org
Search: "Tracking the Companies that Track You Online"
Click on the Listen Now link

ONE LAST THOUGHT

With the growth of the Internet, the nature of privacy has undeniably changed. In addition, the ways people deal with this change are constantly evolving. Here are three examples: The National Do Not Call Registry was implemented in 2003; in Germany, Internet users can opt out of Google's Street View; and in an interview for *The Wall Street Journal*, Google's CEO, Eric Schmidt, suggested that teens change their names upon turning 18 to separate themselves from their youthful mistakes. Can you think of any other ways society can deal with this reduction of privacy without changing the nature of the Internet?

CHAPTER WRITING ASSIGNMENTS

Write a well-developed essay in response to the following prompts. Consult the chapter introduction for guidance in creating your essay.

CONNECTING THE READINGS

1. Both Martin Luther King's "Letter From Birmingham Jail" (1963) and the Center for Immigration Studies at www.cis.org (2011) make different claims about racism, prejudice, and bias. What does each source say about these topics? What progress have we made in these areas in the 48 years between these two "publications"? How do you think we will manage these issues in the future? Organize your responses to these questions in a thoughtful essay.

2. The Internet has helped us make enormous progress as individuals and as a global society. But with these advances come disadvantages, such as the changes Nicholas Carr ("Is Google Making Us Stupid?") observes in our reading habits and the dangers to our social and financial identity that Sullivan ("Online Privacy Fears Are Real") and Kirkpatrick ("Privacy, Facebook, and the Future of the Internet") reveal. Write an essay arguing whether or not the advantages of the Internet are worth the risks we have to take.

3. No matter how much psychological research we do, we are still plagued by suicidal thoughts ("Depression in College Students"), the pain of lost love ("After You've Gone"), and bouts of fear and terror ("Now You Take 'Bambi' or 'Snow White'—That's Scary!") that we cannot thoroughly understand and/or control. What are the relationships between the different types of emotional trauma that these authors discuss? How could a more complete understanding of one of these psychological puzzles help us understand the others?

4. Environmental issues ("Watering Little Sprout") and global warming ("Public Opinion Stunner: Washpost-ABC Poll Finds Strong Support for Global Warming Reductions Despite Relentless Big Oil and Anti-Science Attacks," "An Inconvenient Truth," "Groupthink and the Global-Warming Industry," and "No Plastic Bags, Please") are connected in a number of different ways. What are these connections? Discuss the relationships that you uncover among ideas, and suggest some constructive solutions to any problems that you discover.

MOVING BEYOND THE READINGS

5. We are in the midst of a financial crisis that is a direct result of our individual and collective spending habits. How is our national philosophy of life connected to our natural tendency to acquire things and over-spend? What aspects of our life philosophy led us into our current predicament? What changes should we make in our buying habits to return to a healthier fiscal lifestyle? Discuss these issues of financial responsibility, and argue for a reasonable change of direction in this area—at the individual, state, and national levels.

6. How do you think America's response to people who are struggling in our society helps define our national character? Have some generations been more charitable than others? Write an essay addressing these questions. Be sure to determine a focus before you begin to write.

7. What measures do you take on a regular basis to help save the earth? From what you understand about pollution (air, water, and noise, to name only a few), which type is the most disturbing to you? Do you think we are doing enough as a country to protect ourselves from pollutants? Write an essay in which you discuss this serious national problem, and then explain what other "green" efforts we could engage in to protect our environment.

8. As we all rely more and more on the Internet, including buying, selling, blogging, banking, chatting, emailing, and paying bills, we are increasingly exposed to the dangers of identity theft, cyber bullies, sexual predators, and many other kinds of corruption. How can we protect ourselves in this new Internet age? What precautions should we take now and in the future to keep ourselves safe—both physically and emotionally? Write an essay outlining a clear explanation of the dangers lurking on the Internet and offering a coherent proposal for successfully avoiding the problems you identify.

COMBINING RHETORICAL MODES

9. Being a college student is one of the most exciting times in a person's life. You are expanding your knowledge, questioning your life goals and philosophies, exploring unfamiliar paths, and meeting new people every day. But it is also a vulnerable time because you are processing an enormous amount of information, reconsidering your value system, and generally rethinking your individual self-definition. Do you have any advice for future college students as they navigate this journey? Write a manual for getting the most out of college while staying stable, sane, and emotionally centered.

10. What are your favorite types of movies or books? Why do you like these particular ones? In a well organized essay, explain the reasons for your preferences by analyzing as many of them as possible. You might even discover some new reasons for your choices as you write.

11. A serious problem in the United States, immigration is still not under control. What other problems related to immigration plague our country? What solutions can you propose for these particular problems? How will the solutions work?

12. Songs are a dramatic way to communicate feelings and stories. What are some of your favorite songs, and why do they appeal to you? Do you like the lyrics or the melodies better? What particular qualities make these your favorites?

Image Credits

p. 271 Kevin Schafer/Peter Arnold Images/Photolibrary; **p. 272** iofoto/Shutterstock; **p. 273** StockLite/Shutterstock; **p. 273** Suto Norbert Zsolt/Shutterstock; **p. 275** www.CartoonStock.com; **p. 276** italianestro/Shutterstock; **p. 277** Viktor Koen; **p. 279** LA Times; **p. 278** dubassy/Shutterstock; **p. 278** Joseph McCullar/Shutterstock; **p. 278** Digital N/Shutterstock; **p. 281** www.Cartoon Stock.com; **p. 251** John T Takai/Shutterstock; **p. 283, 322** Mikhail Kokhanchikov/iStockphoto.com; **p. 285** Monkey Business Images/Shutterstock; **p. 293** Fuse/Getty Images; **p. 294** David J. Green/Alamy; **p. 295** Corbis Premium RF/Alamy; **p. 295** Everett Collection; **p. 295** NBCU Photo Bank/AP Images; **p. 297** AP Photo/stf; **p. 298** Mike Keefe, The Denver Post & InToon.com; **p. 299** Wylie Overstreet; **p. 300** Yellowj/Shutterstock; **p. 301** AF archive/Alamy; **p. 301** Penguin Group (USA) Inc.; **p. 302** www. america.gov; **p. 302** AP Photo/Khalid Tanveer; **p. 302** AP Photo/Denis Farrell; **p. 302** Saleha Mallick; **p. 303** AF archive/Alamy; **p. 303** Mary Evans/PARAMOUNT/Ronald Grant/Everett Collection(10307506); **p. 303** AF archive/Alamy; **p. 304** Jaimie Duplass/Shutterstock; **p. 306** Handout/MCT/Newscom; **p. 307** Sony/Playstation/MCT/Newscom; **p. 305** www.CartoonStock. com; **p. 308** JoeFox/Alamy; **p. 309** Diego Cervo/Shutterstock; **p. 312** Zsolt Nyulaszi/Shutterstock; **p. 310** Jonny McCullagh/ Shutterstock; **p. 311** Copyright 1992 by John Gray. Reprinted by permission of Harper Collins Publishers; **p. 314** Greg Wright/ Alamy; **p. 315** Image Courtesy of The Advertising Archives; **p. 316** New York City Department of Health and Mental Hygiene; **p. 317** MOL/Shutterstock; **p. 318** terekhov igor/Shutterstock; **p. 320** Claudio Bravo/Shutterstock; **p. 319** Dariusz Sas/ Shutterstock; **p. 321** oriori/Shutterstock; **p. 323, 370** D. Hurst/Alamy; **p. 325** Randy Glasbergen; **p. 335** Duard van der Westhuizen/Shutterstock; **p. 337** Jose AS Reyes/Shutterstock; **p. 341** David Young-Wolff/Alamy; **p. 338** Alexander Gitlits/ Shutterstock; **p. 336** Monkey Business Images/Shutterstock; **p. 340** KPA/CBI/Sven Hoogerhuis/United Archives GmbH/Alamy; **p. 340** Entertainment Press/Shutterstock; **p. 343** Mira/Alamy; **p. 344** HANDOUT/KRT/Newscom; **p. 345** JHP Attractions/ Alamy; **p. 346** Andersen Ross/Blend Images/Alamy; **p. 353** Monkey Business Images/Shutterstock; **p. 354** Stephen Coburn/ Shutterstock; **p. 356** Photos 12/Alamy; **p. 355** Courtesy of Universal Studios Licensing LLC; **p. 357** Universal Pictures/Everett Collection; **p. 358** Cupertino/Shutterstock; **p. 360** Yuri Arcurs/Shutterstock; **p. 359** Andy Dean Photography/Shutterstock; **p. 359** Lisa F. Young/Shutterstock; **p. 359** Red Images, LLC/Alamy; **p. 359** Snaprender/Shutterstock; **p. 362** Illustration by Jonathan Carlson for TIME; **p. 363** Clifton/imagebroker/Alamy; **p. 364** Andreas Gradin/Shutterstock; **p. 364** Walter G Arce/ Shutterstock; **p. 364** Max Earey/Shutterstock; **p. 364** Dalibor Sevaljevic/Shutterstock; **p. 364** Michael Flachmann; **p. 364** Dainis Derics/Shutterstock; **p. 364** Vitaly M/Shutterstock; **p. 364** J. Henning Buchholz/Shutterstock; **p. 364** Gaertner/Alamy; **p. 364** Aspen Photo/Shutterstock; **p. 364** Close Encounters Photography/Shutterstock; **p. 364** Robert Caplin Robert Caplan Photography/Newscom; **p. 365** www.CartoonStock.com; **p. 366** mark phillips/Alamy; **p. 367** Yuri Arcurs/Shutterstock; **p. 368** Danita Delimont/Alamy; **p. 369** FilmMagic/Getty Images; **p. 371, 410** Ben Earwicker, Garrison Photography www. garrisonphoto.org; **p. 394–395** Foreign Policy; **p. 374** www.CartoonStock.com; **p. 382** Eric Isselée/Shutterstock; **p. 385** Mikhaela B. Reid; **p. 386** "The Read-At-Your-Own-Risk Bookstore" by Roz Chast. Copyright 2002 by Roz Chast, used with permission of The Wylie Agency LLC.; **p. 387** ICP/Alamy; **p. 388** Robert Davies/Alamy; **p. 389** ARENA Creative/Shutterstock; **p. 390** Corbis RF Best/Alamy; **p. 390** D. Hurst/Alamy; **p. 392** Steve Kelley Editorial Cartoon used with the permission of Steve Kelley and Creators Syndicate. All rights reserved.; **p. 393** Alesya/Shutterstock; **p. 396** Mohammed Abidally/Alamy; **p. 397** Sergey Peterman/ Shutterstock; **p. 398** Charles Mistral/Alamy; **p. 400** Travelscape Images/Alamy; **p. 401** K2 images/Shutterstock; **p. 403** Fedor Kondratenko/Shutterstock; **p. 402** Mikael Häggström; **p. 404** Mike Weaver/ABC via Getty Images; **p. 405** Marcelo Santos/Getty Images; **p. 407** stryjek/Shutterstock; **p. 406** Dmitriy Shironosov/Shutterstock; **p. 409** Andrew Shawaf, Pacificcaostnews/Andrew Shawaf, Pacificcaostnews/Newscom; **p. 409** Kevin Perkins/Kevin Perkins, PacificCoastNews/Newscom; **p. 411, 484** Corbis Premium RF/Alamy; **p. 480** Sam Burt Photography/iStockphoto; **p. 415** Public Service Announcement by Peace Corps.; **p. 425** Dmitry Melnikov/Shutterstock; **p. 431** Supri Suharjoto/Shutterstock; **p. 432** william casey /Shutterstock; **p. 426** Peter DaSilva/The New York Times/Redux Pictures; **p. 427** Erin Siegal/Redux; **p. 428** Lebrecht Music and Arts Photo Library/Alamy; **p. 429** Andrzej Tokarski/Alamy; **p. 429** Index Stock/Alamy; **p. 429** D. Hurst/Alamy; **p. 429** Mode Images Limited/Alamy; **p. 429** Jack Sullivan/Alamy; **p. 429** ian nolan/Alamy; **p. 429** amana images inc./Alamy; **p. 434** Paul Fleet/Alamy; **p. 445** Keystone Pictures USA/Alamy; **p. 446** Black Star/Alamy; **p. 450** Maugli/Shutterstock; **p. 453** Black Star/Alamy; **p. 455** Black Star/Alamy; **p. 449** V&A Images/Alamy; **p. 451** AP Photo; **p. 452** Classic Image/Alamy; **p. 458** Shebeko/Shutterstock; **p. 454** tillydesign/ Shutterstock; **p. 443** Center for Immigration Studies; **p. 443** Boris Diakovsky/iStockphoto.com; **p. 444** P_Wei/iStockphoto; **p. 462** Mark Stout Photography/Shutterstock; **p. 464** Karuka/Shutterstock; **p. 465** Supri Suharjoto /Shutterstock; **p. 463** EDHAR/ Shutterstock; **p. 467** www.CartoonStock.com; **p. 459** Pictorial Press Ltd/Alamy; **p. 461** AF archive/Alamy; **p. 461** AF archive/ Alamy; **p. 461** Presselect/Alamy; **p. 461** 2K Games Scripps Howard Photo Service/Newscom; **p. 438** Zurijeta/Shutterstock; **p. 440** CREATISTA/Shutterstock; **p. 442** PhotoAlto/Alamy; **p. 435** Design Pics Inc./Alamy; **p. 437** National Archives; **p. 437** The Ad Council; **p. 437** Steve McCurry/Magnum Photos; **p. 468** Toria/Shutterstock; **p. 472** Supplied by Capital Pictures/ Supplied by Capital Pictures/Newscom; **p. 471** By Bob Englehart www.politicalcartoons.com/Cagle Cartoons, Inc.; **p. 473** Jag_cz/ Shutterstock; **p. 474** DNY59/iStockphoto; **p. 478** Tatiana Popova/Shutterstock; **p. 476** Feng Yu /Shutterstock; **p. 480** Jinx Photography Brands/Alamy; **p. 481** Alexander Sandvoss/Alamy; **p. 479** Guard Dog, Inc.; **p. 483** auremar/Shutterstock

Design Elements:
p. 30 Karen Struthers/Shutterstock; **p. 73** Mauro Saivezzo/Shutterstock; **p. 73** SkillUp/Shutterstock; **p. 72** 1000 Words/ Shutterstock; **p. 72** Ng Yin Jian/Shutterstock

Text Credits

pp. 64–65 Susan Chun, "Officers Describe 9/11 in Memos," CNN.com, August 28, 2003. Courtesy CNN; **p. 60** Timeline of 9/11 attacks, text excerpted from http://archives.cnn.com/2001/US/09/11/chronology.attack/, September 12, 2001. Courtesy CNN; **pp. 68–70** Alice Walker, "Longing to Die of Old Age" from *Living by the Word: Selected Writings 1973–1987* copyright © 1985 by Alice Walker, reprinted by permission of Houghton Mifflin Harcourt Publishing Company; **pp. 76–78** Matthew Brooks Treacy, "She" by Matt Treacy. Copyright © 2010 by Matt Treacy, from *The Norton Pocket Book of Writing by Students*, edited by Melissa A. Goldthwaite. Used by permission of W. W. Norton & Company, Inc.; **pp. 81–82** Simon Rich, "Hey, Look," *The New Yorker*, July 23, 2007. © 2007 by Simon Rich. Reprinted by permission of the author c/o Levine Greenberg Literary Agency, Inc.; **pp. 103–108** Tom Shachtman, excerpt from "Going Away" from *Rumspringa: To Be or Not To Be Amish* by Tom Shachtman. Copyright © 2006 by Tom Shachtman and Stick Figure Productions. Reprinted by permission of North Point Press, a division of Farrar, Straus and Giroux, LLC; **pp. 113–119** Susan Klebold, "I Will Never Know Why," *O, The Oprah Magazine*, November 2009. Reprinted by permission of the author; **pp. 124–126** Garrison Keillor, "After a Fall," *The New Yorker*, June 21, 1982. © 1982 Garrison Keillor. Used with permission. All rights reserved; **pp. 132–134** Sandra Cisneros, "Only Daughter." Copyright © 1990 by Sandra Cisneros. First published in *Glamour*, November 1990. By permission of Susan Bergholz Literary Services, New York, NY and Lamy, NM. All rights reserved; **pp. 149–151** Raquel Levine, "Body Piercing: Stick It Where the Sun Don't Shine," *McGill Tribune*, October 31, 2000. Reprinted by permission of the author; **pp. 163–164** Geneva Reid, "Study: How Twitter Is Hurting Students," *Higher Ed Morning*, October 1, 2009. Reprinted by permission of Progressive Business Publications; **pp. 222–225** Kevin Bonsor and Cristen Conger, "How Human Cloning Will Work," HowStuffWorks.com, April 2, 2001. Text and illustration courtesy of HowStuffWorks.com; **pp. 227–231** 50 Ways to Help the Planet. Reprinted by permission of Wire & Twine; **pp. 233–235** Murray Raphel, "What Makes a Successful Business Person?" *Art Business News*, September 2003. Reprinted by permission of the publisher; **pp. 250–253** Ann Hodgman, "No Wonder They Call Me a Bitch," *Spy: The New York Monthly*, June 1989. © 1989 by Ann Hodgman. Reprinted by permission of the author; **pp. 258–261** Chris Sparling, "The 10 People You'll Find in Any Gym," www.ThatsFit.com, October 2, 2007. Content © 2011 AOL Inc. Used with permission; **pp. 266–270** Judith Viorst, "The Truth About Lying" by Judith Viorst. Copyright © 1981 by Judith Viorst. Originally appeared in *Redbook*. Granted by permission of Lescher & Lescher, Ltd. All rights reserved; **pp. 272–274** Nathan Newberger, "13 Job Interview Mistakes to Avoid," WorkTree.com; **pp. 276–280** David Colker, "A Peek into the Future," *Los Angeles Times*, September 6, 2009. Copyright © 2009 Los Angeles Times. Reprinted with permission; **pp. 293–296** Erma Bombeck, "Grandma" from *At Wit's End* by Erma Bombeck, copyright © 1967 by Newsday, Inc. Used by permission of Doubleday, a division of Random House, Inc.; **pp. 304–307** Robert Workman, "Motion Gaming Review: Kinect vs. Nintendo Wii vs. PlayStation," TechNewsDaily.com, June 23, 2010. Copyright © 2010 TechMediaNetwork. Reprinted by permission; **pp. 309–313** Deborah Tannen, "Sex, Lies, and Conversation," *The Washington Post*, June 24, 1990, **p. C3**, copyright Deborah Tannen. Reprinted by permission; **pp. 318–320** Lynn Neary, © 2009 National Public Radio, Inc. NPR® news report entitled "How E-Books Will Change Reading and Writing" by Lynn Neary was originally broadcast on NPR's *Morning Edition*® December 30, 2009, and is used with the permission of NPR. Any unauthorized duplication is strictly prohibited; **pp. 346–352** *The Millennials: Confident. Connected. Open to Change.* Pew Social & Demographic Trends Project, February 24, 2010. Reprinted with permission. http://pewresearch.org/pubs/1501/millennials-new-survey-generational-personality-upbeat-open-new-ideas-technology-bound; **pp. 358–361** Tom Chiarella, "The Art of the Handshake," *Esquire*, November 1, 2006. © 2006 by Tom Chiarella. Reprinted by permission of the author; **pp. 388–390** Brent Staples, "Black Men and Public Space," *Harper's* Magazine, December 1986. © 1986 by Brent Staples. Reprinted by permission of the author; **pp. 397–399** Erin O'Donnell, "Does Thinking Make It So?" This article originally appeared in the January-February 2009 issue of *Harvard Magazine* (111:3; 13f). © 2009 by Erin O'Donnell. Reprinted by permission of the author; **pp. 401–403** Joel Rose, © 2008 National Public Radio, Inc. NPR® news report entitled "On Reality TV, Less Sleep Means More Drama" by Joel Rose was originally broadcast on NPR's *Morning Edition*® May 14, 2008, and is used with the permission of NPR. Any unauthorized duplication is strictly prohibited; **pp. 425–433** Nicholas Carr, "Is Google Making Us Stupid?" *The Atlantic*, July/August 2008. © 2008 by Nicholas Carr. Reprinted by permission of the author; **pp. 438–440** Stephen King, "Now You Take 'Bambi' or 'Snow White'—That's Scary!" Reprinted With Permission. © Stephen King. All rights reserved. Originally appeared in *TV Guide* (1981); **pp. 445–456** Martin Luther King Jr., "Letter from Birmingham Jail." Reprinted by arrangement with The Heirs to the Estate of Martin Luther King Jr., c/o Writers House as agent for the proprietor New York, NY. Copyright 1963 Dr. Martin Luther King Jr; copyright renewed 1991 Coretta Scott King; **pp. 462–465** Alissa Steiner, "Depression in College Students, http://prizedwriting.ucdavis.edu/past/2007-2008/depression-in-college-students. © Alissa Steiner. Reprinted by permission of the author; **pp. 480–482** Marshall Kirkpatrick, "Privacy, Facebook and the Future of the Internet," www.ReadWriteWeb.com, January 28, 2010. Reprinted by permission of the author.

Index and Glossary of Rhetorical Terms

The numbers after each rhetorical term in this glossary refer to the pages where more information on each term appears.

A

Argument (412–424) is an attempt to persuade someone to take action or to share a particular point of view on a specific issue. It works principally through appeals to logic, emotion, or ethics, or a combination of these rhetorical tools, and deals with topics that can be debated.

Audience (7, 19) is the people for whom a message is intended.

B

Body paragraphs (52, 97) of an essay should explain and support the thesis statement.

C

Causal chain (371) refers to the result of one action causing another.

Cause/effect (370–379) is a form of analysis that examines the reasons for and consequences of events and ideas.

Chronological order (22, 194) means arranging events according to the passage of time—in other words, in the order in which they occurred.

Citations (38) acknowledge the sources of ideas and quotations used in academic papers.

Clustering (17, 18) is a method of drawing or mapping the relationships among ideas.

Coherence (144) is the logical development of an essay or graphic.

Common ground (413, 419) refers to the assumptions or values shared by writers and their readers.

Comparison and contrast (284–292) is one of the traditional rhetorical modes. *Comparison* is a writing technique that examines the similarities between objects or ideas, while *contrast* focuses on their differences.

Conclusion (24–25, 52, 97, 329) is the final part of an essay that brings it to a close.

Concrete words (21) refer to anything we can see, hear, touch, smell, or taste, such as *cars, plants, soap, blankets, bread, cows*, and *windows*.

Critical thinking (4), the most sophisticated form of reasoning, involves taking a complex idea apart, studying its integral pieces, and reassembling the idea with a more thorough understanding of it.

D

Deductive reasoning (419), an argumentative strategy, moves its audience from a broad, general statement to particular examples supporting that statement.

Definition (324–331) is the process of explaining the meaning of a word, object, or idea.

Description (47–53) involves capturing people, places, events, objects, and feelings in words so a reader (or listener) can visualize and respond to them.

Direct quotation (39–40) is the act of using the exact words from a source. Direct quotations in papers must be enclosed within quotation marks and accompanied by a reference to their sources.

Division and classification (239–249) is one of the traditional rhetorical modes. *Division* breaks a subject down into many different subgroups, while *classification* joins together similar subjects into a single category or class.

Documentation (38) is the process of "documenting" or citing sources in a formal paper.

Domains (37) are categories of Web sites. The endings *.com, .edu, .gov,* and *.org* are some of the most common top-level domains.

E

Editing (30–31, 54–56, 99, 143, 193, 246, 290, 331, 379, 421) entails proofreading and correcting mistakes in writing so the final draft conforms to the conventions of standard written English.

Emotional appeals (413–414), also called "pathos," attempt to arouse readers' feelings, instincts, senses, and biases in an effort to get them to agree with an argument.

Ethical appeals (413–414), also called "ethos," involve cultivating a sincere, honest tone that helps establish a writer's reputation as a reliable, credible person who is well informed on the topic under discussion.

Etymology (329) refers to examining the linguistic origins and development of words.

F

Fallacies (419), or flaws in logical arguments, occur most often when a writer or speaker uses faulty evidence, misrepresents evidence, or cites evidence that is irrelevant to an argument.

Figurative language (52–53) means using words imaginatively rather than literally.

G

General to particular (21), the most common method of organizing an essay or paragraph, begins with a general statement and becomes more specific as it progresses.

I

Illustration (139–148) involves giving examples to help communicate ideas.

Inductive reasoning (419) encourages readers to make what is called an "inductive leap" from several particular examples to a single generalization.

Interpretation (4) requires making connections among ideas, drawing inferences from pieces of information, and reaching conclusions about the reading material.

Introduction (24, 52, 97, 329) is the first paragraph of an essay, which should introduce the subject and entice the audience to read further.

J

Journals (33–35) are scholarly publications that contain a collection of articles written by experts in a particular field for others studying the same subject.

L

Logical appeals (412–414), also called "logos," rely on reason and intellect to make their point and are most effective when writers are expecting their readers to disagree with their argument.

Literal level (4) is the foundation of human understanding; it involves knowing the meanings of words and phrases as they work together to form sentences.

M

Metaphors (53) are comparisons between two dissimilar items without the words "like" or "as." See, for example, the caption under David Sipress' cartoon (110): "Daddy works in a magical, faraway land called Academia."

N

Narration (93–102) involves telling stories.

P

Paraphrase (39, 40–41) is a restatement of a passage or idea in the writer's own words.

Particular to general (22) is a method of organizing paragraphs from specific ideas to a general statement.

Peer reviewed articles (36–37) are reviewed or "refereed" anonymously by experts in a particular field.

Plagiarism (39), a serious academic offense, involves using someone else's words or ideas as if they were the writer's own. It comes from the Latin word *plagiarius*, meaning "kidnapper."

Point of view (98) refers to the person, vantage point, and attitude of a writer.

Prereading (7) is the first phase of the reading process during which students prepare to read material by establishing a purpose, making predictions, understanding the title, assessing the audience, and learning about the rhetorical context of an essay (including the author, date and place of publication, and social setting).

Prewriting (15), or preparing to write an essay, involves exploring a subject, choosing a specific topic and generating ideas about it, establishing a purpose, analyzing the audience, and drafting a thesis statement.

Process analysis (188–189) is one of the traditional rhetorical modes that explains an action or an event from beginning to end.

Purpose (17–19) is the writer's reason for doing a project or essay.

Q

QR codes (xv), an abbreviation for "quick response" codes, are two-dimensional barcodes that can be read by smart phones and other barcode readers, taking the user directly to a Web site.

R

Rereading (9) will help students reach a critical understanding of a selection.

Revising (28–30, 53, 99, 143, 193, 244, 289), or "re-seeing," happens when a writer changes words, recasts sentences, and moves whole paragraphs from one place to another.

Rewriting (28–30) involves revising content (development, logic, organization, and coherence) and editing (proofreading and correcting errors in grammar, usage, and sentence structure).

S

Simile (53) is a comparison of two dissimilar items using the words "like" or "as." When Susan Klebold first got the phone call from her husband in "I Will Never Know Why," she says, "I felt as though millions of tiny needles were pricking my skin."

Spatial order (22) means arranging details based on their relationship to each other in space. Beginning at one point and moving detail by detail around a specific area is the simplest way of organizing spatially.

Summarizing (24–25, 41) highlights a selection's main ideas in a coherent paragraph that is much briefer than the original.

Syllogism (419) is a three-step form of reasoning moving from a major premise to a minor premise to a conclusion: Socrates is a man; all men are mortal; therefore, Socrates is mortal.

T

Thesis statement (19, 190, 327–329) is the controlling idea of an essay. It is the main point that all other details in the project will support.

Title (25) is a phrase, usually no more than a few words, that gives a hint about the subject, purpose, or focus of what is to follow.

Topic sentences (20–21) state the controlling idea of each paragraph in an essay.

U

Unity (144) entails a sense of wholeness or interrelatedness achieved by making sure all sentences are related to a main idea.

URL (36), which stands for "uniform resource locator," is the address of a Web site.

Index of Authors and Titles